SOCIAL THEORY TODAY

SOCIAL THEORY TODAY

Edited by Anthony Giddens and
Jonathan H. Turner

STANFORD UNIVERSITY PRESS
STANFORD, CALIFORNIA
1987

Stanford University Press
Stanford, California
©1987 Polity Press
Originating publisher: Polity Press, Cambridge,
  in association with Basil Blackwell, Oxford
First published in the U.S.A. by
  Stanford University Press, 1987
ISBN 0-8047-1397-9
LC 86-63250

Printed in Great Britain by TJ Press Ltd., Padstow

Contents

Introduction

ANTHONY GIDDENS and JONATHAN H. TURNER

This book provides a systematic guide to the leading traditions and trends in social history. We do not take social theory to be the property of any one discipline, for questions about social life and the cultural products of human action stretch across the social sciences and the humanities. Among other problems, the following range of issues are broached by social theorists: the status of the social sciences, especially in relation to the logic of the natural sciences; the nature of the laws or generalizations which can be established; the interpretation of human agency and its differentiation from objects and events in nature; and the character or form of social institutions. Of course, such a bald delineation conceals a host of more specific problems and topics; any definition of social theory is bound to be controversial. The reader looking for consensus over the nature and goals of social theory will thus be disappointed. Indeed this lack of consensus, as several contributions to this book imply, may be endemic to the nature of social science. At the very least, whether there can be a unified framework of social theory or even agreement over its basic preoccupations is itself a contested issue.

Part of our motivation for producing this volume is a growing awareness that there have been important changes taking place in social theory over recent years. Theoretical analysis has always been a variegated enterprise in the social sciences, but for a certain period after the Second World War a particular set of views tended to stand out above the rest and thus commanded a measure of general acceptance. These views were typically influenced by logical empiricism in philosophy. Various interpretations about the character of science were developed by those usually associated with such a standpoint and, despite the imprecision of the label, it denoted several common elements: a suspicion of metaphysics, a desire to define in a clear-cut way what is to count as 'scientific', an emphasis on the testability of concepts and propositions and a sympathy for hypothetico-deductive forms of theory construction.

An essential part of this outlook was the idea of what Neurath called 'unified science', according to which no major logical differences between the natural and social sciences are seen to exist. This viewpoint helped to foster a disinclination to look directly at the logic of the social sciences themselves. For if science in general is guided by a single body of principles, social scientists need only to examine the logical foundations of natural science in order to explicate the nature of their own enterprise. Seen in this light, it is not surprising that many of those working in the social sciences uncritically appropriated the philosophy of natural science associated with logical empiricism to clarify their own tasks. Logical empiricism tended to be seen not as a particular philosophy of science, having potentially questionable assumptions, but as an incontrovertible model of what science is like. Questions of 'interpretation' were repressed in two respects. Natural science was not seen in any basic sense as an interpretative undertaking, since its prime objective was taken to be the formulation of laws, or systems of laws, while the meaning of theories and concepts was presumed to be tied to empirical observations in a direct way. The social sciences in this view are essentially non-interpretative, even though their subject-matter revolves around interpretative processes of culture and communication. As a result, the notion of *Verstehen* – the understanding of meaning – received short shrift both from authors writing in a directly philosophical vein and from most practising social scientists. When *Verstehen* was regarded as relevant, it was viewed as useful only in generating testable theories or hypotheses. Empathic understanding of the outlook and feelings of others, it was held, may assist the social scientific observer in formulating accounts of their conduct, but these accounts should always be formulated in 'operational' terms, or at least in terms of descriptions of observable traits of behaviour which can be tested. *Verstehen* was understood purely as a 'psychological' phenomenon, dependent upon the necessarily intuitive and unreliable discernment of the consciousness of others.

Over the past two decades, however, a dramatic change has occurred. Within the philosophy of natural science, the hold of logical empiricism has waned under the assault of writers such as Kuhn, Toulmin, Lakatos and Hesse. In its place, a 'newer philosophy of science', discarding many of the suppositions of preceding views, has emerged. Summarizing the newer conception boldly, the idea that there can be theory-neutral observations is repudiated, while systems of deductively-linked laws are no longer canonized as the highest ideal of scientific explanation. Most importantly, science is presumed to be an interpretative endeavour, such that problems of meaning, communication and translation are immediately relevant to scientific theories. These developments in the philosophy of natural science have inevitably influenced thinking about the social sciences, while accelerating an increasing disillusionment with the dominant theories of 'mainstream' social science.

The result of such changes has been a proliferation of approaches in theoretical thinking. Traditions of thought that previously had been either little known or ignored have become much more prominent: phenomenology, particularly as associated with the writings of Alfred Schutz; hermeneutics, as developed in the work of such authors as Gadamer and Ricoeur; and critical theory, as represented in recent times by the works of Habermas. Moreover, older traditions of thought, such as symbolic interactionism in the United States and structuralism or post-structuralism in Europe, have become revitalized and examined with new interest. To these one must add more recently developed types of thinking, including ethnomethodology, structuration theory, and the 'theory of practice' associated in particular with Bourdieu. While this emerging diversity of traditions and schools of thought in social theory appears quite stunning, there continues to be something of a 'mainstream', even if it is navigated by fewer than before. Parsonian structural-functionalism, for example, still exerts a strong appeal and, in fact, has undergone a considerable revival recently in the writings of Luhmann, Münch, Alexander, Hayes and others. Social theory has thus come to comprise a varied, often confusing, array of approaches.

In the face of this diversity of approaches, various responses have ensued. At one extreme, many of those whose prime commitment is to empirical research find in the array of squabbling schools and traditions confirmation of what they have believed all along: theoretical debates are of little interest or relevance to those conducting empirical work. If social theorists cannot agree among themselves about the most basic issues, what possible relevance can questions of social theory have for those engaged primarily in empirical research? As a result, there has emerged a rather large split between 'researchers', who may perhaps often still view themselves as 'positivists', and theorists, who now see themselves in many different lights and hues. The dismay of researchers, however, is not shared by all. At the other extreme, many have actively welcomed the diversification of social theory, considering the competition of traditions of thought to be highly desirable. From this standpoint, which has sometimes been influenced by Feyerabend's philosophy of natural science, the proliferation of theoretical traditions represents a way to avoid the dogmatism fostered by an overriding commitment to a single framework of thought. The additional point is sometimes made that the study of human behaviour is necessarily a contested affair; only within a totalitarian society would an unquestioned single framework for the analysis of human social conduct exist.

It would probably be true to say that the majority of those working in the social sciences fall somewhere between these extremes. At a minimum, most would argue that sorting through the divergent claims made by varying theoretical traditions is by no means a fruitless activity. This is certainly the position of the editors of this volume, even though their views differ as to how such an endeavour might best be accomplished. We would also point out that the apparent explosion of competing versions of social theory conceals more consistency and integration between rival viewpoints than may appear at first sight. Several points need to be made here.

First, there may often be more overlap between different approaches than has generally been perceived. The development of ethnomethodology provides a cogent illustration. In the early phases of its formation, ethnomethodology was viewed by opponents and critics alike as radically discrepant from other frameworks of thought within social science. Only now has it become apparent that the writings of those affiliated with ethnomethodology have contributions to make to problems that occupy virtually everyone working in social theory. It has also become quite obvious that there are close similarities between the problems tackled within ethnomethodology and those examined by other theoretical traditions. Thus, for example, the emphasis upon the 'methodological' nature of language-use within the contexts of social life can readily be shown to be relevant to questions of broad significance in social theory.

Second, there are common lines of development shared by a wide range of the theoretical perspectives which have come into prominence over the past two decades. There has been a concern, for instance, to reconceptualize the nature of action. Indeed, many approaches have tended to concentrate so much upon this question that it seemed at one point as though a tide of subjectivism was about to engulf the social sciences. We can now see, however, that a reworking of questions about human action need not lead to an exaggerated emphasis upon subjectivity but, rather, can connect a sophisticated 'theory of the subject' to analyses of a more 'institutional' kind.

Third, it would be difficult to deny that there has been some sort of progress towards resolving issues which previously either appeared intractable or were not analysed in a direct fashion. Thus there was for long a division between naturalistic approaches and those emphasizing *Verstehen*, notwithstanding the sway which the former held over the latter. As a result of convergent developments in a number of traditions of thought, it has become rather evident that the division between *Erklären* (or explanation in terms of causal laws) and *Verstehen* was a misconceived one. *Verstehen* is not, as the logical empiricists insisted, primarily a 'psychological' matter; instead, it is embedded and implicated in all questions about the interpretation of meaning. In the recent literature, these questions have been much explored in relation to both natural and social science; as a result, a definite clarification of matters that previously were quite murky has emerged.

In this book we have tried to cast our net widely, although there are inevitably some gaps. But we believe this volume deals more or less systematically with most of the influential traditions in social theory today. It would be impossible in a brief introduction to analyse in detail the strengths or the shortcomings of all approaches. Instead, we signal some of the salient themes and claims made by the various authors such as to communicate the diversity and vitality of social theory.

What is the Nature of Social Science?

Virtually all of the chapters which follow address this question. As will become evident, there is widespread disagreement over what kind of science, if any, social science is and can be. Defending 'logical positivism', in some sense or another, are George Homans's examination of 'Behaviourism and After', Jonathan Turner's approach in 'Analytical Theorizing' and, if only implicitly, Richard Münch's analysis of 'Parsonian Theory Today'. As Homans has eloquently and forcefully argued for over two decades, sociology can be a science committed to 'covering law' and axiomatic deductive systems. Turner shares this metaphor of a 'covering law' view of sociology, but rejects the possibility of true axiomatic theory. Instead, sociology should seek out abstract laws and use them in loose deductive schemes. Moreover, in Turner's view, abstract laws must be supplemented by analytical models which specify in detail the causal processes operating to connect the variables in an abstract law. Münch argues that Parsonian action theory can be used to generate a 'general frame of reference' which can organize a variety of theoretical and methodological approaches. In terms of methodology, Münch sees ideal-types, idiography, nomological hypotheses and constructivistic models as capable of being understood, and perhaps reconciled, within a more general action frame of reference. Similarly, different ways of explaining events – teleonomic, causal, normative and rational – can be ordered by the action framework. Thus, Münch advocates eclecticism, but it is an eclecticism seemingly committed to a positivistic view of sociology: to generate and test theories in systematic terms.

On the other side of this issue can be found a variety of arguments, most of which revolve around the presumption that the subject-matter of social science precludes the adoption of a natural science orientation. Yet even here there remains a certain ambivalence. For example, Hans Joas's review of the pragmatist roots of interactionism and its elaboration in very diverse directions by the 'Chicago School' is notable on this score. On the one hand, the pragmatic, situational and constructed nature of interaction and, hence, social organization would make the timeless 'laws' and 'generalizations' of positivism impossible. Yet, on the other hand, many interactionists – perhaps including Mead himself – have sought to uncover the basic properties of interaction and to develop universal laws about their operation. operation.

In his lucid analysis of Garfinkel and ethnomethodology John Heritage tends to skirt the question of the 'science' in social science. For while action is indexical, contextual and reflexive, can ethnomethodology develop laws and generalizations about it? Ethnomethodology is not of one voice in its answer to this question – and indeed those associated with it tend to be less explicitly concerned with such matters than most of those working in other traditions. Ethnomethodologists usually advocate the detailed description of empirical processes, apparently bracketing out of consideration just what would constitute 'explanation' and whether descriptions are 'scientific'.

Far less ambivalent on the question of whether or not there can be a natural science of society are Thomas Wilson, Ira Cohen, Jeffrey Alexander and Anthony Giddens. In somewhat different ways, all of these scholars maintain that social science is fundamentally different from natural science. Alexander does not reject outright the idea that laws of social life can be discovered, but he argues forcefully that a consensus could never be reached over these laws and that the nature of social science data can never make them definitive. Social analysis will always, he argues, involve discourse and debate over the presuppositions of theories and the relevance of data for testing these theories.

Wilson makes an even stronger ontological argument. Since social science must take as its topic the emotions, purposes, attitudes and subjective dispositions of actors, theoretical and empirical statements will be 'intensional', involving interpretations of meaning by social analysts. One can create theoretical projects based upon the 'extensional' methods of the natural sciences, but these must be recognized as only heuristically useful. At best, the use of mathematics can 'sort out relations in our data and clarify our ideas about how one theory is related to another in a particular case'. Giddens and Cohen present a similar argument in their respective portrayals of 'structuralism' and 'structuration theory'. Giddens pronounces structuralism and post-structuralism 'dead', arguing that their failure to come to terms with human 'agency', as well as the process by which such agency works to produce, reproduce and change structure, represent major flaws in structural analysis. For in the notion of agency resides the capacity to restructure the social universe, thereby obviating scientific laws depicting this universe.

In presenting a detailed account of Giddens's structuration theory, especially in regard of the notion of *Praxis*, Cohen draws out the fuller implications of the notion of 'agency'. At best, theory can only highlight the 'constitutive potentials of social life' that actors use to produce and reproduce social patterns. Just how these potentials are employed is contextual and historical, making laws and generalizations mutable by the acts of agents. Social science cannot, therefore, be like the natural sciences because its agents can change the very nature of its subject-matter – patterns of social organization.

The chapters by Immanuel Wallerstein and Ralph Miliband appear, on the surface, sympathetic to this view of agency. Indeed, to confront forms of domination through *Praxis* is, of course, the centre-piece of the Marxian tradition. But in his 'World-Systems Analysis', Wallerstein argues that enough energy has been wasted debating the particularistic versus universalistic character of social theory. He sees such debates as 'ponderous'; as an alternative, he proposes that social theory use 'frameworks', such as those in world-systems analysis, that encompass sufficient time and space to see the basic logics or dynamics of social processes. These 'logics' must not be viewed as eternal, since the nature of social organization does indeed change in the long run. Miliband's position is less clear on the question of science. On the one hand, he sees processes of domination as an invariant property of social organization that is the subject of 'class analysis', but, on the other hand, he implies that this property can be eliminated, thereby rendering mutable the very class analysis used to examine it.

Such is the range of opinion. It is clear that the critical rejection of 'logical positivism' has come to predominate in social theory – despite the protests by one editor of this volume. While a 'natural science' view of sociology still has many advocates, they now constitute a minority in social theory as broadly conceived in this volume. Yet the debate is not over, as can be seen in the variety of positions in the chapters to follow.

What is the Basic Subject-matter of Social Theory?

Disagreements over what social theory is, and can be, are reflected in arguments about its basic subject-matter, however conceived. The crux of the debates concerns several interrelated questions: What is 'out there' in the social universe? What are the most fundamental properties of the world? What kind of analysis of these properties is possible and/or appropriate? In asking such questions, old philosophical issues – such as reductionism, realism and nominalism – re-emerge. If we accept Jeffrey Alexander's position, such will always be the case as various authors invoke the support of the 'classics' to buttress their point of view.

In the other chapters of this volume, one can find a full range of opinion about what should be the prime concerns of social theory. Some argue for a micro-analysis of behaviour and interaction in situated contexts, whereas others present a case for more macro approaches concerned with emergent structures; some present a case for a reconciliation of micro- and macro-analyses, whereas others view such syntheses as counter-productive and, at best, premature. Let us briefly review this range of opinion.

In perhaps his strongest statement to date, Homans presents the case for reductionism. The institutions of society 'can be reduced, without residue, to the behaviours of individuals'. At one time, it was possible to interpret such a statement by Homans as merely a strategic argument: the laws of social structure and institutions will be deduced, in an axiomatic system, from those of psychology. But there now appears to be more metaphysical assertiveness in Homans's argument: ultimately, all social reality is behaviour; institutions are *not* anything more than the sum of these constituent behaviours.

As Joas's chapter on 'Symbolic Interactionism' underscores, there is a considerable range of opinion within just this one intellectual tradition on what is fundamental to the social world. The pragmatist roots of symbolic interactionism affirm the importance of human agency where actors construct courses of conduct in concrete situations, but the issue of just what is 'constructed' remains problematic. G.H. Mead emphasized the reproduction of social structures through the behavioural capacities of mind, self, and role-taking, but modern interactionists have been polarized over the question of whether 'structure', *per se*, or processes producing and reproducing such structure, are to be given theoretical priority. For while Mead saw these as two sides of the same conceptual coin, contemporary theorists appear divided on the issue of to what degree structure constrains agency, and vice versa.

As Heritage's review of 'Ethnomethodology' reveals, this ambivalence in interactionism reappears elsewhere. Of course, Heritage and those sympathetic to ethnomethodology would not phrase the issue in these terms, but the message of ethnomethodology is clear: study those interactive processes, especially those revolving around talk and conversation, whereby actors create accounts and a sense of an external, factual world. The most paramount social reality – some believe – is the contextual and indexical interpretation of signs and symbols among situated actors.

Contrasted to this emphasis is Münch's extension of Parsonian functionalism. For while terms like 'meaning' and 'action' are prominent, the real subject-matter of functional theory is complex systems of interrelated actions. For Münch and other Parsonians, reality exists at different system levels which embrace virtually all phases of reality, but, in the end, action-theoretic analysis almost always concentrates on the structure and function of systems and subsystems; their use of various symbolic media; their modes of integration; and their means of adaptation to various environments. Behaviour in concrete settings among individuals becomes subordinate to a view of a majestic social universe of four action systems embedded in an organic, telic and physico-chemical universe.

Cohen's portrayal of Giddens's structuration theory tries to mediate between such disparate views of the social universe. Giddens postulates a 'duality of structure' where structure provides the rules and resources involved in agency, which also reproduces the structural properties of social institutions. Structure is both the medium and the outcome of the day-to-day conduct in which actors engage. For structuration theory, then, agents, action and interaction are constrained by, yet generative of, the structural dimension of social reality.

Jonathan Turner's chapter on 'Analytical Theorizing' is somewhat less optimistic about the possibilities for conceptual integration of institutional and interpersonal analyses. Instead, he argues for an eclectic analysis of microdynamics that incorporates symbolic interactionism, ethnomethodology, behaviourism and other views, but at the same time he advocates a separate conceptualization of macroprocesses that synthesize the insights not only of functional theory but of other structural approaches as well. Efforts at bridging the gap between individual interaction and emergent structures are, in Turner's view, premature. Both levels are equally 'real' but, for now, each requires its own concepts, propositions and models.

More critically-oriented theorists view many of these debates over the subject-matter of sociology with impatience, or perhaps suspicion. For these scholars, the most important reality is that which limits human options and potential through domination and oppression. In this vein, Miliband insists that class domination and class struggles provide the central dynamic of human organization. The fundamental concern of social theory, then, has to be with the analysis of the capacity to control the means of production, administration, communication and coercion in a society. Wallerstein's world-systems approach makes a similar point, but unlike Miliband's class-analytical approach, social formations and the state are not the most important units of analysis. Rather, 'historical systems' stretching across time and space in a variety of forms, ranging from mini-systems to world empires and world economies, should be the central topics of analysis in social theory. For Wallerstein, the power of world economies and empires to constrain and to dominate the actions of individuals, corporate units and 'mini-systems' is the most paramount reality of the social universe.

The Further Development of Social Theory

To a great extent, the pathways and procedures for developing social theory follow from commitments to a particular subject-matter and a philosophy of social science. We can trace a range of convergences and varying trajectories of development here. For example, although Giddens's structuration theory and Münch's version of Parsonian action theory seem to share little in common, they both implicitly advocate a similar theory-building strategy: they construct a conceptual framework that can be used to interpret specific empirical cases. The respective frameworks differ in terms of the substantive properties of the world that they denote and in regard to what kind of explanation each assumes is possible. Yet both are interested in creating 'ontologically-based theory', to use Cohen's description of Giddens's approach. For them, theory is to capture the prime features of human agency and institutional patterns.

Wallerstein appears to advocate the same approach, albeit for a somewhat different subject-matter. Although he rejects the nomothetic–idiographic distinction, he argues basically that 'historical science must *start* with the abstract and move in the direction of the concrete'. As with Giddens and Münch, then, the idea is to use a broad and abstract framework for interpreting concrete historical and empirical events.

Wilson would see such frameworks, even those expressed mathematically, as heuristic devices at best. Moreover, they can never constitute a system from which deductions to empirical events are made, primarily because such deductions will be filled with interpretative content. Yet, like all theorists, Wilson recognizes that one cannot abandon completely the natural science metaphor of modelling, as long as the limitations of this metaphor are recognized.

Alexander would add that the use of such frameworks and heuristic models will inevitably be subject to debate and controversy. Moreover, they will always be underdetermined by data. Hence, theory will be constructed out of a dialogue, typically reaching back to the classics for inspiration and legitimation. As a result, theory will always be developed more at the level of discourse than of empirical confirmation.

Joas's chapter on 'Symbolic Interactionism' and Heritage's portrayal of

'Ethnomethodology' come closest to advocating induction, even though theorists in these traditions might reject such a categorical portrayal. But in essence, they argue that theory must be developed from observations of people's interactions in real-life contexts. Whatever the nature of the theory to be developed from such observations, it must denote what people actually do in situated contexts. That is, concepts, generalizations and frameworks must be empirically grounded in observable processes of interacting individuals.

Turner and Homans in some respects share a common outlook. Homans emphasizes that theory must be about observable behaviour instead of reified entities like structure, but such theory must be formal and deductive. Whether through induction, deduction, abduction or divine inspiration, the goal is to develop abstract axioms that can serve as the covering laws for as wide a range of empirical events as possible. These laws should not be loose frameworks but specific statements about relationships among variables. Turner shares this position, but he recognizes that fully-developed axiomatic theory is probably impossible in social science because of the inability to impose experimental controls. Yet he agrees with Homans that broad conceptual frameworks are too loose and too imprecise to be the endpoint of theorizing. He advocates a creative interplay between abstract laws and analytical models that schematically represent complexes of causal connections among generic classes of variables. The goal is to translate the analytical models into abstract propositions that can be tested, rejected or revised in the light of systematic tests.

Conclusion

Social theory is a most varied enterprise. There is disagreement on some of its most basic concerns: on what kind of social science is possible, on what should be its subject-matter, and on what procedures it should endorse. In the chapters that follow a representative overview of positions on these issues can be found. We have selected scholars and topics carefully in order to provide a systematic guide both to the leading traditions of thought in social theory and to the changes that have occurred over the last two decades. Social theory is in intellectual ferment. For some, this is unsurprising, even unobjectionable, while for others it engenders confusion and stagnation. But for our purposes as editors, the goals have been to represent the diversity of viewpoints that exists and to provide a forum for some of their most prominent representatives to explicate their ideas. We trust that the reader will find *Social Theory Today* a useful guide and reference work on the present state of social theory.

The Centrality of the Classics

JEFFREY C. ALEXANDER

The relationship between social science and the classics is a question which opens up the deepest issues not only in social science but in cultural studies more generally. In the essay which follows I argue for the centrality of the classics in contemporary social science. This position is challenged from what, at first glance, appear to be two entirely different camps. Among social science practitioners, of course, there has always been scepticism toward 'the classics'. Indeed, for those of the positivist persuasion the very question of the relation between social science and the classics leads immediately to another, namely, whether there should be any relationship at all. Why do disciplines which profess to be oriented to the empirical world and to the accumulation of objective knowledge about it need recourse to texts by writers who are long dead and gone? According to the canons of empiricism, after all, whatever is scientifically relevant in these texts should long ago have been either verified and incorporated into contemporary theory, or falsified and cast into the dustbin of history.

Yet it is not only 'hard' positivists who argue against interrelating classical interpretation and contemporary social science; it is humanists as well. Recently there has emerged a powerful argument against the injection of contemporary concerns into the consideration of classical texts. Classical texts, so this argument goes (e.g. Skinner: 1969), must be considered entirely in historical terms. This historicist position on the classics converges with the empiricist, in so far as both camps argue against the intermingling of contemporary social science concerns with the discussion of historical texts.

To answer the questions about the relation between social science and the classics, then, one must think about just exactly what empirical social science is and how it relates to the science of nature. One must also think about what it means to analyse the classics and about what relation this kind of presumptively historical activity might have to the pursuit of contemporary scientific knowledge.

Before pursuing these questions further, however, I will offer a pointed definition of just what a classic is. Classics are earlier works of human exploration which are given a privileged status *vis-à-vis* contemporary explorations in the same field. The concept of privileged status means that contemporary practitioners of the discipline in question believe that they can learn as much about their field through understanding this earlier work as they can from the work of their own contemporaries. To be accorded such a privileged status, moreover, implies that, in the day-to-day work of the average practitioner, this deference is accorded without prior demonstration; it is accepted as a matter of course that, as a classic, such a work establishes fundamental criteria in the particular field. It is because of this privileged position that exegesis and reinterpretation of the classics – within or without a historical context – become conspicuous currents in various disciplines, for what is perceived to be the 'true meaning' of a classical work has broad repercussions. Western theologians have taken the Bible as their classic text, as have those who practise the Judaeo-Christian religious disciplines. For students of English literature, Shakespeare is undoubtedly the author whose work embodies the highest standards in their field. For 500 years, Aristotle and Plato have been accorded a classical status in political theory.

The Empiricist Challenge to the Centrality of the Classics

What stimulates the argument against the classics' centrality from the side of social science seems obvious enough. As I have defined the term, the genre of 'classics' does not exist today in the natural sciences. Whitehead (1974, p. 115), certainly one of this century's most sophisticated philosophers of science, wrote that 'a science which hesitates to forget its founders is lost'. This pronouncement seems undeniably true, in so far, at least, as science is taken in its Anglo-American sense as equivalent to *Naturwissenschaft*. As a historian of science has observed, 'every college freshman knows more physics than Galileo knew, whose claim is higher than any other's to the honor of having founded modern science, and more too than Newton did, whose mind was the most powerful ever to have addressed itself to nature' (Gillispie: 1960, p. 8).

   This fact is undeniable. The problem is, what does it mean? For adherents to the positivist persuasion, it means that in the long run social science too must do without the classics, and in the short run, attention to the classics must be severely delimited. They should be mined simply for empirical information. Exegesis and commentary – which are the sure marks of privileged status – have no place in the social sciences. These conclusions are based on two presumptions. The first is that the absence of classical texts in natural science indicates the latter's purely empirical status; the second is that natural and social science are basically the same. I will argue below that neither of these presumptions is true. Before doing so, however, I will examine the empiricist argument they inform in a more systematic way.

   In an influential essay first formulated forty years ago, Merton (1947, reprinted 1967, pp. 1–38) argued against what he called the merging of the history and systematics of sociological theory. His model for systematic theorizing was the natural sciences. It consisted, apparently, of codifying empirical knowledge and constructing covering laws. What is systematic about scientific theory is that it tests covering laws through experimental procedures and, thereby, steadily accumulates true knowledge. In so far as accumulation occurs, there is no need for classical texts. 'The severest test of truly cumulative knowledge', Merton argues, 'is that run-of-the-mill minds can solve problems today which great minds could not begin to solve earlier'. In a real science, therefore, the 'commemoration of the great contributors of the past is substantially reserved to the history of the discipline' (Merton: 1967a, pp. 27–8). Investigation of earlier figures is a historical activity which has nothing to do with scientific work. This is a job for historians, not social scientists. This radical distinction between science and history is dramatically contrasted by Merton with the situation which holds in the humanities, where 'by direct contrast, each classical work – each poem, drama, novel, essay, or historical work – tends to remain a part of the direct experience of succeeding generations (p. 28).

While Merton acknowledges that sociologists are 'posed between the physical and life scientists and the humanists' his prescription for a position closer to the natural sciences is clear enough. He invokes Weber's confident assertion that 'in science, each of us knows that what he has accomplished will be antiquated in ten, twenty, fifty years' and Weber's insistence that 'every scientific [contribution] asks to be "surpassed" and outdated' (Merton: 1967a, pp. 28–9). That, fifty years after Weber's death, neither Weber's sociological theories nor his assertions about science had actually been 'surpassed' is an irony which, it seems, passes Merton by. To the contrary, he insists that while sociology's intermediate position between science and the humanities may be a fact, it must not be made into a normative position. 'Efforts to straddle scientific and humanistic orientations typically lead to merging the systematics of sociological theory with its history', a merging which, for Merton, is tantamount to making the accumulation of empirical knowledge impossible. The problem, from Merton's point of view, is that sociologists are cross-pressured, a structural position which typically leads to deviance from legitimate role expectations. Most sociologists succumb to these pressures and develop deviant roles. They 'oscillate' between social science and the humanities. Only a few are able to 'adapt to these pressures by acting wholly the scientific role' (Merton: 1967a, p. 29).

It is deviance (my term, not Merton's) from the scientific role which leads to what Merton calls the 'intellectually degenerative tendencies' that merge systematics with history. An attempt at what might be called historical systematics is degenerate because – precisely in the sense in which I have defined a 'classic' – it privileges earlier work. One finds a 'reverence' for 'illustrious ancestors' and an emphasis on 'exegesis' (1967a, p. 30). Worst of all, because it becomes important to understand the meaning of earlier, often difficult works, one finds the emphasis on 'erudition versus originality'.

Merton does not characterize erudite investigation into classical texts as interpretation. To do so, I believe, would imply that such investigation involves a creative theoretical element which is generative (as opposed to degenerative) in the contemporary scientific sense. Generativity would contradict the slavish attitude toward earlier works which Merton sees as inherent in the historical investigation of classical texts, for it is not just reverence but 'uncritical reverence' which he believes to be involved.[1] Interpretation and the creativity it implies would also contradict the mechanistic epistemology which underpins his arguments. For Merton, historical systematics simply provide contemporaries with mirrors in which earlier texts are reflected. They are 'critical summaries', 'mere commentary', 'largely sterile exegesis', 'chronologically ordered set[s] of critical synopses of doctrine' (1967a, pp. 2, 4, 30, 35; cf. p. 9).

Earlier texts, Merton insists, simply should not be looked at in this 'deplorably useless' way. He offers two alternatives, one from the side of systematics, the other from the side of history. From the point of view of social science, he argues that earlier texts must be treated in a utilitarian rather than classical way. True, the present situation is not ideal: there has not been the kind of empirical accumulation which social science has every right to expect. Rather than dwelling on this situation, however, the proper response is to convert new-classic texts into simple sources of data and/or untested theories, that is, to make them into vehicles for further accumulation. They must be treated as sources of 'previously unretrieved information' which can be 'usefully employed as new points of departure'. Such texts can then point toward the scientific future rather than the humanistic past. In this way, the study of earlier texts can itself become scientific. By 'following up and developing theoretical leads', such study can be devoted to 'retrieving relevant cumulative knowledge ... and incorporating it in subsequent formulations (1967a, pp. 30, 35).

The alternative to merging from the point of view of history is, in fact, not much different. Rather than using texts as mines of unretrieved information, the texts can be studied as historical documents in themselves. Once again, the point here is to avoid textual exegesis. 'A genuine *history* of sociological theory', Merton writes, 'must deal with the interplay between theory and such matters as the social origins and statuses of its exponents, the changing social organization of sociology, the changes that diffusion

---

[1] Such a fawning, demeaning attitude to classical authors – the full quote is 'uncritical reverence toward almost any statement made by illustrious ancestors' (Merton: 1967, p. 30) – must be sharply distinguished from the deference and privileged status which accrue to classics according to the definition that I have offered above. I will argue below that while deference defines the formal attitude, continuous critique and reconstruction are what the real substance of historical systematics is all about. Merton's extremism on this matter is typical of those who deny the relevance of classical investigations to social science, for it casts these investigations in an anti-scientific, uncritical light.

brings to ideas, and their relations to the environing social and cultural structure' (p. 35). It is the environment of the ideas, not the ideas themselves, which a good historian of social science should study. The historian's aims, it is assumed, are fully as empirical as those of the sociologist, who studies the same texts for the purposes of accumulation. Merton's rejection of the merging of science and history, then, is based not only on the demand for scientific sociology but for scientific history as well.

I earlier mentioned two assumptions upon which the empiricist challenge to the centrality of the classics depends. The first is that the absence of classics in natural science stems from its empirical and cumulative nature; the second is that in these respects social and natural science are basically the same. In Merton's essay (1967a) against the merging of history and systematics, the empiricist perspective on natural science is an innate assumption that virtually goes without saying. His account of the history of science is a purely progressive one. Rather than a relativistic and historical treatment of earlier scientific texts, which in the spirit of post-Kuhnian sensibilities emphasizes the formative power of supra-scientific cultural and intellectual frameworks, Merton looks on earlier work as a series of 'anticipations', 'adumbrations' and 'prediscoveries' of what is known in the present day (1967a, pp. 8–27). We know, moreover, from Merton's systematic protocols for the sociology of science (e.g. Merton: 1973) that this impression is not a mistake. For Merton, disciplinary and methodological commitments are the only non-empirical factors which impinge on scientific work, and neither of these is conceived as having any direct effect on scientific cognition of the object world.

The oher fundamental assumption upon which Merton's argument rests is that in its primarily empirical referent social science resembles natural science. This second point, however, is a little more difficult for Merton to make. We know from his essay on middle-range theory (Merton: 1967b) – which, not incidentally, immediately follows the work on the merging of history and systematics in Merton's collection, *Social Theory and Social Structure* – that Merton does not view social science as paradigm-bound in Kuhn's sense. Because it is problem- rather than paradigm-driven, social science is organized by empirical specialty rather than by school or tradition. But why, if sociologists are not empiricists, do they straddle science and the humanities? Why, moreover, do they merge history and systematics if they are not intent on forming and sustaining schools? As I have earlier suggested, even while Merton acknowledges these unavoidable facts he insists that they are deviant anomalies, not inherent tendencies. Insisting that 'sociology adopts the orientation and practice of the physical sciences', he claims that social science 'research moves from the frontiers advanced by the cumulative work of past generations' (Merton: 1967a, pp. 29–31).

Indeed, despite the degenerate tendency for engaging in what I have called historical systematics, Merton believes that our knowledge about how to study the history of scientific thought is itself scientific and cumulative! He employs the terminology of progressive science – adumbration, prediscovery, anticipation – to make his case for the right kind of progressive scientific history. Arguing against progressive histories which rest only upon the formal, published descriptions of scientific work, Merton suggests (pp. 4–6) that such accounts rest on a conception of history which 'lags extraordinarily behind long-recognized reality'. It was Bacon who first 'observed' that the process of objective discovery is more creative and intuitive than the formal logic of scientific proof suggests. That there have been independent discoveries of this fact must, according to Merton, confirm it: 'perceptive minds have repeatedly and, it would seem, independently made the same kind of observation'. The scientific theory which covers, or explains, these empirical observations has developed in due course: 'this observation has been generalized' by later thinkers. It is because this empirical logic has held that Merton is confident that the history of science will make inevitable progress, for 'the failure of sociology to distinguish between the history and systematics of theory will eventually be wiped out' (Merton: 1967a, pp. 4–6).

These are the basic assumptions of Merton's – now classic! – argument against the centrality of the classics. There seems, however, to be a third, ancillary one as well, one which is implied by the two central assumptions rather than standing on its own. This is the notion that the meaning of significant earlier texts is there for all to see. I have shown how in condemning historical systematics Merton characterizes it as producing merely summarizing synopses. I have also demonstrated how the sociological history he prefers will focus on the environment of scientific theories rather than on the nature of the ideas themselves. This, by the way, is also the inclination of the challenge to classical centrality which has been issued by the humanities, which I will consider in due course. In the section which immediately follows, however, I direct my argument against the empiricist challenge to classical centrality and the two central assumptions upon which it rests.

The Post-positivist View of Science

The argument against the centrality of the classics assumes that to the degree a discipline is empirical it will be cumulative, and to the degree it is cumulative it will not produce classics. I will argue, to the contrary, that whether a discipline has classics depends not on its empiricism but upon the consensus within that discipline about non-empirical things.

In *Theoretical Logic in Sociology* (Alexander: 1982a, pp. 5–15), I suggested that the positivist persuasion in the social sciences rests on four major postulates. The first is that a radical, epistemological break exists between empirical observations, which are held to be specific and concrete, and non-empirical statements, which are held to be general and abstract. Only because this break is taken for granted can the second postulate be made: more general and abstract concerns – philosophical or metaphysical – do not have fundamental significance for the practice of an empirically-oriented discipline. Third, questions which are of a generalized, abstract and theoretical nature can be evaluated only in relation to empirical observations. This suggests that, whenever possible, theory should be stated in propositional form and, further, that theoretical conflicts are decided through empirical tests and crucial experiments. Finally, because these first three postulates supply no ground for structured scientific disagreement, the fourth postulate suggests that scientific development is 'progressive', that is, linear and cumulative. Differentiation in a scientific field, then, is taken to be the product of specialization in different empirical domains rather than the result of generalized, non-empirical disagreement about how to explain the same empirical domain.

While these four postulates still accurately reflect the common sense of most practising social scientists – especially those of the American variety – they have been sharply challenged by the new wave of post-positivist philosophy, history and, indeed, sociology of natural science which has emerged over the last two decades (Alexander: 1982a, pp. 18–33). Whereas the postulates of the positivist persuasion effectively reduce theory to fact, those of the post-positivist position rehabilitate the theoretical.

1   The empirical data of science are theoretically informed. The fact–theory distinction is neither epistemological nor ontological, that is, it is not a distinction between nature and thought. It is an analytical distinction. As Lakatos (e.g. 1969, p. 156) has written, describing some statements as observations is a manner of speech, not an ontological reference. Analytical distinction refers to observations informed by those theories about which we feel the most certainty.

2   Scientific commitments are not based solely on empirical evidence. As Polanyi (e.g. 1958, p. 92) convincingly demonstrates, the principled rejection of evidence is the very bedrock upon which the continuity of science depends.

3   General, theoretical elaboration is normally dogmatic and horizontal rather than sceptical and progressive. The more generalized the claim, the less Popper's falsification theorem holds. Theoretical formulation does not proceed, as Popper would have it, according to the law of 'the fiercest struggle for survival' (1959, p. 42). To the contrary, when a general theoretical position is confronted with contradictory empirical evidence which cannot be ignored, it proceeds to develop *ad hoc* hypotheses and residual categories (Lakatos: 1969, pp. 168–76). In this manner, new phenomena can be 'explained' without surrendering the general formulations.

4   Fundamental shifts in scientific belief occur only when empirical changes are matched by the availability of convincing theoretical alternatives. Because such theoretical shifts are often in the background, they are less visible to those engaged in scientific work. It is for this reason that empirical data give the appearance of being concretely induced rather than analytically constructed. In truth, however, as Holton observes, the struggle between general theoretical commitments is 'among

the most powerful energizers of empirical research', and it must be placed 'at the heart of major changes in the natural sciences' (1973, pp. 26, 190).

If generalized, non-empirical considerations play such a decisive role, then Merton's first assumption – about the character of natural science – does not hold. Neither, in my view, does his second, for in crucial respects the practices of social and natural science are not particularly alike. This conclusion may seem surprising. Once we have established the non-empirical dimension of natural science, it might seem that the status of classical works would be unchallenged. The fact remains, however, that natural science does not have recourse to classics. The challenge is to explain this fact in a non-empiricist way.

Why There Are No Classics in Natural Science: A Post-positivist View

The epistemology of science does not determine the particular topics to which scientific activity is allocated in any given scientific discipline.[2] Yet, it is precisely the allocation of such activity which is responsible for any discipline's relative empirical 'feel'. Thus, even outspoken anti-empiricists have acknowledged that an explicit focus on empirical questions is what distinguishes natural from human sciences. For example, while Holton has painstakingly demonstrated that arbitrary, supra-empirical 'themata' effect modern physics, he insists that it has never been his intention to argue for the introduction of 'thematic discussions ... into the *practice* of science itself'. Indeed, he suggests that 'only when such questions were ruled out of place in a laboratory did science begin to grow rapidly' (Holton: 1973, pp. 330–1,

---

[2] The distinction I am employing between natural and social science obviously can have only an ideal-typical status. My purpose is to articulate general conditions, not to explain particular disciplinary situations. At the general level, it is certainly fair to say that the conditions for and against having classics broadly correspond with the division between the sciences of nature and the sciences concerned with the actions of human beings. Specific analysis of any particular discipline would require specifying the general conditions in each case. Thus, natural science is typically broken down into the physical and the life sciences. The latter are less subject to mathematization, less consensual, and more often subject to explicit extra-empirical dispute. In some instances this can extend to the point where debate over the classics has a continuing scientific role, as in the dispute over Darwin taking place in evolutionary biology. In the human studies, too, disciplines differ in the degree to which they typically manifest the conditions I will describe. In the United States, for example, economics is less bound to classics than sociology and anthropology, and the relation of history to classics seems constantly in flux. The variation in these empirical cases can be explained in terms of the theoretical conditions I lay out below.

italics added). Even the forthrightly idealist philosopher Collingwood, who has insisted that scientific practice rests upon metaphysical assumptions, allows that 'the scientist's business is not to propound them but only to presuppose them' (Collingwood: 1940, p. 33).

The allocation of scientific activity depends upon what is considered by practitioners to be scientifically problematic. Because in the modern era natural scientists tend to agree about the generalized commitments which inform their craft, it is more empirical questions which usually receive their explicit attention. This, of course, is precisely what allows 'normal science', in Kuhn's phrase (1970), to proceed as an activity of empirical puzzle-solving and specific problem-solutions. Taking normal science to character-ize natural science as such, Habermas, too, has identified consensus as what differentiates 'scientific' as compared to 'non-scientific' activity.

> We term information scientific if and only if an uncompelled and permanent consensus can be obtained with regard to its validity ... The genuine achieve-ment of modern science does not consist primarily in producing truth, that is, correct and cogent statements about what we call reality. Rather, it distinguishes itself from traditional categories of knowledge by a method of arriving at an uncompelled and permanent consensus of this sort about our views. (Habermas: 1972, p. 91)

Only if there is disagreement about the background assumptions which inform a science do these non-empirical issues come explicitly into play. Kuhn calls this a paradigm crisis. It is in such crises, he believes, that there is 'recourse to philosophy and to debate over fundamentals'. (Kuhn: 1970)

It is because attention is usually directed to the empirical dimensions of natural science that classics are absent. The non-empirical dimensions are camouflaged, and it appears that speculative hypotheses can be decided by reference either to sense data which are relatively accessible or to theories whose specificity makes their relevance to such data immediately apparent. Classics, by contrast, imply a privileged position for earlier theories. Earlier theories, not just contemporary ones, are seen as having explanatory status; indeed, classical texts often are considered to be capable of supplying relevant data as well. My point is that natural science is no less a priori than its social counterpart. A non a priori, purely empirical stance is not the explanation for 'classicless' natural science. Rather, it is a matter of the form which the mixture of prior and contingent knowledge takes.

Thus, rather than classics, natural science has what Kuhn called exemp-lars. With this term, Kuhn (1970, p. 182) means concrete examples of successful empirical work: examples of the kind of powerful problem-solutions which define paradigmatic fields. While exemplars embody meta-physical and non-empirical commitments of various kinds, they are in themselves models of how specifically to explain the world. Of necessity, they include definitions and concepts, but they direct those who study them to questions of operationalization and technique. Yet for all their specificity, examplars themselves play an a priori role. They are learned in textbooks and laboratories before neophytes are capable of testing for themselves whether or not they are really true. They are, in other words, internalized because of their privileged position in the socialization process rather than because of their scientific validity. The learning processes are the same in social science; what is different is that social scientists internalize classics at least as often as they internalize exemplars.

The Post-positivist Case for the Classics

The ratio between exemplars and classics is so much different in social science because in its social application science produces so much more disagreement. Because there is persistent and widespread disagreement, the more general background assumptions which remain implicit and relatively invisible in natural science here come vividly into play.[3] The conditions which Kuhn defines for paradigm crisis in the natural sciences are routine in the social. I am not suggesting that there is no 'objective' knowledge in the social sciences, nor even that there is no possibility for successful predictions or covering laws. It is possible, it seems to me, to gain real cumulative knowledge about the world from within different and competing points of view, and even to sustain relatively predictive covering laws from within general orientations which differ in substantial ways. What I am suggesting, however, is that the conditions of social science make consistent agreement about the precise nature of empirical knowledge – let alone agreement about explanatory covering laws – highly unlikely. In social science, therefore, arguments about scientific truth do not refer only to the empirical level. They cut across the full range of non-empirical commitments which sustain competing points of view.

There are cognitive and evaluative reasons for the vast differences in the level of consensus. I will mention here only the most fundamental.

1   In so far as the objects of a science are located in the physical world

---

[3] Mannheim puts this distinction well: 'No one denies the possibility of empirical research nor does anyone maintain that facts do not exist ... We, too, appeal to "facts" for our proof, but the question of the nature of facts is in itself a considerable problem. They exist for the mind always in an intellectual and social context. That they can be understood and formulated implies already the existence of a conceptual apparatus. And if this conceptual apparatus is the same for all the members of a group, the presuppositions (i.e. the possible social and intellectual values), which underlie the individual concepts, never become perceptible. ... However, once the unanimity is broken, the fixed categories which used to give experience its reliable and coherent character undergo an inevitable disintegration. There arise divergent and conflicting modes of thought which (unknown to the thinking subject) order the same facts of experience into different systems of thought, and cause them to be perceived through different logical categories' (Mannheim: 1936, pp. 102–3).

outside of the human mind, its empirical referents can, in principle, more easily be verified through interpersonal communication. In social science, where the objects are either mental states or conditions in which mental states are embedded, the possibility for confusing mental states of the scientific observer with mental states of those observed is endemic.

2   Resistance to simple agreement on empirical referents also emerges from the distinctive evaluative nature of social science. There is a symbiotic relationship between description and evaluation. The findings of social science often carry significant implications for the desirable organization and reorganization of social life. In natural science, by contrast, 'changes in the content of science do not usually imply changes in social structures' (Hagstrom: 1965, p. 285). The ideological implications of social science redound to the very descriptions of the objects of investigation themselves. The very characterization of states of mind or institutions – for example, is society called 'capitalist' or 'industrial', has there been 'proletarianization', 'individuation' or 'atomization' – reflects an estimation of the implication for political values of an explanation of that phenomenon which has not yet occurred. While Mannheim over-estimated evaluative as opposed to cognitive assumptions, he was certainly sensitive to this point. Every definition, he wrote, 'depends necessarily upon one's perspective, i.e. it contains within itself the whole system of thought representing the position of the thinker in question and especially the political evaluations which lie behind this system of thought'. His conclusion, in this regard, seems accurate: 'The very way in which a concept is defined and the nuance in which it is employed already embody to a certain degree a prejudgment concerning the outcome of the chain of ideas built upon it' (Mannheim: 1936, pp. 196–7).

3   Needless to say, in so far as it is difficult, for cognitive and evaluative reasons, to gain consensus about even the simple empirical referents of social science, there will be even less about the abstractions from such concrete referents which form the substance of social theory. Hagstrom suggests (1965, pp. 256–8) that possibilities for scientific consensus significantly depend upon the degree of quantification that is consistent with the discipline's scientific goals. In so far as empirical referents are not clear and abstractions subject to constant dispute, efforts to mathematicize social science can only be efforts at disguising or promoting particular points of view.

4   In so far as neither empirical referents nor covering laws generate agreement, the full range of non-empirical inputs to empirical perception become objects of debate. Because there is such endemic disagreement, moreover, social science will invariably be differentiated by traditions (Shils: 1970) and schools (Tiryakian: 1979). For most members of the social scientific community, it is apparent that such 'extra-scientific' cultural and institutional phenomena are not simply manifestations of disagreement but bases upon which scientific disagreements are promoted and sustained. This realization further sensitizes social scientists to the non-empirical dimensions of their field.

For all of these reasons, discourse – not just explanation – becomes a major feature of the social science field. By discourse, I refer to modes of argument which are more consistently generalized and speculative than are normal scientific discussions. The latter are directed in a more disciplined manner to specific pieces of empirical evidence, to inductive and deductive logics, to explanation through covering laws and to the methods by which these laws can be verified or falsified. Discourse, by contrast, is ratiocinative. It focuses on the process of reasoning rather than the results of immediate experience, and it becomes significant when there is no plain and evident truth. Discourse seeks persuasion through argument rather than prediction. Its persuasiveness is based on such qualities as logical coherence, expansiveness of scope, interpretive insight, value relevance, rhetorical force, beauty, and texture of argument.

Foucault (1973) identifies intellectual, scientific and political practices as 'discourses' in order to deny their merely empirical, inductive status. In this way, he insists that practical activities are historically constituted and shaped by metaphysical understandings that can define an entire epoch. Sociology, too, is a discursive field. Still, one finds here little of the homogeneity that Foucault attributes to such fields; in social science, there are discourses, not a discourse. These discourses are not, moreover, closely linked to the legitimation of power, as Foucault in his later work increasingly claimed. Social scientific discourses are aimed at truth, and they are constantly subjected to rational stipulations about how truth can be arrived at and what truth might be. Here I draw upon Habermas' (e.g. 1984) understanding of discourse as part of an effort that speakers make at achieving undistorted communication. If Habermas underestimates the irrational qualities of communication, let alone action, he certainly has provided a way to conceptualize its rational aspirations. His systematic attempts to identify modes of argument and criteria for arriving at persuasive justification show how rational commitments and the recognition of supra-empirical arguments can be combined. Between the rationalizing discourse of Habermas and the arbitrary discourse of Foucault, this is where the actual field of social science discourse uneasily lies.

It is because of the centrality of discourse that theory in the social sciences is so multivalent and that compulsive efforts (e.g., Wallace 1971) to follow the logic of natural science are so misguided. Those of the positivist persuasion sense the tension between such a multivalent conception and their empiricist point of view. To resolve it they try to privilege 'theory' over 'metatheory', indeed, to exclude theory in favour of 'explanation' narrowly conceived. Thus, complaining that 'far too much social theory consists of the history of ideas and general hero worship of Marx, Weber, [and] Durkheim', Turner argues for 'doing theory as opposed to ... providing yet another metatheoretical analysis of the early theoretical masters'[4] (Turner:

---

[4] This pejorative characterization of metatheory as hero worship recalls Merton's claim of 'uncritical reverence' (1967a, p. 30) which I discussed in note 1. Obsequi-

1986, p. 974). And Stinchcombe describes Marx, Durkheim and Weber as 'those great *empirical* analysts ... who did not work mainly at what we now call *theory*'. He insists that they 'worked out *explanations* of the growth of capitalism, or of class conflict, or of primitive religion'. Rather than being concerned with discursive theory, in his view, 'they used a wide variety of theoretical *methods*' (Stinchcombe: 1968, p. 3, italics added).

These distinctions, however, seem more like 'utopian' efforts to escape from social science than efforts really to understand it. Generalized discourse is central, and theory is inherently multivalent. Indeed, the centrality of discourse and the conditions which produce it make for the overdetermination of social science by theory and its underdetermination by fact. Because there is no clear, indisputable reference for the elements which compose social science, there is no neat translatability between different levels of generality. Formulations at one level do not ramify in clear-cut ways for the other levels of scientific concern. For example, while precise empirical measurements of two variable correlations can sometimes be established, it is rarely possible for such a correlation to prove or disprove a proposition about this interrelationship that is stated in more general terms. The reason is that the existence of empirical and ideological dissensus allows social scientists to operationalize propositions in a variety of different ways.

Let us briefly consider, for example, two of the best recent efforts to move from data to more general theory. In Blau's attempt to test his newly-developed structural theory, for example, he starts with a proposition he calls the size theorem: the notion that a purely ecological variable, group size, determines outgroup relations (Blau, Blum and Schwartz: 1982, p. 46). Drawing from a data set that establishes not only a group's size but its rate of intermarriage, he argues that a relationship between intermarriage rates and group size verifies the size theorem. Why? Because the data demonstrate that 'group size and the proportion outmarried are inversely related' (p. 47). But outmarriage is a datum that does not, in fact, operationalize 'outgroup relations'. It is one type of outgroup relation among many others, and as Blau himself acknowledges at one point in his argument it is a type into which enter factors other than group size. Outgroup relation, in other words, does not have a clear-cut referent. Because of this, the correlation between what is taken to be its indicator and group size cannot verify the general proposition about the relation between group size and outgroup relations. Blau's empirical data, then, are disarticulated from his theory, despite his

---

ousness, of course, is the obverse of scientific scepticism, and it is ultimately in order to deny a scientific role to classical investigations that such negative claims are made. It seems clear, to the contrary, that what I earlier called historical systematics consists of the critical reconstruction of classical theories. Ironically, empiricists like Turner and Merton are able to gain some legitimacy for their accusations because such reconstruction does, in fact, often occur within a framework which explicitly denies any critical ambition. I will try to account for this 'naive attitude' of participants in classical debate in the section which follows.

effort to link them in a theoretically decisive way.

In Lieberson's ambitious study (1980) of black and white immigrants to the United States since 1880, similar problems emerge. Lieberson begins with the less formally stated proposition that the 'heritage of slavery' is responsible for the different achievement levels of black and European immigrants. In order to operationalize this proposition, Lieberson takes two steps. First, he defines heritage in terms of 'lack of opportunity' for former slaves rather than in cultural terms. Second, he identifies opportunity in terms of the data he has developed about varying rates of education and residential segregation. Both these operations, however, are highly contestable. Not only would other social scientists define the heritage of slavery in very different terms, but they might also conceive of opportunities in ways other than education and residence. Because there is, once again, no necessary relationship between the rates Lieberson has identified and differences in opportunities, there can be no certainty about the proposition relating achievement and heritage. While the measured correlations stand on their own, and constitute an empirical contribution in their own right, they cannot test the theories towards which they are aimed.

It is far easier to find examples of the contrasting problem, the overdetermination by theory of empirical 'facts'. In virtually every broader, more theoretically-gauged study, the sampling of empirical data is open to dispute. In *The Protestant Ethic and the Spirit of Capitalism*, for example, Weber's equation of the spirit of capitalism with seventeenth- and eighteenth-century English entrepreneurs has been widely disputed (Weber: 1958). If the Italian capitalists of the early modern city-states are conceived of as manifesting the capitalist spirit (i.e. Trevor-Roper: 1965), then Weber's correlation between capitalists and Puritans is based on a restricted sample and fails to substantiate his theory. In so far as this is true, Weber's empirical data were overselected by his theoretical reference to the Protestant ethic.

In Smelser's famous study, *Social Change in the Industrial Revolution* (1959), a similar distance between general theory and empirical indicator can be found. In his theory, Smelser argues that shifts in familial role divisions, not industrial upheavals *per se*, were responsible for the radical protest activities by English workers which developed in the 1820s. In his narrative historical account, Smelser describes fundamental shifts in family structure as having occurred in the sequence he has suggested. His specific presentations of archival data (Smelser: 1959, pp. 188–99) seem to indicate, however, that these family disturbances did not develop until one or two decades later. Smelser's theoretical concern with the family overdetermined the presentation of his narrative history (and his archival data in turn underdetermined his theory).[5]

---

[5] It demonstrates Smesler's conscientiousness as an historical researcher that he himself presented data that, as it were, went beyond his own theory (in this regard, see Walby 1986). This is not usually the case, for the overdetermination of data by theory usually makes coutervailing data invisible, not only to social scientists them-

In Skocpol's (1979) more recent effort at documenting her historical and comparative theory, the same kind of overdetermination is exercised by a very different theory. Skocpol (p. 18) proposes to take an 'impersonal and nonsubjective viewpoint' on revolutions, which gives causal significance only to 'the institutionally determined situations and relations of groups'. Her search is for the empirical data of revolution and the only a-priority she acknowledges is her commitment to the comparative method (pp. 33–40). When Skocpol acknowledges at various points, however, that local traditions and rights do play a role (e.g. pp. 62, 138), and that political leadership and ideology must (however briefly) be essayed (pp. 161–73), the theoretical overdetermination of her data becomes apparent. Her structural preoccupations have led her to ignore the entire intellectual and cultural context of revolution.[6]

Empirical underdetermination and theoretical overdetermination go hand in hand. From the most specific factual statements up to the most abstract generalizations, social science is essentially contestable. Every conclusion is open to argument by reference to supra-empirical considerations. Here is the specifically social-scientific version of the thematization which, Habermas (1984) has shown, must lay behind every effort at rational argument. Every kind of social scientific statement is subject to the demand for justification by reference to general principles. In other words, I need not – and social scientists as a community simply will not – limit an argument against Blau to an empirical demonstration that structural considerations are only one of several which determine outmarriage; I can, instead, demonstrate that the very stipulation of such structural causation rests upon presuppositions about action which are of an excessively rationalistic kind. In considering Lieberson's work I can bracket the empirical question of the relation between education and objective opportunity in a similar way. Instead, I can try to suggest through discursive argument that Lieberson's exclusive focus on the heritage of slavery reflects ideological considerations and a prior commitment to models generated by conflict theory. In turn, Smelser's work can be effectively criticized in terms of logical adequacy or by demonstrating that his early functionalist model over-emphasizes socialization. And Skocpol's argument – without any reference to empirical material – can be negatively evaluated for the implausible manner in which it limits 'purposive theories' – which she applauds – to the instrumental model of purposive rationality that her theory implies.

To make such arguments – indeed, merely to engage in the kind of discussion in which I have just engaged – is to engage in discourse, not explanation. As Seidman (1986) has emphasized, discourse does not imply the abandonment of claims to truth. Truth claims, after all, need not be limited to the criterion of testable empirical validity (Habermas 1984). Each

---

selves but often to their critics.

[6] Sewell (1985) has forcefully demonstrated this gap in Skocpol's data for the French case.

level of supra-empirical discourse has embedded within it distinctive criteria of truth. These criteria go beyond empirical adequacy to claims about the nature and consequences of presuppositions, the stipulation and adequacy of models, the consequences of ideologies, the meta-implications of models, and the connotations of definitions. Insofar as they become explicit, they are efforts, in short, to rationalize and systematize the intuitively grasped complexities of social analysis and social life. Current disputes between interpretative and causal methodologies, utilitarian and normative conceptions of action, equilibrium and conflict models of societies, radical and conservative theories of change – these are far more than empirical arguments. They reflect efforts by sociologists to articulate criteria for evaluating the 'truth' of different non-empirical domains.

It is no wonder that the discipline's response to important works bears so little resemblance to the neat and confined responses that advocates of the 'logic of science' suggest. Skocpol's *States and Social Revolutions*, for example, has been evaluated at every level of the sociological continuum. The book's presuppositions, ideology, model, method, definitions, concepts and, yes, even its facts have been clarified, disputed, and praised in turn. At stake are the truth criteria Skocpol has employed to justify her positions at each of these levels. Very little of the disciplinary response to this work has involved controlled testing of its hypotheses or the reanalysis of its data. Decisions about the validity of Skocpol's structural approach to revolution certainly will not be decided on these grounds.[7]

[7] In this section I have illustrated the overdetermination of social science by theory, and its underdetermination by fact, by discussing single important works. It could also be illustrated by examining specific 'empirical' subfields. In social science, even the most narrowly defined empirical subfields are subject to tremendous discursive argument. Discussion at a recent national conference on the state of disaster research (Symposium on Social Structure and Disaster: Conception and Measurement, College of William and Mary, Williamsburg, Virginia, May 1986), for example, revealed that even in this very concrete field there is vast disagreement simply about the empirical object of study. 'What is a disaster?' is disputed and argued about by the field's leading researchers. Some argue for a criterion related to objective and calculable facts but disagree over whether these costs should be related to the geographical expanse of the event, the numbers of people involved, or the financial costs of rebuilding. Others argue for criteria that are more subjective but disagree over whether it is the larger society's consensus that a social problem has occurred that is decisive or the perceptions of the victims themselves. Given the extent of such conflict over the simple empirical referent of the field, it is not surprising that sharp discursive disputes rage about every level of the scientific continuum. There are presuppositional disagreements on individual versus social levels of analysis and about economizing versus interpreting actors; there are ideological struggles over whether disaster research should be governed by broad responsibilities to the community or by narrower professional concerns; there are many disputes over definitions, e.g., what is an 'organization?', and over the very value of exercises in definition and taxonomies. For a good summary of these disputes see Drabek 1986 and forthcoming.

When I began this section, I suggested that the proportion of classics to contemporaries is so much greater in social than natural science because endemic disagreement makes the background assumptions of social science more explicit. It is this obvious quality of background assumptions, in turn, that makes discourse so central a quality of social scientific debate. What remains is to explain why this discursive form of argument so often takes a 'classical' turn. The existence of generalized, non-empirical debate does not logically imply any privileged position for earlier works. None the less, the very conditions which make discourse so prominent also make the classics central. There are two reasons for this centrality: the functional, and the intellectual or scientific.

Because disagreement is so rife in social science, serious problems of mutual understanding arise. Without some baseline of minimal understanding, however, communication is impossible. For disagreement to be possible in a coherent, ongoing and consistent way, there must be some basis for a cultural relationship. This can exist only if the participants in a disagreement have a fair idea of what one another is talking about.

This is where the classics come in. The functional necessity for classics develops because of the need for integrating the field of theoretical discourse. By integration, I do not mean cooperation and equilibrium but rather the boundary maintenance, or closure, which allows systems to exist (Luhmann: 1984). It is this functional demand that explains the formation of disciplinary boundaries which from an intellectual standpoint often seem arbitrary. It is the disciplines of social science, and the schools and traditions of which they are composed, which have classics.

To mutually acknowledge a classic is to have a common point of reference. A classic reduces complexity (cf. Luhmann: 1979). It is a symbol which condenses – 'stands for' – a range of diverse general commitments. Condensation, it seems to me, has at least four functional advantages.

In the first place, of course, it simplifies, and thereby facilitates, theoretical discussion. It does so by allowing a very small number of works to substitute for – to represent by a stereotyping or standardizing process – the myriad of finely-graded formulations which are produced in the course of contingent intellectual life. When we discuss the central issues which affect social science in classical terms, we are sacrificing the ability to embrace this finely-graded specificity. We gain, however, something very important. By speaking in terms of the classics, we can be relatively confident that those whom we address will at least know whereof we speak, even if they do not recognize in our discussion their own particular and unique position. It is for this reason that if we wish to make a critical analysis of capitalism we will be more than likely to draw from Marx's work. Similarly, if we wish to evaluate the variety of critical analyses of capitalism which exist today, we will probably typify them by comparing them to Marx's original. Only by so doing can we be relatively confident that others will be able to follow, and perhaps be persuaded by, our ideological and cognitive judgements.

The second functional advantage is that classics allow generalized commitments to be argued without the necessity for making the criteria for their adjudication explicit. Since such criteria are very difficult to formulate, and virtually impossible to gain agreement upon, this concretizing function of the classics is very important. Rather than having to define equilibrium and the nature of systems, one can argue about Parsons, about the relative 'functionality' of his early and later works, about whether his theory (whatever that may be precisely) can actually explain conflict in the real world. Or, rather than explicitly exploring the advantages of an affective or normative perspective on human action, one can argue that such a perspective was, in fact, actually taken by Durkheim's most important works.

The third functional advantage is an ironic one. Because a common classical medium of communication is taken for granted, it becomes possible not to acknowledge the existence of generalized discourse at all. Thus, because the importance of the classics is accepted without argument, it is possible for a social scientist to begin an empirical study – in, for example, industrial sociology – by discussing the treatment of labour in Marx's early writings. While it would be quite illegitimate for him to suggest that non-empirical considerations about human nature, let alone utopian speculations about human possibility, form the baseline for industrial sociology, this is precisely what he has implicitly acknowledged by referring to Marx's work.

Finally, because the condensation provided by the classics gives them such privileged power, reference to the classics becomes important for purely strategic and instrumental reasons. It is in the immediate self-interest of every ambitious social scientist and every rising school to be legitimated *vis-à-vis* the classical founders. Even if no genuine concern for the classics exists, they still must be criticized, re-read, or rediscovered if the discipline's normative criteria for evaluation are to be challenged anew.

These are the functional, or extrinsic, reasons for the privileged status accorded by social science to a small and select number of earlier works. But there are, I believe, intrinsic, genuinely intellectual reasons as well. By intellectual, I mean that certain works are given a classical position because they make a singular and continuing contribution to the science of society. My argument here begins from the proposition that the more generalized a scientific discussion, the less cumulative it can be. Why? Because, while generalized commitments are subject to truth criteria, it is impossible to anchor these criteria in an unequivocal way. Generalized evaluations are sustained less by qualities in the object world – upon which minimum agreement can often be reached – than by the relative tastes and preferences of a particular cultural community. Generalized discourse, then, relies on qualities of personal sensibility – aesthetic, interpretative, philosophical, observational – which are not progressive. In this sense, variations in social science reflect not linear accumulation – an issue which can be calculated temporally – but the essentially random distribution of human ability. Producing great social science is a gift which, like the capacity for creating great art (cf. Nisbet: 1976), varies trans-historically between different societies and different human beings.[8]

Dilthey wrote that 'life as a starting-point and abiding context provides the first basic feature of the structure of the human studies; for they rest on experience, understanding and knowledge of life' (1976, p. 183). Social science, in other words, cannot simply be learned by imitating an empirical problem-solution. Because its object is life, it depends on the scientist's own ability to understand life. It depends on idiosyncratic abilities to experience, to understand and to know. There are, it seems to me, at least three different ways in which such personal knowledge distinguishes itself.

1   Through the interpretation of states of mind.

Any generalization about the structure or causes of a social phenomenon – an institution, religious movement or political event – depends upon some conception of the motives involved. To understand motives accurately, however, requires highly-developed capacities for empathy, insight and interpretation. All other things being equal, the works of social scientists who manifest such capacities to the highest degree become classics to which those with more mundane capacities must refer for insight into the subjective linclinations of humankind. The strength of Durkheim's later 'religious sociology' depends, to an important degree, on his remarkable ability to intuit the cultural meaning and psychological import of ritual behaviour among the Australian Aborigines. Similarly, it is not Goffman's inheritance of interactionist theory or his empirical methods which has made his theorizing so paradigmatic for the micro-analysis of social behaviour; it is his extraordinary sensitivity about the nuances of human behaviour. Few con-temporaries will ever be able to achieve Goffman's level of insight. His works are classical because one must return to them in order to experience

[8] It is idiosyncracy of the capacity for creativity, of course, that is the usual reason cited for the centrality of classics in the arts. In his writing on the formation of canonical literary works, however, Kermode (1985) has shown that this view attributes too much to accurate information about a work and too little to uninformed group opinion and 'irrational' value commitments. The artistic eminence of Botticelli, for example, was re-established in late nineteenth century circles on grounds that have since turned out to be highly spurious. His defenders used arguments whose vagueness and indirection could not, in themselves, have justified his art on aesthetic grounds. In this sense, Kermode introduces functional reasons for canonical works. Indeed, he concludes that 'it is hard to see how the normal operation of learned institutions ... can manage without them' (1985: p. 78). At the same time, Kermode insists that some intrinsic dimension for canonization remains. Thus, while he acknowledges that 'all interpretations are erroneous', he argues that 'some, in relation to their ultimate purpose, are good nevertheless' (1985: p. 91). Why? 'Good enough interpretation is what encourages or enables certain necessary forms of attention. What matters ... is that ways of inducing such forms of attention should continue to exist, even if they are all, in the end, dependent on opinion.' The notion of 'good enough' will be historicized in my discussion of sociological arguments about classics below.

and to understand just what the nature of interactional motivation really is.

2   *Through the reconstruction of the empirical world.*

Because disagreement on background issues makes even the objective empirical referents of social science open to doubt, the complexity of the object world cannot here be reduced via the matrix of consensual disciplinary controls. Hence the social scientist's singular capacity for selection and reconstruction becomes correspondingly important. Here, once again, one finds the same kind of creative and idiosyncratic capacity for representation typically associated with art. As Daw writes about the classics, 'through the creative power of their thought ... they reveal the historical and human continuity which makes their experience representative of ours' (1978, p. 366).

It is not only insightfulness but that evanescent thing, 'quality of mind', upon which the capacity for representation depends. Thus, contemporaries may be able to list the ideal-typical qualities of urban life, but few will be able to understand or represent anonymity and its implications with the richness or vivacity of Simmel himself. Has any Marxist since Marx been able to produce an economic-political history with the subtlety, complexity and apparent conceptual integration of *The Eighteenth Brumaire of Louis Bonaparte*? Indeed, has any social scientist been able to communicate the nature of 'commodities' as well as Marx himself in the first chapter of *Capital*? How many contemporary analyses of feudal society approach the complex and systematic account of economic, religious and political inter-relations which Weber produces in the chapters on patrimonialism and feudalism in *Economy and Society*? This is not to say that in significant respects our knowledge of these phenomena has not surpassed Marx's and Durkheim's own. It is to say, however, that in certain critical respects our knowledge has not. Indeed, the particular ideas I have just cited were so unusual that they simply could not be understood – much less critically evaluated or incorporated – by Marx's and Weber's contemporaries. It has taken generations to recapture, piecemeal, the structure of these arguments, with their intended and unintended implications. This, of course, is exactly what may be said for the most important aesthetic works.

3   *Through the formulation of moral and ideological evaluations.*

The more general a social scientific statement, the more it must provide compelling self-reflection on the meaning of social life. This is its ideological function in the broadest sense of that term. Even if such an ideological reference were undesirable – which in my view it is not – it would not be possible to cleanse even the most scrupulous of social scientific practice of its effects. Effective ideology, moreover (Geertz: 1964), depends not only on a finely-tuned social sensibility but on an aesthetic ability to condense and articulate 'ideological reality' through appropriate rhetorical tropes. Ideological statements, in other words, can assume a classical status as well. The soulless character of rationalized modernity is not just reflected in Weber's concluding pages of *The Protestant Ethic*; it is created by it. To understand rationalized modernity, one cannot merely observe it: one must return to Weber's early work in order to appreciate and experience it once again. Similarly, what is oppressive and suffocating about modernity may never be quite so firmly established as in Marcuse's *One Dimensional Man*.

These functional and intellectual considerations make the classics – not just generalized discourse *per se* – central to the practice of social science. It is because of these considerations that earlier works are accorded a privileged status, that they are so venerated that the meaning attributed to them is often considered equivalent to contemporary scientific knowledge itself. Discourse about a work so privileged becomes a legitimate form of rational scientific dispute; investigation into the 'new meaning' of such texts becomes a legitimate way to point scientific work in a new direction. Which is to say that once a work is 'classicized', its interpretation becomes a key to scientific argument. Indeed, because classics are central to social science, interpretation must be considered as one major form of theoretical argument.

Merton was quite right to suggest that social scientists tend to merge the history and systematics of sociological theory. He was also thoroughly justified in attributing this merging to 'efforts to straddle scientific and humanistic orientations' (Merton: 1967a, p. 29). He was wrong, however, to suggest that the merging, or the straddling which produced it, are pathological. In this sense Merton has not himself been empirical enough. From the beginning of the systematic study of society in ancient Greece, merging and straddling have been endemic to the practice of social science. To read this situation as abnormal reflects unjustified speculative preconceptions, not the empirical facts.

The first unjustified preconception is that social science is a youthful and immature enterprise in comparison to natural science, with the implication that, as it matures, it will grow increasingly to resemble the sciences of nature. I have argued, to the contrary, that there are endemic, irrepressible reasons for the divergence between natural and social science; moreover, the 'maturity' of the latter, it seems to me, has been firmly set for quite a long time. The second preconception is that social science – again, supposedly like its natural science counterpart – is a purely empirical discipline which can shed its discursive and generalized form. I have argued, however, that there is nothing to suggest that such a pristine condition will ever be achieved. Indeed, I have suggested that the science of nature upon which such hopes are modelled can itself never be separated from (usually camouflaged) commitments of an equally generalized kind.

Merton complains that 'almost all sociologists see themselves as qualified to teach and to write the "history" of sociological theory – after all they are acquainted with the classical writings of an earlier day' (1967, p. 2). This, it seems to me, is all to the good. If sociologists did not see themselves as qualified in this way, it would not be merely a 'vulgarized' history of sociology which would be eliminated, but the very practice of sociology itself![9]

Phenomenological Naivety: Why Classical Debates Must Be Deconstructed

In the preceding sections I have made a theoretical argument that the split between history and systematics cannot exist. In the section which follows, I will show empirically that it does not exist. Before doing so, however, I want to acknowledge that there is one place where the split is, after all, very real. This is in the minds of social scientists themselves. It is to this paradox that I devote the present section.

While they continually engage in discourse about classical work, social scientists – on the whole – acknowledge neither that they are doing so in order to make scientific arguments nor that in the process they are committing acts of interpretation. The question of why they are discussing the classics is rarely broached. Instead, the discussion is taken for granted as the most natural kind of professionally-sanctioned activity. As for its theoretical and interpretative character, these possibilities are rarely conceived. As far as the participants are concerned, their effort is simply one of seeing classics as they 'really' are.

This lack of self-awareness is not a reflection of theoretical naivety. To the contrary, it characterizes some of the most sophisticated interpretative discussions that social science has produced.

The most famous example is Parsons's presentation of his convergence thesis in *The Structure of Social Action* (1937). An interpretative *tour de force*, this work argued that all the major social scientific theories in the turn-of-the-century period emphasized the role of social values in the integration of society. Parsons sustained this reading by creative conceptualization and

---

[9] I should also acknowledge that there are significant ambiguities in Merton's essay which make it possible to construe his argument in significantly different ways. (I have found this to be true of his work on middle-range theory as well: see Alexander: 1982a, pp. 11–14.) For example, on the penultimate page of his essay, Merton (1967a, p. 37) suggests the following systematic 'function for the classics': 'changes in current sociological knowledge, problems, and foci of attention enable us to find new ideas in a work we had read before'. He acknowledges, moreover, that these changes could stem from 'recent developments in our own intellectual life'. This could well be read as endorsing just the kind of systematic need for presentist references to the classics (that is, for historical systematics) against which the main part of Merton's essay was written. For this reason, perhaps, Merton immediately qualifies this suggestion with a new version of his empiricist, accumulationist argument. It is because 'each new generation accumulates its own repertoire of knowledge' that 'it comes to see much that is "new" in earlier works'.

dense citation, but what is so striking is that he does not acknowledge that it is an interpretation at all! He insists that he has conducted an empirical inquiry that is 'as much a question of fact as any other' (Parsons: 1937, p. 697). Indeed, rather than being the result of new questions being asked by Parsons himself, it is changes in the object world that have produced Parsons's new analysis of the classics' work. The classics discovered values, and this discovery is the new empirical datum for Parsons's scientific work. His analysis, therefore, 'has followed [largely] from their new empirical discoveries' (Parsons: 1937, p. 721). The same bracketing of theoretical intent and interpretative practice can be seen in the arguments against Parsons's position. In the Preface to *Capitalism and Modern Social Theory* (1972) Giddens presents his neo-Marxian argument as responding to empirical developments like 'recent scholarship' and the discovery of new Marxian texts. Roth (1978, pp. xxxiii–xc) claims that his anti-Parsonian reading of Weber follows from his access to until-recently untranslated sections of Weber's *Economy and Society*, just as Mitzman (1970) argues that his Marcusian re-reading of Weber proceeds from the discovery of new biographical material.

In light of what I have argued above, of course, it is clear that such empiricist self-conceptions serve to obfuscate the relativism which the very centrality of the classics implies. I want to suggest, however, that to provide this camouflage is precisely this self-conception's functional role. If those who engage in classical debates knew that their investigations – whether 'interpretative' or 'historical' – were really theoretical arguments by another name, such arguments could not succeed in reducing complexity. They would feel compelled to justify their positions through direct, systematic discourse. The same holds for empiricist self-conceptions in general, of course. If practitioners were aware and self-conscious about the degree to which their work was guided by presuppositions and the need to reinforce theoretical schools, it would be more difficult to engage in long-term, fruitful theoretical work.

By definition, in other words, social scientists have to adopt in relation to their classics what Husserl (e.g. 1977) called the naive attitude. Immersed in classical formulations and disciplined by what they take to be their legacies, social scientists cannot realize that it is they themselves, through their theoretical interests and their theoretical intentions, who make texts classical and give to each classical text its contemporary meaning. By complaining that the 'concept of the history of theory' which pervades social science 'is in fact neither history nor systematics but a poorly thought out hybrid', Merton himself an empiricist, has once again not been nearly empirical enough. This hybrid, which has for so long been essential to social science, must of necessity be poorly thought out.

I have argued that it is because they express their systematic ambitions through such historical discussions that social scientists need classics. It is this scientific 'intention', in the strict phenomenological sense, which creates the reality of the classics for social scientific life. Husserl showed that the objectivity of social life – its 'realness' *vis-à-vis* the actor – rests upon the actor's ability to bracket, to make invisible to his own consciousness, his intentional creation of objectivity. Similarly, in the discussion of the classics the intentionality of social scientists is hidden not just from outsiders but usually from the actors themselves. The intentions which make the classics what they are – theoretical interests and interpretative practices – are placed in phenomenological brackets. It follows, then, that to explore these theoretical interests and interpretative practices is to exercise what Husserl called the phenomenological reduction. Rather than acceding to common-sense practice and bracketing subjective intention, we must engage in the scientific practice of bracketing the 'objectivity' of the classics themselves. This is a reduction because it seeks to demonstrate that, at any given moment, the 'classics' can be seen as projections of the theoretical and interpretative interests of the actors involved. It is because they can be so reduced that the split between history and systematics does not exist.

Derrida, among others building upon Husserl, has suggested that every text is an intentional construction, not a reflection of some reality. Reflection theory is based on the notion of presence, that a given text can contain – can make present – within itself the key elements of the reality to which it refers, indeed, that there is a reality which is itself present in some ultimate way. If intentionality is acknowledged, however, then it is absence as much as presence which determines the nature of any text. Every description of reality must select from it; by leaving certain elements out it produces not just the 'presences' of what it includes but the absences of what it excludes. The myth of the present text, Derrida suggests, becomes the ideology of the text *qua* text. Texts are considered to be legitimate because they can be trusted to be reflections of the events or ideas they report. If texts rest upon absences, however, they cannot be accepted at face value. It is because they do rest on absences that texts must be deconstructed. 'To "deconstruct" philosophy', Derrida writes at one point, is not only to investigate the history of its key concepts but to determine, from a position which is 'external' to the writer's own, 'what this history has been able to conceal or forbid, constituting itself as history through this repression in which it has a stake' (Derrida: 1981, pp. 6–7, altered translation).

If the centrality of the classics is to be demonstrated, social scientific discussions about the classics must be deconstructed. Only if the subtle interplay between absence and presence is understood can the theoretical function of the classics be seen, much less the interpretative practice through which this theorizing proceeds.

Interpretation of the Classics as Theoretical Argument: Talcott Parsons and his Critics in the Post-war Period

It is possible to conceive sociological theory in the period extending roughly from the Second World War to the early 1980s as possessing a relatively coherent form (Alexander: 1986). The beginning of this period was marked by the emergence of structural-functional theory, and until at least the late 1960s this approach exercised a certain dominance over the scientific field. As early as the late 1950s and early 1960s, however, significant challenges to functionalist theory had developed. By the mid-1970s, functionalism had diminished and its one-time challengers had become dominant tendencies. By the early 1980s, these established orientations had themselves begun to come under scrutiny. At the present time, an entirely new theoretical field may well be in the process of emerging; it may certainly be said that the 'coherent form' of the last forty years is in the process of breaking down.

That this theoretical movement has provided the framework within which 'normal' empirical social science has been conducted is an assumption for all that follows, but I will not try to demonstrate it here (see, e.g., Alexander: forthcoming, 1987). What I do want to argue is that this systematic theoretical movement has informed, and been informed by, far-reaching arguments over the nature and meaning of sociology's classical works.

Throughout the period of the First World War, of course, European theory played a dominant role. In the inter-war period, for a variety of social and intellectual reasons, the locus of sociology began to shift away from Europe toward the United States. In the United States before the Second World War, the Chicago School and institutionalist, quasi-Marxist theorizing played the significant roles. The emphases here were individual interaction, group conflict and the ecological/material environment, and the classics which informed them were American pragmatists like Cooley and Mead, institutionalists like Veblen and Europeans like Simmel. Structural-functionalism emerged against these traditions. It depended not only on the writings of Parsons but also on the work of an unusually wide range of talented students, students whose work had already begun to exert influence in the 1930s. In what follows, however, I will concentrate on Parsons as the leader of the tradition.

It is true, of course, that there were extra-scientific, social reasons which contributed to the positive reception of functionalist work. In the first instance, however, this work was evaluated and received on what were considered to be scientific grounds. As the empiricist perspective would have it, these grounds included the theoretical scope and explanatory power of Parsons's work. But it was not limited to that. Indeed, Parsons did not rest his claim to scientific dominance on his systematic scientific work alone. He rested it on the authority of the classical texts. He argued that the classical texts directed scientific activity toward the kind of systematic theorizing which he himself devised.

When Parsons began his theoretical career in the 1920s, he was himself committed to the blend of pragmatism, evolutionism, and institutionalism which characterized the American tradition (Wearne: 1985). In the work which began the ascent of functionalist theory, however, the classics associated with this tradition were notably absent. In *The Structure of Social Action* (1937), Parsons claimed to define the most important results of the previous

generation of sociological theorizing. Not only were the American pragmatists and institutionalists missing, but so were Simmel and Marx. They
would not be found by systematic sociological theory for many years. The
'presences' in Parsons's reconstruction were Marshall, Pareto, Durkheim
and Weber. Parsons claimed that it was they – and above all Durkheim
and Weber – who formed the classical tradition from which all future
sociology must draw.

It was not only this selection from the field of earlier texts but his
construction of those selected that made Parsons's 1937 work so important.
He argued, somewhat ambiguously to be sure (Alexander: 1983), that these
sociologists had emphasized cultural values and social integration. Because
of the sharpness of his conceptual insight and the density of his textual
argument, Parsons was able to defend this interpretation in an extremely
powerful way. It was his interpretative practice, in other words, not – as
he himself had suggested (see above) – the empirical nature of his discovery,
that made his argument about the classics so successful. This interpretation,
in turn, was informed by theoretical interests. It is only in retrospect that
it has become apparent to the sociological community how incomplete was
Parsons's reading, how it skewed the interpretation of these classical authors
toward the very kind of systematic theoretical argument which Parsons had
later claimed that it in turn justified.

In his crucial discussion of Durkheim's first major work, for example,
Parsons construed the fifth chapter of Book 1 of *The Division of Labor in
Society* – the now famous discussion of the non-contractual elements of
contract – as an argument for normative and cultural control in economic
life. It can be argued, to the contrary (Alexander: 1982b, pp. 124–40), that
Durkheim's intention in this chapter was to underscore the need for a
relatively autonomous, regulatory state. Furthermore, Parsons entirely
ignored Book 2 of *The Division of Labor*, in which Durkheim presented an
ecological, even materialist analysis of the causes of social change. Parsons
also suggested that Durkheim's last work, *The Elementary Forms of Religious
Life*, represented an idealist deviation from the multidimensional treatment
of solidarity which had emerged in his preceding writing. Because Parsons
actually overlooked large parts of this preceding writing, however, he was
hardly in a position to draw this conclusion. It seems much more likely
that Durkheim's later writings were of a piece. If so, the idealism which
Parsons claimed to be a deviation would be broadly characteristic of Durkheim's most mature work. Parsons's hasty reading had the effect of allowing
the one-sided normative emphasis of the last twenty years of Durkheim's
work to escape largely unscathed.

Parsons's interpretation of Durkheim – not despite but because of its
luminous quality – was informed, then, by the theoretical interests which,
in the period after the publication of *Structure*, served to establish the major
lines of functionalist work. This was even more true of his analysis of Weber.
In the first place, Parsons ignored the unresolved tension between normative
and instrumental theorizing which permeates even Weber's sociology of

religion. More significantly, however, he failed even to recognize the substantive political sociology Weber developed in *Economy and Society*: the
historical discussions of the transition from patriarchal household to feudal
and patrimonial systems which revolve almost exclusively around anti-
normative considerations. Only because he ignored this major segment of
Weber's work could Parsons construe Weber's political sociology as focusing
on the problem of legitimacy in moral and symbolic terms.

In the years following the Second World War Parsons's selection and
interpretation of the classics came to be widely accepted. His veneration for
these classical writers was personal and unabashed, and he was instrumental
in convincing his contemporaries to feel the same way. He insisted, at
every step in his subsequent theoretical development, that functional theory
followed logically from the path which these forefathers had laid out. Indeed,
with each new phase of his later theorizing Parsons carefully 'revisited'
Weber and Durkheim, and with each re-reading he found himself able to
understand the promise and problems of their work in terms of the newer
functional framework which was about to appear.

In the long Introduction to his joint translation of Weber's *Theory of Social
and Economic Organization*, Parsons (1947) found that Weber had correctly
emphasized the value context of markets and the cultural backdrop for
authority, but that his theory of bureaucracy had over-emphasized hierarchy
because it neglected socialization and professional norms. These were, of
course, the very subjects of *The Social System* (Parsons: 1951), which appeared
four years later. Similarly, in the midst of his own analysis of the internal
differentiation of social systems, Parsons investigated Durkheim's approach
to social integration (Parsons: 1967). He found that Durkheim was much
more concerned with the differentiation of goals, norms and values than he
had realized in the interpretation of thirty years before. Once again, when
Parsons began the task of conceptualizing an evolutionary theory of social
change, he demonstrated through an extensive investigation of Weber's
sociology of religion that Weber had an evolutionary approach as well, a
point that Bellah (1959), one of Parsons's ablest students, had demonstrated
for Durkheim several years before.

Finally, there is the case of the theorist whose classical status Parsons
came to recognize only at a later date, and whose earlier absence, therefore,
he urgently sought to correct. In Parsons's mature functionalist theorizing,
which first appeared in 1951 with the publication of *The Social System*,
socialization played a major role, and he approached the phenomenon in a
psychoanalytic way. In his Preface to later editions of *The Structure of Social
Action*, Parsons expressed his regret that he had not included Freud in that
selection of classical writers. Indeed, not doing so had by the 1950s become
dangerously anomalous. Because the classics are so central, Parsons's failure
to provide an authoritative discussion of Freud left his psychoanalytic
functionalism open to serious challenge. Anti-functionalist Freudians could
argue that psychoanalytic theory had nothing to do with socialization, that,
to the contrary, it emphasized the disorganization of the personality and its

rebellion against civilization. Beginning in 1952, Parsons (1964a; 1964b; 1955) devoted a series of essays to demonstrating that Freud saw object introjection as the basis for personality development; object introjection, of course, was simply value internalization by another name.

When the theoretical and empirical movement against functionalism emerged in the late 1950s, Parsons's construction of the classics became one of its primary objects. Again, this challenge was not a self-conscious effort at deconstruction, that is, it was not a movement which revealed the theoretical interests behind classical argument as such. It was, rather, an argument aimed for the most part simply at 'setting the historical record straight'. In so far as theoretical interests and interpretative strategies were acknowledged, moreover, they were attributed only to Parsons himself; toward their own investigations his challengers had, of necessity, to keep their naive attitude intact.

It is a testimony to Parsons's power that in the early stages of this process the most gaping absences in his classical construction received the least attention. Hinkle (1963; 1980) defended the legitimacy of early American theory, both institutional and pragmatic, suggesting that it be seen as a sophisticated body of theory in its own right. Yet this argument can actually be seen as defending Parsons's theoretical construction by shoring up his construction of history, as the title to Hinkel's early article – 'Antecedents of the Action Orientation in American Sociology before 1935' – suggests. Coser argued much more aggressively against Parsons's selectivity in his doctoral dissertation on the conflict orientation of early American sociology, pointing to its problem orientation and institutionalist theory. Only a brief summary of this argument, however, ever appeared in print (Coser: 1956, pp. 15–31).

Levine's 1957 doctoral dissertation compared Simmel and Parsons and implied, at the very least, that a rough parity existed between Parsons and an important earlier author whom he had completely ignored. For more than twenty years, however, this dissertation was also unpublished. When it finally saw the light of day – in an offset series devoted to unpublished dissertations and out-of-print books – Levine (1980) made the implications of his introduction of Simmel more critical and explicit. In a new Introduction, he underscored Parsons's decision to drop from the final manuscript of *The Structure of Social Action* a chapter which he had completed on Simmel. This demonstrated, in Levine's view, that Parsons had selected among the classics in a manner to support his 'biased', a priori theoretical interest. Parsons excluded Simmel because to include him would have spread an anti-functionalist influence. While this challenge to absence is justified, of course, what Levine makes of it is not. His argument that simply to include Simmel would be to present an anti-functionalist view rests on the empiricist assumption that Simmel's work has an unequivocal meaning.

The most conspicuous absence in Parsons's construction, however, the figure of Karl Marx, did not receive concerted attention in this early phase. My argument below suggests, indeed, that it was only through disputation within the confines of the Parsonian pantheon and under the guise of 'conflict theory' that Marx first began to be discussed. Only after functionalism had been more or less succeeded by its challengers was Marx explicitly brought into the classical fore. When, in 1968, Zeitlin turned Parsons's construction upside down by arguing that his classical figures were conservatives whose work could only be understood as reactions against Marx, his argument still attracted relatively little attention.[10]

What did become the focus of the emerging anti-functionalist movement was the more subtle absences in Parsons's interpretations of Durkheim, Weber and Freud. The primary theoretical interest here was in restoring a more power-oriented, economically-centred sociological theory; a secondary interest was in restoring the importance of contingent action against what was conceived to be Parsons's focus on collective order as such. Thus, in the mid-1950s, Gouldner (1958) edited the first English translation of Durkheim's *Socialism and Saint-Simon*, a work of the middle period to which Parsons had never referred. Gouldner claimed that this work demonstrated the existence of a radical and materialist Durkheim which was totally at odds with the one of functionalist lore. That his interpretative practice was crude and unsubstantiated compared to Parsons's no doubt explains the book's relative lack of success, but the theoretical interests behind Gouldner's claim are what is important. Giddens (1972) later made the same point in a much more turbulent period and through a more sophisticated interpretation. His argument that Durkheim converged rather than diverged with Marx's economic and institutional focus – indeed, that Durkheim was never concerned with the Parsonian 'problem of order' at all – played a significant role in the movement away from functionalist theory at that later time. In fact, in the process of elaborating the neo-Marxist argument for structural analysis to which he was devoted at the time, Giddens flatly denied Parsons's developmental view of Durkheim's work; inverting Parsons's analysis, he downgraded the *The Elementary Forms* and argued that it was *The Division of Labor* which actually represented Durkheim's most important work. Martindale (1960) and Bendix (1971) argued against Parsons's voluntaristic interpretation in a different way. As Weberians who emphasized power, political movements and contingency, they insisted that Durkheim actually represented an organicist, anti individualist approach.

It was Bendix, of course, who devoted himself to demonstrating that the 'real' Weber had practically nothing in common with the normative portrait to be found in Parsonian work. Bendix claimed that Parsons's Weber rested upon idealist mistranslations of key concepts, for example Parson's characterization of *Herrschaft* as 'imperative coordination' rather than as the 'domination' which a more literal German translation would indicate. He

---

[10] Need I emphasize here that I am only talking about discussion in the discipline of sociology as it is rather narrowly defined? In France and Germany, of course, Marx had never stopped being the focus of widespread intellectual debate. One need think here only of Sartre and the Frankfurt School.

also argued that Parsons underplayed Weber's political sociology and his writings about patrimonial control. For Bendix, this argument over Weber was simply the other side of his effort to construct a historically-specific comparative sociology (e.g. Bendix: 1978). It has been the lifework of Bendix's student, Guenther Roth, to demonstrate this alternative Weber in a more scholarly and detailed way. That there was a clear theoretical ambition behind Roth's (1978) scholarly reconstruction of Weber's *Economy and Society* is demonstrated by his emphasis, in the long Introduction, on the conflict-group orientation of Weber's work. At about the same time, Coser's student, Arthur Mitzman (1970), suggested that, far from being oriented toward values and integration, Weber's mature work must be viewed as a Nietzschean struggle against rational value domination. Earlier, Wrong (1961) had made this revision of Parsons's Freud in a much more explicit way. He had argued that Parsons profoundly under-estimated the emphasis on repression in Freud's conception of the super-ego and the autonomous capacity for anti-social rebellion which Freud gave to the id.

But the mounting effort to break free from the hegemony of functionalist theorizing involved more than finding new ways to interpret the classics and new classics themselves. It also involved the development of theoretical schools which could provide a systematic alternative to what were conceived as functionalism's characteristic emphases. Thus there emerged conflict theory, exchange theory, symbolic interactionism, ethnomethodology and a specifically sociological form of humanistic or radical social theory. These schools had to define their own classics, and they did so not only in opposition to Parsons's interpretations but in opposition to Parsons himself. For in the course of the post-war period which marked Parsons's rise, his own work had become classical in a contemporary sense. It had become enveloped in a numinous charisma such that Parsons's statements came to be venerated in themselves, to be accepted not for their theoretical power but because they were his and his alone. In response, the interpretation of Parsons's work became a minor industry (see Alexander: 1983, pp. 289–310), for to prove that Parsons did or did not say something became equivalent to making a theoretical argument *per se*.

The schools which developed in the wake of the anti-functionalist challenges, therefore, had a double interpretative task. They had to find new classics and they had to get rid of this newly-classicized contemporary. In the establishment of every new theoretical school we can see this double movement. Parsons and the older classics had to be separated. This was accomplished, first, by arguing that the classics were not what Parsons said they were and, second, by arguing that Parsons was not what he was put up to be. When Pope (1973) and his colleagues (Cohen, Hazelrigg and Pope: 1975) called, in a series of widely-discussed essays, for 'de-Parsonizing' the classics, this double-sided intention was neatly expressed.

Consider, for example, the emergence of conflict theory. The key texts in this movement were Rex's *Key Problems in Sociological Theory* (1961), Dahrendorf's *Class and Class Conflict in Industrial Society* (1959) and Coser's *The*

Functions of Social Conflict (1956). In order to argue that systematic sociological theory should be centred on conflict, they had to argue that functionalist theory centred on stability. Rather than arguing this simply at the level of systematic theory or empirical work, each also made the argument through an interpretation of the 'meaning' of Parsons's work. On the one hand, the theoretical interest they brought to this task allowed significant weaknesses in Parsons's work to be revealed; on the other hand, it merely produced a new semiotic field of absences to replace Parsons's own.

Conflict readings of Parsons ignored, for example, the whole series of 'functionalist' essays devoted to power and change which Parsons had published between 1938 and 1950, and, more significantly perhaps, the fact that his theory had turned directly to the problem of change after the publication of *The Social System* in 1951. This destruction of Parsons was symbiotically tied to the construction of Weber and Marx. Rex lauded Marx as an anti-superstructural theorist of conflict; Dahrendorf produced a Weber who was interested only in a theory of coercive power. Coser's construction of the classics differed because he claimed Simmel and Freud for the master theorists of conflict and change. One year before the publication of Coser's book, the groundwork for this argument had been laid in the English-speaking world by Bendix, Parsons's critic from the Weberian side, who published a translation of Simmel's *Conflict and the Web of Group Affiliations* (1955). The most important systematic theorist of the conflict school, Collins (e.g. 1968; 1975; 1986), has continued to challenge the classicization of Parsons and to restructure the older classical tradition in much the same way.

Exchange theory made its first appearance with Homans's (1958) contribution to the issue of the *American Journal of Sociology* commemorating the anniversary of Simmel's birth. After Homas elaborated the systematics of this theory in *Social Behavior* (1961), he defended its legitimacy through reinterpreting the reigning contemporary classic in his presidential address to the American Sociological Association three years later. This address, 'Bringing Men Back In' (Homans: 1964), established a reading of Parsons as 'anti human action' – and of one of his best students (Smelser) as secretly anti-Parsonian – which became the single most important polemical justification for individualistic theorizing in the years which followed. It was not until years later that the classical roots of exchange theory were established in a more positive way through arguments (e.g. Lindenberg: 1983) for the centrality of Adam Smith's political economy.

The interpretative situation of ethnomethodology was at first quite different. Both because Garfinkel's central axioms were – as for many years he was the first to admit – merely succinct paraphrases of earlier phenomenological work, and because his theoretical ambition in those early years was not yet sufficiently developed, Garfinkel (1963) tried at first to force Schütz's work into the classical pantheon beside Weber's and Parsons's. As Garfinkel's intention to create the school of ethnomethodology became explicit, however, his relation to the classics became much more complex. It was not enough to read Schütz in an individualistic way, a manner which camouflaged Schütz's sympathy for Weber's emphasis on social values. References to Schütz's work *per se* became few and far between, for ethno-methodology (Garfinkel: 1984) was in the process of being presented as emerging from empirical studies alone. At the same time, Garfinkel's interpretation of Parsons underwent an inversion. To argue for an alternative to Parsonian theory required Garfinkel to undermine Parsons's classical stature. He was forced to do so in any case, for his shifting theoretical interests caused him to see Parsons in a different way. Garfinkel now insisted that for Parsons actors were 'cultural dopes' who conformed to norms in an unthinking and uncritical way. Henceforth, those who valued the creative and rebellious elements of human action would be compelled to do 'anti-Parsonian' kinds of phenomenological work.

The same effect was produced by Blumer's (1969) scarcely-veiled polemics against Parsonian theory, which helped to resuscitate Mead as a patron for symbolic interactionism (cf. Strauss: 1964). At about the same time, other interactionists (Stone and Farberman: 1967) claimed that Durkheim's later work, far from being an endorsement of the moral order, actually pointed to a *rapprochement* with the individualist thrust of pragmatist thought.

Radical sociology gained ground, particularly in the United States, in much the same way. The key books here, both published in 1970, were Friedrichs's *A Sociology of Sociology* and Gouldner's *The Coming Crisis of Western Sociology*. Operating from within the liberal American context, neither theorist argued directly for the centrality of the classical theorist whom Parsons had left out, that is, for Marx. Instead, they argued against the ideological validity of Parsons. If Parsons could be proved to be on the side of the political Establishment, the possibilities for an alternative and radical sociology would be legitimated thereby. Thus, whereas earlier theorists (e.g. Hacker: 1961) had pointed to the tension between Parsons's supposedly organicist theories and his liberal, reformist ideals, Friedrichs tried to interpret Parsons as an ideologist of the bureaucratic–technocratic state, and Gouldner aligned him with pre-bureaucratic, individualistic capitalism. Gouldner's reinterpretation paved the way for ten years of left-oriented systematic empirical and historical work, much of which emerged in the pages of Gouldner's journal, *Theory and Society*, which tried to 'renew' sociology under the classics of conflict theory, ethnomethodology, and Gouldnerian critical theory. It was not until the end of this period that Gouldner (1980) actually tried to make Marx present in the classical pantheon in an ambitious way. It is revealing of the intimate relation between history and systematics that by the time he had composed this late work – at a time when his theoretical and ideological interests had become distinctly anti-Stalinist – Gouldner had begun to read the contemporary political implications of Parsons's work in a more sympathetically liberal way (Gouldner: 1979; 1980, pp. 355–73).

It seems fitting that the final phase of this destruction of Parsons's construction of the classics involved a historicist attack on the factual foundations of Parsons's 1937 work. This argument maintained that Parsons had distorted the classics because he had pursued a presentist method, that is, the claim was made that his readings of earlier texts were 'biased' because they had not discarded contemporary theoretical concerns in favour of a truly historical account. Jones (1977) claimed that Parsons was ignorant of Durkheim's intellectual milieu, and he suggested that knowledge of this environment revealed a theorist concerned not with general theoretical questions but with the detailed facts of Aboriginal religious life. Camic (1979) and Levine (1980) aimed closer to *Structure*'s theoretical heart. A historically responsible examination of utilitarianism, they suggested, would reveal that it was hardly the individualistic and rationalistic theory against which, Parsons had insisted, the value-oriented theories of classical sociology were correctly aimed. They argued that utilitarianism had itself been a morally-oriented theory and that for this reason Parsons's entire reconstruction of the 'advances' of the classical sociological tradition was flawed in a fundamental way. Their claim was launched, typically, under the banner of historical objectivity, and they presented their accounts as simple expositions which were without theoretical presuppositions. As Hirschman's influential intellectual history had already demonstrated (1977, pp. 108–10), however, it is thoroughly possible for an equally 'objective' investigator to read even Adam Smith's work on moral sentiments as paving the way for the individualistic rationalism of utilitarian thought. Just as with the more systematic efforts which preceded them, these historicist arguments depended on the theoretical interests which lay behind interpretation, not on a neutral reading of the historical literature itself.

With the help of these arguments over the classics, these new theoretical schools came, by the mid-1970s, to be more or less in control of generalized sociological discourse. Parsons's reconstructions no longer compelled. His absent classics had re-emerged; his present classics had been 're-presented' in significant ways. In 1972, Lukes published an intellectual biography of Durkheim which was hailed as the major interpretative work of recent times. In his apparently conscientious review of the disputes over Durkheim's work, Lukes simply failed to engage Parsons's interpretation altogether.

It was only now, when the challenge to Parsons's hegemony was nearly completed, that Marx finally emerged as a classic in his own right. Indeed, for European and younger American theorists Marx seemed the only classic to which social science need have recourse at all. The play of presence and absence in Marx's interpretations held centre stage. Humanists like Avineri (1969) and Lukacians like Ollman (1971) argued for the early Marx, but Althusser's much more systematic and demanding understanding of the centrality of the later work eventually gained wide acceptance (Althusser: 1969; Althusser and Balibar: 1970). Works like the *Grundrisse*, Marx's early draft for *Capital*, were translated and immediately subject to controversy (e.g., compare Nicolaus (1973) with McClellan (1976)[11] in terms of the light of their implications for this interpretative dispute. Whether the early or the later work held pride of place played a crucial role in determining the empirical focus – class formations or ideational superstructures, economic processes or alienation, old or new working classes – of a wide range of investigations.

In England, for example, there emerged a robust movement of empirical work called 'cultural studies' (e.g. Bennett *et al.*: 1981; Clark *et al.*: 1979; Hall *et al.*: 1980). Focusing on symbols and their relation to class and social conflict, this movement took its inspiration (see Cohen: 1980; Hall: 1981) almost entirely from classics within the Marxist tradition, from Williams's distinctively British version to Althusser's more orthodox theorizing about ideological state apparatuses. Neither Durkheim, who in Parsons's construction was the father of symbolic theory, nor Weber, nor indeed Parsons himself, was considered by these British researchers to have exemplary status. An instructive contrast can be found in the American movement of cultural analysis which had earlier crystallized around Bellah's civil religion analysis (e.g. Bellah and Hammond: 1980). Because it had been derived from Durkheim and Parsons, it differed from the British tradition in fundamental empirical, ideological and theoretical ways. Few contrasts provide more compelling evidence for the central force of classical works.

Not only had Parsons's constructions been overthrown but Parsons himself was increasingly absent from the classical scene. In microsociology, debates about Homans, Blumer, Goffman and Garfinkel replaced debates about Parsons; it was disputes over the meaning of their work which were now taken as the equivalents of systematic theorizing. In macrosociology, an amalgam of conflict and critical theories had so powerfully displaced Parsons that the new 'structural' approach could deny non-empirical and classical foundations altogether (e.g. Lieberson: 1980; Skocpol: 1979; Treiman: 1977). A watermark in this declassicization was reached with the publication in 1976 of Giddens's *New Rules of Sociological Method*, which declared not only that Parsons's ideas were inimical to good theory but that Parsons's classics, Durkheim and Weber, were the greatest stumbling-blocks to theoretical progress in the future. Giddens (1979; 1981) set out to develop an entirely different stable of classical figures, and eventually his broom swept out Marx as well.

[11] In 1971, McClellan, who favoured the more phenomenological Marx and the link between early and late writings, produced a translation of some 100 of the more than 800 pages of the *Grundrisse*. In his Introduction (1971, p. 12) he establishes the theoretical relevance of the text which follows: 'The continuity between the *Manuscripts* [i.e. *The Economic and Philosophical Manuscripts* of 1844, which typified the "early" Marx] and *Grundrisse* is evident ... One point in particular emphasizes this continuity: the Grundrisse is as "Hegelian" as the *Paris Manuscripts* [of 1844].' While Nicolaus's translation appeared two years later, it had the obvious scholarly virtue of being annotated and complete. That the document is, none the less, a vehicle to demonstrate his theoretical opposition to the early writings is made clear from the first page of his sixty-page Foreword, which announces that the following manuscipt 'display[s] the key elements in Marx's ... overthrow of the Hegelian philosophy' (Nicolaus: 1973, p. 1).

At this stage, however, it appears that the effort entirely to supersede Parsons's construction should be seen as a pendulum movement rather than a progressive succession. Early efforts to 'stem the tide' which were written entirely from within the Parsonian tradition – Eisenstadt (1968) on Weber, Smelser (1973) on Marx, Bellah (1973) on Durkheim – clearly failed. Yet more recent efforts to maintain not only the centrality of Parsons's classics but his distinctive concern with the cultural dimensions of their theories have been more successful (Alexander: 1982b; Habermas: 1984; Schlüchter: 1981; Seidman: 1983a; Traugott: 1985; Whimpster and Lash: 1986; Wiley: 1987). The depiction of American theory as an individualistic alternative to the collectivism of the European classics has also begun to be sharply questioned (see especially Lewis and Smith (1980), but also Joas (1985)). A movement is even underway to resuscitate the classical stature of Parsons himself. In a remarkable about face, Habermas has argued that 'no social theory can be taken seriously today which does not – at the very least – clarify its relationship to Parsons' (1981, p. 297). My own work (1983; 1985) argues in much the same way, and I suggest that a 'neo-functionalist' tradition based on a reconstructed Parsons and his classical foundations remains possible. Finally, the presuppositions of the 'new structuralism' are being explicated and criticized (Alexander: 1984; Sewell: 1985); indeed, it has begun to be argued not only by theorists (Alexander: forthcoming, 1987b; Thompson: 1985) but by important empirical analysts in this tradition (e.g. Fenton: 1984; Hunt: forthcoming, 1987; O'Connor: 1980; Traugott: 1984) that Durkheim's ideas on structure yet play a significant role.

This examination of classical debate in the post-war period has necessarily been a partial one. If space permitted, for example, the manner in which classical discussions helped to structure the empirical sub-fields of sociology would have to be explored.[12] Even within the confines of my discussion, moreover, I have had the opportunity neither to display the nuances of classical argument nor to demonstrate in a detailed manner how each discussion actually entered systematic theorizing, let alone empirical work. Despite these limitations, however, I believe that my analytical point has been substantially documented. In the major 'systematic' theoretical discussion which marked the post-war period, 'historical' argument about the meaning of classical works played a pivotal role.

In establishing a new pantheon for post-war theoretical discussion, Parsons's investigation of the classical authors was both intellectual and

---

[12] In this regard, see the promising work of Thompson. In 'Rereading the Classics: The Case of Durkheim' (1985; cf. Thompson: forthcoming), he demonstrates how in the development of the field of industrial sociology divergent interpretations of Durkheim's *Division of Labor in Society* have played a major role in specific empirical disputes. I have greatly benefited from Thompson's (1985) theoretical discussion of classical centrality, which in part responded to an earlier version of the present essay.

strategic. By immersing himself in the writings of Durkheim, Pareto and Weber, he gained genuinely new insights into the structure and process of the social world. By arguing that these authors were the only real founders of sociology, moreover, he could undermine the foundations of theories which he had come to consider badly mistaken. Parsons's claim to have 'discovered' the classics was motivated by theoretical interest; at the same time, given the necessary background conditions, his interpretative practice was strong enough to convince the social scientific community that these classical positions actually foreshadowed his own.

The link between historical and contemporary systematics was so strong that Parsons's theoretical hegemony could be challenged only if his version of classical history was overturned as well. An alternative version was established and this occurred as much by re-readings of Parsons's classics as by creating new ones. The intellectual reasons for this are clear enough: with powerful theories there is insight enough for ample interpretative space. But the acceptance of common classics was functionally effective as well, for it allowed post-Parsonian theorists to make their arguments in terms which were more or less widely understood. Ironically, the classicization of Parsons's own work facilitated his theoretical demise, for it, too, provided a relatively well-understood medium through which to argue against the merits of functionalist ideas. Because post-Parsonian theory was built in part upon Parsons, moreover, recent attempts to supersede it have returned not only to earlier classical texts but to Parsons's work as well, and they have done so not only for intellectual but also for strategic reasons.

Humanism and the Classics: Why the Historicist Challenge Is Wrong

To defend the centrality of the classics in a strong way is to argue for an inextricable relationship between contemporary theoretical interests and investigations about the meaning of historical texts. In the first part of this essay I argued for this position in the realm of sociological theory. In the preceding section I have tried to substantiate it by looking at how sociological discussions about the classics actually proceed. In conclusion, I will try to substantiate this position against the challenge which has emerged to classical centrality from within the humanities itself. This is the historicist approach to intellectual history associated with the work of Quentin Skinner, which – often in combination with self-styled Kuhnian histories of science – has made significant intrusions into sociological discussion as well (e.g. Jones: 1979; Peel: 1971; Stocking: 1965).

This challenge is particularly important because it is the humanities which have usually posed the alternative to the social scientific reduction of cultural studies to contemporary empirical intent. In terms of the classics, as Merton himself posed the dichotomy, it has been the humanities which have traditionally defended the uniqueness and permanent importance of the classics' contributions. The humanities are associated with interpretation rather than explanation; it was, after all, from within the humanities that this very distinction was first formalized and advanced. It has been from within the humanistic disciplines, moreover – from nineteenth-century historical studies of religion to contemporary literary theory – that the methodology of interpretation and the investigation and re-investigation of the meaning of classical texts has been most pronounced. Finally, it is the denial of the relevance of textual interpretation for the social sciences which underlies not only the empiricist injunction against the classics but the common sense of classical discussions themselves.

Whereas Merton's injunction against merging history and systematics seeks to cleanse systematics of historical baggage, Skinnerian theory argues against merging in order to purify history of the taint of systematics. The intent is to transform discussions of earlier texts into presuppositionless, purely historical investigations, investigations which would, ironically, be more explanatory than interpretative in form. Yet, while Skinner approaches the problem from an opposite angle, the effect of his argument would be exactly the same. If history can be atheoretical, then theory can be ahistorical. If the classics can be studied without shouldering the burden of interpretation, then interpretation certainly need not intrude into the practice of classicless social science. Skinner provides the kind of intellectual history that Merton needed but could not find.[13] It seems to me, however, that his historical theory suffers from the same abstract, anti-empirical quality as Merton's: it fails to account for the central role of interpretative debate in cultural studies today. It does so, moreover, for much the same reason: it suffers from an empiricism which denies to presuppositions a central role in the study of social life. It makes this claim in the name of defending reason against relativism. In my view, however, it is only by acknowledging a priori interests that reason can bring them to task.

What historicism abhors is the anachronistic introduction of contemporary concerns into the understanding of earlier texts. Skinner complains that this 'priority of paradigms' can result only in 'mythologies' rather than in the discovery of the texts themselves (Skinner: 1969, pp. 6–7). Such a complaint rests, of course, on the implicit claim that the hermeneutical circle can be

---

[13] It is worth noting that the traditional 'history of ideas' is an object of condemnation by Skinner and Merton alike. For both, not surprisingly, it is criticized as being too presentist in nature. In the first section of this essay, I criticized Merton's proposal for an alternative approach to intellectual history as itself pre-Kuhnian in form. Once again, Skinner would provide just the alternative to historical systematics which Merton was unable properly to conceive. What one might call his preferred '*history* of ideas' – as contrasted to the 'history of *ideas*' – perfectly matches the stereotype which empiricist social scientists have of classical inquiry, namely that it is purely historical and because of this irrelevant to contemporary theoretical concerns. Thus, in Turner's attack on 'metatheory', which I noted above, he contrasts 'doing theory' with 'tracing the history of ideas' (1986, p. 974).

broken. What sustains historicism is the belief that the real world, in its pristine and original glory, can be revealed to the investigator if only he knows where and how to look. Historicism provides this knowledge through its emphasis on context and intention. The unmediated availability to cultural studies of intellectual context and authorial intention are the most important assumptions upon which historicism rests. From these follow a third assumption which, while implicit, might well be the most important of all. This is the notion that motivated, historically-situated texts can themselves be read and understood without any particular problem at all. This also, we recall, was precisely the latent assumption in Merton's social scientific attack on the classics. To defend the 'difficulty' of classical texts and their 'relative autonomy' *vis-à-vis* intention and context is, therefore, to defend the practice of interpretation itself. It is, ultimately, just because interpretation is central that a merging of history and systematics must be made. In what follows, I will criticize each of the assumptions upon which historicism rests in turn.

1   *Singular versus infinite context*

Historicism contends that the linguistic conventions of a given period reveal the intellectual universe for any particular historical work. 'It follows from this', Skinner argues, 'that the appropriate methodology for the history of ideas must be concerned, first of all, to delineate the whole range of communications which could have been conventionally performed on the given occasion by the utterance' (Skinner: 1969, p. 49; cf. Jones: 1986, p. 14; Peel: 1971, p. 264; Stocking: 1965, p. 8). No particular misgivings are expressed about the retrievability of this milieu. Jones blithely suggests, for example, that it is possible to achieve 'an understanding of the total sociohistorical context within which sociological theories have emerged' (1977, p. 355). It seems to me, however, that it is precisely this capacity for history to mirror society which must be put into question. If Skinner's nominalism is maintained, then every significant statement in a historical period would have to be recorded and analysed, a clearly impossible task. Total socio-historical context is a chimera. If, on the other hand, a more realist position is assumed, it must be acknowledged that generalizations are made which are necessarily selective. Selection, of course, always involves comparison to some prior standard. There is one anomalous point in Skinner's more recent writing where he seems to recognize that the need for selection refutes the contextualist position he has himself tried to lay out.

> Before we can hope to identify the context which helps to disclose the meaning of a given work, we must already have arrived at an interpretation which serves to suggest what contexts may most profitably be investigated as further aids to interpretation. The relationship between a text and its appropriate

context is in short an instance of the hermeneutic circle. (Skinner: 1976, p. 227)

2 *Transparent versus opaque intention*

Historicism, however, is not a form of social determinism; it seeks to take authorial will fully into account. Context provides only the background for a text; it is the author's own intentions that reveal which conventions he aimed his text to support and supersede. Once again, this claim rests upon an empiricist confidence in the transparency of the social world. Intentions are considered as recoverable as contexts. Skinner is not troubled by the problem of discovering intent; one must simply look at 'what the author himself meant to say' (1969, p. 22). The counter-argument 'that it is actually impossible to recover a writer's motives and intentions' is, Skinner insists, 'straightforwardly false' (1972, p. 400). To find intentions and motive, one needs recourse simply to 'commonplace, but [heretofore] amazingly elusive, facts about the activity of thinking' (Skinner: 1969, p. 30).

It is, of course, exactly the commonplace nature of thinking which has been subject to radical questioning throughout most of the twentieth century. Psychoanalysis has demonstrated that the full intentions of actors are unknown even to themselves, let alone to others who do not know them well. The mind fends off emotional discomfort by constructing defence mechanisms that drastically narrow the actor's conscious understanding (Freud: 1950). While the pseudo-scientific claims of psychoanalysis have been sharply scrutinized, its scepticism toward rational self-understanding has permeated intellectual opinion about interpretation and literary method. For example, it was psychoanalytic ideas which largely inspired the attack by New Criticism on contextual and intentionalist interpretation. Because profound ambiguity lies at the origin of most powerful imaginative works, Empson (1930) argued, texts are filled with unresolved contradictions and readers are forced to invent interpretations about meaning and authorial intent. This points ineluctably to the autonomy of text, for it becomes clear that the author himself is not in conscious control. My own work on the contradictory character of great social theory (e.g. Alexander: 1982b, pp. 301–6, 330–43) suggests, similarly, that 'unconscious deceit' is endemic to such theorizing; in light of this, to pursue the meaning of a theory through the author's conscious intent would surely be barking up the wrong tree.

Inspired not only by psychoanalysis but by cultural theory as well, structuralism and semiotics have made the same point. Arguing against Sartre's intentionalism, Lévi-Strauss insists that structural linguistics demonstrate the existence of a 'totalizing entity' which is 'outside (or beneath) consciousness and will' and that such linguistic formations are prototypes for every cultural text (Lévi-Strauss: 1966, p. 252). Ricoeur argues similarly.

Written discourse is possible, he suggests, only because there are symbolic resources available which transcend situational specificity and immediate intent. For the immediate situation of composition can barely be known by those who encounter written texts after they have been composed: 'The text's career escapes the finite horizon lived by its author. What the text says now matters more than what the author meant to say' (Ricoeur: 1971, p. 534). Hermeneutical philosophy supports this conclusion from the viewpoint of historical method itself. Gadamer argues that whether authorial intent and textual meaning coincide is irrelevant, for intent is something which it is impossible for the historian to recover. Making a virtue of necessity, he expounds a dialogical perspective in which texts can reveal themselves only through interlocution in a historical context: 'The real meaning of a text, as it speaks to the interpreter, does not depend upon the contingency of the author and whom he originally wrote for. It is partly determined also by the historical situation of the interpreter and hence by the totality of the objective course of history' (Gadamer: 1975, p. 264).

3 *Explicit versus multivalent texts*

The unstated assumption which informs historicism's exclusive concentration on context and intention is that it is unnecessary to study the meaning of a text in itself, that is, to concentrate on the text *qua* text. Behind this assumption is a pragmatic, anti-semiotic theory of meaning. Historicists claim that the meaning of any given text is determined and exhausted by its use on a particular occasion. Practice, not textual meaning, becomes the object of investigation: in Skinner's words, 'the *use* of the relevant sentence by a particular agent on a particular occasion with a particular intention (*his* intention) to make a particular *statement*' (1969, p. 50). Inverting Ricoeur, Skinner insists that a text is 'specific to its situation in a way that it can only be naive to try to transcend' (1969, p. 50). This is an agentic, nominalist approach. Texts are means for intellectual action; to study them is to find out 'what genuine historical agents did think' (Skinner: 1969, p. 29).

Yet if context is far from definite and intention impossible to pin down, texts must be given a relative autonomy. They must be studied, that is, as intellectual vehicles in their own right. This is not to deny authorial intention; it is to assert that intention can only be discovered in the text itself. As Hirsch puts it, 'there is a difference between meaning and consciousness of meaning' (1967, p. 22). It is from such beliefs about the complex, camouflaged nature of authorial intention that arguments for textual autonomy emerge, for the intentions of the unconscious author can be discovered only through an independent examination of the text itself. For Ricoeur (1971), texts have a 'surplus of meaning'. Freud (1913) insists on the 'overdetermination' of dream symbolism. Foucault (1970) argues that hidden discourses structure the written documents of history. This extra meaning accrues to a given text because of the organizing principles inherent in that particular cultural form. Ricoeur sees surplus as produced by myth and metaphor. Freud finds overdetermination in such devices of dream construction as displacement and condensation. Foucault's discourses rest on modalities which establish the archaeology of knowledge.

A text is a system of symbols which fixes the meaning of an author as much as the author invests meaning in it. To study the meanings of a particular text, then, one must study that particular system's rules. The investigator must know the rules that govern that particular kind of imaginative activity: how displacement and condensation operate in dreams, how structural logic (Barthes: 1977) underpins the narrative form. These rules, which literary theorists (e.g. Hirsch: 1967, pp. 74, 80) call the rules of genre, are embedded in the consciousness of authors but they are rarely invented by authors themselves. It is, indeed, because they are socially-constituted and -transmitted rules that texts allow interpersonal communication to proceed.

The purpose of critical debate is to make these rules explicit and to show how it is these presuppositions, rather than others, which produce the meaning of texts. If cultural reasoning is bound to be relative, Skinner's attempt to maintain reason by empiricist escape is doomed from the start.[14]

[14] It is precisely this doomed quality of empiricism which explains the series of what can only be called retractions which have been issued by Skinner and his associates in response to the critical debate over their work. Skinner (1972), for example, eventually tried to separate motive from intention, arguing that while the former cannot really be known the latter could. This marked an implicit acknowledgment of the autonomy of texts, for he now argued that intention could be discovered only through an understanding of what the actual act of writing involved. Yet this, too, is further qualified, and in an ambiguous way. Skinner (1972, p. 405) insists that he has 'been concerned only with the ... point that whatever a writer is doing in writing, what he writes must be relevant to interpretation', not that the writer's intention must be the basis of interpretation *per se*. He has reduced his claim to the notion that 'amongst the interpreter's tasks must be the recovery of the writer's intentions in writing what he writes', and he indicates that intention may well be disregarded. While 'it must always be dangerous ... for a critic to override a writer's own explicit statements about what he was doing in a given work', he acknowledges, 'the writer himself may have been self-deceiving about recognizing his intentions, or incompetent at stating them'. The recent work of Jones, Skinner's most important follower in sociology, is also marked by critical equivocations and retractions. He now suggests (Jones: 1986, p. 17), for example, that 'the contextual availability (or unavailability) of descriptive or classificatory terms is not the criterion by which our statements about an historical agent are rendered anachronistic or otherwise'. And he appears to accept the unalterable presentism of textual investigation: 'The practice of social science itself (history included) not only benefits from but repeatedly requires the imposition, upon agents whose beliefs and behavior we wish to understand, of concepts and categories wholly alien to them.' While Jones and Skinner continue to make arguments for the historicist position, if these admissions were seriously taken they would undermine the validity of the position as such. I am grateful to Seidman's (1983b; forthcoming

Reason can be preserved only by making presuppositions explicit and subjecting them to disciplined debate. Standards of evaluation are proposed, not discovered; it is only persuasion which can lead the participants in discourse to accept them as valid. It is for this reason that interpretation and theoretical argument go hand in hand. 'To recognize the impossibility of demonstrating an axiom system', Raymond Aron once wrote, 'is not a defeat of the mind, but the recall of the mind to itself' (1961, p. 106).

Bibliography

Alexander, J. C., 1982a: *Positivism, Presuppositions, and Current Controversies*, vol. 1 of *Theoretical Logic in Sociology*. Berkeley and Los Angeles: University of California Press.

1982b: *The Antinomies of Classical Thought: Marx and Durkheim*. Berkeley and Los Angeles: University of California Press.

1983: *The Modern Reconstruction of Classical Thought: Talcott Parsons*, vol. 4 of *Theoretical Logic in Sociology*. Berkeley and Los Angeles: University of California Press.

1985 (ed.): *Neofunctionalism*. Beverly Hills and London: Sage Publications.

1986: *Twenty lectures on Sociological Theory: Talcott Parsons and his Critics in the Postwar Period*. New York: Columbia University Press.

forthcoming, 1987a: 'Social-Structural Analysis: Presuppositions, Ideologies, Empirical Debates', in his 'Structure and Meaning: Essays in Sociological Theory'. New York: Columbia University Press.

forthcoming, 1987b (ed.): 'Durkheimian Sociology'. New York: Cambridge University Press.

Althusser, L., 1969: *For Marx*. London: New Left Books.

Althusser, L. and Balibar, E., 1970: *Reading 'Capital'*. London: New Left Books.

Aron, R., 1961: 'Max Weber and Michael Polanyi', in M. Grene (ed.), *The Logic of Personal Knowledge: Essays Presented to Michael Polanyi*. Glencoe, Ill.: Free Press, pp. 99–116.

Avineri, S., 1969: *The Social and Political Thought of Karl Marx*. London: Cambridge University Press.

Barthes, R., 1977: 'Introduction to the Structural Analysis of Narratives', in his *Image, Music and Text*. London: Fontana, pp. 79–124.

Bellah, R., 1959: 'Durkheim and History', *American Sociological Review*, 24: 447–61.

1973: 'Introduction', in Bellah (ed.), *Émile Durkheim on Morality and Society*. Chicago: University of Chicago Press, pp. ix–lv.

Bellah, R. and Hammond, P., 1980: *Varieties of Civil Religion*. San Francisco: Harper & Row.

Bendix, R., 1961: *Max Weber: An Intellectual Portrait*. New York: Doubleday Anchor.

1971: 'Two Sociological Traditions', in Bendix and G. Roth, *Scholarship and Partisanship*. Berkeley and Los Angeles: University of California Press, pp. 282–98.

1978: *Kings or People?* Berkeley and Los Angeles: University of California Press.

---

a; forthcoming b) work in this area for bringing to my attention such contradictions and for its illumination of the problems considered in this essay more generally.

Bennett, T. *et al.* (eds), 1981: *Culture, Ideology and Social Process*. London: The Open University Press.

Blau, P. M., Blum, T. C. and Schwartz, J.E ., 1982: 'Heterogeneity and Intermarriage', *American Sociological Review*, 47: 45–62.

Blumer, H., 1969: 'The Methodological Position of Symbolic Interactionism' in his *Symbolic Interactionism*. Englewood Cliffs, Prentice-hall, NJ, pp.. 1–60.

Camic, C., 1979: 'The Utilitarians Revisited', *American Journal of Sociology*, 85: 516–50.

Clarke, J. *et al.* (eds), 1979: *Working Class Culture*. London: Hutchinson Press.

Cohen, J., Hazelrigg, L. and Pope, W., 1975: 'De-Parsonizing Weber: A Critique of Parsons's Interpretation of Weber's Sociology, *American Sociological Review*, 40: 229–41.

Cohen, S., 1980: 'Symbols of Trouble: Introduction to the New Edition', in his *Folk Devils and Moral Panics*. Oxford: Martin Robertson, pp. 1–8.

Collingwood, C., 1940: *Metaphysics*. Oxford: Clarendon Press.

Collins, R., 1968: 'A Comparative Approach to Political Sociology', in R. Bendix (ed.), *State and Society: A Reader in Political Sociology*. Berkeley and Los Angeles: University of California Press, pp. 42–67.

1975: *Conflict Sociology*. New York: Academic Press.

1986: *Weberian Sociological Theory*. New York: Cambridge University Press.

Coser, L., 1956: *The Functions of Social Conflict*. New York: Free Press.

Dahrendorf, R., 1959: *Class and Class Conflict in Industrial Society*. Stanford: Stanford University Press.

Dawe, A., 1978: 'Theories of Social Action', in T. Bottomore and R. Nisbet (eds), *The History of Sociological Analysis*. New York: Basic Books, pp. 362–417.

Derrida, J., 1981: *Positions*. Chicago: University of Chicago Press.

Dilthey, W., 1976: 'The Construction of the Historical World in the Human Studies', in his *Selected Writings*, edited by H. P. Richman. Cambridge, England: Cambridge University Press.

Drabek, Thomas E., 1986: 'Taxonomy and Disaster: Theoretical and Applied Issues', paper presented at the Symposium on 'Social Structure and Disaster: Concept and Measurement,' College of William and Mary, Williamsburg, Virgina.

forthcoming: *Human System Response to Disaster: An Inventory of Sociological Findings*. New York, Hedelberg and Berlin: Springer-Verlag

Eisenstadt, S. N., 1968: 'Charisma and Institution Building: Max Weber and Modern Sociology', in Eisenstadt (ed.), *Max Weber on Charisma and Institution Building*. Chicago: University of Chicago Press, pp. ix–lvi.

Empson, W., 1930: *Seven Types of Ambiguity*. London: Chatto and Windus.

Fenton, S. (ed.), 1984: *Durkheim and Modern Sociology*. London: Cambridge University Press.

Foucault, M., 1970: *The Order of Things*. London: Tavistock Publications.

Freud, A., 1950: *The Ego and the Mechanisms of Defence*. London: International Universities Press.

Freud, S., 1913: *The Interpretation of Dreams*. London: G. Allen.

Friedrichs, R., 1970: *A Sociology of Sociology*. New York: Free Press.

Gadamer, H., 1975: *Truth and Method*. New York: Crossroads.

Garfinkel, H., 1963: 'A Conception of and Experiments with "Trust" as a Condition of Concerted Stable Actions', in O. J. Harvey (ed.), *Motivation and Social Interaction*. New York: Ronald Press, pp. 187–238.

1984: *Studies in Ethnomethodology*. Cambridge, England: Polity Press.

Geertz, C., 1964: 'Ideology as a Cultural System', in D. Apter (ed.), *Ideology and Discontent*. New York: Free Press, pp. 47–76.
Giddens, A., 1971: *Capitalism and Modern Social Theory*. Cambridge, England: Cambridge University Press.
1976: *New Rules of Sociological Method*. New York: Basic Books.
1979: *Central Problems in Social Theory*. Berkeley and Los Angeles: University of California Press.
1981: *A Contemporary Critique of Historical Materialism*. vol. 1. Berkeley and Los Angeles: University of California Press.
Gillispie, C. C., 1960: *The Edge of Objectivity: An Essay in the History of Scientific Ideas*. Princeton: Princeton University Press.
Gouldner, A., 1958: 'Introduction', in E. Durkheim, *Socialism and Saint-Simon*. Yellow Springs, Ohio: Antioch University Press, pp. i–xxiv.
1970: *The Coming Crisis of Western Sociology*. New York: Equinox.
1979: 'Talcott Parsons', *Theory and Society*, 8: 299–301.
1980: *The Two Marxisms*. New York: Seabury.
Habermas, J., 1972: *Knowledge and Human Interests*. Cambridge, England: Polity Press.
1981: *Zur Kritik der Funktionalistischen Vernunft*, vol. 2 of *Theorie des Kommunikativen Handelns*. Frankfurt-on-Main: Suhrkamp.
1984: *Reason and the Rationalization of Society*, vol. 1 of *Theory of Communicative Action*. Cambridge, England: Polity Press.
Hacker, A., 1961: 'Sociology and Ideology', in Max Black (ed.), *The Social Theories of Talcott Parsons*. pp. 289–310.
Hagstrom, W., 1965: *The Scientific Community*. New York: Basic Books.
Hall, S., 1981: 'Cultural Studies: Two Paradigms', in Bennett *et al.*: 1981, pp. 19–37.
Hall, S. *et al.* (eds), 1980: *Culture, Media, Language*. London: Hutchinson.
Hinkle, R., 1963: 'Antecedents of the Action Orientation in American Sociology before 1935', *American Sociological Review*, 28: 705–15.
1980: *Founding Theory of American Sociology, 1881–1915*. London: Routledge and Kegan Paul.
Hirsch, E. D., 1967: *Validity in Interpretation* Bloomington: Indiana University Press.
Hirschman, A., 1977: *The Passions and the Interests*. Princeton: Princeton University Press.
Holton, G., 1973: *Thematic Origins of Scientific Thought: Kepler to Einstein*. Cambridge, Mass.: Harvard University Press.
Homans, G., 1958: 'Social Behavior as Exchange', *American Journal of Sociology*, 62: 597–606.
1961: *Social Behavior: Its Elementary Forms*. New York: Harcourt, Brace.
1964: 'Bringing Men Back In', *American Sociological Review*, 29: 809–18.
Hunt, L., forthcoming, 1987: 'The Sacred and the French Revolution', in J. Alexander, forthcoming, 1987b.
Husserl, E., 1977: *Cartesian Meditations*. The Hague: Martinus Nijhoff. First published 1931.
Joas, H., 1985: *G. H. Mead: A Contemporary Re-Examination of His Thought*. Cambridge, England: Polity Press.
Jones, R. A., 1977: 'On Understanding a Sociological Class', *American Journal of Sociology*, 88: 279–319.
1986: 'Second Thoughts on Privileged Access', *Sociological Theory*, 3 (1): 16–19.

Kermode, Frank, 1985: *Forms of Attention*. Chicago: University of Chicago Press.

Kuhn, T., 1970: *The Structure of Scientific Revolutions*, 2nd edn. Chicago: University of Chicago Press.

Lakatos, I., 1969: 'Criticism and the Methodology of Scientific Research Programmes', *Proceedings of the Aristotelian Society*, 69: 149–86.

Levine, D., 1980: Introduction to the Arno Press edition of *Simmel and Parsons: Two Approaches to the Study of Society* (pp. iii–lxix). New York: Arno Press. First published 1957.

Lévi-Strauss, C., 1966: *The Savage Mind*. Chicago: University of Chicago Press.

Lewis, J. D. and Smith, R., 1980: *American Sociology and Pragmatism: Mead, Chicago Sociology and Symbolic Interactionism*. Chicago: University of Chicago Press.

Lieberson, S., 1980: *A Piece of the Pie*. Berkeley and Los Angeles: University of California Press.

Lindenberg, S., 1983: 'Utility and Morality', *Icyklos*, 36: 450–68.

Luhmann, N., 1979: *Trust and Power*. New York: Wiley.

1984: *The Differentiation of Society*. New York: Columbia University Press.

Lukes, S., 1972: *Émile Durkheim: His Life and Work*. New York: Harper & Row.

Mannheim, K ., 1936: *Ideology and Utopia*. New York: Harcourt, Brace.

Martindale, D., 1960: *The Nature and Types of Sociological Theory*. Cambridge, Mass.

McClellan, D. (ed.), 1971: 'Introduction', in McClellan (ed.), *The Grundrisse: Karl Marx*. New York: Harper & Row, pp. 1–15.

Merton, R. K., 1947: 'Discussion of "The Position of Sociological Theory", *American Sociological Review*, 13 (2): 164–8.

1967a and b: (two essays in 1967) *Social Theory and Social Structure*. New York: Free Press.

1973: 'The Normative Structure of Science', in his *The Sociology of Science*, edited by N. W. Storer. Chicago: University of Chicago Press. First published 1942.

Mitzman, A., 1970: *The Iron Cage*. New York.

Nicholas, M., 1973: 'Foreword' to Karl Marx, *Grundrisse*. New York: Random House, pp. 1–63.

Nisbet, R., 1976: *Sociology as an Art Form*. London: Oxford University Press.

O'Connor, J., 1980: 'The Division of Labor in Society', *Insurgent Sociologist*, 10: 60–8.

Ollman, B., 1971: *Alienation*. London: Cambridge University Press

Parsons, T., 1937: *The Structure of Social Action*. New York: Free Press.

1947: 'Introduction', in M. Weber, *Theory of Social and Economic Organization*. New York: Free Press, pp. 3–86.

1951. *The Social System*. New York: Free Press.

1955: 'Family Structure and the Socialization of the Child', in Parsons *et al.*, *Family, Socialization, and Interaction Process*. New York: Free Press, pp. 35–132.

1964a: 'The Superego and the Theory of Social Systems', in his *Social Structure and Personality*. New York: Free Press, pp. 17–33. First published 1952.

1964b: 'The Father Symbol: An Appraisal in the Light of Psychoanalytic and Sociological Theory', in his *Social Structure and Personality*. New York: Free Press, pp. 34–56.

1967: 'Durkheim's Introduction to the Theory of the Integration of Social Systems', in his *Sociological Theory and Modern Society*. New York: Free Press, pp. 3–34.

Peel, J. D., 1971: *Herbert Spencer*. New York: Basic Books.

Polanyi, M., 1958: *Personal Knowledge*. Chicago: University of Chicago Press.

Pope, W., 1973: 'Classic on Classic: Parsons' Interpretation of Durkheim', *American Sociological Review*, 38: 399–415.

Popper, K., 1949: *The Logic of Scientific Discovery*. New York: Basic Books. First published 1934.

Rex, J., 1961: *Key Problems in Sociological Theory*. London: Routledge and Kegan Paul.

Ricoeur, P., 1971: 'The Model of the Text: Meaningful Action Considered as a Text', *Social Research*, 38: 529–62.

Roth, G., 1978: 'Introduction', in M. Weber, *Economy and Society*, edited by Roth and C. Wittich. Berkeley and Los Angeles: University of California Press, pp. xxvii–cviii. First published 1968.

Schluchter, W., 1981: *The Rise of Western Rationalism: Max Weber's Developmental History*. Berkeley and Los Angeles: University of California Press.

Seidman, S., 1983a: *Liberalism and the Origins of European Social Theory*. Berkeley and Los Angeles: University of California Press.

1983b: 'Beyond Presentism and Historicism: Understanding the History of Social Science', *Sociological Inquiry*, 53: 79–94.

forthcoming a: 'Classics and Contemporaries: The History and Systematics of Sociology Revisited', *History of Sociology*.

forthcoming b: 'Models of Scientific Development in Sociology', *Sociological Theory*.

Sewell, W. jun., 1985: 'Ideologies and Social Revolutions: Reflections on the French Case', *Journal of Modern History*, 57: 57–85.

Shils, E., 1970: 'Tradition, Ecology, and Institution in the History of Sociology', *Daedalus*, 99: 798–820.

Simmel, G., 1955: *Conflict and the Web of Group Affiliations*. New York: Free Press.

Skinner, Q., 1969: 'Meaning and Understanding in the History of Ideas', *History and Theory*, 8: 3–52.

1972: 'Motives, Intentions and the Interpretation of Texts', *New Literary History*, 3: 393–408.

1976: 'Hermeneutics and the Role of History', *New Literary History*, 7: 209–32.

Skocpol, T., 1979: *States and Social Revolutions*. New York: Cambridge University Press.

Smelser, N., 1959: *Social Change in the Industrial Revolution*. Chicago: University of Chicago Press.

1973: 'Introduction', in Smelser (ed.), *Karl Marx on Society and Social Change*. Chicago: University of Chicago Press, pp. vii–xxxvii.

Stinchcombe, A., 1968: *Constructing Social Theories*. Baltimore: Johns Hopkins University Press.

Stocking, G., 1965: 'On the limits of "Presentism" and "Historicism" in the Historiography of the Behavioral Sciences', *Journal of the History of the Behavioral Sciences*, 1: 211–17.

Stone, G. and Farberman, H., 1967: 'On the Edge of Rapprochement: Was Durkheim Moving toward the Perspective of Symbolic Interaction?', *Sociological Quarterly*, 8: 149–64.

Strauss, A., 1964: 'Introduction', in Strauss (ed.), *George Herbert Mead on Social Psychology*. Chicago: University of Chicago Press.

Thompson, K., 1985: 'Rereading the Classics: The Case of Durkheim'. Unpublished paper, Department of Sociology, UCLA, Los Angeles, California.

forthcoming: *Durkheim and Sociological Methods*. Beverly Hills and London: Sage.

Tiryakian, E., 1979: 'The Significance of Schools in the Development of Sociology', in W. E. Snizek *et al.* (eds), *Contemporary Issues in Theory and Research*. Westport, Conn.: Greenwood Press.

Traugott, M., 1984: 'Durkheim and Social Movements', *European Journal of Sociology*, 25: 319–26.

1985: *Armies of the Poor*. Princeton: Princeton University Press.

Treiman, D., 1977: *Occupational Prestige in Comparative Perspective*. New York: Wiley.

Trevor-Roper, H. R., 1965: 'Religion, the Reformation and Social Change', *Historical Studies*, IV: 18–45.

Turner, J., 1986: 'Review: The Theory of Structuration', *American Journal of Sociology*, 91: 969–77.

Walby, Sylvia, 1986: *Patriarchy at Work*. London: Macmillan.

Wallace, Walter L., 1971: *The Logic of Science in Sociology*. Chicago: Aldine.

Wearne, B., 1985: 'The Theory and Scholarship of Talcott Parsons to 1951: A Critical Commentary'. Unpublished doctoral dissertation, Department of Sociology, la Trobe University, Melbourne, Australia.

Weber, M., 1958: *The Protestant Ethic and the Spirit of Capitalism*. First published 1904–5.

Whimpster, S. and Lash, E. (eds), 1986: *Max Weber and Rationality*. London: George Allen and Unwin.

Whitehead, A. N., 1974: 'The Organization of Thought', in his *The Organization of Thought*. Westport, Conn.: Greenwood Press, pp. 105–33. First published 1917.

Wiley, N. (ed.), 1987: *The Marx–Weber Debate*. Beverly Hills and London: Sage.

Wrong, D., 1961: 'The Over-Socialized Conception of Man in Modern Sociology', *American Sociological Review*, 26: 183–93.

Zeitlin, I., 1968: *Ideology and the Development of Sociological Theory*. Englewood Cliffs, NJ: Prentice-Hall.

Behaviourism and After

GEORGE C. HOMANS

I

Behaviourism as first formulated by J. B. Watson and later made more rigorous by B. F. Skinner was once treated as a pariah in psychology and the other social sciences. It is still a pariah to the extent that Skinner has continued to make exaggerated claims for the power it gives people to create a better culture (Skinner: 1971). But the truth of a science is something different from its applicability; as accepted truth behaviourism has ceased to be a pariah: it has become instead a part of the mainstream of psychology, and therefore I shall refer to it hereafter as behavioural psychology. Nor does all modern behavioural psychology derive directly from Skinner. I think especially of the important contributions of Albert Bandura (1969; 1973).

The fundamental insight of behaviourism was strategic: instead of trying to analyse consciousness and states of the mind, scholars could make more progress in psychology by looking at the actions of men and women and at the observable states of people and of their environment to which the actions could be lawfully related. And not just men and women: the propositions of behavioural psychology were first tested experimentally with other higher animals. The behaviourists trusted that neurologists and the like would ultimately discover the characteristics of the central nervous system that made behavioural propositions valid. Behavioural psychology is sometimes distinguished from cognitive psychology, which is concerned with thinking and perceiving. No sharp line can be drawn between the two, since action and perception are inseparable. Indeed perception *is* an action. But here I shall lean toward the behavioural end of the spectrum.

The present essay is concerned with the uses of behavioural psychology in sociology. But many sociologists, including those that dismiss it out of hand, still do not understand what the main tenets of the subject are. I have no space here to write a treatise on psychology. I must grossly simplify, and refer anyone who wants to know more to a good textbook.[1]

First I must make a convenient, though not absolute distinction between *respondent* (reflex) behaviour and what Skinner was the first to call *operant* behaviour. Respondent behaviour is behaviour that can be produced automatically by applying a stimulus to the subject. Examples are the familiar knee-jerk response, and the salivation of Pavlov's dogs upon contact with food. The behaviour is genetic in origin, produced by natural selection, though of course, as Pavlov showed, it can be conditioned to originally neutral stimuli. Respondent behaviour is obviously of the greatest importance. Athletically-effective action, for instance, would be impossible without it. But it is less interesting to sociology, with the exception of the mixed case of emotional behaviour, than operant behaviour.

In operant behaviour, a stimulus does not at once produce a specific kind of action. Instead the higher animals, including man, are possessed by drives (hungers) for foods of different kinds, for water, sex, escape from, or avoidance of, hurtful events, and many others: in fact we do not know how many. The drives differ in strength from one species to another, from individual to individual within a species, and from one circumstance to another within individuals. In so far as one of its drives has not been satisfied, an animal will first display a great increase in activity, simply moving about, exploring and investigating its environment. Activity itself may be a drive. Like the respondents, the drives are genetic in origin, usually, but not always – think of tobacco – selected to help the animal to live and reproduce.

Under natural conditions, and with ordinary good luck, this increased activity will help the animal hit upon some action, which, if it takes it, will be followed by a reduction in the drive. In Skinnerian language this particular action will have been *reinforced*. It is such an action that is called an operant. In unnatural conditions, such as a laboratory box, a hungry, but otherwise untutored animal, such as a pigeon, will explore its cage and sooner or later peck a key the psychologist has put there so that, when the pigeon pecks, a pellet of food will be delivered to it. At this point I must state the first proposition of behavioural psychology, called by its scientific discoverer, E. L. Thorndike, 'the law of effect'. Intuitively humankind has known it throughout history. It is this: if an animal's (or a person's) action is followed by a reward, the person is likely to repeat that action or some approximation thereof. The effect of reward in leading the person to repeat the action justifies saying that the action has been reinforced. Since in one sense the person has learned the action, behavioural psychology is often called *learning theory*. In fact, it does not apply only to learning, since reinforcement tends to maintain a particular action long after it has been learned. Note that the person in question is likely to repeat *any* action that is followed by the reward, even if the link between the two is purely fortuitous, which leaves plenty of room for superstitious behaviour. Some

[1] E.g. Rachlin (1976) or Reynolds (1968).

animals can also learn by imitation. If one of them sees another taking an action that is followed by the latter's obtaining what the former also finds rewarding, the former is likely to take the action itself. Of course it will not continue to do so if, in its case, the reward is not forthcoming. Note in all this a fundamental assumption of behavioural psychology: actions taken in the present feed back to affect future action. Behavioural psychology is thus a fundamentally historical science. The feedbacks often give observers the impression that animals and humans have purposes. Indeed they do. There is no harm in using that word, providing we recognize that 'purpose' in this sense does not imply teleology but cybernetics.

Most research in this field has used rewards that may be consumed, like food, but we must not forget how many rewards are not consumed but are, so to speak, rewarding in themselves. Sex is a good example. Psychologists also speak of negative rewards. Many actions are not followed by rewards but by punishments. Then any actions that allow the animal to escape or avoid the punishment become themselves rewarding. On the other hand, the withdrawal of a reward is punishing, or, in Skinnerian language, *aversive*.

I next introduce what for convenience I take to be the second general proposition of behavioural psychology. If circumstances similar to those that accompanied a person's previously rewarded action recur, the person is likely to repeat the action. These attendant circumstances are usually called *stimuli*. The features of a stimulus that makes it effective vary. Some may be innate, that is, part of the person's genetic inheritance. Some may depend for their effectiveness on the person's ability to recognize the stimulus or the connection between the stimulus and the reward: the person is more apt to be influenced by the stimulus the more closely it is linked in time with the reward. The reward itself is often called a reinforcing stimulus.

Finally, rewards can be acquired, not native. A stimulus that has repeatedly accompanied a rewarded action may itself become a reward and have the same sort of effect on further actions as the original reward. In this way an animal can often learn a long chain of actions leading up to some ultimate reward: a long chain of means to an end. Human beings seem to be able to maintain longer chains of this sort than can other animals.

Some social scientists seem to believe that behavioural psychology ended with Skinner, but like all healthy sciences it has been progressing by fits and starts, and some of the developments have made it increasingly relevant to the understanding of human behaviour. One such fairly recent development must be mentioned here. In his experimental box, Skinner gave his pigeons a single key to peck, varying the frequency of rewards for pecking it and the random ratios or intervals at which the rewards occurred. He then observed the effects of these variables on the pigeons' rate of responding (pecking). He made no effort to control their behaviour when they were not pecking: they might walk about, preen their feathers, etc. Richard Herrnstein, a student of Skinner's, introduced a crucial variation. He put not one but at least two keys in the box, which rewarded at different average rates, though both on random schedules. That is, each was geared to deliver a different average number of pellets per unit of time. Herrnstein discovered that, though it took them some time to reach stable equilibrium, the pigeons would finally settle down to devoting to each key a number of pecks proportional to the key's relative reward (Herrnstein: 1971). Or as he says of the pigeon: 'If it gets 20% of its rewards from the left disc [key], it allocates 20% of its pecks there. If it gets 50% of its rewards from the left, then half the pecks will go there too' (Brown and Herrnstein: 1975, p. 80). Herrnstein showed that the relationship holds for more than two keys. What is more important for my purposes, it has also been shown to hold good of humans – naturally using other actions than pecks. Herrnstein calls this relationship 'the matching law' and now, instead of speaking of 'the law of effect', he speaks of 'the law of relative effect'. This law is of the greatest importance for the understanding of human behaviour, in that many sciences, and notably economics, are concerned with choices between alternative actions and their rewards. The choices need not be conscious.

The matching law is interesting not only for its own sake but because it allows me to introduce a crucial new variable. So far I have been concerned with an animal's degree of *success* in obtaining a reward, measuring success by the frequency with which a repeated action is rewarded. I have also mentioned some of the different kinds of reward but not the different degrees of reward a given unit provides. This variable I call *value*. In the original experiments that led to the matching law, all conditions were kept the same except for the different rates of reward of the two keys. Now consider an experiment with rats pressing levers to get food. The two levers reward at different rates, but now it is easier for the rats to press one lever than the other, because the experimenter has made the other heavier. The rats press the lighter lever more often than the matching law would otherwise call for. Nevertheless a corrective factor can be found that puts the matching law into effect again. Note that pressing the heavier lever is comparatively aversive for the rats, and escape from aversion is rewarding. In short, the corrective factor provides a measure of the value of escape from aversion. The same finding holds good of two levers that offer different kinds of reward, say units of water and pellets of food. Here too a coefficient can be found that makes the matching law still hold good (Brown and Herrnstein: 1975, pp. 81–3).

These results mean that, leaving stimuli aside, there are two kinds of factors that determine how often, in choosing between alternatives, an animal will perform one action rather than another. The first is the relative frequency with which the alternatives are rewarded. This, assuming the reward is greater than zero, I call the *success* proposition. The second is the relative *value* of one reward compared with the other. Differences in value depend on the state of the animal: is it, for instance, suffering from hunger more than from thirst? Over a longer span of time, values may be genetic in origin; they may also be learned by an individual through personal experience, or they may be taught to individuals by other members of their society.

Sometimes an action is followed by both reward and punishment, which takes me back to the rats choosing between the lighter and the heavier lever. They tend to press the heavier lever less often than the matching law would call for. But why do they press it at all? They do so because after all it gets them food. Yet it fatigues them, and fatigue is aversive. In pressing the heavier lever they forgo the reward of avoiding fatigue. I shall, following economics, call a forgone reward a *cost*, and say that the probability of an animal's (including a person's) taking an action varies with its net reward: positive reward minus cost (reward forgone).

Note how much what I have been saying sounds like what the theorists of decision-making in man have called the principle of rational choice: in choosing between alternative actions a person will tend to choose the one for which he perceives the probability of obtaining a particular reward, multiplied by the value of a unit of the reward, is greater. (However, I am not sure that for either rats or humans the proposition holds good exactly for extreme values of the variables.) A person's perception depends on his past experiences of the actions and of the past and present circumstances attending them. I shall return to this principle later, but in my opinion calling the principle 'rational' adds nothing to its meaning, provided we are only concerned with how people do in fact behave. 'Rational' is a normative term, used to persuade people to behave in a certain way.

II

I consider the propositions I have called success, stimulus and value the main propositions of behavioural psychology. There are several refinements of the main propositions and, without doubt, other propositions still to be discovered. At this point I shall introduce only two secondary propositions that a sociologist ought to keep with the main ones in his intellectual kit if he is to understand human social behaviour. I call them secondary because they chiefly influence the value rather than the success factor in behaviour.

The first I have already referred to implicitly. I call it the *deprivation–satiation* proposition. If a person's action is rewarded at a rate higher than some threshold rate, the value of the action's reward will decrease, and therefore, by the value proposition, the frequency with which he performs the action is likely to go down – and the frequency with which he performs some alternative is likely to rise. Thus a person who has been fed to repletion is unlikely for a time to take further action that will get him food. By the same token, if a person has received a reward below some threshold rate, he is likely to increase the frequency of action that might get him that reward. Note that psychologists who experiment with animals try to keep this variable under control and keep the animals thoroughly motivated by always reinforcing behaviour at a rate that will not bring on satiation. In effect the animals are always hungry, as measured by their weight, or similarly deprived of other rewards. The deprivation–satiation proposition may not hold good for what are called *generalized reinforcers*, that is, learned rewards that can themselves be used to obtain a wide variety of more specific rewards. Money is a good example. For most of us it is difficult to become satiated with money unless we are first satiated with all the things money can buy.

The second proposition is usually called the *frustration-aggression* proposition. It describes one of the forms of emotional behaviour, which, for reasons that will become clear later, I shall not dwell on at length here, though it is of the first importance for human social behaviour. If an animal, including man, receives a punishment it did not expect or does not receive a reward it did, it is apt to display what is anthropomorphically described as anger and to exhibit aggressive behaviour, defined by Brown and Herrnstein as 'any behavior likely to cause physical or psychological pain or damage' (Brown and Herrnstein: 1975, p. 202). What the animal 'expects' is at least partly determined by its past experience but partly also by its genetic history: thus most female animals are apt to try to defend their offspring. The aggression is usually addressed to whatever has produced the frustration, as when we kick a door that will not open when it ought to; but at a pinch almost any person or object will do. Many potential targets of aggression are dangerous to attack because they may be able to produce even more damaging counter-aggression. In such a case, a person may, as we say, 'take it out' on some less threatening object, that is, displace his aggression. The value of the results of aggressive behaviour may be measured by the degree to which the aggressor is willing to suffer some damage himself if only he can hurt his target, the degree to which, to use the vernacular again, he is ready 'to cut off his nose to spite his face'. Emotional behaviour, such as aggression, seems to me to partake of the characteristics of both respondent and operant behaviour. On the one hand, it may be automatically released by a frustrating situation. On the other hand, a person may learn to use aggressive action like any operant that is followed by a reward. The reward may be money, status or any number of things. There may also be behaviour that is the mirror opposite of aggression, produced when a person receives a reward he did not expect or fails to receive punishment he did.

These five, admittedly very approximate, propositions should be treated as if they were a system of simultaneous equations, each modifying, depending on the circumstances, the effects of the others.

III

Other developments have further modified the Skinnerian position on behavioural psychology. These have often taken the form of a renewed interest in the relations between genetically-determined behaviour, evolved by natural selection, and learned behaviour, that is, operants and their conditioning. Of course, the characteristics of the nervous systems of animals that make operant conditioning possible themselves evolved through natural selection. But the issues are more specific than that. By studying a few, characteristic drives to which a large number of specific operants could be attached by conditioning, Skinner had unwittingly given an impression that has come to be called the *tabula rasa* view of behaviour. According to this metaphor, the psyche of animals is a blank slate (*tabula rasa*) on which conditioning can inscribe with equal ease almost any kind of behaviour. And indeed animals can learn some surprising actions which none of their kind has ever performed before. Yet matters have turned out to be not quite as simple as the *tabula rasa* view would have them. Skinner's first major work, *The Behavior of Organisms* (1938), was followed much later by the Brelands' paper, entertainingly entitled 'The Misbehavior of Organisms' (1961). The Brelands, students of Skinner's, had become professional animal-trainers and found that operant conditioning did not always work quite in the way Skinner said it would. For instance, they discovered that raccoons, highly intelligent animals, 'reinforced by food for picking up coins seemed determined to engage in coin-washing behavior, though, without water around, it did no apparent good' (Herrnstein: 1977, p. 599). On the *tabula rasa* assumption the raccoons would not have taken time out for coin-washing before cashing in their coins for food. But note that wild raccoons do normally wash such favourite foods as fish. It looks very much as if food-washing were a specifically genetic drive, which can itself, or some semblance of itself, be reinforced. Research has revealed a number of other rather more specific drives than psychologists assumed were implied by the Skinnerian position. I say 'assumed' for I cannot find that Skinner himself took any such position explicitly. These discoveries have not undermined the general principles of behaviourism, but they have made the task of applying them to the explanation of behaviour more complicated.

The question remains open whether the revealed diversity and specificity of drives applies to man also. Herrnstein asks, for instance, whether Lionel Tiger's (1969) notion of male bonding may be an example of such a drive. Tiger 'traces the genetic element to forces in evolution that favored the male bond for purposes of collective aggression against outsiders, for hunting, and for other aspects of social organization that came to depend primarily on the male of the species' (Herrnstein: 1977, p. 597). I am prepared to admit the possibility but do not see how the truth of the hypothesis can be demonstrated. I am able to feel confident only that humans must have a generalized drive, genetically determined but differing in strength from individual to individual, that prepares them to be reinforced under ordinary conditions by interaction with other humans. Unless such a drive existed, it is difficult to understand how 'social' behaviour could be learned or maintained. Man has certainly been for ages a 'social' animal, more similar in this respect to the wolves than to the jackals among the canines.

Again, in some conflict with the blank-slate assumption, it has become clear that animals, including humans, may learn many kinds of behaviour but not learn all of them with equal ease; and the differences in ease of learning may be of genetic origin. Many of these findings may not so much have been newly discovered; psychologists may have been aware of them but kept them in the back of their minds in the excitement of pursuing other discoveries. Their work has been strongly stimulated by that of such biologists as E. O. Wilson, put forward in such books as *Sociobiology* (1975) and *On Human Nature* (1978). Especially important is Wilson's insistence that the old distinction between nature (genetics) and nurture (learning) as explanations of behaviour is a false dichotomy. It is the way nature and nurture interact that counts. Some sociologists have been strongly critical of sociobiology, just as they have been of behaviourism itself, for fear that it will rob sociology of part of its subject-matter. If sociologists continue to reject the findings in these fields, they will bring about the very result they wish to avoid. Scientists of other disciplines will pre-empt the material, and sociologists will have lost much that would have helped them to understand social behaviour. They are defending a Maginot line.

IV

I have felt bound to state, however crudely, the main assumptions and propositions of behavioural psychology. But many social scientists who in fact use behaviourism do not realize that they are doing so. They call it utilitarianism or rational-choice theory. I have already tried to show how rational-choice theory – and I believe I could do the same for utility theory – in fact uses the propositions of behavioural psychology. Such social scientists are like Molière's Monsieur Jourdain, who finally discovered that for forty years he had been speaking prose.[2] Utility or rational-choice theories can be used to explain much human behaviour, but they leave out much that behavioural psychology includes. Accordingly I shall speak of them as 'stripped-down' versions of behaviourism. They often take a person's values (purposes) as given, which may do no harm when the values in question are widespread. But when the values are in the least unusual, they do not ask how a person has acquired them, whether genetically or by learning, or by some combination of the two. Values do not come down to human beings out of the blue. Nor do these other theories take full account of the feedback of the results of a person's actions on his future behaviour: they do not capture the crucial historical character of human behaviour, historical both for individuals and for groups. Finally, neither utility theory nor rational-choice theory pays much attention to emotional behaviour, such as aggression. Efforts to explain human action can rarely afford to neglect such things.

What is in some ways worse, many social scientists take behaviourism to be 'just common sense'. Indeed an ordinary person does not express much

[2] Molière, *Le Bourgeois gentilhomme*, Act II, scene 5.

surprise when he hears that a person whose action has been rewarded is apt to repeat it under similar circumstances. Nor should this itself be surprising, for human beings have been familiar with, and studied their own behaviour, for millennia. They ought to know something about it. To some crude degree the general characteristics of their own behaviour are what they know best, unlike those of the physical sciences, about which they know least. Or rather, they are acquainted with some familiar applications, like the lever, but not with the general propositions of the physical sciences. Only when one goes further than common sense, especially by experimental methods, do the actual complexities of behaviour stand revealed. Moreover, what is 'just common sense' may also be both true and important. The deleterious effect of taking common sense for granted is particularly evident when the social scientist fails to state his general propositions at all. His explanations then become what the logicians call *enthymematic*: their major premises are left unstated. Under these conditions the actual similarities of apparently different kinds of explanations go unrecognized.

V

In explaining individual or social behaviour, behavioural psychology or its stripped-down versions is usually attended, and I believe ought to be attended, by two further doctrines, one individualistic and the other the so-called 'covering law' doctrine of theory. Let me consider them in this order. The propositions of behavioural psychology are propositions about what the behaviours of individual members of a species have in common. In the case of *homo sapiens*, they are propositions about human nature. This does not mean that every individual behaves just like every other. Either by genetic inheritance or by differences in their past experiences – whose effects can often themselves be psychologically explained – people differ in the degree to which they conform to the general propositions. In mathematical language, the equations remain the same; their parameters differ somewhat. Most important for my present purposes, the behavioural propositions remain the same whether a person's actions are rewarded or punished by the natural environment or by some other person or persons. Of course new phenomena emerge when a person does not act alone but interacts with another, but no new propositions are needed to account for them – except of course the new given condition itself: that the behaviour is social. The social is not 'more than the sum' of its individual parts – if indeed that famous expression has any meaning. Certainly the word 'sum' is misleading. In my experience, no statement vexes many of my colleagues more than this. But sooner or later they will have to learn to live with it. The statement does not imply that true emergents cannot exist in other sciences, only that they do not in social science. The statement holds good not only for interaction between two persons but among many.

This position has come to be called *methodological individualism*.[3] I believe that, though certainly not called by this name, it is the position that most people over the centuries have held who have thought about the matter at all. A good, clear and fairly early statement is that of John Stuart Mill in his *A System of Logic*:

> The laws of the phenomena of society are, and can be, nothing but the laws of the actions and passions of human beings united together in the social state. Men, however, in a state of society are still men; their actions and passions are obedient to the laws of individual human nature. Men are not, when brought together, converted into another kind of substance with different properties, as hydrogen and oxygen are different from water ... Human beings in society have no properties but those which are derived from, and may be resolved into, the laws of the nature of individual man. In social phenomena the Composition of Causes is the universal law.
>
> (Mill, *A System of Logic*)

By 'the Composition of Causes' Mill was referring to the fact that social phenomena are the complicated and often unintended resultants – not the mere addition – of the action of many individuals, often behaving at cross-purposes. Note that Mill's statement was programmatic only, since he made no effort to state what 'the laws of individual human nature' are. For me they are the laws of psychology, but in Mill's time psychology had not yet become an observational and experimental science. The chief opponent of methodological individualism was, at least in one of his guises, the great French sociologist, Émile Durkheim, who argued that social phenomena were *sui generis*, irreducible to psychology (Durkheim: 1927, p. 12). His doctrine was once almost universal in sociology. Some sociologists are now beginning to break away from it, even French sociologists, so often unduly loyal to their great men. Thus Raymond Boudon writes in his *La Place du désordre*: 'A fundamental principle of the sociologies of action is that social change ought to be analysed as the resultant of a combination [*ensemble*] of individual actions' (Boudon: 1984, p. 12). The rule does not apply to social change alone.

If the behaviour of human beings, their histories, and their institutions can be analysed without residue into the actions of individuals, then it might seem obvious, as it was to Mill, that the propositions explaining their actions must be propositions about individual human nature, that is, propositions of psychology. (Let me admit at once that, while the analysis can be carried out in principle, it can seldom, and then only roughly, be carried out in practice. At this point some would exclaim, 'Damn principle!') But there are sociologists and even philosophers who accept methodological individualism but deny that it implies what they call psychologism. One such is Karl Popper, who would limit psychology to the *intended* consequences

[3] See esp. Watkins: 1959.

of human actions. He offers an example: 'although some people may claim that a liking for mountains and solitude may be explained psychologically, the fact that, if too many people like the mountains, they cannot enjoy solitude there, is not a psychological fact; but this kind of problem is at the heart of social theory' (Popper: 1964, p. 158). I do not see why enjoyment or the lack of it is not a psychological fact, but I agree that this kind of problem is at the very heart of social theory. Let us consider how the phenomenon is to be explained.

By the success and stimulus propositions of behavioural psychology, two or more persons take actions whose results they expect to find rewarding. In this case, they find solitude rewarding and expect to find it in the mountains: accordingly, they go there. Popper obviously takes as given that they do so at the same time and without knowledge of the actions of the others. Accordingly they all arrive at the mountains together, but by definition this cannot be solitude. And accordingly, all are punished, not rewarded, and this result was not intended by any of them. Here an example of the unintended consequences of human action has been explained by an argument that uses psychological propositions as its major premisses. Thus Popper's argument that psychology is limited to the explanation of intended consequences is simply wrong.

W. G. Runciman offers a weak compromise by stating that sociology is not reducible to psychology but 'dependent' on it (Runciman: 1983, p. 29). Unfortunately he does not offer a clear distinction between dependence and reducibility. As I have already pointed out, some avoid the issue by simply not using the word 'psychology' but speaking of utilitarianism or rational choice instead. They do not thereby escape using psychology in fact.

VI

Behaviourism as applied to sociology is closely related to a particular view of the nature of 'theory'. No word is more often used in sociology than this one, partly because theory, as compared with 'mere data-collection', carries high prestige. It is therefore all the more surprising that few sociologists have spent any time defining what a theory *is*. True, 'theory' is just another word, and a scholar may define it in any way he wishes, provided only that he will stick to the definition he has chosen. But few sociologists have gone even that far. Most sociologists seem to use it in the rough sense of 'generalization', but, however it is defined, it must be more than that. The view of theory adopted here seems to correspond to the one that is accepted in the classical physical sciences, which does not mean that the content, as distinguished from the form, of a theory is the same in physical science as in ours.

The present view of theory is usually called the 'covering law' view, though it really should be put in the plural as 'covering laws'.[4] A theory of a phenomenon is an explanation of it, but 'explanation' too is just another word. An explanation of a phenomenon consists of a deductive system. Such a system consists of a set of propositions, each stating a relationship between two or more variables. It does not just assert that there *is* a relationship, but, at least in a first approximation, what the nature of the relationship is: for instance, x is a positive function of y. Sometimes each of the variables can take only two values: present or absent. For example, if x is present, so also is y. At least one of the propositions is the one to be explained, the *explicandum*. Other propositions may be somewhat more general, and at the top of the system stand propositions that at the moment, though the moment may last a long time, are the most general of all, 'most general' simply meaning that they cannot be derived from the other propositions in the set. These are the propositions that give the covering-law view of theory its name. Other propositions state, as in Euclid, the given conditions (boundary conditions, parameters) to which the general propositions are to be applied. The given conditions can often themselves be explained. The lowest-order propositions, the *explicanda*, are said to be explained when they can be shown to follow logically from the other propositions in the set. Propositions of mathematics, which come from non-contingent theories, may be used to make the deductions, but no scientific theory can consist of non-contingent propositions alone. A contingent proposition is one to whose acceptance data, fact, evidence, etc., are relevant.

Most theories do not have a single *explicandum* but many *explicanda* to be deduced from the covering laws under different given conditions. To speak crudely, we judge a theory to be powerful when from a few covering laws a large number of empirical propositions can be explained. Let me make it plain: the preceding is a description of what a theory ought to look like when completed – and no theory is ever more than provisionally completed. It is not a description of how a theory is arrived at, which may be by many kinds of processes, and which I shall not go into here.[5]

My own efforts to explain the findings that I have encountered in reading and research about behaviour in small groups has led me to the conclusion that their most useful covering laws are those of behavioural psychology. Unlike great scientists I have not had to invent my own covering laws: I can borrow them from the work of others. Moreover I do not think my conclusion is limited to sociology. The covering laws of all the social sciences are those of behavioural psychology. It is easy, for instance, to derive the so-called laws of supply and demand in economics from them. My argument does not in the least imply that sociology will be lost in an undifferentiated social science, athough no doubt there will be overlaps. The reason is that some social sciences will apply behavioural psychology to different given conditions than will others. For instance, the conditions assumed to exist

[4] See esp. Braithwaite: 1953; Hempel: 1965; Nagel: 1961.
[5] But see Holton: 1973.

in the classical market – that no participant need have regular relations with any other participant – are obviously different from those of a working group in industry, where, at least for some time, regular interaction among the members will be the rule. Therefore the kinds of empirical propositions microeconomics is able to explain will be somewhat different from those of microsociology.

When the propositions of one named science can be shown to follow under particular given conditions from those of another, the former are said to be reduced to those of the other. Accordingly, the programme of behaviourism as applied to sociology is often called *psychological reductionism*, and under that name drives many sociologists to fury. Again, they are worried about preserving their identity. Yet other sciences have undergone reduction without apparently feeling any pain. I take it that much chemistry can now be reduced to physics, yet chemistry is well and strong. Practical problems often prevent reduction from bringing about a merger of sciences. Thus thermodynamics can be reduced to statistical mechanics, but we still use thermodynamics for designing heat engines. And we still send rockets to the moon using supposedly superseded Newtonian mechanics. The calculations are simpler than those required by relativity, and in any case the result falls well within the inevitable margin of error on the target.

The programme of behaviourism as applied to sociology consists, then, of three linked sets of ideas: the propositions of behavioural psychology itself, the doctrine of methodological individualism and the covering-law view of theory. It is a programme and – let never the timid fear – the programme can never fully be carried out. Many phenomena it will never be able to explain – but neither will alternative programmes.

VII

Let us now look at the difficulties the programme encounters, what strategies for research it suggests, what it has accomplished, and what further advantages it might offer if adopted more fully.

I shall first deal with one minor ambiguity that the adoption of the view presented here removes from sociology, although, I admit, merely by a change in terminology. At one time the dominant theoretical position in sociology was said to be functionalism. Though the functionalists seldom realized it, there were always two main kinds of functionalism, which I call societal and individualistic functionalism. Societal functionalism tried to explain social institutions by the contributions they made to the survival or equilibrium of the social system of which they were parts. Elsewhere I have diagnosed the weaknesses of this theory;[6] I shall not consider it further here, but turn to individualistic functionalism. Individualistic functionalism

---

[6] E.g., see the index references to 'function' in Homans (1984).

explained much institutional and other behaviour by the functions they performed for individuals, often for many individuals, but still in their character as individuals. The sense of confidence provided by magic was an example. The theory implied that what was functional for someone was what was 'good' for him. Closer consideration found that some things he found 'good' for him were in fact not so: tobacco and some other drugs were examples. If they were not functional in the sense of being good, they certainly were in the sense of being rewarding or reinforcing: action that obtained them was apt to be repeated. In short, for individual functionalism, the word 'function' could be changed to 'reward' without any loss of meaning. With this one change of word, many functional explanations became straightforward individualistic and psychological explanations. An example is Robert Merton's famous 'functional paradigm' that showed, among other things, how in the late nineteenth and early twentieth century, the system that linked urban immigrants with ward-bosses, politicians, and business-men seeking favours from government maintained itself because each pair of the parties concerned provided one another with rewarding behaviour. The explanation is not a special 'functional' one but directly behaviouristic (Merton: 1968, pp. 104–36).

In my view the application of behavioural psychology to sociology is for the time being best pursued by explaining features of social structure that appear again and again in small groups all over the world and can be directly observed when one is making field studies of new groups: norms, cohesion, competition, status, power, leadership, distributive justice and the development of regular channels of communication. The sheer number of such groups forces the researcher's attention on features that are common and so most in need of explanation. I believe that in my own book *Social Behavior: Its Elementary Forms* (1961), I have shown at least in a crude way how these features can be explained on behavioural principles. Groups differ in the degree to which they possess these characteristics, but all groups, including the largest, do possess them. The findings we try to explain are usually only statistically true, because we do not know enough about the characteristics of individual members. We can explain, for instance, why leaders should emerge, but we do not know why particular individuals should do so. When we do know, we of course take these facts into account. I subscribe to this strategy not because I have calculated in the abstract that it is a good one, but because I have had much experience, directly and vicariously, with small groups. As sociologists we would do well to tie down our understanding of these features of small groups before we tackle the unique features of large societies. Such is my hope, but I do not believe in the least that it will be carried out, for scientists *will* pursue what happens to interest them, even at the expense of a good strategy. And I am not sure that they are not correct, for what they lose in strategy, they make up for in motivation.

At the level of what I call elementary social behaviour, the derivation of empirical propositions from the general propositions of behavioural psychology (or, if you prefer, the reduction of the former to the latter) is often straightforward. Long ago, Festinger, Schachter and Back, studying groups living in similar housing units, tested the proposition that, the more cohesive a group was, the more likely were its members to conform to its norms, whatever these might be (Festinger, Schachter and Back: 1950, pp. 61–150). Each variable was measured by a simple questionnaire. Cohesiveness was defined as the proportion of friendship choices the members of a group gave to other members rather than to outsiders, conformity as the number who expressed agreement with important norms. The result could be explained by the fact that people often find agreement with their views rewarding, and reward leads to favourable sentiments between the rewarded and the rewarders. Not a different explanation but simply the other side of the first, might be the following. Friendship with others is rewarding to many people and its loss a punishment. The first punishment members of a group mete out to those who violate their norms is withdrawal of their friendship. But in cohesive groups there is more friendship to lose than in less cohesive ones, and hence there is apt to be less nonconformity in the former. In the explanation, I have tacitly used the value proposition and the frustration-aggression proposition. The authors of the study, though they were all social psychologists, did not mention that they were using behavioural psychology in their explanation. They assumed that they were using common sense. I only wish scholars recognized more often that common sense is often good behavioural psychology, though some of the implications of behavioural psychology go far beyond common sense.

VIII

Already in the explanation of the features of small groups a problem appears that has far wider implications. When I speak of social structures I shall mean any features of groups that persist for any period of time, though the period may not be long. I shall not attempt, nor shall I need to attempt, any more sophisticated definition. Once the structure of a group has emerged and is being maintained by the actions of its members, that structure itself provides contingencies for further behaviour on the part of its members, behaviour that may consolidate the existing structure or give rise to a new one. For instance, once a group has established and is maintaining a status system, an individual member who finds himself at the bottom of the system has no further to fall. His 'falling' in the past was usually caused by his 'bad' behaviour, bad not in any absolute sense, perhaps, but bad according to the norms of the group. But if he is already at the bottom, he incurs no further cost from bad behaviour – he has nothing further to lose – and behaviour that may be rewarding but is otherwise without cost is behaviour he is apt to perform. Yet if he performs it, he only confirms his position at the bottom of the group. This kind of phenomenon goes far to account for the appearance of an under class or *Lumpenproletariat*.

The problem gives rise to a recognizable and important difference among sociologists, which is well treated, together with other matters, in Viktor Vanberg's *Die zwei Soziologien* (1975) – 'The Two Sociologies'. There are those sociologists, like myself, who are most interested in how individuals create social structures, which include, at their most elaborate, the institutions of a society as a whole, such as a legal and political system; and there are those who ask how institutions affect the behaviour of individuals or groups. I am always being reminded by structuralists that the small groups I study are usually parts of larger structures, and the characteristics of the smaller unit are determined in part by the characteristics of the larger. Of course they are. But both sociologies, the effects of individuals on the creation of structures, and the effects of structures on the behaviour of individuals, require for their explanation the same propositions of behavioural psychology. I confess that the creation of institutions, which often have a long past history, may be difficult to explain, for lack of adequate information. Still, when one can observe history in the making, one can always see the behavioural principles at work. Indeed it is often easier to see psychology working in this direction than in the other. It is easy at the small-group level and often at higher ones to see human beings creating structures. It is often not so easy to see the structures affecting the behaviour of individuals, because the process often seems automatic, though it is not. When a red light shows at an intersection, we stop our car; we do not stop to think that our behaviour is the result of psychological principles. A red light is a social structure.

Failure to understand this point is another of the mistakes Karl Popper makes when he argues that methodological individualism does not entail psychologism. He writes: 'In fact, psychology cannot be the basis of social science. First, because it is itself just one of the social sciences: "human nature" varies considerably with the social institutions, and its understanding therefore presupposes an understanding of these institutions' (Popper: 1964, p. 158). The first argument I have been at some pains to refute. Psychology is not just one of the social sciences: it is the one from whose general propositions the empirical propositions of the others can be derived. As for the institutional argument, I would put it the other way around. The understanding of institutions presupposes an understanding of human nature, that is, of the propositions of psychology, though institutions once created react on human behaviour. But the reactions themselves occur in accordance with the characteristics of human nature.

IX

One of the main difficulties in applying the doctrines of behavioural psychology to the explanation of social behaviour is that it is a historical science: a person's behaviour is determined by his past experience in interaction with his present circumstances. We often know a good deal about the latter, but we rarely have enough knowledge of an individual's past to explain other than very roughly his present actions. At times we have enough information to make some difference, especially in the case of historically important individuals whose lives are apt to be recorded. It is surely important in explaining why William the Conqueror invaded England in the face of formidable obstacles to know that he had enjoyed many decades of success in war. According to the success proposition, his conviction that he was likely to succeed again must have been strong. However, I doubt that we shall ever be able to explain convincingly both why he invaded and why he won the battle of Hastings.

This kind of difficulty makes more difference for prediction than for postdiction, though it makes plenty of trouble even there. We can usually explain better what has happened or is happening than predict what will. We sociologists, struggling with our feelings of inferiority, forget there are sciences more respectable than ours that run into the same historical difficulties: geology, for example, or Darwinian evolution. I do not think that Darwinism can predict when a new species will appear, but I bet that when one does it will be able to explain why. Some scientists used to hold that a science that could not predict was no true science. But who would impugn the scientific character of Darwinism? No science should be dismissed because it cannot predict accurately or even predict at all. It will do well enough if it can explain.

It sometimes sounds as if, to use behavioural psychology rigorously in explanation, we should have to know the past history of every individual concerned. Yet psychology can still be applied when one has to deal with a relatively large number of individuals who, for purposes of explanation, may be considered to hold more or less similar values. Let me use another historical example. If I want to explain the rise of the English woollen-cloth industry in the fourteenth century, I begin with the need of the government of England, led by King Edward I, to raise more money from its subjects. This seems to be a universal need of governments. It was especially acute at the end of the thirteenth century because it was a time of inflation, and Edward's intentions were warlike, that is, expensive.

In Edward's time the largest of English exports, both in bulk and value, was raw wool, which went for the most part to Flanders, where it was woven into cloth. Hitherto it had not been taxed. With the advice of his counsellors Edward levied a tax, ultimately called the custom, on the export of wool, and appointed officers to collect the tax. Taxation of wool was apt to be successful in raising money, since bales of wool are bulky in relation to their value and thus not easily smuggled.

The effect of the tax was to raise the cost of manufacturing cloth in Flanders, provided the Flemish merchants could not find an alternative and adequate supply of wool. The chief possibility was Spanish wool, but the cost of transportation to Flanders was high, and the supply may not have been sufficient. England itself had for local needs a small cloth industry of its own. The increased cost of manufacturing in Flanders reduced the relative cost of manufacturing in England. It does not take a great knowledge of economics, which is a branch of utility theory, to account for what happened, and we luckily have a good series of customs records from the fourteenth century to document it. English cloth manufacture increased relative to Flemish, until England became a net exporter of cloth, not wool. There is no reason to believe that King Edward intended his tax to have this effect: he just wanted to raise more money and found wool an easy target for taxation.

The explanation depends on my assuming that there were a number of merchants, Flemish, English, and indeed others, who were concerned with the woollen-cloth trade and that, whatever their other differences, they shared substantially the same sort of values or at least many of them did, so that, though the theory is individualistic, I do not have to take account of every single individual separately.

I have not spelled the explanation out in full, but I have certainly tacitly assumed that the actors, from the king downwards, behaved according to their perceptions of what would be successful in increasing their rewards. The argument is economic; but the rise of the English woollen-cloth industry had long-range social and political effects. It laid the foundation for Britain's leadership in the Industrial Revolution. By the way, I am far from arguing that this explanation alone accounts for England's woollen manufacture. Note that, to produce the explanation, the tacit general propositions about the rewards and success of action must be applied to initial given conditions: that England was at first a large exporter of wool, that England possessed an institution, the kingship, which had effective powers to tax, and so on. These initial conditions may themselves be subject to lengthy explanation, but at some time, for lack of information or only for convenience, the regression on the universe must stop.

The explanation of the results of the behaviour of Edward i and the wool merchants is relatively straightforward, even though the number of merchants was large. It is just as straightforward as the explanation of some of the common features of small groups. For this reason I hesitate to draw any sharp line, on the basis of size of population, between micro and macrosociology. I prefer to use the criterion of complexity of explanation.

Far more complex than the previous examples is such a study as that reported by Raymond Boudon in his book *Effets pervers et ordre social* (1977, pp. 17–130). It includes a study of the relations between a new institutional arrangement, the resulting choices made over time by a very large number of individuals and family groups without systematic communication between them (less, probably, than that between Edward i's merchants), and the aggregate effects produced by these choices. The new institutional arrangement was the provision of free higher education for all qualified Frenchmen and women. Instead of having its intended effect of decreasing the degree of social stratification, it had the opposite – in Boudon's terms, a *perverse effect*. The explanation of this result requires a far greater command of sophisticated statistical methods than does the effect of Edward i's wool tax or the relation between cohesion and conformity in small groups. But no new behavioural principles need be introduced. The *explicandum* is still an aggregate of individual behaviours. I suspect that an increasing number of sociological researches will be of this type.

It is even more difficult to explain in full detail propositions about the relationships between institutions, such as the one, which I believe to be true, that nations with democratic and representative institutions also possess relatively independent judiciaries. The explanation would have to be histori-cal, spreading perhaps over many centuries, requiring attention to each of the two institutions and the changing relations between them. To carry the explanation explicitly back to behavioural principles would require their repetition over and over again for different stages of the historical process, which would be cumbersome and boring – and we are boring enough already. No one is going to undertake this kind of explanation. We would use, as we have used in the past, all sorts of shortcuts. Still, even here, I think it would be useful to state the behavioural principles at least once. They would indicate the often unstated assumptions that are guiding the explanation. They would remind us that historical change is not the result of 'impersonal' forces, such as 'progress', 'increasing differentiation' or 'the development of the forces of production'. The changes are made by people, though the aggregates of their choices may often be summed up in phrases like those above. The people in question may of course be limited in what they can do by conditions that are not 'social' at all but are physical characteristics of the environment. Think what difference the fact that it is an island has made to the history of Britain.

The whole tendency of the argument offered here means that there are no general laws of history *per se*, though many historians have looked for them. There are plenty of historical generalizations, often of great import-ance, that hold good within certain given conditions, but only within these, not across the board. The only fully general historical propositions are propositions about the behaviour of human beings as members of a species. For a good discussion see Raymond Boudon, *La Place du désordre* (1984), and indeed still earlier, Georg Simmel, *Die Probleme der Geschichtsphilosophie* (1907), though he was at a disadvantage because an adequate psychology was not at his disposal. I sometimes think that behavioural psychology is as much of use as a general guide to the nature of explanation in the social sciences as it is in providing the explicit major premisses for actual explanation.

X

The point of view and practice presented here are growing in importance, as shown by the increasing number of scholars that adopt them. True, few use the full panoply of behavioural psychology, but rather its stripped-down form, which they often do not recognize for what it is and which they often refer to instead as utilitarianism or rational-choice theory. But at least they will admit to being methodological individualists, which would have been unthinkable even a few years ago.

To speak only for the moment of sociologists and North Americans, I draw particular attention to the following: much of the work of Robert Hamblin[7] and John H. Kunkel,[8] the too little-known book of John F. Scott, *The Internalization of Norms* (1971), the collection of papers in *Behavioral Theory in Sociology* (Hamblin and Kunkel: 1977), and more recently the book edited by Michael Hechter, *The Microfoundations of Macrosociology* (1983). Though I find him sometimes confused, I believe that Arthur Stinchcombe has the heart of the matter in him. At least in his *Theoretical Methods in Social History* he is willing to say, 'The causal forces that make systematic social change go are people figuring out what to do' (Stinchcombe: 1978, p. 36). The late Richard Emerson I am sure was one of us, though he did not use our language.[9]

In Britain, as I have said, W. G. Runciman (1983) is prepared to admit that sociology is 'dependent' on psychology. And I am ready to recommend, though not always to agree with, Anthony Heath's *Rational Choice and Social Exchange* (1976). Many of these men must always have known what they are now prepared to admit openly. In the past they may have been held back by the fear of only stating common sense. Today common sense about human behaviour has turned into a highly-developed science, in the mainstream of psychology, with much careful experimental work on both animals and humans to its credit. Common sense has become more defensible as it has become so much more than merely common sense.

For reasons not altogether clear to me, more European than American sociologists have adopted to some degree the programme outlined above. Pride of place in time I give to my dear friend Andrzej Malewski and his book *Verhalten und Interaktion* (1967). Malewski, alas, killed himself, I believe in despair for the future of his country, Poland. The West Germans have contributed more than the other Europeans or Americans. Foremost I would place Dr Karl-Dieter Opp, Professor of Sociology at the University of Hamburg, for a whole series of books bearing, some more directly than others, on the programme (Opp: 1970; 1972; 1976; 1978; 1979; 1983; Opp and Hummell: 1973). To Opp's work I would add Enno Schwanenberg, *Soziales Handel* (1970), Werner Raub and Thomas Voss, *Individuelles Handeln und gesellschaftliche Folgen* (1981), Werner Raub, *Rationale Akteure, institutionelle Regelungen und Interdependenzen* (1984), and several papers by Siegwart Lindenberg.[10] In another but very important category I would place Viktor Vanberg's *Die zwei Soziologien* (1975), which I have already cited, and which first made clear to me the relations, including historical relations, between

---

[7] E.g. Hamblin *et al.*: 1971.
[8] E.g. Kunkel: 1975.
[9] See esp. Emerson: 1962.
[10] Conveniently listed in the Bibliography of Raub (1984).

individualistic and what might be called collective sociology, really the relations between individualism and structuralism.

The French have contributed less voluminously but with work of just as high a quality. The pre-eminent figure, whom I have already cited, is Raymond Boudon, especially his two works *Effets pervers et ordre social* (1977) and *La Place du désordre: critiques des théories de changement social* (1984). Since most American sociologists, like most Americans, have not been trained to read foreign languages easily – they suffer from one of the great defects of American education – they are usually not aware of these books, much to their loss.

I have been speaking of sociologists, American and foreign. But in recent years social scientists outside sociology, in economics and political science, have begun to use rational-choice models to explain phenomena not usually treated in their disciplines. (Of course, classical economics itself uses a rational-choice model.) Consider particularly such books as the following and their potential influences on sociology: A. Downs, *An Economic Theory of Democracy* (1957), Mancur Olson, *The Logic of Collective Action* (1965), H. Eylau, *Micro-Macro Political Analysis* (1969), A. O. Hirschman, *Exit, Voice, and Loyalty* (1970), B. Barry, *Sociologists, Economists, and Bureaucracy* (1970), T. Schelling, *Micromotives and Macrobehavior* (1978), and H. Leibenstein, *Beyond Economic Man: A New Foundation for Microeconomics* (1976). This last is not quite what it claims to be, because it still uses a rational-choice theory as microeconomics always did. But it explores some kinds of influences affecting economic choice that are not taken into account in usual economic analysis. If sociologists do not pay attention to these new developments and the kind of theory used in them, they will be in danger of losing some of the most potentially interesting parts of their field to other social science disciplines. I believe that the danger – if it is one – from this quarter is far greater than the much more widely-recognized danger from psychology. Indeed I do not regard the latter as a danger at all.

XI

I end with the present internal state of sociology. It is unfortunately divided into a number of different schools: symbolic interactionism, structuralism, ethnomethodology, conflict theory, dramaturgy (Goffman), and many others, each fiercely asserting its originality and independence from the others. All of them have a number of good empirical findings to their credit. But though they use no word more often than they do 'theory', they are weak in theory, for they do not, with the possible exception of myself, tell us what a theory *is*. Not possessing a doctrine of theory, they do not make explicit their covering laws, which makes it difficult to determine whether the schools are as distinct from one another as they claim to be. My own belief is that they are far less distinct. Consider Mitchell's description of Goffman's approach: 'An effective actor then is not only one who is rewarded for good performances by the acceptance of his audience, but also is one who comes to see a continuity of essentials in his performances and is able to account for himself as more than a mere shell' (Mitchell: 1978, p. 112). This explanation of what makes a good actor embodies an unstated major premiss, and that premiss is one of the general propositions of behavioural psychology: that a person who takes an action which is followed by a reward is apt to repeat that action. Consider for another example Mitchell's description of the work of Harold Garfinkel: 'The issues of ethnomethodology are the issues of communication exchange in that the ethnomethodological search is for the communication processes that lead to a sense of common understanding among people' (Mitchell: 1978, p. 148). But, as I have remarked elsewhere, '"Common understanding" *rewards* people: social life is impossible without it' (Homans: 1982, p. 290). Accordingly ethnomethodology too embodies in its unstated major premisses the success and value propositions of behavioural psychology. I could go on in the same way with the other schools.

One advantage that would accrue to all of us if we accepted and acted upon the covering-law view of theory is that the different schools would have to ask themselves what covering laws they would in fact use if they formalized their theories. I do not want them to do so every time they attempt an explanation. As I have said, that would be repetitious and boring. But I want them to do so at least once. I think that all the schools would find that they would use the principles of behavioural psychology, either in what I have called the stripped-down form or in one that embodies more fully the still-developing experimental findings. By their covering laws shall one recognize the kinship of theories.

The search for the covering laws they have in common would not in the least interfere with their devoting themselves to different areas of empirical research. And the search *conceivably* might help to restore – although I do not believe we ever had it – or, better, create an intellectual unity in our science and encourage us to achieve the oft-stated hope that our findings be cumulative. Except in this one respect, I do not think that my programme would require sociologists to do anything that they are not doing now. I say *conceivably* because at the moment the members of the different schools seem to have more ego invested in their distinctiveness than they can bear to give up.

Bibliography

Bandura, A., 1969: *Principles of Behavior Modification*. New York: Holt, Rinehart and Winston.
    1973: *Aggression: A Social Learning Analysis*. Englewood Cliffs, NJ: Prentice-Hall.
Barry, B., 1970: *Sociologists, Economists, and Bureaucracy*. Chicago: University of Chicago Press.
Boudon, R., 1977: *Effets pervers et ordre social*. Paris: Presses Universitaires de France.

1984: *La Place du désordre: critiques des théories de changement social.* Paris: Presses Universitaires de France. (English translation: Theories of Social Change. Cambridge: Polity Press, 1986).

Braithwaite, R. B., 1953: *Scientific Explanation.* Cambridge, England: Cambridge University Press.

Breland, K. and M., 1961: 'The Misbehavior of Organisms', *American Psychologist,* 16: 681–4.

Brown, R. and Herrnstein, R. J., 1975: *Psychology.* Boston: Little, Brown.

Downs, A., 1957: *An Economic Theory of Democracy.* New York: Harper & Row.

Durkheim, É., 1927: *Les Règles de la méthode sociologique.* Paris: Alcan.

Emerson, R., 1962: 'Power–Dependence Relations', *American Sociological Review,* 22: 31–41.

Eylau, H., 1969: *Micro-Macro Political Analysis: Accents of Inquiry.* Chicago: Aldine.

Festinger, L., Schachter, S. and Back, K., 1950: *Social Pressures in Informal Groups: A Study of Human Factors in Housing.* New York: Harper & Row.

Hamblin, R. T., Buckholdt, D., Ferritor, D., Kozloff, M. and Blackwell, L., 1971: *The Humanization Process: A Social, Behavioral Analysis of Children's Problems.* New York: Wiley–Intersciences.

Hamblin, R. T. and Kunkel, R. H. (eds), 1977: *Behavioral Theory in Sociology: Essays in Honor of George C. Homans.* New Brunswick, NJ: Transaction Books.

Heath, A., 1976: *Rational Choice and Social Exchange: A Critique of Exchange Theory.* Cambridge, England: Cambridge University Press.

Hechter, M. (ed.), 1983: *The Microfoundations of Macrosociology.* Philadelphia: Temple University Press.

Hempel, C. G., 1965: *Aspects of Scientific Explanation and Other Essays in the Philosophy of Science.* New York: Free Press.

Herrnstein, R. J., 1971: 'Quantitative Hedonism', *Journal of Psychiatry,* 8: 399–412.
1977: 'The Evolution of Behaviorism', *American Psychologist,* 32: 593–603.

Hirschman, A. O., 1970: *Exit, Voice, and Loyalty: Responses to Decline in Firms, Organizations, and States.* Cambridge, Mass.: Harvard University Press.

Holton, G., 1973: *Thematic Origins of Scientific Thought, Kepler to Einstein.* Cambridge, Mass.: Harvard University Press.

Homans, G. C. 1961: *Social Behavior: Its Elementary Forms.* New York: Harcourt, Brace. Revised 1974.
1982: 'The Present State of Sociological Theory', *Sociological Quarterly,* 23: 285–99.
1984: *Coming to my Senses: The Autobiography of a Sociologist.* New Brunswick, NJ: Transaction Books.

Kunkel, J. H., 1975: *Behavior, Social Problems and Change: A Social Learning Approach.* Englewood Cliffs, NJ: Prentice-Hall.

Leibenstein, H., 1976: *Beyond Economic Man: A New Foundation for Microeconomics.* Cambridge, Mass.: Harvard University Press.

Malewski, A., 1967: *Verhalten und Interaktion.* Tübingen: Mohr Siebeck. First published in Polish 1964.

Merton, R. K., 1968: *Social Theory and Social Structure,* enlarged edn. New York: Free Press.

Mill, J. S., *A System of Logic,* Book 6, ch. 7, sect. 1.

Mitchell, J. N. 1978: *Social Exchange, Dramaturgy, and Ethnomethodology.* New York: Elsevier.

Nagel, E., 1961: *The Structure of Science: Problems in the Logic of Scientific Explanation.* New York: Harcourt, Brace.

Olson, M. jun., 1965: *The Logic of Collective Action: Public Goods and the Theory of Groups*. Cambridge, Mass.: Harvard University Press.

Opp, K-D., 1970: *Soziales Handeln, Rollen und soziale Systeme: Ein Erklärungsversuch sozialen Verhaltens*. Stuttgart: Enke.

1972: *Verhaltenstheoretische Soziologie: Eine neue sociologische Forschungsrichtung*. Hamburg: Rohwolt.

1976: *Methodologie der Sozialwissenschaften: Einführung in Probleme ihrer Theorienbildung*, revised edn. Hamburg: Rohwolt.

1978: *Theorie sozialer Krisen: Apathie, Protest und kollektives Handeln*. Hamburg: Hoffman und Campe.

1979: *Individualistische Sozialwissenschaft: Arbeitsweise und Probleme individualistisch und kollektivistisch orientierter Sozialwissenschaften*. Stuttgart: Enke.

1983: *Die Entstehung sozialer Normen: Ein Integrationsversuch soziologischer, sozialpsychologischer und ökonomischer Erklärungen*. Tübingen: Mohr Siebeck.

Opp, K.-D. and Hummell, H. J., 1973: *Kritik der Soziologie: Probleme der Erklärung sozialer Prozesse*, 2 vols. Frankfurt-on-Main: Athenäum.

Popper, K. R., 1964: *The Poverty of Historicism*. New York: Harper & Row.

Rachlin, H., 1976: *Introduction to Modern Behaviorism*, 2nd edn. San Francisco: W. H. Freeman.

Raub, W., 1984: *Rationale Akteure, institutionelle Regelungen und Interdependenzen: Untersuchung zu einer erklärenden Soziologie auf strukturell-individualistischer Grundlage*. Frankfurt-on-Main: Peter Lang.

Raub, W. and Voss, T., 1981: *Individuelles Handeln und gesellschaftlicher Folgen: Das individualistische Programm in der Sozialwissenschaften*. Darmstadt: Luchterhand.

Reynolds, G. S., 1968: *A Primer of Operant Conditioning*. Glenview, Ill.: Scott, Foresman.

Runciman, W. G., 1983: *The Methodology of Social Theory*, vol. 1 of *A Treatise on Social Theory*. Cambridge, England: Cambridge University Press.

Schelling, T. C., 1978: *Micromotives and Macrobehavior*. New York: Norton.

Schwanenberg, E., 1970: *Soziales Handel – Die Theorie und ihr Probleme*. Bern: Hans Huber.

Scott, J. F., 1971: *The Internalization of Norms: A Sociological Theory of Moral Commitment*. Englewood Cliffs, NJ: Prentice-Hall.

Simmel, G., 1907: *Die Probleme der Geschichtsphilosophie*. Munich: Dunker und Humblot.

Skinner, B. F., 1938: *The Behaviour of Organisms*. New York: Appleton-Century-Croft.

1971: *Beyond Freedom and Dignity*. New York: Knopf.

Stinchcombe, A. L., 1978: *Theoretical Methods in Social History*. New York: Academic Press.

Tiger, L., 1969: *Men in Groups*. New York: Random House.

Vanberg, V., 1975: *Die zwei Soziologien: Individualismus und Kollektivismus in der Sozialtheorie*. Tübingen: Mohr Siebeck.

Watkins, J. W. N., 1959: 'Historical Explanation in the Social Sciences', in P. Gardiner (ed.), *Theories of History*. Glencoe, Ill.: Free Press, pp. 503–14.

Wilson, E. O., 1975: *Sociobiology*. Cambridge, Mass.: Harvard University Press.

1978: *On Human Nature*. Cambridge, Mass.: Harvard University Press.

Symbolic Interactionism[1]

HANS JOAS

When American sociology set out on its triumphal march around the world after the end of the Second World War, it had passed its own historical turning-point only a short time before. The combination of Lazarsfeld and Merton, as the sociological approach after that turning-point was described (Shils: 1970, p. 794), linked together a quantitatively-oriented and sophisticated empirical social research with a structural-functional theory stripped of its philosophical and historical context and origins and trimmed down to a 'middle range' of application. This combination offered itself as the summing up of all that was valuable from the legacy of the classical European sociologists and as the way of conveying this legacy into the basic store of theory and method of a professionally-safeguarded and cumulative acquisition of knowledge. To be sure, the stability of the discipline's identity was bought at the high price of the suppression of traditions that could be integrated into sociology's new image only with great difficulty. In this regard it is most striking that, although Parsons grappled with the interpretation of Durkheim, Weber and Pareto for hundreds of pages in his first great work, *The Structure of Social Action* (1968a), in that discussion he not only presented a completely inadequate picture of German idealism and Marxism, but even considered the American traditions of social theory as hardly worth mentioning. He literally did not devote a single word to the accomplishments of John Dewey's and George Herbert Mead's pragmatist social philosophy, or to the pioneering methodological achievements of the Chicago School of sociology and the theoretical implications of their large-scale empirical investigations. American ideas and research that were not deemed worthy of attention even in their country of origin could hardly expect to find better treatment outside the United States, given the general leftist or Eurocentric scepticism about American thought.

This does not mean that this tradition has died out completely. In numerous sub-fields of sociology, ranging from research on socialization to

[1] This essay has been translated from the German by Raymond Meyer, Palo Alto, Cal. I would like to thank Anselm Strauss for his helpful comments on the paper.

criminal and urban sociology and including occupational sociology, works of the Chicago tradition play an important role and have contributed to the fruitfulness of investigations carried out in these areas. Scattered fragments of this tradition, such as Mead's conceptions of the self and of role-taking, the 'Thomas theorem' on the effective character of all components of a situation that are regarded as real, and the fundamental notion of the biographical method all belong to the standard stock of sociological knowledge. Certainly, many representatives of this tradition found themselves in relative isolation or had to assume the role of a more or less 'loyal opposition' to the mainstream of sociology. In the sixties, the tradition, especially in the form given it by Herbert Blumer (1969), became the object of an almost fashionable interest. It became so, though, in a theoretically-muddled combination with phenomenological and other approaches that yielded the so-called interpretative approach (Wilson: 1970). In the very recent past, there have been an increasing number of attempts to overcome this tradition's temporary concentration on microsociological phenomena and to achieve an understanding of its premises and principles through an examination of its history.

These attempts have taken two sharply distinct forms. On the one hand, the movement toward the neo-positivist theory of science and behaviourist psychology holds out the promise of overcoming the 'astructural bias' of the symbolic-interactionist tradition.[2] From the standpoint of the history of sociological theory, this line of thought seeks to ensure its validity by attempting to make a metatheoretical conflict between nominalist and realist views the guiding thread for distinguishing the strand of the tradition originating with Peirce and Mead from the one that leads from James, via Dewey, to Blumer.[3] On the other hand, there are the efforts to uncover and extract the macrotheoretical assumptions that had always been implicit in the concrete research carried out within this tradition, and to join them together to make a coherent whole, a theory of 'negotiated order'. In the most recent writings of symbolic interactionists one can also find signs that they are concerning themselves with the ideas of structuralism and post-structuralism (Perinbanayagam: 1985).

No matter how one assesses these different tendencies, they are all indicative of the intent actively to introduce into the general theoretical discussion the legacy of the sociological tradition that has its roots in the Chicago School. This is by no means typical for this school. For many decades, the Chicago tradition was continued less through the elaboration of a systematic

[2] Exemplary statements of this position can be found in McPhail and Rexroat (1979) and Stryker (1980). For a discussion of Stryker's book, see Review Symposium, *Symbolic Interaction*, 5, 1982: 141–72.

[3] See Lewis and Smith: 1980. Several almost completely negative commentaries on this book have appeared, which contain important arguments on the relation between pragmatism and sociology. Some of these are: Blumer: 1983; Johnson and Picou: 1985; Miller: 1982; Rochberg-Halton: 1983.

theory and the tradition's theoretical self-grounding than by means of exemplary research and oral transmission. This fact could itself become a point of reference in the self-understanding of symbolic interactionists, as well as for an account of the history of this school of thought (Rock: 1979). Parsons's silence was, so to speak, repaid in the same currency. It is difficult to say whether this theoretical self-isolation was due to a justified mistrust of analytical construction of theory, in contrast to the symbolic interactionists' own programme of formulating an empirically-grounded theory (Glaser and Strauss: 1967), or simply to the Chicago theorists' inability to oppose to the comprehensive, theoretically and historically broadly-inclusive approaches such as those of Parsons (or of Marxism and critical theory), something even approximately equivalent in scope.

It is from this position that the difficulties of reviewing symbolic interactionism arise. In the following account, one certainly has to define symbolic interactionism as it is generally understood. The name of this line of sociological and sociopsychological research was coined in 1938 by Herbert Blumer (1938). Its focus is processes of interaction – social action that is characterized by an immediately reciprocal orientation – and the investigations of these processes are based on a particular concept of interaction which stresses the symbolic character of social action. The prototypical case is of social relations in which action does not take the form of mere translation of fixed prescriptions into deeds, but in which definitions of the relations are, rather, jointly and reciprocally proposed and established. Social relations are seen, then, not as stabilized once and for all but as open and tied to ongoing common acknowledgement.

Now, it would be entirely inadequate to confine a delineation of symbolic interactionism to this central insight and to the theoretical and methodological preferences arising out of it. The widespread criticism of symbolic interactionism is alone sufficient to make it necessary to go beyond this first level of presentation. Such criticism is directed chiefly against the limitation of symbolic interactionism to phenomena of interpersonal immediacy. However, it also accuses symbolic interactionism of ignoring questions of power and domination. There is imputed to it a view of the complex of macrosocial relations as merely the horizon of life-worldly sociality as well as a complete unawareness of the societal mastery of nature or the fact that societal conditions may become autonomous in relation to the actions and orientations of the participants in social actions. Although many of these criticisms do in fact apply, at least partially, to Herbert Blumer's programme and to the sociologists who follow that programme, their justification is nevertheless doubtful when one considers the breadth of the theoretical and empirical work produced by this line of research.

For the true significance of symbolic interactionism and its potential theoretical fecundity can only be understood when it is viewed against the background of the old Chicago School, which it continues while omitting some aspects of that school's thought. Such a consideration of symbolic interactionism, therefore, constitutes another strand of the following account of that tradition. Symbolic interactionism is regarded as the continuation of certain parts of the thought and work of the loose-knit interdisciplinary network of theoreticians, social researchers and social reformers at the University of Chicago which exercised a determining influence on American sociology between 1890 and 1940, during the discipline's proper phase of institutionalization. To be sure, this school had no unequivocally key theoretician or clearly-outlined programme of research; rather, the Chicago School consisted of a complex nexus of important and less important thinkers and researchers who influenced one another in ways that can now hardly be reconstructed.

An account of this school that wants to include a description of its theoretical system must, then, undertake to reveal and extract the underlying structure of the shared assumptions of the members of this school, and do so without creating a false impression of the school's absolute homogeneity or temporal stability. Yet this is not the principal difficulty. That difficulty lies, rather, in the fact that the Chicago School, which could be described as a combination of pragmatist philosophy, of a politically reformist orientation to the possibilities of democracy under conditions of rapid industrialization and urbanization, and of efforts to make sociology into an empirical science while attaching great importance to pre-scientific sources of experiential knowledge, was itself only a partial realization – from the theoretical standpoint – of the possibilities inherent in the social philosophy of pragmatism.

Hence, the third strand of the present study: the reconstruction of pragmatism as the philosophical source of the Chicago School and of symbolic interactionism. This, of course, does not mean that greater importance or more enduring validity is to be ascribed to the elaboration of philosophical notions as such. What is meant, rather, is that in the philosophy of pragmatism can be found fundamental ideas about the theories of action and social order which have the greatest relevance for the theoretical labours of present-day sociology. These foundations of a theory of action and social order have not been adequately integrated into sociology. The Chicago School and the vital tradition of symbolic interactionism owe a large part of their importance to the transformation of these fundamental ideas into concrete social scientific theory and empirical research. It can be shown, however, that this took place only fragmentarily, and that some of the unsolved problems of this tradition can be solved by means of a reconsideration of its starting-point. The following account thus begins with an analysis of pragmatism's significance for social theory. This is followed by an examination of the most important stages of the development of pragmatism in its sociological form as represented by the work of W. I. Thomas, Robert Park, Herbert Blumer and Everett Hughes, and of the situation at the present time. An assessment of the theoretical yield from this tradition for contemporary construction of theory concludes this examination of the pragmatist school of sociology.

I Pragmatism as the Philosophical Source of the Chicago School

Pragmatism is a philosophy of action. However, it did not develop its model of action as did Parsons and, at least according to the latter's interpretation of them, the classical sociological thinkers, by posing and answering the question: What dimensions must be added to the utilitarian notion of the solitary actor rationally pursuing his ends, if the undeniable but – within the framework of utilitarianism – inexplicable fact of the existence of social order is to be theoretically grasped? Pragmatism is, certainly, no less critical of utilitarianism than were the classical theorists of sociology. It does not, however, attack utilitarianism over the problem of action and social order, but over the problem of action and consciousness. Pragmatism developed the concept of action in order to overcome the Cartesian dualisms. Out of this enterprise there emerged an understanding of intentionality and sociality that differed radically from that of utilitarianism. The concept of rationality and the normative ideal of this mode of thought are theoretically grasped in the idea of self-regulated action. Pragmatism's theory of social order, then, is guided by a conception of social control in the sense of collective self-regulation and problem-solving. This conception of social order is informed by ideas about democracy and the structure of communication within communities of scientists. The actual importance of this type of social order in modern societies poses one of the main problems of pragmatism's political philosophy and of the sociology based on that philosophy. Let us now consider these matters in detail.

The emancipation of the individual from the self-evident validity and authority of received institutions and ideas that took place in the early modern period attained its most extreme and uncompromising expression in the thought of René Descartes. He elevated the individual's right to doubt into the establishment of the self-certainty of the thinking and doubting ego as the firm foundation of a philosophy. Of course, the self-evident, taken-for-granted existence of the world over against the individual consciousness, of the body of the thinking ego as a component of this world and of the other thinking subjects in the world was thereby abolished. An epistemologically-oriented philosophy was thereby able to substantiate its claim to be foundational *vis-à-vis* the sciences. At the same time, though, it incurred the difficult – or impossible – tasks of constituting the world, the body, and the 'you', the subject encountered by the ego, on the basis of the thinking ego. It was against this entire programme that the central idea of pragmatism was directed. The pragmatist places in doubt the meaningfulness of the Cartesian doubt.

> We cannot begin with complete doubt. We must begin with all the prejudices which we actually have when we enter upon the study of philosophy. These prejudices are not to be dispelled by a maxim, for they are things which it

does not occur to us *can* be questioned. Hence this initial skepticism will be a mere self-deception, and not real doubt; and no one who follows the Cartesian method will ever be satisfied until he has formally recovered all those beliefs which in form he has taken up. It is, therefore, as useless a preliminary as going to the North Pole would be in order to get to Constantinople by coming down regularly upon a meridian. A person may, it is true, in the course of his studies, find reason to doubt what he began by believing; but in that case he doubts because he has a positive reason for it, and not on account of the Cartesian maxim. Let us not pretend to doubt in philosophy what we do not doubt in our hearts. (Peirce: 1934, pp. 156ff.)

This critique of the Cartesian doubt is anything but a defence of unquestionable authorities against the emancipatory claim of the thinking ego; it is, though, a plea in defence of *true* doubt, that is, in defence of the anchoring of cognition to real-problem situations. Cartesianism's guiding notion of the solitarily doubting ego is supplanted by the idea of a cooperative search for truth for the purpose of coping with real problems encountered in the course of action. One could be tempted to attribute to this transformation the same historical significance as that accorded the philosophy of Descartes.

The consequences, at least, of this transformation of the guiding idea of philosophical reflection are extremely far-reaching. Indeed, the entire relationship between cognition and reality is changed. The concept of truth no longer expresses a correct representation of reality in cognition, which can be conceived of using the metaphor of a copy; rather, it expresses an increase of the power to act in relation to an environment. All stages of cognition, from sensory perception through to the logical drawing of conclusions and on to self-reflection must now be conceived anew. Charles Peirce had begun to carry out this programme. William James applied it to a great number of problems, chiefly of a religious or existential nature. Led perhaps by his desire to demonstrate the impossibility of finding solutions to these problems that could be made universally binding, James narrowed, and thereby weakened, pragmatism's basic idea in a decisive fashion. In contrast to Peirce, he formulated the criterion for truth in terms of actually occurring results of action rather than those that could generally be expected to occur. In his psychology, James did not take action as his starting-point, but instead the pure stream of conscious experience. He did, however, develop extraordinarily penetrating and impressive analyses showing the selectivity of perception and the apportionment of attention as a function of the subject's purpose. Peirce exercised almost no influence at all on sociologists; James's writings did have influence, but it was very diffuse and manifested itself primarily in a sensitization to the subtleties of subjective experiences. Pragmatism's decisive influence on sociology took place only through John Dewey and George Herbert Mead. These two men, who had initially pursued a programme of 'naturalized' Hegelianism, i.e. Hegelianism recast in terms of the evolutionary processes of nature, and who, like Feuerbach[4], had felt themselves thereby elevated above the Cartesian

---

[4] On Feuerbach, see Honneth and Joas: 1980.

constraints on thought, recognized the crucial importance of a regrounding of pragmatism on the foundation of the biological and social sciences.

This regrounding of pragmatism at first assumed the form of a functionalist psychology. The intent of this psychology was to interpret all psychical operations and processes – and not only the cognitive ones – in terms of their functionality for the solution of problems encountered by subjects in the course of their conduct. This enterprise meant the rejection of traditional epistemological approaches to the interpretation of psychical phenomena as well as a critique of all the psychologies that more or less embody these obsolete philosophical positions. The most famous document of the new approach is John Dewey's trail-blazing article 'The Reflex Arc Concept in Psychology', published in 1896 (Dewey: 1972); its most thorough elaboration, however, is to be found in George Herbert Mead's lengthy, but still almost unknown study, 'The Definition of the Psychical' (1903).

Dewey's critique is directed against a psychology that believes it has found its object in the establishment of law-like causal relations between environmental stimuli and the organism's reactions. Dewey denies that we can legitimately conceive of actions as additively composed of phases of external stimulation, internal processing of the stimulus, and external reaction. To this 'reflex arc model' he opposes the totality of the action: it is the action that determines which stimuli are relevant within the context defined by the action. The elements of an action that are regarded as discrete according to the reflex arc model are, rather, Dewey asserts, functional distinctions within the action; the unity of an action breaks down, and the functionality of these distinctions becomes clear, whenever the execution of an action is interrupted. The sensation enters into the subject's conscious awareness as an external stimulus when its nature is *unknown*; and we become aware of the necessity of a reaction as such when we do *not* know how we should react. Accordingly, Mead defined the psychical as 'that phase of experience within which we are immediately conscious of conflicting impulses which rob the object of its character as object-stimulus, leaving us so far in an attitude of subjectivity; but during which a new object-stimulus appears due to the reconstructive activity which is identified with the subject "I" as distinct from the object "me" (Mead: 1903, p. 109).

Admittedly, Dewey's and Mead's critique, in so far as it is presented here, is principally aimed at theories that reduce action to environmentally-determined conduct. However, the model of action employed in this critique also shows the modification of the meaning of intentionality in comparison with those theories that regard action as the realization of pre-set ends. In pragmatism, precisely because it considers all psychical operations in the light of their functionality for action, it becomes impossible to hold the position that the setting of an end is an act of consciousness *per se* that occurs outside of contexts of action. Rather, the setting of an end can only be the result of reflection on resistances met by conduct that is oriented in a number of different ways. Should it prove impossible to follow simultaneously all the various guiding impulses or compulsions to action, a selection of a dominant motive can take place which then, as an end, dominates the other motives or allows them to become effective only in a subordinate manner.

Such a clear orientation to an end is by no means the usual case, however. By its nature, action is teleological only in a diffuse fashion. Even our perception is shaped by our capacities and possibilities for action. Only under constraint by himself or another, though, will the actor narrow down the wealth of his impulses and sensibility to a clear line of action toward a single end. Dewey and Mead were interested in children's play not only because of their desire to bring about educational reform but because such play also served them as a model of action that was subject to little pressure to achieve unequivocal ends. In their analyses of experimentation, they developed a definition of creative intelligence as the overcoming of action problems through the invention of new possibilities of action; this capacity for invention or creativity, however, presupposes the conscious manipulation of the form of action called play, the 'playing through' of alternative courses of action. At this point in the development of Dewey's and Mead's thought it is already clear that, in comparison to the utilitarian approach, the pragmatist theory of action both opens up new domains of phenomena and makes it necessary to reconceive the known domains, and does so in a way which is unexemplified in the critique made of utilitarianism by the classical sociological thinkers.

Let us now consider briefly three possible objections to the pragmatists' model of action. The criticism that this model narrows the concept of action in an instrumentalist or activist way should have already lost much of its plausibility through the indication above of the significance for pragmatism of play and creativity. This criticism can be refuted most powerfully by means of Dewey's writings on aesthetics (Dewey: 1934) in which it is exactly the subject's passive readiness to experience, and the rounding-off of experience in a present, that are demonstrated. For Dewey, pragmatism was nothing less than a means to criticize those aspects of American life 'which make action an end in itself and which conceive ends too narrowly and too "practically"' (Dewey: 1931, p. 16). Thus the choice of action as the starting-point of philosophical reflection does not mean that the world is degraded to mere material at the disposal of the actors' intentions; this objection is still based on the Cartesian dichotomy, the overcoming of which is precisely what is at issue. Only in action is the qualitative immediacy of the world and of ourselves revealed to us.

The next conceivable objection finds fault with consciousness being bound to the present moment in the pragmatist model of action. This charge can be rebutted by pointing out the central importance of 'habits' in that model. Solutions to action problems are not stored by the actors in their consciousness but employed for new actions, which, being routine in character, run their course outside the actors' consciousness. It is only the new action problem that renders the routines and 'habits' ineffectual and requires new learning.

A third problem, and the most difficult for pragmatist social philosophy, is that the model of action described above is so general that it does not even distinguish the actor's relation to objects of his environment from his relation to his fellow subjects. The transformation of the Cartesian ego into the community constituted by collective problem-solving had at first been only asserted. Peirce had been able, certainly, to link his idea of the critical community of scientists with his theoretical model of action immanently, in so far as he declared all cognition to be symbolic. His theory of signs contains, in addition to the object signified and the qualitative peculiarity of the sign-bearer, an interpreting consciousness belonging to a subject who wants to convey his intention to another or to himself.[5]

Peirce was not able, however, to provide a true theory of the subject that communicates with itself and with others. Cooley had been the first to proclaim the necessity of a 'social' or 'sociological' pragmatism[6] and to develop a theory of the self and its dependence on primary groups. In elaborating this theory, though, he had proceeded in a manner that was still very inconsistent. He did not root consciousness in action with logical rigour, and formulated an emotive rather than a cognitive theory of the self. This problem of arriving at a pragmatist analysis of situations of social interaction and individual self-reflection was the crucial coupling necessary for linking pragmatist philosophy with anti-utilitarian social psychology and sociology. Far more than even Dewey, George Herbert Mead, in his analysis of the origin of human gestural and linguistic communication, was the one who thought through this problem and step by step reached a solution to it. And because he was credited with solving this problem, Mead became the strategically central figure of the Chicago School. This is true regardless of how unimpeachable his solution was and how thoroughly sociologists were acquainted with his thought.

It would be incorrect to understand Mead's contribution[7] as a simple reversal of the relationship between the individual and the collectivity – now to the advantage of the collectivity. The true meaning of his achievement lies, rather, in the fact that he fundamentally changed the way of looking at the problem. Fully in the spirit of pragmatism, he investigated the type of action situation in which a heightened attentiveness to objects of the environment does not suffice to guarantee a successful continuation of the action. What he had in mind was interpersonal action problems. In social situations the actor is himself a source of stimuli for his partner. He must, therefore, be

---

[5] A very interesting account of the pragmatist theory of signs as it differs from the structuralist theory is given in Rochberg-Halton (1982).

[6] Charles H. Cooley ('A social, or perhaps, I should say, a sociological pragmatism remains to be worked out.') quoted in Jandy (1942, p. 110). On Cooley, see Mead's critique in Mead (1930).

[7] See Mead (1934) and Joas (1985a). An important dissertation written under Mead's influence, which helps to understand the significance in contemporary sociology of the change of perspective proposed by Mead, is Bodenhafer (1920–1).

attentive to his own ways of acting, since they elicit reactions from his partner and thereby become conditions for the continuation of his own actions. In this type of situation, not merely consciousness but self-consciousness is functionally required. With this analysis of self-reflectivity, Mead sought to reconstruct pragmatistically the legacy of German idealism.

Mead developed the conditions of the possibility of self-reflectivity out of a theory of the origins of specifically human communication and sociality. In a series of articles written around 1910, he arrives step by step at the fundamentals of the theory of symbolically-mediated interaction. He maintains that the transformation of phases of action into gestural signs makes it possible for an actor to react to his own actions, thereby to represent with his own actions those of others and to cause his own actions to be anticipatorily influenced by the virtual reactions of others. Human behaviour becomes oriented to the possible reactions of others: through symbols, patterns of reciprocal expectations of behaviour are formed, which, however, always remain embedded in the flow of interaction, of the verification of anticipations.

The conceptual results of this innovation are quite well known – the notions of role-taking, of the self, of the generalized other, etc. – and an explanation of them can be omitted here. More important for the purposes of the present account is the fact that Mead undertook to extend his approach into the domain of cognitive problems. On the basis of this social turn of pragmatism,[8] he gives a new interpretation of the constitution of the physical object, of the body image and of subjective temporality. Together, these fragments make it possible to understand action as self-controlled behaviour, and to see a concept of self-control that is not instrumentalistically restricted as pragmatism's concept of rationality.

In particular, Mead establishes the conditions of symbolic interaction and self-reflection. His analyses are guided by a normatively ideal conception of the structure of social order that is based principally on an ideal of democratic self-government combined with Peircean ideas about free and unrestricted communication within the community of scientists. In the central theoretical parts of his work, however, this notion is not used to elaborate a theory of society that could also be put to sociological use. This development is more commonly found in those writings belonging to his political journalism.

John Dewey's writings go further in this regard, especially the discussion in his book *The Public and its Problems* (1927).[9] There Dewey argues in defence of a theory that takes the process of collective action as its starting-point. This action encounters problems and leads to unintended or unanticipated consequences, which must be reflectively 'processed' by the acting

---

[8] I have discussed the constitution of the body image in Joas (1983).

[9] Since most of the standard accounts of pragmatism are not very helpful with regard to the questions of political theory and the possibilities of applying pragmatism in the social sciences, I call attention here to Rucker (1969) and White (1957).

collectivity. Within the framework of communal standards, the consequences of action are perceived, interpreted, assessed and taken into consideration in the preparation of future actions not only by institutions that have specifically been assigned those tasks, but also by all the individuals and collectivities affected by the consequences. In this process of interpreting and assessing the consequences of collective action, communication among all those concerned plays an essential role; everyone affected is motivated to participate in such communication, to manifest that he or she is affected by and concerned with the consequences. Dewey's political philosophy thus does not assume an antagonism between individuals and the state, but instead takes as its starting-point the internal problems of group action. In the public that is founded in group action, as the community of communication made up of all those affected by and concerned with the consequences of such action, both the independent state and the autonomous individual are constituted.

In this theoretical model, communication for the purpose of solving problems of collective concern becomes an essential condition of social order. This becomes even clearer when one compares this notion with the competing theories of social order. Thus conceived, social order does not require the 'like-mindedness' of society's members; human communication links together individual uniqueness and the shared or universal recognition and use of symbolic systems. Dewey's political philosophy is also directed against the Hobbesian tradition of thought, which can conceive of social integration as effected only through the agency of external authorities.

Lastly, Dewey's programme, like the earlier reflections of Cooley, is explicitly opposed to a 'naturalization' of the market and to a conception of it as a self-regulating, problem-solving mechanism. It is precisely the consequences of the interconnection of actions having economic ends that require a collective interpretation and assessment. In the specific way that the notion of 'social control' was used by this group of thinkers, this notion did not refer to a guarantee of social conformity but, rather, to conscious self-regulation, to the idea of self-government effected through the medium of communication and understood as the solving of collective problems. Thus this concept of 'social control' was, in the theory of social order, the equivalent of the concept of 'self-control' in the theory of action.[10] Neither concept was intended for use in value-free description. Rather, they both contained immanent criteria for judging the rationality of actions or of social orders. That does not mean that they were merely evaluative concepts. They were to demonstrate their revelatory power precisely in actual analyses of human actions and societies. On the one hand, pragmatism's social philosophy thus provided a complex of fundamental concepts for social scientific research and theory construction. On the other hand, it ascribed to these very social sciences an enormous moral and political importance. For they were supposed to aid human communities in improving their

[10] On this point, see the outstanding article by Janowitz (1975–6).

potential for collective action and, in a world that had lost all metaphysical certainty, make a decisive contribution to promoting the solidarity of a universal human community that collectively recognizes, discusses and solves the problems of humanity.

II The Development of the Chicago School

Those investigating the theoretical content of the thought and work of the old Chicago School must begin by freeing themselves from several widespread misconceptions about that school if they are to appreciate the real accomplishments of this group of researchers and thinkers.[11]

The first of these misconceptions is that the school had an exclusively empirical orientation and that it not only failed to systematize theoretically the results of its researches, but regarded them as emanations of the objects of research. This assessment is accurate in so far as this school, faithful to the spirit of pragmatism, placed great value on empirical research. In the history of social science, it stands in the middle between the speculative evolutionist social philosophy of sociology's early years and modern empirical social science. It is also true that in retrospect the school for the most part produced a mosaic of quasi-ethnographic studies rather than enduring theoretical treatises. But this fact should not be allowed to give the misleading impression that the works of the school's members do not share an at least implicit theoretical framework. Although it is not exactly identical in each study, nevertheless an implicit general theoretical framework of pragmatism – which was however given hardly any explicit metatheoretical grounding – can be uncovered in the individual substantive theorems of the Chicago School.

Just as mistaken as this assessment is the view that the Chicago School was merely interested in bringing about social reform, or the belief that the specific nature of this school consisted of a more or less secularized Protestant social reformism.[12] In this regard too one could speak of an intermediary position in the history of social science, namely a position between the absence of, and the complete, professionalization of the social sciences. All the central figures of the Chicago School were opposed to social research conducted without professional standards, which merely made the public conscious of the existence and extent of social problems. They were, furthermore, clearly aware that although the professionalization of the social sciences had to be based on improved research methods and a universalistic frame of reference – as opposed to mere reformism – it should not consist

[11] On early American sociology, see Hinkle: 1963; 1980. On the independence of American sociology from the classical European social theorists, see Sutherland: 1978.
[12] Even in the very recent writings of the authors of the first rank, such misinterpretations can be found: see Tenbruck: 1985; Vidich and Lyman: 1985.

of the renunciation of all extra-scientific mandates. Finally, as far as the Christian character of the Chicago School is concerned, it can certainly not be found in the thought and writings of such important members as Thomas and Mead. Nor is it possible to speak meaningfully of a merely secularized form of Christianity, in view of the extremely anti-Puritanical motives of many of the school's members.

A third misassessment regards the Chicago School as the epigoneous result of the study of the writings of European thinkers and the appropriation of their ideas. It is true, certainly, that above all German thought – as it went through the transition from historicism to sociology (represented by Dilthey, Windelband, Rickert, Tönnies and Simmel) – and German ethnology and folk psychology (*Völkerpsychologie*) – which sought to explain the cultural life of nations or peoples – exercised a formative influence on many important figures in the school. Much attention was given to the sociological theories of Durkheim, Tönnies and Simmel. There were, in particular, affinities between members of the school and Simmel, inasmuch as Simmel was searching for a concept of society that would neither reduce society to a mere aggregation of individuals nor reify it into an entity completely transcending individuals.[13] Yet it is completely misleading to regard the ideas of the Chicago School as deriving from the thought of Simmel, or even to assume a general superiority of European social scientific thinking at this time. If the thesis is correct that the theoretical framework of the Chicago School has its origin in the social philosophy of pragmatism, then it will also have been shown that the school had its starting-point in an authentically American school of thought, and not in European philosophy. Even Parsons's later admission that Cooley, Thomas and above all Mead had developed a sociopsychological theory of internalization that constituted an important advance over the classical European social theorists,[14] does not go far enough, as it isolates this accomplishment from the conditions in which it was made and from the consequences resulting from it. That is, the pragmatist critique of rationalistic individualism was not acknowledged in its full breadth.

This fact is expressed most strikingly in the myth of the dominance of Herbert Spencer's utilitarian individualism over pre-Parsonian American sociology. For the period prior to the Chicago School, and for the speculative sociologists outside this school, it is indeed true that a great deal of work was given over to a theoretical modification of Spencer's assertions. However, the fact is that for all the social theorists from this period whose works are still read today – Peirce, James, Baldwin, Mead, Dewey, Cooley, Veblen, Thomas and Park – Spencer was 'more whipping boy than master'.[15] The

[13] On the reception of Simmel in the US, see the comprehensive study by Levine *et al.* (1975–6).

[14] The most important text by Parsons on this complex of themes is his study of Cooley (Parsons: 1968b).

[15] This thesis is advanced most strongly by Wilson (1968), from whom the quotation is taken.

first important textbook of American sociology, W. I. Thomas's *Source Book for Social Origins* (1907), can be understood, in long stretches, as a polemic against Spencer. Since the end of the American Civil War, many American thinkers had renounced allegiance to atomistic individualism and set out on a search for new theoretical and practical models of the formation of community. Their solutions to the problem of a new basis for community took extremely diverse forms and extended from a return to the communitarian ideals of early Puritanism, through a mysticism of nature, attraction to Catholicism, utopian schemes and experiments, and on to a glorification of America's colonial past or of the former conditions in the Southern states. In most instances, the attempt was made to introduce the moral claims of individualism into these models of community.

The way in which pragmatism was transformed into sociology was, of course, determined in a decisive manner by the conditions of American society, of the University of Chicago, and of the political connection of early American sociology to its environing society during the period when it originated, at the beginning of the 1890s and in the years following. In this period, the United States was going through a phase of rapid industrialization and urbanization.[16] The influx of immigrants was enormous; for the most part they came from cultural backgrounds very different from the Protestant tradition. The dissolution of the politically and economically strongly decentralized structure of the United States, together with the simultaneous economic changes *per se*, provided a foundation for a profound modification of the class structure of American society. A part of this change that must be especially mentioned was the rise of a new 'professional' middle class. Politically, these changes were accompanied by many efforts to achieve social reforms, which earned for this epoch the name 'the progressive era'. Common to these reform efforts was the goal of preserving the democratic ideals of the self-government of local communities under the new conditions of a hegemony in American society of the great corporations and the central federal government; this was to be done by developing the ideals of small local communities into a form appropriate to the new urban communities. Chicago was one of the centres of these reformist enterprises. The intellectuals of the Chicago School were closely associated personally with many of these efforts and remained so in large part even during the conservative period of the twenties. The principal themes of the Chicago School were therefore the problems of the modern city, especially of Chicago itself. The choice of the topics of its sociological studies can almost always be accounted for by this focus of concern.

The institutional conditions of the recently-founded University of Chicago favoured an orientation toward research and interdisciplinarity. At this university the emphasis, for the graduate students, was on learning through

---

[16] The best historical account of the social-historical background of the developments mentioned here is given in Wiebe (1967).

research, and for the infrastructure, on cooperatively-conducted research. The establishment of a professional journal, the *American Journal of Sociology*, in 1895 and the publication of textbooks by Thomas and by Park and Burgess gave support to the undertaking of the sociologists at the University of Chicago. There sociology did not find it necessary to struggle for its existence against the *power* of the older disciplines, especially political economy, but was able, under much more favourable conditions than elsewhere, to give its full attention to them *intellectually*, and to demarcate itself from them.[17] It was closely connected with ethnology, with philosophy and educational theory (in the persons and thought of Dewey and Mead), and with the institutionalist, anti-marginalist economics of Thorstein Veblen.

The founders of sociology at the University of Chicago in the strict sense are, with the exception of Albion Small, today forgotten and rightly considered to be of no significance as theorists. Small can be described as a combination of speculative 'systems sociologist' and administrative initiator of empirical sociological research. His own theoretical position, which he apparently did not in any way make a guideline for the empirical sociological research carried out at the University of Chicago, could be called 'collective utilitarianism', that is, it was a theory that accounted for social life through the processes engendered by the conflict among interest groups. Against the force of the pragmatist ideas, though, this approach had little chance of prevailing. In the work of William Isaac Thomas, an early graduate of the University of Chicago who then joined its faculty, there occurred the first important linking of pragmatism and sociological research.

Thomas's intellectual roots lay in ethnography and folk psychology.[18] These two fields of research gathered and investigated materials pertaining to the cultural variety of peoples and eras in a holistic and – compared to introspectionist psychology – 'objective' fashion. Methodologically, Thomas remained faithful to an ethnographic procedure, but now applied to non-exotic objects; theoretically, in the debates around the elaboration of a social psychology, he was interested in a theoretical model that gave close attention to the influence of culture on individual and collective behaviour. In his early writings, he gradually distanced himself from the contemporary notions of a biological determination of racial and sexual differences. The basic

---

[17] On this topic, see Diner: 1975. The most important accounts of the Chicago School are Bulmer (1984), Carey (1975), Faris (1967) and Fisher and Strauss (1978). Those interested in studying this subject further will find helpful the comprehensive bibliography by Kurtz (1984). A very brief but interesting account of a single, although important, aspect of the Chicago tradition is Farberman (1979).

[18] A bibliography of Thomas's publications can be found in Janowitz (1966, pp. 307–10). There is no comprehensive biography of Thomas. Shorter accounts of his life that can be recommended are Janowitz's Introduction to the aforementioned edition of Thomas's writings (Janowitz: 1966, pp. vii–lviii), Coser on Thomas and Znaniecki (Coser: 1977, pp. 511–59), Deegan and Burger (1981) and Zaretsky (1984).

features of his own theoretical model, however, are pragmatist. In the Introduction to his *Source Book for Social Origins* (1909), a central theoretical position was already given to the 'habits' model of action. When confronted with unfamiliar stimuli, habits break down, a state of affairs that constitutes a crisis which can be overcome only by a conscious operation ('attention') on the part of the subject, through which new habits of behaviour originate. He also opposes the concept of control to all the other key concepts then in use, such as imitation, conflict, coercion, contract and 'consciousness of kind'.

More clearly than the pragmatist philosophers, Thomas emphasized the cultural character of behavioural habits and the embedding in a collectivity of even individual initiatives: 'The level of culture of the group limits the power of the mind to meet crisis and readjust' (Thomas: 1909, p. 20). Culture, as Thomas understood it, embraced the most diverse material, technical and cognitive resources of a community. Methodologically, this orientation leads to the search for procedures which make it possible to reconstruct the dynamics of subjective response to, and solution of, action problems. For Thomas, this does not yet mean participant observation or interaction-process analysis, but rather the gathering and interpretation of material about the subjective perspectives of actors. In contrast to Durkheim's maxim in *Rules of Sociological Method*, social facts are not to be explained solely through other social facts. Thus it is not statistical procedures of analysis that are primarily applied; instead individual perceptions and new creations are to be recognized as the mediating link between social facts. Therefore, in sociological studies, materials are to be gathered and examined which approach most closely to the ideal of autobiographical self-presentation and thus to the narrative unity of human existence. Accordingly, for Thomas and the whole Chicago School, a demarcation of their thought and research from psychology did not play an important role, as it did for Durkheim. The theoretical model of a social psychology prevented the identification of psychology with the atomistic individualism they were combating.

Subjective response to, and coping with, the transformation of a 'traditional' society into a 'modern' one was the research topic with which Thomas advanced his reflections furthest, in a combination of theory and empirical research that was admittedly often loose. Quite early in his career, he became interested in the problems of black Americans, of the Jewish socialists in the United States and of the immigrants of various nationalities (Bressler: 1952). His most extensive study dealt with the Polish immigrants (Thomas and Znaniecki: 1926), and became recognized as one of the paradigmatic works of the Chicago School. Thomas followed it with other studies of problems concerning immigrants, as well as of other topics having to do with social adaptation, including one on juvenile prostitutes (Park and Miller: 1921;[19] Thomas: 1923), without, however, making really significant theoretical advances.

---

[19] It is well known that this work was practically written by Thomas.

Thomas's theoretical model, as it is presented chiefly in the preliminary methodological remarks to *The Polish Peasant* (1926) and in other parts of that study, expands the pragmatist model of action in two respects: first, the model is made sociologically more concrete and, second, it is expanded to include collective action. It is made concrete inasmuch as the subjective operation of defining a situation is considered with greater exactitude. Received orientations of conduct are seen as the result of definitions of situations that have previously been successful. With the concept of 'attitude', these definitions are formulated with reference to action and distinguished from the psychology of consciousness. Attention is paid to the social role of the definer of situations. It is clear that these definitions always contain an element of risk. They do not necessarily have to form a unitary coherent system, or to cover all situations equally well. Situations continually arise for which fixed definitions of situations do not suffice. Thomas asserts that it is possible to divide motives of action into four classes. These are: the desire for new experience; for mastery of a situation; for social recognition; and for certitude of identity.

This sketch of a theory of motivation shows that Thomas had gone beyond the notions of instinct psychology without accepting the explanations proposed by psychoanalysis, which he considered to be monocausal. His theory included motives that lay beyond material self-preservation or egoistical pursuit of individual interests, and resembles most strongly the 'humanistic' psychology that was developed later. He made a contribution to the theory of personality with his notion of 'life organization', the subjective shaping of the life course. Using this category he distinguished three personality types: the 'philistine', with a rigid orientation of his life; the 'Bohemian', who has no coherent character structure; and, lastly, with a clearly positive valuation, the creative personality, who is able systematically to guide his own development.

The expansion of the pragmatist model of action to include collective action changes the view of the disintegration of 'traditional' orientations or societies. On this new view, disorganization and crisis always present an opportunity for creative reorganization. Thomas was not a cultural pessimist who saw in the modern era only the disintegration of 'community'. He did not believe in the rigid opposition of strong institutions and anomic loss of orientation; rather, his interest was directed to the collective processes bringing about the formation of new institutions. For him 'the stability of group institutions is thus simply a dynamic equilibrium of processes of disorganization and *reorganization*' (Thomas and Znaniecki: 1926, p. 1130).

This view of society and history made *dépassé* the dichotomous historical categories that had exercised such great influence at the beginning of sociology. No longer was community opposed to society, mechanical to organic solidarity; these oppositions were replaced by continuous processes of institutional disintegration, of the successful or failed formation of new institutions. It was no longer necessary to deny the importance for modern societies of crucial components of earlier societies, such as the family and membership of ethnic groups. These had, to be sure, been changed, but their importance had not necessarily been diminished. The relationship between individual and collective action, or between individual and collective disorganization and reorganization, was explicitly not regarded functionalistically, that is, the opportunity for individual reorganization also existed under conditions of social disorganization. In his empirical research on Polish immigrants, Thomas undertook to investigate the different phases of the crisis-fraught process of adaptation undergone by these immigrants by using empirical materials corresponding to each of the phases (Madge: 1962, pp. 52–87). On the basis of letters, a picture of Polish peasant society was drawn which showed that society from extraordinarily diverse aspects. The disintegration of this society in the spreading industrial capitalism and its first efforts to reorganize itself were documented with articles from Polish newspapers. The personal disorganization of the immigrants was presented with the help of extensive autobiographical material. Information about the social disorganizaton of the immigrant's culture in the United States was gathered from court and parish records. In this way, despite all the problems of the relationship of theory and empirical research, as well as of the elaborateness of theory and methods of empirical research, an impressive pioneering sociological work was written that today must be accorded the status of a classic.

For some time, William Thomas was the most important sociologist of the Chicago School. When, in 1918, he was actually dismissed by his university due to a conspiracy directed against his political and moral nonconformity, his position as unofficial head of the school was filled by a man whom Thomas himself had brought to Chicago a few years before, and who, even prior to their acquaintance, had displayed a very strong affinity with Thomas's orientations and the themes of his thought and research: Robert Park. Until the middle of the thirties, Park was the decisively influential figure in the school. His importance is even greater than that of Thomas, inasmuch as he was effective through his many students and through the organization of research projects, and not just through his own studies.

In light of the many twists and turns of his life, which brought him to a professorship only after he had passed the age of 50, it seems almost as if Park was predestined for the role he played at the University of Chicago.[20] He had, as a student, come under the crucially important influence of John Dewey, had worked for many years as a newspaper reporter, and had obtained a doctoral degree in Germany with a critique, influenced by Simmel, of contemporary crowd psychology, and had published his dissertation in German. Additionally, having been for years a close collaborator

---

[20] Most of the important articles by Park have been published in the three-volume edition of his *Collected Papers* (1950–5). There is excellent secondary literature on Park. Outstanding is Matthews (1977); see also Coser (1977: pp. 357–84) and Turner (1967).

of the black reformer Booker T. Washington, he knew the problems of blacks in the United States better than any other white person of that period. Moreover, these different activities were by no means so unrelated as they might at first appear. Park's creative personality, at least, succeeded in integrating them. From Dewey's philosophy Park had taken over, in particular, the emphasis on democracy as a social order and on public communication as the prerequisite for democracy. His work as a journalist gave him an intimate knowledge of public communication and provided material for his sociological reflections.

Park would later define 'news' as information that is of interest to all because it concerns them, the interpretation of which, however, is still open (Park: 1972). More than Dewey, Park was interested in the empirical reality of the processes by which public opinion is formed, and of the dynamics of the discussion processes which frequently lead to non-consensual results. His passion for giving first-hand reports and his commitment to the blacks in America were both fuelled by a deep hunger for experiences lying outside the narrow cultural and moral confines of the parochial Protestant American milieu. While scarcely any awareness of the plight of blacks in the United States can be found among the majority of progressive intellectuals of the period, Park saw that, prior to the question of the integration of new immigrants into the American society, the existence of a black population made it necessary to reflect on the possibility of 'social control', of democracy under the conditions of cultural heterogeneity. Finally, in his German dissertation Park had undertaken to employ Dewey's concept of democracy as a formal concept in Simmel's sense of the term. By taking this step, Park achieved two things. From the standpoint of the theory of action, the problem of creatively achieving consensus was recognized as being of central importance, and it was shown, counter to the aims of the European crowd psychologists, that there is indeed a possible rationality of collective decision-making processes. What Park did with Dewey's concept, however, also yielded an alternative to the dichotomous theory of historical transformation with its opposed categories of 'community' and 'society'. This alternative was the transformation of traditional communities either into mass societies or into democratically-integrated societies. Park was intensely interested by the creative possibilities both of the masses and of public discussion.

This fact makes it understandable that for him the collective behaviour out of which institutions first emerge, and in which they are changed, became the proper object of sociology. In the large introductory textbook written by Park and Burgess (1921) – the 'green Bible' of American sociologists between the two world wars – sociology is defined as the science of collective behaviour. That does not mean, of course, that individual action is to be ignored or excluded from the domain of sociology, but rather that it is to be understood as collectively constituted in its orientation.

For Park, society does not confront the individual solely as an agency of restraint, of coercion, or of obligation. It is also experienced as a source of inspiration, of an expansion of the self, and of a liberation and enhancement of hidden personal energies. The condition of collective action is the existence of 'collective representations', which are constituted in communication. The focus of such an approach must, therefore, be on the different types of constitution of such collective representations: these extend from systems of religious symbols to public opinion, and also include phenomena such as fashion.

This notion does not take us outside the terrain that is thoroughly familiar to pragmatist social philosophy. The language in which Park and Burgess express these ideas in their textbook is obviously influenced by Durkheim.[21] More strongly than the French theorist, though, they stress the modern and everyday forms of the emergence of collective representations. One might easily conclude that this is little more than a mere formulation of well-known fundamental ideas in a Durkheimian manner and in a way that is closer to empirical reality. This impression disappears, though, when it is recognized that for Park only one of two types of social order is captured by this view of society: the type of 'moral order', of collective action that is regulated with reference to values and meanings. To this type, however, there is opposed another, which Park designates 'biotic' or 'ecological' order.[22] The reason for the introduction of this second type of social order was evidently the difficulty of conceiving – on the basis of its characteristic model of social order – of systematic deviations of the results of collective action from what is collectively intended, or systematically occurring results of uncoordinated action. Park found the archetype for this 'human ecological' theory in plant ecology, which in turn was partially influenced by models of the market economy. These models seemed to him suitable for the scientific representation of processes of competition for scarce resources, and for the resulting reciprocal adaptations and spatial and temporal distributions.

Park's theory was fruitful to the extent that it took seriously the relationship of social processes to their physical environment. This theory was the origin of many impulses, for example for the investigation of the origin and change of function of neighbourhoods and for research on the spatial or regional diffusion of social phenomena. The models used in these studies, however, constantly ran the risk of 'naturalizing' social phenomena and of thereby giving a deterministic interpretation of them. Ralph Turner pointed out this crucial weakness.[23] The distinction of the two types of social order has to do not with different social spheres, but with the intentional or unintentional character of the results of social action.

This fact, however, gives rise to the problem of applying these models of

---

[21] A comparison would have to make use of Durkheim's lectures on pragmatism, in addition to his sociology of religion (Durkheim: 1955). Interpretations of those lectures are given in Joas (1985b) and Stone and Farberman (1967).

[22] For a summary, see Park: 1936.

[23] See the very good critical observations of Turner (1967, p. xxix).

social order and, above all, of their integration to produce a single coherent theory of society. Park's lack of theoretical clarity here leads to a mere combination of a democratically-oriented macrosociology with underlying assumptions of a competition and a struggle for survival that are considered natural. A theory that would reconcile economy and society is not achieved. The gap between the two parts of Park's theory is bridged with evolutionist assumptions about the gradual transformation of the unplanned, competitive sector of societies into the democratically self-determined sector: 'The evolution of society has been the progressive extension of control over nature and the substitution of a moral for the natural order' (Park and Burgess: 1921, p. 511). This implicit view also distorts the idea of 'natural history' and in particular influences the famous 'stage model' of the development of race relations from 'competition' through 'conflict' to mutual 'accommodation' and, finally, 'assimilation'. As Park and his students typically employed these ideas, it was not a matter of ideal types of processes, but of deterministic schemata of stages. As such, of course, they can easily be criticized, whether by drawing attention to ethnocentric features of the way certain phenomena of urbanization are viewed, or by adducing the experience of entirely different courses of development of race relations than that leading to assimilation.[24] Park, though, used the deterministic character of his models for the purposes of a polemic against the unrest of the American blacks and against reformist intellectuals acting on behalf of others.

Obviously, then, it cannot be claimed that Park and his students succeeded in transforming pragmatism into a satisfactory theory of society. About central questions that such a theory must answer in the twentieth century, such as the development of class relations, bureaucracy or international relations, this approach has nothing to say. They did, however, succeed in elaborating a flexible, theoretical and macrosociologically-oriented frame of reference for the many empirical studies of phenomena of everyday life in the modern (American) big city. In the course of the twenties and thirties, a plethora of such studies was carried out that is impressive even today. Some of them have remained famous because of their methods and findings, for example, Nels Anderson's study *The Hobo* (1923), Frederick Thrasher's investigation of criminal youth gangs (1927), or Clifford Shaw's biography of a juvenile criminal (1930). The first sociological studies by black sociologists of the problems of American blacks have their origin in Park's school. In each case it is striking how enormous was the distance from a perception – whether moralistic or social reformist – of the social phenomena from the standpoint of the middle classes. What was produced by Park and his students was a mosaic of studies of metropolitan life full of first-hand descriptions that were of almost literary quality; but it was certainly not a social science methodically progressing by means of the testing of hypotheses or theoretical generalization.

---

[24] For a critique of the race-relations cycle, see also the short report on the last years of Park's life after his departure from Chicago in Cahnman (1978).

Although it is not possible here to discuss in detail the work of other important thinkers of the Chicago School of this period, some of them should at least be mentioned. Chief among them is Park's friend and co-author Ernest Burgess, who, to be sure, tended to an even stronger determinism in his urban sociology than Park. He unequivocally subsumed the sphere of the economy under the ecological model and was a proponent of the famous theory of concentric circles of urban development, which he had based on the case of Chicago. He made an important contribution to the sociology of the family, in which he introduced the view of the family as a processual unity of interacting personalities, without, however, the methodological instruments corresponding to this programme, and under the assumption of the unilinear evolutionary development of the family 'from institution to companionship' (Bogue: 1974). Ellsworth Faris (1937), in many short articles, and very influentially in his teaching, advocated central ideas of pragmatist social philosophy, and made use of them in an original manner principally to criticize behaviouristically reductionist views and the claims of instinct psychology. Louis Wirth,[25] who was influential in the late thirties and the forties, investigated the Jewish ghetto entirely in the manner advocated by Park; on the other hand, though, he proposed a theory of the large city that, completely contrary to the typical approach of Park's school, interpreted life in the large city according to the scheme of the *replacement* of community bonds by societal relations.

It would also be inappropriate to speculate here about the reasons for the much-debated demise of the Chicago School in the thirties.[26] In the context of the present account, it is not the details of the history of sociology that are of interest but the subsequent fortunes of pragmatist theory. How did this theory deal with new problems and with the old, unsolved ones? What became of it after the ebbing of the progressive optimism of the theory's founders about the possibilities of reform? What became of the dualism of moral and biotic orders?

It is customary to see the continuation of this tradition principally in Herbert Blumer's programmatic writings on social psychology. As important as these are, they form too narrow a foundation for examining the tradition's continuation. Thus the eminently inspiring work of Everett Hughes is given equal importance here with that of Blumer. In the writings of these two men, two ways of treating the problems that have been raised can be studied.

Herbert Blumer's work, with its merits and weaknesses, has been of decisive importance for the self-understanding of subsequent generations of proponents of symbolic interactionism. After writing a dissertation in which

[25] See Wirth (1964; 1969); the former volume includes the famous and controversial paper 'Urbanism as a Way of Life' (1964, pp. 60–83), first published in 1938 (Wirth: 1938).

[26] In addition to the general treatments of the Chicago School, see also Kuklick (1973) and Lengermann (1979).

he reviewed the methods of social psychology, Blumer became well known in the thirties in particular through two works (Blumer: 1928; 1939). He examined in an extremely critical manner the relationship between theory and empirical research in Thomas and Znaniecki's study of the Polish peasant; and in an article for a handbook in which he systematized the premises of the tradition of the Chicago School, he invented the name 'symbolic interactionism'. The relationship of theory and empirical research in the social sciences became a subject of life-long interest to Blumer. In opposition to the survey research and professionalized data analysis that was attaining dominance in the social sciences, he developed more and more the thesis that an intimate relation of the social scientist to the object of his investigation was required. For all the sociologists who tended to interpretative methods, to the inclusion in sociological research of subjective experiences, to a use of theoretical concepts that made them more sensitive to empirical reality, his methodological protests and programmes became an extremely important point of reference. Even more than Mead and the other sociological thinkers from whom he had learned, Blumer raised the processual character of all action to a methodological tenet. Phase models of action could never be more than only approximately correct if the continuous re-adaptation to new or changed environmental conditions was just what was characteristic of action. His systematizations also offered an account of the central premises of pragmatist thought that was at a greater remove from philosophy and easier to use for the purposes of the sociological researcher.

In his substantive studies on ethnic topics and on collective behaviour, Blumer strove to go beyond and even to supplant psychologistic and functionalist explanations; also, in contrast to Park, his writings are not guided by evolutionist ideas. If, however, Blumer's work is measured against the questions faced by the contemporary theory of society, then it becomes obvious that his writings simply provide no answer to many of these. The problem implicit in Park's dualism of 'moral' and 'biotic' order is not taken up again in any way. In his version of symbolic interactionism, Blumer confines himself to tackling those problems which lie within the conceptual framework of the 'moral order'. He avoids problems which apparently cannot on principle be located within this framework, or whose assignment to the 'moral order' seem intuitively to be possible only with difficulty. Thus it was possible to consolidate a fruitful paradigm without greatly advancing the confrontation with other theories.

This qualification does not hold for Everett Hughes, the Chicago tradition's leading sociologist of occupations and work.[27] In his work, Park's dualism is preserved, but its form is changed. The distinction between a sector of society that is normatively or communicatively integrated and a societal domain regulated through market processes or the unplanned

---

[27] Everett Hughes's shorter writings have been collected in *The Sociological Eye: Selected Papers* (1971). Two important interpretations of his work are Faught (1980) and Simpson (1972).

interconnections among the results of actions, is transformed in such a way that, although now every organization or institution continues to be analysed using the model of normative integration, the relations among these institutions or organizations appear as competition among collective actors – very similar to the 'collective utilitarianism' that can be found, say, in the theory of Albion Small at the inception of the Chicago School. Hughes regards every institution as a part of an organic system that is not further specified, for which it has certain functions to fulfil but which, as a totality, exhibits no integrative system of values. The concept of collective consciousness is no longer referred to society in its entirety, but applied now only to the individual macroscopic actors. In this position there lies, certainly, an undeniable possibility for fruitful analysis of empirical reality, which was subsequently developed, both within and without the framework of symbolic interactionism, in the theory of reference groups. At the same time, though, this restricted application of the concept of collective consciousness also means the loss of a concept of society as a unitary political and social order.

Like that of Park, Hughes's *oeuvre* includes a great number of small studies and only a few large ones. His importance lay in his ability to maintain a consistent point of view while remaining close to empirical reality, and to make it operative in the research of his students. Also significant were his efforts to guide others to the investigation of institutions as living wholes, and of competition among ethnic groups. Of greatest importance, however, were his studies on occupational sociology. It is not surprising that occupational sociology attracted the attention of the continuators of the Chicago tradition, who were interested in making fruitful use of their ideas about the structure of social order in empirical research. For occupations are the patterns of activities specialized in accordance with a division of labour, in which the mediation, through different interests, relations of forces and processes of negotiations, of a structure that only apparently results from objective constraints is manifested with particular clarity.

Hughes directed his attention especially to the professions, the occupations requiring university training, for the greater latitude they allow individuals to shape their own work makes evident the theoretically-predicted essential feature of the division of labour, namely that it is neither technologically, nor ecologically, nor normatively determined, but can be understood only by reference to the action of the pertinent individuals or occupational groups. Since for Hughes the question of a macrosocietal, institutionalized commonwealth did not arise, he had no difficulty in making the professions the topic of his reflection and research, without holding any simple belief in their self-justification. He examined critically the ideologies of different kinds of professions as means for achieving freedom from control and attaining to high status. He was interested in the techniques and tactics used to avoid undesirable tasks and to conceal mistakes from subordinates and clients. Thus his concentration on professions in which firm guidelines or prescriptions play a minor part, and in which there exists the necessity for those exercising the professions to 'create' their own roles, does not in any way originate in an uncritical attitude toward the ideology of these professions. In the course of Hughes's research studies of industrial work-places were also conducted. In these investigations, the crucial point was that even under the most restrictive conditions, occupational activity cannot be understood without taking into consideration the workers' own definitions of their situation and their struggle for autonomy.

At the beginning of the fifties, the Chicago School, whose dominance had ceased at the end of the thirties, lost its most important representatives at the University of Chicago itself: Ernest Burgess retired, Louis Wirth died, and Herbert Blumer went to California. The end of the Chicago School in the narrower, definitive sense should be dated at this time. The school's intellectual legacy, which was not equally elaborated in all its aspects, was then passed on and developed further along the most diverse paths. The best-known use of this legacy is the elaboration of a symbolic-interactionist social psychology by Tamotsu Shibutani (1961), Anselm Strauss (1959) and Norman Denzin (1977a),[28] as well as of a role-theory and family sociology by, among others, Ralph Turner (1970). The continuation of Hughes's work can be followed in the outstanding sociological studies of the professions, and especially of medicine, by Eliot Freidson (1970), Howard Becker (Becker *et al.*: 1961) and Anselm Strauss. In addition, Becker in large measure opened up a new field of research with his influential study, undertaken completely in the spirit of the Chicago tradition, on 'outsiders' and the genesis of deviant behaviour (Becker: 1963). Gregory Stone and many others have contributed to the sociological understanding and explanation of many phenomena of everyday life (Stone and Farberman: 1970). At the margin of this school stands the brilliant and highly original work of Erving Goffman.[29] If one considers all these topics and researchers together, the picture one sees is certainly that of a vital and viable current of research. However, of these many paths of research only one appears to lead toward an overcoming of the theoretical isolation of this school. This is the one that has developed on the foundation laid chiefly by the studies of Anselm Strauss and that is presented in the writings of younger sociologists as the 'negotiated-order approach'.

The elaboration of this approach, too, was carried out entirely in the empirical style of the Chicago tradition: on the whole, by means of themati-cally-limited, specific case studies rather than through mere elaboration of concepts. The starting-point for the development of this approach can be located where the research on professions conducted by members of the Chicago School, chiefly in the studies of hospitals, led to a distinct perspec-tive regarding the sociology of organizations.[30] It was initially the reaction

[28] A good overview is given by Lauer and Handel (1977).

[29] As Goffman's work cannot be explained by means of the premises of prag-matism, I only mention it here.

[30] Examples of this research are Strauss *et al.* (1963) and Bucher and Stelling (1969).

to a process of change, namely the increase in the number of types of professionals carrying out their professional activities within complex organizations, that brought about a shift of interest away from the 'professions' to the 'professional organizations'. In the analysis of the 'hospital' as a typical example of such an organization, the models of organizational sociology of the rationalist-bureaucratic and functionalist types proved to be inadequate. The structures of the division of labour within the hospitals proved to be, from the outset, quite indefinite, the goals non-specific, and the rules equivocal. Only a continuous process of tacit agreements, unofficial arrangements and official decisions among the various professional groups concerned, parts of professional groups and individuals regarding the strategy of the total organization and the way it divides up work makes the functioning of such an organization possible. From this is derived the general principle asserted by this sociology of organizations: that organizations are to be conceptualized as 'ongoing systems of negotiation'.

According to this theory, organizations are not formations structured by univocal, normative rules; the action performed within them is not determined by a mere application of prescriptions or guidelines free of all intervention by the actor's self. Reflection and dialogue are required not just for the alteration of rules and norms, but also for their maintenance and reproduction. For their existence, organizations are dependent on their continuous reconstitution in action; they reproduce themselves in and through the medium of action. Goals and strategies of organizations are a matter of controversy; agreement can assume many different forms, including those of intentional or knowingly-tolerated intermingling of goals and plurality of goals. Every agreement is of a conditional and transitory character. The actors themselves have theories, drawn from their everyday experience, about the nature, scope and probable success of negotiation processes. If this holds good even for relatively formal organizations, then it is all the more true of more loosely-structured social formations. It is not the tracing out of static structures, but the reconstruction of reciprocal processes of definition extending over time that becomes, then, the central task for a sociology of organizations that is striving to be compatible with the premises of symbolic interactionism regarding social psychology and personality theory, and to regain thereby the possibility of achieving the more comprehensive goals of a transformation of pragmatism within sociology.

Such a sociology of organizations is, to be sure, only a first step along this path. The importance of negotiation processes in formal organizations is not merely asserted against an incorrect understanding of this social form; more far-reaching is the claim that almost all types of social order are misinterpreted if the role of negotiation processes is left out of consideration. Wherever neither absolute consensus nor pure force obtains, such processes can be found, and complete consensus and pure force are only limiting cases and not prototypes of social life (see Maines and Charlton: 1985, p. 295).

The utilization of this insight, however, can take different directions. For example, one can attempt to distinguish the different dimensions of negotiation processes in order to become more sensitive to them in empirical studies. Anselm Strauss, in his book *Negotiations* (1979), has made an attempt to work out such a conceptual grid, although it is in many respects still very preliminary.[31] The dimensions he lists include the number of participants, their relevant experience, and whether they are speaking only for themselves or represent collectivities. He then points out that negotiations can be non-recurring or can take place repeatedly, that they can recur at regular intervals or be ordered in determinate sequences. Further, the difference in power among the participating actors is significant. Other dimensions are the importance that the negotiation has for the participants, and that it does not have to be equally great for all of them; the visibility of the negotiation for other than the immediate partners in the negotiation; the number and complexity of the objects of the negotiation; and the options of the partners in the negotiation other than the implementation of consensual decisions, i.e. in case the negotiation is broken off.

This enumeration makes it clear that this approach is not concerned with asserting the existence of an ideal consensuality regarding social regulations in which power, conflict and structural constraints play no role. That would be a gross misunderstanding. What is to be demonstrated is, rather, how the results of earlier actions must be taken into consideration even by the actor himself, both individually and collectively, both consensually and conflictually, and that this assimilation and assessment itself takes place under structural conditions which can, in their turn, be traced back to earlier negotiation processes and intended or unintended results of action.

A schema of the dimensions of negotiation processes is, at first, neutral with respect to the societal sphere in which these processes occur, as well as in relation to the question of the significance of these dimensions for the functioning of societies. A second direction in which the 'negotiated order' approach has been elaborated can thus be characterized as the inclusion, in addition to the 'professional organization', of other objects of research and the accomplishment thereby of the gradual enlargement of the approach's macrosociological capability.

Studies which are quite different from one another share this aim. The course followed by political decision-making, for example, almost literally forces itself on the attention of the researcher seeking an object for this approach (Hall: 1972). Not only the formal and substantive determination of the relations among professional groups in existing institutions, but also the constitution of the structure of professions and of the system of societal division of labour in general are made an object of study by Eliot Freidson (1975–6). Some researchers, for example Harvey Farberman (1975) and Norman Denzin (1977b), have directed their attention to selected market phenomena and have shown that these remain incomprehensible without reference to the intermediation of negotiation processes. Gary Alan Fine and Sherryl Kleinman (1983) have extended symbolic interactionism's field

[31] In addition to Maines and Charlton (1985), for overviews see Fine (1984) and Maines (1977).

of attention beyond small groups and organizations to encompass personal networks, to the investigation of which they have also made an original contribution.

Common to all these scattered undertakings is that they have yielded macrosociological studies or fragments of theory without lapsing into the naturalization of the processes investigated into a 'biotic order'. More than the theory of democracy in pragmatism's social philosophy, they insist not only on the normative but also on the empirical explosive power of an examination of the features of social life that appear under the conditions of democracy. For the most part, however, these studies are still only miniature portraits, not great tableaux of the present period treating matters of political and historical importance. None the less, the threshold leading to a theory of society as a whole and to the understanding of forms of social integration, such as the market in which independence from collective decisions is institutionalized, has been crossed. Further progress along this path, however, cannot be made without confronting the great schools of theory on these topics. Yet it is to just these schools that the philosophical foundation laid by pragmatism, its extensively-elaborated social psychology and microsociology, as well as the basic principles of the 'negotiated order' approach, pose a theoretical challenge.

III An Assessment

An assessment of the theoretical fruits of the sociological school deriving from pragmatism and a contrast of this school with the other major currents of sociology at the present time cannot be succinctly formulated unless the many different problems addressed by the theories and research of the competing schools are restricted to a few fundamental questions. The most compelling suggestion on this point is to be found in the Parsonian tradition. According to this proposal, it is the questons of action and of social order as an ordered nexus of actions that make up the central and unavoidable metatheoretical problems of sociology.[32] These problems are metatheoretical because they do not concern the development of empirically tenable special theories for selected domains of phenomena, but questions dealing with the conceptual definition and description of the domain of sociology or the social sciences in general. These questions can be said to be unavoidable because, although not every sociological theory concerns itself with them explicitly, none can do without at least implicit assumptions about the nature of action and of social order. Metatheoretical reflection in this sense throws these more or less implicit assumptions into clear relief and requires their grounding. If one accepts this definition of the logical status of the theory of action and of social order, then the reality and the inherent possibilities of pragmatism can be related to competing or complementary schools of sociology on these two planes.

[32] The clearest account of this position is to be found in Alexander (1982).

As it has been presented above, pragmatism's theory of action is radically different from the models of a sociological utilitarianism. In their exclusive recognition of rational action, these models are incapable of giving an account of activities deviating from this model of rationality other than as deficient modes of action. They produce a residual category of non-rational action which does not permit the reconstruction of the phenomenal diversity of action. The transcending of this utilitarian position, which is constitutive of sociology – implicitly in the works of the classical social theorists (Weber, Durkheim and Pareto) and explicitly in the writings of Parsons – has continued to be shaped by the polemic with which it began. It is thus characterized by a concentration on the normative dimension, which certainly represents progress beyond utilitarianism but runs the risk of misunderstanding the role of norms in the dynamics of real action. In contrast, symbolic interactionism assumes neither the consistency nor the deterministic character of internalized norms. The great counter-tradition to academic sociology, Marxism, is incomprehensible, at least in its origin, without its foundation in its own theory of action, in the 'expressionistic'[33] concept of work according to which work effects the embodiment of the worker's labour-power and skills in the product of his work. However, many of those who contributed to the development of this tradition as a theory of society and history disregarded this foundation of Marxism. There has been hardly any elaboration of the notions of *'Praxis'*, of 'activity' and of 'labour' (or 'work') nor a relating of them to the problems addressed by the sociological theory of action.

Even the most creative new approach to the sociological theory of action, which transcends utilitarianism, the normativist critique of utilitarianism and traditional Marxism: Jürgen Habermas's theory of communicative action (1981), does not achieve a comprehensive revision of the sociological theory of action. The opposition of a communicative concept of rationality to the deficiencies of an instrumentalist understanding of rationality has the effect of excluding many dimensions of action which can be found in the history of social thought.[34] The unsolved problem in this connection is how the sociological theory of action can be integrated with the theoretical fecundity of pragmatism and the traditions of the philosophy of *Praxis*, and with the expressionistic notion of work.[35] For the solution of this problem, pragmatism continues to be of central importance. For it has prepared the way not simply to take as a model for the sociological theory of action the purposively acting individual who has mastery over his own body and is autonomous in relation to his fellow human beings and to the environment, but instead to explain the conditions of the possibility of this type of 'actor'. For this clarification, the literature of symbolic interactionism supplies a

---

[33] On this 'expressionist' tradition cf. Berlin (1980) and Taylor (1975).

[34] For a critical examination of this theory of action, see Joas: 1986. The two other most important new approaches in the theory of action at present are, in my opinion, Castoriadis (1987) and Giddens (1984). On Giddens, see Joas: forthcoming.

[35] As an account of the different philosophical traditions that have elaborated the concept of action, Bernstein (1971) remains unexcelled.

wealth of material.   Because pragmatism introduced the concept of action as a means to attain to a new view of the relationship between action and consciousness, that is, as a means to pass beyond and to supersede the philosophy of consciousness, it is also able to withstand the offensive of structuralism and post-structuralism, while recognizing some cogency in their arguments, and to safeguard the dimension of human action.[36]

On the level of the theory of social order, the theory of action of the pragmatist, or symbolic-interactionist, tradition compels a relativizing of utilitarian and functionalist models. A relativizing only, since the pragmatic usefulness and explanatory value of these models in many cases are not disputed but, rather, the claim made in sociology for their comprehensive validity. Substantively speaking, the only theory that will be able to avoid falling into functionalism is one which, in its theory of social order, takes collective action as its point of departure and develops a comprehensive typology of its forms, ranging from totemistic ritual to successful democratic self-government and ideal discourse. Sociological analysis is thereby centred on forms of collective processing of intentional and unintentional results of action, on the collective constitution of normative regulations and collective procedures for dealing with normative conflicts. In this regard, too, the tradition of symbolic interactionism offers important material in the categories of collective behaviour and social movement, of the determination of social structures by negotiation, and of democracy as a type of social order. Often, though, these notions have been elaborated, in the manner of a 'qualitative empiricism', in the investigation of objects of slight macrosociological relevance. The analytical richness of symbolic interactionism thus remains unutilized for a diagnosis of the present time that is politically oriented and that takes the era's historical development and context into consideration. This must change, if the tradition wants again to play the role that the social philosophy of pragmatism once, in its beginning, had for its own present.

[36] Referring to the parallels between James and Nietzsche, Richard Rorty has made the following statement: 'James and Nietzsche make parallel criticisms of nineteenth-century thought. Further, James' version is preferable, for it avoids the "metaphysical" elements in Nietzsche which Heidegger criticizes, and for that matter, the "metaphysical" elements in Heidegger which Derrida criticizes. On my view, James and Dewey were not only waiting at the end of the dialectical road which analytic philosophy travelled, but are waiting at the end of the road which, for example, Foucault and Deleuze are currently travelling' (Rorty: 1982, p. xviii).

Bibliography

Alexander, J., 1982: *Positivism, Presuppositions, and Current Controversies*, vol. 1 of *Theoretical Logic in Sociology*. Berkeley and Los Angeles: University of California Press.

Anderson, N., 1923: *The Hobo*. Chicago: University of Chicago Press.

Becker, H., 1963: *Outsiders: Studies in the Sociology of Deviance*. London: Macmillan.

Becker, H. *et al.*, 1961: *Boys in White*. Chicago: University of Chicago Press.

Berlin, I., 1980: *Against the Current*. London: Hogarth Press.

Bernstein, R., 1971: *Praxis and Action*. Philadelphia: Duckworth.

Blumer, H., 1928: 'The Method of Social Psychology', Doctoral dissertation, University of Chicago.

1938: 'Social Psychology', in E. P. Schmidt (ed.), *Man and Society*, New York, pp. 144–98.

1939: 'An Appraisal of Thomas and Znaniecki's "The Polish Peasant in Europe and America"', *Critiques of Research in the Social Sciences*. I. New York: Transaction.

1969: *Symbolic Interactionism: Perspective and Method*. Englewood Cliffs, NJ: Prentice-Hall.

1983: 'Going Astray with a Logical Scheme', *Studies in Symbolic Interaction*, 6: 123–38.

Bodenhafer, W., 1920–1: 'The Comparative Role of the Group Concept in Ward's "Dynamic Sociology"and Contemporary American Sociology', *American Journal of Sociology*, 26: 273–314, 425–74, 583–600, 716–43.

Bogue, D. J. (ed.), 1974: *The Basic Writings of Ernest W. Burgess*. Chicago: University of Chicago Press.

Bressler, M., 1952: 'Selected Family Patterns in W. I. Thomas's Unfinished Study of the "Bintl Brief"', *American Sociological Review*, 17: 563–71.

Bucher, R. and Stelling, J., 1969: 'Characteristics of Professional Organizations', *Journal of Health and Social Behavior*, 10: 3–15.

Bulmer, M., 1984: *The Chicago School of Sociology: Institutionalization, Diversity, and the Rise of Sociology*. Chicago: University of Chicago Press.

Cahnman, W. J., 1978: 'Robert E. Park at Fisk', *Journal of the History of the Behavioral Sciences*, 14: 328–36.

Carey, J. T., 1975: *Sociology and Public Affairs: The Chicago School*. London.

Castoriadis, C., 1987: *The Imaginary Institution of Society*, Cambridge, England: Polity Press.

Coser, L., 1977: *Masters of Sociological Thought*. New York: Harcourt, Brace, Jovanovich.

Deegan, M. J. and Burger, J. S., 1981: 'W. I. Thomas and Social Reform: His Work and Writings', *Journal of the History of the Behavioral Sciences*, 17: 114–25.

Denzin, N., 1977a: *Childhood Socialization: Studies in the Development of Language, Social Behavior, and Identity*. San Francisco: Jossey-Bass.

1977b: 'Notes on the Criminogenic Hypothesis: A Case Study of the American Liquor Industry', *American Sociological Review*, 42: 905–20.

Dewey, J., 1927: *The Public and its Problems*. New York: Henry Holt.

1931: 'The Development of American Pragmatism', in *John Dewey, Philosophy and Civilization*. New York: Minton, Balch, pp. 13–35.

1934: *Art as Experience*. New York: Minton, Balch.

1972: 'The Reflex Arc Concept in Psychology', in *The Early Works*, vol. 5. Carbondale, Ill.: pp. 96–109. First published 1896.

Diner, S. J., 1975: 'Department and Discipline: The Department of Sociology at the University of Chicago 1892–1920', *Minerva*, 13: 514–53.

Durkheim, E., 1955: *Pragmatism et Sociologie*. Paris: Alcan.

Farberman, H., 1975: 'A Criminogenic Market Structure: The Automobile Industry', *Sociological Quarterly*, 16: 438–57.

1979: 'The Chicago School: Continuities in Urban Sociology', *Studies in Symbolic Interaction*, 2: 3–20.

Faris, E., 1937: *The Nature of Human Nature*. Chicago: University of Chicago Press.

Faris, R. E. L., 1967: *Chicago Sociology 1920–32*. Chicago: University of Chicago Press.

Faught, J., 1980: 'Presuppositions of the Chicago School in the Work of Everett Hughes', *The American Sociologist*, 15: 72–82.

Fine, G.A., 1984: 'Negotiated Orders and Organization Cultures', *Annual Review of Sociology*, 10: 239–62.

Fine, G. A. and Kleinman, S., 1983: 'Network and Meaning: An Interactionist Approach to Structure', *Studies in Symbolic Interaction*, 6: 97–110.

Fisher, B. and Strauss, A., 1978: 'Interactionism', in T. Bottomore and R. Nisbet (eds), *A History of Sociological Analysis*. New York: Oxford University Press.

Freidson, E., 1970: *Profession of Medicine: A Study of the Sociology of Applied Knowledge*. New York.

1975–6: 'The Division of Labor as Social Interaction', *Social Problems*, 23: 304–13.

Giddens, A., 1984: *The Constitution of Society*. Cambridge, England: Polity Press.

Glaser, B. and Strauss, A., 1967: *The Discovery of Grounded Theory: Strategies for Qualitative Research*. New York: Sociology Press.

Habermas, J., 1981: *Theorie des kommunikativen Handelns*, 2 vols. Frankfurt-on-Main: English translation, *Reason and the Rationalization of Society*, vol. 1 of *Theory of Communicative Action*. Cambridge, England: Polity Press, 1984.

Hall, P. M., 1972: 'A Symbolic Interactionist Analysis of Politics', *Sociological Inquiry*, 42: 35–75.

Hinkle, R. C., 1963: 'Antecedents of the Action Orientation in American Sociology before 1935', *American Sociological Review*, 28: 705–15.

1980: *Founding Theory of American Sociology 1881–1915*. Boston: Methuen.

Honneth, A. and Joas, H., 1980: *Soziales Handeln und menschliche Natur: Anthropologische Grundlagen der Sozialwissenschaften*. Frankfurt-on-Main. English edn. Cambridge: forthcoming, 1987.

Hughes, E., 1971: *The Sociological Eye: Selected Papers of Everett Hughes*. Chicago: University of Chicago Press.

Jandy, E. C., 1942: *Charles H. Cooley: His Life and his Social Theory*. New York: Hippocrene Books.

Janowitz, M. (ed.), 1966: W. I. Thomas *On Social Organization and Social Personality*. Chicago: University of Chicago Press.

1975–6: 'Sociological Theory and Social Control'', *American Journal of Sociology*, 81: 82–108.

Joas, H., 1983: 'The Intersubjective Constitution of the Body Image', *Human Studies*, 6: 197–204.

1985a: *G. H. Mead: A Contemporary Re-examination of his Thought*. Cambridge, England: Polity Press.

1985b: 'Durkheim und der Pragmatismus: Bewusstseinspsychologie und die soziale Konstitution der Kategorien', *Kölner Zeitschrift für Soziologie und Sozialpsychologie*, 37, 411–30.

1986: 'Die unglückliche Ehe von Hermeneutik und Funktionalismus', in A. Honneth and Joas (eds), *Kommunikatives Handeln*. Frankfurt-on-Main: Suhrkamp.

forthcoming: 'Giddens' theory of structuration', *International Sociology*, 2.

Johnson, G. and Picou, J. S., 1985: 'The Foundations of Symbolic Interactionism Reconsidered', in H. J. Helle and S. N. Eisenstadt (eds), *Microsociological Theory: Perspectives on Sociological Theory*, vol. 2. London, pp. 54–70.

Kuklick, H., 1973: 'A "Scientific Revolution": Sociological Theory in the United States 1930–45', *Sociological Inquiry*, 43: 3–22.

Kurtz, L. R., 1984: *Evaluating Chicago Sociology*. Chicago: University of Chicago Press.

Lauer, R. and Handel, W., 1977: *Social Psychology: The Theory and Application of Symbolic Interactionism*. Boston: P.-H.

Lengermann, P., 1979: 'The Founding of the *American Sociological Review*: The Anatomy of a Rebellion', *American Sociological Review*, 44: 185–98.

Levine, D. N. *et al.*, 1975–6: 'Simmel's influence on American Sociology', *American Journal of Sociology*, 81: 813–45, 1112–32.

Lewis, J. D. and Smith, R. L., 1980: *American Sociology and Pragmatism: Mead, Chicago Sociology, and Symbolic Interaction*. Chicago: University of Chicago Press.

Madge, J., 1962: *The Origins of Scientific Sociology*. New York: Free Press.

Maines, D., 1977: 'Social Organization and Social Structure in Symbolic Interactionist Thought', *Annual Review of Sociology*, 3: 235–59.

Maines, D. and Charlton, J., 1985: 'The Negotiated Order Approach to the Analysis of the Social Organization', *Studies in Symbolic Interaction*, supplement 1, *Foundations of Interpretative Sociology*, edited by H. Farberman and R. Perinbanayagam, pp. 271–308.

Matthews, F. H., 1977: *Quest for an American Sociology: Robert E. Park and the Chicago School*. Montreal: McGill-Queens University Press.

McPhail, C. and Rexroat, C., 1979: 'Mead vs. Blumer: The Divergent Methodological Perspectives of Social Behaviorism and Symbolic Interactionism', *American Sociological Review*, 44: 449–67.

Mead, G. H., 1903: 'The Definition of the Psychical', *Decennial Publications of the University of Chicago*, First Series, vol. 3. Chicago: University of Chicago Press, pp. 77–112.

1930: 'Cooley's Contribution to American Social Thought', *American Journal of Sociology*, 35: 693–706.

1934: *Mind, Self, and Society*, edited by Charles W. Morris. Chicago: University of Chicago Press.

Miller, D. L., 1982: Review, *Journal of the History of Sociology*, 4: 108–14.

Park, R. E., 1936: 'Human Ecology', *American Journal of Sociology*, 42: 1–15.

1950–55: *Collected Papers*, 3 vols. Glencoe, Ill.: Free Press.

1972: *The Crowd and the Public*. Chicago: University of Chicago Press. First published in 1904 as *Masse und Publikum: Eine methodologische and soziologische Untersuchung*. Bern.

Park, R. E., and Burgess, E. W., 1921: *Introduction to the Science of Sociology*. Chicago: University of Chicago Press.

Park, R. E. and Miller, H.A., 1921: *Old World Traits Transplanted*. New York.

Parsons, T., 1968a: *The Structure of Social Action*, 2 vols. New York: Free Press. First published 1937.

1968b: 'Cooley and the Problem of Internalization', in Albert J. Reiss (ed.), *Cooley and Sociological Analysis*. Ann Arbor. pp. 48–67.

Peirce, C. S., 1934: 'Some Consequences of Four Incapacities', in *Collected Papers*, edited by C. Hartshorne and P. Weiss, vol. 5. Cambridge, Mass.: Harvard University Press.

Perinbanayagam, R. S., 1985: *Signifying Acts: Structure and Meaning in Everyday Life*. Carbondale, Ill.: S. Illinois University Press.

Rochberg-Halton, E., 1982: 'Situation, Structure and the Context of Meaning', *Sociological Quarterly*, 23: 455–76.

1983: 'The Real Nature of Pragmatism and Chicago Sociology', *Studies in Symbolic Interaction*, 6: 139–54.

Rock, P., 1979: *The Making of Symbolic Interactionism*. London: Rowman.

Rorty, R., 1982: *Consequences of Pragmatism: Essays 1972–1980*. Minneapolis: University of Minneapolis Press.

Rucker, D., 1969: *The Chicago Pragmatists*. Minneapolis: University of Minneapolis Press.

Shaw, C., 1930: *A Delinquent Boy's Own Story*. Chicago: University of Chicago Press.

Shibutani, T., 1961: *Society and Personality: An Interactionist Approach to Social Psychology*. Englewood Cliffs, NJ: Prentice-Hall.

Shils, E., 1970: 'Tradition, Ecology, and Institution in the History of Sociology', *Daedalus*, 99: 760–825.

Simpson, T. H., 1972: 'Continuities in the Sociology of Everett Hughes', *Sociological Quarterly*, 13: 547–59.

Stone, G. and Farberman, H., 1967: 'On the Edge of Rapprochement: Was Durkheim Moving towards the Perspective of Symbolic Interaction?', *Sociological Quarterly*, 8: 149–64.

1970 (eds): *Social Psychology through Symbolic Interaction*. Waltham, Mass.

Strauss, A., 1959: *Mirrors and Masks: The Search for Identity*. Glencoe, Ill.: Sociology Press.

1979: *Negotiations*. San Francisco: Jossey-Bass.

Strauss, A. *et al.*, 1963: 'The Hospital and its Negotiated Order', in E. Freidson (ed.), *The Hospital in Modern Society*. New York, pp. 147–69.

Stryker, S., 1980: *Symbolic Interactionism: A Social Structural Vision*. Menloe Park: Benjamin Cummings.

Sutherland, D. E., 1978: 'Who now Reads European Sociology? Reflections on the Relationship between European and American Sociology', *Journal of the History of Sociology*, 1: 35–66.

Taylor, C., 1975: *Hegel*. Cambridge, England: University of Chicago Press.

Tenbruck, F. H., 1985: 'G. H. Mead und die Ursprünge der Soziologie in Deutschland und Amerika: Ein Kapital über die Gültigkeit und Vergleichbarkeit soziologischer Theorien', in H. Joas (ed.), *Das Problem der Intersubjektivität: Neuere Beiträge zum Werk G. H. Meads*. Frankfurt-on-Main, pp. 179–243.

Thomas, W. I. (ed.), 1907: *Source Book for Social Origins*. Boston.

1923: *The Unadjusted Girl*. Boston.

Thomas, W. I. and Znaniecki, F., 1926: *The Polish Peasant in Europe and America*, 2 vols. New York: University of Illinois Press.

Thrasher, F., 1927: *The Gang*. Chicago: University of Chicago Press.

Turner, R., 1967: 'Introduction', in R. Park, *On Social Control and Collective Behavior* Chicago: University of Chicago Press. pp. ix–xlvi.

1970: *Family Interaction*. New York.

Vidich, A. J. and Lyman, S. M., 1985. *American Sociology: Worldly Rejections of Religion and their Directions*. New Haven, Conn.: Yale University Press.

White, M., 1957: *Social Thought in America: The Revolt Against Formalism*. Boston: Oxford.

Wiebe, R. H., 1967: *The Search for Order 1877–1920*. New York: Greenwood.

Wilson, R., 1968: *In Quest of Community: Social Philosophy in the United States 1860–1920*. New York: Knopf.

Wilson, T. P., 1970: 'Concepts of Interaction and Forms of Sociological Explanation', *American Sociological Review*, 35: 697–710.

Wirth, L., 1938: 'Urbanism as a Way of Life', *American Journal of Sociology*, 44: 1–24.

1964: *On Cities and Social Life: Selected Papers of Louis Wirth*. Chicago: University of Chicago Press.

1969: *The Ghetto*. Chicago: University of Chicago Press. First published 1928.

Zaretsky, E., 1984: 'Introduction' in W. I. Thomas and F. Znaniecki, *The Polish Peasant in Europe and America*, abridged edn. Urbana, Ill.: University of Illinois Press. pp. 1–53.

Parsonian Theory Today: In Search of a New Synthesis[1]

RICHARD MÜNCH

Introduction

At the present time the Parsonian theoretical tradition is undergoing a remarkable renewal. Although this tradition was pronounced dead by many sociologists during the seventies, the eighties have brought forth, to some astonishment, several new approaches which build on Parsonian theory to carry it onward to a new level. One should note, though, that this development has its origins in the seventies. This was a decade in which there was a curious parallel between the assumed decline of Parsonianism and the simultaneous increase in the number of contributions dealing with Talcott Parsons's work whose authors were primarily younger members of the academic world. The approaches developed during this period have made it evident that a new generation of sociologists are once again taking up the Parsonian theoretical tradition, but in a new way and with a critical and constructive attitude.

Thus it is not as surprising as it would at first sight appear that a breakthrough has occurred in the renewal of the Parsonian theoretical tradition during the eighties. The outstanding event sparking off this revivification was the testimonial collection produced by Jan J. Loubser, Rainer C. Baum, Andrew Effrat and Victor M. Lidz in 1976, *Explorations in General Theory in Social Science*, which impressively documents the vitality welling up again in Parsonian theory (Loubser *et al.*, 1976)[2]. From among

[1] I am grateful to Neil Johnson for translating this article from the German original.

[2] For important contributions pre-dating the testimonial collection, see Bershady: 1973; Black: 1961; Inkeles and Barber: 1973; Mitchell: 1967; Rocher: 1974; Schwanenberg: 1970; 1971; Turner: 1974; 1978; Turner and Beeghley: 1974. For important literature concurrent with the collection, and the rush of work which followed, see Adriaansens: 1980; Alexander: 1985; Almarez: 1981; Bourricaud: 1976; Berger: 1977; Buxton: 1982; Genov: 1982; Loh: 1980; Menzies: 1977;

the very many treatises following on from that, which also provide a firm basis for the theory's renewal, the extensive work of Jeffrey C. Alexander is particularly prominent, especially his four volumes on *Theoretical Logic in Sociology* which appeared in 1982 and 1983.[3] In Europe, too, new links have been forged with the work of Talcott Parsons. Niklas Luhmann, for example, has been extraordinarily successful in developing a new conception of systems theory (Luhmann: 1974; 1977; 1978; 1980; 1984). Jürgen Habermas, by reflecting critically upon Parsonian systems theory, has built a comprehensive paradigm for the analysis of modern society (Habermas: 1981a; 1981b). Wolfgang Schluchter has incorporated crucial elements of Parsons's work into his renewal of Weberian sociology (Schluchter: 1979; 1980). The author of this essay has endeavoured to give a fresh interpretation of Parsonian theory from a Kantian perspective and to formulate it anew (Münch: 1980; 1981a; 1981b; 1982b; 1982c; 1983a; 1983b; 1984; 1986; see also Alexander: 1984).

What all these attempts have in common is that they refer to the current state of theoretical development in seeking a new synthesis, just as Parsons had intended in 1937 with his first major work, *The Structure of Social Action* (1968), by both preserving and replacing positivism and idealism in a voluntaristic theory of action. At the current stage of development of the theory in general, this involves employing all the critiques of Parsons's approach and all the alternative theoretical approaches formulated since the late fifties in order to overcome the imbalances of Parsons's theory; at the same time, the content of his theory which is accepted as correct needs to be used as a frame of reference in determining the scope and limits of the new approaches. In this way Parsonian theory can enter into a fruitful, interpenetrative relationship with the competing theoretical approaches, enabling it to generate new theoretical formulations.

This present essay is designed to indicate, in programmatic fashion, the new way forward for the development of the Parsonian tradition shown by, on the one hand, the mutual penetration of the tracing of Parsonian theory back to its abstract foundations and, on the other, the application of competing theoretical approaches in formulating the theory on more specialized levels. I hark back to Parsons's own point of departure in *The Structure of Social Action* by terming this approach 'voluntaristic action theory'. The theoretical analysis of modern institutions will be taken as an example in clarifying this approach. The institutions referred to include the economy, the polity (with its own specific institutions of the constitution, the legal system, the executive, the bureaucracy and the political market), the modern societal community with civil rights as its basis, and the cultural institutions, such as those of science and the professions and those involved in the

---

Miebach: 1984; Proctor: 1980: Saurwein: 1984; Savage: 1981; Sciulli: 1984; Sciulli and Gerstein: 1985; Stichweh: 1980; Tiryakian: 1979–80; Turner and Beeghley: 1981.

[3] See also Alexander: 1978; 1982–3.

formation of public consensus and in intellectual discourse. The question one faces in each case is what theoretical approach should be employed to investigate such institutions.

In subjecting modern institutions to theoretical analysis, we need at our disposal a comprehensive theory of action capable of incorporating within itself the two fundamental streams in Western thought, positivism and idealism. We may differentiate such a theory, as a voluntaristic theory of action, from positivistic or idealistic action theories. Positivism's and idealism's one-sided aspects need to be overcome on both metatheoretical and object-theoretical levels (Münch: 1982b; cf. Alexander: 1982; Miebach: 1984; Parsons: 1968, pp. 757–75; Parsons and Platt: 1973, pp. 7–102). On a metatheoretical level, I shall initially attempt to integrate idiographic, ideal-typical, nomological and constructivist methodological approaches. Each of these procedural forms can be conceived of in a positivistic or an idealistic variant. The next step is to forge a link between the positivistic methods of causal and teleonomic explanation and idealistic methods concerned with the normative and the life-world or with rational interpretation. The task on the object-theoretical level is to integrate utilitarianism and conflict theory – variants of positivism – with normative life-world sociology and the rationalistic theory of culture, as variants of idealism. Finally, integration must be achieved between the theories of social stability and those of social change, micro and macrosociology, individualism and collectivism, action theory and systems theory.

With the intention of developing a comprehensive paradigm able to integrate the different metatheoretical and object-theoretical procedural approaches, I begin by constructing an abstract action space within the confines of which all action takes place. The second step involves determining how to proceed metatheoretically according to the dimensions of the action space: that is, determining methods and explanations. In the third step an object-theoretical action frame of reference, a model of factors controlling action in distinguishable areas of the action space, is constructed. In the fourth step, the subsystems of action need to be determined by way of systems theory. The fifth step is intended to make explicit the various methodological applications of the object-theoretical frame of reference. Once the paradigm of a voluntaristic theory of action has been formally introduced the sixth step can be taken, in which the limits of particular metatheoretical and object-theoretical approaches and the ways in which they can be integrated are indicated.

I   Basic Elements of the Theoretical Frame of Reference

All scientific study strives to recognize how the world is ordered. This is no less true of the scientific study of human action (Bershady: 1973; Kant: 1956; Münch: 1982b, pp. 17–58; 1982c, pp. 709–39; Parsons: 1954; Whitehead: 1956). This analytical problem of order in the world must be strictly delimited in relation to the empirical problem of stability or change in concrete societies. Equally, the interest in gaining knowledge of the analytical order of the world (of action) has nothing at all to do with interest in the stability of concrete societies.[4] The intermingling of these two levels where there should be a fundamental distinction – between analytical order and empirical stability – is a widespread phenomenon which leads to such erroneous dichotomizations as theory of change versus theory of stability, conflict theory versus the theory of order or integration, individualism versus collectivism and action theory versus systems theory.

Phenomena in reality, and hence also in action, can vary from total unpredictability (contingency) to total predictability (orderedness). We base predictions of events upon antecedents which we expect to have certain consequences. The number of antecedents involved can range from maximum complexity (a multiplicity with many interdependencies) to maximum simplicity (one single antecedent), and the consequences range from maximum contingency and minimum predictability (an infinite number of consequences) to minimum contingency or maximum predictability (only one possible consequence). On this basis we can construct a system of coordinates in which the vertical axis (ordinate) represents the complexity of antecedents and the horizontal axis (abscissa) represents the contingency of consequences. At the four extremes of this system of coordinates are the points determining the four fields in which events are ordered (Münch: 1982b, pp. 98–109, 224–6, 242–52):

1   maximum complexity of antecedents and maximum contingency of consequences;
2   maximum complexity of antecedents and minimum contingency of consequences;
3   minimum complexity of antecedents and maximum contingency of consequences;
4   minimum complexity of antecedents and minimum contingency of consequences.

If we wish to apply this system of coordinates to human action, we must begin with the first definitional characteristic distinguishing human action from mere reaction to causal impulses or instinctive response to stimuli, i.e. with meaningfulness. On the level of meaningfulness human action is guided by symbols whose meaning is interpreted by actors. In this case, then, relations between antecedents and consequences are those between symbols and the actions which can be subsumed under them. We can also take the various interpretations which symbols allow as belonging to the category of actions. Here, too, a system of coordinates can be constructed in order to define the action space. The ordinate now represents symbolic complexity

---

[4] This is shown by Alexander: 1982, pp. 90–4.

and the abscissa the contingency of action. The action space is delineated by four extreme points defining their respective fields of action:

1   maximum symbolic complexity and maximum contingency of action;
2   maximum symbolic complexity and minimum contingency of action;
3   minimum symbolic complexity and maximum contingency of action;
4   minimum symbolic complexity and minimum contingency of action.

II   Methods and Explanations

With this system of coordinates it is possible, in corresponding fashion and taking the metatheoretical level first, to explicate four discrete methods and four discrete explanations although, of course, it is possible for less extreme combinations to exist between them.

The following four methodological procedures should be distinguished (see figure 1).

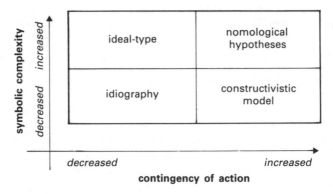

Figure 1   Methodological procedures.

1   The nomological method attempts to formulate scientific laws independently of symbolic complexity and the contingency of action. It investigates laws in action contexts which, as such, are totally open.
2   The ideal-typical method proceeds selectively. With regard to the complexity of symbols guiding action in different directions, it picks out one quite specific, selective interpretation of the symbols which exercise relatively unambiguous control over action.
3   Constructivist-model construction reduces the complexity of the symbolic world to a simplified set of abstract symbols which guide action in general, but on a concrete level imply that action is highly contingent and has a minimum of predictability.

4   The idiographic method describes action in closed societal contexts in which both symbolic complexity and the contingency of action are reduced by a self-evident but particularized life-world.

As regards explanations, the following four types can be distinguished (see figure 2).

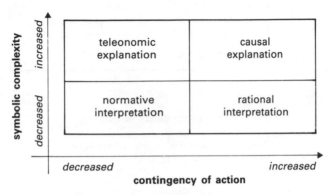

Figure 2   Explanations.

1   Causal explanation applies latent causal laws, independently of the complexity of the symbolic world and the contingency of action, to the explanation of action.
2   Teleonomic explanation attempts, regardless of the symbolic world's complexity, to explain a latent directedness, and hence restricted contingency, in action.
3   Rational interpretation sees action as being deduced according to simple, general principles from a set of premisses and initial conditions for those premisses. The general principles (low symbolic complexity) admit of a multiplicity of actions (high contingency of action) which will depend upon concrete circumstances.
4   Normative interpretation reads action in terms of an established normative symbolic pattern. Knowledge of a particularized life-world (low symbolic complexity) allows action to be unequivocally predicted (low contingency of action).

III   Basic Assumptions of Action Theory

On an object-theoretical level we can formulate a frame of reference out of the factors guiding action in the four discrete action fields (Münch: 1982b, pp. 234–52; Parsons: 1968, pp. 43–86) (see figure 3).

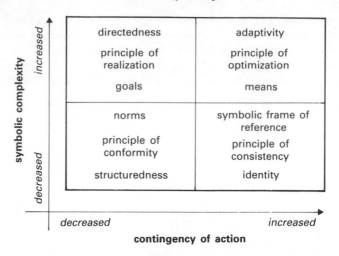

Figure 3   The action frame of reference.

1   Means enhance the variability and adaptivity of action and allow maximum symbolic complexity to be combined with maximum contingency of action. This is the zone where action has adaptivity and is governed by the principle of the optimization of goals.

2   Goals lend directedness to action, thus reducing the contingency of action in spite of the symbolic alternatives which could be conceived of. This is the zone where action has directedness, and occurs in accordance with the principle of realization and the maximization of goals.

3   Symbolic frames of reference give action its identity. The symbolic world is simplified by abstraction, but the contingency of the action which can be subsumed under it remains high. This is the zone where action has identity, and it occurs in accordance with the principle of consistency within a frame of reference.

4   Norms are responsible for action conforming to regular patterns. In this instance the symbolic world is normatively simplified and, at the same time, action which conforms to the prevailing norms is unequivocally determined. This is the zone where action has structuredness and obeys the principle of conformity to norms.

IV   Basic Assumptions of Systems Theory

Action theory can be extended in systems-theoretical terms if we subdivide to find subsystems and their respective environments which correspond to

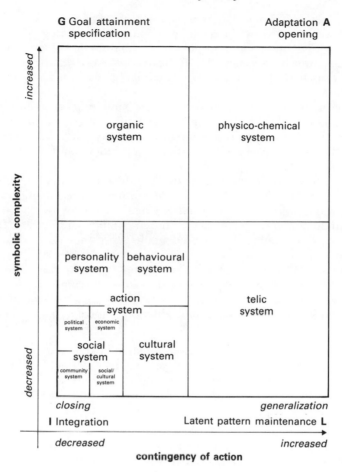

Figure 4   The human condition.

the fields of action in the action space. The subsystems are characterized by particular functions and their associated structures and processes, and also by generalized media which control these processes. Depending on the level involved, and working from the highest downwards, the generalized media are oriented to, respectively, categories of orientation and the standards of evaluation applied to them, meaning patterns and standards of value, or value principles and standards of coordination (Münch: 1982b, pp. 123–67).

The most abstract stage in the analysis comprises the anthropological level of the human condition. The following subsystems can be distinguished on this level (Parsons: 1978) (see figure 4).

1   The physico-chemical system is made up of physical and chemical processes controlled by the medium of empirical ordering. It fulfils the function of adaptation and opening by combining maximum complexity and maximum contingency (**A**). The category of orientation is causality, and the associated standard of evaluation is the adequacy of causal explanations.

2   The organic system is founded upon organic processes controlled by the medium of health. It fulfils the function of goal attainment and specification by combining maximum complexity and minimum contingency (**G**). The category of orientation is teleonomy, and the standard of evaluation is diagnosis.

3   The telic system comprises the transcendental conditions of meaningful human existence controlled by the medium of transcendental ordering. It fulfils the function of latent pattern maintenance and generalization by combining minimum complexity and maximum contingency (**L**). The category of orientation is transcendentality, and the standard of evaluation is transcendental discourse.

4   The action system is based upon action, controlled by meaning. It fulfils the function of integration and closing by combining minimum complexity and minimum contingency (**I**). The category of orientation is generativity, and the standard of evaluation is interpretation (*Verstehen*).

The second systems level is the general system of action, and this too can be divided up internally according to the four fields of action (Loubser *et al.*: 1976, vol. 1; Parsons: 1951; 1959; 1964; Parsons and Bates: 1956; Parsons and Platt: 1973, pp. 7–102; Parsons and Shils: 1951).

1   The behavioural system is composed of stimulus–response linkages and cognitive schemata controlled by the medium of intelligence. It fulfils the function of adaptation together with the opening up of the scope for action by combining maximum symbolic complexity and maximum contingency of action (**A**). The meaning pattern to which intelligence relates comprises grounds for cognitive validity and significance, and the standard of value is cognitive rationality.

2   The personality system encompasses personal dispositions controlled by personal performance capacity. It fulfils the function of goal attainment and specification of the scope for action by combining maximum symbolic complexity with minimum contingency of action (**G**). The meaning pattern is the internalization of relevant meaning by the personality, and the standard of value is the means–end rationality of action.

3   The cultural system is built upon symbols controlled by definitions of the situation. It fulfils the function of latent pattern maintenance and generalization of the scope for action by combining minimum symbolic complexity and maximum contingency of action (**L**). The meaning pattern is shaped by the human condition's constitutive grounds of meaning,

and the standard of value is the meaningfulness of action in a cultural frame of reference.

4   The social system is defined by social action, controlled by affective attachment. It fulfils the function of integration and the closing of the scope for action by combining minimum symbolic complexity with minimum contingency of action (**I**). The relevant meaning pattern is the institutionalization of meaning in social systems, and the standard of value is the unity in meaning of the social actors' identities.

The inner structure of the social system can in turn be differentiated into four subsystems in line with the fields into which the action space is divided. They are distinguishable according to the structure of social interaction and to the corresponding generalized media which control social action. In an ideal case, the use of the generalized media is regulated by a special normative order. The social subsystems and the corresponding generalized media are associated with distinguishable general value principles and with standards of coordination used to assess the realization of those principles (Loubser *et al.*: 1976, vol. 2; Parsons: 1961, 1967, 1977; Parsons and Smelser: 1956).[5]

1   The economic system is determined by acts of competition and exchange in a market; economic action is controlled by money as regulated by an order of property. It fulfils the function of allocating resources and preferences and as such is a concretization of the function of adaptation and the opening up of the scope for action by combining maximum symbolic complexity and maximum contingency of action. The value principle applying to money is utility, and the standard of coordination is the solvency of economic enterprises.

2   The political system is founded upon authority. Political action is controlled by power as regulated in an order of authority. It fulfils the function of collective decision-making and is a concretization of the function of goal attainment and a specification of the scope for action by combining maximum symbolic complexity with minimum contingency of action (**G**). The value principle for political power is political effectiveness as expressed in decision-making ability, and the standard of coordination is the acceptance and observance of decisions.

3   The social-cultural system derives from discourse, conductd with arguments (value commitments) as regulated by an order of discourse. It fulfils the function of constructing symbols in a socially binding manner and is a concretization of the function of latent pattern maintenance and a generalization of the scope for action by combining minimum symbolic complexity and maximum contingency of action (**L**). The value principle relating to arguments (value commitments) is the integrity of patterns of

[5] See also Parsons's essays, 'On the Concept of Political Power', 'On the Concept of Influence' and 'On the Concept of Value Commitments' (1969, pp. 352–404, 405–48,   439–72).

symbols, and the standard of coordination is the consistency of symbol systems.

4   The community system is built upon the foundation of mutual attachment, controlled by influence, and based on the commitment to a community and its norms as regulated by a communal order. It fulfils the function of the maintenance of solidarity and is a concretization of the function of integration and the closing of the scope for action by combining minimum symbolic complexity and minimum contingency of action (**I**). The value principle for influence based on commitment is the solidarity of community members, and the standard of coordination is social consensus.

All subsystems are functionally specialized systems requiring structures adequate to the fulfilment of their functions; in addition, they are not self-sufficient but depend upon the performance of complementary functions by the other subsystems. A necessary requirement for this is that the performance of functions should be interchanged with the aid of generalized media and that mediating subsystems should develop in the zones of interpenetration between the systems. A society represents a concrete and relatively self-sufficient social system. If it is to maintain its unity, there must be internal interpenetration between its subsystems, and it must 'adapt' to its environment, that is there must be external interpenetration too. The society's environment can be subdivided according to the dimensions of the action space as follows: **A**, articulation of interests, learning, physico-chemical processes; **G**, goals set by individuals and groups, individuals' personal dispositions, organic structures; **L**, social-cultural discourse, cultural symbols, transcendental conditions; **I**, particularized communities.

The relations between the action subsystems, and between the society and its environment, vary depending upon how coherent the systems are and upon the type of order inherent in them, as well as upon the mediating systems' level of development and their type of order.

(a) If adaptive subsystems are relatively strongly developed this has a dynamizing effect on the other subsystems and causes them to accommodate the adaptive subsystems, i.e. norms, values and goals are accommodated to interests and/or means.

(b) If goal-directed subsystems are relatively strongly developed this has a selective effect on the other subsystems and causes them to be dominated through compulsion, i.e. values, norms and interests/means are forcibly dominated by goals and the power standing behind them.

(c) If integrative subsystems are relatively strongly developed this has a limiting effect on the other systems and leads to them being enchained, i.e. values, goals and interests/means are enchained by norms.

(d) If structure-maintaining subsystems are relatively strongly developed this has a generalizing effect on the other subsystems so that all of them are defined but without concrete control, i.e. norms, goals and interests/means are subsumed under generally applicable values.

How much certain subsystems might dominate, with the effects upon other subsystems described above, depends upon the relative development of the subsystems themselves and of the mediating systems. The following constellations are conceivable.

(a) All subsystems and mediating systems are poorly developed: the result is an underdeveloped and malintegrated action system.
(b) All subsystems are poorly developed, but the mediating systems are more strongly developed: the result is an underdeveloped but integrated action system.
(c) The subsystems are strongly developed, but the mediating systems are poorly developed: the result is conflict.
(d) One subsystem is strongly developed, but the others and the mediating systems poorly developed: the result is the dominance of that one subsystem over the others.
(e) One subsystem is strongly developed, the others more poorly developed, but the mediating systems are well advanced: the result is that the strong subsystem overrides the others.
(f) All subsystems and mediating systems are strongly developed: the result is a highly developed, differentiated and integrated system of action.

How the action system is integrated is in turn a product of the structure of the mediating systems.

(a) Exchange produces open and unstable integration.
(b) Authority causes integration which is compulsively enforced through domination.
(c) Communal association leads to a conformist and immobile integration.
(d) Discourse implies integration through reconciliation.
(e) The combination of exchange, authority, communal association and discourse according to their analytical order as mediating systems is the main precondition for the interpenetration of strongly-developed subsystems. These latter are themselves a necessary condition for interpenetration as realized by the mediating systems.

V Forms of Application of the Theoretical Frame of Reference

With the aid of this comprehensive paradigm we are able to proceed constructivistically, ideal-typically, nomologically or idiographically.

1   A constructivist model is available to us in the shape of the entire frame of reference. In terms of action theory, it represents a closed model of interdependent factors which, in any given situation, guide action in particular fields of the action space. In terms of systems theory, the frame of reference is a closed model of interdependent subsystems in an environment defined according to the dimensions of the action space. In this instance the emphasis is upon abstraction (**L**).

2   Ideal-types can be constructed by selecting particular fields and factors of action or particular subsystems and functions. It is important that the selective nature of this procedure is immediately apparent from the frame of reference's point of view and that the interdependence of the ideal-typical structures and processes with the other factors of action and subsystems can be demonstrated. Max Weber's types of action serve as an example: they selectively define quite specific factors controlling action, yet without being arranged in a model which might throw light on their special characteristics and their mutual relations. Weber distinguishes between instrumentally (means-end) rational, value-rational, affectual and traditional action. Their unique characteristics and interdependence emerge more clearly than they did in Weber's own work if we interpret them as representing different fields of action in the action space. Instrumentally-rational action leads into the field of adaptivity, value-rational action into the field of identity, affectual action into the field of directedness and traditional action into the field of structuredness. Ideal-types are specifications of the general frame of reference (**G**).

3   Nomological hypotheses give expression to structural relations. Without our frame of reference the following four basic hypotheses can be formulated.

(i)   The more action is controlled by exchange, utility orientation, money, learning, intelligence and physico-chemical processes, then in turn the more frequently and rapidly an institutional order will change but the less an order will be enforced, will retain any continuity or will conform to regular patterns.

(ii) The more action is controlled by authority, by orientation to goals and by power, personal dispositions, performance capacity and organic processes, then in turn the more one institutional order is enforced against other alternatives but the less it will change situationally, retain any continuity or conform to regular patterns.

(iii) The more action is controlled by discourse, orientation to universal principles, arguments, symbols, definitions of the situation and transcendental conditions, then in turn the more an institutional order will retain continuity but the less it will change situationally, be concretized and enforced or conform to regular patterns.

(iv) The more action is controlled by communal association, orientation to norms, influence based on commitments, obligation through solidarity, and affective attachment, then in turn the more an institutional order will conform to regular patterns but the less it will change situationally, be concretely enforced against its alternatives or maintain its continuity.

Nomological hypotheses relate to the field of opening in the action space (**A**).

4 In idiographic accounts we use the language of the paradigm. More specifically, we can indicate with the aid of the frame of reference which factors in action, subsystems, structures and functions in individual societies carry special weight and dominate in relation to others, what frictions exist beween subsystems and what gaps there are in the institutional order. Idiographic descriptions are attuned to the field where the scope for action is closed (**I**).

VI The Scope and Limits of Specific Approaches in Metatheory and Object Theory

Having thus far given a formal presentation of the paradigm for a voluntaristic theory of action, this perspective will now be adopted in a detailed examination of the scope and limits of specific metatheoretical and object-theoretical approaches and of their integration into the voluntaristic paradigm. The following metatheoretical approaches and explanations on the metatheoretical level will be discussed: (**a**) idiographic, ideal-typical, nomological and constructivist methods; (**b**) causal, teleonomic, normatively interpretative and rationally interpretative explanation. On the object-theoretical level, our concern is with the scope, limits and integration of the following approaches: (**c**) utilitarianism and conflict theory as variants of positivism, and normativism and cultural rationalism as variants of idealism; (**d**) the explanation of stability and change in institutions; (**e**) micro and macrosociology; (**f**) individualism and collectivism; (**g**) action theory and systems theory. Finally, (**h**) the emergence of modern law will be discussed as an example of systems analysis founded in action theory.

(a) Idiographic, ideal typical, nomological and constructivist methods

If we examine modern institutions using the frame of reference of voluntaristic action theory, we go beyond a merely *idiographic* description and explanation of the institutions. The latter method would have to make an interpretative explanation of an institution's uniqueness within a concrete society at a particular point in time, looking outwards from the context of the life-world in that particular society (Collingwood: 1946; Dilthey: 1970; Husserl: 1928; Schütz: 1962; Schütz and Luckmann: 1979). Historical casuistry predominates, with no opportunity to trace hypothesized functional relations back to universally verifiable knowledge or to point out deficiencies, alternative procedures and further developments associated with a model ranging beyond the individual case under study. Positivist empiricism differs

from this idealistic variant of empiricism in that it offers a historical explanation by collecting quantifiable historical data (Best and Mann: 1977;
Clubb and Scheuch: 1980; Flora: 1974; Imhof: 1980). However, when
such collections of historical data serve as the sole methodological basis the
problem is the same, namely, that nothing can be said about functional
relations, deficiencies, alternative procedures or further developments.

Nor should our examination be based solely on the deliberately selective
construction of positivistic or idealistic *ideal-types* in the manner of Max
Weber.[6] In this case too, functional relations, deficiencies, alternative procedures and further developments cannot be generally established. An ideal-
type, ultimately, is an arbitrary selection of a phenomenon's characteristics
from among the manifold qualities present in reality, without any attempt
to place it in any superordinate relationship. This can easily lead to distortions and hasty conclusions which cannot be corrected in the absence of
more universal knowledge, even though the distortions occur during a
'conscious' process. There is no superordinate analytical order.

Another method which is inadequate if applied in isolation is historical
explanation by way of *nomological* hypotheses, whether in its positivistic
variant centred around natural laws or in its idealistic one with a normative
emphasis (Dray: 1957; Goldstein: 1972; Hempel: 1965a; 1966; Nagel:
1960; Schmid: 1979). The former lacks both access to action's meaningful
aspects and any superordinate analytical order, and the latter lacks universal
order. As a rule, positivistic explanations are sought in utilitarian and
conflict-theoretical approaches. This means that the relation to the normative and the life-world and the cultural interrelations in which institutional
orders are involved are either completely eliminated or are reduced to
constellations of interests or power. The substantive quality of institutions
then goes by the board. In the absence of any superordinate analytical
order it is impossible to place the special ways in which factors work, and
the reciprocal relations between different nomological hypotheses, in any
further structured framework. The question of which hypotheses should be
applied to which problem is wide open: there is a veritable jumble of
competing hypotheses.

Finally, positivistic or idealistic *constructivism* is a method which, for all its
special relevance here, still ought not to become an object in itself (Kambartel: 1976; Lorenzen: 1974). It is restricted to constructing abstract models
which are then tested under the sole criterion of their internal consistency.
Under such circumstances it is of course easy for historical concretization
to be missing, along with any application to reality. If pursued as an end
in itself, constructivism leads ultimately to 'neo Platonism' (Albert: 1965).
Examples can be found in constructions of developmental logic in its idealistic, materialistic and indeed dialectic variants. The theory of rationalization

---

[6] Here, see Burger: 1976; Henrich: 1952; Parsons: 1968, pp. 579–639; Prewo:
1979; Schelting: 1934, pp. 325–43, 354–61; Tenbruck: 1959; Watkins: 1952;
Weber: 1973; Weiss: 1975.

as used in explaining the formation of modern institutions undoubtedly displays this kind of developmental logic.

If we wish to avoid the distortions arising from these different methods, we need to choose a procedure which integrates them all within a more comprehensive frame of reference. We need to work constructivistically, ideal-typically, nomologically and idiographically at one and the same time. This does not necessarily rule out the possibility of giving priority to one method in particular (depending on the type of knowledge one is seeking to enlarge) and then supplementing it by making at least some use of the others. When making a historical investigation of an individual case, for example, one tends to utilize the idiographic method. Even here, though, if the research is not guided by a constructive frame of reference, ideal-types and nomological hypotheses, it will amount to no more than blind empirical work with no order to it. Sociological investigation differs from historical scrutiny in that it strives to achieve a greater order in knowledge at the expense of the variety of individual cases. It is for this reason that a constructive frame of reference is especially important, thought it must be expanded by ideal-types, nomological hypotheses and idiographic-empirical accounts.

In the investigation of modern institutions we need to adopt a sociological approach, and therefore our first requirement is for a comprehensive frame of reference. The constructivist method, construing general patterns inherent in modern institutions, is pre-eminent here. We use this method with the conviction that sociological knowledge without the achievement of such ordering will inevitably remain blind. Just as intuition and empirical observation are blind without concepts and a theoretical frame of reference, so too the concepts and theoretical frame of reference are empty without intuition and empirical observation (Kant: 1956, pp. 294–349). If we wish to be faithful to this maxim of Kant, a constructivistic method is as indispensable in investigating modern institutions as it is elsewhere, but, again, this must not become mere constructivism for its own sake. It must be compelled to work side by side with idiographic/empirical considerations to provide for empirical testing, with ideal-typical considerations to allow specification toward particular sections of reality and with nomological ones to explain phenomena observed.

(b) Causal, teleonomic, normatively interpretative and rationally interpretative explanation

Another question arising on the metatheoretical level is the controversy between the idealistic method of interpretation (*Verstehen*) and the positivistic one of explanation (Parsons: 1968, pp. 579–639; Weber: 1973). Here, too, we should not have to choose between the one method and the other, but should find a way of proceeding which integrates the two. Institutions consist of a pattern of norms. In analysing their relations of meaning –

whether internally, or externally in relation to other institutions, culture in general and the life-world of communities – we have need of interpretation through *Verstehen*. Likewise, the placing of these institutions in a more universal pattern is attributable to this form of interpretation. Yet interpretation is also to the fore in explaining the actions of individual and collective actors in a situation. Any such actor's intentional action should be interpreted as being derived from a choice made according to a certain principle under given initial conditions consisting of means, conditions (situation), ends, norms and a frame of reference. The underlying principles the actor can follow are the optimization of goals, the maximization and attainment of one goal, conformity to norms or consistency within a frame of reference, or, again, an ordered pattern incorporating all of these. The link between the initial conditions and the intention implicit in the action is a relation of meaning which can be appreciated through interpretation, and not a causal relation; the only aspect which is causal or quasi-causal in nature is the direct effect conditions have upon the action carried out.

The more the object of investigation is determined by levels of action which are far removed from symbolic structures (culture and the life-world) and constitute conditions which the actor cannot change by argument, the more his action is causally or quasi-causally determined and should be explained accordingly. This also applies to the relation between relatively rigid and established structures of interaction or institutional structures, on the one hand, and particular frequencies of given types of action on the other. The links between features of the social structure and rates of suicide investigated by Émile Durkheim (1973) are classic examples of quasi-causal relationships. They are also exemplified in Max Weber's demonstration of the relation between the spread of ascetic Protestantism and the existence of *rational* capitalism as a form of capitalism subject to normative order (Weber: 1973). However, it is not causal laws running their predictable course without any human reflection which are under discussion, but natural laws which are only quasi-causal in character. Apart from establishing statistically significant correlations and allowing for determining factors by comparison, in order to test for causal adequacy Weber and Durkheim alike expended considerable effort to discover the relation of meaning between the symbolic features of the social structure concerned and the intentions of the actors. Max Weber emphasized the meaning connection between the Protestant ethic and capitalist norms in order to ascertain the adequacy of the hypothesized relation on the level of meaning. Émile Durkheim analysed suicide as a meaningfully understandable action under conditions of, respectively, a lack of order in the personality system (anomic suicide), social isolation and the individual search for meaning (egoistic suicide), and communal responsibility (altruistic suicide).

The fact that meaning structures accessible to human reflection underlie what at first sight appear to be inexorable laws means that they can also be undermined and changed by human beings. This is why such relations are described as *quasi*-causal. For example, the meaning connection between the Protestant ethic and capitalism can be portrayed as a problem in discourse, with the result that changes occur in the justifiability of economic structures. In close proximity to quasi-causal relations, as far as their effect on the frequency of actions and the characteristics of social orders are concerned, are interest constellations and power structures. Here, actors are strategic in what they do, and if they act communicatively at all then it is only on a superordinate level, meaning that their action is largely determined by external conditions. The frequency with which actors generate negative external effects for each other when they act self-interestedly or make use of power in large, interdependent circles of interaction is a necessary consequence which the actors can only overcome if they transfer from strategic to communicative action.

The investigation of modern institutions is not to remain restricted to the level of meaning structures, nor to the level of interest and power structures or to that of individual action, and if institutions are to be seen as meaning structures which interrelate not only with other meaning structures but also with interest and power structures, then a comprehensive approach demands the formulation of quasi-nomological hypotheses which can be measured against the criterion of the causal adequacy of statements on relations and applied through quasi-causal explanation. Yet the investigation also demands interpretations (through *Verstehen*) of meaning relations and ways of acting oriented to the criterion of the adequacy of assertions concerning relations on the level of meaning.

Another method of explanation may be used, particularly where we are investigating concretely-delineated systems of action to which we can attribute an unequivocal underlying purpose, as in the case of organizations. Here we require a comprehensive model of the functions which such systems need to fulfil if they are effectively to attain their goals in the environment. It is then possible to give a *functional* explanation for the relation between goal attainment and the fulfilment of required functions within a system. If the system manages to maintain goal attainment constantly we are able to deduce *functionalistically* the existence of the structures required for the purpose. If it has the means to control inputs from the environment with regard to the extent to which they allow goal attainment to be held over time then, whenever disruptions due to the environment occur, particular processes can be explained *teleonomically* as being responsible for restoring the position of goal attainment (Hempel: 1965b; Münch: 1976, pp. 111–59; Nagel: 1956). Of the three explanatory variants, the one most likely to play a part in the analysis of institutions is functional explanation. This involves viewing an institution as the normative pattern of a concrete system of interactions related to one particular goal (function), and indicating which structures, i.e. patterns of interaction, need to be developed in order to achieve the goal (fulfil the function) in question; the extent of a system's goal attainment (function fulfilment) can be ascertained by a measure of how marked the required patterns of interaction are.

(c) Utilitarianism, conflict theory, normativism and cultural rationalism

I turn now to object theory. Here we need to overcome the limitations of the two variants of positivism, utilitarianism and conflict theory, and of the two of idealism, normative life-world sociology and the rationalistic theory of culture.

A *utilitarian* viewpoint would have to make the formation of modern institutions attributable to the utility calculations of the actors involved.[7] This, without doubt, is a difficult undertaking. Any attempts so far made in this direction have invariably confined themselves to the simple question of whether the very existence of social order or laws of property is beneficial when set against the possibility of their non-existence. However, in larger circles of interaction even this question cannot be answered on the basis of individual utility considerations, as the actors in this situation succumb to a prisoner's dilemma. This approach provides no opportunity for establishing anything substantial about modern institutions or about the significance for their stability and development of cultural traditions and discursive argument. According to this approach, institutions are situated in a cultural and communal vacuum.

Similar problems apply to explanations of modern institutions through *conflict theory* (Bendix: 1964; 1978; Collins: 1968; 1975; Coser: 1956; 1967; Dahrendorf: 1959; 1961). The question of how they originated is reduced, in this theory's authoritarian variant, to one of the size and strength of the battalions which could be mobilized on their behalf or, in its liberal variant, to the existence of a precarious and transient equilibrium of power between societal groups. This raises the question of how, in this perspective, one is supposed to regard the continuity of such political institutions as those of Britain and the United States, which were supported neither by a power structure which remained stable throughout nor by any continuous power equilibrium. Conflict theoreticians frequently tend to ignore those foundations of controlled conflict which do not in themselves contain any elements of conflict, namely the cultural and communal foundations, in just the same way that the utilitarians fail to notice the non-contractual, i.e. cultural and communal, foundations underlying the closing of contracts in one's own interest. Conflict theory precludes statements about the substantive characteristics of institutions, unless we are prepared to look into the cultural traditions of those who support them. However, this in itself is to overstep the limits of conflict theory in the direction of a sociology of culture and the life-world.

From the perspective of *normativistic* life-world sociology, modern institutions appear to be an expression of the particularized life-world of specific societies, and as such to be normatively closed (Berger and Luckmann:

[7] See, among others, Becker: 1976; Buchanan: 1975; North and Thomas: 1973; for a criticism of these see Münch: 1983b, pp. 45–76.

1966; Collingwood: 1946; Schütz and Luckmann: 1979).[8] Each institution
has to be understood and interpreted from its own particular position in
the interrelations of life. Its formation and structure, in terms of meaning,
have to be cemented into the structure of the life-world of a concrete society.
The objection to this approach from a rationalistic perspective is that it
provides no hint of an explanation for the development of universal institutional patterns. Institutions remain particularized life-interrelations confined to themselves. It is equally impossible to provide a critique of
institutions from the perspective of more generally valid normative patterns.
Other factors which cannot be grasped within the normativistic framework
are those inducing change in institutions, such as learning processes and
market behaviour. The same is true of factors allowing concrete institutional
norms to be enforced even though they are not an integral part of any
existing tradition, or of factors which might actually allow tradition to be
broken, such as the mobilization of power, and charisma.

The *rationalistic* theory of culture regards modern institutions as the product of a cultural process of rationalization which is in turn converted into
the societal rationalization of institutions (Habermas: 1981a; Tenbruck:
1975; Schluchter: 1979). Rationalizations in the spheres of the economy,
polity and communal relations are interpreted as specifications of a general
cultural pattern of rationality. Rationalization refers here to the tendency
of culture to become intellectualized, the economy and business life to
become economically rationalized, politics to become bureaucratized and
politicized and community relations to become formalized and objectivized.
It frequently remains unclear as to whether institutions are penetrated and
shaped by cultural rationalization or whether cultural impulses spur on the
rationalization of institutional spheres according to their own laws. What
cannot be grasped in this approach's frame of reference are the institutional
particularisms resulting from any given society's life-world tradition; nor,
equally, can it explain the situational, open and undirected changes to
which institutions are subjected by the articulation of interests, by learning
processes and by exchange relations, nor can it explain instances of the
enforcement of institutional norms without general, cultural legitimation
and before rational justifications have been established.

Instead of the restricted viewpoints of the sociological approaches outlined
above, we need a comprehensive paradigm with a frame of reference in
which appropriate assumptions from all those approaches are preserved
while, at the same time, their limitations are recognized. An integrated
paradigm is required to encompass the various institutional fields where
the individual approaches do provide adequate explanations. The following
fields can be distinguished (see figure 5).

---

[8] For a conjunction of the normative/life-world and the conflict-theoretical
approaches, cf. Haferkamp: 1980; 1981.

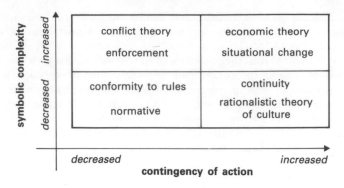

Figure 5   Theoretical paradigms and aspects of institutional orders.

1 *Situational change* in specific institutional norms occurs as a result of learning processes, the interchange of interests, and utility orientations. This is the domain of utilitarian positivism.

2 The *enforcement* of specific institutional norms in the face of opposition depends upon the mobilization of power and upon authority and charisma. This is where the power and conflict theory's variant of positivism is appropriate.

3 The observance of *regular patterns* in institutional action and the *social binding power* of institutional norms are bound up with the roots they have in a community's life-world tradition. This is the field of normativistic idealism.

4 The *continuity* of institutions is a consequence of the generalization of their norms in discursive procedures of argument. This is the sphere where explanatory power rests with rationalistic idealism.

(d) Explanation of stability and change in institutions

With a suitable paradigm which integrates specific approaches into a generally valid frame of reference, it ought to be possible to explain not only change in institutions, but also their stability or consolidation (Alexander: 1981; Eisenstadt: 1973; Parsons: 1961, pp. 70–9; Smelser: 1963). Change does not signify mere chaos, but the transformation of an institutional pattern from one point in time, t_1, to another, t_2. This transformation has effects in all the fields of action which have been discussed. At t_1 an institutional pattern initially has its foundations in consolidation upon communal tradition. This pattern is subjected to undirected pressure for change by learning processes, the articulation of interests, and utility orientations, while directed pressure for change comes from discursive argument questioning the validity of institutional patterns. Both of these processes have the effect of undermining the tradition concerned. If orderly procedures are available the institutional pattern can be adjusted step by step, by opening and discursive generalization. In the absence of such procedures, a break with tradition is necessary which must rely on the mobilization of power and on charisma (Eisenstadt: 1968; Shils: 1975, pp. 127–34, 256–75; Weber: 1976, pp. 140–8, 654 87). However, if this is to lead to a new institutional pattern, processes of traditionalization and communal consolidation need to establish the necessary social binding power as the step-by-step adjustments take place. In the case of a break in tradition, a new traditionalizing process is again necessary to secure social binding power; furthermore, discursive justifications are needed to guarantee the continuity of the new pattern. In this sense any change in an institution t_1 and t_2 that is not mere chaos invariably relies on processes whereby institutions are eased open, generalized, enforced and newly consolidated. In consequence, a theory is needed which can grasp these different processes and the nature of their effects on action within one integrated paradigm.

One particular form of change is the evolution of sociocultural patterns (Giesen: 1980; Parsons: 1966; 1971a; Giesen: 1982; Schmid: 1982).[9] For this purpose we can take cultural patterns to be a genetic code which during the process of sociocultural evolution obeys, *internally*, a logic of rational argument and, as determined by this logic alone, approaches a cultural pattern with increasing universal validity. *Externally*, this cultural pattern has to be converted into particular institutional patterns by interpretative procedures. In this respect, the institutional patterns represent genotypes of the cultural pattern shaped by genetic construction. The handing down of tradition and socialization ensures the institutional pattern's reproduction, whereas innovations provide for variations and hence facilitate change. The institutional patterns gained by interpretation are then further specified to become institutional norms. These are the concretely existing institutions which can be described as phenotypes, and as such they are exposed to an *external* selection process by their environment.

We can understand an institution to be a specified normative pattern whose 'successful survival' is influenced by how it is rooted in a community's life-world tradition, by enforcement through the mobilization of power and through charisma, and by adaptation to situationally changing learning experiences, interests and utility calculations. The institutions which have thus been socioculturally stabilized then again determine the make-up of the cultural pattern, meaning that the evolution of this pattern not only proceeds according to an internal logic of cultural rationalization, but is also subjected to external selective processes. Which factors are foremost as the evolution unfolds depends on how strongly they are shaped by appropriate structures and on the reciprocal relations between them, which can range from dominance and accommodation through mutual isolation and reconciliation to interpenetration.

[9] See also Parsons's essays 'Evolutionary Universals in Society' (1967, pp. 490–520) and 'Comparative Studies and Evolutionary Change' (1977, pp. 279–320).

The evolutionary perspective has a part to play in the consideration of modern institutions to the extent that those institutions possess a specific cultural pattern representing an interpretation of the general Western pattern of culture (rationality, activism, freedom, equality). This institutional pattern is specified in institutional norms which are subjected to the process of selection by anchoring in tradition, by the mobilization of power and charisma and by learning processes and utility calculations.

(e) Micro and macrosociology

In addition to the integrating effects we have already asked of it, a comprehensive paradigm must also allow micro and macro-levels to be considered on an integrated basis.[10] This distinction can only be a relative one made according to the size of unit being investigated. On the level of social action we can regard situative interaction between two actors as a microphenomenon. For example, the interaction occurring in a concrete situation between a buyer and a seller of a certain commodity is a microphenomenon provided all we are looking at is the commodity itself and the mutual orientations of the exchanging parties. However, as soon as we also take account of the effects this may have for third parties, how they react and how the exchanging parties orient themselves to this, we have already begun to investigate a larger social unit which then, in *relative* terms, appears to be a macrophenomenon. Similarly the fact that, when they effect their transaction, the two parties follow a normative pattern which they share in common with a larger market community, or that they observe rules enforced by a superordinate body as binding on all acts of exchange, is a macrophenomenon reaching beyond the immediate interactive dyad. The same is ultimately also true of the language in which they communicate, unless it is a private language between the two parties rather than one spoken by a larger community.

From the foregoing we see that, as a rule, any concrete action involves a complex interweaving of micro-interaction and macro-relations, so that both perspectives need to be brought into the analysis. To the extent that institutions are patterns of interactions valid for a larger circle of people, they should be treated as macrophenomena. On the other hand, they are microphenomena as specifications of a broader cultural pattern. In turn, the action of two interacting parties oriented toward institutions includes purely situational elements within it which, when set against the macro-level of the institutions, define the micro-level of institutionally-oriented action. One particular institution, such as a modern democracy, is a microphenomenon in relation to the social system of society in its entirety. Thus whether a micro- or macro-analysis should be carried out depends on the

[10] See here Blau: 1975; Brodbeck: 1958; Collins: 1981; Homans: 1961; Lindenberg: 1977; O'Neill: 1973; Parsons: 1971b; Sztompka: 1979, pp. 83–128, 287–323; Turk and Simpson: 1971; Wippler: 1978.

perspective applied. In any event, the concrete investigation of an institution must range from micro-interaction right through to the nature of the inter-weaving on overall societal and overall cultural levels. The same applies to our example of the analysis of modern institutions. What is needed here is a model in which larger units are systematically constructed from combinations of smaller ones.

(f) Individualism and collectivism

The theoretical dichotomy between individualism and collectivism is also inappropriate here (Alexander: 1982, pp. 90–112; Parsons: 1968, pp. 43–125). Institutions should be interpreted as patterns for collective orders, that is, as seen from the aspect of consolidated conformity to rules, they consist of norms which are commonly shared in a collectivity (a community) and are maintained by mutual attachment in solidarity. Both those who violate norms and those injured as a result can assume that the community members will maintain solidarity in ensuring that the norms' binding power remains intact. The violator must expect to be subjected to sanctions, whereas the injured party can expect help through solidarity. The prime basis for the binding power of norms is not the sanctions invoked when they are broken, but the mutual attachment in solidarity inherent in the common sharing of the norms, which is a prerequisite for the equitable sanctioning invoked by norm violations. Otherwise, any sanctioning which takes place can be countered by opposing sanctions. In this sense institutions have a *collective* basis for their conformity to regular patterns.

In contrast to communal association in solidarity, other factors do not have the same singular effect of consolidating norms. Discursive argument tends to bring about the universalization and hence alteration of particularized life-world norms. The spontaneous articulation of interests and individual actors' utility orientations can create coincidental orders but these are situational and short-lived; in the long run, these are factors which have the effect of dissolving order. The use of power only facilitates the enforcement of rules if there is a clear power gradient, but even then it is invariably pushed aside either because the holder of power has no need of rules for himself/herself or because the power gradient is transformed. The power equilibrium involved is an extremely precarious state of affairs and as such is virtually as unstable as the coincidental complementarity of interests. Even though institutions, as far as their consolidated regular patterns are concerned, cannot rely on factors such as these, that is nevertheless not to say that they are dispensable, for institutions are not covered by consolidated regular patterns alone. In as far as they undergo any process of universalization they are reliant upon discursive procedures; their ability to change depends on the opening effect of interest and utility orientations and, to assert themselves, they need the use of power, and charisma.

It is indeed the case that the aspect of consolidated regular patterns in institutions is based upon collective attachment in sharing and maintaining norms. Yet this does not mean that the individual actor has no place in the paradigm underlying our analysis. All we mean is that individual utility orientation among a large number of actors is incapable of producing any order in social action other than a coincidental and unstable one. At the same time, however, the concept of the individual actor is extended. Strictly individualistic approaches without exception locate the roots of the individual's motivation to follow collective rules in the individual rather than in any communal involvement and attachment or in any socialization. The radical variant of utilitarianism thus reduces the possibility of collective order to coincidental complementarity of interests (Buchanan: 1975; Locke: 1963, esp. Book 2, paras 95–122; Smith: 1937). The non-radical variant generally postulates a *naturally* given sense of social sympathy in each individual (Hume: 1966; Smith: 1966). The individualistic variants of pragmatism and symbolic interactionism also assume, at least in evolutionary terms, that there is a given solidarity in individuals which precedes communal attachment and socialization (Joas: 1980; Lewis and Smith: 1980; Mead: 1972; Peirce: 1958; 1960). The collectivist solution to the problem of order sees the emergence of a collective moral order only as the result of the individual's communal attachment and socialization within the community. As part of the same process, however, it is only then that an individual personality develops which reaches beyond the structure of organic drives, and that cultural identity and autonomy develop which stretch beyond the confines of particularized groups (Münch: 1981a, pp. 311–54; 1982b, pp. 364–426).

The *concrete* individual embraces all of these aspects: structure of needs, personality, membership of the collectivity and cultural identity. A collective order in this case is naturally based on the unification of the individuals involved who, in their communal association, put a normatively-consolidated imprint, which all of them carry, on their own need structures, free personal development and cultural identity, whereas need structures and personalities are not shared and their cultural identity reaches out beyond the limits set by communal norms and can thus subject those norms to critical reflection. The collective order relies upon individuals' abilities to step beyond the confines of their organic needs and personal dispositions to adopt the wider standpoint of collective solidarity.

A comprehensive paradigm can be neither purely individualistic nor purely collectivistic; instead, it must take up within itself the tension between these two components. This tension finds expression primarily in the concept of voluntaristic order. This is an order which is conditional upon the interpenetration of the organic structure of needs, personal dispositions, collective attachment and cultural identity. In all of these four aspects, we can speak of the individual's orientations to action. In this extended sense, I proceed in individualistic terms. However, orderedness in action cannot be reduced to the coincidental complementarity of needs and dispositions, but derives from communal association. In this sense, I adopt a collectivistic procedure. It is useful at this point to draw a distinction between the individual as a concrete actor who acts intentionally, combining all orientations to action in a specific way in any particular situation, and the individual personality, individual organism and individual behavioural system which are merely analytical aspects of the individual. Equally, an intentionally acting collective actor such as a group, a commercial undertaking, a club or association and, indeed, a society, must be set apart from collective communal association which is an analytically definable aspect of social systems (Parsons: 1968, p. 337).

(g) Action theory and systems theory

The final dichotomy which needs to be avoided is that between action theory and systems theory.[11] The two need to be incorporated as differing perspectives into the one frame of reference. In the perspective of action theory, the object of investigation is an individual or collective actor whose action takes place in a situation that comprises given conditions and available means, is directed towards ends and is oriented to norms and a general frame of reference. The actor derives an intended action, following a certain principle of action or a combination of such principles ordered in a certain way, from perceptions of the situation, the frame of reference, ends and norms. We may explain how this derivation is made by way of interpretation (*Verstehen*).

It is also possible, from an action-theoretical perspective, to solve the problem of order in action. One must ask what influence the basic elements of action (ends, situation, norms, frame of reference) exert upon the orderedness of action. Ends give action directedness, but one which is dependent upon the power at the actor's disposal. Means and conditions give it situational variability, but not any constant, stable order. General frames of reference merely cause action to have an abstract identity, with high variability on more superficial levels. Norms alone produce consolidated regular patterns in action. This is equally true for both action in general and social action in particular. Norms cannot be established by individuals alone, as this would make them synonymous with ends and dependent on individual power for their effectiveness. It is only in the form of commonly-shared rules upheld by attachment in solidarity that norms can convey a constant, stable orderedness to action in general and to social action in particular.

A first step toward the extension of action theory by systems theory is taken when subsystems of action are distinguished according to an appropriate systematic framework encompassing dimensions and aspects of action and the analytical order associated with that framework. In this case the

---

[11] See here Adriaansens: 1980; Bershady: 1973; Dubin: 1967; Gerstein: 1975; Habermas: 1981a, vol. 2, pp. 297–443; Menzies: 1977; Münch: 1982b, pp. 193–214; Parsons, 'Pattern Variables Revisited: A Response to Robert Dubin' (1967, pp. 192–219); Savage: 1981.

basic elements of action are attributed to particular structures and processes which can be delineated as subsystems of action and which have reciprocal interchange relations of special significance for the order underlying action. Three levels can be distinguished here: the human condition, the general level of action and social action. On the anthropological level of the human condition, the human organism determines the goals, physico-chemical processes allow for situational adaptation, the meaningful definition of action brings order, and transcendental conditions for meaningful human existence represent a general frame of reference. On the general action level, goals are set through the formation and development of personal dispositions and performance capacity, situational adaptation is a product of adaptive learn-ing processes and intelligence, attachment to norms is a product of social bonding and affective attachment, and the orientation to a general frame of reference is the product of cultural symbolization and definitions of the situation. On the level of social action, goals are set by authority as a decision-making procedure and by political power, situational adaptation follows from the economic allocation of resources and preferences and from money, attachment to norms is based on communal association and commitments to norms, and the orientation to a general frame of reference is brought by communication in argumentative discourse.

The greater the extent to which the subsystems of action are not only analytically separable but also concretely differentiated from each other, the more in turn the order underlying action is a product not only of the subsystems' different contributions but also of the interrelations among them. None of these subsystems is self-sufficient; all of them rely on the provision of 'factors' and 'products' from the other subsystems in order to be able to fulfil these functions.

Let us take the social subsystem of collective goal-setting and decision-making as an example. The subsystem encompasses decision-making pro-cedures and the processes resulting from them, as well as the enforcement of decisions by means of political power. The selection and enforcement of decisions is something which does flow from the above structures and processes; what does not, however, is their social binding power, legitimacy and realizability. For decisions to have social binding power demands that commitments from the societal community be mobilized, for them to attain legitimacy requires discursive societal-cultural justification, and for them to be realizable, resources must be mobilized from the economic system. The political subsystem's relation to the other social subsystems is not in this respect understood in terms of one concrete system having to adapt natural-istically to a complex environment. Rather, the reciprocal interchange of factors and products is postulated as essential if subsystems are to fulfil their special functions, and is interpreted as a form of interpenetration.

The political system does not function in a naturalistic sense but as interdependent and meaningful social actions oriented to collective decision-making. The more these actions have a density of interdependence among themselves which is relatively greater than the density of their interdependence with actions which are oriented differently, the more they can be delimited from other actions as a concrete system. As we know, if the system's delineation is to be lasting, there must be a normative order for a political institution. We may speak of the system fulfilling its function if collective decisions in accordance with articulated needs are reached within these interdependent and normatively-governed political interactions. Although it is not a self-sufficient social subsystem but one specialized to suit a certain function, the political system is nevertheless dependent for the fulfilment of its function on the economic mobilization of resources and on social-cultural legitimation and communal attachment, which are in turn themselves dependent on the effects of political decision-making (Münch: 1982a).

The only area where the interchange portrayed here may have quasi-naturalistic aspects is in the political system's relation to economic resource mobilization, at least to the extent that collective decision-making must accommodate itself to the realities of available material resources, which it does in an instrumental and technical way. However, in so far as the interchange is also conducted between role-carriers from the political and economic sectors then here too elements of meaningful communication are involved. The latter apply exclusively in the case of the cultural legitimation of political decision-making procedures and the decisions resulting from them. The essential requirement for such a process is that the procedures and resulting decisions are rationally grounded by discursive argument, which is what holds together social-cultural discourse and political decisions. In concrete terms this means that politicians cannot simply rest their decision-making procedures and resulting decisions on factually existing power but have to justify them with regard to generally valid values and norms. Conversely, the procedures and resulting decisions are invariably subject to social-cultural criticism by intellectuals. Thus the political system's relation with its social-cultural 'environment' is not a quasi-naturalistic but a discursive one. Nor is its relation with the environment of communities quasi-naturalistic in character. In this case the central issue is the social binding force of decision-making procedures and the resulting decisions. To ensure that this applies, the relevant social communities must be drawn into the decision-making process and become a common carrier of the procedural rules at least. This provides for communal association and for communication within a life-world.

In the form of systems-theoretical consideration discussed above, there is no trace of any naturalization or technologization of communication. Moreover, the interchange relations between the social subsystems should not be understood as economic exchange relations. Intellectuals do not barter cultural legitimation of decision-making procedures and of actual decisions in return for the collective decisions themselves. To interpret interchange relations in such a way would be absurd. What is meant here is that politicians, for example, only obtain the legitimation they need for decision-making procedures and the resulting decisions if they ensure that they are rationally grounded, which means they cannot avoid taking account of social-cultural discussions. Put more vividly, they have to step outside the purely political context to subject themselves to the rules of social-cultural discourse if they are to achieve legitimation and justification for their decision-making procedures and ultimate decisions. Conversely, intellectuals need to make an effort to mobilize power in decision-making processes if they wish to see their abstract ideals converted into concrete decisions. To do this they have to step outside the sphere of mere discussion and enter the political arena.

This form of interchange between the political and social-cultural systems is facilitated by the formation of mediating systems in the systems' zones of interpenetration. Political constitutions, for example, can be understood as social-cultural subsystems of political systems in which political decisions are subordinate to social-cultural discursive procedures. Likewise the professional complex can be understood as a subsystem of the social-cultural system in which interpretations of meaning, norms, expressions and knowledge are transferred to collective decisions on the basis of professional authority. The corresponding subsystems in the other zones of interpenetration mediate in a similar way in the interchange of factors and products between the social-cultural, communal, political and economic-action systems.

It would be a further step in the direction of system-environment analysis if the 'survival' of a system's normative structure – the norms of political decision-making procedures, for example – were to be interpreted as signifying that the system had adapted to its environment (cf. Buckley: 1967; Luhmann: 1970; Sztompka: 1974). Yet even this kind of perspective cannot be interpreted naturalistically on the level of meaningful action. Neither the system's structure – meaningful interactions – nor its environment are built solely upon non-meaningful phenomena. Let us again consider the political system as an example. Its immediate environment consists of utility-oriented articulations of interest, social-cultural discussions, and communities. As applied to these dimensions, environmental 'adaptation' signifies the development of subsystems which open up the decision-making procedures to utility-oriented articulations of interests (the political market), subsume them under generally valid values and norms (the constitution) and bind them to the life-world of communities (legal system), and which can also execute decisions even if there is a wide variety of preferences (the administration). At least as far as culture and communities are concerned, 'adaptation' in this situation is only possible by way of discourse and communication.

The same can be said of the 'adaptation' of society, which we can understand as a concrete social system not specialized to suit any particular social function and in this sense relatively self-sufficient in *social* terms.[12] A

[12] See here Parsons's essay, 'Social Systems' (1977, pp. 177–203), esp. pp. 182–3.

society's environment is only partly made up of material resources and demands; this dimension, on the other hand, is the only one where that society's adaptation to the environment has a naturalistic character through the development of technology and economic resource and preference allocation. For society is also situated in an environment of social communities which it needs to tie into itself through *societal* communal association. Only communication among the groups involved and between representatives of the societal decision-making centre and these groups can make adaptation possible. Another environment to be taken into account is the cultural area to which the society belongs. In this case the discursive foundation of the societal culture in relation to the wider culture is imperative. Finally, the goals set by societal and extra-societal groups also represent an environment in relation to which society needs to prove its ability to develop and assert collective goals. This means that political decision-making procedures are an essential requirement.

If the demands made by these very different environments increase, the society's 'adaptation' to them calls for the formation of appropriate subsystems 'functionally' specialized toward dealing with specific environmental demands. They then make up zones of interpenetration between society and the environment. Being functionally specialized, however, the subsystems have to rely on the interchange of factors and products not only to fulfil their own functions but also to be able to maintain the society's existence as a concrete unit. This interchange of factors and products again has to be mediated by further subsystems in the internal, societal zones of interpenetration. These continue to proliferate the more the functionally specialized subsystems for their part 'adapt' to their internal societal environment. In all these cases, the relation between system and environment only has a naturalistic character when it comes to the system's adaptation to material and organic conditions. Even the relations to articulations of interests and to established goals are quasi-naturalistic at the most, and permeated by processes of communication. The relations in the cultural and communal dimensions are inconceivable without communication. This is how we should regard the interchange relations between the social subsystems which are the components of a paradigm of interchange (Baum: 1976a; 1976b; Gould: 1976; Johnson: 1973; Münch: 1982c, esp. pp. 796–806).[13]

(h) An example of systems analysis founded in action theory: the emergence of modern law

The wish to explain the development of modern law solely as a result of the necessities of maintaining systems as their environment becomes

---

[13] See also Parsons's essays, 'On the Concept of Political Power', 'On the Concept of Influence', 'On the Concept of Value Commitments' and 'Social Structure and the Symbolic Media of Interchange' (1977, pp. 204–28).

increasingly complex is one which falls well short of its target.[14] The problem begins with the usual explanation for increased environmental complexity, namely systems differentiation. Can the development of modern law really be understood as a process of differentiation providing the basis for the law itself to achieve an unprecedented degree of autonomy, proceeding solely according to its own inner laws? The formula trips off sociologists' tongues so glibly that they have completely ceased to reflect on what it actually means. One should be clear about the background of such a development, namely the predominance of common law, giving expression to principles a community accepts without question. Common law obeys the logic of communal association and is thus bound to commitment to the community and to the limits of that same community. It is relatively rigid, and limited in the extent to which it can undergo change, can be specified to fit particular purposes or can be generalized beyond the boundaries of the community.

The increased complexity of the environment is far too general an event to be able to explain precisely the process of the differentiation of the law from communal action. Though the 'complexity' of society certainly did increase as cities and trade blossomed anew in the Middle Ages, such surges in complexity repeatedly occurred in the wake of more widespread commercial activity in India and China, yet without resulting in any comparable rationalization of the law. Max Weber stressed this clearly enough. Weber tells us, however, that there were three primary factors contributing to the development of modern rational law: an independent profession of lawyers and jurists oriented solely to its own system of logic, capitalist interested parties wishing to assess their opportunities for gain, and monarchs and princes striving for a unified control of their domains in opposition to existing disparate estates (Weber: 1972, pp. 437–8; 1976: pp. 398–9, 401, 416–22, 487–8, 490–1, 502, 506). That is, the law was subjected by the jurists to a process of rationalization (abstraction, analytical sharpness of concepts, freedom from contradiction, formalism). If we assume that the law's function is to regulate social interaction by way of norms, these regulations are generalized to such an extent by rationalization that they are applicable to considerably broader interaction contexts than communal action alone. This is the explanation for the universal applicability of modern law.

However, the law has also come under the influence of utilitarian interests wishing to rationalize business relations in order to enhance their profit opportunities. The law is thus subjected to a constant process of change as new situations and interests press for new regulations. This serves to explain why rapidity of change is a characteristic of modern law. Finally, institutions vested with political authority (monarchs, princes, governments, parliaments, bureaucracies) are intent on subjugating their respective

[14] See Teubner and Willke: 1984, esp. pp. 9–13, 15–16, 19–24; see also Luhmann: 1972; 1984.

domains to uniform control and on breaking down particularized claims to authority or sources of resistance, and thus represent a force acting towards the systematic unification of the law and towards its enforcement in a uniform way, even in the face of resistance (Münch: 1984, pp. 380–446).

Generalization, dependence on interests, and uniform systematization and enforcement, all reaching beyond the context of purely communal action, are three hallmarks of modern law which distinguish it from common law and in this sense include a process of differentiation from the original particularized, rigid common law which was limited in its effectiveness. However, it is a process which runs in three totally different directions, none of which in any way lead to a unidimensional inner logic of legal development. Moreover, even though the common law tradition loses some significance it does not become altogether insignificant, and does not do so at all in the Anglo-Saxon legal sphere. The legal tradition, as the characteristic of common law, remains the source of the law's self-evident obligatory power. If it is not anchored in this way to the collective legal convictions of a legal community – one which can vary in the pluralism of its structure – politically-established law, too, will be devoid of any binding power which is *felt to be obligatory*. The law's differentiation as it emerges from pure common law renders its development accessible to the logic of rules of thought, to the pluralism of economic interests and to the goal-setting and unification associated with a central, political legislative process. It is drawn away from communal action and into the spheres of cultural and scientific thought, of economic interchange and of the exertion of political power; as such it occupies a new position as a zone of interpenetration between these extreme fields of action.

When compared to common law, modern law is determined by a greater variety of different factors and represents the space where they collide and engage in a continued struggle for supremacy. For fundamental differences in the actual course taken by the differentiation process, one need look no further than the development of European law as against that of Anglo-Saxon law.

In Europe, formulation of the law has always been in the hands of university-trained legal theorists. It has been subjected to especially thorough rationalization which has led to a radical breach in the particularism associated with common law. In the main, the university-trained jurists were employed as civil servants, meaning that the state was able to enforce its concern to achieve a purposeful, uniform control over its sphere of authority. The great moves to codify the law issued from this union of state and bureaucracy, giving shape to generalization and to purposeful, uniform enforcement as a hallmark of modern law. In comparison, economic interests played a secondary role, though they cannot be entirely ignored. As codified law developed it always did so against a background of complaints that it was out of touch with reality. Juristic rationalism and political legislators together steadily supplanted the tradition of common law.

The Anglo-Saxon legal sphere is a different matter. There, common law remains an essential part of the legal system to this day. Anglo-Saxon law is rooted in the collective legal convictions of the legal community, yet its primordial self-evidence is always lost if new societal groups come forward with interests and convictions which have not yet filtered into the communal legal consensus. Common sense in such situations is merely a dominating consensus, but an endangered one.

Anglo-Saxon law has been subjected to comparatively little rationalization by jurists. It has been shaped by legal *practitioners* interacting directly with their economically-motivated clients. Accordingly, the law has been quicker to adapt to changing constellations of economic interests and represents a conjunction of the binding power of common law and situational adaptation to new interests. Unification to suit the purposes of political bodies, however, is far less marked than it is in Europe. In the absence of any comparable alliance between legal theoreticians and the political legislature, the law lacks an equivalent degree of codification to form a uniform system, even though it is certainly possible to identify a – somewhat weaker – trend in this direction.

Modern law, then, has undergone a development which, though it certainly differentiates it from common law, has not by any means made it into a unidimensional system proceeding according to its own logic. Rather, it represents a zone of interpenetration between rational thought, the political formulation of statutes, the economic articulation of interests and the collective convictions of the legal community, with whatever degree of pluralism. Thus, though their individual weightings vary, modern law combines characteristics as different from each other as rationality, collective binding authority, uniform enforcement, and change according to interest constellations. One cannot grasp the nature and extent of its development by regarding such characteristics as subject solely to a quasi-naturalistic and completely unspecified process whereby modern law's own complexity is raised in response to increased complexity of the environment.

In such an approach, any action-theoretical basis, and hence any access to the cultural differences in the development of the law, are altogether lacking. To adopt an action-theoretical orientation, one would have to understand the development of certain characteristics of the law (rationality, binding authority, uniform enforcement, and change dependent on interests) as the results of how certain actors carry out their actions according to certain principles, thus influencing how the law is shaped (see figure 6). Legal theoreticians orient their actions towards rational laws of thought (the principle of consistency), political bodies orient theirs towards instrumental control over their domain (the principle of realization), economic interests act according to the maximization of profit (principle of optimization), and to the extent that we feel ourselves to be members of a legal community we follow the norms which have always applied to social intercourse (principle of conformity). In the perspective adopted by systems theory, all these specifications of the concrete development of the law are suppressed to the point of being unrecognizable by the logic of systems development.

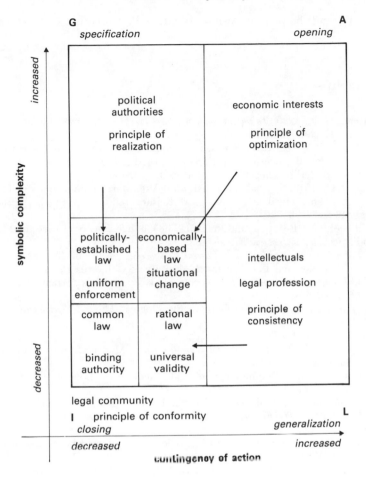

G   A
specification   *opening*

political
authorities   economic interests

principle of   principle of
realization   optimization

politically-   economically-
established   based
law   law   intellectuals
situational
uniform   change   legal profession
enforcement
principle of
common   rational   consistency
law   law

binding   universal
authority   validity

legal community

I   principle of conformity   L
closing   *generalization*

decreased   *increased*

contingency of action

Figure 6   The development of modern law in its social environment.

Conclusion

I have endeavoured to show programmatically how cross-fertilization
between Parsonian theory and competing theoretical approaches can allow
us to make progress along the road toward a new synthesis. What is
important now is the willingness to continue along this path by way of
mutual criticism that is prepared to appreciate the alternative points of
view, and then to apply this in concrete practical research. The aim is not
simply to incorporate competing theoretical approaches within the paradigm
of Parsonian theory as it already exists, but to achieve a *new* synthesis

reaching beyond the present position of either Parsonianism or its competitors.

Bibliography

Adriaansens, H. P., 1980: *Talcott Parsons and the Conceptual Dilemma*. London: Routledge and Kegan Paul.

Albert, H., 1965: 'Modell-Platonismus: Der neoklassische Stil des ökonischen Denkens in kritischer Beleuchtung', in E. Topitsch (ed.), *Logik der Sozialwissenschaften*. Cologne and Berlin: Kiepenheuer & Witsch, pp. 406–34.

Alexander, J. C., 1978: 'Formal and Substantive Voluntarism in the Work of Talcott Parsons: A Theoretical and Ideological Reinterpretation', *American Sociological Review*, 43: 177–98.

　　1981: 'Revolution, Reaction, and Reform: The Change Theory of Parsons' Middle Period', *Sociological Inquiry*, 51: 267–80.

　　1982: *Positivism, Presuppositions and Current Controversies*, vol. 1 of *Theoretical Logic in Sociology*. Berkeley and Los Angeles: University of California Press.

　　1982–3: *Theoretical Logic in Sociology*, 4 vols. Berkeley and Los Angeles: University of California Press.

　　1984: 'The Parsons Revival in German Sociological Theory', *Sociological Theory*, 2: 394–412.

　　1985 (ed.): *Neofunctionalism*. Beverly Hills: Sage.

Almaraz, J., 1981: *La Teoría sociológica de Talcott Parsons*. Madrid: Centro de Investigaciones Sociológica.

Baum, R. C., 1976a: 'Communication and Media', in Loubser *et al.*: 1976, pp. 53–56.

　　1976b: 'On Societal Media Dynamics', in Loubser *et al.*: 1976, pp. 579–608.

Becker, G. S., 1976: *The Economic Approach to Human Behavior*. Chicago: University of Chicago Press.

Bendix, R., 1964: *Nation-Building and Citizenship: Studies of our Changing Social Order*. New York: Wiley.

　　1978: *Kings or People: Power and the Mandate to Rule*. Berkeley and Los Angeles: University of California Press.

Berger, P. L. and Luckmann, T., 1966: *The Social Construction of Reality*. Garden City, New York: Doubleday.

Bershady, H. J., 1973: *Ideology and Social Knowledge*. Oxford: Basil Blackwell.

Best, H. and Mann, R. (eds), 1977: *Quantitative Methoden in der historischsozialwissenschaftlichen*. Stuttgart: Klett-Cotta.

Black, M. (ed.), 1961: *The Social Theories of Talcott Parsons: A Critical Examination*. Englewood Cliffs, NJ: Prentice-Hall.

Blau, P. M. (ed.), 1975: *Approaches to the Study of Social Structure*. New York: Free Press.

Bourricaud, F., 1976: *Understanding Talcott Parsons*. Morristown: General Learning Press.

Bourricaud, F., 1976: *L'individualisme institutionnel: Essai sur la sociologie de Talcott Parsons*. Paris: Presses Universitaires de France.

Brodbeck, M., 1958: 'Methodological Individualism: Definition and Reduction', *Philosophy of Science*, 25: 1–22.

Buchanan, J. M., 1975: *The Limits of Liberty: Between Anarchy and Leviathan.* Chicago: University of Chicago Press.

Buckley, W., 1967: *Sociology and Modern Systems Theory.* Englewood Cliffs, NJ: Prentice-Hall.

Burger, T., 1976: *Max Weber's Theory of Concept Formation: History, Laws, and Idealtypes.* Durham, NC: Duke University Press.

1977: 'Talcott Parsons, the Problem of Order in Society, and the Program of Analytical Sociology', *American Journal of Sociology*, 83: 320–34.

Buxton, W., 1982: *Parsonian Theory in Historical Perspective.* Fredericton: University of New Brunswick.

Clubb, J. M. and Scheuch, E. K. (eds), 1980: *Historical Social Research.* Stuttgart: Klett-Cotta.

Collingwood, R. G., 1946: *The Idea of History.* Oxford: Clarendon Press.

Collins, R., 1968: 'A Comparative Approach to Political Sociology', in Bendix (ed.), *State and Society: A Reader in Comparative Political Sociology*, Berkeley and Los Angeles: University of California Press, pp. 42–67.

1975: *Conflict Sociology: Toward an Explanatory Science.* New York: Academic Press.

1981: 'The Microfoundations of Microsociology, *American Journal of Sociology*. 86: 984–1014.

Coser, L., 1956: *The Functions of Social Conflict.* New York: Free Press.

1967: *Continuities in the Study of Social Conflict.* New York: Free Press.

Dahrendorf, R., 1959: *Class and Class Conflict in Industrial Society.* Stanford: Stanford University Press.

1961: *Gesellschaft und Freiheit.* Munich: Piper.

Dilthey, W., 1970: *Der Aufbau der geschichtlichen Welt in den Geisteswissenschaften*, edited by M. Riedel. Frankfurt-on-Main: Suhrkamp.

Dray, W., 1957: *Laws and Explanation in History.* Oxford: Clarendon Press.

Dubin, R., 1967: 'Parsons' Actor: Continuities in Social Theory', in Parsons: 1967, pp. 521–36.

Durkheim, É., 1973: *Le Suicide.* Paris: Presses Universitaires de France. First published 1897.

Eisenstadt, S. N., 1968: 'Charisma and Institution Building: Max Weber and Modern Sociology', in Weber, *On Charisma and Institution Building*, edited by Eisenstadt. Chicago: University of Chicago Press, pp. ix lvi.

1973: *Tradition, Change and Modernity.* New York: Wiley.

Flora, P., 1974: *Modernisierungsforschung.* Opladen: Westdeutscher Verlag.

Genov, N., 1982: *Talcott Parsons and Theoretical Sociology.* Sofia: Publishing House of the Bulgarian Academy of Sciences.

Gerstein, D. R., 1975: 'A Note on the Continuity of Parsonian Action Theory', *Sociological Inquiry*, 45: 11–15.

Giesen, B., 1980: *Makrosoziologie: Eine evolutionstheoretische Einführung.* Hamburg: Hoffman and Campe.

Goldstein, L., 1972: 'Theorien in der Geschichtsforschung', in H. Albert (ed.), *Theorie und Realität.* Tübingen: Mohr Siebeck, pp. 289–315.

Gould, M., 1976: 'Systems Analysis, Macrosociology, and the Generalized Media of Social Action', in Loubser *et al.*: 1976, pp. 470–506.

Habermas, J., 1981a: *Theorie des Kommunikativen Handelns*, 2 vols. Frankfurt-on-Main: Suhrkamp. English translation, *Theory of Communicative Action*, vol. 1, *Reason and the Rationalization of Society.* Cambridge, England: Polity Press, 1984.

1981b: 'Problems of Theory Construction', *Sociological Inquiry*, 51: 173–96.

Haferkamp, H., 1980: *Herrschaft und Strafrecht*. Opladen: Westdeutscher Verlag.
  1981: 'Entstehung und Entwicklung von Normen', Archiv für Rechts- und Sozial-philosophie, 67: 217–32.
Hempel, C. G., 1965a: *Aspects of Scientific Explanation*. New York: Free Press.
  1965b: 'The Logic of Functional Analysis', in his *Aspects of Scientific Explanation*, New York: Free Press, pp. 297–30.
  1966: 'Explanation in Science and in History', in W. H. Dray (ed.), *Philosophical Analysis and History*. New York: Harper & Row, pp. 95–126.
Henrich, D., 1952: *Die Einheit der Wissenschaftslehre Max Webers*. Tübingen: Mohr Siebeck.
Homans, G. C., 1961: *Social Behavior: Its Elementary Forms*. New York: Harcourt, Brace and World.
Hume, D., 1966: *Enquiries Concerning the Human Understanding and Concerning the Principles of Morals*, edited by L. A. Selby-Bigge. Oxford: Clarendon Press. First published 1748–51.
Husserl, E., 1928: *Logische Untersuchungen*. Halle: M. Niemeyer. First published 1900–1.
Imhof, A. E., 1980: *Einführung in die historische Demographie*. Munich: Beck.
Inkeles, A. and Barber, B. (eds), 1973: *Stability and Social Change*. Boston: Little, Brown.
Joas, H., 1980: *Praktische Intersubjektivität: Die Entwicklung des Werkes von George Herbert Mead*. Frankfurt-on-Main: Suhrkamp.
Johnson, H.M., 1973: 'The Generalized Symbolic Media in Parsons' Theory', *Sociology and Social Research*, 57: 208–21.
Kambartel, F., 1976: *Erfahrung und Struktur: Bausteine zu einer Kritik des Empirismus und Formalismus*. Frankfurt-on-Main: Suhrkamp. First published 1968.
Kant, I., 1956: *Kritik der reinen Vernunft*. Hamburg: Meiner. First published 1781.
Lewis, J. D. and Smith, R. L., 1980: *American Sociology and Pragmatism: Mead, Chicago Sociology, and Symbolic Interactionism*. Chicago: University of Chicago Press.
Lindenberg, S., 1977: 'Individuelle Effekte, kollektive Phänomene und das Problem der Transformation', in K. Eichner and W. Habermehl (eds), *Probleme der Erklärung sozialen Verhaltens*. Meisenheim: Hain, pp. 46–84.
Locke, J., 1963: 'Two Treatises on Government', in Locke, *The Works*, vol. 5. Aalen, W. Germany: Scientia. First published 1690.
Loh, W., 1980: 'AGIL-Dimensionen im Spätwerk von T. Parsons und Kombinatorik', *Kölner Zeitschrift für Soziologie und Sozialpsychologie*, 32: 130–43.
Lorenzen, P., 1974: *Konstruktive Wissenschaftstheorie*. Frankfurt-on-Main: Suhrkamp.
Loubser, J. J., Baum, R. C., Effrat, A., and Lidz, V. M. (eds), 1976: *Explorations in General Theory in Social Science: Essays in Honor of Talcott Parsons*, 2 vols. New York: Free Press.
Luhmann, N., 1970: *Soziologische Aufklärung*, vol. 1. Opladen: Westdeutscher Verlag.
  1972: *Rechtssoziologie*. Reinbek bei Hamburg: Rowohlt.
  1974: 'Einführende Bemerkungen zu einer Theorie symbolisch generalisierter Kommunikationsmedien', *Zeitschrift für Soziologie*, 3: 236–55.
  1977: 'Interpenetration – Zum Verhältnis personaler und sozialer Systeme', *Zeitschrift für Soziologie*, 6: 62–76.
  1978: 'Interpenetration bei Parsons', *Zeitschrift für Soziologie*, 7: 299–302.
  1980: 'Talcott Parsons – Zur Zukunft eines Theorieprogramms', *Zeitschrift für Soziologie*, 9: 5–17.
  1984: *Soziale Systeme: Grundriss einer allgemeinen Theorie*. Frankfurt-on-Main: Suhrkamp.

Mead, G. H., 1972: *Mind, Self, and Society from the Standpoint of a Social Behaviorist.* Chicago: University of Chicago Press. First published 1934.

Menzies, K., 1977: *Talcott Parsons and the Social Image of Man.* London: Routledge and Kegan Paul.

Miebach, B., 1984: *Strukturalistische Handlungstheorie: Zum Verhältnis von soziologischer Theorie und empirischer Forschung im Werk Talcott Parsons.* Opladen: Westdeutscher Verlag.

Mitchell, W. C., 1967: *Sociological Analysis and Politics: The Theories of Talcott Parsons.* Englewood Cliffs, NJ: Prentice-Hall.

Münch, R., 1976: *Theorie sozialer Systeme: Eine Einführung in Grundbegriffe, Grundannahmen und logische Struktur.* Opladen: Westdeutscher Verlag.

1980: 'Über Parsons zu Weber: von der Theorie der Rationalisierung zur Theorie der Interpenetration', *Zeitschrift für Soziologie,* 9: 18–53.

1981a: 'Socialization and Personality Development from the Point of View of Action Theory: The Legacy of Émile Durkheim', *Sociological Inquiry,* 51: 311–54.

1981b: 'Talcott Parsons and the Theory of Action I: The Structure of the Kantian Core', *American Journal of Sociology,* 86: 709–39.

1982a: *Basale Soziologie: Soziologie der Politik.* Opladen: Westdeutscher Verlag.

1982b: *Theorie des Handelns: Zur Rekonstruktion der Beiträge von Talcott Parsons, Émile Durkheim und Max Weber.* Frankfurt-on-Main: Suhrkamp.

1982c: 'Talcott Parsons and the Theory of Action II: The Continuity of the Development', *American Journal of Sociology,* 87: 771–826.

1983a: 'Modern Science and Technology: Differentiation or Interpenetration?', *International Journal of Comparative Sociology,* 24: 157–75.

1983b: 'From Pure Methodological Individualism to Poor Sociological Utilitarianism: A Critique of an Avoidable Alliance', *Canadian Journal of Sociology,* 8: 45–76.

1984: *Die Struktur der Moderne: Grundmuster und differentielle Gestaltung des institutionellen Aufbaus der modernen Gesellschaften.* Frankfurt-on-Main: Suhrkamp.

1986: *Die Kultur der Moderne: Ihre Entwicklung in England, Amerika, Frankreich und Deutschland.* Frankfurt-on-Main: Suhrkamp.

Nagel, E., 1956: 'A Formalization of Functionalism', in his *Logic without Metaphysics.* New York: Free Press, pp. 247–83.

1960: 'Determination in History', *Philosophy and Phenomenological Research,* 20: 291–317.

North, D. C. and Thomas, R. P., 1973: *The Rise of the Western World.* Cambridge, England: Cambridge University Press.

O'Neill, J. (ed.), 1973: *Modes of Individualism and Collectivism.* London: Heinemann.

Parsons, T., 1951: *The Social System.* Glencoe, Ill.: Free Press.

1954: 'The Present Position and Prospects of Systematic Theory in Sociology', in his *Essays in Sociological Theory.* New York: Free Press, pp. 212–37.

1959: 'An Approach to Psychological Theory in Terms of the Theory of Action', in S. Koch (ed.), *Psychology: A Study of a Science,* vol. 3. New York: McGraw-Hill, pp. 612–711.

1961: 'An Outline of the Social System', in Parsons, E. A. Shils, K. D. Naegele and J. R. Pitts (eds), *Theories of Society.* New York: Free Press, pp. 30–79.

1964: *Social Structure and Personality.* New York: Free Press.

1966: *Societies: Evolutionary and Comparative Perspectives.* Englewood Cliffs, NJ: Prentice-Hall.

1967: *Sociological Theory and Modern Society.* New York: Free Press.

1968: *The Structure of Social Action.* New York: Free Press. First published 1937.

1969: *Politics and Social Structure*. New York: Free Press.

1971a: *The System of Modern Societies*. Englewood Cliffs, NJ: Prentice-Hall.

1971b: 'Levels of Organization and the Meditation of Social Interaction', in H. Turk and R. L. Simpson (eds), *Institutions and Social Exchange*. Indianapolis: Bobbs-Merill, pp. 23–35.

1977: *Social Systems and the Evolution of Action Theory*. New York: Free Press.

1978: 'A Paradigm of the Human Condition', in his *Action Theory and the Human Condition*. New York: Free Press, pp. 352–43.

Parsons, T. and Bales, R. F., 1956: *Family Socialization and Interaction Process*. London: Routledge and Kegan Paul.

Parsons, T. and Platt, G. M., 1973: *The American University*. Cambridge, Mass.: Harvard University Press.

Parsons, T. and Shils, E. A. (eds), 1951: 'Values, Motives and Systems of Actions', in their *Toward a General Theory of Action*. Cambridge, Mass.: Harvard University Press, pp. 45–275.

Parsons, T. and Smelser, N. J., 1956: *Economy and Society*. New York: Free Press.

Peirce, C. S., 1958: *Collected Papers*, vols 7–8, edited by A. Burks. Cambridge, Mass.: Harvard University Press. First published 1931–35.

Peirce, C. S., 1960: *Collected Papers*, vols 1–4, edited by C. Hartshorne and P. Weiss. Cambridge, Mass.: Harvard University Press. First published 1931–35.

Prewo, R., 1979: *Max Webers Wissenschaftsprogramm: Versuch einer methodischen Neuerschliessung*. Frankfurt-on-Main: Suhrkamp.

Proctor, I., 1980: 'Parsons' Early Voluntarism', *Sociological Inquiry*, 48: 37–48.

Rocher, G., 1974: *Talcott Parsons and American Sociology*. London: Nelson.

Saurwein, K. H., forthcoming: 'Das ökonomische Element in der soziologischen Theorie Talcott Parsons'. Doctoral dissertation, University of Düsseldorf, 1984.

Savage, P., 1981: *The Theories of Talcott Parsons*. New York: St Martin's.

Schelting, A. V., 1934: *Max Webers Wissenschaftslehre: Das logische Problem der historischen Kulturerkenntnis. Die Grenzen der Soziologie des Wissens*. Tübingen: Mohr Siebeck.

Schluchter, W., 1979: *Entwicklung des okzidentalen Rationalismus: Eine Analyse von Max Webers Gesellschaftsgeschichte*. Tübingen: Mohr Siebeck.

1980 (ed.): *Verhalten Handeln und System: Talcott Parsons' Beitrag zur Entwicklung der Sozialwissenschaften*. Frankfurt-on-Main: Suhrkamp.

Schmid, M., 1979: *Handlungsrationalität: Kritik einer dogmatischen Handlungswissenschaft*. Munich: Finck.

1982: *Theorie sozialen Wandels*. Opladen: Westdeutscher Verlag.

Schutz, A., 1962: *Collected Papers*, vol. 1. The Hague: Martinus Nijhoff.

Schutz, A. and Luckmann, T., 1979: *Strukturen der Lebenswelt*. Frankfurt-on-Main: Suhrkamp.

Schwanenberg, E., 1970: *Soziales Handeln – Die Theorie und ihr Problem*. Berne: Huber.

1971: 'The Two Problems of Order in Parsons' Theory: An Analysis from Within', *Social Forces*, 49: 569–81.

Sciulli, D., 1984: 'Talcott Parsons' Analytical Critique of Marxism's Concept of Alienation', *American Journal of Sociology*, 90: 514–40.

Sciulli, D. and Gerstein, D., 1985: 'Social Theory and Talcott Parsons in the 1980s', *Annual Review of Sociology*, 11: 369–87.

Shils, E., 1975: *Center and Periphery: Essays in Microsociology*. Chicago: University of Chicago Press.

Smelser, N. S., 1963: *Theory of Collective Behavior*. New York: Free Press.

Smith, A., 1937: *The Wealth of Nations*. New York: Modern Library. First published 1776.

1966: *The Theory of Moral Sentiments*. New York: Bohn. First published 1759.

Stichweh, R., 1980: 'Rationalität bei Parsons', *Zeitschrift für Soziologie*, 9: 54–78.

Sztompka, P., 1974: *System and Function: Toward a Theory of Society*. New York: Academic Press.

1979: *Sociological Dilemmas: Toward a Dialectic Paradigm*. New York: Academic Press.

Tenbruck, F. H., 1959: 'Die Genesis der Methodologie Max Webers', *Kölner Zeitschrift für Soziologie und Sozialpsychologie*, 11: 573–630.

1975: 'Das Werk Max Webers', *Kölner Zeitschrift für Soziologie und Sozialpsychologie*, 27: 663–702.

Teubner, G. and Willkie, H., 1984: 'Kontext und Autonomie: Gesellschaftliche Selbststeuerung durch reflexives Recht', *Zeitschrift für Rechtssoziologie*, 6: 4–35.

Tiryakian, E. A., 1979–80: 'Post-Parsonian Sociology', *Humboldt Journal of Social Relations*, 7: 17–32.

Turk, H. and Simpson, R. L. (eds), 1971: *Institutions and Social Exchange*. Indianapolis: Bobbs-Merill.

Turner, J. H., 1974: 'Persistent Issues in Parsonian Action Theory', *Sociological Inquiry*, 44: 61–3.

1978: *The Structure of Sociological Theory*. Homewood, Ill.: Dorsey. First published 1974.

Turner, J. H. and Beeghley, L., 1974: 'Current Folklore in the Criticism of Parsonian Action Theory', *Sociological Inquiry*, 4: 47–55.

1981: *The Emergence of Sociological Theory*. Homewood, Ill.: Dorsey.

Watkins, J. W. N., 1952: 'Idealtypes and Historical Explanation', *British Journal of Sociology*, 3: 22–43.

Weber, M., 1972: *Gesammelte Aufsätze zur Religionssoziologie*, vol. 1. Tübingen, Mohr Siebeck. First published 1920.

1973: *Gesammelte Aufsätze zur Wissenschaftslehre*. Tübingen: Mohr Siebeck. First published 1922.

1976: *Wirtschaft und Gesellschaft*. Tübingen: Mohr Siebeck. First published 1922.

Weiss, J., 1975: *Max Webers Grundlegung der Soziologie*. Munich: Ullstein.

Whitehead, A. N., 1967: *Science and the Modern World*. New York: Macmillan. First published 1925.

Wippler, R., 1978: 'Nicht-intendierte soziale Folgen individueller Handlungen', *Soziale Welt*, 29: 155–79.

Analytical Theorizing
JONATHAN H. TURNER

The term 'analytical' is admittedly vague, but I use it here to describe a range of theoretical approaches which make the following assumptions: there is an external universe 'out there' which exists independently of our conceptualizations of it; this universe reveals certain timeless, universal and invariant properties; the goal of sociological theory is to isolate these generic properties and understand their operation. These assertions invite, I am afraid, an avalanche of criticism and immediately immerse theoretical activity into a philosophical debate which, by its nature, is unresolvable. Indeed, social theorists have spent far too much time defending or attacking the position of analytical theorizing, and as a result, they have neglected the main task of all theory: to understand how the social world operates. I do not want to be yet another Brer Rabbit who is pulled into this philosophical quagmire, but let me at least frame, in general terms, some of the philosophical issues.

The Philosophical Debate

Analytical theory assumes that, in A. R. Radcliffe-Brown's words, a 'natural science of society' is possible (Radcliffe-Brown: 1948). This argument was given its most forceful expression by the titular founder of sociology, Auguste Comte, who argued that sociology could be a 'positivistic science'. Thus, analytical theory and positivism are closely allied, but the nature of this alliance is obscured by the fact that portrayals of positivism vary considerably. Unlike some recent portrayals of positivism that associate this term with 'raw empiricism', Comte argued that 'no real observation of any kind of phenomenon is possible, except in as far as it is first directed, and finally interpreted, by some theory' (Comte: 1830–42, p. 242). Indeed, Comte saw as a 'great hindrance ... the empiricism which is introduced into [positivism] by those who, in the name of impartiality, would interdict the use of any theory whatever' (p. 242). Thus, positivism means the use of theory to interpret empirical events and, conversely, the reliance on observation to assess the plausibility of theory. But what is the nature of theory in Comte's positivism? The opening pages of his *Positive Philosophy* inform us.

> The first characteristic of Positive philosophy is that it regards all phenomena as subject to invariable natural *Laws*. Our business is – seeing how vain is any research into what are called *Causes*, whether first or final – to pursue an accurate discovery of these Laws, with a view to reducing them to the smallest possible number. By speculating upon causes, we could solve no difficulty about origin and purpose. Our real business is to analyze accurately the circumstances of phenomena, and to connect them by the natural relations of succession and resemblance. The best illustration of this is in the case of the doctrine of Gravitation (Comte: 1830–42, pp. 5–6).

The above quotation makes a number of critical points. First, sociological theory involves the search for abstract natural laws. There should be relatively few laws; and one principal goal of theoretical activity is to reduce the number of laws so that only basic, fundamental and invariant properties of the universe are subject to theoretical analysis.

Second, causal and functional analysis are inappropriate. Here, Comte seems to accept David Hume's analysis of the impossibility of determining the cause of phenomena, but he adds a similar warning about analysis of phenomena in terms of the purposes, ends or needs that they serve. Sadly, sociology ignored Comte's warning. Indeed, Émile Durkheim was to 'stand Comte on his head' in 1895 with the publication of *The Rules of the Sociological Method* which argued for both causal and functional analysis (Durkheim: 1983). I think that we would have been far wiser, as a theoretical discipline, to follow Comte's 'old rules of the sociological method' rather than Durkheim's proposal; and as I will indicate shortly, we certainly should not follow Giddens's and others' proposals for 'New Rules' of the sociological method (Giddens: 1977). Unfortunately, sociological theory was to follow Durkheim's rather than Comte's advice and, more recently, a variety of anti-positivist treatises. The overall result is to divert and dilute theorizing in sociology.

Third, sociological laws should be modelled after the physics of Comte's time, but the form of the laws is left rather vague. Terms like 'natural relations of succession and resemblance' are imprecise, especially since causal concerns have been eliminated. In dealing with this vagueness, more modern portrayals of positivism in philosophy have somewhat misinterpreted Comte's programme and inserted rigid criteria for formulating the 'natural relations' of phenomena (e.g., see Carnap: 1966; Hempel: 1965). This new positivism is often preceded by the modifier 'logical' and takes the following form (Keat and Orry: 1975): abstract laws express regularities in the universe; such laws 'explain' events when they predict what will occur in a specific empirical case; the vehicle of this explanation is 'logical deductions' from the law (the *explanas*) to a set of empirical phenomena (the *explicandum*); such 'logical deductions' take the form of using the laws as a premiss, inserting statements which 'connect' or 'attach' the law to a general class of empirical phenomena and then making a prediction about what is expected to occur for one specific empirical case within this general class of phenomena; and if the prediction is not confirmed by the empirical case, the theory is re-assessed, although there is disagreement here over whether the theory is now 'falsified' (Popper: 1959; 1969) or whether its failure to be 'confirmed' merely requires a serious re-examination of the theory (Lakatos: 1970).

This view of positivism 'fills in' Comte's points of vagueness with excessively restrictive criteria which most analytical theorists do not, and cannot, follow. True, they often pay lip-service to them in their moments of philosophical/methodological reflection, but in their actual work they do not adhere to them. There are good reasons for this inability to follow the straitjacket of logical positivism and they are fundamental to analytical theorizing. Let me elaborate on these.

First, the criterion of prediction is unrealistic. When scientists must work in natural empirical systems, prediction is difficult, since controls cannot be imposed on the effects of extraneous variables. These extraneous forces may be unknown or unmeasurable with current methodologies, and even if they are known or measurable, there may be moral and political reasons for not imposing controls. This situation is true not just for social scientists but for all natural scientists. In recognizing the difficulties of prediction, however, I do not propose that we abandon efforts to be a natural science, any more than geology and biology re-assess their scientific worth when they cannot, respectively, predict earthquakes or speciation.

Second, the rejection of causality is a great weakness in some forms of positivism, whether Comte's or the versions of more modern philosophers. Such a rejection is acceptable when logical deductions from premises to conclusion can be the criterion of explanation, but analytical theory must also be concerned with the processes that operate to connect phenomena. That is, it is important to know why, how and in what ways invariant properties of the universe operate. Such concerns will require the analysis of underlying social processes and, invariably, of causality. Depending on the theorist, causality may or may not be part of the formal laws, but it cannot be ignored (Keat and Urry: 1975).

Third, logical positivism assumes that the calculuses by which 'deductions' from premises to conclusions, or from *explanas* to *explicandum*, are made are unambiguous and clear. In fact, they are not. Much of what constitutes a 'deductive system' in all scientific theory is folk-reasoning, and highly discursive. For example, the synthetic theory of evolution is discursive, although some portions of it (such as genetics) can be stated with a degree of precision. But when this theory is used to explain events, the application is not in terms of strict adherence to a calculus but, rather, in conformity with what 'seems reasonable' to a community of scholars. Having asserted this, however, I am not advocating retreat into a version of currently fashionable hermeneutics or relativism.

These considerations require that sociological theory loosen the requirements of logical positivism. We should still view as our goal the isolation and understanding of invariant, fundamental and basic features of the social universe, but we should not be intellectual fascists about it. Moreover, analytical theory must not be concerned with regularities *per se* but with the 'why' and 'how' of invariant regularities. Thus, my view of theory, which is shared by most analytical theorists, is this: we can develop abstract laws of invariant properties of the universe, but such laws will need to be supplemented by scenarios (models, descriptions, analogies) of the under-lying processes of these properties. Moreover, explanation is in most cases not going to involve precise predictions and deductions, primarily because experimental controls are not possible in the tests of most theories. Expla-nation will consist, instead, of a more discursive use of abstract propositions and models to understand specific events. Deduction will be loose, and even metaphorical. And it will naturally be subject to argument and debate. But, sociology is not unique here; most sciences operate this way. While Thomas Kuhn's analysis is highly flawed, it did emphasize the social-political charac-ter of theories (Kuhn: 1970). But again, we do not need to abandon our search for invariant properties any more than physics has after recognizing that many formulations are stated, initially at least, rather loosely and that they are subject to political negotiation within a scientific community.

Let me close this section on the philosophical debate with a brief comment on the criticisms of positivism, even my rather relaxed portrayal of its tenets. One criticism is that theoretical statements are not so much descriptions or analyses of an independent, external reality as creations and constructions of the scientist. Theory is not about a reality 'out there', but rather it is a product of scientists' interests or their sense of aesthetics. A variant of this criticism is that theories are never tested against the 'hard facts' of an external world because the 'facts' themselves are also related to the scientists' interests and to the research protocols that are politically acceptable to a scientific community. Moreover, facts will be interpreted, or ignored, in light of the interests of scientists. The overall result, critics argue, is that the presumed self-correcting process of theory-hypothesis testing in science is an illusion.

My sense is that there is an important point to this criticism, but it is rather dramatically overstated. All concepts are, of course, reifications in some sense; all 'facts' are biased by our methods; and all facts are interpreted to some extent. But despite these problems, knowledge about the universe has been accumulated. This knowledge could not be wholly subjective or biased: otherwise, nuclear weapons would not explode, thermometers would not work, aeroplanes would not fly, and so on. If we took theory-building seriously in sociology, knowledge about the social universe would accumu-late, albeit along the muddled path that it has in the 'hard sciences'. Thus, in the long run, the world out there does impose itself as a corrective to theoretical knowledge.

A second general line of criticism of the analytical approach that I am advocating is more specific to the social sciences and concerns the substantive nature of the social universe. There are numerous variants of this argument but the central point is this: the very nature of the universe is alterable by virtue of human beings' capacity for thought, reflection and action. Laws about an invariant world are irrelevant or at least time-bound in social science because the social universe is constantly restructuring itself through the reflexive acts of humans. Moreover, humans can use social science theories to restructure the universe in ways that obviate the relevance of such laws (see, e.g., Giddens 1984). At best, then, laws and other theoretical tools such as modelling are temporal and pertinent to a specific historical period; at worst, they are never useful since the basic nature of the social universe is constantly reshaped.

Many who have made this charge – from Marx to Giddens – have violated it in their own work. For example, there would be little reason to pore over Marx, as contemporary theorists are wont to do, unless we sense that he unlocked some of the basic, generic and invariant dynamics of power. Or, why would Giddens (1981; 1984) bother to develop a 'theory of structuration' which posits relations among invariant properties of the universe, unless he sensed that he had penetrated beneath the surface historical changes to the core of human action, interaction and organization?

Many who make this charge confuse law and empirical generalization. Of course actual social systems change, as do solar, biological, geological and chemical systems in the empirical universe. But these changes do not alter, respectively, the laws of gravity, speciation, entropy, force/diffusion or the periodic table. Indeed, change occurs in accordance with these laws. Humans have always acted, interacted, differentiated and coordinated their social relations; these are some of the invariant properties of human organization and these are what our most abstract laws must address. Capitalism, nuclear families, caste systems, urbanization and other historical events are, of course, variable, but they are *not* the subject-matter of theory, as many would argue. Thus, while the structure of the social universe is constantly changing, the fundamental dynamics underlying this structure are not.

A third line of criticism of analytical theorizing comes from critical theorists (see, e.g., Habermas: 1972) who argue that positivism sees existing conditions as the way the social universe *must be* and, as a result, it cannot propose alternatives to the existing status quo. In their concern with lawful regularities that pertain to the way the universe is currently structured, positivists ideologically support existing conditions of human domination. Value-free science thus becomes a tool for supporting the interests of those who benefit most from existing social arrangements.

This criticism has some merit, but the critical theorist's alternative to positivism is to generate formulations which often have little foundation in the operative dynamics of the universe. Much critical theory, for example, is either pessimistic critique and/or construction of hopelessly naive utopias (see, e.g., Habermas: 1981).

Moreover, I think that this critique is based upon a view of positivism which is deficient. Theory should not merely describe existing structures but uncover the underlying dynamics of these structures. Rather than 'theories of' capitalism, bureaucracy, urbanization and other empirical events, we need, respectively, theories of production, task organization, spatial destruction and other generic processes. Historical cases and empirical manifestations are not the subject-matter of laws; they are the place to test the plausibility of laws. For example, descriptions of regularities in capitalist economies are the data (not the theory) for testing the implications of abstract laws of production.

It can be argued, of course, that such 'laws of production' uncritically accept the status quo, but I would counter that patterns of human organization require production to be sustained and, hence, represent a generic property of human organization rather than a blind affirmation of the status quo. Much critical theory fails to recognize that there are invariant properties which theorists cannot 'wish away' with their utopias. Karl Marx made this mistake in 1848 by assuming that concentrated power 'withers away' in differentiated systems (Marx and Engels: 1971); more recently, Jürgen Habermas (1970; 1981) has proposed a utopian view of communicative action that under-emphasizes the extent to which *all* interaction is inherently distorted in complex systems.

My point here is twofold. First, if we look for invariant properties, we are less likely to make statements supportive of the status quo. Second, to assume that there are no invariant properties invites theory which increasingly fails to recognize that the world is not easily bent and, in some cases, can never be bent to the theorist's ideological fancies and fantasies.

It is not wise to delve any further into these philosophical questions. The position of analytical theorizing on these questions is clear. The real debate within analytical theory is over the best strategy for developing theoretical statements about the basic properties of the social universe.

The Varying Strategies of Analytical Theorizing

There are, I believe, four basic approaches to building sociological theory:[1] metatheoretical schemes; analytical schemes; propositional schemes; and modelling schemes. However, there are contradictory variants within these basic approaches, and so in actual practice there are considerably more than four. None the less, the variants will be examined under these four general headings.

Metatheorizing

Many in sociology argue that for theory to be productive, it is essential to block out the basic 'presuppositions' that should guide theoretical activity.

---

[1] For a more detailed analysis see Turner: 1985b; 1986, ch. 1.

That is, before adequate theorizing can occur, it is necessary to address such fundamental questions as: what is the nature of human activity, human interaction, human organization? What is the most appropriate set of procedures for developing theory and what kind of theory is possible? What are the central issues or critical problems on which sociological theory should concentrate? And so on. Such questions and the rather long treatises (e.g. Alexander: 1982–3) that they encourage pull theory into the old and unresolvable philosophical debates – idealism versus materialism, induction versus deduction, subjectivism versus objectivism, and the like.

What makes these treatises 'meta' – that is, 'coming after' or 'subsequent to', as the dictionary informs us – is that these philosophical issues are raised in the context of yet one more re-analysis of the 'great theorists', the favourite targets being Karl Marx, Max Weber, Émile Durkheim and, more recently, Talcott Parsons. Although these works are always scholarly, filled with long footnotes and relevant quotations, my sense is that they often suffocate theoretical activity. They embroil theory in unresolvable philosophical issues and they easily become scholastic treatises that lose sight of the goal of all theory: to explain how the social universe works. Thus, metatheorizing is interesting philosophy and, at times, a fascinating history of ideas, but it is not theory and it is not easily used in analytical theorizing.

Analytical schemes

A great deal of theorizing in sociology involves the construction of abstract systems of categories that presumably denote key properties of the universe and crucial relations among these properties. In essence, such schemes are typologies that map the important dynamics of the universe. Abstract concepts dissect the basic properties of the universe and then order these properties in a way that is presumed to offer insight into the structure and dynamics of the universe. Explanation of specific events is achieved when the scheme can be used to interpret some specific empirical process. Such interpretations are of two basic kinds: when the place or niche of an empirical event in the category system is found, then the empirical event is considered to be explained;[2] or, when the scheme can be used to construct a descriptive scenario of why and how events in an empirical situation transpired, then these events are seen as explained.[3]

These somewhat different views of explanation by analytical schemes reflect two contradictory approaches: 'naturalistic analytical schemes' and 'sensitizing analytical schemes'. The first assumes that the ordering of concepts in the scheme represents an 'analytical accentuation' of the ordering of the universe (Parsons: 1937); as a consequence of this isomorphism, explanation is usually seen as involving the discovery of the place of an

---

[2] See, for examples, Parsons: 1937; 1961; 1966; 1971a; 1971b; 1978.
[3] For examples, see Blumer (1969) and Giddens (1984).

empirical event in the scheme. The second approach usually rejects positivism as well as naturalism and argues that the system of concepts is only provisional and sensitizing (Blumer: 1969; Giddens: 1984). Since the universe will change, conceptual schemes must also change; at best, they can provide a useful way to interpret empirical events at a particular point in time.

Those following the naturalistic variant often argue in a vein similar to metatheorists: the analytical scheme is a necessary prerequisite for other kinds of theoretical activity (e.g. Münch: 1982). For until one has a scheme which denotes and orders at an analytical level the properties of the universe, it is difficult to know what to theorize about. Thus, for some, naturalistic analytical schemes are a necessary preliminary to the propositional and modelling approaches for developing sociological theory. In contrast, those employing sensitizing analytical schemes typically reject the search for universal laws as fruitless, since these laws will be obviated as the fundamental nature of the world changes (Giddens: 1977; 1984).

Propositional schemes

Propositional schemes revolve around statements that connect variables to one another. That is, propositions state the form of the relation between two or more variable properties of the social universe. Propositional schemes vary widely and can be grouped into three general types: 'axiomatic schemes', 'formal schemes' and 'empirical schemes'.

Axiomatic theorizing involves deductions, in terms of a precise calculus, from abstract axioms that contain precisely-defined concepts to an empirical event. Explanation consists of determining that an empirical event is 'covered' by one or more axioms. In actual fact, however, axiomatic theory is rarely possible in those sciences that cannot exert laboratory controls, define concepts in terms of 'exact classes' and use a formal calculus such as logic or mathematics (Freese: 1980). While sociologists (e.g. Emerson: 1972; Homans: 1974) often use the vocabulary of axiomatic theory – axioms, theorems, corollaries – they are rarely in a position to meet the requirements of true axiomatic theory. Instead, they engage in formal theorizing (Freese: 1980).

Formal theorizing is 'watered-down' axiomatic theorizing. Abstract laws are articulated and, in what is often a rough and discursive manner, 'deductions' to empirical events are made. Explanation consists of visualizing an empirical event as an instance or manifestation of the more abstract law. The goal of theorizing is thus to develop elementary laws or principles about basic properties of the universe.

The third type of propositional scheme – the empirical – is not really theory at all. But many theorists and researchers consider it to be so and therefore I must mention this kind of activity. Indeed, many critics of analytical theorizing use examples of empirical propositional schemes to indict positivism. For instance, I have already alluded to the tendency of the critics of positivism to confuse abstract law about a generic phenomenon and generalization about a set of empirical events. This assertion that empirical generalizations are laws is then used to mount a rejection of positivism: there are no timeless laws because empirical events always change. Such a conclusion is based upon the inability of critics to recognize the difference between an empirical generalization and an abstract law. But even among those sympathetic to positivism, there is a tendency to confuse what is to be explained (the empirical generalization) with what is to explain (the abstract law). This confusion takes several forms.

One is to elevate the humble empirical generalization to the status of a 'law', as is the case with 'Golden's law', which merely reports that industrialization and literacy are positively correlated. Another is to follow Robert Merton's famous advocacy for 'theories of the middle range' where the goal is to develop some generalizations for a substantive area – say, urbanization, organizational control, deviance, socialization or some other substantive topic (Merton: 1968). Such 'theories' are, in fact, empirical generalizations whose regularities require a more abstract formulation to explain them. Yet a good many sociologists believe that these 'middle range' propositions are theories, despite their empirical character.

Thus, much propositional activity will not be useful to theory-building. The conditions necessary for axiomatic theory can rarely be met, and empirical propositions are not, by their nature, sufficiently abstract to be theoretical. Of the various propositional approaches, my view is that formal theory will be the most useful approach for developing analytical theory.

Modelling schemes

The use of the term 'model' is highly ambiguous in the social sciences. In the more mature sciences, a model is a way to represent visually a phenomenon in a way that exposes its underlying properties and their interconnections. In social theory, modelling involves a variety of activities, ranging from the construction of formal equations and computer simulations to graphic representations of relations among phenomena. I will restrict my usage of the term to theorizing in which concepts and their relations are presented as a visual picture that maps properties of the social universe and their interrelations.

A model, then, is a diagrammatic representation of events that includes: concepts that denote and highlight certain features of the universe; the arrangement of these concepts in visual space so as to reflect the ordering of events in the universe; symbols that mark the nature of connections among concepts. In sociological theory, two types of models are generally constructed: 'abstract-analytical models' and 'empirical-causal models'.

Abstract-analytical models develop context-free concepts – for example, concepts pertaining to production, centralization of power, differentiation, and the like – and then represent their relations in a visual picture. Such relations are usually expressed in causal terms, but these causal connections are complex, involving varying weights and patterns (such as feedback loops, cycles, mutual effects and other non-linear connective representations).

In contrast, empirical-causal models are usually statements of correlation among measured variables, ordered in a linear and temporal sequence. The object is 'to explain variance' in a dependent variable in terms of a series of independent and intervening variables (Blalock: 1964; Duncan: 1966). Such exercises are, in reality, empirical description because the concepts in the model are measured variables for a particular empirical case. Yet, despite their lack of abstraction, they are often considered 'theoretical'. Thus, as with empirical propositional schemes, these more empirical models will be much less useful in theory-building than the analytical ones. Much like their propositional counterparts, causal models are regularities in data that require a more abstract theory to explain them.

This completes my review of various strategies for building sociological theory. As is evident, I see only some of these as appropriate for analytical theorizing and for theorizing in general. Let me now complete this review with a more explicit assessment of their relative merits.

Relative merits of diverse theoretical strategies

From an analytical viewpoint, theory should, first of all, be abstract and not tied to the particulars of an historical/empirical case. Hence, empirical modelling and empirical propositional schemes are not theory, but regularities in the data that require a theory to explain them. They are an *explicandum* in search of an *explanas*. Second, analytical theorizing emphasizes that theories must be tested against the facts, and thus metatheoretical schemes and elaborate analytical schemes are not theory proper. Whereas metatheory is highly philosophical and impossible to test, sensitizing analytical schemes can be used as starting-points for building testable theory. If the anti-positivist tenets of their practitioners can be ignored, such sensitizing analytical schemes provide a sound place to *begin* conceptualizing basic classes of variables that can be incorporated into testable propositions and models. This is also possible with naturalistic analytical schemes, but more difficult because they tend to become excessively concerned with their own architectural majesty. Finally, in contrast to some analytical theorists, I think that theory must involve more than abstract statements of regularities: it must address the issue of causality, but not the simple causality of empirical models. My view is that analytical models provide an important supplement to abstract propositions because they map the complex causal connections – direct and indirect effects, feedback loops, reciprocal effects, etc. – among the concepts in propositions. Without such models, it is difficult to know what processes and mechanisms are involved in creating the relations that are specified in a proposition.

In light of these considerations, then, analytical theory must be abstract; it must denote generic properties of the universe; it must be testable or capable of generating testable propositions; and it cannot ignore causality, process and operative mechanisms. The best approach to theory-building in sociology is thus a combination of sensitizing analytical schemes, abstract formal propositions and analytical models (Turner: 1986). This is where the most creative synergy is; and while various analytical theorists tend to emphasize one over the other, it is the *simultaneous* use of all three approaches that offers the most potential for developing a 'natural science of society'. Figure 1 portrays in somewhat idealized form my argument.[4]

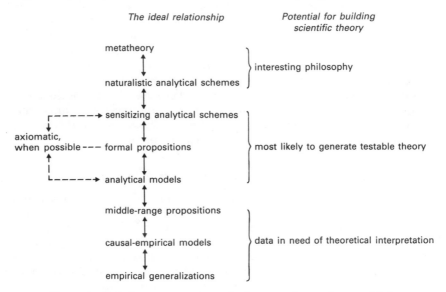

Figure 1   Relations among theoretical approaches and potential for building theory.

As is evident, one place to begin theorizing is by constructing sensitizing analytical schemes that denote in a provisional manner key properties of the social universe. By itself such activity is unproductive since the scheme cannot be tested. Rather, it can only be used to 'interpret' events. In my view, this is inadequate: it is also necessary to generate from the scheme abstract and testable propositions and, at the same time, to model the processes that operate to connect the concepts in the propositions. This exercise itself, regardless of empirical tests, can force revision of the sensitizing scheme. Or, construction of an analytical model can encourage rethinking of a proposition. The critical point here is that these three activities are mutually reinforcing; this is what I mean by 'creative synergy'.

In contrast, naturalistic analytical schemes and metatheorizing tend to

---

[4] See Turner (1985b; 1986) for more detailed portrayal of the elements in figure 1.

be too philosophical and detached from the actual workings of the world. They become overly reified and either concerned with their architecture or obsessed with their scholastic capacity to 'resolve' philosophical issues. Yet I do not consider these to be unimportant activities but, rather, as being useful only *after* we have developed laws and models in which we have confidence. Then, more philosophical discussion is useful and can force re-examination of laws and propositions. But without these laws and propositions, analytical schemes and metatheorizing become self-sustaining philosophical treatises. The vehicle for connecting propositions and models to more formal analytical schemes and metatheory is the sensitizing analytical scheme. These sensitizing schemes, when used to stimulate the formulation of propositions and when re-assessed in light of tests of propositions, can provide empirically-informed presuppositions for more complex naturalistic schemes and for metatheorizing. In turn, when metatheory and naturalistic schemes have been built from a propositional base, they can provide useful insights that force assessment of existing propositions and models. Yet without this attachment to testable theory, analytical schemes and metatheory float away into the reified and rarified world of philosophical speculation and debate.

On the more empirical side of theory-building, middle-range propositions that are, in essence, empirical generalizations for an entire substantive area can be useful as one way of testing more abstract theories. Such middle-range 'theories' order research findings for whole classes of empirical phenomena, and hence provide a consolidated set of data that can shed light on a theoretical law and model. Empirical-causal models can explicate the temporal processes that operate to connect variables in middle-range theories or a simple empirical generalization. As such, they can help to assess the plausibility of analytical models and abstract propositions. But without the abstract laws and models these more empirical approaches will not help to build theory. For if uninformed by abstract laws and formal models, then middle range theories, causal models and empirical generaliz ations are constructed *ad hoc*, without concern for whether or not they illustrate an underlying dynamic of the universe. Only infrequently does one make inductions from these empirical formats and create theory, for the reality of theory-building is the other way around: theory first, then assessment with data. Of course, with such focused data comes an assessment of the theory. But when one starts with the particulars, one rarely rises above them.

Such is my position and that of most analytical theorists. Start with sensitizing schemes, propositions and models, and only then move on to the formal collection of data or to metatheorizing and scheme-building. Although most analytical theorists would agree with this kind of strategic statement, there is considerable disagreement over the substance of analytical theorizing.

Substantive Debate in Analytical Theorizing

The substantive debate in analytical theory is over the issue of what theory should be about. What are the most important properties of the social universe? Which of these should be studied first, or is more fundamental? How are microprocesses of action and interaction to be reconciled with macrodynamics of differentiation and integration of populations? These are the kinds of questions that consume analytical theory, and although they are obviously important, sociological theorists have spent far too much time debating them. Fortunately, there have also been more creative efforts to theorize, that is, to assert what is an important property in the social universe, to develop a sensitizing analytical scheme to frame the important questions, to develop abstract concepts and propositions and to construct analytical models to denote the operative mechanisms and processes inhering in this property.

I cannot review all of these theoretical efforts and so, instead, I propose to present my views on the basic properties of the universe and to illustrate the type of analytical theorizing that I feel will be most productive. In so doing, I will summarize most of the theoretical work in analytical theory, since my approach is highly eclectic and borrows heavily from others. But I should add several points of caution. First, I selectively borrow and, hence, do not do full justice to those from whom I take ideas. Second, I quite willingly take from those who might not consider themselves analytical theorists; in fact, they might well consider themselves hostile to the kind of theorizing that I advocate. With these qualifications, let me begin.

A sensitizing scheme for the analysis of human organization

As mentioned earlier, most naturalistic analytical schemes are too complex. Moreover, they tend to become ever more elaborate as new dimensions of reality are incorporated into the constantly proliferating system of categories and as new elements in the scheme are reconciled with older ones. Sensitizing analytical schemes also suffer from this tendency to become more elaborate, adding concepts and specifying new analytical connections. The more complex that analytical schemes become, I feel, the less their utility. In my view, complexity should be handled at the propositional and modelling level, not in the overarching conceptual framework. Thus, a sensitizing analytical scheme should merely denote generic *classes* of variables, with specific propositions and models filling in the details. Therefore, the sensitizing scheme proposed in figure 2 is far simpler than existing ones, although it does become more complex as each of its elements is analysed in more detail.

One reason for the complexity of existing schemes is that they try to do too much. They typically seek to account for 'everything, all at once' (Turner: 1984, ch. 1). Yet sciences have not progressed very far in their

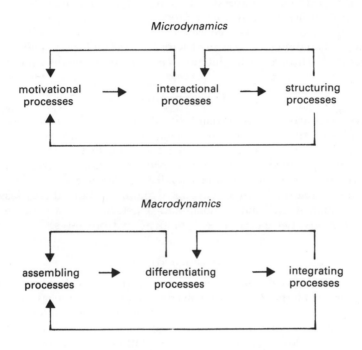

Figure 2　A sensitizing scheme for analytical theorizing.

early stages by trying to achieve premature comprehensiveness. This push for comprehensiveness is reflected in the recent resurgence of interest in the micro–macro 'link', or 'gap' as it is often called (Alexander *et al*.: 1986; Knorr Cetina and Cicourel: 1981; Turner: 1983). Theorists now want to explain everything – micro and macro – all at once, despite the fact that neither microprocesses of interaction among individuals in situations or macrodynamics of aggregations of people have been adequately conceptualized. My view is that all this concern over understanding the micro-basis of the macro, and vice versa, is premature. Figure 1 proposes to retain the division between macro and microsociology, at least for the time being. Thus, there is a 'gap' between micro and macroprocesses and, except in the most metaphorical way, I do not propose to fill it.

With respect to microprocesses, I see three classes of dynamics as critical in analytical theorizing: those 'energizing' or 'pushing' individuals to interact (note that I do not say 'act' which has received too much conceptual emphasis in sociology) (Turner: 1985a); those operating on individuals as they mutually adjust their conduct towards each other; and those structuring chains of interaction over time and across space. As the arrows indicate, these microprocesses are interrelated, each operating as a parameter for the others. In regard to macroprocesses, I see three types of dynamics as central to analytical theorizing: assembling processes determining the number of actors (whether individuals or collectivities) and their distribution in time and space; differentiation processes of actors in time and space; and integrating processes coordinating the interactions of actors over time and space.

Microdynamics

As I have suggested, analytical complexity should be added at the modelling level, and sometimes at the propositional level, because only here can theoretical ideas have a chance of being tested against the facts (with all the problems presented by the critics of positivism duly noted and rejected, at least in their extreme and intellectually debilitating form). Thus, the task of micro-analysis is to specify the dynamics of the three classes of variables – motivational, interactional and structuring – in abstract models and propositions. Let me begin with motivational processes.

Motivational processes

The explicit conceptualization of 'motives' has fallen into abeyance in theorizing because of all the problems involved in analysing and measuring 'what drives people' and 'makes them do things'. Instead, sociologists have talked about behaviour, action and interaction in ways that mask the extent to which they are addressing the issue of motivation. In so doing, they have obscured the analysis of both motivation and interaction. It is more useful to separate these analytically by presenting a simple model of what 'pushes', 'drives', 'energizes' and 'directs' people to interact with each other in certain ways. Admittedly, these terms are vague, but none the less they communicate my general intent.

There are four motivational processes in all situations of interaction: those processes involved in sustaining 'ontological security' (Giddens: 1984), or the implicit need to reduce anxiety and achieve a sense of trust with others; those revolving around the maintenance of what some interactionists term a 'core' self-conception, or the reaffirmation of one's central and basic definition of oneself as a certain type of being; those concerning what utilitarian economics and behavioural exchange theorists view as efforts of individuals to 'make a profit' or augment their material, symbolic, political or psychic resources in situations (Homans: 1974); and those dealing with what ethnomethodologists have at times termed 'facticity', or the presumption that the world has an obdurate or factual character and order (Garfinkel: 1984). These four processes correspond, respectively, to various conceptions of motivation in the psychoanalytic (Erikson: 1950), symbolic interactionist (Kuhn and McPartland: 1954), behavioural/utilitarian (Homans: 1974) and ethnomethodological traditions (Garfinkel: 1984). Typically these have been seen as antagonistic approaches, with certain notable exceptions (e.g. Collins: 1975; Giddens: 1984; Shibutani: 1968). In figure 3, an analytical model outlining the principal interrelations among these four processes is presented.

At the right-hand side of figure 3, I emphasize that all interaction is motivated by exchange considerations. People want to feel that they have increased their level of resources in exchange for the expenditure of energy and investment of resources. Naturally, the nature of resources can vary, but analytical exchange theories usually view power, prestige, approval and, at times, material well-being as the most generic. Thus, from the point of view of most contemporary exchange perspectives, individuals are 'driven' to seek some profit in terms of these classes of resources, and so much interaction involves negotiation over power, prestige and approval (and occasionally material benefits). I will not outline the arguments of exchange theory here, since they are well known, but the basic principles of exchange theory are, I feel, a good summary of *one* motivational process.

Another motivational process is also part of interpersonal exchanges: talk and conversation. I think that Collins (1986) is correct in his view that this is a major resource, as opposed to vehicle or medium, in interaction. That is, people 'spend' talk and conversation in hopes of receiving not just power (deference), prestige or approval, but also rewarding talk *per se*. Indeed, people negotiate over conversational resources as actively as they do over the other resources. Out of such conversations, they develop a 'sense' and 'feeling' of satisfaction, or what Collins has termed 'emotion'. That is, people spend and augment their 'emotional capital' in their conversational exchanges. Thus talk is not only a medium by which power, prestige and approval are transmitted; it is also a resource in itself.

Negotiations over conversational resources involve more than exchange, however. There is also a process of trying to 'fill in' and 'interpret' what is occurring in an interaction. A situation does not 'feel right' without the capacity to use words, non-verbal gestures, features of a setting and other cues to achieve a fuller 'sense' of 'what is being talked about' and 'what is going on'. As Garfinkel (1984) first emphasized, much of what occurs in an interaction involves interpretations of gestures in light of the context of interaction. People use implicit stocks of knowledge and understanding to interpret a conversation in order to feel comfortable in an interaction context. And they employ a variety of 'folk' or 'ethno' methods to generate a sense that each understands the other and that they are experiencing a similar world. Thus, in addition to an exchange of resources, conversations are negotiations over 'what is going on'; when this sense of mutual ageement on the nature of a situation is disrupted, as was evident in Garfinkel's famous 'breaching experiments', individuals work very hard to 'repair' the sense that they share, experience and participate in a common world. When individuals cannot sustain a sense of a common and shared universe, their anxiety increases; the sense of trust so necessary for ontological security is eroded, which, in turn, activates people to re-interpret and renegotiate their conversational exchanges. Such negotiations have the ironic consequence of sustaining anxiety, but if participants can use 'ethno' methods to achieve a

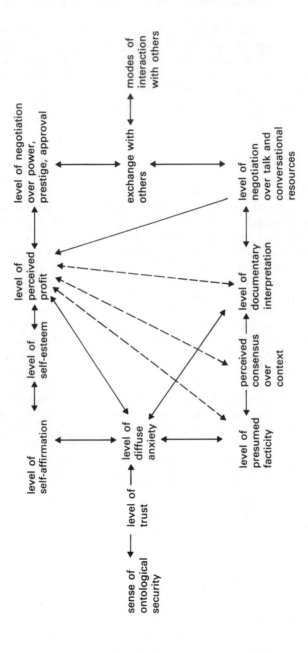

Figure 3   The dynamics of interpersonal motivation.

sense and presumption that they share a similar factual world, then anxiety is reduced. Hence, a need for 'facticity' is a powerful motivational force in human interaction, as is indicated by the processes shown at the bottom of figure 3.

Turning back to the top of figure 3, yet another motivating force in interaction is the effort to sustain a conception of oneself as a certain kind of person. This is done primarily through exchange relations revolving around power, prestige, approval and, at times, material well-being, as well as those concerning the receipt of emotional capital in conversations. Thus, if people sense that they receive a 'psychic profit' in their exchanges, they will also sustain their self-esteem, which I see as the major mechanism mediating between their 'core self' (Kuhn and Hickman: 1956) and exchange outcomes. As the dotted arrows indicate, a secondary process in sustaining a 'profit' is the dynamics leading to a sense of facticity. To the extent that achieving facticity is problematic, individuals will not feel that they have 'profited' from an interaction, and hence they will have difficulty sustaining their self-esteem and self-conception in that situation. Whether from this secondary source or simply from the inability to enhance emotional capital or extract approval, deference and prestige, a failure to confirm self creates anxiety which, in turn, disrupts the trust (in oneself) so essential to ontological security.

The details of this model cannot be explored here, but it does try to pull together diverse analytical traditions into a more synthetic view of motivational dynamics. In closing, let me illustrate my overall theoretical strategy by using the model to develop several abstract 'laws of motivation'.

I The level of motivational energy of individuals in an interaction situation is an inverse function of the degree to which individuals fail to (*a*) achieve a sense of ontological security, (*b*) develop a presumption of facticity, (*c*) affirm their core self and (*d*) achieve a sense of resource augmentation.

II The form, direction and intensity of interaction in a situation will be a positive function of the relative salience of (*a*), (*b*), (*c*) and (*d*) above as well as of the absolute levels of (*a*), (*b*), (*c*) and (*d*) above.

These two principles state, at an abstract level, the general way in which people are 'energized' to interact. Obviously the propositions do not specify the processes of motivation, as does the model in figure 3. Thus, I think that the analytical model provides necessary details about the mechanisms (that is, anxiety, self-esteem, profit, consensus over context, documentary interpretation and negotiation). I would, of course, insert these into the propositions, but then the laws lose their simplicity and parsimony which for many purposes (such as their use in a deductive calculus) is desirable. Thus, as I indicated earlier, there is a creative interplay between abstract laws and analytical models. One without the other leaves something to be desired: the model is too complex to be tested as a whole (and hence its conversion to simple laws is essential), but the simple laws do not delineate the complex causal processes and mechanisms that underlie the relations specified in the law (thus the need to supplement laws with abstract analytical models).

Interactional processes

The next element in the sensitizing scheme presented in figure 2 is the process of interaction itself. The key issue is this: what occurs as people mutually signal each other and interpret each other's gestures? Figure 4 outlines the critical processes: the use of stocks of implicit knowledge (Schütz: 1967) or 'stock-making' in my terms, to engage in a variety of signalling processes, notably stage-making (Goffman: 1959), role-making (Turner: 1962), claim-making (Habermas: 1981), and account-making (Garfinkel: 1984), and the use of stocks of knowledge, or 'stock-taking', to perform a number of interpretative processes, particularly account-taking (Garfinkel: 1984), claim-taking (Habermas: 1981), role-taking (Mead: 1934), and type-taking (Schütz: 1967). I cannot provide a detailed discussion of these processes, especially since the model in figure 4 draws from very diverse theoretical traditions, but let me enumerate on the processes that are delineated.

As George Herbert Mead was the first to recognize explicitly, interaction is a 'conversation of gestures'. People signal their respective courses of action (consciously and unconsciously) by emitting gestures, and at the same time, they interpret the gestures of others. Out of this simultaneous process of signalling and interpreting, people adjust their respective lines of conduct, with the pattern of such an adjustment being a function of the motivational processes discussed above. In order to signal and interpret, actors draw upon what Alfred Schütz termed 'stock knowledge at hand', or the stores of explicit and implicit meanings, conceptions, procedures, rules, attitudes and understanding that individuals acquire as they live, grow-up and participate in ongoing social relations. In order to signal, individuals stock-*make* in that they draw upon these stocks of knowledge to make or construct a line of conduct for themselves. Reciprocally, in order to interpret the gestures of others, individuals must stock-*take* in that they must take from their stocks of knowledge in order to 'make sense' of others' signals. This simultaneous process of stock-making and stock-taking is often implicit and unconscious. Yet, when signals are not acknowledged by others, when such signals cannot be easily interpreted or when motives for ontological security, self-affirmation, resource augmentation and facticity are not being met (see proposition II), then these processes of stock-making and stock-taking become much more explicit.

The middle sections of the model in figure 4 attempt to reconcile the early insights of Mead and Schütz with what are sometimes viewed as antagonistic traditions. These traditions are not antagonistic, however, because each has something to contribute to a synthetic view of interaction.

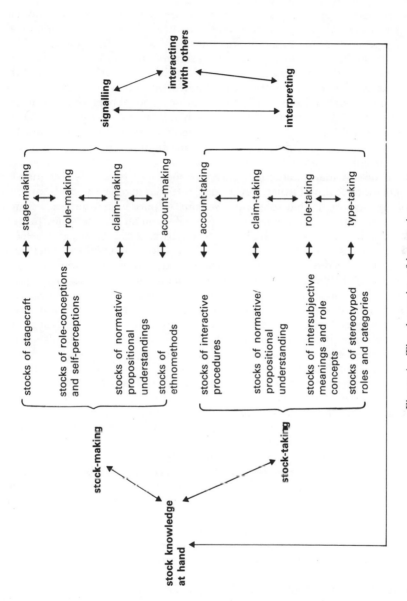

Figure 4 The dynamics of interaction.

Let me document this compatibility by discussing each of the elements outlined in the middle sections of figure 4.

As Goffman was the first to conceptualize explicitly and as Giddens (1984) has more recently done, interaction always involves 'stage-making'. People possess understandings about 'stagecraft' in that they 'know', at least implicitly, about such matters as the relative positioning of actors, the movement to and from front and backstage regions, and other aspects of the demography of space. By their positioning in space, or by their movement in space, people signal to others their intentions and expectations. Without this capacity to draw from stocks of knowledge and make for themselves a 'stage presence', interaction would be difficult, since individuals could not use their respective positions and movements in space to tell others about their respective actions.

Much of the manipulation of this positioning in space is designed to facilitate what Ralph Turner has termed role-making, or the orchestration of gestures to signal what role one is seeking to play in a situation. In such role-making activities, humans do not rely solely on stagecraft. They possess stocks of 'role conceptions' which denote syndromes of gestures and behavioural sequences associated with a particular line of conduct. Such role concepts can become very finely-tuned in that, for example, we can not only distinguish someone as playing a 'student role,' but also *what kind* of student role (serious, scholarly, athletic, social, etc.). People thus possess a vast repertoire of role concepts and from this repertoire, they seek to make a role for themselves by orchestrating their emission of gestures. Just which roles they make for themselves is, of course, circumscribed not only by the existing structure (students cannot be professors, for instance) but also by their stocks of self-perceptions and definitions. Thus, humans select from their repertoire of roles those which are consistent with their stocks of self-perceptions and definitions. Some of these self-perceptions follow from core self-conceptions that motivate interaction, but humans also possess stocks of more peripheral and situational images of themselves. For example, a person may recognize without great loss of self-esteem and degradation of core self that he or she is not good at sports, and as a consequence this person will make a role that corresponds to a self-image of poor proficiency in 'game situations'. Without this capacity to make roles, interaction would be unduly stressful and time-consuming, since individuals could not assume that their orchestration of gestures signalled a particular line of conduct to others. But with common conceptions of various types of roles, individuals can signal their intentions and trust that others will recognize what they are up to, without having constantly to re-signal their proposed line of conduct.

While I find much of Jürgen Habermas's 'critical project' excessively ideological, idealized and, at times, sociologically naive, his discussion of the 'ideal speech act' and 'communicative action' (Habermas: 1981) has none the less uncovered a basic dynamic in human interaction: the process of making 'validity claims'. As individuals interact, they make 'validity claims' that others can accept or challenge. Such claims involve assertions, typically implicit but at times explicit, about the authenticity and sincerity of gestures as manifestations of subjective experiences; about the efficiency and effectiveness of gestures as indicators of means to an end; and about the correctness of actions in terms of relevant norms. I do not share Habermas's ideological view that such claim-making (and the challenge and discourse that can ensue) are the essence of human liberation from forms of domination, but I do think that interaction involves a subtle and typically implicit process whereby each party 'asserts' that they are sincere, efficient and correct. Such claims are related to role-making efforts but they also draw upon shared stocks of knowledge about norms, understandings of sincere behaviour and culturally-agreed upon connections between means–ends.

The final signalling process is related to claim-making, but more directly to stocks of 'ethno' methods such as the 'et cetera principle', conversational sequences, normal forms and other folk practices (Cicourel: 1973; Heritage: 1984) which individuals use to create a *sense* of a social order. Thus, signalling always involves a process of 'account-making' in which individuals implicitly use various folk methods or procedures for convincing others that they share a common factual world. Garfinkel's breaching experiments (1963; 1984) as well as other analyses of conversations[5] indicate that such procedures are crucial for an interaction to proceed smoothly; when the use of these 'ethno' methods does not occur or when they are not understood or accepted, then the interaction becomes problematic. Thus, much of what individuals signal to others involves an effort to make an account of what is real and factual in the situation.

Simultaneous to these four signalling processes – stage-making, role-making, claim-making and account-making – are reciprocal processes of interpreting the signals emitted by others. Moreover to some degree humans also interpret their own signals, and thus interaction involves a reflexive monitoring of one's own as well as others' gestures.

Account-making goes side by side with 'account-taking', in which the signals of others as well as one's own, especially those pertaining to stocks of interpretative understandings, are used to develop a set of implicit presumptions about the background features of an interaction setting. That is, actors interpret certain classes of signals (i.e. folk methods) in order to 'fill in' and 'make sense' of what others are doing as well as to provide for themselves a sense, perhaps somewhat illusory, that they and other(s) share a common universe.

Related to such 'ethnomethodizing', if I can invent yet another word in a field filled with linguistic innovation, is the other side of Habermas's claim-making: 'claim-taking'. That is, the 'validity claims' of others (and oneself) as to sincerity, correctness and means–ends effectiveness are interpreted in light of stocks of normative understandings, means–ends formula

---

[5] See, for a review, Heritage: 1984.

and genre of authenticity. Such interpretation can lead to an acceptance of claims, or it can involve 'challenges' to any one or all three types of validity claims. If the latter occurs, then counter claim-making is signalled and the interaction will cycle around claim-making and claim-taking processes until validity claims by all parties are accepted (or one set of claims is simply imposed upon others through the capacity for coercion or for control of resources).

The third interpretative process is that first conceptualized by Mead as 'role-taking' and 'taking-the-role-of-the-other', or what Schütz termed 'reciprocity of perspectives'. The gestures or signals of others are used to put oneself in another's position or to assume his or her perspective. Such role-taking occurs on several levels, however. One is the converse of role-making where stocks of role conceptions are used to determine what role others are playing. Another, deeper level is the use of stocks of agreed understandings about how people typically act in various types of situations to fill in the background features necessary to understand why a person is behaving in a certain way. Together, these two levels of role-taking by individuals can provide a perspective on others' likely modes and directions of conduct.

At times, interaction involves what Schütz termed 'typification' or interaction in terms of 'ideal-types'. For much interaction involves placing others into stereotyped categories and then interacting with them as non-persons or ideals. Thus, role-taking can shift into 'type-taking' when a situation does not call for sensitive and finely-tuned interpretations of others' motives, feelings and attitudes. As type-taking occurs, the other interpretative processes of role-taking, claim-taking and account-taking decrease because, in essence, they are 'preprogrammed' into the stocks of stereotyped roles and categories that are used to type-take.

In sum, then, I see interaction as a dual and simultaneous process of signalling and interpreting, drawing from stocks of knowledge that individuals have acquired. Different theoretical approaches have emphasized varying aspects of this basic process, but none alone captures the full dynamics of interaction. The model in figure 4 attempts to pull these various approaches together into a more unified approach that views the processes of interpretation and signalling as interrelated. To complete this synthesis of diverse approaches to interactional processes in analytical theory, let me reformulate the key elements of the model into a few 'laws of interaction'.

III   The degree of interaction by individuals is a situation in a joint and positive function of their respective levels of (*a*) signalling and (*b*) interpreting.
(*a*)   The degree of signalling is a joint and positive function of the degree of stage-making, role-making, claim-making and account-making.
(*b*)   The degree of interpreting is a joint and positive function of the degree of account-taking, claim-taking, role-taking and type-taking.
IV   The degree of mutual accommodation and cooperation among indi-

viduals in an interaction situation is a positive function of the degree to which they share common stocks of knowledge and use these in their signalling and interpreting.

Structuring processes

Most interaction occurs within an existing structure which has been built up and sustained by previous interactions. Such structures are best viewed as constraining parameters (Blau: 1977) in that they circumscribe the staging activities of individuals by locating them within physical spaces; restrict the kinds of validating processes – that is, claims and challenges – that can occur; provide the contextual base for accounting activities that allows people to create a sense of reality; dictate the kinds of role-making that are possible; provide cues for the nature of role-taking; and organize people and their activities in ways that encourage (or discourage) mutual typification.

Yet, because individuals evidence distinct motivational profiles and because existing structures provide only parameters for the staging, validating, accounting, role-taking, role-making and typifying, there is always some potential for the restructuring of situations. The basic processes involved in such restructuring are, however, the same as those for sustaining an existing structure, and so we can use the same models and propositions to understand both structuring and restructuring. In figure 5, I present my views on the dynamics of these processes.

I will begin by outlining just what 'structure' is. First, it is a process, not a thing. To use the currently fashionable terms, it is 'produced' and 'reproduced' by individuals in interaction. Second, structure refers to the ordering of interactions across time and in space (Collins: 1975; Giddens: 1981; 1984). The time dimension can denote processes that order interactions for a particular set of individuals, but more important is the organization of interactions for *successive sets* of individuals who, as each passes through the existing structural parameters, reproduce these parameters. Third, such reproduction of structure is, as the right-hand side of figure 5 emphasizes, determined by the capacity of individuals in interaction to 'regionalize', 'routinize', 'normatize', 'ritualize' and 'categorize' their joint activities. Thus, structure is both the process and product of staging, validating, accounting, role-taking, role-making and typifying activities. These interactive processes produce (or reproduce) structure when they enable individuals to regionalize, routinize, normatize, ritualize and categorize their joint actions. Let me now analyse these five processes on the right-hand side of figure 5 in more detail.

As individuals stage-make (see figure 4), they negotiate over the utilization of space. They decide such questions as who occupies what territory, who can move where and how frequently, and who can come and go in space, and other similar issues of interactive demography and ecology. If actors

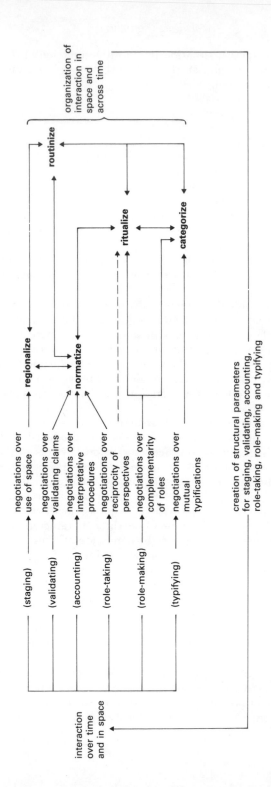

Figure 5 The process of structuring.

can agree on such issues, they regionalize their interaction in that their spatial distribution and mobility become patterned. Negotiations over space are, of course, facilitated when there are physical props, such as streets, corridors, buildings, rooms and offices, to constrain negotiations. Equally important, however, are normative agreements over what these props as well as interpersonal signals 'mean' to individuals. That is, regionalization involves rules, agreements and understandings about who can occupy what space, who can hold 'desirable' space and who can move in space (hence the arrow from 'normatize' to 'regionalize' in figure 5). Another important force, which is related to normatization but is also an independent factor in its own right, is routinization. Regionalization of activities is greatly facilitated when joint actions are routinized in that individuals do approximately the same things (move, gesture, talk, etc.) at the same time in the same space.

Conversely, both routinization and normatization are facilitated by regionalization. There is, then, mutual feedback among these processes. Routines facilitate the ordering of space, but once ordered, routines are easy to sustain (of course, if spatial order is disrupted, so are routines). Norms allow distributions in space to be interpreted, while guiding the joint activities of individuals occupying varying points in space; but once interactions are regionalized, the maintenance of the normative system is encouraged (conversely, if spatial order is disrupted, so will be the normative structure).

As is evident in figure 5, the creation of norms, or to 'normatize' as I call it, is critical to the process of structuring. Unfortunately, the concept of 'norm' has become unfashionable in social theory, primarily because of its association with functionalism. I propose that we retain this concept, but use it in ways that move beyond simple assumptions that for 'each status position there are attendant norms' or that 'roles are enactments of normative expectations'. Both of these assumptions are at times true, but they are more of a special case of normative interaction than the rule. As figure 5 emphasizes, I see norms as a process revolving around validating, accounting and role-taking. As people negotiate over what is proper, authentic and efficient (validating), as they negotiate over the proper interpretative procedures or 'ethno' methods for creating a sense of common reality (accounting), and as they try to put themselves in others' places and assume their perspective (role-taking), they *do* develop implicit and provisionally binding agreements about how they are to interact and adjust their conduct to each other. If humans could not do this, interaction would be too much work, for we would constantly and incessantly be negotiating over proper conduct. The development of these implicit agreements is facilitated by regionalization, routinization and ritualization (the latter concept denoting stereotyped sequences of gestures among interactants). Such norms become part of people's stocks of knowledge and they are used in appropriate contexts. Indeed, much role-taking, accounting and validating revolves around people's efforts to interpret in a particular situation which norms are being taken from stocks of knowledge.

Routines are also an important process in structuring. If sets of actors engage in more or less the same sequences of behaviour over time and in space, then the organization of interaction is greatly facilitated. Conversely, routines are influenced by the other structuring processes of regionalization, normatization, ritualization and categorization. When activities are ordered in space, it is easier to establish routines. If there are agreements over norms, then creating routines is encouraged. If interaction can also be ritualized so that people's encounters involve stereotyped sequences of gestures, then routines can be sustained without much 'interpersonal work' (that is, active and self-conscious signalling and interpreting). And when actors can effectively categorize each other as non-persons and thereby interact without great efforts at signalling and interpreting, then routines can be more readily established and maintained.

Rituals are another critical element in structuring. For when actors can open, sustain and close interaction in situations with stereotyped talk and gesturing, interaction can proceed more smoothly and become more readily ordered. Just what rituals to perform, how to perform them and when to perform them is normatively determined. But rituals are also the result of routinization and categorization. If actors can place each other in simple categories, then their interaction will be ritualized, involving predictable opening and closing gestures, with a typical form of conversation and gesturing between the opening and closing rituals. Similarly, routine activities encourage rituals, for as individuals seek to sustain their established routines they try to ritualize interaction so as to keep it from intruding (through having to do 'interpersonal' work) into their routines. But perhaps most important, rituals are related to role-making individuals negotiate over their respective roles, and if they can negotiate complementary roles, then they can ritualize much of their interaction. This is especially likely to be the case when the respective roles are unequal in terms of power (Collins: 1975).

The final basic structuring process is categorization which emerges out of people's negotiations over how mutually to typify one another and their relationship. This process of categorizing each other and each relationship is facilitated by successful role-making and by routinization as well as by ritualization of the relation. Categorization allows individuals to treat each other as non-persons and to avoid the time and energy involved in sensitive and finely-tuned signalling and interpreting. In this way, their interaction can proceed smoothly across time (in repeated encounters) and in space (without renegotiating who should be where).

I cannot explore here all of the subtleties of these five processes, but the arrows in figure 5 indicate how I would approach a more detailed analysis (Turner: forthcoming a). As people mutually signal and interpret, they are engaged in staging, validating, accounting, role-taking, role-making and typifying which, respectively, involve negotiations over space, validity claims, interpretative procedures, reciprocity of perspectives, respective roles and mutual typifications. Out of these processes come the structuring processes of regionalization, routinization, normatization, ritualization and categorization which organize interaction over time and in space. In turn, these structuring processes serve as structural parameters that constrain and circumscribe the interactive processes of staging, validating, accounting, role-taking, role-making and typifying. Such is, in general terms, my view of the process of structuring which incorporates much of the work in analytical theorizing on micro-interactive interpretations of 'social structure'. Let me complete my review by offering a few 'laws of structuring'.

V   The degree of structuring of interaction is a positive and additive function of the degree to which that interaction can be (*a*) regionalized, (*b*) routinized, (*c*) normatized, (*d*) ritualized and (*e*) categorized.

(*a*) The degree of regionalization of interaction is a positive and additive function of the degree to which individuals can successfully negotiate over the use of space and routinize as well as normatize their joint activities.

(*b*) The degree of routinization of interaction is a positive and additive function of the degree to which individuals can normatize, regionalize, ritualize and categorize their joint activities.

(*c*) The degree of normatization of interaction is a positive and additive function of the degree to which individuals can successfully negotiate over validity claims, interpretative procedures and reciprocity of perspectives, and regionalize, routinize and ritualize their joint activities.

(*d*) The degree of ritualization of interaction is a positive and additive function of the degree to which individuals can successfully negotiate over reciprocity of perspectives as well as complementarity of roles, and normatize, routinize and categorize their joint activities.

(*e*) The degree of categorization of interaction is a positive and additive function of the degree to which individuals can successfully negotiate over mutual typifications as well as complementarity of roles, and ritualize as well as routinize their joint activities.

This completes my review of theoretical work in analytical theory on microdynamics. Obviously, I have taken ideas from scholars who would object to being classified as analytical theorists, but to the extent that analytical theory addresses the question of microprocesses, figures 3, 4 and 5 as well as propositions I–V capture the thrust of this theorizing. With some notable exceptions (e.g. Collins: 1975; 1986; Giddens: 1984; Turner: 1980), analytical theorizing has concentrated on macrodynamics, preferring to take interaction as a 'given', as 'random processes' (e.g. Mayhew and Leringen: 1976) or as a 'rate' (Blau: 1977). Let me now turn to this more macro-approach.

Macrodynamics

A clear consensus over just what constitutes 'macroreality' does not exist in sociological theorizing. Some macrosociologists view it as the analysis of structural properties, independent of those processes occurring among individuals (e.g. Blau: 1977; Mayhew: 1981). Others see macrosociology as the analysis of the various ways that micro-units are aggregated to form large-scale organizational and societal processes (e.g. Collins: 1975; 1986). Critics typically see all macro-analysis as a reification or hypostatization (Knorr-Cetina and Cicourel: 1981). Yet despite these kinds of criticism and the apparent conceptual confusion over the microbasis of social structure, it is still difficult to deny a simple fact of social life: human populations grow and aggregate into large numbers and create complex social forms that stretch across vast geographical regions and over considerable periods of time. To assert, as many do, that such forms can be analysed solely in terms of the constituent acts and interactions of individuals is misleading. Such reductionist approaches produce conceptual anarchy, for one can never see 'the wood for the trees', or even the trees through the branches.

There is no doubt, of course, that macroprocesses involve interactions among individuals, but it is often wise to bracket these out of analysis. For just as it is useful to ignore for most analytical purposes the respiratory and circulatory physiology of the human anatomy when studying many properties of interaction, so it is reasonable to ignore, for many purposes, individuals, individual acts and individual interactions. Naturally, knowing just what people do as they regionalize, routinize, normatize, ritualize and categorize their interactions (see figure 5) can serve as a useful *supplement* to macro-analysis, but such inquiry cannot substitute for pure macro-analysis where concern is with the processes by which larger numbers of actors are assembled, differentiated and integrated (see figure 2). Such is my position and that of most analytical theorists (Turner: 1983).

In figure 6, my views on the most basic and fundamental macrodynamics of human organization are delineated. I have grouped these dynamics, as in figure 2, under three constituent processes: *assemblage*, or the accretion of individuals and their productive capacities in space; *differentiation*, or the number of different sub-units and cultural symbols among members of an assembled population; and *integration*, or the degree to which relations among sub-units of an assembled population are coordinated. Unlike my analysis of microprocesses, however, I have not broken these down into three separate models. Rather, I have created one composite model which, if broken down, could be articulated in more detail. I plan to undertake such an analysis in the near future (Turner: forthcoming b), but for my present purposes the model is presented in its simplified form.

Processes of assemblage

Early sociological theorists, particularly Herbert Spencer (1905) and Émile Durkheim (1935), understood these dynamics well. They recognized that the growth of a population, its aggregation in delimited space and its modes of production are interrelated. Their analysis focused primarily on societies, but the relations among these processes hold for all other units of analysis as well. The pattern of interconnection is indicated by the direction of the arrows in figure 6: size/growth and production are mutually reinforcing, with each feeding back and increasing the values of the other, especially when values for material, organizational and technological resources are high; aggregation is related to size/growth and levels of production, and while there is some feedback between these forces, it is secondary and not indicated in this simplified version of the model. These specific processes of interconnection could be modelled in more detail, but I will not do so here.

In turn, each of these three processes is related to other forces, listed on the far left of figure 6. Aggregation is related to the available space and the way in which such space is currently organized (as well as to the existing patterns of social organization of subgroups: note arrow at top of figure 6). Growth/size is connected to the net rate of immigration into a population, the rate of indigenous population increase (reproduction), and external incorporation (i.e. mergers, conquests, alliances, etc.). Production is related to the level of relevant resources, primarily material, organizational, technological and political (note feedback arrow at bottom of figure 6). To summarize these processes as a simple set of 'laws of assemblage', I offer the following.

VI The level of assemblage for a population is a multiplicative function of its (a) size and rate of growth, (b) degree of ecological concentration and (c) level of production (a clear tautology, obviated below).
(a) The size and rate of growth of a population is an additive and positive function of external influx, internal increase, external incorporation and level of production.
(b) The degree of aggregation of a population is a positive and additive function of its size and rate of growth, level of production, capacity to organize space and the number and diversity of its subgroupings, while being an inverse function of the amount of available space.
(c) The level of production for a population is a positive multiplicative function of its size and rate of growth, level of material, organizational and technological resources and capacity to mobilize power.

The process of differentiation

Increases in aggregation, size/rate of growth, and production escalate the level of competition over resources among social units. Such competition

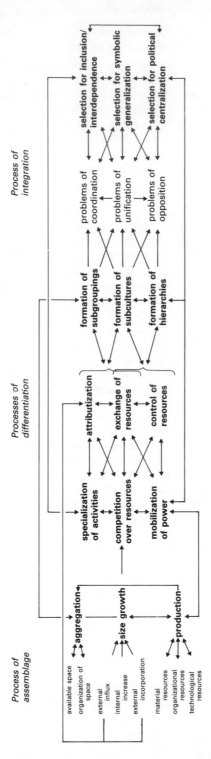

Figure 6 The process of assemblage, differentiation and integration.

sets in motion, as both Spencer and Durkheim emphasized, the process of differentiation among individuals and sub-units of organization in a population. This differentiation is the result of two mutually reinforcing cycles: one revolving around the processes of competition, specialization, exchange and the development of distinctive attributes, or what I term 'attributization', and the other around competition, exchange, power and control of resources. In turn, these two cycles produce three interrelated forms of differentiation: subgroups or heterogeneity, subcultures or symbolic diversity and hierarchies or inequalities (Blau: 1977). Before analysing these basic forms of differentiation, however, let me return to the mutually reinforcing cycles that produce them.

Competition and exchange are reciprocally related. Competition will, over time, produce exchange relations among differentiated actors, and conversely, exchange relations will, initially at least, increase the level of competition (Blau: 1966). Exchange and competition both produce specialization of activities (Durkheim: 1935; Spencer: 1905) since some can 'outcompete' others and force differentiation of activities and since exchange relations create pressures for actors to specialize in the provision for each other of different resources (Emerson: 1972). Competition, exchange and specialization all operate to create distinctive attributes – resource levels, activities, symbols and other parameters – among actors (Blau: 1977). Moreover, the assemblage processes of external influx and incorporation can also operate to make actors distinctive, since new members of a population can come from diverse systems (note arrow at top of figure 6). In turn, such distinctiveness encourages exchange of different resources, competition and specialization.

This cycle is reinforced and intensified by the mutually reinforcing effects of competition, exchange, mobilization of power and control of resources. Competition and exchange always involve efforts to mobilize power (Blau: 1966); and such mobilization increases, for a while at least, competition and exchange. Out of this positive feedback system, some actors are able to use power to control those resources – symbolic, material, organizational, etc. – that will increase their power, their capacity to engage in exchange and their ability to compete. And, as the arrow at the bottom of figure 6 indicates, existing patterns of political centralization operate to increase both mobilization of power and control of resources. In turn, these processes of mobilization and control escalate the level of specialization and the development of distinctive attributes because they accelerate, to a point, competition and encourage exchange.

Many of the reciprocal causal effects in these two cycles are either curvilinear or gradual *s*-functions. That is, they increase their respective values up to a point, and then level off or decline. Part of the reason for this pattern of relation resides in the self-transforming processes inhering in these cycles. For example, exchange increases competition, but once power has been mobilized and respective control of resources established, the exchange is more likely to become institutionalized (Blau: 1966) and balanced (Emerson: 1972), thereby decreasing competition. Or, to take another example, competition increases the mobilization of power and the resulting control of resources, but once these are increased, this power and control can be used to suppress competition, at least for a while. What these examples illustrate is that there are many subprocesses to those delineated in figure 6 which can also be modelled in a finely-tuned analysis, but for my purposes here these more specific processes need only be mentioned.

Out of these two cycles come three basic forms of differentiation: the formation of subgroups whose internal solidarity is high and whose network structure is dense relative to other subgroups; the formation of distinctive subcultures whose stocks of knowledge and repertoires of symbols differ from each other and whose distinctiveness is both a cause and effect of subgroup formation; and the formation of hierarchies which vary in terms of the respective shares of material, political and cultural resources that various actors hold and the extent to which correlations in the distribution of resources are 'superimposed' (Dahrendorf: 1958; 1959), 'correlated' (Lenski: 1966) or 'consolidated' (Blau: 1977). Thus, the degree of differentiation of a population is defined in terms of the number of subgroups, subcultures and hierarchies, and the more differentiation, then the greater are problems of coordination or integration for a population. Before moving to this third macroprocess, however, let me reformulate this discussion in terms of a few 'laws of differentiation'.

VII   The level of differentiation in a population is a positive and multiplicative function of the number of (*a*) subgroupings, (*b*) subcultures and (*c*) hierarchies evident in that population (an obvious tautology, which is obviated below).

(*a*) The number of subgroupings in a population is a curvilinear and multiplicative function of the level of exchange, competition, specialization and attributization among members of that population, while being a positive function of the number of subcultures in, and the rate of external influx/incorporation into, that population.

(*b*) The number of subcultures in a population is an additive and an *s*-function of the level of competition, exchange, specialization, attributization, mobilization of power and control of resources, while being a positive function of the formation of subgroupings and hierarchies.

(*c*) The number of hierarchies in a population is an inverse function of the mobilization of power and control of resources and a positive function of competition, exchange and formation of subcultures, with the degree of consolidation of hierarchies being a positive function of the mobilization of power and control of resources and a negative function of competition and exchange.

Integrating processes

The concept of 'integration' is admittedly vague, if not evaluative (that is, integration is 'good' and malintegration is 'bad'), but it is still useful as a label for several interrelated processes. For me, integration is a concept which varies along three separate dimensions: the degree of coordination among social units; the degree of symbolic unification among social units; and the degree of opposition and conflict among social units.

Viewed in these terms, the critical theoretical question becomes: what conditions promote or retard coordination, symbolic unification and opposition/conflict? In general terms, the existence *per se* of subgroupings, subcultures and hierarchies increases, respectively, problems of structural coordination, symbolic unification and conflictual opposition. Thus, inherent in the process of differentiation are problems of integration among variously differentiated units. Such problems set in motion 'selection pressures' for resolving such problems, but as the history of any society, organization, community or other macro-unit documents, the existence of such pressures does not guarantee selection for integrating processes. Indeed, in the long run, *all* patterns of organization disintegrate. None the less, in most macro-analytical theory, emphasis is on selection for structural and cultural forms that resolve, in varying degrees, problems of structural coordination, symbolic unification and conflictual opposition.

On the right-hand side of figure 6, I have outlined the critical processes of integration. Subgroup formation and subcultures create problems of coordination which, in turn, generate pressures for structural inclusion (subunits inside of ever more inclusive units)[6] and structural interdependence (overlapping membership as well as functional dependencies). The formation of subcultures and subgroups also poses, as Durkheim (1935) emphasized, the problem, of unifying a population with a 'common conscience' and 'collective conscience', or more generally, with common symbols (language, values, beliefs, norms, stocks of knowledge, etc.). The creation of hierarchies intensifies these problems. Conversely, such unification problems can also escalate selection pressures for structures resolving problems of coordination and opposition associated with hierarchies and subgroups.

The net effect of these problems of symbolic unification is to generate selection pressures for symbolic generalization, or the development of abstract and highly-generalized systems of symbols (values, beliefs, linguistic codes, stocks of knowledge) that can supplement the symbolic diversity of subgroups, subcultures and hierarchies. Durkheim called this process the 'enfeeblement of the collective conscience' and worried about the anomic consequences of highly-abstracted cultural codes, whereas Parsons (1966) termed it 'value generalization' and saw it as an integrating process that would allow for further social differentiation. They are both correct in this

---

[6] For a more detailed analysis, see Wallace: 1983.

sense: if generalized cultural codes are not compatible, salient or relevant to the more specific cultural codes of classes, subcultures or subgroups, then they aggravate problems of unification, but if they are compatible and salient, then they promote integration of subgroups, classes and subcultures. Thus, as the reciprocal arrows in figure 6 indicate, symbolic generalization can be a double-edged sword: it is essential for integration of differentiated systems but it is frequently inadequate to the task, and at times it aggravates not only problems of unification, but those of coordination and opposition as well.

Hierarchies among social units, especially when consolidated, correlated or superimposed, create problems of opposition, as all versions of conflict theory emphasize.[7] Such opposition can be intensified when there are few generalized symbols, but hierarchies also generate pressures for political centralization, in either of two ways. First, existing élites will politically centralize to control opposition and, second, if they are unsuccessful and the losers in conflict, the new élite will centralize power to consolidate its position and suppress remnants of the old hierarchy. Typically, appeals are made to generalized symbols (i.e. ideologies, values, beliefs) to legitimate these efforts and, if successful, they facilitate the centralization of power by creating legitimated authority. But as the long feedback arrow at the bottom of figure 6 underlines, these processes will set in motion the very forces that produce opposition. And as the arrows on the far right of the figure indicate, centralized power not only quells, for a time, opposition, it is also essential to structural inclusion and interdependence, since these involve regulation and control in terms of power and/or authority (Rueschemeyer: 1977). Indeed, the existence of inclusion and interdependence, as well as of generalized symbols, encourages political centralization. As the feedback arrow at the top of figure 6 highlights, politically-regulated inclusion and interdependence facilitate further specialization of activities. This increase in specialization sets in motion those dynamics creating escalated problems of symbolic unification and coordination that lead to more political centralization which, in the long run, generates opposition (as emphasized by the feedback arrow at the bottom of figure 6).[8]

Thus, inhering in the dynamics of integration are forces that increase differentiation and problems of integration. In all systems at some time in their history these problems escalate to a point where the social order collapses, only to be re-assembled in altered form. Such are, I think, the principal implications of the causal effects, cycles and feedback loops delineated in figure 6. Let me close this review of the right-hand sections of figure 6 by offering a few 'laws of integration'.

VIII   The greater is the degree of differentiation of a population into

---

[7] See Turner (1986) for a summary.

[8] For an empirical illustration and analysis of these processes, see Kelley and Klein: 1977.

subgroupings, subcultures and consolidated hierarchies, the greater are problems of structural coordination, symbolic unification and conflictual opposition in that population.

IX   The greater are the problems of coordination, unification and opposition in a population, the greater are selection pressures for structural inclusion/interdependence, symbolic generalization and political centralization in that population.

X   The more a population is integrated through political centralization, generalized symbols and patterns of interdependence/inclusion, the more likely is that population to increase its degree of differentiation and, hence, to intensify problems of coordination, unification and opposition.

Analytical Theorizing: Problems and Prospects

The major problem with analytical theorizing is that it exists within a hostile intellectual environment. Most social theorists, as is evident from the essays in this volume, would not accept the assumptions on the opening page of this chapter. Most social theorists would disagree that there are generic, timeless and universal properties of social organization; and most would not see the goal of theory as isolating these properties and developing abstract laws and models about their operation. There is, in my view, far too much scepticism, historicism, relativism and solipsism in social theory, and as a consequence theory typically involves discussions of issues and persons rather than of the operative dynamics of the social universe.

My proposal in this essay is to go back to Auguste Comte's original vision of sociology as a science. In this advocacy, I have outlined a general strategy: construct sensitizing analytical schemes, abstract laws and abstract analytical models; use each of these three analytical strategies as a corrective for the other two; then, test the abstract propositions as a check on their plausibility. I have illustrated this strategy by presenting my own views on micro-interactive and macrostructural processes. These views are only provisional and preliminary, and they have only been presented in outline form. Even so, my approach is eclectic and does bring together diverse scholars' work, and hence the models and propositions presented in this chapter do represent a schematic summary of analytical theorizing in contemporary sociology. The best prospects for sociology reside in further efforts to build this kind of analytical theory.

Bibliography

Alexander, J. C., 1982–3: *Theoretical Logic in Sociology*, 4 vols. Berkeley and Los Angeles: University of California Press.

Alexander, J. C., *et al.*, 1986: *The Micro–Macro Link*. Berkeley and Los Angeles: University of California Press.

Blalock, H. M., 1964: *Causal Inferences in Nonexperimental Research*. Chapel Hill: University of North Carolina Press.

Blau, P. M., 1966: *Exchange and Power in Social Life*. New York: Wiley.

    1977: *Inequality and Heterogeneity: A Primitive Theory of Social Structure*. New York: Free Press.

Blumer, H., 1969: *Symbolic Interaction: Perspective and Method*. Englewood Cliffs: Prentice-Hall.

Carnap, R., 1966: *Philosophical Foundations of Physics*. New York: Basic Books.

Cicourel, A. V., 1973: *Cognitive Sociology*. London: Macmillan.

Collins, R., 1975: *Conflict Sociology*. New York: Academic Press.

    1986: 'Interaction Ritual Chains, Power and Property', in Alexander *et al.*: 1986.

Comte, A., 1830–42: *A System of Positive Philosophy*. Paris: Bachelier.

Dahrendorf, R., 1958: 'Toward a Theory of Social Conflict', *Journal of Conflict Resolution*, 7: 170–83.

    1959: *Class and Class Conflict in Industrial Society*. Stanford: Stanford University Press.

Duncan, O. D., 1966: 'Path Analysis: Sociological Examples', *American Sociological Review*, 72: 1–10.

Durkheim, É., 1935: *The Division of Labor in Society*. New York: Macmillan. First published 1893.

    1938: *The Rules of the Sociological Method*. New York: Free Press.

Emerson, R., 1972: 'Exchange Theory: Part 2', in J. Berger, M. Zelditch and B. Anderson (eds), *Sociological Theories in Progress*. vol. 2. Boston: Houghton Mifflin.

Erikson, E., 1950: *Childhood and Society*. New York: Norton.

Freese, L., 1980: 'Formal Theorizing', *Annual Review of Sociology*, 6: 187–212.

Garfinkel, H., 1963: 'A Conception of, and Experiments with, "Trust" as a Condition of Stable Concerted Actions', in O. J. Harvey (ed.), *Motivation and Social Interaction*. New York: Ronald Press.

    1984: *Studies in Ethnomethodology*. Cambridge, England: Polity Press.

Giddens, A., 1977: *New Rules of the Sociological Method*. New York: Basic Books.

    1981: *Central Problems in Social Theory*. London: Macmillan.

    1984: *The Constitution of Society*. Cambridge, England: Polity Press.

Goffman, E., 1959: *The Presentation of Self in Everyday Life*. New York: Doubleday.

Habermas, J., 1970: 'On Systematically-Distorted Communication', *Inquiry*, 13: 205–18.

    1972: *Knowledge and Human Interests*. Cambridge, England: Polity Press.

    1981: *Theory of Communicative Action* 2 vols. London: Heinemann. Vol. 1, *Reason and the Rationalization of Society*, also published by Polity Press, Cambridge, England, 1984.

Hempel, C. G., 1965: *Aspects of Scientific Explanation*. New York: Free Press.

Heritage, J., 1984: *Garfinkel and Ethnomethodology*. Cambridge, England: Polity Press.

Homans, G. C., 1974: *Social Behavior: Its Elementary Forms*, revised edn. New York: Harcourt, Brace.

Keat, R. and Urry, J., 1975: *Social Theory as Science*. London: Routledge and Kegan Paul.

Kelley, J. and Klein, H. S., 1977: 'Revolution and the Rebirth of Inequality', *American Journal of Sociology*, 83: 78–99.

Knorr-Cetina, K. D. and Cicourel, A. V. (eds), 1981: *Advances in Social Theory and Methodology, Toward an Integration of Micro- and Macro-Sociologies*. London: Routledge and Kegan Paul.

Kuhn, M. H. and McPartland, T. S., 1954: 'An Empirical Investigation of Self-Attitudes', *American Sociological Review*, 19: 68–96.

Kuhn, M. S. and Hickman, C. A., 1956: *Individuals, Groups, and Economic Behavior*. New York: Dryden Press.

Kuhn, T., 1970: *The Structure of Scientific Revolutions*, 2nd edn. Chicago: University of Chicago Press.

Lakatos, I., 1970: 'Falsification and the Methodology of Scientific Research Programmes', in Lakatos and H. Musgrave (eds), *Criticism and the Growth of Scientific Knowledge*. Cambridge, England: Cambridge University Press.

Lenski, G., 1966: *Power and Privilege*. New York: McGraw-Hill.

Marx, K. and Engels, F., 1971: *The Communist Manifesto*. New York: International Publishers.

Mayhew, B. H., 1981: 'Structuralism versus Individualism', *Social Forces*, 59: 627–48.

Mayhew, B. H. and Levinger, R., 1976: 'Size and Density of Interaction in Human Aggregates', *American Journal of Sociology*, 82: 86–110.

Mead, G. H., 1934: *Mind, Self and Society*. Chicago: University of Chicago Press.

Merton, R. K., 1968: *Social Theory and Social Structure*. New York: Free Press.

Münch, R., 1982: *Theory of Action: Reconstructing the Contributions of Talcott Parsons, Émile Durkheim and Max Weber*, 2 vols. Frankfurt-on-Main: Suhrkamp.

Parsons, T., 1937: *The Structure of Social Action*. New York: McGraw-Hill.

    1961: 'An Outline of the Social System', in Parsons *et al.* (eds), *Theories of Society*. New York: Free Press.

    1966: *Societies: Evolutionary and Comparative Perspectives*. Englewood Cliffs, NJ: Prentice-Hall

    1971a: *The System of Modern Societies*. Englewood Cliffs NJ: Prentice-Hall.

    1971b: 'Some Problems in General Theory', in J. C. McKinney and E. C. Tiryakian (eds), *Theoretical Sociology: Perspectives and Developments*. New York: Appleton-Century-Crofts.

    1978: *Action Theory and the Human Condition*. New York: Free Press.

Popper, K. R., 1959: *The Logic of Scientific Discovery*. London: Hutchinson.

    1969: *Conjectures and Refutations*. London: Routledge and Kegan Paul.

Radcliffe-Brown, A. R., 1948: *A Natural Science of Society*. Glencoe, Ill.: Free Press.

Rueschemeyer, D., 1977: 'Structural Differentiation, Efficiency and Power', *American Journal of Sociology*, 83: 1–25.

Schütz, A., 1967: *The Phenomenology of the Social World*. Evanston: Northwestern University Press. First published 1932.

Shibutani, T., 1968: 'A Cybernetic Approach to Motivation', in W. Buckley (ed.), *Modern Systems Research for the Behavioral Scientist: A Sourcebook*. Chicago: Aldine.

Spencer, H., 1905: *Principles of Sociology*. New York: Appleton. First published in serial form 1874–96.

Turner, J.H., 1983: 'Theoretical Strategies for Linking Micro and Macro Processes: An Evaluation of Seven Approaches', *Western Sociological Review*, 14: 4–15.

1984: *Societal Stratification: A Theoretical Analysis*. New York: Columbia University Press, ch. 1.

1985a: 'The Concept of "Action" in Sociological Analysis', in G. Seebass and R. Tuomela (eds), *Social Action*. Dordrecht: D. Reidel, pp. 61–87.

1985b: 'In Defense of Positivism', *Sociological Theory*, 4.

1986: *The Structure of Sociological Theory*, 4th edn. Homewood, Ill.: Dorsey Press.

forthcoming a: 'The Structure of Social Interaction'.

forthcoming b: 'Macro Dynamics'.

Turner, R. H., 1962: 'Role-Taking: Process versus Conformity', in A. M. Rose (ed.), *Human Behaviour and Social Processes*. Boston: Houghton Mifflin.

1980: 'A Strategy for Developing an Integrated Role Theory', *Humboldt Journal of Social Relations*, 7: 128–39.

Wallace, W. L., 1983: *Principles of Scientific Sociology*. New York: Aldine.

Structuralism, Post-structuralism and the Production of Culture

ANTHONY GIDDENS

Structuralism, and post-structuralism also, are dead traditions of thought. Notwithstanding the promise they held in the fresh bloom of youth, they have ultimately failed to generate the revolution in philosophical under-standing and social theory that was once their pledge. In this discussion, I shall seek not so much to write their obituary as to indicate what they have bequeathed to us today in respect of intellectual possessions which still might be put to good use. For although they did not transform our intellec-tual universe in the manner so often claimed, they none the less drew to our attention some problems of considerable and durable significance.

Of course, many have doubted that there ever was a coherent enough body of thought to be designated by the name 'structuralism', let alone the even vaguer appellation 'post-structuralism' (see Runciman: 1970). After all, most of the leading figures ordinarily lumped under these labels have rejected these terms as applying meaningfully to their own endeavours. Saussure, commonly regarded as the founder of structuralist linguistics, barely uses the term 'structure' at all in his work (Saussure: 1974). Lévi-Strauss at one time actively promoted the cause of both 'structural anthropo-logy' and 'structuralism' more generally, but has become more cautious in characterizing his approach in these ways over the latter part of his career. Barthes may have in his early writings drawn fairly heavily from Lévi-Strauss, but later on any such connections became quite remote. Foucault, Lacan, Althusser and Derrida diverge radically both from the main ideas of Saussure and Lévi-Strauss and from one another. The homogeneity needed to speak of a distinct tradition of thought might appear to be almost completely lacking.

But for all their diversity there are a number of themes that crop up in the works of all these authors. Moreover, with the exception of Saussure, all are French and have been involved in networks of mutual influence and contact. In using the terms 'structuralism' and 'post-structuralism' in what follows, I have in mind Saussure and Lévi-Strauss as belonging to the first category, with the others in the second. 'Post-structuralist' is admittedly a fairly loose label for a cluster of authors who, while reacting against some of the distinctive emphases of earlier structuralist thought, at the same time take over some of those very ideas in their own work. Thus while they handle these themes in diverse ways, the following can be said to be persistent, and definitive, characteristics of structuralism and post-structuralism: the thesis that linguistics, or more accurately, certain aspects of particular versions of linguistics, are of key importance to philosophy and social theory as a whole; an emphasis upon the relational nature of totalities, connected with the thesis of the arbitrary character of the sign, together with a stress upon the primacy of signifiers over what is signified; the decentring of the subject; a peculiar concern with the nature of writing, and therefore with textual materials; and an interest in the character of temporality as somehow constitutively involved with the nature of objects and events. There is not a single one of these themes which does not bear upon issues of importance for social theory today. Equally, however, there is not one in respect of which the views of any of the writers listed above could be said to be acceptable.

Problems of Linguistics

Structuralism was of course originally both a movement within linguistics and an endeavour to demonstrate the significance of concepts and methods of linguistics for a wide variety of issues in the humanities and social sciences. Saussure's distinction between *langue* and *parole* may justly be regarded as the key idea in structuralist linguistics. The distinction removes the study of 'language' from the sphere of the contingent and the contextual. As an overall structural form, language is to be separated from the multifarious uses to which particular speech acts may be put. *Parole* is what Saussure calls the 'executive side of language', while *langue* is 'a system of signs in which the only essential thing is the union of meanings and acoustic images' (Saussure: 1974). Language is thus an idealized system, inferred from but nevertheless independent of the particular uses to which speech is put. The actual sound contents of language are in a way irrelevant to the analysis of *langue*, because the concern is with the formal relations between sounds, or marks, not with their actual substance. Although in Saussure a certain mentalism and reliance upon psychology remain, in principle linguistics becomes clearly separable from other disciplines concerned with the study of human activity. Phonemics becomes also clearly differentiated from phonetics, the latter being of relatively marginal importance to the main core of linguistic analysis.

There is an inconsistency at the heart of Saussure's conception of *langue*. On the one hand, language is regarded as ultimately a psychological phenomenon, organized in terms of mental properties. On the other – as Saussure's seeming indebtedness to Durkheim would indicate – language is a collective product, a system of social representations. As critics have pointed out, if language is essentially a psychological reality, signs are no longer arbitrary. Since the relations that constitute language would be patterned in terms of characteristics of mind, they would have a determinate form controlled by mental processes. Thus if language is looked at as a mental reality the sign is by no means arbitrary and its meaning is by no means defined by its relations with contemporaneous elements of the language (Clarke: 1981, p. 123).

Broadly speaking, most forms of structuralist linguistics have opted for the 'psychological' rather than the 'social' version of *langue*. It was by adopting this approach that Chomsky was able to effect a fusion of ideas drawn from European linguistics with notions taken from the 'behaviourist structuralism' of Bloomfield, Harris and others within linguistics in the United States. Bloomfield and Harris sought to separate linguistics completely from any kind of mentalism or psychology (Bloomfield: 1957; Harris: 1951). For them the aim of linguistics is to analyse language so far as possible solely as sequences of regularized sounds. Attention is not to be concentrated upon the interpretative involvements of speakers with language-use. While this standpoint at first sight seems substantially distinct from Saussurian linguistics, and while indeed its leading advocates rejected the differentiation of *langue* from *parole*, there are certainly some underlying affinities, which Chomsky was able to bring out. Redefining the distinction of *langue* and *parole* as one of competence and performance, and dissociating himself in a radical way from the behaviourism of Bloomfield and Harris, Chomsky was able to reconnect a mentalistic basis for language with an elaborated model of formal linguistics. Given the differentiation which is made between competence and performance, Chomskyan linguistics necessarily accords a central significance to syntax (see, e.g., Chomsky: 1968). Its objective is not to explicate all utterances of the speakers within a particular language community, but only the syntactical structures of an idealized language speaker. Chomsky's theory reintroduces interpretation, because the identification of syntactical correctness depends upon what is deemed acceptable by language speakers. It also gives a certain priority to the creative components of language, in the sense that the competent speaker is able to generate an indefinite corpus of syntactically acceptable sentences. It is arguable that the Chomskyan competence–performance distinction is in some respects superior to the *langue–parole* differentiation, because Chomsky at least has a model of the linguistic agent. As Chomsky points out, criticizing Saussure, the latter treated *langue* mainly as a repository of 'word-like elements' and 'fixed phrases', contrasting it to the more flexible character of *parole*. What is missing is an account of the 'mediating term' between *langue* and *parole*. The agent is for Chomsky the locus of what he regards as the 'rule-governed creativity' of language as a system (Chomsky: 1964, p. 23).

Chomsky's transformational grammar is one approach influenced by some of the emphases of Saussure; another is the linguistics of the Prague School, which through Jakobson was the main influence upon Lévi-Strauss. Broadly speaking one can say that the Prague group follows the 'social' conception of *langue* rather than the 'psychological' one. Whereas Chomsky's linguistics focuses upon the competence of the individual speaker, the linguistics of the Prague School concentrates above all upon language as a communicative medium. Thus semantics is not completely severed from syntactics, and the nature of *langue* expresses relations of meaning. As Trubetzkoy claims, linguistics should investigate 'which phonic differences are linked, in the language under consideration, with differences of meaning, how these differentiating elements or marks are related to one another, and according to what rules they combine to form words and phrases' (Trubetzkoy: 1969, p. 12). Stress upon the use of language as communication, combined with an emphasis on meaning, would seem to compromise the autonomous character of linguistics as specified by Saussure (and Chomsky). For it would appear that language would then have to be analysed in the institutions of social life. Certainly the Prague linguists dissociated themselves from the inflexible distinction between *langue* and *parole* drawn by Saussure and from the associated division between the synchronic and the diachronic. In spite of this, the distinctive emphasis of the Prague group tended to be upon phonology, where the sound system of language can be studied without attention to the external connotations of meaning. Jakobson's early work in particular pursued the idea that a 'phonological revolution' (Lévi-Strauss's term) could be produced by analysing phonemes in terms of oppositions which are the constituent features of language as a whole. Although this was justified on methodological rather than epistemological grounds, the result was again to return linguistics to the study of the internal structures of *langue* (Jakobson: 1971).

Lévi-Strauss and Barthes have each at various times seen the main basis for structuralism as consisting of the application of procedures of linguistics to other areas of analysis. Lévi-Strauss regards structuralist linguistics as both supplying modes of analysis that are applicable elsewhere and providing substantive clues to the nature of the human mind. In *The Elementary Structures* he explicitly compares his objectives with those of phonological linguistics, and adds that linguists and social scientists 'do not merely apply the same methods, but are studying the same thing' (1969a: p. 493). For structural linguistics allows us to discern what he later came to regard as 'fundamental and objective realities consisting of systems of relations which are the products of unconscious thought processes' (Lévi-Strauss: 1968, p. 58). As Culler points out, regarding linguistics as of central importance to structuralism generally carries several implications. First, linguistics seems to provide a rigour lacking elsewhere in the humanities and social sciences. Second, linguistics offers a number of basic concepts which seem to be capable of much wider application than that involved in the framework of their origin – *langue* and *parole* in particular, perhaps, but also the associated distinctions of the syntagmatic from the paradigmatic, signifier from signified, the idea of the arbitrary nature of the sign, and so on. Third, linguistics appears to provide a series of general guidelines for the formulation of semiotic programmes. Such a notion was of course sketched out by Saussure and developed in some detail by Jakobson and others.

Because of the connections between structuralist linguistics and structuralism more generally, it is often held that structuralism has participated in the general 'linguistic turn' characteristic of modern philosophy and social theory. However, this is a specious conclusion, for reasons I shall now indicate. On the one hand, the hopes that were pinned on linguistics for providing general models of procedure that could be applied very widely now quite plainly appear to be misplaced. On the other, the 'linguistic turn', at least in its most valuable forms, does not involve an extension of ideas taken from the study of language to other aspects of human activity, but rather explores the intersection between language and the constitution of social practices. The relevant considerations here concern both the critique of structuralist linguistics as an approach to the analysis of language itself, and the critical appraisal of the importation of notions taken from this version of linguistics into other areas of the explication of human behaviour.

Many criticisms, of course, have been made of Saussure's version of linguistics – or at any rate, that portrayal of it which has come down to us through the medium of his students – including those offered cogently by Chomsky. There is no point in rehearsing these in any detail here. Most significant for the lines of argument to be developed later in this discussion are the shortcomings shared by virtually all forms of structuralist linguistics, including that of Chomsky. These concern above all the isolation of language, or of certain features taken to be fundamental to the structure and properties of language, from the social environments of language-use. Thus, while Chomsky recognizes, and even accentuates, the creative capabilities of human subjects, this creative quality is attributed to characteristics of the human mind, not to conscious agents carrying out their day-to-day activities in the context of social institutions. As one observer puts it, 'the creative power of the subject has to be taken away as soon as it is acknowledged and given to a mechanism inscribed in the biological constitution of the mind' (Clarke: 1980, p. 171). Although it is in many ways the most developed and sophisticated form of structural linguistics, Chomsky's theory of language has proved essentially defective in respect of the understanding of quite elementary features of language. These defects do not centre so much upon the unsatisfactory nature of the division drawn between syntactics and semantics as upon the identification of the core features of linguistic competence. In Chomsky's view, the idealized language speaker is able unconsciously to grasp rules making possible the production and understanding of any or all grammatical sentences in a language. But this is not really an appropriate model of competence. Someone who might in any given context produce any sentence at all, however syntactically correct, would be treated as distinctly aberrant. Linguistic competence involves not only the syntactical mastery of sentences, but mastery of the circumstances in which particular types of sentence are appropriate. In Hymes's words: 'he or she acquires competence as to when to speak, when not, and as to what to talk about with whom, when, where, in what manner' (Hymes: 1972, p. 277). In other words, mastery of the language is inseparable from mastery of the variety of contexts in which language is used.

The works of authors as diverse as Wittgenstein and Garfinkel have made us aware of what this involves, both for understanding the nature of language and for grasping the character of social life. Knowing a language certainly means knowing syntactical rules but, equally importantly, to know a language is to acquire a range of methodological devices involved both with the production of utterances themselves and with the constitution and reconstitution of social life in the daily contexts of social activity (Giddens: 1984, ch. 1). It is not just that to know a language is to know a form of life, or rather a multiplicity of interweaving forms of life: to know a form of life is to be able to deploy certain methodical strategies geared to indexical qualities of the contexts in which social practices are carried out. In this understanding of language, linguistics neither has the degree of self-sufficiency which Saussure, the Prague School, Chomsky and others have claimed, nor does it make much sense to hold, as Lévi-Strauss has sometimes asserted, that social life is 'like a language'. Linguistics cannot provide a model for analysing the nature of either agency or social institutions, because it is in a basic sense only explicable through an understanding of these. The 'linguistic turn' can be seen as a turn away from linguistics, conceived as an independently-formed discipline, towards examining the mutual co-ordination of language and *Praxis*.

The Relational Nature of Totalities

In Saussure's doctrines, the relational character of *langue* is closely connected with the thesis of the arbitrary character of the sign, and with a stress upon the significance of signifiers as compared with the more traditional preoccupation with signifieds. It is often remarked that Saussure's differentiation of *langue* from *parole*, according priority to the former over the latter, reflects Durkheim's assertion that the qualities of social wholes are more than the sum of their parts. But this is surely wrong, and under-estimates the subtlety with which Saussure designates the systemic form of *langue*. In explicating *langue* as a system of differences, Saussure reformulates the nature of both what the 'whole' is and what its 'parts' are, indicating that each is only defined in terms of the other. To say that language is a system without positive terms, that is, formed through the differences recognized to exist between sounds or marks, shows that the 'parts' are only such in virtue of the self-same characteristics that compose the 'whole'. The insight is a fundamental one in so far as it demonstrates that the linguistic totality does not 'exist' in the contexts of the use of language. The totality is not 'present' in the instantiations which are its traces.

The tie between this view and the notion of the arbitrary character of the sign is easily specified. The assertion of the arbitrary nature of the sign can be read as a critique of object theories of meaning and of theories of ostensive reference. But this critique does not stem from the kinds of demonstration which Wittgenstein, Quine and other later philosophers were to make that the use of lexical items cannot be said to 'correspond' to objects or events in the world. Saussure's criticism is based wholly upon the idea of the constitution of *langue* through difference. Because a word only derives its meaning from the differences established between it and other words, words cannot 'mean' their objects. Language is form, not substance, and is only able to generate meaning by the internal play of differences. This is therefore just as much the case with the relation between words – or sentences – and the mental states which might accompany them, as it is of the relation between words and external objects and events.

The emphasis upon the constitution of the totality through difference might appear to lead away from signifiers rather than toward them. For what matters is not whatever is used to signify, but only the differences that create the 'spacing' between them. However, a concentration on the properties of signifiers tends to flow rather readily from Saussure's views, because of the rejection that there is anything 'underneath' language which explains its character (apart from the vague presumption of some kind of innate mental qualities). While the actual substance comprising signifiers is unimportant, without the differences which sounds, marks or other material differentiations create no meanings of any kind could exist. The programme of semiotics is hence certainly not just an adjunct to linguistics in the Saussurian formulation, but is necessarily coextensive with the exploration of *langue* itself.

The relational character of wholes, the arbitrary nature of the sign, and the notion of difference are concepts which run through structuralist and post-structuralist perspectives as a whole. At the same time they are the source of the main features that separate the structuralist authors from their post-structuralist successors. Jakobson and Lévi-Strauss provide clear cases of the direct utilization of the Saussurian idea of the relational character of totalities. For the former, structuralism is defined in terms of the study of phenomena 'treated not as a mechanical agglomeration, but as a structural whole' (Jakobson: 1971, p. 711). Lévi-Strauss writes even more emphatically when he claims: 'authentic structuralism seeks ... above all to grasp the intrinsic properties of certain kinds of order. The properties express nothing which would be external to them' (Lévi-Strauss: 1971, pp. 561–2). However, Jakobson's own criticisms of Saussure make it clear that the principle of the identification of relations through difference is separable from the assertion that *langue* is a clearly definable whole. The boundaries of the 'whole' that is Saussure's *langue*, or that is Chomsky's linguistic corpus known to a competent speaker, are exceedingly difficult to draw. It can therefore be argued that more important than the principle of establishing the coherence of the totality is the endeavour to examine the nature of difference itself. Within linguistics, Jakobson established the beginning of such an endeavour in his attempt to focus upon the basic structuring properties of codes rather than on the parameters of these codes themselves.

Derrida's philosophy radicalizes this much further. His disavowal of the 'metaphysics of presence' derives directly from his treatment of the idea of difference as constitutive, not only of modes of signification, but of existence in general (Derrida: 1976; 1978). Derrida will have nothing of the search for universal properties of mind, or indeed of any attempt to construct a systematic philosophy at all. In his discussion of Lévi-Strauss and structuralism in the social sciences, Derrida emphasizes the unrealizable character of Lévi-Strauss's programme, deriving this from contradictions supposedly implicit in Lévi-Strauss's own text. Lévi-Strauss's exploration of oral cultures is paradoxically itself a form of Western 'logocentrism'. Derrida's critique of the metaphysics of presence is derived more or less directly from an exploration of the implications of the idea of difference as first indicated by Saussure and contrasted with notions of negation involved in the work of Hegel, Freud and others. Because of his distinction between *langue* and *parole*, Saussure was able to treat the idea of difference as involved with a 'virtual system' out of time. The transmutation of the Saussurian version of difference into Derrida's *différance* is made by introducing the temporal element. To differ is also to defer. If this is so, Derrida asks, how can anything, such as forms of signification, be considered as presences? Saussure's writings already contain the notion of the 'absent totality' which is language. In this idea of totality, however, there is still in Derrida's view a lingering nostalgia for presence. All signification operates through traces: memory traces in the brain, the fading of sounds as they are uttered, and the traces that writing leaves.

Derrida's reversal of the usual priority accorded to speaking over writing vigorously pursues a preoccupation with signifiers at the expense of the signified. This is also in some part derived from an immanent critique of Saussure. Speech, Derrida claims, seems to represent a moment in which form and meaning are present simultaneously. Once we see, however, as Saussure himself demonstrates, that this cannot be so, then we are led to question the presumption that speech is the most elemental expression of language. As I hear myself speak, it seems as though the words uttered are simply vehicles for my thoughts, consciousness being clothed in and given expression by language. Access to the inner contents of consciousness is regarded as the real basis of the meanings inherent in language, which writing can only hope indirectly to recapture. At key parts in his arguments about the structuring of language through difference, however, Saussure abandons sound units in favour of examples from writing. Thus, for instance, any particular letter of the alphabet, he points out, may be written in varying ways; all that matters is that it is distinct from other letters that could potentially be confused with it. Writing emerges as the best illustration of difference. The characteristics of absence and deferment involved in the nature of written texts indicate the conditions of signification in general. Speech 'personalizes' language by connecting it with the thoughts of the speaker. In fact language is essentially anonymous, never the property of individual speakers and depends for its form upon its recursive properties. Of course, Derrida does not intend by this to accord a primacy to actual writing over instances of speech, which would make little sense, if only for the reason that writing is in historical terms such a relatively recent development compared with the prevalence of oral cultures. Rather, language is a 'proto-writing' (*archi-écriture*), a process of the temporal spacing and repetition of signifying phenomena. Proto-writing, Derrida argues, 'is *invoked* by the themes of the arbitrariness of the sign and of difference', but it 'can never be recognized as the *object of science*'.[2] That is to say, it is not to be the object of investigation of a sort of non-logocentric linguistics.

The notion of the arbitrary character of the sign is responsible not only for some of the strengths but also for the enduring weaknesses that run through structuralist and post-structuralist traditions of thought. As formulated by Saussure, the doctrine of the arbitrary character of the sign has itself a somewhat arbitrary aspect. The term 'arbitrary' is not a particularly happy one for the phenomenon at issue. As Saussure himself fully accepted, the conventions involved in language-use are certainly not arbitrary in the sense that the language user is free to choose whatever utterances he or she might care to make. On the contrary, accepted usage has a strongly binding force. But more important is that the thesis of the arbitrary nature of the sign is in the end rather obscure, especially in so far as it bears upon the nature of the signified rather than upon that of the signifier. If Saussure merely meant to claim that words have only a conventional connection with whatever objects they might be used to designate or refer to, it is so obvious as to be uninteresting. If – as quite often seems to be the case in Saussure's argument – the arbitrary nature of the sign is the same as the idea that language is constituted through difference, it is true that this has implications for the nature of meaning, but these implications are not pursued because the nature of signifieds is left largely unexplicated. Saussure evidently wished to claim that the meaning of a word is not the object to which that word might be used to refer, but since he nowhere analyses the nature of reference, this claim remains essentially unelucidated philosophically. The result is the confusion noted by Benveniste. As Benveniste observes:

> even though Saussure said that the idea of 'sister' is not connected to the signifier s-ö-r [*soeur*], he was not thinking any less of the *reality of the notion*. When he spoke of the difference b-ö-f [*boeuf*] and o-k-s [ox], was referring in spite of himself to the fact that these two terms apply to the same *reality*. Here, then, is the *thing*, expressly excluded at first from the definition of the sign, now creeping into it by a detour. (Benveniste: 1971, p. 44)

[2] Quoted in Culler: 1979.

Saussure's writings promoted a 'retreat into the code' which has ever since been characteristic both of structuralist and post-structuralist authors. That is to say, the discovery that the component elements of *langue* only have identity through their differentiation within the overall system serves to drag language away from whatever connections of reference it might have with the object world. Structuralist and post-structuralist thought alike have consistently failed to generate an account of reference, and it is surely not by chance that these traditions of thought have concentrated their attention so much upon the internal organization of texts, in which the play of signifiers can be analysed as an inside affair (see Giddens: 1979, chs 1ff.). It is important to see that while the 'retreat into the code' was promoted by the Saussurian emphases, as these were modified and adapted by subsequent authors, this 'retreat' was never really established by philosophical argument. It derived from the assimilation of the doctrine of the arbitrary nature of the sign and of that of the role of difference.

Derrida's writings are in some ways the most sophisticated outcome of the transition from structuralism to post-structuralism. Although Derrida's works seem on first contact to be quite alien to Anglo-Saxon eyes, there are some rather close affinities between them and views expressed by the later Wittgenstein. Derrida's disavowal of the 'metaphysics of presence' is by no means entirely dissimilar, either in its objectives or in its methods, from Wittgenstein's attempt to puncture the aspirations of metaphysics in *Philsophical Investigations* (1953). For both authors the goals of metaphysics cannot simply be re-examined or updated; they have to be 'deconstructed' rather than 'reconstructed' because they rest upon mistaken premisses. In both cases it is suggested that this is because of a misapprehension about the nature of reality. There are no essences to be captured by appropriate linguistic formulations. Wittgenstein is as firm as Derrida that neither words nor sentences involve some sort of corresponding mental images which supply their meaning, any more than do the objects or events in the external world to which words can be used to refer. While Wittgenstein would no doubt protest against Derrida's ambitious extension of the concept of writing, he would agree with the latter that language is not to be interpreted in terms of the subjective meanings of individual agents. Wittgenstein's rejection of the 'private language' argument is obviously not directly an analogue of Derrida's embrace of the idea of writing, but in both instances language is necessarily an 'anonymous' production and thus in an important sense 'subjectless'.

Whether Wittgenstein would have had much regard for the idea of difference is, to say the least, debatable. None the less, in his elaboration of the notion of language games the 'spacing' of utterances and activities is plainly central. Both the recursive and the relational character of language are stressed. However, it seems indisputable that the main lines of development of Wittgensteinian philosophy are more defensible than those worked out within post-structuralism. Rather than promoting a 'retreat into the code' Wittgenstein seeks to understand the relational character of signification in the context of social practices. His resolute preoccupation with ordinary language tends to inhibit a concern with poetics, art or literature. But there do not seem to be any distinctively logical barriers to extending Wittgenstein's ideas into these domains, while the account of language and meaning which can be generated from Wittgenstein's philosophy (or at least from certain basic notions contained within it) are more sophisticated than those available within structuralism and post-structuralism (a matter I shall develop further below).

The unsatisfactory character of the thesis of the arbitrary form of the sign, as diffused into structuralist and post-structuralist traditions, has radically impoverished the accounts of meaning such traditions have been able to offer. A preoccupation with signifiers at the expense of the signified is in large part an emphasis enforced by this circumstance. For Wittgenstein the meaning of lexical items is to be found in the intermeshing of language and practice, within the complex of language games involved in forms of life. While no doubt this view, as formulated by Wittgenstein himself, leaves aside certain fundamental problems of meaning – in particular in what sense, if at all, the understanding of meaning implies a grasp of the truth-conditions of certain classes of assertions – it is surely a perspective of considerable fruitfulness.

The Decentring of the Subject

Although the phrase 'the decentring of the subject' has come to be peculiarly associated with structuralism and post-structuralism, the ideas involved derive from wider sources. As structuralist and post-structuralist authors themselves are fond of pointing out, psychoanalysis had already shown the ego not to be master in its own home, its characteristics only being revealed by way of a detour through the unconscious. Although this was not the interpretation which Sartre made, Heidegger's writings from *Being and Time* onwards can be taken to assert the primacy of being over consciousness (Heidegger: 1978). Moreover, there is more than a diffuse connection between Freud, Heidegger and Nietzsche. Indeed the writings of each of these authors tend to figure prominently in the work of those associated with post-structuralism. This having been said, it is evident that we can discern the origins of the notion of the 'decentred subject' in Saussure.

According to Saussure, language is a system of signs, constituted by differences, with an arbitrary relation to objects. If this includes objects in the external world, it must also embrace the characteristics of the producer of language, the speaker. Just as the meaning of 'tree' is not the object tree, so the meaning of terms that refer to human subjectivity, most particularly the 'I' of the thinking or acting subject, cannot be the states of consciousness of that subject. Like any other term in a language, 'I' is only constituted as a sign by virtue of its differences from 'you', 'we', 'they', etc. Since the 'I' has sense only by virtue of being an element in an 'anonymous' totality, there can be no question of according it some distinctive philosophical privilege. In Saussure this idea is not developed in a direct way; moreover Saussure's own views are somewhat confusing in light of the persistence of a certain mentalism in his writings. It was therefore left to others to develop what Saussure left largely implicit, and they did not hesitate to do so: there is probably no theme which appears more persistently in the literature of structuralism and post-structuralism.

Lévi-Strauss has written less explicitly about the decentring of the subject than have most of his successors. None the less in certain respects his writings have been the main mediating link between Saussure and criticisms of 'humanism' in post-structuralist philosophy. Referring to his analysis of myths, Lévi-Strauss observes in a celebrated statement that he claims to show 'not how men think in myths, but how myths operate in men's minds without their being aware of the fact'; or again, 'myths signify the mind which evolves them by making use of the world of which it is itself a part' (Lévi-Strauss: 1969b, pp. 12, 341). There is no 'I think' in this characterization of the human mind. The unconscious categories of mind are the constitutive backdrop against which sentiments of selfhood exist. Consciousness is made possible by structures of mind that are not immediately available to it.

The decentring of the subject emerges in various guises in the post-structuralist literature. In Foucault's discussion of the beginnings and end of the 'age of man' it is primarily a set of historical observations about the development of Western philosophy and of Western culture as a whole. In Barthes, it is a series of claims about the nature of authors in relation to their texts. In Lacan, it is part of an attempt to rework the main concepts of psychoanalysis, giving of course especial attention to the idea that the unconscious exemplifies certain features of language. All these clearly share a critical attitude toward Cartesianism and to every philosophy (such as certain versions of phenomenology) that treats consciousness as a datum upon which the foundations of claims to knowledge may be established. 'I think, therefore I am' is disqualified on a number of grounds. The 'I' is not immediately available to itself, deriving its identity as it does from its involvement in a system of signification. The 'I' is not the expression of some core of continuous selfhood that is its basis. The 'being' suggested in the 'I am' is not given through the capability of the subject to use the concept 'I'. What Lacan calls the 'discourse of the Other' is taken to be source both of the capability of the subject to employ 'I' and of the assertion of existence in 'I am'. As Lacan puts it: 'the Other is, therefore, the locus in which is constituted the I who speaks to him who hears, that which is said by the one being already the reply, the other deciding to hear it whether the one has or has not spoken' (Lacan: 1977, p. 453).

All the above authors agree upon the irrelevance of the author to the interpretation of texts. The writer is not a presence somehow to be uncovered behind the text. Just as the primacy accorded to the author is a historical expression of the individualism of the Age of Man, so the 'I' of the author is a grammatical form rather than a flesh-and-blood agent. Since the text is organized in terms of the internal play of signifiers, what its originator or originators intended to put into it is more or less irrelevant to our understanding of it. Authors are to be found everywhere in their texts and consequently nowhere: as Barthes puts it, 'a text is ... a multi-dimensional space in which a variety of writings, none of them original, blend and clash' (Barthes: 1977, p. 146). Once more, of course, this is not a conclusion which is specifically the province of structuralism or post-structuralism. The view of the 'autonomy' of texts reached by Gadamer, drawing primarily upon Heidegger, is in some respects directly comparable with that reached within the French traditions of thought (Gadamer: 1975). In neither case is it believed that the author has some kind of privileged relation to his or her text. Both textual analysis and literary criticism therefore must break in a clear-cut fashion with 'intentionalist' perspectives.

The theme of the decentring of the subject is without doubt one which must be taken seriously by anyone interested in modern philosophy or social theory. But while the basic perspective surely must be accepted, the particular mode in which it is elaborated within structuralism and post-structuralism remains defective. To reject the idea that consciousness, whether consciousness of self or the sensory registering of the external world, can provide a foundation for knowledge, is to participate in one of the major transitions in modern philosophy. Those forms of philosophy, and therefore modes of social analysis based on them, which presume an unmediated access to consciousness are by now thoroughly discredited. Since some schools of philosophical thought, most notably phenomenology, have been closely associated with such philosophical standpoints, the rejection of those standpoints unavoidably compromises those schools of thought also. But structuralist and post-structuralist accounts of the decentring of the subject are inevitably closely tied to the versions of language and the unconscious associated with structuralist linguistics and its influence. The detour needed to recover the 'I' is not only taken very largely through language, but is in addition filtered through a particular theory of language as well. If we regard language as situated in social practices, and if we reject the structuralist and post structuralist distinction between consciousness and the unconscious, we reach a different conception of the human subject – as agent. Again, this is a theme to which I shall later return.

Writing and the Text

Comparing Wittgenstein and Derrida, it is worth considering why the latter gives such a fundamental priority to the theme of writing, whereas in the former a concern with the significance of writing is largely absent. Derrida's preoccupation with writing is closely connected with his rejection of the metaphysics of presence. In Derrida's words:

no element can function as a sign without relating to another element which itself is not simply present. This linkage means that each 'element' – phoneme or grapheme – is constituted with reference to the trace in it of the other elements of the sequence ... Nothing, in either the elements or the system, is anywhere ever simply present or absent (Derrida: 1981, p. 92)

Thus, in Derrida's view, it is mistaken to suppose that writing is a particular mode of giving expression to speech. Writing – in the extended sense which Derrida attributes to the term – expresses more clearly than speech the relational nature of signification as constituted both in space and in time. We might more accurately speak of the timing and spacing of signification, rather than of its 'occurrence' in a given context. There are similarities with what Wittgenstein has to say here, both in respect of the 'deconstruction' of metaphysical questions about time and space and in respect of the mode in which it is suggested that time-space is constitutive of the identity of objects or events. In commenting critically upon St Augustine's reflections on the nature of time, Wittgenstein argues that the puzzles with which Augustine grappled are empty of content because they rest upon the mistaken attribution of an essence to temporality. It is actually the 'grammar' of time that needs elucidating. Time has no essence, and there is no abstract formulation that can therefore convey its nature. We can only experience and observe temporality in the unfolding of events. It might be argued that Wittgenstein does not in fact take the next step, and like Derrida (and before him Heidegger) treat time-space as constitutive of events and objects. But I think there is no other way of making sense of Wittgenstein's philosophy save by presuming this to be intrinsic to the analyses he develops.

Wittgenstein's struggles with form – his disinclination to write in a narrative style, and the seemingly disorganized character of the *Philosophical Investigations* – have a definite affinity with Derrida's use of various sorts of graphic innovations. For both writers wish to give expression to views that are refractory to being 'described'. Both assert that it is not the presence of some sort of reality, physical or mental, which serves to anchor the meaningful components of systems of signification.

The limitations of Derrida's view of writing can be understood when we consider what is involved in his 'timing' and 'spacing'. Derrida's conception of 'writing' is a direct development of Saussure's separation of the signifier from an external world of objects and events. Derrida participates in the 'retreat into the text', the universe of signifiers, characteristic of structuralist and post-structuralist traditions of thought as a whole. His 'text' is that of the play of differences intrinsic to signification as such. Although the notion of *différance* makes it possible for Derrida to comprehend temporality, his treatment of space is purely nominal. Or to put things another way, although he talks of 'timing' and 'spacing', to all intents and purposes these are the same. The 'extending' of writing is involved in the spacing of sounds or marks, but this is the very same phenomenon as their temporal differentiation. Wittgenstein's portrayal of the relational character of signification as expressed in the organization of social practices, however, does not involve the collapsing of time into space. Time-space enters into the structuring of signification not through the 'flat' dimension of writing – even conceptualized as proto-writing – but through the contextuality of social practices themselves. For a long while, philosophers influenced by Wittgenstein were misled by the idea that the meaning of words or utterances consists in their use. For from this it might seem to follow that we simply substitute 'use' for the objects to which words were held to correspond in previous theories of meaning. But what is at issue is not 'use', but the process of *using* words and phrases in contexts of social conduct. Meaning is not constructed by the play of signifiers, but by the intersection of the production of signifiers with objects and events in the world, focused and organized through the acting individual. If this view is basically correct, as I hold it to be, the priority which Derrida gives to writing over speech has to be questioned. For speech – or rather talk – recovers a priority over other media of signification. Talk, carried on in day-to-day contexts of activity, is the fundamental 'carrier' of signification, because it operates in saturated behavioural and conceptual contexts. Writing (in its more narrow conventional sense) has certain distinctive properties that can be precisely explicated only by contrasting them with the character of day-to-day talk. The constitution of meaning in such talk is the condition, moreover, of the signifying properties of writing and texts.

Derrida's emphasis upon writing informs a whole philosophy. But there are three other, more modest, senses in which a preoccupation with writing tends to be generated by structuralist and post-structuralist traditions. One concerns the link between writing and power. In both Lévi-Strauss and Foucault, this theme is explored through the relation between orality and writing. Lévi-Strauss's structuralist method is supposed to apply only to oral cultures. Societies without writing are 'cold cultures' because they exist within a framework of reiterated tradition, passed on by example and by word of mouth. Civilizations presume the existence of writing, which is first and foremost a medium of administrative power, not simply a novel way of expressing what was previously formulated in speech. Writing not only generates 'history', it demands new modes of adjustment to both the social and the material world. Society and nature come to be seen in terms of dynamism and transformation, no longer in terms of the saturation of the present by the past. In Lévi-Strauss's work, this theme is never developed in any detail, since he does not offer an analysis of civilizations. Rather, societies with writing form a backdrop against which the distinctive characteristics of oral cultures can more easily be pin-pointed.

In Foucault, a concern with the links between writing, orality and power is more direct and more extensively spelled out. Foucault shows that the discourse of the social sciences and psychiatry does not simply form a set of theories and findings about a 'given' subject-matter. On the contrary, the concepts and generalizations developed in these disciplines come to constitute new fields for the operation of power. Such fields of power are codified through and dependent upon writing. The keeping of written records – as for example in the recording of the proceedings of law courts or of psychiatric case histories – is integral to the forms of disciplinary organization which Foucault seeks to analyse.

At the same time as, through the recording of events, writing 'makes history', those whose activities do not come to the attention of the record-keepers are excluded from 'history'. That is to say, that while of course their activities comprise 'history' in the sense of the elapsing of events, neither their actions nor their ideas form part of that reflexive appropriation of the past that is written history. Thus as Foucault points out in *I, Paul Rivière* (1978), the case record of the criminal or the vagrant is one of the few means that those not ordinarily written into history have of figuring in its field of discourse.

A second sense in which the theme of writing constantly recurs in structuralism and post-structuralism is simply in the guise of a fascination with texts generally. In formulating the outlines of a programme for semiology, Saussure initiated the possibility of a study of sign systems that goes well beyond textual materials. The call for the development of semiology was not ignored, and many subsequent works developed the idea that any cultural difference can provide a means of signification. But although the idea of a unified discipline of semiology, or semiotics, has its advocates, on the whole it has to be said that the study of cultural signs remains a rather stunted enterprise. Those influenced by structuralism and post-structuralism continue to return to the text as their main preoccupation. It is surely not by chance that these traditions of thought have had more influence in the field of literature than in any other domain.

The absorption with texts symbolizes some of the greatest strengths, and at the same time the most consistent weaknesses, of structuralist and post-structuralist traditions. On the one hand, it has allowed authors within these traditions to develop analyses that have no rivals in Anglo-Saxon philosophy. The theory of the text is both made central to certain elementary philosophical issues and elucidated through consideration of those issues. Apart from those within the relatively-specialized field of literary criticism, English-speaking philosophers and social theorists have made very little contribution to such discussion. On the other hand, the overriding concern with texts reflects limitations in accounts of the nature of signification that can be traced from Saussure onwards. The thesis of the arbitrary character of the sign, as Saussure developed it, tends to elide the difference between texts which claim to deliver some veridical description of the world and those that are fictional. The positive value of such an elision is readily demonstrated, for example, in the subtle treatments of the use of figurative mechanisms in scientific texts. Its weaknesses are apparent in respect of the basic issue that has haunted these traditions: how to relate the text back to an exterior world. Not only have structuralist and post-structuralist traditions failed to generate satisfactory accounts of reference that would make sense of scientific achievements, they have become more or less completely cut off from the study of ordinary talk. Ordinary talk is precisely that 'medium of living in the world' in which reference and meaning interlace. I believe such to be the case, at least, and I think that pursuing this issue allows us to come to terms with some of the most deep-seated deficiencies of structuralism and post-structuralism.

A third sense in which these traditions of thought tend to produce a concern with writing is in respect of writing as an active process. The term 'writing' is ambiguous, since it can refer to what is actually recorded in a given medium or to the actual process of bringing about that recording. In respect of the second of these meanings, writing has also come to take on a particular significance as the penning of books of imagination or invention. The 'writer', or literary author, tends to be accorded a special esteem in modern culture. In fastening upon the theme of the 'author', structuralists and post-structuralists have been able to make major contributions to our understanding of cultural production. Here, obviously, there is a major overlap with the more general theme of the decentring of the subject. The source of the 'creativity' displayed in texts is not to be discovered in the individual or individuals who wrote them. The text generates its own free play of signifiers, constantly open to appropriation and re-appropriation by different generations of readers. There are interesting connections here also between structuralism, post-structuralism and the latter-day development of hermeneutics. In the work of Gadamer and others, as I have mentioned previously, we also find an affirmation of the autonomy of the text from its author and an emphasis on the multiplicity of readings that texts can generate. The processes of writing and reading become closely intertwined, with reading viewed as the temporary stabilization of the indefinite range of meanings generated by processes of writing. But again we find characteristic weaknesses. Writing is sometimes portrayed as though texts wrote themselves; the relegation of the author to the role of a shadowy adjunct to writing is manifestly unsatisfactory. We can accept the significance of the theme of the decentring of the subject, and therefore the need to construct what an 'author' is. But we shall have no proper grasp of the process of writing unless we manage to recombine satisfactorily the elements that have been decentred. Structuralism and post-structuralism have in my view been unable to generate satisfactory accounts of human agency, in large part because of shortcomings that have already been noted, and this weakness reappears in the shape of the tendency to equate the production of texts with their inner 'productivity'.

History and Temporality

In Saussure's writings, it might seem as though the theme of temporality is thoroughly repressed. For after all, Saussure's greatest innovation was to treat *langue* as existing out of time. Whereas previous forms of linguistics had concentrated upon tracing changes in the usage of linguistic items,

Saussure placed language as a system at the forefront of linguistic analysis. *Langue* does not exist in a time-space context: it is built up inferentially from the actual practices of language users. Of course, Saussure did recognize a differentiation between the synchronic study involved in the analysis of *langue* and the diachronic analysis involved in tracing out actual changes in linguistic usage. Whether or not Saussure himself intended to give priority to synchrony over diachrony, it is certainly true that much of the subsequent attraction of his writings has concerned the diagnosis of properties of *langue*. Paradoxically, however, it is just this emphasis which has tended to stimulate a recurrent concern with temporality within structuralist and post-structuralist thought.

Some of the issues involved here are brought out rather clearly in the work of Lévi-Strauss. The methodological repression of time involved in Saussure's conception of *langue* is translated by Lévi-Strauss into the substantive repression of time involved in the codes organized through myth. Myths do not so much take temporality out of social life as provide for a particular mobilization of time separating it from what is later understood as 'history'. Lévi-Strauss's notion of reversible time is deliberately contrasted to the movement of time in history, where 'history' is understood as the linear charting of social change (Lévi-Strauss: 1966). As Lévi-Strauss has effectively emphasized in his debate with Sartre, a preoccupation with history is not necessarily the same thing as a concern with time. The Marxian adage that 'human beings make history' actually expresses the dynamism of a particular culture rather than representing a portrayal of the past existence of humanity as a whole. 'Hot' cultures exist in dynamic interchange with their environment, and mobilize themselves internally in the pursuit of social transformation. Modern culture very substantially accelerates this dynamism. History for us therefore becomes the linear unfolding of dates, within which certain forms of change are mapped out. Oral cultures are genuinely 'prehistoric' when contrasted to such dynamism. For them, time is not mobilized as history. The writing of history is thus associated with that very historicity which separates hot cultures from their oral forerunners.

While Lévi-Strauss's conception of the structures of the human mind has often been criticized for being unhistorical, it might be more accurate to see him as seeking to provide a subtle and nuanced account of what history is in relation to temporality. Lévi-Strauss has sometimes even been said to be 'anti-historical', but this surely fails to discern the subtlety with which his discussion contrasts time and history. Structuralism, in its Lévi-Straussian form, has certainly not proved to be refractory to history as some have claimed. Lévi-Strauss is effectively carrying out what Foucault was later to call an 'archaeology', digging below the historical consciousness of hot cultures to unearth the ground of temporality characterizing those forms of culture dominating human 'history'.

In Derrida, temporality of course appears as fundamental to the critique of the metaphysics of presence. To differ is also to defer, and time is regarded as inseparable from the nature of signification. The sliding of presence into absence becomes the very medium of understanding temporality. Here the concern is not so much with 'history', real or written, but with the understanding of being as becoming. Time is for Derrida bound up with the very nature of his appraisals of the limitations of structuralism as practised by Lévi-Strauss. It is intrinsically part of the process whereby signification generates a play of meanings (Culler: 1979). In replacing, in Culler's phrase, the 'anguish of infinite regress by the pleasure of infinite creation', Derrida affirms the evanescence of processes of meaning: everything should be understood 'as an active movement, a process of demotivating, rather than the structure given once and for all' (Derrida: 1981, p. 103). I have already criticized this view, but would add that the tendency to reduce time to the spacing of signification effectively precludes a satisfactory treatment of the time-space relations within which the signifying practices occur.

Foucault writes as a historian, and it is in his work above all that the themes of temporality and structural analysis are explored. Foucault's critique of 'continuous history' is in his view closely related to the necessity of decentring the subject. Not only does history have no overall teleology, it is in an important sense not the result of the action of human subjects. Human beings do not make history; rather, history makes human beings. That is, the nature of human subjectivity is formed in and through processes of historical development. Continuous history depends upon:

> the certainty that time will dispense nothing without restoring it in a reconstituted unity; the promise that one day the subject – in the form of historical consciousness – will once again be able to appropriate, to bring back under its sway, all those things that are kept at a distance by difference, and find in them what might be called its abode. (Foucault: 1973, p. 12)

Foucault's style of writing history, therefore, does not flow along with chronological time. Nor does it depend upon the narrative description of a sequence of events. Reading Foucault is an uncomfortable experience for those accustomed to more orthodox modes of writing history. Topics are not discussed in a temporal order and there are breaks in the description when the reader expects continuity. Very little indication is given of whatever causal influences might be at work in the shifts or changes which Foucault analyses. Obscure though his epistemological reflections might often be, Foucault makes it clear enough that this historical style derives from a particular view both of time and of the historical nature of writing about history. The past is not an area of study formed by the secretion of time. If the elapsing of past time has any form at all, it is that of the interweaving of layers of epistemic organization, layers which need to be unearthed by means of 'archaeology'. There is more than an echo of Lévi-Strauss in Foucault's view that history is one form of knowledge among others – and of course, like other forms of knowledge, a mode of mobilizing power.

To have separated time from history, to have shown that there are properties of signification systems that exist outside time-space, and to have connected these with a re-examination of the nature of the human subject – these are major achievements of structuralism and post-structuralism. But in these respects, as in the others previously discussed, the results are not completely satisfying. Foucault's manner of writing history has a definite shock value. But in spite of his elaborate methodological discussions, the mode in which he practises history remains highly idiosyncratic. No real unification is achieved between the diagnosis of epistemes as existing 'out of time' and the generative processes involved in historical organization and change. Having decentred the subject, Foucault is no more able to develop a cogent account of human agency than are other writers in structuralist and post-structuralist traditions. That 'history has no subject' can readily be accepted. But Foucault's history tends to have no active subjects at all. It is history with the agency removed. The individuals who appear in Foucault's analyses seem impotent to determine their own destinies. Moreover, that reflexive appropriation of history basic to history in modern culture does not appear at the level of the agents themselves. The historian is a reflective being, aware of the influence of the writing of history upon the determination of the present. But this quality of self-understanding is seemingly not extended to historical agents themselves.

Signification, Cultural Production and Writing

A theory of cultural production cannot be properly developed unless we possess an adequate account of the nature of human agents. In demanding a 'theory of the subject' in place of the presumption that subjectivity is the unmediated ground of experience, structuralism and post-structuralism have made a major contribution, albeit one which is not unique to these traditions of thought. But it is essential to insist upon the need for an interpretation of the agent rather than the subject, and of agency rather than subjectivity alone. 'Subjects' are first and foremost agents. In explicating human agency, two elements which tend to be either lacking or downplayed in structuralist accounts need to be brought to the fore. One is what I have elsewhere called 'practical consciousness', the other is the contextuality of action. Structuralist thinking tends to operate in terms of a contrast between the conscious and the unconscious. For Lévi-Strauss and Lacan, the unconscious is the 'other face' of language. It is what cannot be said in words, but makes such saying possible. Now, we may agree that a concept of the unconscious is necessary in providing a comprehensive account of why human agents act as they do. We may also accept that the relation between what can and what cannot be put into words is of elementary significance in human activity. However, if, unlike structuralism and post-structuralism, we seek to grasp human life within frameworks of practical action, we reach a different view from that characteristic of these schools of thought. What cannot be put into words, as Wittgenstein proposes, is what has to be *done*. Human action does not unfold as the result of programmed impulses. Rather, human beings reflexively monitor what they do as an intrinsic part of what it is that they do. Such monitoring is ordinarily not expressed discursively. It is carried on at the level of practical consciousness. It is none the less extraordinarily elaborate and is a chronic feature of even the most trivial of human activities.

In speaking of the contextuality of action, I mean to rework the differentiation between presence and absence. Human social life may be understood in terms of relations between individuals 'moving' in time-space, linking both action and context, and differing contexts, with one another. Contexts form 'settings' of action, whose qualities agents routinely draw upon in the course of orienting what they do and what they say to one another (Giddens: 1984, ch. 1). Common awareness of these settings of action forms an anchoring element in the 'mutual knowledge' whereby agents make sense of what others say and do. Context should not be identified with what makes a particular segment of action idiosyncratic. Settings of action and interaction, distributed across time-space and reproduced in the 'reversible time' of day-to-day activities, are integral to the structured form which both social life and language possess.

In this view, signification is presumed to be saturated in the settings of practical action. The meanings engendered within language would not exist were it not for the situated, yet reproduced, nature of social practices. Timing and spacing are basic to the generation and sustaining of meaning, both in the ordering of settings and in the reflexive use of such settings to formulate verbal interchange. Rather than 'speech', which sounds formal, we should refer here to 'talk'. Talk, the casual exchange of conversation in the settings of day-to-day social life, is the grounding of all the more elaborate and formalized aspects of language-use – or so I want to argue here. Talk, as Garfinkel has done more than anyone else to show, operates through the indexicality of context and through the 'methodological devices' which agents use to produce a 'meaningful' social world (Garfinkel: 1984). Indexicality should not be identified with context-dependence. Such an identification was one of the main problems facing the early elaboration of ethnomethodological studies. Indexicality refers just as much to the use of setting in order to produce context-freedom as it does to the use of items specific to a particular time and place in the generation of meaning. The fact that meaning is produced and sustained through the use of methodological devices is fundamental to correcting the lapses of structuralism and post-structuralism. Meaning is not built into the codes or sets of differences associated with *langue*. The use of 'et cetera' clauses, formulating and other methodological devices, organizes meaning contextually. A competent language user has not merely mastered sets of syntactical and semantic rules, but the gamut of conventions involved in 'going on' in day-to-day contexts of social activity.

Cultural analysis focuses on the relation between discourse and what I shall henceforth call 'cultural objects'. By cultural objects, I mean artifacts which escape from contexts of presence/state but which are distinct from

objects generally in so far as they incorporate 'extended' forms of signification. Texts are the principal type of cultural object in this definition;
however in modern times we have to add media of electronic communication.
There are definite ways in which cultural objects contrast with the 'carrying'
of language as talk. We can enumerate these characteristics as follows.

1   Cultural objects involve a distancing of 'producer' from 'consumer'.
This quality is shared with all material artifacts. All artifacts, not just
cultural objects, involve a process of 'interpretation' in some part distinct
from that implied in the monitoring of talk in contexts of co-presence.
In ordinary talk, individuals routinely employ a diversity of aspects of
setting in order to understand others and to 'gear' what they themselves
say to such a process of understanding. The interpretation of cultural
objects occurs without certain elements of the mutual knowledge involved
in co-presence within a setting, and without the coordinated monitoring
which co-present individuals carry out as part of ongoing talk.
2   As a consequence of this, the 'consumer' or receiver becomes more
important than the producer in the interpretative process. In contexts of
co-presence, the production and interpretation of speech acts tend to be
closely intertwined, as part of the serial and participatory nature of
conversation.
3   Cultural objects, as distinct from artifacts in general, involve the
following characteristics.

(a) *A durable medium of transmission across contexts.* 'Medium' should be
    taken to refer both to the physical substance of the cultural object
    and to the means of its dissemination across different contexts.
(b) *A means of storage.* In the case of cultural objects this involves *encoding*.
    'Storage' means here the leaving of traces whereby information can
    be 'rescued' from the evanescence of talk. Information cannot be
    stored as material resources can be stored. Information is stored –
    just as structuralist and post-structuralists state – as the specification
    of differences. 'Encoding' refers to the ordered properties of differences
    between traces.
(c) *A means of retrieval.* To retrieve information is to have a mastery of
    the forms of encoding it incorporates. Retrieval presumes a human
    agent who possesses certain skills such as literacy. It may also, at
    least in modern times, involve the use of mechanical devices without
    which access to the encoded material is unavailable.

The nature of cultural objects can only be understood in relation to talk.
It is accepted by everyone that there is a close relation between culture,
language and communication. According to the foregoing observations, this
relation should be understood in terms of the basic role which talk, in
contexts of practical action and co-presence, plays in the generation and

sustaining of meaning. Language is a means of communication, but communication is not the 'objective' of talk. Rather talk expresses, and is expressed in, the variegated range of activities which it informs. The significance of cultural or informational objects is that they introduce new mediations between culture, language and communication. In talk, the agent and the setting are the means whereby culture is linked to communication. In contexts of practical action, communication through talk always has to be 'worked upon' by participants, although most of such 'work' is done routinely as part of the process of reflexive monitoring in practical monitoring. Cultural objects break this symmetry. Since language as 'carried' by cultural objects is no longer talk, it loses its saturation in the referential properties which language-use has in the contexts of day-to-day action. As a visible or recoverable trace, separated from the immediacy of contexts of talk, the signifier becomes of peculiar significance. The preoccupation of structuralism and post-structuralism with writing and with the signifier at the expense of the signified can surely be traced to this. The differentiation of the signifier from practical contexts of action at the same time places a new premium upon communication, as a result of the greater effort at interpretation that is necessary. Communication is no longer more or less taken for granted as a result of the methodological processes involved in the sustaining of conversations. More defined and explicit hermeneutic tasks have to be undertaken in order to forge the communicative link between the cultural object and its interpreter. Given that this is so, it is not surprising that as a formal discipline hermeneutics arose from difficulties involved in the interpretation of texts. If a hermeneutic element has never been particularly pronounced in structuralism or post-structuralism, it is because signification has been primarily dealt with in terms of the internal organization of codes, or as the play of signifiers, rather than as the 'recovery of meaning'.

What is writing, and how far does writing itself contribute to the autonomy of texts? What relation, if any, do authors' intentions in writing texts have to the interpretation subsequently made of them? Should a 'theory of text' essentially be a theory of reading? These are all questions that have to be confronted in the wake of the impact of structuralism and post-structuralism, which has at a minimum compelled us to look at them in a new way.

We cannot best explicate what language or signification are through writing. In this, Derrida is wrong. We should assert the priority not of speech, but of talk, over writing. But this should not lead us to suppose that writing is simply a 'representation' of talk. For reasons already mentioned, it cannot be so. Just as the invention of writing introduced something new into history, the production of texts involves qualities distinct from those carried within day-to-day talk. The origins of writing are certainly relevant to grasping its generic significance. Writing did not first of all emerge as a means of describing objects or events in the world. Writing was originally purely a mode of recording – storage in its pure form. In the early agrarian states, writing was an administrative device, making possible the coordination of material resources and human action across time and space. Writing was never therefore a 'translation' of the verbal into the visual. It signalled and expressed new modes of the coordination of activities in time-space. The earliest texts – lists, collations of items – have no author. More important than the people who produced them is who they were produced *for* and what uses were made of them (Giddens: 1981).

This strongly suggests that writing diverges from talk not just in terms of the intrinsic characteristics of each, but in terms of the broader forms of social organization in which each is involved. Writing in a certain sense gives a primacy to 'spacing' over 'timing' that is absent in talk. This is surely more important than the simple fact that writing is visual and talk is auditory. Talk (contrary to Saussure's view) is sequential and serial, rather than linear. Writing has no temporal differentiation, although obviously such differentiation is involved in any process of the reading of a text. The spatial order of writing, on the other hand, since it is 'out of time' does not impose upon the reader the same constraints of sequencing which are involved in talk. That is to say, the reader need not follow a text straight through, but can look at the end before the beginning, and so on.

Once it proceeds beyond simple listing, writing opens itself out to 'art' in ways in which talk does not. Even the most trivial forms of day-to-day talk involve immense skill and presume a great deal of learning. Talk can become art in the sense in which particular forms of convention or contrivance may be employed to secure certain expressive or communicative ends. Story-telling, displays of wit, rhetoric and drama exist in all types of society. The 'success' of these verbal forms, however, is directly involved with their performance in contexts of co-presence. Conceived of as a process of production, rather than as of a given form, writing as art has rather different characteristics. Writing is not a performance to an audience. The skills of a writer do not depend upon his or her capability to employ the qualities available in contexts of co-presence to influence others in desired ways. Talk is necessarily an individualized production, moreover, in a manner in which writing is not. Speech has a serial character, because only one speaker can talk at any particular time in a given context of co-presence. In the case of writing, it is usually irrelevant to any of the terms in which the 'success' of a text might be judged whether one individual or many were involved in its production. Texts of any length have to be produced across periods of time, which may be very prolonged. While 'work' goes into the construction of meaning in even the most casual of conversations, a text tends to be a 'work' in a more protracted sense. It is a 'labour', in which discipline and originality may commingle in the fashioning of the spacing of writing.

Ordinary language is 'open' in an important sense. Most of the words and phrases used in everyday talk do not have precise lexical definitions. But as Wittgenstein showed, ordinary language is not thereby necessarily vague or indefinite. What gives ordinary language its precision is its use in context. Settings of talk are used by participants to define the nature of what is said. The openness of writing is rather different – something which may be obscured by the fact that similar linguistic forms, such as metaphor and metonymy, may be used in both talk and writing. The openness of writing derives from the 'suspension' of reference involved in it. We have to be careful to specify what this means. Writing can be and more often than not is used to refer to objects and events in the world. This is very obviously the case, for example, in respect of a list. The referential properties of writing do not depend – although they are always parasitic upon – the referential qualities of talk. Meaning and reference are ordinarily closely combined in talk, not because talk is in any way primarily oriented toward description, but because it is carried on and organized within practical contexts of action. That is to say, meaning is sustained through the constant connecting of talk with the modalities of day-to-day experience. The referential properties of writing cannot be connected with settings in this way. Consequently, even the most bluntly and coldly referential of statements can be read rhetorically or figuratively, and vice versa. As examples of Japanese *haiku* demonstrate, if demonstration is needed, a list may very readily be read as a poem.

All these considerations are relevant to the question of the autonomy of texts. The traditional issue of how far a text can be understood without reference to the intentions of its author is one which can be approached both in the light of these considerations and in light of the account of agency indicated earlier. Agents, as Schütz puts it, have overall projects in terms of which the intentionality of their activities is organized (Schütz: 1972). The writing of a text may involve just such a project or projects. That is, an author will have a certain range of objectives in mind in producing a given text. However, these are unlikely to be as relevant to the understanding of a text as to the process of reflexive monitoring involved in the labour that goes into the text's construction. A text, to repeat, is a 'work' in the sense that it involves a chronic process of 'monitored' production. An 'author' is therefore neither an amalgam of intentions, nor a series of deposits or traces left in the text. Rather, the author is a producer working in specific settings of practical action.

This does not resolve the issue that has polarized discussion of the nature of texts, the question of how far there is a 'correct' interpretation of a text which can be fixed in relation to the intentions of its author. As against 'textual relativism', Hirsch and others have argued that the author's intention provides a basis for recovering the original meaning of a text. Now 'intention' here can only be understood as 'project' in Schütz's sense. But we can easily see that the projects which lead an author to produce a text are likely to be only marginally relevant to anyone reading that text. Authors may choose to write a given text for a range of particular motives to gain fame, to make money, for self-satisfaction, and so on. Moreover, it does not make much sense to ask what a text as a whole 'means'. We are much more likely to ask what an author meant by a particular sentence or paragraph, or what arguments are threaded through a text, than we are to ask what a text as a whole means: this is entirely consonant with the way in which we deploy the phrase 'what did you mean?' in day-to-day talk. When we examine this type of question, as addressed to texts, it is fairly clear that nothing is being asked about the particular producer. If one were to ask, 'what did Marx mean by such-and-such a section of *Capital*?', Marx's characteristics as an individual are unlikely to be invoked. We could in most cases replace this query with the more anonymous question, 'what did the author mean?' In ordinary talk, when we ask 'what did *x* mean by that?', probably we most usually mean 'what did he or she mean to accomplish by saying *x*?' That is, we address the issue of the illocutionary force of what is said. But the question might also imply 'what did he or she mean to communicate?' 'Meaning' in this sense implies, as Grice says, that the speaker 'intended the utterance *x* to produce an effect upon another or others by means of their recognising this to be his intention' (Grice: 1957; see also Grice: 1982). 'Meaning' here equals communicative intent and it can be shown that such intent can be discerned only when participants in a given context of interaction share forms of mutual knowledge. In ordinary talk, communicative intent can be checked by direct interrogation and by reformulation on the part of the original speaker. There seems no reason to deny that we can interrogate a text in like manner. That is, we can ask what was the communicative intent involved in a given section of a text. Where the author is unavailable, we can seek to answer such a question by investigating the forms of mutual knowledge implied in what the author wrote. This entails in turn that there are criteria for the accuracy of interpretations.

But these criteria, and the types of material that must be known to confirm them, are complicated. They essentially involve enquiring into the settings of production of the text as a work. They mean knowing a good deal about the way in which the author set out to produce the text and the intellectual resources drawn upon in its production. But they also involve knowing about the audience to whom the text was primarily addressed. Skinner and others have quite rightly pointed to the significance of this latter emphasis, which does not in any way deny the inherent autonomy of texts (Skinner: 1969). Texts are written within various conventions of form, style and readership. 'How' the reader is to take the text is 'worked upon' by the author in its production.

Structuralist and post-structuralist discussions of the 'disappearance of the author' have been valuable in several respects. We are led to recognize that many texts do not have 'authors' in the sense in which most of the works discussed in modern literary criticism do. This is not just true of texts written in the pre-modern period – biblical texts, sagas, archives, and so on. It is also true of the vast majority of texts which circulate in modern societies. Records, files, case histories, bills – these characteristically do not have authors, in the sense that they are not attributed to one individual, may indeed be the product of several hands, and no one thinks it worthwhile ordinarily to enquire into which specific individuals produced them. It is obvious enough that the conditions of their production as texts have to be grasped both in relation to characteristics shared with artefacts in general and in terms of features of writing previously discussed. All artefacts which have a durable character can become more or less completely separated both from the contexts of their initial production and from the projects of those who created them. All artifacts similarly may be put to purposes, or even 'interpreted', in ways of which their producers may never have dreamed. All texts turn the openness of language away from the modes in which, in talk, closure and fixity are achieved. How open to multiple interpretations a text is probably has little to do with the intrinsic nature of the text itself. Here we have to make the transition to an account of the readings which texts may help to engender. Most of the observations made about understanding the production of texts in relation to the reflexive monitoring of action also apply to reading. No text is read in isolation; all reading occurs within frameworks of 'intertextuality' as well as in settings that involve drawing upon mutual knowledge. Several recent approaches, that only partly if at all derive from structuralism and post-structuralism, are promising in respect of developing accounts of reading. An example is Jauss's 'reception aesthetics' (Jauss: 1974). In this view, a reader approaches a text with a 'horizon of expectations' without which the text would make no sense. According to Jauss, understanding the relation between works and their readers involves answering several questions. We must know what readers understand of the particular genre within which the work is written. We have to know about the reader's knowledge of previous texts similar to the one in question. And we must have a sense of the differentiation between practical talk and poetic language, something likely to shift between different places and different cultural settings. Since all authors are also presumably readers, such discussion has to be closely integrated with explication of the production of texts.

Conclusion

I make no claim in this analysis to have covered all the significant themes raised by the traditions of structuralism and post-structuralism. There are many divergencies between the ideas of the authors to whom I have referred which I have simply ignored or glossed over. I have sought to portray the contributions of structuralism and post-structuralism in broad strokes, in order to suggest some general questions which they raise for social theory today. No doubt the assertion that these traditions have proved incapable of handling the very issues they have brought to the fore is contentious. I hope, however, both to have justified this allegation and to have shown how some of those issues might more satisfactorily be analysed.

Bibliography

Barthes, R., 1977: 'The Death of the Author', in *Image-Music-Text*. Glasgow: Fontana.
Benveniste, E., 1971: 'The Nature of the Linguistic Sign', in *Problems in General Linguistics*. Florida: University of Miami Press.
Bloomfield, M., 1957: *Language*. London: George Allen and Unwin.
Chomsky, N., 1964: *Current Issues in Linguistic Theory*. The Hague: Mouton.
    1968: *Language and Mind*. New York: Harcourt, Brace.
Clarke, S., 1981: *The Foundations of Structuralism*. Sussex: Harvester.
Culler, J., 1975: *Structuralist Poetics*. London: Routledge and Kegan Paul.
    1979: 'Jacques Derrida', in J. Sturrock (ed.), *Structuralism and Since*. Oxford: Oxford University Press.
Derrida, J., 1976: *Of Grammatology*. Baltimore: Johns Hopkins University Press.
    1978: *Writing and Difference*. London: Routledge and Kegan Paul.
    1981: *Positions*. London: Athlone.
Foucault, M., 1972: *The Archaeology of Knowledge*. New York: Pantheon.
    1978: *I, Pierre Rivière: A Case of Patricide in the 19th Century*. Harmondsworth, Middlesex: Penguin.
Gadamer, H., 1975: *Truth and Method*. London: Sheed and Ward.
Garfinkel, H., 1984: *Studies in Ethnomethodology*. Cambridge, England: Polity Press.
Giddens, A., 1979: *Central Problems in Social Theory*. London: Macmillan.
    1981: *A Contemporary Critique of Historical Materialism*, vol. 1. London: Macmillan.
    1984: *The Constitution of Society*. Cambridge, England: Polity Press.
Grice, H. P., 1957: 'Meaning', *Philosophical Review*, 66.
    1982: 'Meaning Revisited', in N. V. Smith (ed.), *Mutual Knowledge*. London: Academic Press.
Harris, Z., 1951: *Methods in Structural Linguistics*. Chicago: University of Chicago Press.
Heidegger, M., 1978: *Being and Time*. Oxford: Basil Blackwell.
Hymes, D. H., 1972: 'On Communicative Competence', in J. B. Pride and J. Holmes (eds), *Sociolinguistics*. Harmondsworth, Middlesex: Penguin.
Jakobson, R., 1971: *Word and Language*. The Hague: Mouton.
Jauss, H. R., 1974: 'Literary History as a Challenge to Literary Theory', in R. Cohen (ed.), *New Directions in Literary Theory*. Baltimore: Johns Hopkins University Press.
Lacan, J., 1977: *Écrits*. London: Tavistock.
Lévi-Strauss, C., 1966: *The Savage Mind*. Chicago: University of Chicago Press.
    1968: *Structural Anthropology*. London: Allen Lane.
    1969a: *The Elementary Structures of Kinship*. London: Eyre and Spottiswoode.
    1969b: *The Raw and the Cooked*. London: Cape.
    1971: *L'homme nu*. Paris: Plon.
Runciman, W. G., 1970: 'What is Structuralism?', in *Sociology in its Place*. Cambridge, England: Cambridge University Press.
Saussure, F. de, 1974: *Course in General Linguistics*. London: Fontana.
Schütz, A., 1972: *The Phenomenology of the Social World*. London: Heinemann.
Skinner, Q., 1969: 'Meaning and Understanding in the History of Ideas', *History and Theory*, 8: pp. 3–53.

Trubetzkoy, N., 1969: *Principles of Phonology*. Berkeley and Los Angeles: University of California Press.

Wittgenstein, L., 1953: *Philosophical Investigations*. Oxford: Basil Blackwell.

Ethnomethodology[1]

JOHN C. HERITAGE

With the first publication in 1967 of Harold Garfinkel's *Studies in Ethnomethodology* (1984) a new and distinctive approach to sociological analysis emerged into the public domain. The new perspective rapidly gained adherents and stimulated an increasingly diverse and influential range of empirical work. But, although Garfinkel's writings were immediately recognized as significant,[2] ethnomethodology did not find a ready or full-hearted acceptance within the sociological community. Indeed it might be said of Garfinkel that, like Durkheim before him, his ideas have been paid 'the tribute of unrelenting criticism'.[3] The initial responses to ethnomethodology contained a variety of objections, many of which were strongly incompatible with one another, and the result was a period in which discussions of the new perspective were apt to generate more heat than light.

A number of factors contributed towards this outcome. Garfinkel's writings are highly compressed and, at times, opaque and cryptic. Although they contain powerful underlying theoretical continuities, these are not systematically articulated in terms of classical sociological reference points. There has thus been scope for considerable confusion and misunderstanding among adherents as well as detractors of the enterprise. Moreover *Studies in Ethnomethodology* emerged during a period of chaotic upheaval in the social sciences in which the previously dominant Parsonian structural-functional

[1] I would like to thank Tom Wilson for his valuable comments on an earlier draft of this paper.

[2] The significance of *Studies in Ethnomethodology* was clearly recognized by the allocation of a three-part review symposium to it by the *American Sociological Review* (see Swanson, Wallace and Coleman: 1968).

[3] The phrase is Steven Lukes's (Lukes: 1973, p. 2). The parallels with the reception of Durkheim's work are surprisingly extensive. Like Durkheimian sociology, ethnomethodology has been critically represented as embodying almost every conceivable political persuasion, as expressing an immense variety of (often diametrically opposed) conceptual standpoints and as advocating conceptions every bit as absurd as that of the 'group mind' with which Durkheim was arraigned at the beginning of this century (cf. Lukes: 1973, pp. 2–3, 497ff.).

paradigm was an early sociological casualty. Because Garfinkel's complex writings became public property at this moment of rapid and confusing theoretical change, his seminal theorizing and extraordinary empirical investigations were often misrepresented and trivialized.[4] The unhappy consequence was that ethnomethodology came to be construed as 'a method without a substance' (Coser: 1975) or, worse still, as a vehicle for the denial of social organization itself – a kind of 'anything goes' sociology. The inevitable outcome was that Garfinkel's investigations, whose initial impetus derived from a most penetrating critique of the Parsonian corpus which had been undertaken long before the tide had turned against structural-functionalism, were lost in the welter of charge and counter-charge. Small wonder then that Garfinkel, who disdained to intervene in the fray, declared early on that the very term 'ethnomethodology' had become a shibboleth that had acquired a life of its own (Garfinkel: 1974, p. 18).

Garfinkel's lifelong theoretical endeavours have been directed at a range of conceptual issues which have always been central topics of sociology. These issues – the theory of social action, the nature of intersubjectivity and the social constitution of knowledge – are complex and tightly interwoven. Because the conceptual formulation of these issues has wide theoretical and methodological ramifications in the conceptualization of social organization, they represent a central site of theoretical innovation within the discipline. Garfinkel has approached this domain through a persistent series of explorations of the elementary properties of practical reasoning and practical actions. In the course of these studies, he has sought to divorce the theory of action from its traditional preoccupation with motivational issues and to recentre it on the knowledgeable ways in which, whether consciously or not,[5] social actors recognize, produce and reproduce social

---

[4] Anthony Giddens's writings (Giddens 1976; 1979; 1984) have been a consistent exception to the generally negative tone of response to ethnomethodology. A widespread pattern of misinterpretation of the field was concretized by an apparently authoritative, but highly misleading, paper by Attewell (1972) (see Peyrot: 1982; Zimmerman: 1976 for clear critical discussions of this source). Attewell's paper embodied many of the misunderstandings which subsequently reappeared in articles by, among others, Coser (1975), Mayrl (1973), McSweeney (1973), Mennell (1976) and Phillips (1978). By the end of the 1970s the climate of misunderstanding was so densely developed that sophisticated interventions such as that by O'Keefe (1979) did not succeed in clearing the air. Useful efforts at clarification by practising ethnomethodologists include Coulter (1971; 1973; 1974), Maynard and Wilson (1980), Peyrot (1982), Wieder (1977), Wilson and Zimmerman (1979) and Zimmerman (1976; 1978). Monograph-length secondary accounts of ethnomethodology now include Benson and Hughes (1983), Handel (1982), Heritage (1984a), Leiter (1980), Mehan and Wood (1975) and Sharrock and Anderson (1986).

[5] There are, of course, many levels of 'consciousness' with respect to the organization of everyday life. Moreover an actor may be consciously oriented to a phenomenon without being able to formulate the object of orientation in so many words. Garfinkel uses the term 'seen but unnoticed' to refer to orientation without conscious awareness to aspects of social organization.

actions and social structures. This stress on the knowledgeability of actors, however, places a new premium on uncovering the ways in which social actors analyse their circumstances and can share an intersubjective under-standing of them. Here Garfinkel's researches came to focus on the unavoid-ably contextual character of ordinary understandings and with this focus came an appreciation of the extraordinarily complex and detailed ways in which the contexts of events furnish resources for their interpretation.

The new approach additionally required that the analyses of action and knowledge be fully integrated with one another. This integration was achieved by Garfinkel's replacement of the prevailing motivational approach to the analysis of social action with a *procedural* approach to the topic and was programmatically summarized in his primary recommendation that 'the activities whereby members produce and manage settings of organized everyday affairs are identical with members' procedures for making those settings "account-able"' (Garfinkel: 1984a, p. 1). From this basis, it became possible to address the practices and process of specific social institutions in a new way and to open up new attitudes to processes of linguistic communication. And, still more broadly, it became possible to gain a new understanding and treatment of people's subscription to, and grasp of, the socially accountable realities in which they are enmeshed.

It is these topics which have provided a substantial measure of the substance of the work done by Garfinkel and his collaborators. The results of this work constitute a most profound and challenging re-orientation of these fundamental aspects of sociological theory and one, moreover, which has issued in a strong programme of empirical inquiry. The aim of this chapter is to situate Garfinkel's theoretical researches by references to the context of social theory out of which they emerged, to give an account of the main ways in which his thinking has led to a reconceptualization of the nature of social action and social organization and to outline some of the main kinds of empirical research that have emerged as a result of his initiatives.

Re-thinking the Theory of Action

Between 1946 and 1952 Garfinkel trained as a sociologist under the super-vision of Talcott Parsons. In 1946 Parsons had assumed the chair of the newly formed Department of Social Relations at Harvard University and his leadership stimulated a concerted effort to forward the development of systematic sociological theory. The goal was to link the disciplines of psy-chology, sociology and anthropology within a single overarching theoretical framework which had been sketched out in *The Structure of Social Action* (Parsons: 1937) as the 'voluntaristic theory of action'. The results of this effort were to be highly influential. Notwithstanding piecemeal criticisms of the Parsonian theoretical edifice, it came to dominate English-speaking sociological theory for the two decades following the Second World War. It was in this highly-charged theoretical atmosphere that Garfinkel developed a critique of the new theoretical framework at the very moment it was emerging from the Harvard department. The critique struck at the deepest presuppositions of the Parsonian corpus and has, in effect, taken nearly thirty years to surface in contemporary discussions of social theory.

The Parsonian theory of action which Garfinkel encountered during his years at Harvard was essentially a theory of the motivation of action and was dominated by two fundamental preoccupations. The first is that human life is not to be understood as merely a matter of passive adaptation to environmental pressures. On the contrary, it is a central feature of human society and history that ordinary men and women engage in costly striving to realize goals – often of a non-materal kind – in the face of powerful obstacles. This first preoccupation – Parsons's 'voluntaristic metaphysic' (Procter: 1978; Scott: 1963) – is one which stresses the subjective direction of effort in the pursuit of normatively-valued ends. Parsons's second preoccupation was derived from Hobbes's famous discussion of chaos in the 'state of nature'. The Hobbesian 'problem of order', as Parsons formulated it, raises the question of how the active strivings of social actors can be reconciled with one another in such a way that social relations will not be dominated by the exercise of force and fraud (Parsons: 1937, p. 92). In theoretical terms, then, the motivational question which dominates the Parsonian theory of action is how to allow for social actors who actively pursue a range of ends while simultaneously providing for a mechanism that avoids the problem of order posed by Hobbes.

As is well known, Parsons's solution, although expressed as the outcome of the famous 'convergence' among the European social theorists, was essentially derived from Durkheim. It embodied the proposal that moral values which are internalized during the course of socialization can exert a powerful influence, both on the ends of action and on the means by which these ends are sought. To the extent to which these values are institutionalized within a society – ultimately, in the form of a central value system – social cohesion will emerge in the sharing of goals and expectations and hence as patterns of coordinated activity.[6]

These proposals were fleshed out, in subsequent publications from the Harvard department, with the now-familiar tripartite analytical division of social organization into cultural, social and personality systems; the conception of institutional role requirements specified in terms of the 'pattern variables'; the internalization of values as the motivating 'need-dispositions'

---

[6] As Parsons and Shils put it in 1951, 'institutionalization itself must be regarded as the fundamental integrative mechanism of social systems. It is through internalization of common patterns of value orientation that a system of social interaction can be stabilized (Parsons and Shils: 1951, p. 150).

of the personality system; and the famous discussion of the 'double contingency' of social interaction with its 'two-fold binding-in processes'.[7]

It is striking that, while critics have argued variously that Parsons tended to over-estimate the extent to which normative consensus is an empirical characteristic of societies (Dahrendorf: 1958; Gouldner: 1970), that social integration is not to be confused with system integration (Lockwood: 1964) and that other motivational factors should be given more weight in the analysis of social action (Wrong: 1961), the basic emphasis of Parsonian theory on the motivational aspects of action has remained virtually unchallenged.[8] Yet Parsons had emphasized motivational issues virtually to the exclusion of any concern with the understandings in terms of which social actors coordinate their actions and guide them over their course. In this critical sense, Parsons had failed to construct a theory of *action* at all but had, instead, constructed only a theory of dispositions to act. Central to any genuine analysis of social action is a conceptualization of the knowledge which the actors bring to bear on their circumstances.[9] This requires solutions to questions concerning the nature and properties of the knowledge which it is appropriate to attribute to social actors, and of how that knowledge is employed by them and is to be analytically treated within the theory of action. And it was on these crucial issues that Garfinkel came, during the immediate post-war period, to depart from the Parsonian viewpoint in a most fundamental way.

In Parsons's writings, the issue of the actor's knowledge is generally given relatively little emphasis but it none the less exerts a profound underlying influence on his theorizing through the medium of his discussion of rationality.[10] For Parsons, the actor's rationality is determined by assessing the extent to which the actor's actions are based on the application of a knowledge base which is compatible with scientific knowledge (Parsons: 1937, p. 58). Where such compatibility is present, the action will be judged as 'intrinsically rational' and the actor's explanation of the action – in being consistent with a scientific explanation of it – must necessarily be counted as scientifically adequate.

---

[7] As Parsons summarized the overall claim, 'the integration of a set of common value patterns with the internalized need-disposition structure of the constituent personalities is the core phenomenon of the dynamics of social systems. That the stability of any social system except the most evanescent interaction process is dependent on a degree of such integration may be said to be the fundamental dynamic theorem of sociology' (Parsons: 1951, p. 42).

[8] In part, this was because the theory united major strands of the styles of sociological and psychological theorizing which have prevailed well into the post-war period. Indeed Parsons repeatedly noted the convergence of Durkheim and Freud on the phenomenon of internalization in support of his claims.

[9] This position has also recently been strongly urged by Giddens (see, e.g., Giddens: 1979, pp. 253–4).

[10] Cf. Garfinkel (1952, pp. 91ff.; 1984h) and Heritage (1984a, pp. 22–33) for discussion of this issue.

In the majority of cases, however, actors' explanations of their actions will not coincide with the scientist's and in these cases, Parsons proposes, the actors' explanations may be discounted. In these instances a scientific explanation of the actors' actions will be couched in terms of the motivating role of internalized norms and values. A radical gulf is thus created between rational actions with their self-subsistent reasons and non-rational actions in which the actors' reasoning is discounted in favour of causal normative explanations of conduct. This gulf is compounded by Parsons's repeatedly expressed view (e.g. Parsons: 1937, pp. 403–5; 1951, p. 37) that, if moral values are to be an effective prophylactic against Hobbesian chaos, the members of a social order will not be capable of an instrumental orientation toward the normative elements which they have internalized. For such an orientation could give rise to Machiavellian calculation which, if generalized, would undermine the moral constitution of society and leave social order dependent on unstable coalitions of interest. The cumulative effect of these provisions was to marginalize the knowledgeability of social actors to a remarkable degree and to treat the actors, in Garfinkel's memorable phrase, as 'judgemental dopes' (Garfinkel: 1984, p. 68) whose understanding and reasoning in concrete situations of action are irrelevant to an analytical approach to social action.[11]

In developing an alternative to Parsons's approach to the analysis of social action, Garfinkel drew extensively on the work of Alfred Schutz who, in a long series of theoretical writings, had created an unanswerable case for the inclusion of a treatment of the actors' knowledge within the theory of action. From his earliest writings, Schutz had stressed that the social world is interpreted in terms of common-sense categories and constructs which are largely social in origin. These constructs are the resources with which social actors interpret their situations of action, grasp the intentions and motivations of others, achieve intersubjective understandings and co-

---

[11] Garfinkel's (1952) critique of the Parsonian framework began from the theory of knowledge on which it was based. Parsons, he argued, had founded his analysis on a neo-Kantian epistemological framework ('analytic realism' – Parsons: 1937, pp. 730ff.) premised on the assumption that accurate knowledge of the external world is gained by the application of the logico-empirical canons of scientific inquiry through a process of successive approximation. The theory implies that successful social action is based on accurate knowledge and therefore obliges its proponents to account for the persistence of inadequate knowledge and non-rational action in a social world in which, *ex hypothesi*, the actors would be more successful if they adopted a more scientific standpoint. The voluntaristic theory, of course, met this requirement with a causal explanation of 'non-rational' actions couched, *inter alia*, in terms of normative dispositions. Two consequences flowed from this neo-Kantian conceptualization of knowledge. First, scientific rationality is treated as the fundamental standard in terms of which actors' knowledge and judgements are to be evaluated and, second, the intrinsic properties of the actors' 'non-rational' judgements can be ignored in favour of attempts to give causal explanations of how such 'non-rational' actions are persistently undertaken notwithstanding their deficiencies.

ordinated actions and, more generally, navigate the social world. Their contents and properties plainly require systematic investigation at both the theoretical and the empirical level. Indeed, Schutz asserted, the contents and properties of these constructs cannot be bypassed without the loss of the basic foundations of social theory – its reference to the social world of everyday life and experience which is the only ultimate guarantee that 'the world of social reality will not be replaced by a fictional non-existing world created by the scientific observer' (Schutz: 1964a, p. 8).

At the theoretical level, Schutz had set out a number of important properties of common-sense knowledge and cognition. First, the world of everyday life is one which is permeated by what Schutz terms the '*epoché* of the natural attitude' (Schutz: 1962c, p. 229). In ordinary life, there is a general *suspension of doubt* that things might not be as they seem or that past experience may not be a reliable guide to the present. The objectivity and typicality of ordinary objects and events is grasped on a taken-for-granted basis. Second, Schutz proposed that the objects to which the actor orients are actively constituted in the stream of experience through a series of subjective operations. Of particular significance in this context is the notion that the construction (or constitution) of both natural and social objects is necessarily continuously updated through endlessly renewed 'syntheses of identification'. It is in this way that objects are stabilized as 'self-same' objects despite changes in the physical perspectives from which they are viewed and, in the case of animate objects, despite their changing shapes and varied behavioural manifestations.

Third, Schutz argued that all the objects of the social world are constituted within a framework of 'familiarity and pre-acquaintanceship' (Schutz: 1962a, p. 7) supplied by a 'stock of knowledge at hand' which is overwhelmingly social in origin. Fourth, this stock of social constructs is held in typified form (1962a, p. 7). The typified knowledge in terms of which actors analyse the social world is approximate and revisable but, within the attitude of everyday life in which the constructs serve as pragmatic resources for the organization of action, any general doubt as to their validity and usefulness remains suspended. Finally, Schutz proposed that intersubjective understanding between actors is achieved through an active process in which the participants assume 'the general thesis of the reciprocity of perspectives' (1962a, pp. 11–13), i.e. that notwithstanding the different perspectives, biographies and motivations which lead to the actors having non-identical experiences of the world, they can none the less treat their experiences as 'identical for all practical purposes'.

To this account of the properties of common-sense knowledge, Schutz added the important rider that common-sense knowledge is organized as a highly uneven patchwork in which 'clear and distinct experiences are intermingled with vague conjectures; suppositions and prejudices cross well-proven evidences; motives, means and ends, as well as causes and effects, are strung together without clear understanding of their real connections' and 'nowhere have we a guarantee of the reliability of all these assumptions by which we are governed' (Schutz: 1964b, pp. 72–3). There is little comparison between the characteristic features of scientific and common-sense knowledge. Schutz argues, and ideally-rational actions are not to be sought for in the common-sense world in which, indeed, 'actions are at best partially rational and that rationality has many degrees' (1962a, p. 3).

Explicitly developing this analysis, Garfinkel proposed that, if mundane social actions were premised on the characteristic features of scientific rationality, the result would not be successful activity but, rather, inactivity, disorganization and anomie (Garfinkel: 1952; 1984, pp. 270–1). A scientifically adequate orientation to the events of the social world is thus far from being an ideal strategy for dealing with the flow of ordinary events. Its imposition as a standard with which to evaluate actors' judgements is therefore wholly unwarranted and, Garfinkel insisted, it is both unnecessary and inhibiting in analysing the properties of practical action (Garfinkel: 1984, pp. 280–1). Moreover, if ideal conceptions of rational action are dropped from the picture, the way is open to begin investigations based on the properties of the actor's actual knowledge in the making of reasonable choices among courses of action, i.e. 'the operations of judgement, choice, assessment of outcomes, and so on that he does in fact employ' (Garfinkel: 1952, p. 117).

With this last proposal, Garfinkel established a new territory for sociological analysis: the study of properties of practical common-sense reasoning in mundane situations of action. Moreover the proposal embodied a rejection of the use of scientific rationality as a central point of comparison in the analysis of mundane reasoning. Yet the programme of study that would issue from this proposal was by no means self-evident. Previous models of social action from the utilitarians onwards had routinely used the properties of scientific knowledge and activity as the basis from which to portray the extent to which daily life departed from these features. Devoid of such a comparative yardstick, how were the properties of common-sense knowledge and action to be described?

Garfinkel approached the problem with a variation on the phenomenological procedure of 'bracketing' (cf. Psathas: 1980; Schutz: 1962b). Rather than beginning with a privileged version of social structure to which the participants are treated as orienting with various degrees of error, this procedure involves the analyst in suspending any and all commitments to privileged versions of social structure – including the versions held by both the analyst and the participants – in favour of studying *how* the participants create, assemble, produce and reproduce the social structures to which they orient. This is the famous policy of 'ethnomethodological indifference' (Garfinkel and Sacks: 1970) which has created such misunderstanding and argument. At bottom, it simply involves studying the systematic properties of practical reasoning and practical action while refraining from judgements which have the effect of endorsing or undermining them. Within the 'brackets' the practical activities and their properties are examined with as few presuppositions, and as dispassionately, as possible.[12]

Projected within these brackets, the concrete investigations reported in *Studies in Ethnomethodology* (1984) contain two main avenues of approach to the study of practical reasoning and action. First, with the breaching experiments, Garfinkel developed Schutz's proposal that social actors must assume the 'general thesis of the reciprocity of perspectives' into a series of investigations into how the mutual intelligibility of ordinary activity is achieved and maintained. Second, he devised a range of demonstrations of the role of common-sense knowledge in the achievement of ordinary understandings of actions, events and artifacts. This knowledge was shown to be highly complex, to draw upon contextual resources which bear immensely varied relations to the focal matters they illuminate, to be unavoidably relied upon as a resource and to be strongly 'trusted' as such.

Thus the issue which Garfinkel made empirically problematic is the fact that the actors *somehow* know what they are doing and know it in common with one another. Garfinkel's empirical researches into the properties of ordinary actions and ordinary understandings were thus begun in the midst of the events of action. Granted that there is an order of events to be found, the question becomes that of 'how men, isolated yet simultaneously in an odd communion, go about the business of constructing, testing, maintaining, altering, validating, questioning, defining an order *together*' (Garfinkel: 1952, p. 114). It was this new *'cognitive problem of order'*, construed as a constituent feature of the analysis of social action, which Garfinkel set about researching and which is fundamental to the inception of ethnomethodology.

Investigating the Properties of Practical Actions: The Breaching Experiments

In beginning his investigations of the properties of common-sense knowledge and action, Garfinkel argued that the social actor responds 'not only to the perceived behaviour, feelings, motives, relationships and other socially organized features of life around him' but also to the 'perceived normality of these events' (Garfinkel: 1963, p. 188).[13] However, his approach to the

---

[12] While the policy as expressed amounts to a clear statement of good scientific procedure, it may not be easy to carry out. It may be difficult to remain detached from the common-sense beliefs and presuppositions which analysts necessarily share with other social participants and to avoid making judgements about the rationality of other social actors. Moreover the social sciences are replete with theoretical systems the terms of which intrinsically embody such beliefs and judgements and it is in this latter context that the radicalism of Garfinkel's procedure manifests itself.

[13] Garfinkel defined the 'perceived normality' of events by reference to the following features: 'the *perceived formal* features that environing events have for the perceiver as instances of a class of events, i.e. *typicality*; their 'chances' of occurrence, i.e. *likelihood*; their *comparability* with past or future events; the conditions of their occurrences, i.e. *causal texture*; their place in a set of means-ends relationships, i.e.

latter did not commence with an attempt to characterize the subjective outlooks of social actors.[14] Rather, he began from the assumption that the 'perceived normality' of social events can be investigated from the 'outside' by experimental manipulations of sequences of actions. Such manipulations could be used to determine the conditions under which events can be treated as perceivedly normal and to locate procedures by which social actors might seek to 'normalize' discrepancies between expected and actual events. In practical terms, this meant starting with an established context of interaction and seeing what could be done to disrupt it. As Garfinkel later summarized the rationale for this procedure,

> the operations that one would have to perform in order to multiply the senseless features of perceived environments; to produce and sustain bewilderment, consternation and confusion; to produce the socially structured affects of anxiety, shame, guilt and indignation should tell us something about how the structures of everyday activities are ordinarily and routinely produced and maintained. (Garfinkel: 1984b, pp. 37–8)

The outcome of this approach took the form of a long series of ingenious and variegated breaching experiments (Garfinkel: 1952; 1963; 1984b).

In the published studies, Garfinkel began by considering the case of games. Games, he observed, have a set of basic rules which define the range of legally-possible game events. A set of basic rules is constitutive of a game in that modifications of the set modify the identity of the game that is being played. Knowledge of the rules and the presumption of their reciprocally binding character allow each player to use the rules 'as a scheme for recognizing and interpreting the other players' as well as his own behavioral displays as events of game conduct' (Garfinkel: 1963, p. 190). Thus in a context of 'trust' in which the players take the basic rules of the game for granted as a definition of the situation and of their relationship to other players (1963, pp. 193–4),

> the basic rules provide a behavior's *sense* as an action. They are the terms in which a player decides whether or not he has correctly identified 'What happened.' 'Subjective meaning' is 'attached' to a behavior in terms of these rules. (Garfinkel: 1963, p. 195)

Given these features, games are relatively easy to disrupt and Garfinkel

---

instrumental efficacy; their necessity according to a natural or moral order, i.e. *moral requiredness*' (Garfinkel: 1963, p. 188).

[14] As Garfinkel puts its, 'I shall exercise a theorist's preference and say that meaningful events are entirely and exclusively events in a person's behavioral environment ... Hence there is no reason to look under the skull since nothing of interest is to be found there except brains. The 'skin' of the person will be left intact. Instead questions will be confined to the operations that can be performed upon events that are 'scenic' to the person' (Garfinkel: 1963, p. 190).

reports an exercise in which the game of 'tick-tack-toe' (British 'noughts and crosses') was breached by experimenters who, having asked the subject to make the first move, erased the mark, moved it to another cell and then made their own move while avoiding any indication that something unusual was being done. In over 250 trials, 95 per cent of the experimental subjects evinced some reaction to this behaviour and over 75 per cent actively objected to it or demanded an explanation of it. The experiment showed decisively that the discrepant behaviours motivated immediate attempts at normalization. Most significantly, it also showed that those who sought to normalize the discrepancy by altering the framework in terms of which the events were understood, for example by assuming that the experiment was intended as a joke or as the initiation of a new game, evinced the least disturbance. By contrast, those who sought to normalize the event while holding fast to the original rules of the game as a constitutive order of events showed most disturbance. Thus the interpretative frameworks which were used in order to determine 'what had occurred' had a dramatic impact on the actions and the sentiments of the participants.

However, while it is relatively easy to describe and breach the understandings which are constitutive of games, it is less easy to translate the exercise into the realm of ordinary social action.[15] In pursuit of this latter goal, Garfinkel drew extensively on Schutz's analysis of the constitutive expectancies of everyday life (see esp. Garfinkel: 1963, pp. 209–17; 1984b, pp. 53–65). In particular, he sought to show that actions which breached the fundamental presupposition of the reciprocity of perspectives would result in the kind of bewilderment, anger and vigorous attempts to restore the situation that were found in the experiments with games. The procedure he adopted was to have experimenters insist that their co-interactants clarify the sense of their commonplace remarks without giving any indication that anything unusual was going on. The results of this procedure were spectacular and have become so widely known that one simple protocol will serve to illustrate the kind of outcome that emerged:

> The subject was telling the experimenter, a member of the subject's car pool, about having had a flat tyre while going to work the previous day.
> S: 'I had a flat tyre.'
> E: 'What do you mean, you had a flat tyre?'
> She appeared momentarily stunned. Then she answered in a hostile way: 'What do you mean "What do you mean?" A flat tyre is a flat tyre. That is what I meant. Nothing special. What a crazy question!' (Garfinkel: 1984b, p. 42)

In many other cases, subjects responded to the breaching moves with this kind of anger or, alternatively, with requests for explanations of the

---

[15] Garfinkel describes various important differences between game and 'real life' situations (Garfinkel: 1963, pp. 206–9).

experimenters' behaviour, with attempts to interpret the breaching moves as jokes and, in one of the reproduced protocols, with inactivity.

In both the experiments with games and in real settings, the 'perceived normality' of events was made seriously problematic and, in both cases, this was done through an undermining of 'a set of "more fundamental" presuppositions in terms of which behavioral instances are attended by actors as instances of *intended* actions that a group member assumes "anyone can see"' (Garfinkel: 1963, p. 198). Thus the observations about games could be generalized to a considerable extent:

> When the work with games was begun, we took for granted that the omnirelev-
> ance of normative regulation was peculiar to games … When, however,
> incongruity-inducing procedures were applied in 'real life' situations, it was
> unnerving to find the seeming endless variety of events that lent themselves
> to the production of really nasty surprises. These events ranged from those
> that, according to sociological commonsense, were 'critical', like standing very,
> very close to a person while otherwise maintaining an innocuous conversation,
> to others that acccording to sociological commonsense were 'trivial', like saying
> 'hello' at the termination of a conversation … It was conjectured therefore
> that *all* actions as perceived events may have a constitutive structure, and
> that perhaps it is the threat to the normative order of events as such that is
> the critical variable in evoking indignation. (Garfinkel: 1963, p. 198)

The implications of these observations are very great. If all actions can be analysed in terms of their constitutive structures and the latter are visible – even if in a 'seen but unnoticed' fashion – in the organization of action itself, then the way lies open to a detailed structural analysis of that organization. And this way will not centre on the motivations of social actions but, rather, on the procedural bases through which they are produced and understood – the ways in which the actions themselves betray their own analysability. And, in such a context, the motivations and other 'subjective' factors which are ordinarily understood to lie behind actions can, when analysed from a social scientific perspective, be understood as available to the actors by virtue of a combination of contextual knowledge and their tacit grasp of the procedural structure of their own activities.[16]

Investigating the Analysability of Action

In spite of the range of discussions of 'context' which occupy the pages of *Studies in Ethnomethodology*, it is still easy to lose sight of the extent to which the contextuality of ordinary actions is demonstrated to be a crucial resource through which they are understood. For example, in an introductory dis-

---

[16] From this point of view, the actor's 'intuition' can be treated as the capacity for coordinated inference based on a grasp of behavioural detail and contextual background.

cussion of how a husband and wife made sense of a conversation, Garfinkel noted the extent to which each interpreted the utterances of the other by reference to their place in a serial order and by imputing a background of matters that were assumed to be known in common (Garfinkel: 1984b, pp. 38–42). In a procedure in which students were asked to spend time in their homes viewing events from the perspective of boarders, Garfinkel reported that, under this instruction, the students deleted the familiar, biographically-furnished assumptions in terms of which family members and their activities were normally described. In consequence, almost all the students 'behaviourized' their reports of the family scenes.[17] In the course of practising their new mode of observation, they became uncomfortably aware of the precise details of behaviour and also of 'quarrelling, bickering and hostile motivations' which, they generally asserted, did not represent a 'true' picture of the family. Many of the students reported being relieved to restore the normal texture of background understandings to their interpretation of events (Garfinkel: 1984b, pp. 44–9). Here the deletion of a set of contextual assumptions radically altered the way in which events were perceived and reported.

In other contexts, the relevance of 'background knowledge' was just as critical in interpreting the nature of events and actions. In a study based on special clinic records designed to develop a model of a psychiatric clinic's procedures for treating outpatients, Garfinkel found that the coders of the raw records were assuming contextual knowledge of the clinic's procedures in order to facilitate the coding process in this case, the 'contextual knowledge' being invoked comprised assumptions about the clinic's procedures – the very phenomena which the study was designed to determine. These assumptions, Garfinkel stresses, were not invoked to resolve ambiguities in the records. Instead,

> such presupposed knowledge seemed necessary and was most deliberately consulted whenever, for whatever reasons, the coders needed to be satisfied that they had coded 'what really happened'. *This was so regardless of whether or not they had encountered 'ambiguous' folder contents.* (Garfinkel: 1984a, p. 20)

In these and other investigations which Garfinkel reports, the contextuality of actions and events is always an imputed contextuality and its imputation is, in turn, a key element in making sense of the actions, i.e. of their accountability. But if the invoking of contextual matters is inevitably part and parcel of the sense that is made of events, how are contextual matters invoked?

In his essay 'Commonsense Knowledge of Social Structures' (Garfinkel: 1984c), Garfinkel elaborated a major process which, he proposed, is impli-

---

[17] The students thus tended to exceed their assignment by deleting aspects of their common-sense knowledge of social structures in addition to the family biographical particulars.

cated in many aspects of the interpretation of action. Following Mannheim (1952), he termed this process 'the documentary method of interpretation' and observed that

> the method consists of treating an actual appearance as 'the document of', as 'pointing to', as 'standing on behalf of' a presupposed underlying pattern. Not only is the underlying pattern derived from its individual documentary evidences, but the individual documentary evidences, in their turn, are interpreted on the basis of 'what is known' about the underlying pattern. Each is used to elaborate the other. (Garfinkel: 1984c, p. 78)

This process, whose workings are readily apparent, for example, in the interpretation of gestalt figures, is also involved, Garfinkel observes, in 'recognizing such common occurrences and objects as mailmen, friendly gestures and promises' (1984c, p. 78).

Garfinkel developed his discussion of the documentary method in the context of a study which was designed to exaggerate its features. Students were invited to participate in a novel form of counselling. Its procedure involved the separation of student and counsellor in adjoining rooms connected by intercom. The student was required to outline the background of the problem for which advice was being sought and then to pose a series of questions which could be answered in a 'yes/no' fashion. In between each question and its answer, the subject was asked to disconnect the intercom and tape-record his or her reflections on what had been said. At the end of the exchanges the subjects were asked to give their impressions of them and were subsequently interviewed. Unknown to the subjects, the 'counsellors'' responses to their questions were determined through a table of random numbers and the experiment had been devised to see how they made sense of responses having, on the face of it, a merely random consistency.[18]

In his discussion of the events of this study, Garfinkel stresses the extent to which the subjects were able to complete the exchange and to summarize and evaluate the 'advice they had been given' (Garfinkel: 1984c, pp. 89–94). Notwithstanding the randomness of the advisers' responses, the students did not treat them as such. Instead, they viewed the responses of the advisers as motivated by the questions and found that they could see 'what the adviser had in mind'. The subjects located the content of the 'advice' they received by examining particular contents of their own questions and elaborating those contents over a series of exchanges so as to secure and maintain, as far as was possible, a consistent pattern of 'advice'. They interpreted the meaning of the 'advice' by reference to their own common-sense knowledge of various aspects of normatively-valued collectivity memberships – knowledge which they presupposed was held in common with the adviser. Moreover they evaluated the advice as 'reasonable' or 'unreasonable'

---

[18] For detailed protocols of events arising from this procedure, see Garfinkel: 1984c, pp. 80–8; McHugh: 1968).

through a procedure of assigning 'perceivedly normal values' (see note 13) to what the advisers proposed.

Above all, the subjects devoted considerable efforts to maintaining the interaction as one involving a pattern of advice-giving. To this end, both the 'pattern of advice' and the 'underlying problem to which it was directed' were repeatedly accommodated to each present answer 'so as to maintain the "course of advice", to elaborate what had "really been advised" previously, and to motivate the new possibilities as emerging features of the problem' (1984c, pp. 89–94). In dealing with incomplete, inappropriate or contradictory answers, the subjects often elected to wait and see if later answers would clarify the situation, or 'found a reason' that 'made good sense' of the response, or they concluded that the adviser had 'changed his mind' or 'learned something new' between responses, that he was insufficiently acquainted with the details of the problem, or that the question was badly put, etc. In short, the subjects used every means at their disposal, *ad hoc*, so as to maintain a commitment to the exchanges as a course of advice involving the participation of trustworthy and properly-motivated advisers.

Several conclusions can readily be drawn from this study. The first is simply to acknowledge the enormous range of presuppositions, knowledge elements, inferences and contextual features that were used as resources to maintain a consistent sense of the central events of the exchanges. While the term 'the documentary method of interpretation' identifies a general process of understanding, it is salutary to recognize that an indefinitely large range of matters are grist to its processual mill. Relatedly, it is clear that at any given stage in the proceedings the subjects' understandings of what was going on were provisional, 'loose' and subject to revision. Although they were based both on the application of detailed knowledge and on the use of inferences which operated 'in detail' over the particulars of the exchanges, the subjects' inferences could not be interpreted as the products of clear-cut rules or algorithms unambiguously applied. Garfinkel has repeatedly shown that the application of rules invariably involves the use of *ad hoc* devices, such as 'unless', 'etcetera' and 'let it pass',[19] and undoubtedly these devices were implemented in the subjects' interpretations of their 'counselling' sessions. Finally it is worth noting once again the extent to which presupposed 'underlying patterns' (i.e. that the exchanges involved 'counselling' and were intelligible as such) were repeatedly and extendedly given the benefit of the doubt despite the existence of appearances that argued to the contrary. In accordance with Schutz's account of the 'natural attitude', the participants did indeed suspend for as long as possible any emerging doubts they may have entertained about the character of the exchanges.

With these observations made, however, there is also an important sense

---

[19] See, *inter alia*, Garfinkel (1984a, pp. 2–4, 18–24) as well as the whole of Garfinkel (1984c).

in which the results of the 'student counselling' experiment stand in a strikingly paradoxical relation with the results of the 'breaching' experiments discussed in the previous section. The subjects of the counselling experiment persisted in the belief that they were getting realistic 'counselling' and were exceptionally ingenious in invoking *ad hoc* considerations to sustain this sense of what was going on. By contrast, the subjects of the breaching experiments very rapidly abandoned any attempt to make sense of what was going on and instead responded almost immediately with outrage and hostility to the actions of the experimenters.

The clue to these two alternative responses appears to lie in the extent to which the subjects were able to interpret the experimenters' behaviour as intelligible and reasonable. As long as the experimenters produced behaviour that could be *procedurally* fitted[20] to the context in which it occurred, the subjects were prepared to respond on the basis of 'trust' and let it pass on a reading that would 'make sense'. Once, however, the experimenters produced behaviour which could not be so fitted, the behaviour was immediately sanctioned.

Yet although the subjects were often disconcerted and bewildered during these experiments, it is significant that they did *not* analyse the behaviour of the 'breaching' experimenters as meaningless, random or unmotivated. Garfinkel's breaching experiments were originally designed, in effect, to immobilize the documentary method of interpretation and create scenes of total inactivity and anomie. In fact, however, they rarely did so. The 'documentary method' remained at work and the subjects were able to respond to what was happening to them. Indeed the subjects' predominantly hostile reactions betrayed their analyses of the experimenters' behaviour as motivated by presently undisclosed – though probably disagreeable – intentions.[21]

[20] Garfinkel stresses that all understanding is procedurally or methodically founded. As he puts it, 'For the conduct of their daily affairs, persons take for granted that what is said will be made out according to methods that the parties use to make out what they are saying for its clear, consistent, coherent, understandable, or planful character, i.e. as subject to some rule's jurisdiction – in a word, as rational. To see the 'sense' of what is said is to accord to what is said its character 'as a rule'. *'Shared agreement' refers to various social methods for accomplishing the member's recognition that something was said-according-to-a-rule and not the demonstrable matching of substantive matters. The appropriate image of a common understanding is therefore an operation rather than a common intersection of overlapping sets'* (Garfinkel: 1984a, p. 30).

[21] Significantly, the experimenter's unusual conduct routinely evoked attempts at explanation in terms of motives or intentions which Garfinkel repeatedly documents. For example, (1) in a chess game in which, before making a move, Garfinkel switched the physical positions of identical pieces – e.g. two pawns – thus creating no material change in the state of the game, subjects none the less 'would speak of the obscurity of my motives' (Garfinkel: 1963, p. 199). (2) Similarly, after many of the breaching procedures, both the subjects and the experimenters found it difficult to renormalize their habitual expectations even after the experimental character of

Central, then, to the analysability of action is the phenomenon of *procedural trust*. The participants enter any situation of action with a set of interpretative procedures which they will use, largely unconsciously, to determine a specific sense for particular, located social actions. But where such sense cannot be achieved, the participants may not necessarily abandon the procedural bases of their understandings. Rather they may use those same procedural bases as the grounds on which to judge social actions as *departures* from 'normal sensible' behaviour, as negatively motivated and as morally sanctionable. The procedures through which action is interpreted are thus *doubly constitutive* of the activities they organize. They provide both for the intelligibility of perceivedly normal conduct and for the visibility of conduct which deviates from this. The interpretative procedures thus have some striking properties. Not only are they capable of flexible implementation so as to permit a range of behaviour to be assimilated into a given underlying pattern, they are also usable to create the visibility of actions that deviate from their dictates as motivated or 'wilful', and hence as meaningful.

In turn this means that the set of interpretative procedures through which action is rendered intelligible have the remarkable property of totally 'covering' the field of action. There is thus no uncategorizable action – even if, at the limits of discussion, some of the more drastic departures from 'perceivedly normal' behaviour are placed in the residual category of 'insane'. This 'double constitution' property of interpretative procedures has immense significance for the analysis of ordinary social action, to which we now turn.

Norms and Action: Normative Determination versus Moral Accountability

Within the major sociological perspectives concerned with the analysis of social action, it has been traditional to treat the occurrence of ordinary actions as rule-governed (Wilson: 1971) or as determined by moral norms and, in this way, to specify the primary mechanism through which collectivi-

---

the procedure had been revealed (see Garfinkel: 1984b, pp. 48–9, 52–3). They continued to question the experimenter's motives, often complaining, '"all right, it was an experiment, but why did you have to choose *me*". Characteristically, subject and experimenter wanted some further resolution than the explanation furnished but were uncertain about what it could or should consist of' (1984b, pp. 72–3). (3) Again, in the student-counselling experiment, Garfinkel found that the students could not escape the search for motivation to account for the pattern of the experimenter's behaviour: 'Subjects found it very difficult to grasp the implications of randomness in the utterances. A predetermined utterance was treated as deceit in the answers instead of as an utterance that was decided beforehand and that occurred independently of the subject's questions and interests' (1984c, p. 91). The (secondarily elaborative) treatment of deviant behaviour as specially-motivated behaviour is a central factor in the maintenance of normative expectations as interpretative resources in ordinary contexts of action.

ties shape and constrain the activities of their members.[22] In Parsons's influential account of this process, moral norms are internalized to constitute the need-dispositions of individuals in a socialization process which essentially involves conditioning through the administration of rewards and punishments. What is lost in this analysis is any principled approach to the reasoning of ordinary actors in situations of action. The social actor is treated as a 'judgemental dope', i.e.

> the man-in-the-sociologist's society who produces the stable features of the society by acting in compliance with pre-established and legitimate alternatives of action that the common culture provides.

And hence

> the person's use of commonsense knowledge of social structures over the temporal 'succession' of here and now situations are treated as epiphenomenal. (Garfinkel: 1984b, p. 68)

What is lost by the 'judgemental dope' formulation is a conception of social actors who use their interpretative resources to make out the character of the circumstances in which they find themselves and, as part of that process, determine how possible courses of action will be evaluated relative to the normative order of events in which they are enmeshed. What is lost, in short, is an analysis of social action built in terms of what is central to the participants – the mutual intelligibility and moral accountability of action. Garfinkel's treatment of the role of norms in social action is one which makes them central to both the recognizability and the moral accountability of action. Such a treatment involves a major reconceptualization of traditional conceptions of the role of norms in social activity. None the less once these elements are placed at the centre of the analysis a radically different, but theoretically coherent and empirically fruitful, approach to the analysis of action emerges.

1 The situation of action.

An initial reconceptualization within the theory of action which is required by Garfinkel's results concerns the situation of action itself. In the Parsonian analysis and, more generally, the 'normative paradigm' (Wilson: 1971), shared norms function as stable linkages between situations and the actions which are required under given situational conditions. Essentially 'given situations' – initially recognized by the participants independently of normative considerations – are viewed as calling up specific normative dispositions and expectations which issue in behaviour of a particular kind. The norma-

---

[22] As Wilson (1971, p. 66) has noted, both conflict and consensus theories have shared this assumption and have primarily disagreed on the extent to which a normative consensus exists and social integration is engendered by the consensus.

tive model of concerted action thus requires not only that the actors have had similar normative training but also that they share common perceptions of the empirical situations in which they are placed. If this latter condition is met, the actors can be treated as placed in contexts which, through the medium of the appropriate norms, are determinative of their joint actions. In this analysis, each situation is treated as discrete and anterior to action and as determining action in a 'container-contained' kind of way.[23] Within this framework, the constitutive role of time in the organization of activity as a temporal sequence is ignored. There is no possibility here of the interpretative role of retrospective-prospective temporal perspectives which, Garfinkel shows, are central to understanding even an elementary conversation (Garfinkel: 1984b, pp. 38–42). And, more generally, the theory tends to treat the temporal relationship between a situation and the actions it generates as occurring within the confines of a single 'fat moment' (Garfinkel: 1952, p. 147).

But this view of the relationship between an action and its context is quite inconsistent with Garfinkel's findings about the operations of the documentary method of interpretation in ordinary situations of action. For it will be recollected that his findings were that not only does the context of action influence what the action is thought to consist of, but the component actions too contribute to a developing sense of the situation of action itself.[24] 'Action' and 'context' are mutually elaborative and mutually determinative elements in a simultaneous equation that the actors are continually solving and re-solving to determine the nature of the events in which they are placed. Thus the 'circumstances' of an action cannot properly be analysable as grossly anterior to a subsequent set of actions which they 'enfold'. As the presumptive, but not incorrigible, basis on which actions are both premised and interpreted, the 'circumstances' should, rather, be construed as the developing and transformable products of their constituent actions.

2 The norm–situation link.
A related issue for the analysis of action arises from a consideration of the relationship between the norms by which actions are 'determined' and the situations to which those norms apply. The central problem here is that every situation of action differs – to a greater or lesser extent – from every other and that, in principle therefore, the social world consists of an indefinitely large number of differentiable situations of action.[25] But although the normative paradigm works from the presumption of a domain

[23] This usage is drawn from Burke (1945).

[24] See in particular Garfinkel's analyses of the process by which a simple conversation is understood (Garfinkel: 1984b, pp. 38–42) and of the characteristics of the understandings in the student-counselling experiment (1984c, pp. 89–94).

[25] Thus every situation of action is uniquely and, as Sacks (1963) noted, indefinitely describable.

of discrete situations from which actions will be generated through the operation of norms, the model is threatened by the prospect of an indefinitely large array of unique contexts of action.[26] It is clear that normative prescriptions do not exist for each situation of action for, if they did, each prescription would lapse from use after a single application. Such an outcome, if it were conceivable, would undermine the very concept of a rule of conduct and would render the sharing of such a rule unimaginable.

But if internalized norms or rules are to be determinative of action across diverse states of affairs, the normative theorist must, as a crucial component in the specification of the theory, be able to identify the domain of situations in which they will apply. Yet it is a commonplace of post-Wittgensteinian philosophy of action that the boundaries of such categories are negotiable and revisable through the actors' usages, which are negotiable, rather than deterministic, in character.[27] In short, as the legal theorist H. L. A. Hart has observed, 'Particular fact situations do not await us already marked off from each other and labelled as instances of the general rule, the application of which is in question; nor can the rule itself step forward to claim its own instances' (Hart: 1961, p. 123). Instances of the application of rules are decided by the participants in light of the particulars of the situations in which they find themselves. Moreover, given that the situations in which a rule may be applied will vary in specific details, the characteristic *sense* of the rule's application in each set of circumstances will also differ. It is this issue which, *inter alia*, Garfinkel addresses in his recommended policy of refusing

> serious consideration to the prevailing proposal that ... rational properties of practical activities be assessed, recognized, categorized, described by using a rule or a standard obtained outside actual settings within which such properties are recognized, used, produced and talked about by settings' members. (Garfinkel: 1984a, p. 33)

Thus in both these problem areas – the domain of actions to which given norms apply and the concrete application of norms to specific situational contexts – there is sufficient slippage to undermine fatally the credibility of normative determinism as a model of action. This does not mean that normative expectations are insignificant in the organization of action. Rather it suggests that their role will have to be reconsidered.

In contrast to the normatively deterministic model of action described above, Garfinkel's researches suggest an alternative analysis which is founded on a notion of the normative accountability of action. Within this viewpoint the actors' normative expectations are treated not as regulative

---

[26] For the normative paradigm, the problematic relationship between general moral norms and a diverse set of unique action situations manifests itself as a variation on the problem of universals.

[27] See Barnes (1984a, 1984b) for a lucid discussion of some of the issues involved.

or determinative of actions whose recognizability is treated as independent of the norm, but rather as playing a constitutive role in the actors' recognition of what the actions consist of. Thus temporal successions of actions are grasped and portrayed as related to one another by reference primarily to sets of normative expectations. It is through such a medium that a sequence of actions – such as a series of questions and answers – can be rendered 'observable-reportable' or 'accountable', for example, as a classroom lesson. However, for a lesson to observably-reportably occur, a set of actions which are recognizably its 'component activities' must be produced in particular patterned arrangements or sequences. Only if this condition is met can the event be continuously assembled as a recognizable 'lesson' over the temporarily extended course of its production.

Within the event itself, the component actions will be produced by participants who will inevitably have a grasp, if only tacit, of the specific contextual moments in which they should act and of how various possible courses of action will fulfil or disappoint the constitutive expectancies attached to those moments. Each successive action is thus visible – through the norms which are collectively constitutive of 'what a school lesson consists of' – as a maintenance of, or a departure from, the constitutive expectancies of school lessons. Thus the 'situation of action' – the lesson – is most effectively viewed as the presupposition, project and product of its own constituent actions. As Garfinkel puts it, 'the policy is recommended that any social setting be viewed as self-organizing with respect to the intelligible character of its own appearances' (1984a, p. 33). Moreover, each constituent action will be analysed as an establishment, adjustment, restoration, alteration or breach of the 'classroom context' and will be found to have been so analysed in and of its own production or, as Garfinkel puts it, 'reflexively' or 'incarnately'.[28] It follows that, even in a setting such as a classroom in which the regulative role of norms or rules of conduct might seem to be self-evident, there is a much more fundamental *constitutive* role for the norms of classroom activity. This constitutive role is particularly apparent when the norms are breached, and in two ways.

1   Self-evidently it is the norms of classroom conduct which are, through the property of double constitution, constitutive in the actors' awareness of activities which depart from them. The norms of classroom conduct are thus, inevitably, the vehicles through which conduct that, for example, challenges or undermines or ridicules the teacher's role can conceivably be achieved. The visibility of such conduct is available to all participants who have an awareness of the norms – and where their authors can be held to have such awareness, they can thereby be held morally accountable as agents for their actions.[29]

---

[28] For example, an 'insolent' response to a teacher's question does not have to be named as such before its character can be recognized; on the contrary, its character has to be recognized before it can be so named.

2   The precise character of such departures from the norm is available in detail from an analysis of their contexts – which will necessarily elaborate their sense as actions. And it is through this detailed analysis that departures can be accountably treated as voluntary or involuntary, as constructive or sanctionable, etc.

3 *The binding character of norms.*

A central tenet of the Parsonian analysis of normative constraint is that social actors will find it difficult or impossible to maintain a calculative orientation to the norms which they have internalized. Once internalized, norms become need-dispositions of personality which drive action in largely unrationalized and prescribed ways, and it is this which establishes their binding character.

For Garfinkel, by contrast, normative conventions are primarily to be understood as resources for establishing and maintaining the intelligibility of a field of action. As the breaching experiments showed, regardless of what actions take place the actors will attempt to make sense of them by reference to the norms, and in those cases where the action cannot be held to comply with a normative convention, it can none the less be treated as a *departure* from it. Such departures can, in turn, be given 'secondarily elaborative' treatments in which particular (often negative) motives and intentions may be invoked to interpret them.[30] Moreover normative conventions can, in the breach, be resources for transforming situations of action, redefining the social identities in play within them, etc.

These interpretations, however, generally presume that (*contra* Parsons) the normative conventions applicable to a situation of action are cognitively available to all concerned and thus that the 'deviant' is generally one who 'should have known better' and 'could have done otherwise'. Conventional notions of responsibility for action (and the sanctionability of action) rest on this presumption. All of these understandings depend upon the actor's capacity to adopt a reflexive and, on occasion, a calculative orientation to normative conventions. Thus in the Garfinkelian account, which places no particular significance on a history of rewards and punishments as a guarantee that social participants will be driven by normative conventions, it may none the less be argued that it is the reflexive anticipation of the analysability and moral accountability of departures from norms which inhibits their production (Garfinkel: 1984c, pp. 66–70). In the cognitive analysis of norms developed by Garfinkel in which normative conventions constitute

---

[29] This point is nicely illustrated in the following observation by Peter French about an infant class. A child who was engaged in looking down a simple microscope was asked by his teacher 'What can you see?' Looking up, the child replied, 'Have a look'. French remarked that all the children in the class he observed had learned to avoid such responses by the third week of their first term in school.

[30] See note 21 and Heritage: 1984a, pp. 115–20, 209–12.

publicly-available frameworks for the analysis of conduct, reflexive anticipation of how deviant conduct will be analysable may, rather than undermining dispositions to comply with norms as suggested by Parsons, supply
the actor with 'good reasons' for normatively appropriate behaviour.[31]

4 The maintenance of normative frameworks.
A final major area in which the Garfinkelian perspective entails a revision
of the normatively deterministic approach to the theory of action arises from
a consideration of the reproduction or persistence of normative expectations.
Notwithstanding the power of Parsons's discussion of the 'double contingency' of interaction and the 'two-fold binding-in' of normative expectations,
there are surprising lacunae in his account of how norms persist as sources
of conduct. For norms represent ideal standards of conduct which actors
may, in the nature of things, readily fall short of or depart from. Parsons's
account assumes both internalization and an unremitting sanctioning process as the basis on which norms are sustained, but his account offers no
other elementary processes through which the persistence of norms might
be ensured. This is a serious weakness, for, given the ideal character of
norms and the rationalizing capabilities of social actors, deviations and
derelictions may often go unsanctioned either by conscience or by the
reactions of others. And, to the extent that this is frequently the case, a
process in which normative expectations undergo entropic degeneration
might be expected. In short, the question arises of how normative standards
are maintained as standards under circumstances in which they may be
breached relatively frequently and without sanction.

The normative accountability approach to the analysis of action offers an
economical solution to this question. It was proposed earlier that, through
their property of double constitution, norms are invoked in the recognition
of both conforming and deviant actions. Additionally it was noted that, for
social actors, while conforming actions are rarely the objects of additional
explanation, deviant actions are usually explained through a variety of
'secondarily elaborative' accounts which make reference to the circumstances
of the action or the character and to the motives or intentions of the doer.
Thus in the case of normative expectations, there are only two sets of
possibilities. Either the norm is complied with, or deviance from it both
triggers and requires an account in terms of some 'special' motive or context.
In the first case the norm effectively furnishes a self-subsistent explanation

---

[31] The notion that the actor's anticipation of how conduct will be construed is an
important consideration influencing choice among courses of action goes back to
C. Wright Mills's classic 'Situated Actions and Vocabularies of Motive' (Mills:
1940). As Garfinkel put the underlying issue in his doctoral dissertation: 'The big
question is not whether actors understand each other or not. The fact is that they
do understand each other, that they *will* understand each other, but the catch is
that they will understand each other regardless of how they *would* be understood'
(Garfinkel: 1952, p. 367).

for the action. In the second, the norm motivates the search for the special conditions that can explain why it was not met. *In either case, the norm is cognitively preserved as the primary interpretative base in terms of which the action, whether conforming or deviant, is understood.*[32] Hence norms can stand outside the fall of events and thus be proof against erosion by actions which fall short of or deviate from their dictates.

To grasp this presuppositional and constitutive role of norms in the production and recognition of action is to identify a central source of stability in the reproductive maintenance of social institutions. It is also to recognize the chronic interpenetration between the factual and moral orders that exists within the viewpoint of ordinary actors. The latter are routinely engaged in the moral constitution of social events through a framework of normative expectations which, in seen but unnoticed ways, they ceaselessly maintain as incorrigible.

In sum, the Garfinkelian view of action, which stresses its moral accountability through the medium of normative conventions, is one which departs from the normatively deterministic viewpoint at each of the key points listed above.

1 It avoids reifying the situation of action into a standardized and determining context of activity. As Garfinkel observes,

Social science theorists ... have used the fact of standardization to conceive the character and consequences of actions that comply with standardized expectancies. Generally they have acknowledged but otherwise neglected the fact that by these same actions persons discover, create and sustain this standardization. (Garfinkel: 1984b, p. 67)

Instead, the situation of action is treated as an essentially transformable context of activity that is unavoidably maintained, altered or restored in and through the courses of action which are conventionally said to occur 'within it' but which, more realistically, may be said to constitute and reconstitute it in a continuous process of renewal.

2 The norms through which situations and their component actions are recognized are to be understood not as rigid templates, but as elastic and revisable resources which are adjusted and altered over the course of their application to concrete contexts. In this sense the specific character of ordinary actions is grasped through 'accommodative work' (Garfinkel: 1963, p. 187) and is always recognized, as Garfinkel elsewhere puts it, for 'another first time' (1984a, p. 9).

3 Rather than treating norms as drivers of behaviour, normative con-

---

[32] This issue is central to Pollner's (1974a; forthcoming) analysis of mundane reasoning and to Mulkay and Gilbert's analysis of error accounts in scientific discourse (see Gilbert and Mulkay: 1984, ch. 4; Mulkay and Gilbert: 1982). See also Heritage (1984a, pp. 209ff.) for a more elaborate discussion.

ventions are construed, within the Garfinkelian view, as a major source
of the cognitive resources through which settings of action are rendered
both intelligible and morally accountable. In particular, they provide for
the visibility of both appropriate and deviant behaviour: they provide
for the secondary analysability of deviant behaviour in terms of meaning
and motive; and reflexive awareness of how deviant behaviour will be
analysed can motivate normatively appropriate behaviour. Cognitive
awareness of normative frameworks is presumed when social participants
treat conduct as intelligible and morally accountable regardless of
whether that conduct complies with or departs from norms. The secondary analysability of departures from normative conventions, however,
may tend in general to motivate compliant conduct.

4   Normative conventions are treated as presuppositional to the fields
of action which they render intelligible and accountable. Their maintenance is, at one and the same time, the presupposition, process and
product of their use to interpret ordinary scenes of social activity (cf.
Pollner: 1974a). It is this status which gives them immense stability as
institutional bases of action that are simultaneously cognitive and moral
in character.

Taken together, these considerations represent a major re-orientation of
the Parsonian conception of action that has prevailed during the post-war
era. The new centrality given to the procedural bases of action, the nature
of the actors' understandings of the circumstances in which they are located,
and the reflexive properties of action has stimulated a great deal of empirical
work which has been exploited to shed new light on old problems. Perhaps
most importantly, the normative accountability view of human action has
proved to be an open and generative source of accumulating insights in the
nature of social organization. It has been central in new understandings of
the role of language in social action, the nature of intersubjectivity in human
conduct, the institutional foundations of the generation and implementation
of knowledge, and an increasingly detailed account of the nature of social
interaction. It is to these themes that we now turn.

Language and Accountability

Garfinkel's proposal that 'the activities whereby members produce and
manage settings of organized everyday affairs are identical with members'
procedures for making those settings account-able' (1984a, p. 1) is not, of
course, to be understood as proposing that ordinary descriptive accounts
provide unproblematic access to the nature of the activities they describe.
Nor is it to be understood as asserting that the analysis of verbal accounts
of action can in any way substitute for the analysis of action itself. On the
contrary, his use of the term 'account-able' as a synonym for 'observable-
reportable' (1984a, p. 1; 1974, p. 17) means that his observation is

addressed to the way any setting of activity can be grasped as patterned in and through the unfolding character of its constituent actions, irrespective of whether this patterning is (or even can be) given linguistic formulation. Social actions do not have to be baptised with language for their intelligibility and implicativeness to be available to the participants. Garfinkel often uses the example of queueing to illustrate the ways in which a group of people, simply by standing in a particular spatial relationship to one another, mutely constitute a small-scale social institution and establish sets of expectations and moral obligations *vis-à-vis* one another.

Granted this inherent or 'incarnate' intelligibility of social activity, what then is the relationship between events and the verbal accounts which bring them to descriptive formulation? In his treatment of accounts, Garfinkel was concerned to get away from the view that descriptive accounts are *transparent* and thus leave ordinary understandings of the objects and events they depict unaltered by the fact of their having been described. And he also seeks to undermine the view that describing and other forms of speaking are, as it were, inert with respect to the settings in which they occur. Such a notion of description is explicit in theories that stress the representative function of language and the correspondences between words and things, and it is implicit in forms of practical social scientific research that treat the reports of social actors as data which unproblematically index underlying social realities.

Against both of these positions, Garfinkel emphasizes the extent to which ordinary accounts have a 'loose' fit to the circumstances they depict. The nature of the fit between accounts and their circumstances is established through an active course of interpretative work. The rational features of accounts, he asserts, '*consist* of what members do with, what they "make of" the accounts in the socially organized actual occasions of their use' (1984a, pp. 3–4). Accounts are thus *indexical expressions*. They are not to be treated as external to or independent of the contexts in which they are employed.

The term 'indexical expression' has been the object of significant misunderstanding in discussions of ethnomethodology. The term itself derives from the literature of logic and linguistics, where it is used to describe expressions (such as 'he', 'this', 'today', etc.) that require contextual knowledge in order to recover their referents (see Levinson: 1983, pp. 45–96). This origin has been a potent source of confusion in sociological responses to Garfinkel's proposals, and in two main ways. First, it will be apparent that in its logico-linguistic usage, the term has a relatively narrow, technical meaning. In his usage, by contrast, Garfinkel dramatically widened the sense of the term. His proposal is that every use of language *without exception* is informed by contextual attachments. Thus, even where a sentence is being produced as purely descriptive of a state of affairs, contextual features of the sentence will have to be invoked in order to see that, after all, it is intended as a description and not, for example, as an irony, a joke or a metaphor.

The second source of confusion is closely related to the first. In the logico-linguistic literature, indexical expressions have attracted interest because, as Garfinkel (1984a, pp. 4–7) notes, they constitute obstacles to the use of fully-formalized analytical techniques in a variety of disciplines. This background has been incorporated into the inappropriate view that ordinary actions are concerned with the problem of 'remedying' indexical expressions (Attewell: 1972; Phillips: 1978). This has led to the creation of an incorrect understanding of the role of language in social relations. For, in contexts of ordinary language-use, social participants clearly *exploit* the indexical characteristics of talk in a wide variety of ways (see, among others, Heritage: 1984a, pp. 142–57; Schegloff: 1984). The indexical properties of accounts are thus a resource rather than an obstacle to sense-making in ordinary social contexts.

The indexical properties of accounts ultimately arise from their character as actions. Accounts are inextricably tied to the occasions of their use, Garfinkel asserts, because the accounts are '*features* of the socially organized occasions of their use' (Garfinkel: 1984a, pp. 4–7). Ordinary accountings are thus not 'time out' from actions. They are not the moments at which action ceases and commentary on action takes its place. Nor are accounts disembodied events that stand outside the activities in which they are temporally enmeshed. Rather they are actions in their own right and, like other actions, they inevitably contribute to the setting of which they are a part, and, again like other actions, they are interpreted and understood procedurally. Moreover, accounts are contextually interpreted through the reflexively elaborative procedures of the documentary method of interpretation. As Garfinkel and Sacks summarize the position, 'a description, for example, in the ways it may be a constituent part of the circumstances it describes, in endless ways and unavoidably, elaborates those circumstances and is elaborated by them' (Garfinkel and Sacks: 1970, p. 338). Accounts, then, are subject to the same circumstantial and interpretative contingencies as the actions to which they are oriented. For, to repeat, accounts are actions and the important thing about them is that they are used in an immensely varied range of ways to manage ordinary settings of activity. Accounts, therefore, are not a terminus for social scientific investigation, they are, rather, a point of departure for it.

Garfinkel's view of language and social relations is thus one which opens up completely new fields of investigation while raising profound and complex questions about the nature of speech, speaking and other forms of communicative action. Inevitably, this treatment generates more problems than it resolves. This is entirely to the good. The older views of language rendered it as a transparent, unresearchable entity. Garfinkel's observations 'naturalize' language and place the analysis of accounts and accounting practices on a par with the analysis of other forms of practical action. Within this view, language is understood as a resource through which social participants intervene in action situations, but the 'frameworks' and 'mechanics' through which words are assembled into accounts and these accounts are 'attached' to real-world situations remain open to empirical study. As valuable analyses of the variety of ways in which ordinary accountings are invoked in the maintenance of social worlds, the reader is recommended to examine Wieder's classic study (1974) of the use of the 'convict code' as an accounting scheme in a 'half-way house' for paroled narcotics addicts and Gilbert and Mulkay's study (1984) of the ways in which scientists depict a contemporary field of biochemical research. Each of these studies, which defy summary in a short essay, readily reveals the gains in sociological insight which can be made from abandoning the traditional representative view of language in investigating forms of social organization.

Dimensions of Empirical Research in Ethnomethodology

1 Social structures as 'normal environments'

One of the first, and most prominent, lines of development deriving from Garfinkel's initiatives focused on typification or normalization as a characteristic of common-sense reasoning and judgement. This focus was, in part, a legacy from the phenomenological writings of Schutz, who had stressed the role of consciousness as a typifying agency and characterized everyday language as 'the typifying medium *par excellence*' and as a 'treasure house of ready-made preconstituted types' (Schutz: 1962a, p. 14). This theme was taken up and stressed by Cicourel in his discussion of 'normal form typification' as a methodological issue (Cicourel: 1972, pp. 254–6) and is of course thematically embedded in Garfinkel's discussions of 'perceived normality' as a property of cultural objects and events and in his discussions of mundane accountability and the documentary method.

In the empirical analyses which stemmed from the typification theme, the main emphasis of research fell on the underlying assumptions and presuppositions of particular typification frameworks, the concrete procedures and considerations informing the assimilation of objects and events into categories and the roles of such categories in particular social environments. Much of this empirical work emerged in the field of deviance or dealt with related bureaucratic decision-making procedures that are implemented in the 'processing of people'. The superficial affinity with the labelling perspective (Becker: 1963) was considerable, not least because of the large substantive overlap between the two approaches. None the less, the two perspectives differed on two related and critical issues. First, the ethnomethodological studies avoided the nominalistic labelling premiss that deviance was constituted by societal reactions *tout court* (cf. Pollner: 1974b) and, second, they rejected as over-simple the labelling theorists' concentration on the distinction between the correctly and incorrectly labelled. Instead the ethnomethodological studies focused directly upon the organizational practices and contingencies of the defining process and accepted that normalizing expectancies were an irremediable feature of its operation.[33]

An early exemplar of this approach was David Sudnow's well-known study, 'Normal Crimes' (1965). Here Sudnow showed in considerable detail that Californian public lawyers' common-sense constructs of typical offenders and patterns of offence commission effectively shaped their approaches to plea bargaining and hence substantial aspects of the administration of justice.[34] In particular he showed that the constructs were used to determine the appropriateness of entering into plea-bargaining activities. In interviews with defendants, they were used to epitomize the defendants as 'cases' in ways that presupposed their guilt. And these same constructs strongly influenced the type of charge that was finally arrived at in exchange for the 'guilty' plea, subject only, Sudnow showed, to a further consideration: the issue of what sentence this type of 'normal' offence should get as its 'due'. The categories of crime which were used by the legal representatives were, to say the least, underdetermined by the legal code. As Sudnow observes,

> in their actual use, categories of crime ... are ... the shorthand reference terms for that knowledge of the social structure and its criminal events upon which the task of practically organizing the work of 'representation' is premised. That knowledge includes, embodied within what burglary, petty theft, narcotics violations, child molestation and the rest *actually stand for*, knowledge of modes of criminal activity, ecological characteristics of the community, patterns of daily slum life, psychological and social biographies of offenders, criminal histories and futures. (Sudnow: 1965, p. 275)

Through the use of this knowledge with its routinization and typification of 'normal crimes', Sudnow argued, the administration of justice had become subject to a process of informal bureaucratization that was not depicted in the Californian criminal code.

In parallel with Sudnow's study, a substantial number of ethnomethodological investigations carried out during the 1960s showed that a large and previously unsuspected range of contextual considerations could be invoked in constituting or modifying normal bureaucratic decisions or courses of action. Closely associated with this was the recognition that members of bureaucracies are not only able, but positively obliged, to invoke and interpret bureaucratic rules and procedures in *ad hoc* ways and that this, in turn, is an important source of discretionary power. The necessity of producing *ad hoc* interpretations of even very clear-cut rules of procedure was elegantly demonstrated by Zimmerman (1969a) in a study of the activities

---

[33] See Pollner (1974b) for a critique of the labelling perspective from an ethnomethodological viewpoint. The ethnomethodological conclusion that all procedures for locating deviance are ultimately constituent features of the deviance they thus render accountable was a proximate point of departure for a radical eruption out of ethnomethodology by Alan Blum and Peter McHugh and their associates into a totalizing moral critique of social relations. See McHugh *et al.* (1974) for a collection of papers and Heritage (1975) for an attempt at appraisal.

[34] For a valuable study of the particulars of the plea-bargaining process itself, see Maynard: 1984.

of receptionists in a state welfare agency. The receptionists, who used a highly specific procedure to allocate a smooth flow of claimants to case officers, were obliged to depart from the procedure under a number of contingencies. In such cases, the receptionists' actions were defensible and defended by the claim that the objectives of the procedure were more effectively satisfied by departing from it than adhering to it. As Zimmerman put it, 'the notion of action-in-accord-with-a-rule is a matter not of compliance or non-compliance *per se* but of the various ways in which persons *satisfy* themselves and others concerning what is or is not "reasonable" compliance in particular situations' (1970, p. 23).

In related papers arising from the same research project, Zimmerman disclosed a range of ways in which documented claims and verbal accounts were interpreted through procedures which closely resembled those of Garfinkel's coders (see p. 236). Like the coders, the case officers were often able, at a glance, to 'see the system' in the documentary evidence that formed the basis for claims. When the documents appeared problematic, conceptions of the 'ways in which the documents could have been produced' (Zimmerman: 1969a) furnished an open set of resources through which the officials could arrive at determinate and warrantable decisions. Other studies, too, demonstrated the extent to which the processing of people is subject to interpretative practices in which the discretionary invocation of contextual matters can play a crucial role. In the field of education, studies of pupil-counselling (Cicourel and Kitsuse: 1963) and of the application of tests and other courses of treatment (Cicourel *et al.*: 1974; Leiter: 1976) have documented these processes in substantial measure and Bittner's work (see esp. Bittner: 1967a) illustrates parallel processes in the work of practical policing.[35]

While the above studies show the extent and range of ways in which background information characteristically enters into ordinary bureaucratic decision-making, Garfinkel's famous study '"Good" Organizational Reasons for "Bad" Clinic Records' (1984f) takes the argument a step further. The point of departure for this study was the fact that a preliminary investigation of a psychiatric clinic's records showed that, while entries were regularly made, they were insufficiently detailed for even quite elementary social scientific uses. This raised the question of why such incomplete, vague and elliptical records should none the less be kept. Garfinkel's conclusion was that the records were kept as a resource with which to depict relations between the patients and clinic personnel as appropriate fulfilments of a 'therapeutic contract'. The absence of detail, he proposed, served as a

---

[35] The demonstration of related processes across the range of social science procedures has, of course, been a long-term project of Cicourel's writings from Cicourel (1964) onwards. As Handel (see 1982, pp. 112ff.) has noted, this project is expressed in the two-pronged character of much of Cicourel's empirical work, which is simultaneously substantive and concerned with the practical social science reasoning underlying the substantive conclusions.

defensive resource by ensuring that the records could only be competently read by entitled personnel who would interpret them in terms of their understandings of typical clinic procedures. The records consisted of 'a single free field of elements' whose unavoidable contextualization by reference to typical aspects of clinic practice would inevitably serve to justify the practices and procedures that had been carried out (Garfinkel: 1984f, p. 201). Thus, not only is 'normalized' background information a constituent feature of bureaucratic decision-making, but bureaucracies can defend themselves against an unknown range of future difficulties by the production of records which, almost unavoidably, will be defensively exploited through this very fact.

Perhaps the best known of the ethnomethodological studies dealing with organizational processes have been those that cast doubt on the value of official statistics for the conduct of sociological research. Most prominent among these have been Cicourel's study (1968) of the processing of juvenile offenders and the work by Douglas (1967) and Atkinson (1978) on the investigation of suicide. These writers stressed the extent to which background knowledge enters into the constitution of the judgements that make up the official statistics and argued that studies based on official statistics were likely to recover the assumptions which had been built into the defining process by the legal agencies but were unlikely to recover causal factors that had not already been actively or passively acted upon by the agencies themselves.

Thus in his well-known study of juvenile justice, Cicourel showed that the officials concerned associated juvenile delinquency with marriage break-down in the offenders' homes. It was assumed that offenders from broken homes, lacking parental guidance and correction, would be likely to commit more serious offences in the future. In accordance with this assumption, juvenile offences committed by children from broken homes were treated more seriously than similar offences by children from 'two-parent families'. This differential treatment was apparent in a variety of statistics dealing with each stage of the law-enforcement process. Offences by children from broken homes appeared more often in official reports, were more commonly dealt with by the courts and were more commonly given custodial sentences. It is clear that if the disposition of juvenile cases is strongly influenced by such presumptions which thereby become built into the crime statistics, the statistics of 'juvenile crime' cannot be a valid resource with which to pursue social scientific objectives. For the statistics will not give a representative depiction of the incidence of juvenile crime and cannot be used to assess the role of social characteristics (such as broken homes) as causal factors in crime-generation.

Cicourel proposed that internal police records are also of dubious social scientific value. Having studied the processes through which the officials concerned created dossiers on their juvenile subjects, Cicourel argued, drawing on Shibutani's studies (1966) of rumour, that such dossiers embodied a process of progressive typification in which case details became more concise, selective and consistent with the assumptions and objectives of the law-enforcement agencies.

In the case of both sets of information – the statistics and the dossiers – Cicourel concluded that a circular process was occurring in which fundamental presumptions about juveniles were being built into the records which, in turn, were being used to argue for the validity of the presumptions. A rather similar conclusion was arrived at by Douglas (1967) and Atkinson (1978) with respect to the interpretation of suicide statistics. Thus Douglas proposed that the kinds of sociological factors normally used to explain the variations in suicide rates may themselves influence the social processes through which deaths come to be recorded as suicides (Douglas: 1967, pp. 163–231). In particular, he argued that social integration will be positively associated with attempts to conceal suicide which, to the extent that they are successful, will influence the measurement of suicide rates.

Atkinson's study focused on the role of British coroners and their officers in the investigative process. He found that the officials concerned with the certification of death have relatively well-defined conceptions of 'typical suicides', 'typical suicidal biographies', and that such factors as the mode of death and the dead person's immediate life circumstances formed the material out of which formulaic 'recipe knowledge' of forms of suicide was constructed. These conceptions, which embrace and, in some cases, closely resemble social scientific hypotheses on the causation of suicide, are subsequently built into the suicide statistics through the investigative procedures of coroners and their officials. Thus studies of official suicide statistics, Atkinson proposes, are inevitably – if unknowingly – engaged in decoding the common-sense theories of suicide which were constitutive in the recognition of individual cases and hence, cumulatively, in the statistics as a whole.

All of the work described in this section has focused on the normalizing and typifying processes which are characteristic of organizational activity in all its variety. Notwithstanding the controversial nature of the last-mentioned studies, it would be a mistake to conclude, as some have done, that the work described in this section has only a methodological relevance, and a negative one at that. The work on normalization was undertaken in the wake of Garfinkel's proposal that the 'perceived normality' of social events is the product of active work. The application of this notion to organizational processes has not only confirmed the original insight. It has also given rise to new levels of understanding that have positively informed a wide range of sociological investigations, including many which are not themselves ethnomethodological. Moreover, the studies of organizational processes described here have shown the profound extent to which the normalizing procedures are embedded in what may be termed 'organizational exigencies'. Again and again the studies show finely-detailed connections between the routine normalizing activities that make up the daily work of the organizations on the one hand and the social arrangements of the organizations, with their obligations and their 'considerations', on the other.

The studies show the extent to which the normalizing activities were tied to

> the terms of employment, to various internal and external chains of reportage, supervision, and review, and to similar organizationally supplied 'priorities of relevances' for assessments of what 'realistically', 'practically', or 'reasonably' needed to be done or could be done, how quickly, with what resources, seeing whom, talking about what, for how long and so on. (Garfinkel: 1984a, p. 13).

In the process, these studies have begun to establish a new sociology of knowledge which is freed from the strait-jacket of prescriptive rationality and in which the reflexive ties between the social constitution of knowledge and the institutional contexts in which that knowledge is generated and maintained are given their full weight as sociological phenomena.

2 Conversation analysis

Conversation analysis[36] has developed over the past fifteen years as a vigorous and distinctive aspect of ethnomethodology. During this time the perspective has given rise to a very substantial research literature which is strikingly cumulative and interlocking. Of all the research streams of ethnomethodology, conversation analysis is perhaps the one most occupied with the direct analysis of social action. From the outset, the approach has been resolutely empirical. Rather than speculating about idealized characteristics of social action, conversation analysts have directed their empirical investigations towards 'actual, particular social actions and organized sequences of them' (Schegloff: 1980, p. 151). The outcome has been remarkable. A large literature has developed which contains results of great scope and cumulative power and which has had a considerable impact on the neighbouring disciplines of social psychology, linguistics and cognitive science.

The basic research posture of conversation analysis was collaboratively developed in a series of papers by Sacks, Schegloff and Jefferson. Their analyses, like other ethnomethodological studies, focused on the methods or procedures by which ordinary social participants conduct their interactional

---

[36] The term 'conversation analysis' is preferred to the somtimes-used conversational analysis because, within this field, conversation is the object of investigation. The field began to emerge in the late 1960s with the publication of Schegloff (1968) and the widespread circulation of Sacks's unpublished lectures (Sacks: 1964–72). Although no monograph-length introductions are available, summary outlines are contained in Atkinson and Drew (1979, pp. 34–81), Heritage (1984a, pp. 233–92), Levinson (1983, pp. 284–370) and West and Zimmerman (1982). Collections of published studies include Atkinson and Heritage: 1984; Psathas: 1979; Schenkein: 1978; *Sociology*: 1978; Zimmerman and West: 1980. See Heritage (1985) for a lengthy bibliography.

affairs.[37] All evidence for the participants' orientation to, or use of, these procedures was to be derived solely from the behaviour of the participants in the ordinary circumstances of their lives. As Schegloff and Sacks summarized the orientation:

> We have proceeded on the assumption ... that insofar as the materials we worked with exhibited orderliness, they did so not only to us, indeed not in the first place for us, but for the co-participants who had produced them. If the materials ... were orderly, they were so because they had been methodically produced by the members of society for one another. (Schegloff and Sacks: 1973, p. 290).

This posture plainly entails the use of naturalistic methods of study, but the choice of subject-matter was initially not particularly principled. Indeed, as Sacks recalled, the initial motivation to study ordinary conversation was methodological, reflecting a desire to see if the organizational details of naturally occurring interaction could be subjected to formal description (Sacks: 1984a, p. 26). It was the success of this venture that led to a more intensely substantive interest in the details of interaction.

Despite the fact that Sacks and his co-workers began studying ordinary conversation almost by accident, conversation analysts have maintained a primary research focus on ordinary, mundane interaction rather than, for example, the 'institutionalized' interaction of the courtroom or the business organization. There are good reasons for this approach. Not only is 'ordinary conversation' the predominant medium of interaction in the social world, it is also the primary form of interaction to which, with whatever simplifications,[38] the child is first exposed and through which socialization proceeds. There is thus every reason to suppose that the basic forms of mundane talk constitute a kind of benchmark against which other more formal or 'institutional' types of interaction are recognized and experienced. And indeed, more recent studies of 'institutional' interaction do show systematic variations and restrictions on forms of action relative to ordinary conversation (see, e.g., Atkinson: 1982; Atkinson and Drew: 1979; Drew: 1984; Heritage: 1984b; Maynard: 1984; Mehan: 1979). Thus mundane conversation represents a broad and flexible domain of primary interactional practices. In approaching it, conversation analysts have, where possible,

[37] Both Sacks and Schegloff underwent graduate training with Goffman and their approach to studying the common-sense reasoning underlying ordinary actions may reflect convergent influences from both Garfinkel and Goffman. Both may be said to have departed from Goffman's example in the extent to which they abandoned ethnographic styles of analysis and reportage in favour of increasingly systematic efforts to render both the logic and the practical reasoning informing conversational interaction explicit.

[38] See, for example, Bruner (1983), Ochs and Schieffelin (1979) and Snow and Ferguson (1977) for accounts of some aspects of the simplifications which accompany mothers' speech to young children.

focused on interaction between peers with an underlying research strategy of uncovering what is systematic about social interaction in the broadest range of 'unmarked' interaction contexts. In turn this approach offers the best hope of determining what is distinctive about interactions involving, for example, the specialisms of the school or the hospital or the asymmetries of status, gender, ethnicity, etc.

As already mentioned, conversation analysis was developed as a naturalistic programme of research. In pursuit of its goals, every effort is made to maintain a direct focus on the specifics of interaction which is naturally occurring and uncontaminated by interventions from the researcher.[39] This research strategy is strongly maintained and is associated with the view (see pp. 241–2) that social actions and the social settings to which they stand in a reflexive relationship are established in and through the details of interaction. Research procedures which result in the loss of detail or its contamination are therefore to be avoided as far as possible.

The central objective of conversation analysis is to uncover the social competences which underlie social interaction, that is, the procedures and expectations through which interaction is produced and understood.[40] A number of assumptions are made in pursuit of this task. First, it is assumed that interaction is organized by reference to institutionalized procedures which, for analytical purposes, can be treated as structures in their own right (cf. Schegloff: 1986). Second, it is assumed that contributions to interaction are both context-shaped, in that actions cannot be adequately understood without reference to the context of preceding actions to which they are generally understood to respond, and context-renewing, in that each current action will propose a current here-and-now definition of the situation to which subsequent talk will be oriented. Finally, as noted above, it is assumed that social actions work *in detail* and hence that the specific details of interaction cannot simply be ignored as insignificant without damaging the prospects for coherent and effective analyses.

At its inception, conversation analysis was developed in two major dimensions. First, arising from both Garfinkel's and Sacks's concern with descriptive accounting (Garfinkel: 1984; Garfinkel and Sacks: 1970; Sacks: 1963) there emerged a number of papers on particular lexical formulations and

---

[39] The following procedures are thus avoided by researchers in conversation analysis as involving unwarranted departures from the use of naturally occurring data: experimental procedures involving the observer in the direction or manipulation of behaviour; the use of pre-coded schedules to categorize behaviour directly in the field or on tape; the use of interviewing as a substitute for natural observation; the creation of data through invented or imagined 'vignettes'.

[40] As in other areas of ethnomethodology, conversation analysts have begun from Garfinkel's proposal that both the production and the recognition of courses of action are informed by a *common* set of methods or procedures. As Garfinkel puts the point: 'the activities whereby members produce and manage settings of organized everyday affairs are identical with members' procedures for making those settings 'account-able' (1984a, p. 1).

referring expressions (e.g. Sacks: 1973; 1975; Sacks and Schegloff: 1979; Schegloff: 1972) of which the most influential derived from Sacks's research on communications to a suicide prevention centre and in his work on membership categorization devices (Sacks: 1972a; 1972b). The second, simultaneously emerging dimension of conversation-analytical research focused on the sequential organization of interaction and it was this second dimension which came to assume increasing prominence in conversation-analytical publications after 1972. The best known of these latter publications centred on the management of conversational turn-taking (Sacks, Schegloff and Jefferson: 1974) and the related problems of securing coordinated entry to (Schegloff: 1968), exit from (Schegloff and Sacks: 1973) and suspension of (Sacks: 1974) turn-taking procedures for conversation. These papers were the first to show a detailed and systematic set of procedures for turn-taking that was consistent with a wide variety of basic facts about interaction. In so doing they established completely new standards of rigour and comprehensiveness in the study of social interaction and, as a result, they became highly influential. Moreover the studies introduced further analytical concepts for the study of interaction which were not confined in their significance to the study of turn-taking *per se*.

The most important of these concepts was that of the *adjacency pair*. This concept embodies the observation that certain kinds of activities (such as greetings and farewells, questions and answers, etc.) are conventionally organized as pairs such that the production of a first member of the pair both projects and requires that a second, complementary action should be produced 'next' by the recipient of the first. The concept unlocked a number of aspects of the reasoning procedures informing interaction. It suggested ways in which social participants can find projected 'next' actions to be noticeably or non-trivially absent (Sacks: 1972b; Schegloff: 1972). It also indicated how second actions that were unrelated to a first could be understood as misaligned or in error. And, perhaps most importantly, it suggested how second speakers could be treated as normatively accountable for failures to respond, faulty responses and other interactional mishaps – thus intimating an inbuilt motivation for competent conversational performance (see also Sacks *et al.*: 1974, pp. 727–8). Although the adjacency-pair notion was developed in the context of paired actions (such as greetings and farewells) that were clearly geared to turn-taking contingencies, the concept obviously had a broader applicability.

At a further level, the concept suggested a primary mechanism through which intersubjective understanding is maintained in interaction. For, to the extent that 'next' actions can be found to be fitted to the prior first-pair part, they can be treated as displaying understandings of the first-pair parts that are appropriate to the fit. Thus second-pair parts not only accomplish (or fail to accomplish) the relevant next action, in so doing they also display a public understanding of the prior utterance to which they are directed, and that understanding is available for 'third turn' confirmation, comment, correction, etc., by the producer of the first-pair part. Thus adjacent positioning provides a resource for the continuous updating of inter-subjective understandings. Moreover it is by means of adjacent positioning, as Schegloff and Sacks (1973) observed, that various forms of failures can be recognized and that appreciations and corrections etc. can be understandably attempted.

In sum, the unpacking of the adjacency-pair concept considerably developed and particularized some important elements of what Garfinkel has referred to as the 'incarnate accountability' of action. The general pattern of analytical reasoning that was sketched out in these papers has subsequently been applied to an ever-expanding range of interactional activities. These latter have included non-verbal conduct including the organization of a range of features of gaze and body movement (Goodwin: 1981; Heath: 1986), the 'preferential' organization of alternative courses of conduct (Davidson: 1984; Pomerantz: 1978; 1984; Schegloff, Jefferson and Sacks: 1977) and a wide range of more particular topic areas (see Heritage: 1985 for details).

In the past five years or so, conversation analysis has begun to branch out from its 'baseline' in mundane conversational activity toward studies of interaction in a range of institutional settings involving strongly-defined social roles, such as classrooms, courtrooms, news interviews, doctor–patient and other institutionally-regulated forms of interaction.[41] This work exhibits certain differences from the original foundational work in conversation. While 'pure' conversational interaction has been shown to be organized in terms of formal principles which permit cumulative findings of considerable abstractness and power, studies of interaction in institutional settings presently exhibit a more 'piecemeal' aspect. As noted above, institutional interaction seems to involve specific narrowings and re-specifications of the range of options that are operative in conversational interaction. More importantly, these narrowings and re-specifications are *conventional* in character: they are culturally variable, they are sometimes subject to legal constraints, and they are discursively justifiable and justified by reference to considerations of, *inter alia*, task, equity and efficiency in ways that mundane conversational practices manifestly are not. Associated with these conventions are differing participation frameworks (Goffman: 1981) with their

[41] See McHoul (1978) and Mehan (1979) for classroom interaction; Atkinson and Drew (1979), Drew (1984) and Pomerantz and Atkinson (1984) for approaches to courtroom data, Maynard (1984) for studies of plea-bargaining interaction, and Eglin and Wideman (forthcoming), Sharrock and Turner (1978), Watson (forthcoming) and Whalen and Zimmerman (forthcoming) and Zimmerman (n.d.) for a range of studies of interaction involving the police. For doctor–patient interaction, among a large literature, see West (1984) and the contributions to Fisher and Todd (1983). Conversation-analytical principles have also been extended into the analysis of political speeches, e.g. Atkinson (1984) and Heritage and Greatbatch (1986).

associated rights and obligations, different footings and differential patterns of opportunity and power.

A basic point of departure for some of the more recent studies in institutional interaction has been Sacks, Schegloff and Jefferson's comparative discussion of different turn-taking systems (1974: pp. 729–30). Since then analyses by McHoul (1978), Mehan (1979), Atkinson and Drew (1979) and Greatbatch (1985) have detailed the forms of turn-taking which are characteristic in classroom, courtroom and news-interview interactions. These studies converge in suggesting that the relatively restricted patterns of conduct characteristic of these settings are the product of turn-type pre-allocation (Atkinson and Drew: 1979) and that this form of turn-taking has a pervasive influence both on the range and design of the interactional activities which the different parties routinely undertake and on the detailed management of such encounters (see also Schegloff: forthcoming). Other studies of institutional interaction are concerned with investigating the management of particular activities in a range of settings[42] and with the patterning of power imbalances in interactional conduct.[43]

Because institutional interaction is conventionalized and culturally variable, the studies that deal with it are less interlocking than the 'pure' conversation-analytical work from which they derive. None the less there is an underlying coherence of perspective which informs the field. This derives both from the fundamentals of the ethnomethodological viewpoint and from the ways in which that viewpoint is particularized by the use of conversation-analytical techniques. Based on the recognition that institutional roles are created and maintained through specific patterns of interaction, this work carries a considerable and growing potential for applied and policy-oriented studies, a potential which was by no means apparent at the inception of conversation analysis.

Taken as a whole, conversation analysis has evolved into a powerful and productive field of study which has been widely influential both inside and outside its home discipline of sociology. Its contribution to social science has already been substantial, not only in the analysis of action and the development of new methodological techniques but also in raising the general level of sociological sensitivity and awareness to the detailed organization of social conduct. There is every reason to suppose that its growth and development will continue in the coming years.

3 Studies of work

In the final section of this essay, we briefly consider a newly emerging phase of research by Garfinkel and his collaborators which is generically termed the 'studies of work'. Although the term was originally intended to

---

[42] See Heritage (1985) for details.

[43] See, in particular, the work by West and Zimmerman (West: 1979; West and Zimmerman: 1977; 1983; Zimmerman and West: 1980).

embrace the widest range of naturally-organized ordinary activities, the studies which have been published thus far primarily deal with 'work' in the narrower sense of occupational activity. These studies have focused in particular on the activities of physical scientists and mathematicians (e.g. Garfinkel, Lynch and Livingston: 1981; Livingston: 1986; Lynch: 1982; 1985a; 1985b; Lynch, Livingston and Garfinkel: 1983), though investigations of a broader range of work activity are scheduled for publication shortly (Garfinkel: forthcoming).

Adumbrated by ethnomethodological investigations of work activities in a range of concrete contexts (e.g. Garfinkel: 1967; Wieder: 1974; Zimmerman: 1969a; 1969b) the new studies of work depart from their forerunners in their focus on the specific competences which comprise ordinary occupational activities. Their objective is to examine what an occupational activity consists of, and they respond to this question on a complex analytical and empirical basis.

Garfinkel introduced the 'studies of work' programme by noting that many social scientific studies have tended to be 'about' rather than 'of' occupations (Garfinkel *et al.*: 1981, pp. 132–3). He has drawn attention to the fact that while many studies of occupations have much to report about such sociologically-formulated social characteristics of the participants as their income, ethnicity, class position, role relations, etc., these studies are not informative about the fundamental activities which make the occupations significant in the first place. The occupations involve the creation of various forms of valued outcomes often drawing upon complex skills and bodies of knowledge, yet little is known about what is involved. The 'studies of work' programme thus embodies the recognition that there is a descriptive vacuum at the centre of sociological analyses of occupations.

Garfinkel often recalls, as a way of highlighting the problem, an exchange between Fred Strodtbeck and Edward Shils. When Strodtbeck wanted to use Bales's 'Interaction Process Analysis' to study jury deliberations, Shils objected that while the analysis would convey the ways in which the jury functioned as a small group it would not give access to how the jury functioned as a jury (Garfinkel *et al.*: 1981, p. 133). Shils's complaint raises a fundamental issue. Social scientists should be able to describe the practices which are distinctive and important about an occupation or activity. And this in turn means raising the question of what Garfinkel terms the 'quiddity' or 'just whatness' of social practices: just what does competent work in the biological sciences consist of (cf. Lynch: 1985a), what is it to demonstrate a mathematical theorem (Livingston: 1986), or to play something that is recognizably jazz music (Sudnow: 1978)?

It is important to recognize that any attempt to address this question will involve a wide range of research activities. Some of these will have a pronounced 'deconstructive' component: there is no reason to expect that either the statements of occupational practitioners or the normative philosophies of occupations will furnish the resources out of which an analysis that is adequate to its subject-matter can be fashioned, for such accounts routinely gloss over or conceal the practical work involved in the accomplish-ment of occupational or scientific goals.[44] At the same time the 'work' of occupations (and indeed of other social activities) inherently embodies conceptualizations of 'relevant considerations' relative to the work in ques-tion that are intrinsic to and embedded within the actual concrete practices of practitioners. Thus this subject-matter – embracing analyses of naturally-theorized and naturally-organized work practices – can ultimately be addressed only through analyses based in empirical materials.

The task of analysis is approached by starting with what the *occupational practitioners* recognize as belonging to a domain of work activities and work competences. These activities are predominantly treated through examining concrete features of occupational practices, normally in the form of taped or documentary records. Thus competences are exclusively treated *from within*, that is, as recognized and acted upon by the practitioners in ordinary settings of work activity. Within this framework, as Lynch *et al.* point out, the analyses centre on the ways in which the logical and reasoned character of occupational actions is made publicly available through

> orders of intersubjectively accountable details; the order of spoken utterances
> by different parties in conversation, the compositional order of manipulated
> materials at the laboratory bench, or the transitive order of written materials
> on a page of text. (Lynch *et al.*: 1983, p. 206)

The complex interweaving of temporal organization into the substantive practices of competent occupational practitioners has formed a particularly valuable point of entry into studies of their properties.

What is being attempted here is a substantial departure from existing sociological practice and very much more complex than it may appear at first sight. The methodological issues which surround the 'studies of work' programme – such as determining the scope and dimensions of occupational actions, finding ways of depicting their 'units' and 'segments', establishing criteria of adequacy in depicting their naturally-theoretic commitments, etc. – are considerably more thorny and complicated than, for example, those which are involved in conversation analysis. And the studies of work have involved the use of a variety of research methods, including a range of ethnographic techniques, forms of textual analysis, conversation-analytical procedures, and others. This methodological pluralism is a response to the fact that occupational domains may be manifested in a variety of ways – for example, in bodily and conversational activity for which a video record-ing might be the most appropriate mode of analytical access, but also in documentary records of various kinds requiring different methods of approach.

[44] See the discussion of this issue in Garfinkel *et al.* (1981) and in Holton's (1981) response to it. Further discussion of the ways in which written formulations of scientific findings both obscure and depend upon underlying work-site competences may be found in Garfinkel (1985) and Livingston (1986).

Regardless of the particular procedures that are employed, Garfinkel proposes that the studies of work should be disciplined by what he terms the 'unique adequacy requirement'. This requirement arises out of the fact that occupational skills and scientific knowledge have advanced through the development of practices and techniques which are commonly highly specific to particular tasks or objectives. This specificity imposes considerable demands on any researcher who wishes to investigate them. For example, any analysis of the correspondence of a law firm which fails to recognize that many elements of legal phraseology have a particular legal status which has been tested in the courts will inevitably fail to grasp the nature of this aspect of legal work. Similarly, an ethnographic study of a scientific laboratory conducted by someone who is not competent in the relevant scientific field is unlikely to yield much that is instructive about the organization of its scientific practice. In sum, much of what is carried out within an occupation – which, from the practitioner's point of view, may range from the familiar and instantly recognizable to the esoteric – is likely to be opaque to an outside observer. Accordingly, Garfinkel advocates that all forms of investigation be carried out within the 'unique adequacy requirement' – the requirement that the researcher be a competent practitioner in the domain of activities under investigation. This requirement, he proposes, optimizes the chances that the fundamental research objective of the 'studies of work' programme will be realized, namely that the constituent details of occupationally competent activities will be depicted with as much precision and specificity as possible.

The new studies of work represent a substantial extension of the preoccupations which have been at the centre of Garfinkel's work for the past twenty years. Each of these studies involves the maintenance of ethnomethodological indifference: the activities of brain scientists, mathematicians or jazz pianists are presented without celebration, irony or relativization and without transforming their technical features or downgrading their achievements. By the same token, the new studies also express an important continuity in Garfinkel's sociological programme. From his earliest writings, Garfinkel has rejected any approach to sociological analysis that was premised on a distinction between rational and non-rational actions and that meted out different explanatory treatments to each. As we have seen, such an approach was central to Parsonian theorizing. The notion that rational actions are their own explanation, while non-rational actions can be explained by reference to the deterministic influence of moral norms resulted in a loss of analytical purchase on the accountable, reasonable features of ordinary activities. Equally, however, it led to the conclusion that highly-rationalized scientific activities lay outside the remit of sociological investigation.[45] Garfinkel's theoretical perspective advocates the restoration of

---

[45] A parallel position was adopted by Bloor (1976) who coined the term 'sociology of error' to characterize sociological perspectives which excluded science as an object of investigation on epistemological grounds. For a range of related positions in the

both of these domains to serious sociological study and it is in the 'studies of work' programme in particular that he and his collaborators have broached the second domain in earnest.

The relentless focus of these studies – a focus which inevitably defies the task of an overview – is on the specific, discoverable, material practices which make up these activities. Their objective, therefore, is detailed descriptions of naturally-organized social practices which, like observations in the natural sciences, can be reproduced, checked, evaluated and form the basis for naturalistic study and conjecture. Their revolutionary character lies simply in the fact that, before Garfinkel raised the issue, the question of depicting just what the business of ordinary work activity consists of had never been raised as a serious descriptive task. The studies so far published are of great intrinsic interest and, if the development of related fields such as conversation analysis is any guide, they promise a theoretical and practical relevance which is no less substantial.

Conclusion

Any assessment of the contribution of ethnomethodology to the contemporary state of sociology must inevitably begin with the wholesale transformation of the theory of action that was initiated in Garfinkel's researches. The essential moves in this process were, first, the decision to study the characteristics of the reasoning and the rationales which, at whatever level of conscious orientation, enter into choices among courses of action. This decision was, secondly, an unconditional one in the sense that the reasoning was to be studied regardless of the extent to which it appeared rational when viewed from the outside. Studying practical reasoning in this way means, thirdly, looking at the rationales of action from within the contexts in which they are used. And, as we have seen, this means bracketing questions of their ultimate validity or effectiveness in favour of looking quite simply at how they work out in practice. It has also, fourthly, meant studying social processes as naturalistically as possible for, if the rationales are employed (and make specific kinds of sense) only in particular circumstances, their articulation with the contexts in which they are used can only be explored naturalistically.

These proposals have struck some commentators less as an approach to the analysis of action, than as explorations of subjective consciousness or, at best, as avenues toward the study of social cognition. This is not an appropriate understanding of Garfinkel's initiative. His entire approach to the analysis of action and its rationales is premised on the public account-

---

sociology of science, see the contributions to Collins (1981) and to Knorr-Cetina and Mulkay (1983). Latour and Woolgar's (1979) study of laboratory science converges in atmosphere, though not in specific orientations, with the 'study of work' programme.

ability of action. Each social action is a recognizable commentary on, and intervention in, the setting of activity in which it occurs. Its specific character as commentary and intervention (i.e. its public accountability) has a procedural basis. It is the product of procedures or methods which are socially shared and used. These methods are numerous, reticulated and complexly interrelated. None the less, since they form the fundamental framework through which action will be interpreted, they will inevitably inform the *design and production* of action as well as its interpretation. Thus it is the procedural basis of action which bridges the gap between cognition and action, both practically for the actors and theoretically for the social scientist.

Viewed in this context, Garfinkel's theoretical writings represent an extraordinary achievement. For they embody a grasp of the foundations of social action, intersubjective understanding and social organization in a single core phenomenon: the methodically accountable character of ordinary social activity. From the Harvard years onwards, Garfinkel has occupied a wholly original analytical position in relation to the topics of social action and social order. In the intervening years, he has worked to give this vision practical demonstration, coherent shape and depth of penetration. The vision has proved to be a fecund one inspiring, and finding confirmation in, the hundreds of conversation-analytical and related studies which have appeared in the past decade.

As a dialectical correlate to this analysis of action as based on methodical knowledge, Garfinkel has also stressed that, regardless of how specialized or technical it is, the knowledge which is used in everyday settings cannot be analysed independently of the courses of action through which it is acted upon, maintained and validated. This theme emerges particularly strongly in the studies of organizational activity which he has both undertaken and inspired and is surfacing in still stronger form in the more recent studies of work. The studies of action and the analyses of knowledge practices thus represent complementary aspects of the same programme of investigation.

Above all, these studies, in all their facets, have sought to turn attention away from prematurely-theorized conceptions of the social world and towards the empirical phenomena of social activity in all their richness and diversity. In this way they express Garfinkel's continuing stand against 'all attempts, no matter how thoughtful, to specify an examinable practice by detailing a generality'.

Bibliography

Atkinson, J. M., 1978: *Discovering Suicide: Studies in the Social Organization of Sudden Death*. London: Macmillan.
    1982: 'Understanding Formality: Notes on the Categorization and Production of "Formal" Interaction', *British Journal of Sociology*, 33: 86–117.
    1984: *Our Masters' Voices: Studies in the Language and Body Language of Politics*. London: Methuen.

Atkinson, J. M. and Drew, P., 1979: *Order in Court: The Organization of Verbal Interaction in Judicial Settings*. London: Macmillan.

Atkinson, J.M. and Heritage, J. (eds), 1984: *Structures of Social Action: Studies in Conversation Analysis*. Cambridge, England: Cambridge University Press.

Attewell, P., 1972: 'Ethnomethodology since Garfinkel', *Theory and Society*, 1: 179–210.

Barnes, B., 1984a: *T. S. Kuhn and Social Science*. London: Macmillan.

1984b: 'On the Extension of Concepts and the Growth of Knowledge', *Sociological Review*, 30: 23–44.

Becker, H., 1963: *Outsiders*. New York: Free Press.

Benson, D. and Hughes, J., 1983: *The Perspective of Ethnomethodology*. London: Longman.

Bittner, E., 1967a: 'The Police on Skid-row: A Study of Peace-keeping', *American Sociological Review*, 32: 699–715.

1967b: 'Police Discretion in the Emergency Apprehension of Mentally-Ill Persons, *Social Problems*, 14: 278–92.

Bloor, D., 1976: *Knowledge and Social Imagery*. London: Routledge and Kegan Paul.

Brown, P. and Levinson, S., 1978: 'Universals in Language Usage: Politeness Phenomena, in E. Goody (ed.), *Questions and Politeness: Strategies in Social Interaction*. Cambridge, England: Cambridge University Press, pp. 56–289.

Bruner, J., 1983: *Child's Talk: Learning to Use Language*. Oxford: Oxford University Press.

Burke, K., 1945: *A Grammar of Motives*. Englewood Cliffs, NJ: Prentice-Hall.

Cicourel, A. V., 1964: *Method and Measurement in Sociology*. New York: Free Press.

1968: *The Social Organization of Juvenile Justice*. New York: Wiley.

1972: 'Basic and Normative Rules in the Negotiation of Status and Role', in Sudnow: 1972, pp. 229–58.

Cicourel, A. and Kitsuse, J., 1963: *The Educational Decision Makers*. New York: Bobbs-Merrill.

Cicourel, A. *et al.*, 1974: *Language Use and School Performance*. New York: Wiley.

Collins, H. M. (ed.), 1981: 'Knowledge and Controversy: Studies of Modern Natural Science', *Social Studies of Science*, special issue, 11 (1).

Coser, L., 1975: 'Presidential Address: Two Methods in Search of a Substance', *American Sociological Review*, 40: 691–700.

Coulter, J., 1971: 'Decontextualized Meanings: Current Approaches to *verstehende* Investigations', *Sociological Review*, 19: 301–33.

1973: 'Language and the Conceptualization of Meaning', *Sociology*, 7: 173–89.

1974: 'The Ethnomethodological Programme in Contemporary Sociology', *The Human Context*, 6: 103–22.

Dahrendorf, R., 1958: 'Out of Utopia', *American Journal of Sociology*, 64: 115–27.

Davidson, J., 1984: 'Subsequent Versions of Invitations, Offers, Requests and Proposals Dealing with Potential or Actual Rejection', in Atkinson and Heritage: 1984, pp. 102–28.

Douglas, J., 1967: *The Social Meanings of Suicide*. Princeton: Princeton University Press.

1971 (ed.): *Understanding Everyday Life*. London: Routledge and Kegan Paul.

Drew, P., 1984: 'Analyzing the Use of Language in Courtroom Interaction', in T. van Dijk (ed.), *Discourse and Dialogue*, vol. 3 of *A Handbook of Discourse Analysis*. New York: Academic Press, pp. 133–47.

Eglin, P. and Wideman, D., forthcoming: 'Inequality in Professional Service

Encounters: Verbal Strategies of Control versus Task Performance in Calls to the Police', *Zeitschrift für Soziologie*.

Garfinkel, H., 1952: 'The Perception of the Other: A Study in Social Order'. Unpublished doctoral dissertation. Harvard University.

1963: 'A Conception of, and Experiments with, "Trust" as a Condition of Stable Concerted Actions', in O. J. Harvey (ed.), *Motivation and Social Interaction*. New York: Ronald Press, pp. 187–238.

1967: 'Practical Sociological Reasoning: Some Features of the Work of the Los Angeles Suicide Prevention Center', in E. S. Schneidman (ed.), *Essays in Self-Destruction*. New York: International Science Press, pp. 171–87.

1974: 'On the Origins of the Term "Ethnomethodology"', in R. Turner (ed.), *Ethnomethodology*. Harmondsworth, Middlesex: Penguin, pp. 15–18.

1984: *Studies in Ethnomethodology*. Cambridge, England: Polity Press.

1984a: 'What is Ethnomethodology?' in Garfinkel: 1984, pp. 1–34.

1984b: 'Studies of the Routine Grounds of Everyday Activities', in Garfinkel: 1984, pp. 35–75. (Reprinted with revisions from *Social Problems*, 11: 225–50.)

1984c: 'Commonsense Knowledge of Social Structures: The Documentary Method of Interpretation in Lay and Professional Fact-Finding', in Garfinkel: 1984, pp. 76–103. (Reprinted from J. M. Sher (ed.), *Theories of the Mind*. New York: Free Press, 1962.)

1984d: 'Some Rules of Correct Decision Making that Jurors Respect', in Garfinkel: 1984, pp. 104–15.

1984e: 'Passing and the Managed Achievement of Sexual Status in an Intersexed Person', part 1, in Garfinkel: 1984, pp. 116–85.

1984f: '"Good" Organizational Reasons for "Bad" Clinic Records', in Garfinkel: 1984, pp. 186–207.

1984g: 'Methodological Adequacy in the Quantitative Study of Selection Criteria and Selection Practices in Psychiatric Outpatient Clinics', in Garfinkel: 1984, pp. 208–61.

1984h: 'The Rational Properties of Commonsense and Scientific Activities', in Garfinkel: 1984, pp. 262–84. (Reprinted from *Behavioural Science*, 5: 72–83.)

1985: Interview with B. Jules-Rosette, *Sociétés*, 1 (5): 35–9.

(forthcoming): 'A Manual for the Study of Naturally-Organized Ordinary Activities', 3 vols. London: Routledge and Kegan Paul.

Garfinkel, H., Lynch, M. and Livingston, E., 1981: 'The Work of a Discovering Science Construed with Materials from the Optically Discovered Pulsar', *Philosophy of the Social Sciences*, 11: 131–58.

Garfinkel, H. and Sacks, H., 1970: 'On Formal Structures of Practical Actions', in J. C. McKinney and E. A. Tiryakian (eds), *Theoretical Sociology*. New York: Appleton-Century-Crofts, pp. 338–66.

Giddens, A., 1976: *New Rules of Sociological Method*. London: Hutchinson.

1979: *Central Problems in Social Theory*. London: Macmillan.

1984: *The Constitution of Society*. Cambridge, England: Polity Press.

Gilbert, N. and Mulkay, M., 1984: *Opening Pandora's Box: An Analysis of Scientists' Discourse*. Cambridge, England: Cambridge University Press.

Goffman, E., 1981: 'Footing', in E. Goffman, *Forms of Talk*. Oxford: Basil Blackwell.

Goodwin, C., 1981: *Conversational Organization: Interaction between Speakers and Hearers*. New York: Academic Press.

Gouldner, A., 1970: *The Coming Crisis of Western Sociology*. New York: Basic Books.

Greatbatch, D., 1985: 'The Social Organization of News-Interview Interaction'.

Unpublished doctoral dissertation, University of Warwick.

Handel, W., 1982: *Ethnomethodology: How People Make Sense*. Englewood Cliffs, NJ: Prentice-Hall.

Hart, H. L. A., 1961: *The Concept of Law*. Oxford: Oxford University Press.

Heath, C., 1986: *The Partnership: Essays in the Social Organization of Speech and Body Movement in the Medical Consultation*. Cambridge, England: Cambridge University Press.

Heritage, J., 1975: 'Community and Practicality in Sociology and Beyond', *Sociology*, 9: 329–39.

1984a: *Garfinkel and Ethnomethodology*. Cambridge, England: Polity Press.

1984b: 'Analyzing News Interviews: Aspects of the Production of Talk for an Overhearing Audience', in T. van Dijk (ed.), *Discourse and Dialogue*, vol. 3 of *A Handbook of Discourse Analysis*. New York: Academic Press, pp. 95–117.

1985: 'Recent Developments in Conversation Analysis', *Sociolinguistics*, 15: 1–19.

Heritage, J. and Greatbatch, D., 1986: 'Generating Applause: A Study of Rhetoric and Response at Party Political Conferences'. *American Journal of Sociology*, 92: 110–57.

Holton, G., 1981: 'Comments on Professor Harold Garfinkel's Paper', *Philosophy of the Social Sciences*, 11: 159–61.

Knorr-Cetina, K. and Mulkay, M. (eds), 1983: *Science Observed*. London: Sage.

Latour, B. and Woolgar, S., 1979: *Laboratory Life: The Social Construction of Scientific Facts*. London: Sage.

Leiter, K., 1976: 'Teachers' Use of Background Knowledge to Interpret Test Scores', *Sociology of Education*, 49: 59–65.

1980: *A Primer on Ethnomethodology*. New York: Oxford University Press.

Levinson, S., 1983: *Pragmatics*. Cambridge, England: Cambridge University Press.

Livingston, E., 1986: *Ethnomethodological Foundations of Mathematics*. London: Routledge and Kegan Paul.

Lockwood, D., 1964: 'Social Integration and System Integration', in G. K. Zollschan and W. Hirsch (eds), *Explorations in Social Change*. London: Routledge and Kegan Paul.

Lukes, S., 1973: *Émile Durkheim*. Harmondsworth, Middlesex: Peregrine.

Lynch, M., 1982: 'Technical Work and Critical Inquiry: Investigations in a Scientific Laboratory', *Social Studies of Science*, 12: 499–534.

1985a: *Art and Artifact in Laboratory Science*. London: Routledge and Kegan Paul.

1985b: 'Discipline and the Material Form of Images: An Analysis of Scientific Visibility', *Social Studies of Science*, 15: 37–66.

Lynch, M., Livingston, E. and Garfinkel, H., 1983: 'Temporal Order in Laboratory Work', in Knorr-Cetina and Mulkay: 1983, pp. 205–38.

Mannheim, K., 1952: 'On the Interpretation of *Weltanschauung*', in his *Essays on the Sociology of Knowledge*, translated and edited by P. Kecskemeti. London: Routledge and Kegan Paul, pp. 33–83.

Maynard, D., 1984: *Inside Plea Bargaining: The Language of Negotiation*. New York: Plenum.

Maynard, D. and Wilson, T., 1980: 'On the Reification of Social Structure' in S. G. McNall and G. N. Howe (eds), *Current Perspectives in Social Theory: A Research Annual*. Greenwich, Conn.: JAI Press, pp. 287–322.

Mayrl, W., 1973: 'Ethnomethodology: Sociology without Society', *Catalyst*, 7: 15–28.

McHoul, A., 1978: 'The Organization of Turns at Formal Talk in the Classroom', *Language in Society*, 7: 183–213.

McHugh, P., 1968: *Defining the Situation*. New York: Bobbs-Merrill.

McHugh, P., Raffel, S., Foss, D. C., and Blum, A., 1974: *On the Beginning of Sociological Inquiry*. London: Routledge and Kegan Paul.

McSweeney, W., 1973: 'Meaning, Context and Situation', *European Journal of Sociology*, 14: 137–53.

Mehan, H., 1979: *Learning Lessons: Social Organization in the Classroom*. Cambridge, Mass.: Harvard University Press.

Mehan, H. and Wood, H., 1975: *The Reality of Ethnomethodology*. New York: Wiley.

Mennell, S., 1976: 'Ethnomethodology and the New *Methodenstreit*', in D. C. Thorns (ed.), *New Directions in Sociology*. Newton Abbott: David and Charles.

Mills, C. W., 1940: 'Situated Actions and Vocabularies of Motives', *American Journal of Sociology*, 5: 904–13.

Mulkay, M. and Gilbert, G. N., 1982: 'Accounting for Error', *Sociology*, 16: 165–83.

Ochs, E. and Schieffelin, B., 1979: *Developmental Pragmatics*. New York: Academic Press.

O'Keefe, D. J., 1979: 'Ethnomethodology', *Journal for the Theory of Social Behaviour*, 9: 187–219.

Parsons, T., 1937: *The Structure of Social Action*. New York: McGraw-Hill.

1951: *The Social System*. New York: Free Press.

Parsons, T. *et al.*, 1951: *Toward a General Theory of Action*. Cambridge, Mass.: Harvard University Press.

Peyrot, M., 1982: 'Understanding Ethnomethodology: A Remedy for Some Common Misconceptions', *Human Studies*, 5: 261–83.

Phillips, J., 1978: 'Some Problems in Locating Practices', *Sociology*, 12: 56–77.

Pollner, M., 1974a: 'Mundane Reasoning', *Philosophy of the Social Sciences*, 4: 35–54.

1974b: 'Sociological and Commonsense Models of the Labelling Process', in Turner: 1974, pp. 27–40.

1975: '"The Very Coinage of Your Brain": The Anatomy of Reality Disjunctures', *Philosophy of the Social Sciences*, 5: 411–30.

forthcoming: *Mundane Reason: Reality in Everyday and Sociological Discourse*. Cambridge, England: Cambridge University Press.

Pomerantz, A., 1978: 'Compliment Responses: Notes on the Co-operation of Multiple Constraints', in Schenkein: 1978, pp. 79–112.

1984: 'Agreeing and Disagreeing with Assessments', in Atkinson and Heritage: 1984, pp. 57–101.

Pomerantz, A. and Atkinson, J. M., 1984: 'Ethnomethodology, Conversation Analysis and the Study of Courtroom Behaviour', in D. J. Muller, D. E. Blackman and A. J. Chapman (eds), *Topics in Psychology and Law*. Chichester: Wiley, pp. 283–97.

Procter, I., 1978: 'Parsons's Early Voluntarism', *Sociological Inquiry*, 48: 37–48.

Psathas, G. (ed.), 1979: *Everyday Language: Studies in Ethnomethodology*. New York: Irvington Press.

1980: 'Approaches to the Study of the World of Everyday life', *Human Studies*, 3: 3–17.

Sacks, H., 1963: 'Sociological Description', *Berkeley Journal of Sociology*, 8: 1–16.

1964–72: Unpublished lectures, University of California at Irvine. (Transcribed and indexed by G. Jefferson.)

1972a: 'An Initial Investigation of the Usability of Conversational Data for Doing Sociology' in Sudnow: 1972, pp. 31–74.

1972b: 'On the Analyzability of Stories by Children', in J. J. Gumperz and D. Hymes (eds), *Directions in Sociolinguistics*. New York: Holt, Rinehart and Winston, pp. 325–45.

1973: 'On Some Puns with Some Intimations', in R. W. Shuy (ed.), *Report of the Twenty-Third Annual Round Table Meeting on Linguistics and Language Studies.* Washington DC: Georgetown University Press, pp. 135–44.

1974: 'An Analysis of the Course of a Joke's Telling in Conversation', in R. Bauman and J. Sherzer (eds), *Explorations in the Ethnography of Speaking.* Cambridge, England: Cambridge University Press, pp. 337–53.

1975: 'Everyone has to lie', in M. Sanches and B. Blount (eds), *Sociocultural Dimensions of Language Use.* New York: Academic Press, pp. 57–80.

1978: 'Some Technical Considerations of a Dirty Joke', in Schenkein: 1978, pp. 249–70.

1979: 'Hotrodder: A Revolutionary Category', in Psathas: 1979, pp. 7–14.

1984a: 'Methodological remarks', in Atkinson and Heritage: 1984, pp. 21–7.

1984b: 'On doing "being ordinary"', in Atkinson and Heritage: 1984: pp. 413–29.

Sacks, H. and Schegloff, E. A., 1979: 'Two Preferences in the Organization of Reference to Persons in Conversation and Their Interaction', in Psathas: 1979: pp. 15–21.

Sacks, H., Schegloff, E. A. and Jefferson, G., 1974: 'A Simplest Systematics for the Organization of Turn-taking in Conversation', *Language*, 50: 696–735.

Schegloff, E. A., 1968: 'Sequencing in Conversational Openings', *American Anthropologist*, 70: 1075–95.

1972: 'Notes on Conversational Practice: Formulating Place', in Sudnow: 1972, pp. 75–119.

1980: 'Preliminaries to Preliminaries: "Can I Ask You a Question?"', *Sociological Inquiry*, 50: 104–52.

1984: 'On Some Questions and Ambiguities in Conversation', in Atkinson and Heritage: 1984, pp. 28–52.

1986: 'Between Macro and Micro: Contexts and Other Connections', in J. Alexander, B. Giesen, R. Munch and N. Smelser (eds), *The Micro–Macro Link.* Berkeley and Los Angeles: University of California Press.

Schegloff, E. A., Jefferson, G. and Sacks, H. 1977: 'The Preference for Self-correction in the Organization of Repair in Conversation', *Language*, 53: 361–82.

Schegloff, E. A. and Sacks, H., 1973: 'Opening up Closings', *Semiotica*, 7: 289–327.

Schenkein, J. (ed.), 1978: *Studies in the Organization of Conversational Interaction.* New York: Academic Press.

Schutz, A., 1962a: 'Commonsense and Scientific Interpretations of Human Action', in his *Collected Papers*, vol. 1. The Hague: Martinus Nijhoff, pp. 3–47.

1962b: 'Some Leading Concepts of Phenomenology', in his *Collected Papers*, vol. 1. The Hague: Martinus Nijhoff, pp. 99–117.

1962c: 'On Multiple Realities', in his *Collected Papers*, vol. 1. The Hague: Martinus Nijhoff, pp. 207–59.

1964a: 'The Social World and the Theory of Social Action', in his *Collected Papers*, vol. 2. The Hague: Martinus Nijhoff, pp. 3–19.

1964b: 'The Problem of Rationality in the Social World', in his *Collected Papers*, vol. 2. The Hague: Martinus Nijhoff, pp. 64–90.

Scott, J. F., 1963: 'The Changing Foundations of the Parsonian Action Scheme', *American Sociological Review*, 28: 716–35.

Sharrock, W. and Anderson, R., 1986: *The Ethnomethodologists.* London: Tavistock.

Sharrock, W. and Turner, R., 1978: 'A Conversational Environment for Equivocality', in Schenkein: 1978, pp. 173–97.

Shibutani, T., 1966: *Improvised News: A Sociological Study of Rumor.* Indianapolis: Bobbs-Merrill.

Skinner, Q., 1978: *The Foundations of Modern Political Thought: The Renaissance*. Cambridge, England: Cambridge University Press.
Snow, C. and Ferguson, C. A., 1977: *Talking to Children*. Cambridge, England: Cambridge University Press.
Sociology, 1978: *Language and Practical Reasoning*, special issue, 12 (1).
Sudnow, D., 1965: 'Normal Crimes', *Social Problems*, 12: 255–76.
  1972 (ed.): *Studies in Social Interaction*. New York: Free Press.
  1978: *Ways of the Hand*. Cambridge, Mass.: Harvard University Press.
Swanson, G., Wallace, A. and Coleman, J., 1968: 'Review Symposium of Harold Garfinkel, *Studies in Ethnomethodology*', *American Sociological Review*, 33: 122–30.
Turner, R. (ed.), 1974: *Ethnomethodology*. Harmondsworth, Middlesex: Penguin.
Watson, D. R., forthcoming: 'Some Features of the Elicitation of Confession in Murder Interrogations', in G. Psathas (ed.), *Interactional Competence*. New York: Erlbaum.
West, C., 1979: 'Against our Will: Male Interruptions of Females in Cross-sex Conversation', in J. Orsanu, M. K. Slater and L. L. Adler (eds), *Language, Sex and Gender*. Annals of the New York Academy of Sciences, vol. 327, pp. 81–97.
  1984: *Routine Complications: Troubles with Talk between Doctors and Patients*. Indiana: Indiana University Press.
West, C. and Zimmerman, D. H., 1977: 'Women's Place in Everyday Talk: Reflections on Parent-Child Interaction'. *Social Problems*, 24: 521–9.
  1982: 'Conversation Analysis', in K. R. Scherer and P. Ekman (eds), *Handbook of Methods in Nonverbal Behaviour Research*. Cambridge, England: Cambridge University Press, pp. 506–41.
  1983: 'Small Insults: A Study of Interruptions in Cross-sex Conversations with Unacquainted Persons', in B. Thorne, C. Kramerae and N. Henley (eds), *Language, Gender and Society*. Rowley, Mass.: Newbury House, pp. 102–17.
Wieder, L., 1974: *Language and Social Reality*. The Hague: Mouton.
  1977: 'Ethnomethodology and Ethnosociology', *Mid-American Review of Sociology*, 2: 1–18.
Wilson, T. P., 1971: 'Normative and Interpretative Paradigms in Sociology', in Douglas: 1971, pp. 57–79.
Wilson, T. P. and Zimmerman, D. H., 1979: 'Ethnomethodology, Sociology and Theory', *Humboldt Journal of Social Relations*, 7: 52–88.
Wrong, D., 1961: 'The Oversocialized Conception of Man in Modern Sociology', *American Sociological Review*, 26: 183–93.
Zimmerman, D. H., 1969a: 'Record-keeping and the Intake Process in a Public Welfare Agency', in S. Wheeler (ed.), *On Record: Files and Dossiers in American Life*. Beverly Hills: Sage.
  1969b: 'Tasks and Troubles: The Practical Bases of Work Activities in a Public Assistance Agency', in D. H. Hansen (ed.), *Explorations in Sociology and Counselling*. New York: Houghton Mifflin.
  1971: 'The Practicalities of Rule Use', in Douglas: 1971, pp. 221–38.
  1976: 'A Reply to Professor Coser', *American Sociologist*, 11: 4–13.
  1978: 'Ethnomethodology', *American Sociologist*, 13: 6–15.
  (n.d.): 'Talk and its Occasion: The Case of Calling the Police'. Mimeo, University of California, Santa Barbara.
Zimmerman, D. H. and West, C. (eds), 1980: *Language and Social Interaction, Sociological Inquiry*, special issue, 50 (3–4).

Structuration Theory and Social *Praxis*[1]

IRA J. COHEN

'Human beings make their own history, but not in circumstances of their own choosing' (Marx: 1963, p. 15)[2] is an aphorism that appears more cogent in the preface to most works on social theory than it does in the conclusions. There is, of course, a substantial body of theory and research that illuminates various processes and procedures through which social action is produced, but such works generally neglect the implication of historically-inherited collective circumstances in the course and outcome of social conduct, and make no mention of the constitution of social collectivities. Theory and research that capture the contours of collectivities have been fundamental objectives of social science since its inception, but accounts of social action incorporated in such works are typically designed to stress the intrusion of structural or systemic circumstances into the consciousness of actors or the domains in which activity occurs, while the practices through which the production of social life takes place remain unaddressed. The numerous analytical arguments and methodological procedures that have been advanced to ascribe priority to either social action or the properties of collectivities are difficult to sustain when considered in light of two textbook truisms: the existence of collectivities exhibiting specific properties and particular configurations depends upon the transaction of determinate forms of conduct; conversely, social conduct is carried out in different ways in historically-specific types of collectivities. The only plausible conclusion once these maxims are conjoined, is that properties of collectivities and procedures of action in some way presuppose one another in the reality of social life. To ascribe priority *ab initio* to structure or action appears mistaken and misleading when it is recognized that the two are interwoven whenever human beings make their own history.

If it were a simple matter to reconcile action and collectivities in a single

[1] I wish to thank Susan Hekman and Reggie Feiner Cohen for their helpful comments on earlier drafts of this essay.
[2] For variations on this theme, see Simmel (1950, pp. 12–13) and Vico (1968, p. 382, para. 1108).

social theory, then the discrimination between these themes would never have arisen. But it is especially difficult to embark upon this project in an era when so many disparate theories and traditions of research have attracted adherents on both sides of the divide. It is to the credit of Anthony Giddens to have accepted the burdens which this project entails, as part of a larger programme devised to produce a comprehensive re-orientation of the theoretical agenda in social science.[3] Structuration theory, the fruit of this project, reconstructs the wisdom of an array of theories which range beyond all national and disciplinary boundaries, and simultaneously poses a challenging alternative. The extraordinary diversity of the schools of thought which are subjected to positive critiques in his writings, as well as the scope and detail of structuration theory itself, set Giddens apart from other scholars who are engaged in similar efforts.[4]

Anything more than a concise summary of the reconciliation of action and collectivities provided in the tightly woven tenets of structuration theory would surpass the space allotted to this essay.[5] Rather than following this route I shall focus on a series of themes and issues, all but one of which involve Giddens's account of social *Praxis*: the production and reproduction of social life. One of the most significant contributions of structuration theory, beyond the reconciliation of action and collectivities, is to disengage social theory from the dilemmas inherent in both positivism and theories of social action that have absorbed the attention of scholars, without ever being fully resolved, throughout much of the twentieth century. Giddens has remained cognizant of these dilemmas throughout his writings on structuration theory. Yet despite, or perhaps because of, the extraordinary breadth of his work there is much to be said in order to consolidate and elaborate the relation of structuration theory to both schools of thought. The first section of this essay begins by expanding the new concern of structuration theory with the ontological constitution of social life, a development which is fundamental not only to the contrast between structuration theory and positivism but also to the overall status of Giddens's project.[6] Positivistic social theory embodies an ontological principle, the principle of uniformity, that presumes the existence of trans-historical regularities. Subsequently, I establish why Giddens's account of human agency and social practices implies a thoroughgoing denial that uniformities of *Praxis* even exist. The question of regularities also looms large in the second section of this essay, where my objective is to demonstrate how structuration theory surmounts the inadequate provision for regularities of *Praxis* that occurs in

---

[3] For early statements of Giddens's larger programme, see Giddens (1976, p. 7) and 'Introduction: Some Issues in the Social Sciences Today', in Giddens (1977).

[4] Scholars engaged in similar efforts include Roy Bhaskar, Pierre Bourdieu, Randall Collins, Rom Harré and Kenneth Gergen.

[5] A comprehensive discussion of structuration theory will be presented in Cohen: forthcoming.

[6] See also Cohen (1986).

most theories of action by virtue of their restricted focus on social conduct *in situ*. Giddens's reconciliation of action and structure will be discussed from this standpoint, and it will also be shown how his views on regularities of conduct take into account many of the major concerns that have made theorists of action hesitant to undertake a similar approach. The last section turns to a praxiologically-oriented critique of Giddens's account of social relations. I suggest that his account collapses several important distinctions and that it neglects altogether the category of anchored social relations, which is of basic significance in a wide variety of social settings.

Structuration Theory and Positivism

Although there is presently no canonical doctrine known as positivism, the term continues to make sense in so far as it refers to principles that assume or assert that methods which couple nomic propositions with empirical observation are suitable for the formation of knowledge across all domains of scientific inquiry. Given the extent to which positivism as so defined has influenced the course of development in modern social theory – an influence which extends beyond the development of positivistic theories to theories that presuppose objections to positivistic doctrine – it may seem curious that Giddens has not launched structuration theory through a critical encounter with positivistic principles. His writings establish beyond any doubt that he is quite familiar with these principles and the full array of criticisms that have been lodged against them both in the philosophy of science and in social theory *per se*.[7] However, rather than entering into a confrontation with positivism and positivistic social theory, Giddens has chosen to develop the insights which are fundamental to structuration theory in response to theories and schools of thought that already stand at some remove from positivistic points of view. Proceeding in this way has enabled him to avoid diversion into the thicket of issues in which those who debate the merits and liabilities of positivistic social science remain entangled. But a more fundamental reason why positivism does not provide a suitable backdrop for his work is that the issues of structuration theory are of a different order than those which absorb the attention of positivistic social theorists.

From epistemology to ontology

The invocation of positivistic principles in the development of social theory is the most obvious expression of an enduring concern throughout the field

[7] See Giddens (1974; 1976, ch. 4; 1979, pp. 242–4) and Giddens, 'Positivism and its Critics' (1977, ch. 1).

for preferred forms of knowledge and epistemological legitimacy.[8] While Giddens has a number of important proposals regarding the nature and critical intent of social scientific knowledge,[9] he is unwilling to shape his inquiries to conform to a predetermined set of epistemological principles. Instead, he takes his bearings from central problems concerning the subject-matter of social scientific knowledge. To concentrate upon epistemological issues, he argues,

> draws attention away from the more 'ontological' concerns of social theory and it is these upon which structuration theory primarily concentrates. Rather than becoming preoccupied with epistemological disputes and with the question of whether or not anything like 'epistemology' in its time-honoured sense can be formulated at all, those working in social theory, I suggest, should be concerned first and foremost with reworking conceptions of human being and human doing, social reproduction and social transformation. (Giddens: 1984, p. xx)

Social theorists grown weary with the seemingly endless round of debates about appropriate forms of knowledge may welcome Giddens's decision to initiate structuration theory along ontological lines. While subject-matter and methodological principles inevitably stand in a reciprocal relation, neither domain can be reduced to the other without residuum, and each must be granted a degree of autonomy if imagination and insight are to thrive. But despite this autonomy, the objectives Giddens pursues in the formation of an ontological theory of the constitution of social life do not stand apart from the concerns of social science at large. To the contrary, the main purpose of social theory from his point of view is to inform theories of substantive structures and social processes and to serve the prosecution of empirical research (Giddens: 1984, p. xvii).

By casting his conceptions of social phenomena in ontological terms, Giddens obviously contravenes positivist injunctions against metaphysical postulates. The revocation of these injunctions is one of the liberating consequences of the post-positivist or post-empiricist revolution in the philosophy of science. But some caution is in order. In the first place, if positivism is in decline in the philosophy of science, it remains an influential doctrine in social scientific circles, particularly in the United States.[10] In the second

---

[8] While this quest for legitimacy is easily identified in the works of classical and contemporary positivistic social scientists, a thoroughgoing historical investigation of the agenda-setting consequences of this quest remains to be written. A model for a study of this kind is provided in Jeffrey T. Bergner's work (1981) on the influence of neo-Kantian epistemology upon the development of social science.

[9] See Giddens: 1976, ch. 4; 1979, ch. 7; 1984: ch. 6. For an extension of the methodological implications of structuration theory, see Cohen: 1984.

[10] Any list of major American social scientists is bound to include at least some of the following positivists: Peter Blau, Hubert Blalock, Ronald Burt, James Coleman, George Homans, Jonathan Turner, Walter Wallace, Harrison White and Morris Zelditch.

place, the post-empiricist revolution does not invalidate some of the most prominent concerns that lead positivists to be wary of metaphysical insights.

One of the principal objectives pursued by the progenitors of positivism was to expunge from social thought all theories and methods that ascribe effective agency or consequence in the course or character of social life to abstract forces or qualities conceived exclusively in metaphysical terms. These hypostatized modes of theorizing exemplified in many social-contract theories and carried to an extreme in the works of Hegel convey edifying insights that continue to inspire new developments in ethical and political philosophy. Yet such explanations of social phenomena generally involve deductions of the necessity or inevitability of historical circumstances and events from the metaphysical mechanisms which are purported to regulate social life at large. In one of the earliest condemnations of this strategy, Auguste Comte – who was by no means innocent of the faults he identified in the works of others – characterized the speculative spirit of metaphysical theories as 'at once ideal in its course, absolute in its conception, and arbitrary in its application' (Comte: 1893, vol. 2, Book 6, ch. 3, p. 57). Over a century later, Comte's pronouncement reverberates in the works of his successors. Thus, Robert Merton seeks to dampen an enthusiasm for master conceptual schemes by suggesting that they verge toward the large philosophical systems of the past which, despite their varied suggestiveness, remain scientifically sterile.[11]

There is wisdom in these objections which should not be dismissed no matter how much one may disagree with positivistic social theorists on other grounds. To attribute agency or consequence to hypostatized metaphysical forces or qualities is to distort the formation of substantive theories as well as empirical investigations of social processes. The diversity that is evident across different societies and civilizations must be trimmed and shaped to preserve the fundamental metaphysical insights. For the same reason, historical discontinuities that are inconsistent with these insights must be set aside or suppressed. While few modern social theorists recommend such procedures, they remain evident in many theories of social evolution as well as in theories that postulate fundamental 'needs', or the priority of material or ideal factors as ubiquitous characteristics of all collectivities. Restrictions of this kind irritate not only positivistic social theorists, but all social scientists who refuse to subordinate their inquiries in deference to canonical doctrines and systems of thought.

Post-empiricist philosophers of science certainly do not sustain hypostatized modes of metaphysical theorizing. Yet they do claim that metaphysical or ontological conceptions of the subject matter of investigation in any given scientific domain are required to fill the void created by the underdetermination of theories by fact. Without entering into the details of the complex arguments that have been advanced in this regard, it is useful to mention

---

[11] Merton, 'On Sociological Theories of the Middle Range', in Merton (1968), p. 51. These remarks generalize Merton's criticism of the works of Talcott Parsons.

the views of some of the leading figures in post-empiricist philosophy.[12]

The turn to metaphysics is evident even in the early works of Karl Popper. The disengagement of scientific discovery from empirical inquiry, which is fundamental to Popper's thought, leads him to acknowledge that the process of discovery is impossible without faith in certain metaphysical ideas which are unwarranted from an empirical point of view (Popper: 1968, p. 38). Several decades later Thomas Kuhn expounds a similar point in an introductory passage to *The Structure of Scientific Revolutions*.

> Effective research scarcely begins before a scientific community thinks it has acquired firm answers to questions like the following: What are the fundamental entities of which the universe is composed? How do these interact with each other and with the senses? What questions may legitimately be asked about such entities and what techniques employed in seeking solutions? (Kuhn: 1970, pp. 4–5)

While Kuhn summarizes what unmistakably are metaphysical questions regarding the constitution of the subject-matter investigated by members of a scientific community,[13] his main concerns revolve around the socio-historical dimensions of scientific practices. However, his views are ratified by post-empiricist scholars, who take a more methodological slant. According to Imre Lakatos, at the centre of a scientific 'research programme' there is a 'hard core' as well as a 'positive heuristic', both of which can be formulated in metaphysical terms (Lakatos: 1978, vol. 1, pp. 47–52, 110–11, 115). The success of a 'research programme' as evaluated by Lakatos depends upon the capacity of its metaphysical elements to inspire satisfactory explanations of empirical research (Lakatos: 1978, vol. 1, pp. 48–52). Although Larry Laudan differs from Lakatos on a number of central issues, he proposes a similar view of the place of metaphysical conceptions in scientific inquiry. What he terms 'research traditions' incorporate metaphysical commitments to an ontology that specifies in a general way the types of fundamental entities in a given domain and the modes in which these entities interact. Specific theories explain empirical problems in terms reducible to this ontology (Laudan: 1977, p. 79). Roy Bhaskar offers an account of the significance of ontological entities in a realist theory of science that is far more robust than the accounts proposed by Kuhn, Lakatos and Laudan. Adopting a transcendental perspective, Bhaskar argues that beneath empirically demonstrable patterns of events there must be mechanisms conceivable in ontological terms that interact to constitute the actual states and happenings of the world. In his view, such mechanisms

---

[12] For summaries of post-empiricist philosophy, see Alexander (1982, pp. 18–33) and Giddens, 'Positivism and its Critics' (1977, ch. 1); for a commentary on metaphysics in social theory, see Cohen: 1968, pp. 5–6, 11–13.

[13] For a commentary on the significance of metaphysics in Kuhn's notoriously ambiguous use of the term 'paradigm', see Masterman: 1970, p. 65.

are the 'intransitive objects' of scientific theory (Bhaskar: 1978, pp. 45–56).

To explore further the status of ontological assumptions would be an epistemological digression of the sort Giddens suggests social theorists would do well to avoid. However, it is immediately evident that unlike metaphysical modes of theorizing, post-empiricist accounts discourage the hypostatization of abstract forces or qualities by distinguishing between ontological conceptions of fundamental entities or mechanisms on the one hand, and substantive theory and empirical research on the other. The ontological element of scientific theory can be understood as a series of internally consistent insights into the trans-historical *potentials* of the phenomena that constitute a domain of inquiry, i.e. the fundamental processes and properties that may be activated or realized in numerous different ways on different occasions. These potentials are irrefutable on empirical grounds because they are formulated without regard to their manifestations in the empirical flux of events. Yet for the same reason, the development of substantive theories is required to determine how these processes and properties operate and appear in any given context, and these theories are subject to empirical refutation. A primary consideration in the formulation of ontological concepts of this kind must be to allow the widest possible latitude for the diversity and contingencies that may occur in different settings. Therefore, hypostatized accounts of the trans-historical determination of circumstances or the universal trajectories of events are neither necessary nor desirable. To the contrary, an acceptable ontology of potentials may be sufficiently flexible to allow for the development of a variety of different substantive theories addressed to the same subject-matter.

Structuration theory is thoroughly consistent with this post-empiricist view of the nature and objectives of ontological insights. *The structurationist ontology is addressed exclusively to the constitutive potentials of social life: the generic human capacities and fundamental conditions through which the course and outcomes of social processes and events are generated and shaped in a manifold of empirically distinguishable ways.* The absence of hypostatization in structuration theory is evident in the extent to which Giddens refrains from imposing any substantive restrictions on his ontological concepts. These concepts do not attribute trans-historical priority to specific practices or processes of social production and reproduction; no universal 'needs' are postulated either for collectivities or social actors; and Giddens vigorously insists that all modes of theory that postulate or imply any functional teleology or universal trajectory of social evolution are misleading and incorrect.[14]

Although a comprehensive documentation of the preceding claims will not be advanced in this essay, the ontological flexibility of Giddens's conceptions of social *Praxis* will be highlighted in later sections. However, there is

---

[14] For Giddens's arguments against functionalist teleology, see his 'Functionalism après la lutte' (1977, ch. 2); for his arguments against evolutionary aspects of Marx's work, see Giddens: 1981a, ch. 3; for his arguments against other forms of evolutionary theory, see Giddens: 1984, ch. 5.

one general point that deserves special mention here. Commentators who quarrel with the absence of systematically-related propositions in Giddens's writings on structuration theory[15] overlook the hypostatization of social life that would result were he to proceed in this way. Because structuration theory concentrates upon the production and reproduction of society by social agents themselves, a systematization of ontological propositions would entail some degree of trans-historical systematization in the processes and outcomes of social *Praxis* as well. But the absence of systematic propositions is not only a matter of methodological prudence. It is evident throughout Giddens's writings that he has a deep respect for the protean capacities of social agents to reproduce and transform their own historical circumstances.[16] Social agents, not social theorists, produce, sustain and alter whatever degree of 'systemness' exists in society (Giddens: 1981a, pp. 41–8; 1984, pp. 164–5). Hence, to the degree that sets of systematically-related propositions are in order, this is a matter for substantive theories addressed to specific types of socio-historical circumstances. This point of view, of course, is directly opposed to the pervasive reliance on systemic modes of analysis in Talcott Parsons's 'general theory'.

From the principle of uniformity to the production of social life

Since the various interpretations of positivist doctrine involve philosophical reconstructions of methods for the development and acceptance of theory and evidence drawn from diverse case studies in the natural sciences, positivist social scientists have generally not adopted these doctrines on ontological grounds. If positivist procedures were without implications for the constitution of the subject-matter in any given domain of inquiry, then it might be possible to formulate structuration theory in accordance with these methods. But, as such theorists of action as Alfred Schütz and Aaron Cicourel have demonstrated, positivist doctrines do intrude on how social scientists conceive of the constitution of social life (see Cicourel: 1964; Schütz; 1962, pp. 3–47). Their arguments indicate that positivist strategies of observation and measurement neglect and distort the complex subjective rationalities and strategies that comprise fundamental aspects of human social *Praxis*. This point is consistent with the account of social *Praxis* incorporated in structuration theory. However, the reason for structuration theory's departure from positivism runs somewhat deeper than this, arriving ultimately at a dissent from one of positivism's primordial assumptions.

There are certain respects in which my development of this issue intersects Roy Bhaskar's critique of positivism, but I shall proceed independently, for two reasons. First, Bhaskar's critique presupposes the transcendental strat-

---

[15] See Archer (1982) and McLennan (1984); a reply to McLennan is presented in Cohen (1986).
[16] See esp. Giddens: 1981a.

egy he incorporates in his realist theory of science. While other elements of Bhaskar's philosophy of science might be reconciled with structuration theory, it remains unclear whether it is either necessary or useful to accept the burdens involved in the defence of Bhaskar's transcendental reasoning. Second, Bhaskar is intent on preserving analogies between the constitution of natural domains and the domains of social life, with the important proviso that social structures – which he takes as the mechanisms that generate social life – are produced through social *Praxis* and hence may be only relatively enduring.[17] By contrast, my discussion of the discrepancy between positivism and structuration theory accentuates a fundamental discontinuity between nature and society, one that turns directly on the characteristics of social *Praxis per se*.

Robert Merton articulates the conventional wisdom of most positivist social scientists when he asserts that a knowledge of the logic or methodology of scientific procedure does not contain or imply the particular content of sociological theory.[18] The sheer variety of the conceptions of social phenomena that have been developed in conformity with positivist principles would seem to suggest that Merton is correct. Individualist theories of social behaviour and exchange as well as holistic theories of social structure, incorporating varying degrees of emphasis on idealist or materialist factors, are all represented within the positivist tradition. Yet Merton himself, in an early essay on the sociology of science, presents a lucid account of an ontological assumption that contradicts his assertion of the thematic neutrality of the logic of science.

> The *basic* assumption in modern science 'is a widespread, instinctive conviction in the existence of an *Order of Things*, and in particular an Order of Nature'. This belief, this faith, for at least since Hume it must be recognized as such, is simply 'impervious to the demand for a consistent rationality'. In the systems of scientific thought of Galileo, Newton, and of their successors, the testimony of experiment is the ultimate criterion of truth, but the very notion of experiment is ruled out without the prior assumption that Nature constitutes an intelligible order, so that when appropriate questions are asked, she will answer, so to speak. Hence this assumption is final and absolute.[19]

In proposing this view, Merton quotes from commentary by A. N. Whitehead. According to Whitehead, the belief in the order of nature presumes that all phenomena are the result of recurrences in nature, exemplifications of general principles which reign throughout the natural order. This belief did not originate in scientific method, but arose well before the advent of modern science (Whitehead: 1925, pp. 3ff.). Stephen Toulmin provides a

---

[17] See Bhaskar: 1979, pp. 47–9; for Bhaskar's comments on differences of emphasis between his work and structuration theory, see Bhaskar: 1983, p. 85.

[18] See here Merton, 'The Bearing of Sociological Theory on Empirical Research', in Merton (1968), pp. 140–1.

[19] Merton, 'Puritanism, Pietism, and Science', in Merton (1968), p. 635–6.

summary statement of what this belief involves. The typical scientist, he suggests, 'begins with the conviction that things are not just happening (not even just-happening-regularly) but rather that some fixed set of laws or patterns or mechanisms accounts for Nature's following the course it does, and that his understanding of these should guide his expectations' (Toulmin: 1961, p. 45). Karl Popper fixes the status of this principle of the uniformity of nature when he notes that 'it expresses the metaphysical faith in the existence of regularities in our world' (Popper: 1968, p. 252; see also p. 278).

It is important to recognize that the principle of uniformity does not provide a comprehensive set of insights into the subject-matter at issue in any given theory. In the first place, this principle is clearly insufficient in itself to establish anything about specific kinds of patterns or mechanisms. Second, no specific account of causation or teleology is implied. Finally, the principle of uniformity by no means requires that empirical circumstances and events must occur in the same way under all conditions: conjunctions of uniformities may result in rare or unprecedented outcomes in any given instance. The only point upon which the principle insists is the existence of a trans-historical order of forces or relations between entities, and it is to this that scientific inquiry should be addressed.

The principle of uniformity is often used as a warrant for inductive methods of theory construction, and a uniformitarian 'extensionalist argument' has been shown by Thomas Wilson to be embedded in the philosophical foundations of mathematical methods also.[20] But since a belief in the uniform order of nature originates prior to modern science, the principle of uniformity cannot be treated simply as a methodological artifact. To the contrary, unless positivist science is to be seen as a quixotic enterprise, methodological directives to develop and employ propositions that take the form of statements addressed to universal regularities – whether or not these are rigorously nomological – must presume the existence of uniformities in the subject-matter at hand.

Most positivist social theorists appear to have adopted the principle of uniformity through their acceptance of methodological directives of this kind, but a few have implied or proposed an awareness of these ontological implications of positivist methods. Thus Walter Wallace, whose recent work marks him as one of the most sophisticated positivist theorists in the present era, invokes Popper's contention that the principle of uniformity is a metaphysical belief, and then declares: just as 'astrophysicists assume that the same processes (whether these processes are known or not) that prevail now and here on Earth prevail across the cosmos and throughout all past and future time, ... similarly, sociologists assume that the same processes

---

[20] For a critical discussion of the principles of uniformity as employed in inductive philosophies of science, see Hansen: 1969, chs 21, 25. A critique of the related 'extensionist' arguments in mathematical methods for theory construction is presented in Wilson (1984).

(again whether known or not) prevail across all societies, past, present and future' (Wallace: 1983, p. 461).

Social theorists who propose or accept a positivist strategy for theory construction imply a commitment to the principle of uniformity on methodological grounds. But a uniformitarian outlook is characteristic of many other theories as well. Those functionalist theories that can be reconstructed in the nomothetic manner proposed by Carl Hempel (1965) and Ernest Nagel (1957) can certainly be included in this group. Harold Bershady (1973) has established that a drive to establish universal laws is embedded in the works of Talcott Parsons. Merton's well-known proposal for the development of theories of the middle range may seem to steer clear of the principle of uniformity, but this would be true only if his conception of these theories limited their scope to historically-bounded collectivities and processes. As it is, Merton denies the historical specificity of middle-range theories and holds only that they are limited to a determinate range of conceptual issues. The ultimate goal remains to consolidate these theories into a progressively more general conceptual scheme.[21]

Whether or not the principle of uniformity is ever contradicted in nature, common experience suggests that a multitude of natural regularities operate in similar ways under the same conditions, whenever and wherever they occur. A question then arises that is much older than social theory in the modern era: is social life continuous with nature, or can it be distinguished from nature on determinate grounds? Giddens establishes his position on this issue in the opening pages of his first book on structuration theory:

> The difference between society and nature is that nature is ... not produced by man ... While not made by any single person, society is created and recreated afresh, if not *ex nihilo*, by the participants in every social encounter. The *production of society* is a skilled performance, sustained and 'made to happen' by human beings. (Giddens: 1976, p. 15)

While Giddens establishes an unequivocal distinction between nature and society, it is not immediately evident where he stands on the principle of uniformity. That he resists a uniformitarian outlook is made abundantly clear in his objections to all forms of universal generalizations (Giddens: 1976, pp. 153–4; 1979, pp. 242–4; 1984: pp. xviii–xix, 343–7). What remains to be considered is why he adopts this stance. In dealing with this issue, I shall concentrate on elements of Giddens's account of the constitution of social agency and social practices, and bracket, for the time being, issues regarding social reproduction and the reconciliation of structure and action. These brackets will be removed in the next section of this essay. No reference will be made to the interests or motives that dispose or impel social agents or actors – the terms are interchangeable – who engage in social practices.

---

[21] Merton, 'On Sociological Theories of the Middle Range', in Merton (1968), pp. 45, 51.

This follows from Giddens's contention that while social theory must con-
serve an interest in the subject as a reasoning, acting being, the subject
must also be 'decentred' in favour of a more central concern with social
conduct (Giddens: 1979, p. 47; 1984: p. xxii).

A line of thought promulgated by Max Weber and sustained in a substantially altered form by Talcott Parsons holds that human action fundamentally involves the meanings and motives that actors associate with their
behaviour. The problem with social action thus conceived is that the performance of social activities is not taken into account. Sociologists who
concentrate upon the production of social action represent a considerable
improvement in this regard, yet there is still an over-emphasis upon discursive aspects of conduct in their work. For example, ethnomethodologists
who stress the rational accountability of practical actions concentrate upon
conversational practices at the expense of non-discursive aspects of the
production of social activities. An intrinsic association between action and
communication is also presupposed in symbolic interactionism.

While Giddens accepts that conversation and the negotiation of meaning
are prominent characteristics of social practices, his conception of human
agency shifts attention to a more basic aspect of all human conduct, the
power to intervene in a course of events or state of affairs (see Giddens:
1976, pp. 110–11; 1979, p. 88; 1984, pp. 14–16). This connection between
agency and power logically precedes and informs Giddens's account of social
practices. Indeed, power in this generic sense is logically prior to all matters
regarding subjectivity or the reflexive monitoring of conduct (Giddens:
1979, p. 92; 1984: p. 15). This is because social agency depends solely
upon the capability of actors to 'make a difference' in the production of
definite outcomes, regardless of whether or not they intend (are aware) that
these outcomes occur. Since 'to make a difference' is to transform some
aspect of a process or event, agency in structuration theory is equated with
transformative capacity.

As matters stand there is nothing in this account of agency to deny the
existence of social uniformities. If social agency results in determinate
outcomes, then the same can be said of the colliding billiard balls in
illustrations of Newtonian mechanics, of cells that divide during mitosis,
and so forth. But from a uniformitarian standpoint the production of natural
outcomes is not under the control of the entities involved. With a limited
allowance for higher species in the animal kingdom, the operations and
interactions among elements and objects in nature are said to result from
the interplay between their indigenous properties and exogenous circumstances. A distinguishing feature of the exercise of social agency, on the
other hand, is that the interventions undertaken by social agents are, to
some greater or lesser extent, always under their own control. As Giddens
insists, at any phase in any given sequence of conduct any agent could have
acted in a manner somehow different than she or he did (Giddens: 1979,
pp. 92, 267, n. 15; 1981a, p. 53; 1984, p. 9). To the extent that this point is
granted it becomes difficult to presume that social activity will be produced

everywhere and always in a manner that corresponds to the order of nature. In principle, any given pattern of social conduct may be altered by the actors who are engaged in its production. This is not to deny that much of social life is comprised of regularities in conduct (see below), but it does prohibit conceiving these regularities as elements of a trans-historical order of uniformities.

It has been argued that Giddens's contention that agents 'could have acted otherwise' implies that all actors exploit a generous degree of freedom in their conduct (Archer: 1982, pp. 459–60; Carlstein: 1981, pp. 52–3). As Giddens has now indicated at length, structuration theory directs a great deal of attention to both social and material constraints that any individual agent may be unable to change. Hence, it makes ample allowance for the limited set of options available for the exercise of agency in any given set of circumstances (see Giddens: 1984, pp. 169–80). It is beyond the concerns of this essay to adumbrate these constraints. It is germane, however, to draw implications from the structurationist conception of agency with regard to determinism and freedom (NB not free will, since agency stands prior to subjectivity).

In addressing this issue, it is important to bear in mind what has been said about the substantial leeway that ontological theories should allow for the diversity of situations and events to which they can be applied. Adopting a fixed position on the degree of freedom or constraint in the exercise of agency prior to the development of substantive theory and empirical research would be to restrict the scope of structuration theory. Giddens's contention that enablements and constraints in the exercise of agency will vary considerably in different historical circumstance (Giddens: 1984, p. 179) signifies an unwillingness to estabish an *a priori* position on questions of freedom or determinism. Considered in this light, the proviso that, in principle, agents are always capable of 'acting otherwise', represents only a denial of a thoroughgoing determinism of agency by forces to which the agent must respond automatically. But if structuration theory denies a thoroughgoing determinism, it stands equally opposed to unqualified freedom. There are two ways in which to establish this point. First, Giddens argues that in every social relation there is a dialectic of control involving the asymmetrical access to and manipulation of the media (resources) through which agents influence one another's behaviour. It is central to this concept that no agent engaged in interaction is ever completely autonomous (Giddens: 1981a, pp. 61–3; 1984, p. 16). Second, to make a point that anticipates subsequent discussion on the production and reproduction of social activity, the latitude of freedom of agency crucially depends upon the range of practices that an agent is competent to perform. However great this range may be, unqualified freedom is denied because no agent is sufficiently skilled to perform every type of practice that his or her fellow actors have mastered. Thus, the conception of agency in structuration theory resists the polarities of both thoroughgoing determinism and unqualified freedom, while preserving all possibilities between these extremes.

The historical diversity of social practices

While the structurationist conception of social agency provides fundamental grounds for denying the transposition of the principle of uniformity from nature to social life, this point can be elaborated by turning to Giddens's account of social practices. The capability of intervention is activated in these practices and they 'make a difference' to the course and outcome of social activities, activities that may involve the sequential and interactive organization of numerous practices undertaken by others.

A prominent aspect of Giddens's distinction betwen nature and society is that the production of social life is a *skilled* performance. Social practices can be understood as skilful procedures, methods or techniques appropriately performed by social agents (cf. Giddens, 1984, pp. 20–2). This definition suggests a correspondence with the concerns of ethnomethodologists. However, as previously noted, while Giddens considers Garfinkel's investigations of the rational accountability of action to be highly significant to an understanding of social conduct, he does not limit his account of practices to discursive accounting practices *per se*.[22] There are a variety of practices that may be conducted in the absence of others, such as attending to matters of personal cleanliness and appearance, or voting by secret ballot. Moreover, as Erving Goffman has demonstrated in exquisite detail, many subtle but consequential modes of physical gesture and bodily posture resist reduction to conversational practices.

If social life is distinguished from nature by the performance of social practices, then the basis for this distinction consists of the skills and resources required to perform any given practice. It is in addressing the constitution of praxiological skills that human consciousness first arises as a major theme in structuration theory. However, the specific mode of consciousness, i.e. *practical consciousness* of social skills, must be distinguished from *discursive consciousness*, i.e. the level of awareness determined by the ability to put things into words (Giddens: 1984, pp. 41–5).[23] The distinctive quality of practical consciousness is that agents need be only tacitly aware of the skills they have mastered, although it is generally possible to concentrate discursive attention on these skills when the occasion arises. By stressing actors' tacit awareness of skills and procedures, Giddens is able to propose that practices can be performed without being directly motivated – indeed he claims that much day-to-day conduct occurs in this manner (1979, pp. 59, 218; 1984, p. 6).

The awareness of procedures of action can be conceived as a form of knowledge, i.e. a knowledge of 'how to do something', or 'how to go on'. Clarifying Alfred Schütz's conception of 'stocks of knowledge', Giddens refers

[22] See Giddens (1984, pp. 77–83) for pertinent remarks on this point.
[23] See also Giddens: 1979, pp. 57, 73; as Giddens makes clear in these remarks, practical consciousness must also be distinguished from the unconscious.

to *mutual knowledge*: a knowledge that is shared by all who are competent to engage in or recognize the appropriate performance of a social practice or range of practices (1976, pp. 88–9, 107; 1979, pp. 73, 84, 251–3; 1984, p. 4). Both social practices and mutual knowledge are initially conceived in unitary terms. However, for analytical purposes they may be dealt with as a series of rules. Since these rules refer to tacitly understood social procedures, they are to be distinguished from legal codes, bureaucratic regulations and other rules that are discursively formulated. Two aspects of rules can be identified, although both are always intricately interwoven in knowledge and practice. The semantic aspect of rules refers to the qualitative and procedural meaning of practices, the locales associated with their performance and some (not all) of their likely outcomes. The normative aspect of rules refers to the same practices, locales and outcomes from the standpoint of the rights and obligations that establish their legitimate or illegitimate nature as well as the appropriate and inappropriate ways in which practices may be carried out (Giddens; 1976, pp. 104–10; 1979, pp. 81–8; 1984, pp. 16–25).

Since social agency involves interventions that alter or transform social events, i.e. that contribute to their production, there must be an aspect of social practices that refers to how this influence is exercised. Giddens introduces the notion of resources to serve this end. Resources are the facilities or bases of power to which the agent has access, and which she or he manipulates to influence the course of interaction with others. It is important here to bear in mind what has been said about the dialectic of control. But it should also be understood that the manipulation of resources does not occur in discrete practices; their mobilization always involves both semantic and normative aspects of mutual knowledge. Conversely, resources provide the means whereby these semantic and normative rules are actualized. Two categories of resources, which again are subtly interwoven in concrete practices, may be distinguished in analytical terms. Authoritative resources are capabilities that generate command over people (life chances, spatio-temporal positioning, organization and relations between human beings). Allocative resources are capabilities that generate command over material objects (raw materials, means of production, produced goods) (Giddens: 1976, p. 112; 1979, pp. 91–4; 1981a, pp. 40–63).

Unlike social agency, there is nothing in the structurationist conception of social practices that logically entails a rejection of the principles of uniformity. Nevertheless, the burden that a uniformitarian theory of social practices must assume would tax the limits of the most resolute and ingenious positivist. To transpose the principle of uniformity from nature to social practices would require postulates to the effect that: social actors in all historical eras and across all civilizations are knowledgeable about similar procedures of action; that they construe and apply the semantic and normative aspects of these procedures in the same way; and that they have access to the same kinds of resources. These are daunting propositions to uphold. They imply far more than the claim that human beings everywhere have similar needs. Needs (e.g. food, shelter, sex, nurture of the young) can be fulfilled through a variety of different practices, and there may be considerable variation in the degree and kind of satisfaction that results when these practices are carried out. What these uniformitarian postulates actually imply is nothing less than the reduction of historical diversity to fundamental forms of social conduct in the production of social life.

I know of no positivist theorist who has succeeded in identifying transhistorical uniformities in social *Praxis*. Even George Homans, whose positivist credentials are beyond question, suggests that the 'historicity' of human behaviour and institutions poses difficulties for the type of scientific explanation to which he is committed (Homans: 1974, p. 41). Homans, of course, confines his theoretical propositions to the reinforcement or suppression of social behaviour based upon the rewards and punishment received by social actors. This behaviourist theory is in itself controversial, and it most certainly runs counter to the tenets of structuration theory. But for the present purposes it is sufficient to note that Homans, in effect, reduces the problem of 'historicity' at the start of his work by bracketing the content of behavioural norms and, *ipso facto*, the historical diversity of conduct (Homans: 1974, p. 2).

Giddens refuses to deny historical diversity as a fundamental characteristic of social practices. Human beings, he observes, are unlike animals because they are not biologically programmed to produce social life, although obviously some allowance must be made for the universal qualities of the human organism (Giddens: 1976, p. 160; 1979, p. 244; 1984, pp. 216–17, 174). In the absence of many instinctive forms of activity it is difficult to imagine any alternative mechanism that would provide for transhistorical regularities of conduct. Moreover, unlike natural processes, it is not intuitively obvious that many uniformities of practice actually exist. Indeed, on the basis of immediate appearances, the variability of practices between geographically and historically remote civilizations and societies seems far more pronounced than their broad similarities.

The polymorphic diversity of human practices is one important reason why Giddens holds that the concept of agency cannot be fully elucidated apart from historically-specific modes of activity (1979, p. 56). In structuration theory the types of resources to which agents have access and the knowledgeable skills involved in the practices they perform, as well as their discursive knowledge of broader social conditions, always exist within determinate historical and spatial bounds. It may seem paradoxical to affirm the historical variability of social *Praxis* in ontological terms. Ontology, after all, refers only to those aspects of a subject-matter that exist wherever it is found. Yet here again it must be underscored that structuration theory provides an *ontology of potentials*. It maintains that one potential possessed by all social agents is the ability to produce historical variations in their own forms of conduct. Because this ability is presented as a potential, it is equally consistent to hold that it is not always exercised.

The obligation incurred in adopting this position is that no aspect of social

Praxis conceived in ontological terms can refer to historically determinate processes or events. This is exactly how Giddens develops his account of social *Praxis* in structuration theory. Consider, for example, his analytical distinction between rules and resources as characteristic features of all social practices. Neither of these concepts logically entail any historical content. While allocative resources involve the control of material items, and rules are inherently idealist in nature, Giddens makes no claim that either factor must figure more prominently than the other in the production of historical activities and events. Finally, unlike Talcott Parsons, Giddens does not propose any necessary systemic configuration of rules and resources that must be employed in the analysis of historical instances of social conduct. By refraining from stipulations regarding the content, priority and systematic relations between rules and resources, Giddens preserves the greatest poss- ible latitude for historical variation. Investigators who draw upon the struc- turationist ontology are therefore free to address these issues in different ways, depending on the specific forms of practice carried out in any given historical domain and the theoretical issues they wish to pursue in their works. The only substantive postulate of structuration theory they must honour is that all historical practices and circumstances are subject to change.

Regularities of *Praxis*

In many quarters of modern social science a denial of positivist methods, and of the uniformitarian outlook they entail, is associated with a suppression of interest in social regularities. This is especially the case for theories and research devoted to the production of social action. While the existence of regularities of *Praxis* is acknowledged in virtually all of the numerous programmes in this field, there has been a pronounced tendency, beginning with Weber's idiographically-oriented definition of social action, to focus upon the generation and meaning of instances or forms of activity within the boundaries of the settings within which they occur. As I will indicate below, even such scholars as Peter Winch and Randall Collins, who have attempted to address regularities of conduct, ultimately remain wedded to a view of social action *in situ*, and for this reason they fail to provide adequate accounts of how regularities are reproduced.

While structuration theory requires a rejection of the principle of uniform- ity, it is equally opposed to the insufficiencies of latter-day theories of action as regards the nature and reproduction of regularities of *Praxis*. Giddens, of course, has derived many insights from these theories. But unlike them, he emphasizes that generalizations ultimately based upon the reproduction and consequences of historically-bounded forms of conduct are highly relevant to social analysis (Giddens: 1979, pp. 242–4; 1984, pp. 343–7). However, Giddens's commentaries on theories of action have not accentuated the problem of regularities, although a critique of this problem is implied in his remarks on the closely related issue of the neglect by theorists of action of the structural properties of collectivities.[24] The connection between these points can be summarized in terms of the reconciliation of structure and action provided in one of Giddens's central concepts, the duality of structure. That is, to neglect the reproduction of regularities in practice makes it impossible to determine how enduring structural properties are generated and sustained; conversely, to neglect structural properties makes it impossible to determine the circumstances that agents require to reproduce such regularities.

There are advantages to be gained by elaborating Giddens's account of the reproduction of regularities in the duality of structure against the backdrop of a critique of the problem of regularities in theories of action. In the first place, it affords the opportunity to clarify the nature and significance of these regularities in structuration theory. Second, it is possible to discuss how Giddens takes account of some of the legitimate concerns that have made theorists of action hesitant to deal with the reproduction of regularities. I shall begin by presenting a brief and highly selective consideration of the problem of regularities in the works of four of the most innovative students of social action: Herbert Blumer, Harold Garfinkel, Peter Winch and Randall Collins.[25]

The problem of regularities in theories of action

While George Herbert Mead inspired the development of symbolic interactionism, Herbert Blumer must be acknowledged as the founder of the Chicago School, which comprises the dominant trend within this tradition. The Chicago School's neglect of structural issues has been dealt with by both exponents and critics.[26] Here I shall summarize only those aspects of Blumer's thought that relate directly to the problem of regularities.

What often goes unnoticed in Blumer's work is that he does make some allowance for stable and repetitive sequences of interaction. Most situations people encounter, he suggests, are 'structured' through definitions and interpretations they have previously acquired. Serious consideration of what this contention implies might have led Blumer to conceive of transsituational properties of interaction from a collective viewpoint. However, in his most well-known essays Blumer does not follow this route. Instead, his comments on regularized situations and encounters appear as points of departure for discussions of the significance of 'undefined' situations and novel forms of interactive alignments (Blumer: 1969, pp. 17ff., 86).

It is fundamental to Blumer's perspective on interaction that social acts

[24] See Giddens: 1976, esp. pp. 126–9; see also his 'Hermeneutics, Ethnomethodology, and Problems of Interpretative Analysis', in Giddens (1977, ch. 4), and Giddens: 1982.

[25] The omission from this discussion of individualist theorists (e.g. Alfred Schütz) is in keeping with the 'decentring' of the subject in structuration theory.

[26] For summaries, see Maines (1977, pp. 235–7) and Meltzer *et al.* (1975, ch. 3).

are generated through symbolically-mediated behaviour between actors. He asserts that it is quite common in modern societies for situations to occur in which the actions of participants are not regularized and in which the symbols of interpretation shift and vary. Such actions depart or surpass the structural dimensions of the social organizations in which they occur. At times Blumer also holds open the possibility of situational novelty in universal, and hence ontological, terms (1969, pp. 18, 88–9). But whatever the status of this point, Blumer's persistent sensitivity to the possibility of novelty in situated conduct corresponds with his methodological proposal for investigators to consider the distinctive, unique and particular characteristics of every 'object of inquiry' before inferring what it shares in common with other 'objects' in conceptual terms (1969, pp. 148–9). His emphasis upon 'undefined' situations coupled with this methodological proposal effectively enjoin a reduction of the purview of symbolic interactionism to situated instances of social conduct.

Blumer's regard for innovations in interaction should not be dismissed. If agents were unable to originate new forms of activity then it would be impossible to account for the extraordinary variation in social conduct that has been exhibited in the course of human history. But even members of the Chicago School have become dissatisfied with the impediments to the study of regularities and collective aspects of social life that necessarily result from Blumer's reductive point of view. Proposals now exist to merge symbolic interactionism with the trans-situational concerns of semiotics (see MacCannel: 1976; Perinbanayagam: 1985). Until now there has been little dialogue between symbolic interactionism and structuration theory. While a semiotically-informed symbolic interactionism would probably continue to differ from structuration theory on a number of salient points, it would create openings for fruitful exchanges in the future.

As in Blumer's works, there is a strand of thought in Harold Garfinkel's original formulation of the ethnomethodological research programme that might lead to an interest in the reproduction of regularities of social practices. This is made evident when Garfinkel suggests that members of a society maintain standardized expectations about the character and consequences of social action. But by the same token 'members' cannot be regarded as 'judgemental dopes' who merely conform to existent standards. To the contrary, Garfinkel insists that standardized actions are discovered, created and sustained by social actors during the course of these actions themselves (Garfinkel: 1984, pp. 66–7). It is consistent with this point for Garfinkel (with Harvey Sacks) to propose that everyday activities exhibit a formal structure independent of any given cohort of actors, but produced and recognized as the practical, situated accomplishment of the members of a particular cohort (Garfinkel and Sacks: 1970, p. 346). This proposal suggests two possible lines of inquiry: the practices and procedures by which the standardized features of forms of activity are produced may be thematisised, or attention may be confined to the production and recognition of these forms in particular situations (cf. Garfinkel: 1984, p. 10). While ethnomethodologists engaged in conversational analysis have advanced along the first of these lines, Garfinkel and others have pursued the second, more situated and specific approach.

This reversion to the situation stems from Garfinkel's conception of the production of accounts and contexts as summarized in the notions of indexicality and reflexivity. Indexicality means that all items raised for discussion are inherently equivocal apart from the accounting procedures through which they are assembled as particular features of an ethnographic context. This context is composed of items indexed during the previous course of discussion. Hence the accounts produced by 'members' are reflexively tied to the socially-organized occasion where they are generated. Whatever is typical or potentially repetitive does not depend upon any 'context-in-general' but rather upon the reflexive indexicality of the accounts generated through the use of methods in situated instances of conduct (Garfinkel: 1984, pp. 4–10).

As John Heritage has recently demonstrated, Garfinkel's emphasis upon the production of indexical accounts in situated contexts is coextensive with a finitist perspective in which every use of concepts, rules, typifications, etc., must ultimately be referred to specific, local, contingent determinants (Heritage: 1984, pp. 120–9).[27] Since Garfinkel acknowledges an 'enormous standardization' (Garfinkel: 1984, pp. 9–10) in how organized interaction is accomplished and recognized, this finitism does not imply Blumer's caution on the contingent possibility of novelty in forms of conduct. It stems instead from an insistence on rigorous attention to nuance and detail that is a hallmark of ethnomethodological research.

Garfinkel's finitist deference to the complexity of social *Praxis* is expressed in a series of methodological policies that effectively foreclose an interest in social reproduction. These proposals stipulate that every feature of any case of inquiry be addressed as a particular, located, organization of practices; that such practices be viewed as contingent accomplishments; and that every setting be viewed as self-organizing with respect to its intelligibility and representation of social order (Garfinkel: 1984, pp. 32–4). The effect of these policies is to place methodological brackets around questions of both the reproducibility of social practices and the intrusion of enduring properties of collectivities into locally-organized methods and procedures. (Garfinkel's well-known policy of 'ethnomethodological indifference' also brackets the consequences of social conduct (Garfinkel and Sacks: 1970, p. 345).) Hence, while Garfinkel may acknowledge an 'enormous standardization' in how activities are organized, at the same time he also recommends that instances of common activities be recognized for purposes of inquiry as 'another first time' (Garfinkel: 1984, p. 10).[28]

---

[27] My remarks on ethnomethodology have been illuminated by Heritage's study. However, Heritage finds more merit than I in Garfinkel's finitist approach to social action.

[28] Recently a few ethnomethodologists have begun to set these brackets aside: see

A shift of concern from the generation of specific instances of situated conduct to reproduced forms of conduct is evident in the work of Peter Winch. Winch's post-Wittgensteinian conception of the objectives of social science underscores the point that when participation in a general kind of activity occurs, the participants rely upon rules which specify what is to count as 'doing the same kind of thing' in relation to that activity. All participants have learned of these activities in similar ways, and the rules on which they draw can thus be said to rest upon a context of common activity within a social group (Winch: 1958, pp. 83–7).

This might suggest that Winch concentrates upon how established regularities of conduct are reproduced through a reliance upon commonly-shared rules. Yet the objectives Winch upholds for social science actually move in an entirely different direction. Instead of entertaining questions about social *Praxis* as a process of social reproduction, Winch proposes to accept 'forms of life' as they stand. Social scientists, Winch believes, should study modes of conduct in order to understand them, i.e. in order to give accounts of the nature of social phenomena. Shared rules of conduct become sociologically relevant as criteria to identify and elucidate these general kinds of activity (Winch: 1958, pp. 40ff., 86–7). This standpoint in very general respects draws Winch toward the position of European philosophers of hermeneutics such as Hans-Georg Gadamer.[29]

That empirical inquiry in the social sciences must rely upon interpretative accounts justified by the criteria participants use to recognize their own activities is accepted as a methodological necessity in structuration theory.[30] But social scientists cannot rest content with the elucidation of recurrent forms of conduct. They must also be concerned with the procedures of reproduction and social transformation as well as with the consequences that ensue from general kinds of activities. Therefore, while Winch's notion of rules verges on becoming a concept that can be dealt with from a trans-situational point of view, because he overlooks these topics, established rules which provide for the reproduction of regularities merely form the boundary of his approach (Giddens: 1976, p. 51).

Randall Collins's recently-published works on the 'microfoundations' of 'macrosociology' offer a useful counterpoint to Winch's approach (Collins: 1981a; 1981b). Like Winch, Collins accepts the iterative nature of social activities. But unlike Winch, Collins retains a central interest in the processes through which forms of conduct are reproduced, by absorbing analytical insights from Erving Goffman as well as from several leading ethnomethodo-

---

Maynard and Wilson (1980) and Wilson and Zimmerman (1979–80). Giddens has expressed an appreciation of this work in Giddens (1984, pp. 332–3).

[29] The affinities and antimonies between European hermeneutics and the Wittgensteinian approach to social analysis exemplified by Winch are discussed in Apel (1967) and Thompson (1981, pp. 118–20).

[30] On this point, see Cohen: 1984; this study expands upon Giddens's methodological conception of the 'double hermeneutic'.

logists. But the most pronounced point of contrast between Collins and Winch is that Collins denies that trans-situational rules of conduct contribute to the constitution of persistent modes of social activity.

One of Collins's central contentions is that all varieties of 'macrostructure' can be translated and reduced to quantitative aggregations, distributions and configurations of 'micro-events'. Collins is led to this position by the ethnomethodological strategy of ultra-detailed empirical research. Transposing this strategy into a theoretical key, Collins suggests that while individuals within 'microsituations' may harbour 'macroviews' and make 'macroreferences' in their conversations, such views and references are merely aggregates of their moment-by-moment sensory and subjective experiences, glossed or reified in thought and discourse. Since all social reality is 'micro-experience', Collins denies that social rules, norms and values are appropriately conceived on a 'macrostructural' basis (Collins: 1981a, p. 105; 1981b, pp. 991, 995).

A problem Collins must now resolve is: in the absence of trans-situational rules or norms, how can an account of reproduction of regularities be adduced from situated instances of repetitive conduct? Although he acknowledges that cultural resources and emotional dispositions enter into the reproduction of or change in patterns of interpersonal relations, he does not propose either phenomenon as the bedrock for an account of social reproduction. Cultural resources are topics of conversation invoking a common cognitive reality among participants in interaction. But this must be balanced against one of Collins's crucial claims, which is that human beings operate within a very limited range of cognitive capacities (Collins: 1981a, p. 103; 1981b, p. 995). Extrapolating from Collins's arguments, it also appears that while emotions provide propensities (e.g. confidence, warmth, enthusiasm) to act in certain ways, such propensities cannot account for the specific kinds of activity reproduced in any given situation. Ultimately, Collins provides a basis for reproduction by introducing a surprising materialist twist into conventional ethnomethodological views of the contextuality of social activities. 'The microreality of any "social structure"', he contends, 'is some patterns of repetitive associations among people in relation to some physical object or place ... because human cognitive capacities do not allow people to organize in any other way' (Collins: 1981b, p. 996). 'The repetitive behaviors ... are primarily based upon the *physical* plane' (1981a, p. 103).

Giddens has made a number of objections to Collins's approach, but he has not dealt with this materialist account of social reproduction (Giddens: 1984, pp. 140–2). To anticipate later discussion, it should be noted that the physical aspects of social locales play a prominent role in social reproduction from the standpoint of structuration theory. But Collins's reduction of the reproduction of conduct to repeated instances of activity in the same physical circumstances overlooks the following: while material objects and the physical capacities and appearance of the human body may constrain certain forms of conduct and facilitate others, these material circumstances in and of themselves do not provide social actors with the competence to reproduce social conduct time after time in the same type of setting. Indeed, in many physical settings the same actors may undertake different activities on different occasions (e.g. in family kitchens, on city streets). Moreover, some modes of conduct are less restricted by material requisites than others. Given face-to-face propinquity, actors may converse, hold meetings, and so forth, in a wide (but not unlimited) range of settings. Given modern means of communication and transport even bodily co-presence is unnecessary for many significant forms of interaction to be carried out (see below). But in all cases, unless actors sustain a knowledge of how general forms of conduct are appropriately performed in suitable locales on an ongoing basis, they will be unable to reproduce these activities as a matter of course in their day-to-day lives. Acknowledgement that social agents sustain an ongoing awareness of social skills and procedures requires a greater respect for human cognitive capacities than Collins allows. It equally suggests that an adequate approach to social reproduction cannot avoid some reference to trans-situational rules for these skills and procedures.

Social institutions: practice and context

A summary of the items outlined in the preceding sections yields a series of issues that are addressed in Giddens's account of the reproduction of regularities of *Praxis*. As opposed to Blumer and Garfinkel, Giddens places great emphasis upon persistently-repeated forms of conduct; as opposed to Winch, Giddens concentrates directly upon how forms of conduct are reproduced; and as opposed to Collins, Giddens ascribes great importance to trans-situational rules and human cognitive capacities. But these scholars also raise points with which Giddens must contend. The account of reproduced forms of conduct Giddens presents in structuration theory sustains Garfinkel's concern for the reflexive elaboration of context and action while incorporating Collins's regard for the physical settings of conduct. In the duality of structure Giddens establishes how social practices are reproduced but also preserves Blumer's insistence upon the opportunities for innovation.

The absence of an adequate conception of reproduced forms of conduct in many theories of social action stands behind Giddens's call for an *institutional theory of everyday life* (Giddens: 1979, p. 81; 1981b, pp. 164–5). The term 'institutional' is not used here in a casual manner but has a programmatic intent. The concept of social institutions in structuration theory specifically refers to routinized practices that are carried out or recognized by the majority of members of a collectivity (cf. Giddens: 1979, p. 80; 1981b, p. 164; 1984, p. 17).

Most social scientists acknowledge pervasive and enduring repetition of customary practices in tribal societies and other small-scale groups. But the extraordinary diversity of social practices in modern Western civilization obscures the extent to which institutionalized routines are constitutive of the daily transaction of events. Some mundane but nevertheless highly

consequential modes of conduct are reproduced throughout Western civilization and beyond, for example coordination by mensurable clock-time and
the Gregorian calendar, the use of money and other instruments of credit.
Other routines involving the use of language, formal political procedures,
culinary conventions, etc., are essential to the course and cycle of social
events in specific societies or a small group of societies. Less extensive
domains in which institutionalized forms of conduct are reproduced include
particular social classes as well as age-specific, gender-specific, ethnic and
regional groups.

An emphasis upon reflexive contextuality as an integral element of social
encounters is sustained in Giddens's account of social institutions, although
he departs from Garfinkel by absorbing Goffman's insights into the many
aspects of contextuality that are established in non-verbal gestures. However, unlike either scholar, Giddens emphasizes the point that agents can
constitute the meaningful context and content of social conduct in an
institutionalized manner (1979, pp. 83–4; 1984, p. 119). To accept that
context and conduct may be reproduced necessarily entails a rejection of
the finitist methodological policy that Garfinkel recommends, but it does
not deny the utility of adopting a finitist perspective for certain purposes.
In the first place, while reproduced practices exhibit a certain degree of
consistency that allows them to be conceived as institutionalized regularities,
many of the more subtle aspects of their reproduction may remain unknown,
for example the sequencing and timing of procedures of interaction. The
finitist concentration upon the empirical investigation of individual situations of the reproduction of such practices continues to be the most
appropriate way in which these subtle, yet often highly significant, aspects
of *Praxis* can be discovered and analysed. The results of such studies
ultimately deepen our understanding of how regularities of *Praxis* are reproduced. Second, every instance in which the reproduction of practices and
contexts occurs manifests certain idiosyncracies such as differences in personal mannerisms, as well as local references to determinate circumstances
and affairs. Whenever these or other particulars of specific situations are at
issue, finitist inquiries are obviously in order.

The physical aspects of social settings play a prominent part in the
reproduction of institutional activities. Giddens accepts that the nature
and contours of physical objects, material boundaries and the corporeal
characteristics of the human body shape and facilitate the reproduction of
both context and conduct. Unlike Collins, Giddens proposes that physical
circumstances always interweave with social routines in reproduced practices. The physical aspects of settings do not simply impinge upon social
conduct; instead, they are mobilized and categorized during the course of
social action and interaction (Giddens: 1976, pp. 106–7; 1979, pp. 206–7).

What is implied here is a synthesis of idealist and materialist factors in
social reproduction. The reflexive attention to the context of social encounters (which Giddens (1984, pp. 46–7) considers to be an active process of
perceptual organization) coupled with conversational procedures may be

conceived in idealist terms. Modern means of communication permit a limited degree of contextuality to be generated by agents who are not physically co-present. But the most well-developed modes of contextuality are generated by agents who are in close proximity to one another. Here agents are in a position to perceive the doings of others, and to perceive that others are perceiving them as well. Diffuse forms of contextuality that may be sustained on this basis can be distinguished from the more intensive forms of context reciprocally generated by conversational and non-verbal procedures in face-to-face encounters (Giddens: 1984, pp. 67–73).

The concept of *locale* in structuration theory joins perceptual and conversational procedures to the material circumstances of social conduct. Locales may be designated by the physical circumstances and human artifacts associated with institutionalized activities, but the concept of locale specifically refers to the way in which these material aspects of social settings are used during the course of social routines (Giddens: 1976, pp. 106–7; 1979, pp. 206–7; 1981a, pp. 39, 161; 1984, pp. 118–19). This view departs from Collins by suggesting that material circumstances may have a variable influence on the transaction of conduct. While many practices inherently involve the use of items in specific settings (e.g. agricultural and industrial production), other practices may involve the use of items that are not fixed to one spatial location. However, even in the latter case determinate material boundaries are generally required so that agents can establish a reflexive awareness and engage in discourse. For example, academics find it difficult to create the context for their lectures before large classes held outdoors.

The reproduction of action and structure in the duality of structure

Giddens's account of the reproduction of institutional practices in the duality of structure provides a basis for his reconciliation of action and structure. It thus represents a dramatic departure not only from prevailing theories of action but also from theories that concentrate upon the properties of social collectivities. Although contrasts between this account and theories of action will be discussed here, it is important to mention an item in Giddens's concept of collectivities that will be bracketed for present purposes. In structuration theory the patterning of relations in collectivities is constituted by interrelated (but politically asymmetrical) practices reproduced across time and space in various locales. (The term structuration refers to the reproduction of social relations across time and space as transacted in the duality of structure.) Consistent with the ontological flexibility of structuration theory at large, Giddens holds open for substantive inquiry all questions regarding specific systemic patterns as well as the degree to which systems are stable, organized and permeable. However, he does draw a basic distinction between two modes of integration. Social integration concerns reciprocities of practices on the level of face-to-face interaction. System integration refers to reciprocal relations between those who are physically absent. In this essay I shall address the reproduction of practices in the duality of structure without taking this distinction into account, and concentrate upon the reproduction of individual practices in a system of indeterminate dimensions. I shall have more to say about Giddens's conception of social relations in subsequent remarks.

According to Giddens, the duality of structure refers to:

> the essential recursiveness of social life as constituted in social practices. Structure is both medium and outcome of the reproduction of practices. Structure enters simultaneously into the constitution of social practices, and 'exists' in the generating moments of this constitution. (Giddens: 1979, p. 4)

It should be evident that none of the theorists of action discussed in this essay are able to propose a similar point of view. What is more noteworthy, however, is that in their comments on the conditions associated with regularities of conduct each of these theorists, with the exception of Collins, mentions an insight that figures prominently in Giddens's conception of the duality of structure. Both Blumer and Garfinkel acknowledge in passing that common understandings or expectations are drawn upon and made manifest in and through the procedures whereby 'structured' modes of conduct are repeatedly undertaken during the routine course of everyday life. Winch makes a similar point in terms more in keeping with structuration theory when he suggests that established forms of activity are undertaken by agents on the basis of rules they have learned in the past. In the duality of structure Giddens expands upon his own conception of how rules are implicated in the performances of social practices (see above). Rules now appear as generalizable procedures that are drawn upon in the reproduction of regularities of *Praxis*, a process of reproduction that serves to regenerate these rules as established features of historically-bounded social domains.

Considered against the backdrop of the pre-eminent concern of action theorists with situated instances and forms of social conduct, Giddens's most significant contribution in the duality of structure is to treat rules regarding regularities of conduct as structural properties of social collectivities. Because of the central role that this insight plays in the overall development of structuration theory it deserves to be clarified with the greatest precision. Since rules are made manifest only when institutionalized practices are reproduced (see below), they cannot be conceived exclusively in holistic terms. Nevertheless, if rules are to be identified in collective terms they must be irreducible without remainder to individual situations where specific instances of conduct are carried out.[31] Irreducibility here implies that rules of conduct (procedures of actions) are trans-situational in the sense that they are involved in forms of conduct that are: (1) reproduced and recognized many times over during the routine activities undertaken by members

---

[31] This is a modification of the criterion of irreducibility developed by Mandelbaum (1955).

of a collectivity; (2) reproduced and recognized for a considerable period in the history of that group. Where these criteria apply rules of conduct may be conceived as trans-situational properties of a collectivity that enter into the reproduction of institutionalized conduct.

Giddens's conception of rules of conduct can be shown to conform to both these criteria. To elaborate this point it is useful to return to the notion of mutual knowledge, which, as has been indicated in the previous discussion, subsumes the semantic and normative aspects of rules regarding the appropriate performance of social practices. Consider now the characteristics of mutual knowledge pertaining to institutionalized practices reproduced on numerous occasions by numerous agents in daily life. It should be evident that this knowledge cannot be thoroughly reduced to any specific situation of conduct. Indeed, at the same moment agents in different settings may draw upon the same form of mutual knowledge to reproduce the same general kind of activity.

The case studies of deviant practices that have been instrumental in the early development of symbolic interactionism and ethnomethodology are somewhat misleading in this regard. From a structural viewpoint the most prominent rules of conduct are those which are most commonly instituted in everyday practices. A useful thought experiment to determine the structural significance of rules is to imagine what difference it would make to the routine transaction of social events if agents ceased to perform the practices associated with a determinate category of mutual knowledge. Thus, to take a Durkheimian example, if it is correct to ascribe a great structural significance in Western civilization to rules concerning the rights and duties of individuals, then the removal of practices in which these rules are in play would make it difficult to sustain the routine course of social events. Such practices might range from subtle procedures of self-assertion and tactful respect for the doings of anonymous individuals, to more obvious ways in which the civic rights and obligations of individuals are exercised and fulfilled.

Mutual knowledge of rules of social *Praxis* also conforms to the criterion of historical persistence. A prerequisite here is that this knowledgeability must be associated with practices carried out in a collectivity beyond the lifetime of any agent or any cohort of agents (Giddens: 1984, p. 170). A second prerequisite is the designation of means whereby mutual knowledge is preserved and transported across time and space between situations where such practices are reproduced. Giddens's insight considerably extends the incidental references by Blumer and Garfinkel to the common understandings agents bring to 'structured' forms of conduct. 'Memory traces' of how things are done, he suggests, provide the basic means by which mutual knowledge is 'stored' by social agents (1979, p. 64; 1981a, p. 35). The type of memory at issue here should not be confused with self-reflective recall of past experiences and events. Memory in the latter sense can be verbally expressed and therefore corresponds to what Giddens terms discursive consciousness. Mutual knowledge is fundamentally sustained and recalled in a tacit manner on the level of practical consciousness.

Theorists of action have provided few insights into the exercise of power. However, it is important to note that resources as well as rules are considered by Giddens to be structural properties of collectivities. In a broader discussion of the structuration of power it would be necessary to consider the significance Giddens ascribes to the storage of authoritative and allocative resources as well as to the dialectic of control. For present purposes, however, it is sufficient to mention that resources conceived as properties of collectivities do not exert an independent influence upon the reproduction of practices in the duality of structure. Instead, the meshing of rules and resources in institutionalized conduct results in what Giddens terms *strategies of control*: the ways in which agents apply knowledge about the manipulation of the resources to which they have access in order to reproduce their strategic autonomy over the actions of others (Giddens: 1981a, pp. 61–4; 1985, ch. 1). While resources may be conceptualized as structural properties of collectivities for analytical purposes, strategies of control represent aspects of *Praxis* that are reproduced in the duality structure.

To say that social routines are reproduced in the duality of structure is not to claim that the routinization of social life is inevitable. Social practices do not reproduce themselves, social agents do, and from the standpoint of structuration theory social agents are always seen to retain the capability to act otherwise than they do. Giddens preserves this crucial qualification when he notes: 'all action exists in continuity with the past, which supplies *the means of its initiation*' (1979, p. 70, italics added). Mutual knowledge and resources conceived in structural terms establish the continuity with the past to which Giddens refers, but they serve only as the media for the reproduction of institutonalized practices and contexts. *There is no guarantee that agents will reproduce regularities of conduct as they previously have done.* For this reason Giddens makes it a matter of principle that 'the concept of social reproduction ... is not explanatory: all reproduction is contingent and historical' (1981a, p. 27).

The contingencies of reproduction to which Giddens refers incorporate Blumer's concern for the possibility of innovation in social conduct. But this is only one of several ways in which agents may depart from established routines. First, agents may make mistakes which constitute situational improprieties or cultural lapses. However, the frequency of these errors is necessarily limited. As Giddens notes, if there is any continuity to social life, actors must be right most of the time (Giddens: 1984, p. 90). Second, actors who retain the competence and capacity to reproduce routine practices may refrain from doing so. In certain respects this forbearance itself may comprise a skilful course of conduct (e.g. strikes, tactful neglect of situational improprieties). But the alteration of established modes of conduct, the possibility of novelty from Blumer's point of view, undoubtedly represents the most significant contingency of social reproduction. The production of unprecedented forms of conduct provides the praxiological basis for social transformation. It is therefore extremely important to note that

Giddens conceives the possibility for change as inherent in every act of social reproduction (1976, p. 102). But it is equally significant that continuities of conduct always accompany and facilitate the generation of discontinuities in social *Praxis*. Indeed, many institutionalized routines continue to be reproduced even during the most radical episodes of social change (1979, pp. 216–17; 1984, pp. 26, 87).

It is fundamental to the duality of structure that the structural properties of collectivities (rules and resources) not only serve as the media of social reproduction but are also reproduced as an *outcome* of this process. None of the theories of action discussed in this essay exhibits a concern for the outcomes of social activity. (On the other hand, collectivist theorists such as Durkheim, who emphasize structural properties that 'emerge' from social conduct, fail to supply an adequate account of social *Praxis*.) But the claim that structural properties are reproduced in routine practices needs precise clarification.

As is indicated in Giddens's summary definition of the duality of structure quoted above, structure 'exists' in a manifest form only when it is instantiated in social practices. It otherwise persists between instances of social reproduction only as 'memory traces' sustained by knowledgeable social agents. To say that structure is reproduced in the duality of structure means that structure is *reconstituted* in each instance where a pervasive and enduring practice is reproduced. This reconstitution of structure reinforces agents' familiarity with established cognitive outlooks (Giddens: 1979, p. 128; 1984, p. 104). That is, it reinforces the mutual knowledge of rules and of the strategies of control of resources associated with these practices, both for those who actually participate in them and for those who recognize that these practices are being performed. This point applies equally to the reproduction of context. In every instance where agents reflexively monitor physical, social and temporal elements of their circumstances in a routine manner, they reflexively regenerate the contextual relevance of these elements (Giddens: 1979, pp. 83–4). Of course no single act of social reproduction is sufficient in itself to reconstitute structural properties. But the continual repetition and recognition of familiar modes of conduct by numerous members of a social collectivity or group embed an awareness of these practices deep within their tacit memory of the familiar features of social *Praxis* in the circumstances of their daily lives. Conversely, when certain forms of conduct cease or are transformed, the mutual knowledge of the specific configuration of rules and resources associated with these practices begins to lapse and fade. Gradually, through the passing of the generations, the only way to retrieve knowledge of the structuration of these practices is through whatever historical documentation may have been preserved.

While it has not been my purpose here to discuss the connection between the reproduction of social life in the duality of structure and the subjective dispositions of social agents, two points of clarification should be mentioned. First, since structuration theory places so much emphasis upon the reproduction of institutionalized routines, it is incumbent upon Giddens to specify in a generic sense why social agents are disposed to undertake similar types of practice on numerous occasions. Although Giddens proposes that many practices are undertaken by social agents on a tacit basis, without any direct motivation, he also acknowledges that specific interests and long-term projects may impel agents to act as they do. It should also be acknowledged that the material milieux of action, the exercise of sanctions as strategies of control, and the constitution and configuration of the practices that prevail within any given social system may constrain possibilities for alternative modes of conduct (Giddens: 1984, pp. 174–9). But Giddens also suggests that, underlying all routine practices, agents develop an unconscious sense of trust in the fabric of social activities and the object world that comprise the course and circumstances of their daily lives. This sense of *ontological security* serves to connect the agents' unconscious 'basic security system' to the routine procedures of social reproduction.[32] However, given Giddens's allowance for contingencies in *Praxis*, it should be stressed that dispositions to engage in institutionalized conduct can be resisted by agents on a variety of grounds.

The second point concerns whether agents must intend (i.e. be aware) that their mundane social practices serve to reconstitute social structure.[33] Giddens contends that such need not be, and often is not, the case. The basis for this contention is established in the ascription of priority to agency over consciousness in the performance of social activity (see above). Agents may 'make a difference' by contributing to the reproduction of structure without even a tacit awareness that they do so. But this unintentional reproduction of structure is not a logical necessity. It remains possible for agents to thematisize the contributions they make to ongoing circumstances, and to alter their practices on the basis of these insights. The inherently critical role played by social scientific knowledge from the standpoint of structuration theory logically follows from this point.

The Concept of Social Relations: A Critical Assessment

Since this essay has been confined to the praxiological dimensions of structuration theory, it is out of the question to offer an evaluation of the degree to which this theory succeeds in providing a comprehensive ontology of social life; instead, I propose a critique of Giddens's conception of social relations. These matters are not only significant for an adequate account of social *Praxis*, they are also consequential for topics in structuration theory beyond those currently under discussion.

From the standpoint of the duality of structure, practices that are institu-

---

[32] For a more extended discussion of the relation of the unconscious to social routine, see Giddens: 1984, ch. 2.

[33] For a more extended discussion of intentionality, see Giddens: 1984, pp. 8, 13.

tionalized throughout a group reproduce specific structural properties that have a very broad extension throughout that collectivity. However, social relations cannot be grasped on this basis. Social relations must always involve differentiations of identity and practice between individual agents, as well as among and between various groups. To further complicate matters, social relations need not involve agents who are physically co-present. Indeed, as previously mentioned, social relations between those who are physically absent are presupposed in Giddens's conception of social systems. Nevertheless, consistent with the emphasis upon the duality of structure in structuration theory, social relations must be conceived in terms of the recursive reproduction of structural properties and forms of social *Praxis*, that is, social relations are 'structured' by means of rules embedded in practices of interaction.

Giddens's conception of social relations addresses the structuration of practices in social systems. The 'positioning' of practices is crucial to this conception in several respects, two of which are particularly important. The first is the positioning of agents in the regions of large-scale collectivities and totalities. Positioning in this sense involves the differentiation and interrelation of practices associated with social locales. Drawing upon important, albeit hitherto little-known, work in time-geography by Thorsten Hagerstrand, Alan Pred and other scholars, Giddens develops a novel approach to time-space positioning. While I shall not deal with this work here, its significance to Giddens's thought should not be underestimated.[34]

While social locales are reproduced as contextual settings in social relations, something more must be said about the social structuring of relations *per se*. Here Giddens provides for a second mode of positioning, a positioning that is bound up in his conceptual account of the constitution of social relations.

> Social relations are ... involved in the structuring of interaction but are also the main 'building blocks' around which institutions are articulated in system integration ... Social relations concern the 'positioning' of individuals within a 'social space' of symbolic categories and ties. Rules involved in social positions are normally to do with the specification of rights and obligations relevant to persons having a particular social identity. The normative aspects of such rules, in other words, are particularly pronounced, but all previously stated characteristics of rules [see above] apply to them too. (Giddens: 1984, p. 89)

It is evident that social relations are identities, rights and obligations that are embedded in institutionalized practices and sustained in the practical consciousness of social agents. The notion of position as it is used here is meant to replace standard conceptions of social role. Giddens reserves the term 'role' for encounters where agents are co-present in a determinate locale and where normative definitions of 'expected' modes of conduct are

[34] For an exposition of this work, see Giddens: 1984, pp. 84–5, ch. 3.

strongly pronounced. Relations here tend toward a more clear-cut closure than in social systems at large. The concept of social position is then freed to refer to less well-defined identities (e.g. age, gender, skin pigmentation) associated with a broader range of modes of conduct (Giddens: 1984, pp. 83–4; see also Giddens: 1979, p. 117). To emphasize the structural properties of positioning in social relations, Giddens adopts Roy Bhaskar's term, 'position-practice relations' (Giddens: 1984, p. 83; see also Bhaskar: 1979, pp. 51–2).

Giddens's emphasis upon position-practices in social relations is a substantial advance upon the over-socialized conception of social role exhibited in many works on social theory. But the distinction he draws between social roles and position-practices is more problematic. Social relations in modern social systems are highly differentiated in a multitude of ways. In my view the distinction between social roles and position-practices compresses too many dimensions of social interaction to provide a satisfactory categorical basis for this diversity. Consider, for example, social relations in bureaucracies, many of which are characterized by strongly-pronounced normative expectations. On this basis they might be classified as roles. Yet it is often the case that bureaucratic officials exercise their rights and fulfil their obligations to one another while in separate offices or, more remotely, separate branches of the organization. Their relations here do not correspond to Giddens's concept of roles, but rather to position-practices. Another ambiguity arises with regard to social relations as exemplified by the interaction between blacks and whites in the United States during the early part of the twentieth century. Once again the normative expectations involved in social interaction are sufficiently pronounced to allow for the concept of roles to apply, but the well-defined identities and the 'closure' of relations Giddens associates with roles need not, and very often did not, exist.

These examples suggest that the concepts of role and position-practice relations in general are best conceived not as alternatives but as polar extremes. There appear to be three dimensions of social relations that have been compressed into the distinction between role and position-practice relations: the degree of determination of 'expected' modes of conduct; the degree to which conduct occurs in circumstances of co-presence; and the degree of 'closure' of relations. Each of these dimensions is useful to the study of social relations from a praxiological view point, and the concept of role which involves extreme positions on each of these dimensions is useful as it stands. But it is quite possible to build a series of further concepts from these dimensions of position-practice relations. Coupled with concepts already in place regarding the time-space regionalization of social systems, such concepts would add more flexibility and precision to the study of social relations, and thus of social systems also.

The neglect of anchored relations

There is one category of social relations that is of great significance but which is not captured by the distinction between general social positions and determinate social roles. I refer to what Erving Goffman terms *anchored relations*. Goffman suggests that such relations involve a binding whereby agents identify one another on a personal basis. These relations are particularly distinctive in that they involve reciprocal acknowledgements between agents that an irrevocable framework of mutual knowing has been established between them, and this framework organizes their experience of one another. Goffman therefore contrasts relations that are anchored in this way with anonymous forms of social relations (Goffman: 1971, p. 189; see also Goffman: 1983, p. 13). Family relations are the obvious example, but Goffman includes a much broader range of anchored relations by making 'acquaintanceship' the limiting case (1971, p. 205; 1983, p. 13), and a spectrum of increasingly intimate relations may also be included here. But, one must not confuse intimacy with harmony. Rivalries and feuds can be anchored in mutual knowing just as much as more amicable forms of social relations.

Goffman presents no equivalent to the duality of structure; indeed his argument against a 'strong coupling' of structure and action is based upon a finitism that resembles Harold Garfinkel's position (see Goffman: 1983, pp. 11–12). Nevertheless, he does assume that anchored relations are 'structure-building' entities that may often have their own 'natural' history (Goffman: 1971, p. 190; 1983, p. 13). Moreover, Goffman devotes most of his attention, with his inimitable eye for subtlety and detail, to the forms of practice through which the mutual knowing in anchored relations is established and sustained. Thus, with regard to the principles of structuration theory, it seems perfectly appropriate to consider anchored relations as involving a recursive reproduction of structure and action in the duality of structure.

The closest Giddens has so far come to presenting a concept of 'anchored relations' is in the concept of social roles. But while social roles involve a closure based upon the propinquity and identity of agents, Giddens makes no mention of the framework of personal knowledge agents establish and reproduce in anchored relations. Hence it is feasible to propose unanchored role relations between agents who maintain impersonal identities, as for example those between traffic warden and motorist when a parking-ticket is issued, or between teachers and parents who meet to discuss the education of a child.

Anchored social relations are far too important to the course of social life to be neglected in structuration theory. The need to take them into account is particularly acute in the study of family life. Indeed, it is impossible to account for family relations on any other basis. Anchored family relations are crucibles within which many powerful emotions are forged and fused throughout the life cycle of family members. The ramifications of such relations thus extend to the very core of human experience in many basic respects. The significance of anchored relations is also evident in the constitution of collectivities, as is illustrated in the recent interest in interpersonal relations between members of the capitalist class in the United States and Great Britain. Anchored relations figure prominently too in the investigation of small-scale communities, scientific research groups, and so on.

Structuration theory is quite new, and no doubt there will be many critical issues in addition to those I raise here that will be discussed in the future. What is beyond dispute is that Giddens has succeeded in bringing the production and reproduction of social life into the centre of concerns in social theory. In this essay I have sought to demonstrate a number of respects in which the emphasis upon social *Praxis* in structuration theory represents a departure from prevailing theories and theoretical traditions. The topics I have raised here certainly do not exhaust the matter. Critical discussion of structuration theory may continue for some time, but so too will the discovery of the many ways in which it illuminates the constitution of social life.

Bibliography

Alexander, J. C., 1982: *Positivism, Presuppositions, and Current Controversies*, vol. 1 of his *Theoretical Logic in Sociology*, 4 vols. Berkeley and Los Angeles: University of California Press.

Apel, K. O., 1967: *Analytic Philosophy of Language and the Geisteswissenschaften*. Dordrecht: D. Reidel.

Archer, M. S., 1982: 'Structuration versus Morphogenesis: On Combining Structure and Action', *British Journal of Sociology*, 3: 445–83.

Bergner, J. T., 1981: *The Origin of Formalism in Social Science*. Chicago: University of Chicago Press.

Bershady, H., 1973: *Ideology and Social Knowledge*. Oxford: Basil Blackwell.

Bhaskar, R., 1978: *A Realist Theory of Science*. Sussex: Harvester.
    1979: *The Possibility of Naturalism: A Philosophical Critique of the Contemporary Human Sciences*. Atlantic Highlands, NJ: Humanities.
    1983: 'Beef, Structure, and Place: Notes from a Critical Naturalist Perspective', *Journal for the Theory of Social Behavior*, 13.

Blumer, H., 1969: *Symbolic Interactionism: Perspective and Method*. Englewood Cliffs, NJ: Prentice-Hall.

Carlstein, T., 1981: 'The Sociology of Structuration in Time and Space: A Time-Geographic Assessment of Giddens's Theory', *Svensk Geografisk Arsbok,*. 57: pp. 41–57.

Cicourel, A., 1964: *Method and Measurement in Sociology*. New York: Free Press.

Cohen, I. J., 1984: 'Participant Observation and Professional Sociology: Transposing and Transforming Descriptions of Everyday Life', *Current Perspectives in Social Theory*, 5: 71–100.
    1986: 'The Status of Structuration Theory: A Reply to McLennan', *Theory, Culture, and Society*, 3: 123–34.
    forthcoming: *Structuration Theory*. London: Macmillan; New York: St Martin's.

Cohen, P. S., 1968: *Modern Social Theory*. London: Heinemann.

Collins, R., 1981a: 'Micro-translation as a Theory-building Structure', in K. Knorr-

Cetina and A. V. Cicourel (eds), *Advances in Social Theory and Methodology: Towards an Integration of Micro- and Macro-Sociologies*. London: Routledge and Kegan Paul, pp. 81–108.

1981b: 'On the Microfoundations of Macrosociology', *American Journal of Sociology*, 86: 984–1014.

Comte, A., 1893: *The Positivist Philosophy*, translated by Harriet Martineau, 2 vols. London: Routledge and Kegan Paul.

Garfinkel, H., 1984: *Studies in Ethnomethodology*. Cambridge, England: Polity Press.

Garfinkel, H. and Sacks, H., 1970: 'On Formal Structures of Practical Actions', in J. C. McKinney and E. A. Tiryakian (eds), *Theoretical Sociology*. New York: Appleton-Century-Croft. pp. 326–38.

Giddens, A., 1974: 'Introduction', in Giddens (ed.), *Positivism and Sociology*. London: Heinemann, pp. 1–22.

1976: *New Rules of Sociological Method: A Positive Critique of Interpretative Sociologies*. London: Hutchinson; New York: Basic Books.

1977: *Studies in Social and Political Theory*. London: Hutchinson; New York: Basic Books.

1979: *Central Problems in Social Theory: Action, Structure, and Contradiction in Social Analysis*. London: Macmillan; Berkeley and Los Angeles: University of California Press.

1981a: *Power, Property and the State*, vol. 1 of *A Contemporary Critique of Historical Materialism*. London: Macmillan; Berkeley and Los Angeles: University of California Press.

1981b: 'Agency, Institution, and Time-Space Analysis', in K. Knorr-Cetina and A. V. Cicourel, *Advances in Social Theory and Methodology: Towards an Integration of Micro- and Macro-Sociologies*. London: Routledge and Kegan Paul.

1982: 'Hermeneutics and Social Theory', in his *Profiles and Critiques in Social Theory*. London: Macmillan; Berkeley and Los Angeles: University of California Press, pp. 1–17.

1984: *The Constitution of Society: Outline of the Theory of Structuration*. Cambridge, England: Polity Press.

1985: *The Nation-State and Violence*, vol. 2 of *Critique of Historical Materialism*. Cambridge, England: Polity Press.

Goffman, E., 1971: *Relations in Public: Microstudies of the Public Order*. New York: Basic Books.

1983: 'The Interaction Order', *American Sociological Review*, 48: pp. 1–17.

Hansen, N., 1969: *Perception and Discovery: An Introduction to Scientific Inquiry*. San Francisco: Freeman, Cooper and Co.

Hempel, C., 1965: 'The Logic of Functional Analysis', in his *Aspects of Scientific Explanation and Other Essays in the Philosophy of Science*. New York: Free Press, pp. 297–330.

Heritage, J., 1984: *Garfinkel and Ethnomethodology*. Cambridge, England: Polity Press.

Homans, G. C., 1974: *Social Behavior: Its Elementary Forms*, revised edn. New York: Harcourt, Brace.

Kuhn, T. S., 1970: *The Structure of Scientific Revolutions*, 2nd edn. Chicago: University of Chicago Press.

Lakatos, I., 1978: *The Methodology of Scientific Research Programmes*, 2 vols. Cambridge, England: Cambridge University Press.

Laudan, L., 1977: *Progress and its Problems: Towards a Theory of Scientific Growth*. Berkeley and Los Angeles: University of California Press.

MacCannel, D., 1976: 'The Past and Future of Symbolic Interactionism', *Semiotica*, 16: 99–114.

Maines, D. R., 1977: 'Social Organization and Social Structure in Symbolic Interactionist Thought', *Annual Review of Sociology*, 3: pp. 235–59.

Mandelbaum, M., 1955: 'Societal Facts', *British Journal of Sociology*, 5: 305–17.

Marx, K., 1963: *The Eighteenth Brumaire of Louis Bonaparte*. New York: International Publishers.

Masterman, M., 1970: 'The Nature of a Paradigm', in I. Lakatos and A. Musgrave (eds), *Criticism and the Growth of Knowledge*. Cambridge, England: Cambridge University Press. pp. 59–89.

Maynard, D. W. and Wilson, T. P., 1980: 'On the Reification of Social Structure', *Current Perspectives in Social Theory*, 1: 287–322.

McLennan, G., 1984: 'Critical of Positive Theory? A Comment on the Status of Anthony Giddens's Social Theory', *Theory, Culture, and Society*, 2: 23–9.

Meltzer, B. N., Petras, J.W. and Reynolds, L. T., 1975: *Symbolic Interactionism: Genesis, Varieties and Criticism*. London: Routledge and Kegan Paul.

Merton, R. K., 1968: *Social Theory and Social Structure*, enlarged edn. New York: Free Press.

Nagel, E., 'A Formalization of Functionalism', in his *Logic Without Metaphysics*. New York: Free Press, pp. 247–83.

Perinbanayagam, R. S., 1985: *Signifying Acts: Structure and Meaning in Everyday Life*. Carbondale, Ill.: Southern Illinois University Press.

Popper, K. R., 1968: *The Logic of Scientific Discovery*. New York: Harper & Row.

Schütz, A., 1962: 'Common-sense and Scientific Interpretation of Human Action', in his *The Problem of Social Reality*, vol. 1 of *Collected Papers*, edited by M. Nathanson. The Hague: Martinus Nijhoff, pp. 3–47.

Simmel, G., 1950: 'The Field of Sociology', in K. H. Wolff (ed.), *The Sociology of Georg Simmel*. New York: Macmillan. pp. 3–25.

Thompson, J. B., 1981: *Critical Hermeneutics: A Study in the Thought of Paul Ricoeur and Jürgen Habermas*. Cambridge, England: Cambridge University Press.

Toulmin, S., 1961: *Foresight and Understanding: An Enquiry into the Aims of Science*. New York: Harper & Row.

Vico, G., 1968: *The New Science*. Ithaca: Cornell University Press.

Wallace, W., 1983: *Principles of Scientific Sociology*. New York: Aldine.

Whitehead, A. N., 1925: *Science and the Modern World*. New York: Free Press.

Wilson, T. P., 1984: 'On the Role of Mathematics in the Social Sciences', *Journal for Mathematical Sociology*, 10: 221–39.

Wilson, T. P. and Zimmerman, D. H., 1979–80: 'Ethnomethodolgy and Social Theory', *Humboldt Journal of Social Relations*, 7: 52–83.

Winch, P., 1958: *The Idea of Social Science and its Relation to Philosophy*. New York: Humanities.

World-Systems Analysis

IMMANUEL WALLERSTEIN

'World-systems analysis' is not a theory about the social world, or about part of it. It is a protest against the ways in which social scientific inquiry was structured for all of us at its inception in the middle of the nineteenth century. This mode of inquiry has come to be a set of often-unquestioned a priori assumptions. World-systems analysis maintains that this mode of social scientific inquiry, practised worldwide, has had the effect of closing off rather than opening up many of the most important or the most interesting questions. In wearing the blinkers which the nineteenth century constructed, we are unable to perform the social task we wish to perform and that the rest of the world wishes us to perform, which is to present rationally the real historical alternatives that lie before us. World-systems analysis was born as moral, and in its broadest sense, political, protest. However, it is on the basis of scientific claims, that is, on the basis of claims related to the possibilities of systematic knowledge about social reality, that world-systems analysis challenges the prevailing mode of inquiry.

This is a debate, then, about fundamentals, and such debates are always difficult. First of all, most participants have deep commitments about fundamentals. Second, it is seldom the case that any clear, or at least any simple, empirical test can resolve or even clarify the issues. The empirical debate has to be addressed at a very complex and holistic level. Does the sum of derived theorizing starting from one or another set of premisses encompass known descriptions of reality in a more 'satisfactory' manner? This involves us in all sorts of secondary dilemmas. Our known 'descriptions' of reality are to some extent a function of our premisses; future 'descriptions' may of course transform our sense of reality. Does the 'theorizing' said today to encompass reality really encompass it? And last but not least, what does it mean to encompass reality 'in a satisfactory manner'? Is this latter criterion anything more than an aesthetic adjunct?

Not only are debates about fundamentals frustrating for all these reasons, but each side has a built-in handicap. The defenders of existing views must 'explain away' the anomalies, hence our present challenge. But the challengers must offer convincing 'data' in a situation where, compared to the 150 years or so of traditional social scientific inquiry, they have had far less time to accumulate appropriately-relevant 'data'. In a subject-matter inherently recalcitrant to experimental manipulation, 'data' cannot be accumulated rapidly. So a dispute about fundamentals may be thought of as analogous to a heavyweight championship bout, but without a referee and between two somewhat dyspeptic boxers, each with his left hand tied behind his back. It may be fun to watch, but is it boxing? Is it science?

And who will decide? In some sense, the spectators will decide – and probably not by watching the boxers, but by fighting it out themselves. So why bother? Because the boxers are part of the spectators, who are of course all boxers.

Lest we get lost in analogies, let me return to the discussion of fundamentals. I propose to take seven common assumptions of social scientific inquiry and indicate what it is that makes me feel uncomfortable about them. I shall then explore whether alternative (or even opposing) assumptions are not as plausible or more plausible and indicate the direction in which these alternative assumptions would lead us.

I

The social sciences are constituted of a number of 'disciplines' which are intellectually-coherent groupings of subject-matter distinct from each other.

These disciplines are most frequently listed as anthropology, economics, political science and sociology. There are, to be sure, potential additions to this list, such as geography. Whether history is or is not a social science is a matter of some controversy, and we shall return to this later (see section II). There is a similar debate about psychology, or at least about social psychology.

It has been a growing fashion, since at least 1945, to deplore the unnecessary barriers between the 'disciplines' and to endorse the merits of 'interdisciplinary' research and/or teaching. This has been argued on two counts. One is the assertion that the analysis of some 'problem areas' can benefit from an approach combining the perspectives of many disciplines. It is said, for example, that if we wish to study 'labour', pooling the knowledge offered by the disciplines of economics, political science and sociology might be of great advantage. The logic of such an approach leads to multidisciplinary teams, or to a single scholar 'learning several disciplines', at least in so far as they relate to 'labour'.

The second presumed basis for 'interdisciplinary' research is slightly different. As we pursue our collective inquiry it becomes clear, it is argued, that some of our subject-matter is 'at the borderline' of two or more disciplines. 'Linguistics', for example, may be located at such a 'border'. The logic of such an approach may lead eventually to the development of a new 'autonomous discipline', which in many ways is what has been happening to the study of linguistics during the last thirty years.

We know that there are multiple disciplines, since there are multiple academic departments in universities around the world, graduate degrees in these disciplines and national and international associations of scholars of these disciplines. That is, we know *politically* that different disciplines exist. They have organizations with boundaries, structures and personnel to defend their collective interests and ensure their collective reproduction. But this tells us nothing about the validity of the *intellectual* claims to separateness, claims which presumably justify the organizational networks.

The lauding of the merits of interdisciplinary work in the social sciences has so far not significantly undermined the strengths of the organizational apparatuses that shield the separate disciplines. Indeed, the contrary may be true: what has enhanced the claim of each discipline to represent a separately coherent level of analysis linked to appropriate methodologies is the constant assertion by practitioners of the various disciplines that each has something to learn from the other which it could not know by pursuing its own level of analysis with its specific methodologies, and that this 'other' knowledge is pertinent and significant to the resolution of the intellectual problems on which each is working. Interdisciplinary work is in no sense an intellectual critique *per se* of the existing compartmentalization of social science, and lacks in any case the political clout to affect the existing institutional structures.

But are the various social scientific disciplines really 'disciplines'? For a word so widely used, what constitutes a 'discipline' is seldom discussed. There is no entry for this term in the *International Encyclopaedia of the Social Sciences* nor in the *Encyclopaedia of Philosophy* nor in the *Encyclopaedia Britannica*. We do better by going to the *Oxford English Dictionary*, which tell us that:

> Etymologically, *discipline*, as pertaining to the disciple or scholar, is antithetical to *doctrine*, the property of the doctor or teacher; hence, in the history of the words, *doctrine* is more concerned with abstract theory, and *discipline* with practice or exercise.

But having reminded us of the term's origins, the *OED* does no better for us in the actual definition than describing it as 'a branch of instruction or education; a department of learning or knowledge; a science or art in its educational aspect'. The emphasis here seems to be on the reproduction of knowledge (or at least its dissemination) and not on its production. But surely the concept, 'discipline', cannot be unrelated to the process of producing knowledge?

The history of the social sciences is quite clear, at least in broad brush strokes. Once, there were no social sciences, or only 'predecessors'. Then slowly but steadily there emerged over the course of the nineteenth century a set of names, and then of departments, degrees and associations, that by 1945 (although sometimes earlier) had crystallized into the categories we use today. There were other 'names' which were discarded and which presumably involved different 'groupings' of 'subject-matter'. What is, or was, encompassed by such terms as 'moral economy' or *Staatswissenschaft* is not entirely clear. This is not because their advocates were insufficiently clear-thinking but because a 'discipline' in some real sense defines itself over a long run in its practice. An interrupted practice means an unfulfilled discipline. For example, the famous quadripartite subdivision of anthropology (physical anthropology, social or cultural anthropology, archaeology and linguistics) was (and to some extent still is) a 'practice' rather than a 'doctrine'. It then became a doctrine, taught and justified by doctors or teachers. But did the whole add up to a coherent, defensible level of analysis or mode of analysis, or just to segregated subject-matter?

We know where all these divisions of subject-matter came from. They derive intellectually from the dominant liberal ideology of the nineteenth century which argued that state and market, politics and economics, were analytically separate (and largely self-contained) domains, each with their particular rules ('logics'). Society was adjured to keep them separate, and scholars studied them separately. Since there seemed to be many realities that apparently were neither in the domain of the market nor in that of the state, these realities were placed in a residual grab-bag which took on as compensation the grand name of sociology. There was a sense in which sociology was thought to explain the seemingly 'irrational' phenomena that economics and political science were unable to account for. Finally, since there were people beyond the realm of the civilized world – remote, and with whom it was difficult to communicate – the study of such peoples encompassed special rules and special training, which took on the somewhat polemical name of anthropology.

We know the historical origins of the fields. We know their intellectual itineraries, which have been complex and variegated, especially since 1945. And we know why they have run into 'boundary' difficulties. As the real world evolved, the contact line between 'primitive' and 'civilized', 'political' and 'economic', blurred. Scholarly poaching became commonplace. The poachers kept moving the fences, without however breaking them down.

The question before us today is whether there are any criteria which can be used to assert in a relatively clear and defensible way boundaries between the four presumed disciplines of anthropology, economics, political science and sociology. World-systems analysis responds with an unequivocal 'no' to this question. All the presumed criteria – level of analysis, subject-matter, methods, theoretical assumptions – either are no longer true in practice or, if sustained, are barriers to further knowledge rather than stimuli to its creation.

Or, put another way, the differences between permissible topics, methods, theories or theorizing *within* any of the so-called 'disciplines' are far greater than the differences *among* them. This means in practice that the overlap is substantial and, in terms of the historical evolution of all these fields, is increasing all the time. The time has come to cut through this intellectual morass by saying that these four disciplines are but a single one. This is not to say that all social scientists should be doing identical work. There is every need for, and likelihood of, specialization in 'fields of inquiry'. But let us remember the one significant organizational example we have. Somewhere in the period 1945–55, two hitherto organizationally separate 'disciplines', botany and zoology, merged into a single discipline called biology. Since that time, biology has been a flourishing discipline and has generated many sub-fields, but none of them, as far as I know, bears the name or has the contours of botany or zoology.

The argument of world-systems analysis is straightforward. The three presumed arenas of collective human action – the economic, the political and the social or sociocultural – are not autonomous arenas of social action. They do not have separate 'logics'. More importantly, the intermeshing of constraints, options, decisions, norms and 'rationalities' is such that no useful research model can isolate 'factors' according to the categories of economic, political and social, and treat only one kind of variable, implicitly holding the others constant. We are arguing that there is a single 'set of rules' or a single 'set of constraints' within which these various structures operate.

The case of the virtually total overlap of the presumed domains of sociology and anthropology is even stronger. By what stretch of the imagination can one assert that Elliot Liebow's *Tally Corner* and William F. Whyte's *Street-Corner Society* – both 'classic' works, one written by an 'anthropologist' and the other by a 'sociologist' – are works in two different 'disciplines'? It would not be hard, as every reader knows, to assemble a long list of such examples.

II

> History is the study of, the explanation of, the particular as it really happened in the past. Social science is the statement of the universal set of rules by which human/social behaviour is explained.

This is the famous distinction between idiographic and nomothetic modes of analysis, which are considered to be antithetical. The 'hard' version of this antithesis is to argue that only one of the modes (which one varies according to one's views) is legitimate or interesting or even 'possible'. This 'hard' version is what the *Methodenstreit* was about. The 'soft' version sees these two modes as two ways of cutting into social reality. Though undertaken separately, differently and for dissimilar (even opposing) purposes, it would be fruitful for the world of scholarship to combine the two modes. This 'soft' view is comparable to arguing the merits of 'interdisciplinary' work in the social sciences. By asserting the merits of combining two approaches, the intellectual legitimacy of viewing them as two separate modes is reinforced.

The strongest arguments of the idiographic and nomothetic schools both seem plausible. The argument of the idiographic school is the ancient doctrine that 'all is flux'. If everything is always changing, then any generalization purporting to apply to two or more presumably comparable phenomena is never true. All that one can do is to understand emphatically a sequence of events. Conversely, the argument of the nomothetic school is that it is manifest that the real world (including the social world) is not a set of random happenings. If so, there must be rules that describe 'regularities', in which case there is a domain for scientific activity.

The strongest critiques of each side about the other are also plausible. The nomothetic critique of the idiographic view is that any recounting of 'past happenings' is by definition a selection from reality (as it really happened) and therefore implies criteria of selection and categories of description. These criteria and categories are based on unavowed but none the less real generalizations that are akin to scientific laws. The critique of the nomothetic view is that it neglects those transformational phenomena (due in part to the reflexiveness of social reality) which makes it impossible to 'repeat' structural arrangements.

There are various ways of dealing with these mutual criticisms. One way is the path of 'combining' history and the social sciences. The historian is said to serve the social scientist by providing the latter with wider, deeper sets of data from which to induce his law-like generalizations. The social scientist is said to serve the historian by offering him the results of research, reasonably-demonstrated generalizations that offer insight into the explication of a particular sequence of events.

The problem with this neat division of intellectual labour is that it presumes the possibility of isolating 'sequences' subject to 'historical' analysis and small 'universes' subject to 'social scientific' analysis. In practice, however, one person's sequence is another's universe, and the neutral observer is in some quandary as to how to distinguish between the two on purely logical as opposed to, say, stylistic or presentational grounds.

The problem however is deeper than that. Is there a meaningful difference between sequence and universe, between history and social science? Are they two activities or one? Synchrony is akin to a geometric dimension. One can describe it logically, but it can be drawn only falsely on paper. In geometry, a point, a line or a plane can be drawn only in three (or four) dimensions. So is it in 'social science'. Synchrony is a conceptual limit, not a socially usable category. All description has time, and the only question is how wide a band is immediately relevant. Similarly, unique sequence is only describable in non-unique categories. All conceptual language presumes comparisons among universes. Just as we cannot literally 'draw' a point, so we cannot literally 'describe' a unique 'event'. The drawing, the description, has thickness or complex generalization.

Since this is an inextricable logical dilemma, the solution must be sought on heuristic grounds. World-systems analysis offers the heuristic value of the *via media* between trans-historical generalizations and particularistic narrations. It argues that, as our format tends toward either extreme, it tends toward an exposition of minimal interest and minimal utility. It argues that the optimal method is to pursue analysis within systemic frameworks, long enough in time and large enough in space to contain governing 'logics' which 'determine' the largest part of sequential reality, while simultaneously recognizing and taking into account that these systemic frameworks have beginnings and ends and are therefore not to be conceived of as 'eternal' phenomena. This implies, then, that at every instant we look both for the framework (the 'cyclical rhythms' of the system), which we describe conceptually, and for the patterns of internal transformation (the 'secular trends' of the system) that will eventually bring about the demise of the system, which we describe sequentially. This implies that the task is singular. There is neither historian nor social scientist, but only a historical social scientist who analyses the general laws of particular systems and the particular sequences through which these systems have gone (the grammatical tense here deliberately not being the so-called ethnographic present). We are then faced with the issue of determining the 'unit of analysis' within which we must work, which brings us to our third premiss.

III

Human beings are organized in entities we may call societies, which constitute the fundamental social frameworks within which human life is lived.

No concept is more pervasive in modern social science than society, and no concept is used more automatically and unreflectively than society, despite the countless pages devoted to its definition. The textbook definitions revolve around the question: 'What is a society?', whereas the arguments we have just made about the unity of historical social science lead us to ask a different question: 'When and where is a society?'

'Societies' are concrete. Furthermore, society is a term which we might do well to discard because of its conceptual history and hence its virtually ineradicable and profoundly misleading connotations. Society is a term whose current usage in history and the social sciences is coeval with the institutional emergence of modern social science in the nineteenth century. Society is one half of an antithetic tandem in which the other is the state. The French Revolution was a cultural watershed in the ideological history of the modern world-system in that it led to the widespread acceptance of the idea that social change rather than social stasis is normal, both in the normative and in the statistical sense of the word. It thereby posed the intellectual problem of how to regulate, speed up, slow down, or otherwise affect this normal process of change and evolution.

The emergence of social science as an institutionalized social activity was one of the major systemic responses to this intellectual problem. Social science has come to represent the rationalist ideology that if one understands the process (whether idiographically or, more commonly, nomothetically) one can affect it in some morally positive manner. (Even 'conservatives', dedicated to containing change, could broadly assent to this approach.)

The political implications of such an enterprise escaped (and escapes) no one. This is of course why social science has remained to this day 'controversial'. But it is also why in the nineteenth century the concept 'society' was opposed to that of 'state'. The multiple sovereign states that had been and were being constituted were the obvious focuses of political activity. They seemed the locus of effective social control, and therefore the arena in which social change could be affected and effected. The standard nineteenth-century approach to the intellectual-political issue was concerned with the question of how to 'reconcile' society and state. In this formulation, the state could be observed and analysed directly. It operated through formal institutions by way of known (constitutional) rules. The 'society' was taken to mean that tissue of manners and customs that held a group of people together without, despite or against formal rules. In some sense 'society' represented something more enduring and 'deeper' than the state, less manipulable and certainly more elusive.

There has ever since been enormous debate about how society and state relate to each other, which one was or should be subordinate to the other, and which incarnated the higher moral values. In the process we have become accustomed to thinking that the boundaries of a society and of a state are synonymous, or if not should (and eventually would) be made so. Thus, without explicitly asserting this theoretically, historians and social scientists have come to see current sovereign states (projected hypothetically backward in time) as the basic social entities within which social life is conducted. There was some sporadic resistance to this view on the part of anthropologists, but they resisted in the name of a putative earlier political-cultural entity whose importance remained primary, many of them asserted, for large segments of the world's population.

Thus, by the back door, and unanalysed, a whole historiography and a whole theory of the modern world crept in as the substratum of both history and social science. We live in states. There is a society underlying each state. States have histories and therefore traditions. Above all, since change is normal, it is states that normally change or develop. They change their mode of production; they urbanize; they have social problems; they prosper or decline. They have the boundaries, inside of which factors are 'internal' and outside of which they are 'external'. They are 'logically' independent entities such that, for statistical purposes, they can be 'compared'.

This image of social reality was not a fantasy, and so it was possible for both idiographic and nomothetic theorists to proceed with reasonable aplomb using these assumptions about society and state, and to come up with some plausible findings. The only problem was that, as time went on, more and more 'anomalies' seemed to be unexplained within this framework, and more and more lacunae (of uninvestigated zones of human activity) seemed to emerge.

World-systems analysis makes the unit of analysis a subject of debate. Where and when do the entities within which social life occurs exist? It substitutes for the term 'society' the term 'historical system'. Of course, this is a mere semantic substitution. But it rids us of the central connotation that 'society' has acquired, its link to 'state', and therefore of the presupposition about the 'where' and 'when'. Furthermore, 'historical system' as a term underlines the unity of historical social science. The entity is simultaneously systemic and historical.

Having opened up the question of the unit of analysis, there is no simple answer. I myself have put forth the tentative hypothesis that there have been three known forms or varieties of historical systems, which I have called mini-systems, world-empires and world-economies. I have also suggested that it is not unthinkable that we could identify other forms or varieties.

I have argued two things about the varieties of historical systems: one concerns the link of 'logic' and form; the other concerns the history of the coexistence of forms. In terms of form, I have taken as the defining boundaries of a historical system those within which the system and the people within it are regularly reproduced by means of some kind of ongoing division of labour. I argue that empirically there have been three such modes. The 'mini-systems', so-called because they are small in space and probably relatively brief in time (a life-span of about six generations), are highly homogeneous in terms of cultural and governing structures. The basic logic is one of 'reciprocity' in exchanges. The 'world empires' are vast political structures (at least at the apex of the process of expansion and contraction which seems to be their fate) and encompass a wide variety of 'cultural' patterns. The basic logic of the system is the extraction of tribute from otherwise locally self-administered direct producers (mostly rural) that is passed upward to the centre and redistributed to a thin but crucial network of officials. The 'world economies' are vast uneven chains of integrated production structures dissected by multiple political structures. The basic logic is that the accumulated surplus is distributed unequally in favour of those able to achieve various kinds of temporary monopolies in the market networks. This is a 'capitalist' logic.

The history of the coexistence of forms can be construed as follows. In the pre-agricultural era, there were a multiplicity of mini-systems whose constant death may have been largely a function of ecological mishaps plus the splitting of groups grown too large. Our knowledge is very limited. There was no writing and we are confined to archaeological reconstructions. In the period between, say, 8000 BC and 1500 AD, there coexisted on the earth at any one time multiple historical systems of all three varieties. The world empire was the 'strong' form of that era, since whenever one expanded it destroyed and/or absorbed both mini-systems and world-economies and whenever one contracted it opened up space for the re-creation of mini-systems and world economies. Most of what we call the 'history' of this period is the history of such world-empires, which is understandable, since they bred the cultural scribes to record what was going on. World economies were a 'weak' form, individual ones never surviving long. This is because they either disintegrated or were absorbed by or transformed into a world empire (by the internal expansion of a single political unit).

Around 1500, one such world economy managed to escape this fate. For reasons that need to be explained, the 'modern world-system' was born out of the consolidation of a world economy. Hence it had time to achieve its full development as a capitalist system. By *its* inner logic, this capitalist world economy then expanded to cover the entire globe, absorbing in the process all existing mini-systems and world empires. Hence by the late nineteenth century, for the first time ever, there existed only one historical system on the globe. We are still in that situation today.

I have sketched my hypotheses about the forms and the history of the coexistence of historical systems. They do not constitute world-systems analysis. They are a set of hypotheses within world-systems analysis, open to debate, refinement, rejection. The crucial issue is that defining and explicating the units of analysis – the historical systems – becomes a central object of the scientific enterprise.

Within the discussion I have just related there lies hidden a further debate about the modern world and its defining characteristics. This is a debate in which the two main versions of nineteenth-century thought – classical liberalism and classical Marxism – share certain crucial premises about the nature of capitalism.

IV

Capitalism is a system based on competition between free producers using free labour with free commodities, 'free' meaning its availability for sale and purchase on a market.

Constraints on such freedoms, wherever they exist, are leftovers from an incomplete evolutionary process and mean, to the extent that they exist, that a zone or an enterprise is 'less capitalist' than if there were no such constraints. This is essentially the view of Adam Smith. Smith thought of the capitalist system as the only system consonant with 'human nature', and saw alternative systems as the imposition of unnatural and undesirable constraints on social existence. But this too was essentially the view of Karl Marx. In characterizing the system, Marx placed particular emphasis on the importance of free labour. He did not regard the capitalist system as eternally natural, and he did not consider it desirable. But he did regard it as a normal stage of humanity's historical development.

Most liberals and Marxists of the last 150 years have regarded this picture of 'competitive capitalism' as an accurate description of the capitalist norm, and have therefore discussed all historical situations that involved non-free labour/producers/commodities as deviations from this norm and thus as phenomena to be explained. The norm has largely reflected an idealized portrait of what was thought to be the quintessential exemplar of the norm – England after the 'Industrial Revolution', where proletarian workers (essentially landless, toolless urban workers) laboured in factories owned by bourgeois entrepreneurs (essentially private owners of the capital stock of these factories). The owner purchased the labour-power of (paid wages to) the workers – primarily adult males – who had no real alternative, in terms of survival, than to seek wage-work. No one has ever pretended that all work situations were of this model. But both liberals and Marxists have tended to regard any situation that varied from this model as less capitalist to the extent that it varied.

If each work situation could be classified on a degree-of-capitalism scale, as it were, then each state, as the locus of such work situations, can be designated as falling somewhere on that scale. The economic structure of a state, then, can be seen as 'more' or 'less' capitalist, and the state structure itself can be viewed as reasonably congruent with the degree of capitalism in the economy, or as inconsistent with it – in which case we might expect it somehow to change over time in the direction of greater congruence.

What is to be made of work situations that are less than fully capitalist under this definition? They can be seen as reflecting a not-yet-capitalist situation in a state that will eventually see capitalist structures become dominant. Or they can be seen as anomalous continuances from the past in a state where capitalist structures are dominant.

How the 'dominance' of a particular way of structuring the work units within a spatial entity (the state) can be determined has never been entirely clear. In a famous US Supreme Court decision, Justice William Brennan wrote of the definition of pornography: 'I know it when I see it'. In a sense, both liberals and Marxists have defined dominance of capitalism in a similar fashion: they knew it when they saw it. Obviously, there is implicitly a quantitative criterion in this approach. But in so far as there is such a counting of heads, it is crucial to know what heads are being counted. And thereby hangs a tale.

A distinction was made between productive and unproductive labour. Although the exact definitions of the physiocrats, Saint-Simon and Marx were quite different, they all wished to define certain kinds of 'economic activity' as non-work, that is, as non-productive. This has created an enormous and very useful loophole in the definition of capitalism. If among the various kinds of activity eliminated as non-productive fall a significant number which do not meet the model of a capitalist work-situation – the most obvious but certainly not the only example, is housework – then it becomes far easier to argue that the 'majority' of work situations in some countries are of the kinds described in the model, and thus we really do have some 'capitalist' countries in terms of the definition. All this manipulation is scarcely necessary were the deduced 'norm' in fact the statistical norm. But it was not, and is not. The situation of free labourers working for wages in the enterprises of free producers is a minority situation in the modern world.

This is certainly true if our unit of analysis is the world economy. It is probably true, or largely true, even if we undertake the analysis within the framework of single highly-industrialized states in the twentieth century.

When a deduced 'norm' turns out not to be the statistical norm, that is, when the situation abounds with exceptions (anomalies, residues), then we ought to wonder whether the definition of the norm serves any useful function. World-systems analysis argues that the capitalist world-economy is a particular historical system. Therefore if we want to ascertain the norms, that is, the mode of functioning of this concrete system, the optimal way is to look at the historical evolution of this system. If we find, as we do, that the system seems to contain wide areas of wage and non-wage labour, wide areas of commodified and non-commodified goods and wide areas of alienable and non-alienable forms of property and capital, then we should at the very least wonder whether this 'combination' or mixture of the so-called free and the non-free is not itself the defining feature of capitalism as a historical system.

Once the question is opened up, there are no simple answers. We discover that the proportions of the mixes are uneven, spatially and temporally. We may then search for structures that maintain the stability of any particular mix of mixes (the cyclical trends again) as well as for underlying pressures that may be transforming, over time, the mix of mixes (the secular trends). The anomalies now become not exceptions to be explained away but patterns to be analysed, so inverting the psychology of the scientific effort. We must conclude that the definition of capitalism that dominated the nineteenth-century thought of both liberals and Marxists accounts for the central historiographical insight that has been bequeathed to us.

V

The end of the eighteenth and the beginning of the nineteenth century represent a crucial turning-point in the history of the world, in that the capitalists finally achieved state-societal power in the key states.

The two great 'events' that occurred in this period, the Industrial Revolution in England and the French Revolution, were, it is argued, crucial in the development of social scientific theory. A simple bibliographical check will verify that a remarkably large proportion of world history has been devoted to these two 'events'. Furthermore, an even larger proportion has been devoted to analysing other 'situations' in terms of how they measure up to these two 'events'.

The link between the historical centrality accorded these two 'events' and the prevailing definition of capitalism is not difficult to elucidate. We have already pointed out that the concept of degrees of capitalism leads necessarily to an implicit exercise in quantification so that we can ascertain when capitalism becomes 'dominant'. This theory assumed that a mismatch between 'economic' dominance and state-societal power is possible, and that it can be overcome.

The Industrial Revolution and the French Revolution are of interest because they presumably represent the overcoming of a mismatch. The French Revolution highlights the political arena. According to the now strongly-challenged but long predominant 'social interpretation', the French Revolution was the moment when the bourgeoisie ousted the feudal aristocracy from state power and thereby transformed the pre-capitalist *ancien régime* into a capitalist state. The Industrial Revolution highlights the fruits of such a transformation. Once the capitalists achieve state power (or in Smithian terms reduce the interference of the state) then it is possible to expand significantly the triumphal possibilities of a capitalist system.

Given these assumptions, it is possible to treat both these phenomena as 'events' and to concentrate on the details of what happened and why they happened in that particular way. Books on the Industrial Revolution typically debate which factor (or factors) was more important to its occurrence, what its precise dating was and which of the various features encompassed by the term was the most consequential for future transformations. Books on the French Revolution typically debate when it started and ended, what factor or factors triggered it, which groups were involved in key processes and how and when there were alterations in the cast of characters, and what legacy the Revolution left.

Of course such a close and ultimately idiographic scrutiny of these 'events' inevitably breeds scepticism. Increasingly there are voices doubting how revolutionary the revolutions were. None the less, virtually all these analyses (of both believers and sceptics) presume the analytical frame of reference that led to these two 'events' being singled out in the first place: the assumption that capitalism (or its surrogate, individual freedom) had in some sense to 'triumph' at some point within particular states.

Furthermore, lest one think that history is central only to historians, we should notice how it immediately became central to the analytical exercises of social scientists. The idea of *the* 'Industrial Revolution' has been transformed into the process of *an* 'industrial revolution' or of 'industrialization' and bred a whole family of sub-categories and therefore of sub-issues: the idea of a 'take-off', the notions of both 'pre-industrial' and 'post-industrial' societies, and so on. The idea of the 'bourgeois revolution' has become the analysis of when and how a 'bourgeois revolution' (or the middle classes in power) could or would occur. I do not suggest that these debates are not about the real world. Clearly, twentieth-century Brazil can be discussed in terms of industrialization, or of the role of the national bourgeoisie, or of the relation of the middle classes to the military. But once again, key assumptions are being made which should be examined.

What world-systems analysis calls for is an evaluation of the centrality of these purportedly key 'events' in terms of the long *duré* of the historical system within which they occurred. If the unit of analysis of the modern world-system is the capitalist world-economy (and this remains an 'if'), then we will need to ask whether the received categorical distinctions – agriculture and industry, landowner and industrialist – do or do not represent a *leitmotiv* around which the historical development centred. We can only be in a post-industrial phase if there was an industrial phase. There can only be disjunctures of the tenants of state power and economic power if we are dealing with analytically-separable groups. All these categories are now so deep in our subconscious that we can scarcely talk about the world without using them. World-systems analysis argues that the categories that inform our history were historically formed (and for the most part only a century or so ago). It is time that they were re-opened for examination.

Of course, this prevailing history is itself informed by the dominant metaphysics of the modern world. The triumph of this modern metaphysics required a long struggle. But triumph it did, in the Enlightenment, which brings us to the sixth premiss.

VI

Human history is progressive, and inevitably so.

To be sure, the idea of progress has had its detractors, but they have for two centuries been in a distinct minority. I do *not* count in this minority all those who have criticized the *naive* view of progress and have concentrated their efforts on explaining the so-called irrational. These people have been making rational the irrational. Nor do I include the growing number of disabused believers who embrace a sort of hopelessness or despair about progress. They are rather like lapsed Catholics in a Graham Greene novel, always searching for the faith they once had.

The true conservatives, the ones who do not believe that systematic change or improvement in the world is a desirable or fruitful collective activity, are actually quite rare in the modern world. But notice once again how the dominant assumptions have circumscribed the sceptics and the opponents. To the notion that progress is inevitable, the only response seems to have been despair: despair because the thesis is incorrect, or despair because it is correct.

World-systems analysis wants to remove the idea of progress from the status of a trajectory and open it up as an analytical variable. There may be better and there may be worse historical systems (and we can debate the criteria by which to judge). It is not at all certain that there has been a linear trend – upward, downward or straightforward. Perhaps the trend line is uneven, or perhaps indeterminate. Were this conceded to be possible, a whole new arena of intellectual analysis is immediately opened up. If the world has had multiple instances of, and types of, historical systems, and if all historical systems have beginnings and ends, then we will want to know something about the process by which there occurs a succession (in time-space) of historical systems.

This has typically been discussed as the problem of 'transitions', but transitions have been analysed within the framework of linear transformations. We detail the process of the transformation toward some inevitable end-point which we presume to be, to have been, the only real historical alternative. But suppose the construction of new historical systems is a stochastic process. Then we have a totally new arena of intellectual activity before us.

The debate of 'free will' versus 'determinism' is a hoary one. But it has been traditionally pursued as an either–or proposition. What the re-opening of the issue of transitions does – transitions as really occurring, transitions as moving toward uncertain outcomes – is to suggest a different formulation of this debate. Perhaps it is the case that what we call 'determinism' is largely the process internal to historical systems in which the 'logic' of the system is translated into a set of self-moving, self-reinforcing institutional structures that 'determine' the long-term trajectory. But perhaps it is also the case that what we call 'free will' occurs largely in the process of 'transition' when, precisely because of the breakdown of these very structures, the real historical choices are wide and difficult to predict.

This would then turn our collective attention to the study of precisely how these stochastic processes work. Perhaps they will turn out not to be stochastic at all but have an inner hidden key, or perhaps the inner key is some process that keeps these processes stochastic (that is, not really subject to human manipulation). Or perhaps, least acceptable to the present inhabitants of the globe no doubt, God plays dice. We shall not know unless we look. We may of course not know even then. But how do we look? This brings us to the last and deepest of the assumptions, the assumptions concerning the nature of science.

VII

Science is the search for the rules which summarize most succinctly why everything is the way it is and how things happen.

Modern science is not a child of the nineteenth century. It goes back at least to the sixteenth, perhaps to the thirteenth, century. It has come down strongly on the determinist side of the equation, on the side of linearity and concision. Scientists have brought more and more domains of the universe under their aegis, the world of man being no doubt the last such domain. It was in the name of this tradition that nomothetic social science asserted itself.

The methodology that nomothetic social science adopted emulated the basic principles of its socially successful predecessor, the natural sciences:

systematic and precise empirical inquiry, then induction leading to theories. The more elegant the theory, the more advanced the science. Practical applications would of course follow. Nomothetic social science has been haunted by its inadequacies – in a comparison with physics – but sustained by its certainty that science was cumulative and unilinear.

In our doubts concerning the previous assumptions there has been implicit – it should now be clear – another view of science. If we reject the utility of the nomothetic–idiographic distinction, then we are casting doubt on the usefulness of the Newtonian view of science. We do not do this, as the idiographers did, on the basis of the peculiarity of social inquiry (humans as reflexive actors). We doubt its utility for the natural sciences as well (and indeed there has emerged in the last two decades a thrust toward a non-linear natural science, wherein stochastic processes are central).

Specifically, in terms of what we have been calling historical social science, we raise the question of whether the method of going from the concrete to the abstract, from the particular to the universal, should not be inverted. Perhaps historical social science must *start* with the abstract and move in the direction of the concrete, ending with a coherent interpretation of the processes of particular historical systems that accounts plausibly for how they followed a particular concrete historical path. The determinate is not the simple but the complex, indeed the hyper-complex. And of course no concrete situation is more complex than the long moments of transition when the simpler constraints collapse.

History and social science took their current dominant forms at the moment of fullest unchallenged triumph of the logic of our present historical system. They are children of that logic. We are now however living in the long moment of transition wherein the contradictions of that system have made it impossible to continue to adjust its machinery. We are living in a period of real historical choice. And this period is incomprehensible on the basis of the assumptions of that system.

World-systems analysis is a call for the construction of a historical social science that feels comfortable with the uncertainties of transition, that contributes to the transformation of the world by illuminating the choices without appealing to the crutch of a belief in the inevitable triumph of good. World-systems analysis is a call to open the shutters that prevent us from exploring many arenas of the real world. World-systems analysis is not a paradigm of historical social science. It is a call for a debate about the paradigm.

Class Analysis[1]

RALPH MILIBAND

I

The notion of class analysis, in its classical Marxist form, embodies a very large claim, namely that it constitutes a uniquely powerful organizing principle of social and political analysis, and that it provides the best available method to give theoretical and empirical meaning and coherence to the vast accumulation of data of every kind which make up the historical record and the present life of society. My purpose in this essay is to argue that, contrary to much current opinion, not least in many parts of the Left, the claim is justified; but I propose to do so on the basis of a somewhat modified version of the Marxist 'model' of class analysis.

Marx himself, it may be recalled, sarcastically warned in a letter of 1877 against any attempt to use 'as one's master key a general historico-philosophical theory, the supreme virtue of which consists in being super-historical'.[2] The warning is well taken, but I do not believe that the kind of class analysis proposed here falls under the label 'super-historical' or 'historico-philosophical'; on the contrary, it is firmly grounded in historical and contemporary reality.

For his part, Engels, writing two years after Marx's death, proclaimed that,

> it was precisely Marx who had first discovered the great law of motion of history, the law according to which all historical struggles, whether they proceed in the political, religious, philosophical or some other ideological domain, are in fact the more or less clear expression of struggles of social classes. (Engels: 1950, p. 223)

This law, Engels added, in typical Engels fashion, had 'the same significance

[1] I am grateful to Anthony Giddens for some very useful comments on this essay.
[2] K. Marx to *Otechestvenniye Zapiski*, November 1877, in Marx and Engels: 1956, p. 379.

for history as the law of the transformation of energy had for natural science'.

Reference to 'laws' in relation to human affairs (or reference to the authority of Engels for that matter) are at present rather unfashionable. On the Right, any talk of such 'laws' in history or the social sciences is alleged to betoken an intolerably doctrinaire arrogance which points straight in the direction of the Gulag Archipelago, and much of the Marxist Left has itself been seized by great doubt about how much could properly be claimed for historical materialism as a tool of analysis. Also, class analysis has come more and more frequently to be denounced from within the Left as a simplistic 'class reductionism', quite unable to account for crucial features of social reality such as patriarchy, racism, nationalism, state-building, Communist systems, and so on. For reasons to be discussed as I proceed, I believe these strictures to be misconceived, and I wish to reiterate at the outset the conviction which informs this essay, namely that class analysis, properly understood, does constitute a theoretical construct of incomparable value.

II

The point of departure of class analysis in Marxism is the famous passage in the *Communist Manifesto* in which Marx and Engels declared that 'the history of all hitherto existing society is the history of class struggle'.

> Freeman and slave, patrician and plebeian, lord and serf, guild master and journeyman – in a word, oppressor and oppressed, stood in constant opposition to one another, carried on an uninterrupted, now hidden, now open fight, a fight that each time ended either in a revolutionary re-constitution of society at large or in the common ruin of the contending classes. (Marx and Engels: 1976, p. 482)

On this view, class analysis is in effect *class struggle analysis*: it is a mode of analysis which proceeds from the belief that class struggle has constituted the crucial fact of social life from the remote past to the present. It is primarily concerned with the basis and mechanisms of that struggle, with the character of the protagonists, the forms which the struggle takes, the reasons for the differences in these forms from period to period in any one society, and between societies, the ideological constructs under which the struggle is waged and other such questions which may serve to illuminate diverse facets of social life and processes.

In the classical Marxist view, the protagonists in class struggle are the owners of the means of production on the one hand and the producers on the other, and these protagonists are locked in a conflict which is inherent, 'structurally' determined and implicit in their respective location in the process of production. The owners are ineluctably driven to try and extract the greatest amount of surplus labour which it is possible to extract from the producers in the given historical conditions, whereas the producers are similarly driven to try and minimize that amount and to produce under the least onerous conditions possible. The decisive importance which Marx attached to this relationship between owners and producers for the whole organization and life of society is clearly brought out in another familiar passage from *Capital*.

> It is in each case the direct relationship of the owners of the conditions of production to the immediate producers ... in which we find the innermost secret, the hidden basis of the entire social edifice, and hence also the political form of the relationship of sovereignty and dependence. (Marx: 1981, p. 927)

Essentially, the relationship between owners and producers is one of *exploitation*, a term which has very strong normative connotations, but which can also be used in a technical sense to denote the appropriation of surplus labour and the allocation of the surplus product by people over whom the producers have little or no control, in a process of production over which the producers have little or no control either. Exploitation is not of course peculiar to capitalism. As Marx noted,[3]

> capital did not invent surplus labour. Wherever a part of society possesses the monopoly of the means of production, the worker, free or unfree, must add to the labour-time necessary for his own maintenance an extra quantity of labour-time in order to produce the means of subsistence for the owner of the means of production. (Marx: 1976, p. 344)

However, and as Marx himself saw, the matter of the appropriation and allocation of surplus labour is rather more complicated than these formulations suggest. All societies need to appropriate a part of the product from the producers for such purposes as the maintenance of the young, the sick and the old, investment for further production and later distribution, the provision of collective services, and so on. In a classless society, however, appropriation would occur *only* for these purposes. In other words, no part of the product would be appropriated by virtue of ownership rights or privileged position or without the freely-given agreement of the producers. In such circumstances, the appropriation of surplus labour and the allocation of part of the product to recipients other than the producers would not be exploitation.

---

[3] Marx also noted that 'what distinguishes the various economic formations of society – the distinction between for example a society based on slave-labour and a society based on wage-labour – is the form in which this surplus labour is in each case extorted from the immediate producer, the worker' (Marx: 1976, p. 325).

III

The Marxist emphasis on the extraction of surplus labour as the crucial aspect of social life seems to me to be entirely justified. The problem, however, is that the focus of analysis which is thereby provided is too narrow and tends to occlude, or at least to cast into shadow, a linked feature of the process of exploitation, namely *domination*. Class analysis, I propose to argue here, is basically concerned with a process of class domination and class subordination that is an essential condition of the process of exploitation; or, to put the point the other way round, exploitation, in the sense in which it has been defined here, has always been the main purpose of domination. On the other hand, exploitation in this sense has by no means been the *only* purpose of domination: patriarchy, for instance, as one form of domination, provides other advantages to its beneficiaries than the extraction of surplus labour.

The example of patriarchy suggests the reason for using the focus of domination in class analysis, for it widens the framework within which class relations and class struggle are considered and thus encompasses various aspects which the exclusive focus on exploitation tends to obscure or leave out of account. Also, this wider focus relates the phenomenon of exploitation to its wider social and political context and removes from it a certain 'economistic' narrowness which the exclusive emphasis on exploitation encourages.

In no way is this to be taken as a devaluation of the importance of exploitation. Exploitation *is* of crucial importance, but it is domination which makes it possible. Nor does the emphasis on domination in the least imply a departure from Marx's own perspective. On the contrary, it serves to illuminate the theme which is at the very core of Marx's thought and striving, the need to create a 'truly human society' from which relations of domination and coercion have been abolished. It is this concern with domination, and with the exploitation which it makes possible, that informs every page of *Capital*, a work which could well be called a treatise on domination under the capitalist mode of production.

In a recent work, Erik Olin Wright argues in terms which suggest that the stress on domination is somehow incompatible with the stress on exploitation. He refers to a tendency in 'neo-Marxist conceptualizations of class structure' to 'substitute domination for exploitation' and speaks of a 'shift to a domination-centred concept of class'; and he expresses the fear that 'domination-centred concepts of class tend to slide into the "multiple-oppressions" approach to understanding society ... Class, then, becomes just one of many oppressions, with no particular centrality to social and historical analysis' (Wright: 1985, pp. 56, 57).

But such consequences do not necessarily follow from the stress on domination, and they are certainly not intended to follow from it here. Exploitation remains the essential purpose of domination. But the focus on domination does have the advantages detailed earlier and it also permits a more comprehensive and realistic appreciation and identification of the protagonists in class struggle. With this focus, the dominant class in class society is no longer solely defined in terms of the ownership of the means of production. Properly speaking, a dominant class in any class society is constituted by virtue of its effective control over three main sources of domination: the means of production, where control may involve (and has usually involved) the ownership of these means but need not necessarily do so; the means of state administration and coercion; and the main means of communication and consent.

Each of these three forms a part of one structure of domination. A class that owns or controls the means of production must also have adequate assurance, at the least, of the goodwill and protection of those who control the means of administration and coercion; and those who control the state must be able to rely on the cooperation of those who own or control the means of production. Control of the main means of communication and consent is likely to follow from control of the other two.

In this instance too, emphasis on the notion of control is in no way intended to devalue the importance of ownership: it clearly remains of fundamental importance in the life of capitalist society and pervades every aspect of it, and it remains the main source of managerial power in medium and small capitalist enterprises. But it is not an essential prerequisite for control of the main sources of power in capitalist society – corporate power and state power.

Effective control for the purpose of exploitation is perfectly possible without personal ownership: although churchmen in the Middle Ages did not own the land they controlled, this lack of personal ownership did not in the least prevent them from extracting surplus labour from the producers under their control. The same point, in a contemporary setting, applies to the top executives and managers of large corporations, who may own no more than a small part, or no part, of the firms they control. What was wrong with the 'managerial revolution' thesis was not that it pointed to a process of 'managerialization' in large-scale capitalist enterprises (although it exaggerated the rapidity of the process), but that it attributed to top executives and managers very different purposes from those of owner-entrepreneurs and managers; also managers of state enterprises are perfectly able to act as extractors of surplus labour, even though they do not own any part of the enterprises they control.

The state itself is a major extractor of surplus labour, both as employer and as tax collector; it is able to engage in the process of extraction by virtue of its control of state power, without any question of personal ownership intervening in that process. Taxation has always been and remains today a crucial aspect of the process of surplus extraction, and requires not ownership but the effective control of the means of administration and coercion.

IV

In the conditions of contemporary capitalism, economic power, meaning in effect the control of corporate power, and state power, meaning the control of the means of state administration and coercion, are institutionally separate, even though the links between the two forms of power are many and intimate. As a result of this institutional separation, what (borrowing from C. Wright Mills) will here be called the 'power elite' of advanced capitalist societies is made up of two distinct elements. On the one hand, there are the people who control the few hundred largest industrial, financial and commercial enterprises in the private sector of the economy, to which may be added those who control the media industry in the private sector (and who may of course include some of the people who control other capitalist sectors). On the other hand, there are the people who control the commanding positions in the state system – presidents, prime ministers and their immediate collaborators, the top people in the civil service, in the military and the police, in the judiciary and (at least in some systems, such as the American) in the legislature – and this element also includes people who control public or state enterprises and the media in the public sector.[4]

This power elite constitutes the top layer of the dominant class in these societies. The other, and much larger, part of that class also has two distinct elements: on the one hand, the people who own and control a large number of medium-sized firms forming a vast scatter of very diverse enterprises, dwarfed by the corporate giants yet constituting a substantial part of total capitalist activity; on the other, a large professional class of men and women (mainly men), made up of lawyers, accountants, scientists, architects, doctors, middle-rank civil servants and military personnel, senior teachers and administrators in higher education, public relations experts, and many others. They form the upper levels of the 'credentialized' part of the social structure and many are employed, full-time or part-time, by capitalist enterprises or the state, or work independently of either.

Together, the business and professional elements of this part of the dominant class make up the bourgeoisie of the advanced capitalist societies of today – what is commonly and misleadingly called the 'middle class' or 'upper middle class'. This bourgeoisie is distinguished from the power elite by virtue of the fact that it does not have anything like its power. Neverthe-

---

[4] In *The Power Elite* (1956), Mills described the power elite in the United States as being composed of three different elements: the 'chief executives' of the 'hundred or so corporations which, measured by sales and capital, are the largest' (p. 126); the 'political directorate' – in effect the people in charge of the main 'command posts' of the state; and the top people in the military. In my understanding of it, I see no good reason to turn the military into a separate and quasi-autonomous element in the power elite: it would be more accurate to see it as part of the state system.

less, it is part of the dominant class because its members do exercise a great deal of power and influence in economic, social, political and cultural terms, not only in society at large but in various parts of the state as well. It is among them, and in the power elite, that are to be found the people who own a very disproportionate part of personal wealth, and it is the dominant class as a whole which is at the upper and uppermost levels of the income scale. It is also mainly from the ranks of the bourgeoisie that are recruited the members of the power elite, and it is to its ranks that return the members of the power elite who have ceased, by reason of age or demotion, to be part of it.

Obviously, the dominant class is far from homogeneous: but then, no class is. There are important differences and conflicts to be found not only between capitalist interests and the state but also within them. The capitalist class comprises different, and often conflictual, 'fractions' and groupings. Quite pronounced disagreements and clashes constantly occur between different segments of the state system: top civil servants and their political 'masters', the military and the government, the judiciary or the legislature and the executive, central and subcentral government. At least this is the case in the capitalist-democratic regimes which have in this century been characteristic of most advanced capitalist societies. These conflicts are hidden from the light of day in authoritarian regimes, but they do nevertheless endure in such regimes.

Still, despite the differences and conflicts which beset dominant classes, they usually remain sufficiently cohesive to ensure that their common purposes are effectively defended and advanced. This is particularly true of the power elite; there are more 'class traitors' in the bourgeoisie, though they remain a relatively small minority. Many of the differences in the power elite are little more than the froth of politics, news today, gone tomorrow, and are afforded much of their brief notoriety by 'commentators' in search of sensation. Other differences may be more serious and involve important policy choices. But all such differences and conflicts generally pall into relative insignificance when compared with the vast and crucial areas of agreement between most members of the dominant classes. For whereas such people may disagree on what precisely they do want, they very firmly agree on what they do not want and this encompasses anything that might appear to them to threaten the structure of power, privilege and property of which they are the main beneficiaries. The power elite and the vast majority of the bourgeoisie of advanced capitalist countries (as indeed of all other capitalist countries, whatever their stage of development) are all but unanimous on this score, to say nothing of their opposition to 'communism', a term which has been given a sufficient degree of elasticity to cover any abhorrent challenge.

Nor, it should be added, has the high degree of ideological and political congruity which is characteristic of dominant classes in advanced capitalist countries been greatly affected by the arrival into the state system of social democratic governments. Such intrusions may cause strain and difficulties, but have never fatally impaired the partnership (with the exception of Chile) between corporate power and state power.[5] The reason for this is very simple, namely that social democratic governments have always been prepared to retreat from their purposes and policies and to accommodate corporate power. Should a socialist government be elected and insist on carrying out the fundamental transformations in the structure of wealth and power to which it was pledged, it would find the partnership dissolved and replaced by implacable hostility and opposition, and it would need to forge a new partnership, this time with the subordinate class. The script for this 'scenario' has not so far been written: the 'scenario' itself belongs to the 1990s and possibly beyond.

However this may be, the dominant class constitutes one of the two major, 'fundamental' classes which class analysis needs to take into account. The other is the subordinate class of capitalist society, which comprises the vast majority of its population and of which the largest part is made up, at least in the conditions of advanced capitalism, of workers and their dependents – the 'working class', properly speaking, an extremely variegated, diverse class, divided on the basis of occupation, skill, gender, race, ethnicity, religion, ideology, etc.

Such divisions are clearly of great political importance and have weighed very heavily on the history of capitalist societies, let alone labour movements, and more will be said about this presently. But the point that needs to be made here is that the currently fashionable notion that 'the working class' is dwindling rests on a misconception of what the term means. The industrial, manufacturing component of the working class is indeed diminishing, but the working class as a whole, the people whose exclusive *source of income* is the sale of their labour-power (or who mainly rely on transfer payments by the state), whose *level of income* puts them in the lower and lowest 'income groups', whose *individual power and responsibility at work and beyond* is low or virtually non-existent – this class of people has increased, not diminished, over the years. The working class in this sense is made up of blue-collar and white-collar workers and their dependents, and of a variety of men and women in 'service' and distributive occupations. Whatever consciousness they may or may not have of their 'proletarian' status, they constitute a very large majority of the population.

The dominant class and the working class represent respectively the apex and the base of the pyramid characteristic of the social structure of advanced capitalist societies. Between them, there is also to be found a substantial petty bourgeoisie, and this class too is composed of two distinct elements or subclasses; first, a disparate range of small businessmen, shopkeepers, tradesmen and self-employed artisans, who are the minnows of capitalist enterprise; and second, a large and constantly growing subclass of semi-professional, supervisory men and women engaged as salaried employees in

[5] For a discussion of the notion of 'partnership' in this context, see Miliband: 1983; 1985.

capitalist enterprises, or in the administrative, welfare, control, coercive and service agencies of the state – social workers, local government officials, and the like. Though at a different level of the social pyramid than the working class, such people too are properly speaking part of the subordinate population of advanced capitalist societies. No more than in the case of the working class does this mean that they are politically unimportant; it only means that the amount of *individual* power and responsibility that they have is very limited. Nor does the fact that they are part of the subordinate population mean that they are necesarily *conscious* of their subordinate position. The notion of consciousness raises altogether different issues than the question of their 'objective' position in society. All that needs to be said about this here is that the petty bourgeoisie engaged in small-scale enterprise has, generally speaking, been of quite pronounced right-wing disposition, whereas the sub-professional and supervisory petty bourgeoisie has constituted a new 'aristocracy of labour', a substantial part of whose members are of a leftist disposition.

To complete the picture, mention must be made of an 'underclass' at the very bottom of the pyramid, issued from the working class and in some ways still part of it, yet also distinct from it: the more or less permanently unemployed, the members of the working class who are elderly, chronically sick or handicapped, and those unable for other reasons to find their way into the 'labour market'.

Obviously, the people located at different points of the pyramid are not totally immobile: there is some movement, fairly limited, upwards, and some movement downwards, and the different levels of the pyramid are not separated by rigid lines of division. But neither social mobility nor blurred boundaries change the fact that the pyramid is a hard, solid reality and that the differences between the class situated at the upper levels of the pyramid, and the classes situated at its lower levels are very great indeed in terms of wealth, income, power, responsibility, style and quality of life and everything else that makes up the texture of existence. This may be deplored, or praised, or declared to be regrettable but inevitable, or viewed in some other such way. What cannot or should not be done is to ignore the existence of such divisions and the crucial importance they have for the life of the society in which they occur.

V

Given the social structure and mode of production and advanced capitalist societies, the tasks of class analysis are quite plain. First, class analysis involves the detailed identification of the classes and subclasses which make up these societies – in other words, the tracing of a 'social map' that is as detailed and as accurate as possible and includes the many complexities which surround the nature of class. Second, class analysis must demonstrate the precise structures and mechanisms of domination and exploitation in these societies and the different ways in which surplus labour is extracted, appropriated and allocated. Third, and relatedly, class analysis must be concerned with the conflict between classes, pre-eminently between capital and the state on the one side and labour on the other, although it must also pay close attention to the pressures exercised by other classes and groupings, such as different sections of the petty bourgeoisie, or social movements with specific grievances and demands.

The struggles with which class analysis is concerned assume a multiplicity of forms and expressions, but they can nevertheless be placed under two general categories. On the one hand, the dominant class naturally seeks above all else to defend, maintain and strengthen the social order, and does so (with the utmost conviction and sincerity) in the name of the national interest, freedom, democracy, or whatever. This dominant class is what may properly (indeed literally) be called the leading conservative class in society, which does not of course mean that other classes may not be conservative or may not include many people wedded to the conservative cause. On the other hand, the subordinate class, or at least the activist minority within it (an important distinction), is involved in a permanent process of pressure from below which always takes one of two forms. It is exercised *either* to modify or improve the conditions in which subordination is experienced *or* to bring about the end of subordination altogether. The first is mainly concerned with improvements and reforms, local or national, large or small, within the framework of capitalism and does not seek to go beyond that framework. The second does, and is in this sense a revolutionary enterprise. The labour movements of advanced capitalist countries have for the most part sought to exercise the first of these forms of pressure. It is also possible to envisage forms of pressure which, though 'reformist' in character, nevertheless have revolutionary purposes in so far as the reforms are intended to achieve in due course the fundamental, 'revolutionary' transformation of the social order. This kind of 'revolutionary reformism' was theoretically the path traced by European social democracy before 1914, but it is not the path which it has subsequently followed.[6]

It is clearly not the case that the dominant class and its allies are conservative in the sense that they always reject all reforms. Their purpose is to defend and strengthen the existing social order and this may well involve the acceptance of reform as the price to be paid for the containment and subduance of pressure from below, where other classes and subclasses may in any case have strong conservative dispositions. None the less, class struggle and pressure from above have been, and must reasonably be expected to be, designed to achieve conservative purposes and the defeat of anti-conservative ones, whereas pressure from below must equally reasonably be expected to have as its purpose the achievement of change in the ways suggested earlier. It is the opposition and struggle generated by these contradictory purposes which is the crucial fact of social life.

[6] On this, see for example Liebman: 1986.

This is the basic framework of class analysis, and it may be useful at this point to indicate what is entailed by the class analysis of 'pressure from above' and 'pressure from below'. The two are of course intertwined and constantly react upon each other, but they nevertheless have their own and differing fields of concern and action.

To begin with pressure from above, class analysis is concerned with the ways in which the struggle for 'hegemony', for the 'hearts and minds' of subordinate populations, is waged, or, to put the matter somewhat differently, how the ideological and political 'socialization' of subordinate populations into the existing social system occurs. A vast array of persons and institutions play a part in this process: newspapers and other publications, radio, television, the cinema and the theatre, churches, parties, associations and lobbies, schools, intellectuals and other 'managers of consent' and, not least, the state – in short, whatever in the social system makes a contribution, large or small, to the strengthening of the social order and the containment or defeat of the 'counter-hegemonic' forces which a system of domination and exploitation necessarily engenders.

Another and obvious area of investigation for class analysis is the ways in which dominant classes seek to use the political system for their own purposes. The most important such institution is the state, for it plays a unique and indispensable role in the defence and strengthening of the social order; no other institution is capable of intervening with the same effect in the life of society. However 'non-interventionist' the state may wish to be in economic life, it nevertheless plays a crucial role in this realm, not least in order to attenuate the social costs of capitalist enterprise, which it is in the nature of such enterprise to ignore. It is also the state which is ultimately responsible for the welfare and collective services which, whatever else they may be intended to achieve, also serve to ensure the maintenance and reproduction of an efficient labour-force on the one hand and the attenuation of grievances and pressure from below on the other. The state is now deeply involved in propaganda, indoctrination and the 'engineering of consent' and, crucially, it is also in charge of the vast apparatus of coercion and repression which is inevitably at work in class society.

Class analysis provides an explanation of state action in these realms in terms of the role which the state seeks to fulfil in the maintenance of the social order, which of course means the maintenance of a social order based upon class domination and exploitation. It is in these terms also that class analysis explains a phenomenon which is one of the most notable features in the development of capitalism in the twentieth century, the growth of 'statism', meaning the constant expansion of state power, the 'statization' of society. This is often attributed, following Weber, to some technologically-based tendency toward 'bureaucratization' in 'modern' society, but the 'statization' which has occurred in advanced capitalist societies is better explained in terms of class relations and the state's involvement in the maintenance and defence of the given class system.

It is also worth noting that conservative attempts in recent years, in the form of 'Thatcherism' or 'Reaganism', to 'roll back the state' are only directed at a particular kind of 'statism', namely public enterprise, the regulation of private enterprise and welfare services. 'Rolling back the state' in these areas is best seen as a form of class struggle from above, designed to help capitalist enterprise and, through the erosion of welfare provisions, to reduce the independence and resilience of the working class. Nor in any case do any of these policies in the least reduce the vital role which the state plays in economic life by way of its financial policies and the many actions it takes on behalf of capitalist enterprise. There are facets of 'statism' that are greatly strengthened rather than weakened by 'Thatcherism' and 'Reaganism', predominantly the repressive surveillance-and-control functions of the state and the inflation of state power to the detriment of citizen rights. Here too, class analysis is an indispensable tool for the adequate understanding of this version of conservatism in an age of more or less permanent capitalist crisis.

Class analysis is also deeply concerned with the crucial and unremitting struggle from above to impose upon the producers the disciplines which are required to make possible the extraction of surplus labour, a process which occurs at the point of production and at the site of work but which depends also upon a whole range of social and political conditions. Such include a requisite degree of 'hegemonic' control, an adequate imposition of managerial authority, itself backed by the repressive power of the state, division and fragmentation in the ranks of the producers and, not least, domestic arrangements by way of unwaged domestic labour which caters for many essential needs outside work and which makes it possible for the producers to accomplish their tasks at work.

In relation to class struggle and pressure from below, we must return first of all to the distinction that was made earlier between struggles for the modification and improvement of the conditions in which subordination and exploitation are experienced, and the struggle for the abolition of subordination altogether. Marx believed that the working class must inevitably (and within a not-too-distant future) be moved to adopt the second of these alternatives. He was obviously wrong, but whether he was wrong absolutely or in his timing remains a matter of argument. At any rate, such pressure in the last hundred years, which roughly spans the period of existence of the modern labour movement, has been pre-eminently 'reformist' in character.

This is not to under-estimate the intensity of the struggles even for 'trade union' and quite limited purposes, or to overlook the fact that large parts of the working class of advanced capitalist countries have frequently voted, particularly since the Second World War, for parties pledged to bring about a wholesale transformation of these societies, albeit within the existing constitutional and legal framework. Nor is it to ignore the not infrequent occasions when, in periods of great stress and crisis, working-class movements or parts of working-class movements have assumed a quasi-revolutionary or revolutionary character, as in the immediate aftermath of the First World War or in the European Resistance in the Second World War. However, when all such qualifications have been duly noted, the fact remains that revolutionary formations have for the most part been firmly pushed back to the periphery of working-class politics.

In these countries, the stage has been mainly occupied by agencies of the labour movement, the trade unions and political parties, whose whole mode of being has been explicitly and intensely 'reformist' – and even this may be something of an exaggeration, given the strong transformative aspect of 'reformism'. What pressure from below, intense class struggle and the threat of class struggle have achieved by way of reform has undoubtedly served to attenuate the harshness of class domination and exploitation for many parts of the subordinate population, and notably for organized labour; and it has, by way of the extension of collective and welfare services, of civic and political rights, and of influence on the climate in which power is exercised at work and beyond, served the subordinate population as a whole. But it is also the case that the structure of property, privilege and power in these societies has remained relatively safe from the assault by labour and that the pressures exercised from below against these structures has been nothing as fierce as had been confidently expected by Marx and later Marxists.

The reasons for this are of crucial interest for class analysis. So far, Marxists have tended to explain the phenomenon by invoking a whole series of factors: economic growth, reform itself, the crumbs of imperialism, the impact of the 'aristocracy of labour' on the labour movement, divisions in the working class exacerbated by capital and the state, the weight of tradition, ideological manipulation, false consciousness, the actions of labour leaders, and so on. But however important any or all of these factors might be, they would need to be supplemented by another, of massive weight, namely the influence of capitalist democracy upon labour movements. For capitalist democracy, in the hundred years or so in which it has developed in advanced capitalist countries, has proved to be a system of extraordinary flexibility, resilience and absorptive power, and has played a fundamental role in the containment and defusing of pressure from below. Quite apart from anything else, the existence of capitalist democracy has ensured that those who sought to exercise pressure from below did not for the most part feel that they had to look further than the existing constitutional and political system to achieve their purposes. The question here is not whether they were right or wrong: the limits of capitalist democracy in terms of radical reform are much more severe than 'reformism' has been willing to contemplate. But be that as it may, the predominance of 'reformist' dispositions in the working class and the labour movement of advanced capitalist countries, notwithstanding all the derelictions and shortcomings and crises that have marked the history of advanced capitalism, must surely be attributed to a political system deemed capable of affording remedy and reform. Nothing could have been more important in helping to confine pressure from below into manageable channels and to ensure the 'routinization' and reduction of conflict.[7]

Capitalist democracy has in this context given its full weight to the influence exercised by 'reformist' labour leaders. For the framework of capitalist democracy vastly enhances the role of these leaders as advocates of 'moderation', gradualism, conciliation and compromise and lends added plausibility to their approach in the eyes of their members and followers. The organizations which these leaders control thus become charged with considerable ambiguity: on the one hand, these organizations are mobilizing agencies, 'aggregating' and 'articulating' grievances and demands; on the other hand, however, they also regularly turn themselves into demobilizing agencies, concerned to contain and even reduce pressure from below and to combat the influence of their militant and radical members. In this perspective, and however it may be judged, the role which those in effective charge of these organizations have had in fostering and enhancing the 'reformist' propensities of labour movements, and in countering the influence of the revolutionary Left, cannot be over-estimated.

I have already suggested that class analysis makes possible a rational and coherent explanation of class struggle as it is conducted both from above and from below. Given the crucial role which class struggle plays in the life of class society, this means that class analysis can provide a rational and coherent explanation of the general dynamic of social life. It also provides a fundamental, essential criterion whereby the role played in class relations and class struggle by people, institutions and ideological constructs of the most varied kind may be assessed. People, institutions and ideological constructs are affected by their social context to some degree or another, and 'social context' must be taken to have as its largest ingredient the state of class relations. But people, institutions and ideological constructs are not only affected by their social context: they also affect it, to some degree or another. The question which class analysis asks is: what role or place do people and agencies and ideas have in class relations and class struggle? It is not the *only* question which may be asked about them, but it is nevertheless an important one whose answer permits an illumination of their nature and function in class-divided societies. The answer, as in the case of agencies of labour, may be ambiguous rather than straightforward, but that too is illuminating. It may also be the case that the question does not admit of an answer, because it is of no relevance: there *are* manifestations of life in society, whether expressed in institutions or intellectual productions, which cannot reasonably be said to have any bearing on class relations, even though they are themselves affected by their social context. The experience of Communist regimes, with monopolistic party systems seeking to

---

[7] I have tried to show this in relation to Britain in *Capitalist Democracy in Britain* (Miliband: 1982).

encompass and control all manifestations of social life and to suppress those deemed to be on the wrong side of the class struggle, shows well enough how fraught the question can be. But this is not a sufficient reason for not asking it, for not to ask it is to turn away from an essential aspect of social analysis. What is made of the answer is not itself determined by the nature of the question.

VI

I have so far referred to class analysis in a purely national context. But it is a mode of analysis which is as relevant to the international context in which societies have their being as to the national one.

It must first be noted that the ever-greater 'internationalization' of the economies of the capitalist world does not change the fact that the dominant classes in each capitalist country remain in being. Nor is that fact changed by the emergence of vast and powerful 'multinational' conglomerates. These corporate giants are 'multinational' in the sense that their operations extend over many countries, but they are in essence *national* firms (mainly American, followed by British, with Canadian, French, German, Japanese, Dutch and one or two others trailing a long way behind) controlled by people who form part of the dominant class of their own society. The 'internationalization' of capital must obviously affect the ways in which capital and the state in each separate country operate, but what they do internationally is dictated by precisely the same purposes which move them in relation to internal matters, namely the defence of a 'national interest' naturally conceived in terms which make it synonymous with the interests of the dominant class. However, these interests have, in the twentieth century, acquired a more pronounced global reach, not only through the internationalization of capital but on larger political grounds concerned with the emergence of 'communism' on the world scene from the time of the Bolshevik Revolution onwards.

In this perspective, class analysis involves the charting of international relations since 1917 in terms of the twin concern of dominant classes in advanced capitalist countries: first, to defend the 'national interest' against all other capitalist states and second, to prevent the spread of 'communism' anywhere in the world. It was these concerns, and notably the latter, that decisively shaped the character and substance of international relations in the years between the two world wars, and the struggle against 'communism' has been even more decisive in shaping international relations since 1945.

In this struggle, the Western powers have encountered the Soviet Union in so far as the Soviet Union, for its own purposes, has accorded help to revolutionary movements or regimes; the struggle is thus made to appear as primarily one between states, each pursuing its own 'national interest'. But this is no more than appearance: the basis of the struggle and its inner dynamic are provided by the determination of advanced capitalist countries, under the leadership of the United States, to wage a global struggle, by economic, political, ideological and military means, against all movements bent on revolutionary change or radical reform. On this view, international relations since 1917, and particularly since 1945, have been shaped by class struggle on a world scale. It is a view which provides a more reasonable and coherent explanation of international relations in the twentieth century than alternative explanations based on traditional views of conflict between states or on the 'madness' or irrationality of people in power.

VII

How far, if at all, is class analysis relevant to Communist regimes? The question arises because all the societies over which these regimes preside have undergone a revolutionary transformation in their system of power, property and privilege, and their whole class structure has in consequence been radically changed. What is at issue is what kind of social structure has been built on the ruins of the old, and whether that structure is susceptible to class analysis.

An answer to that question must begin with the fact that a dominant class or stratum does exist in all these societies. It does not seem to me to matter much whether 'class' or 'stratum' is used to denote the people in question, notwithstanding the fierceness of the controversies which have raged over these terms.[8] The important point is the fact of domination, exercised by virtue of the control of the means of production, the means of administration and coercion and the means of communication, vested in a relatively small number of people in the (monopolistic) party and the state. Here, too, it is necessary to distinguish between a power elite, made up of the people who occupy the leading positions in the party and the state (or more accurately the party-state), and the rest of the dominant class which, under the ultimate direction of the party-state leadership, occupy positions of high responsibility in the party, the state and society at large.

A fundamental difference between Communist regimes and capitalist ones is that it is exclusively location in the uppermost reaches of the party and the state that determines membership of the power elite – no element of

---

[8] Insistence, notably by Trotsky and later Trotskyists, that the people in controlling positions in the Soviet Union were not a dominant class but a dominant stratum is largely derived from the fact that their power and position are not based on their ownership of property and capital and they cannot perpetuate themselves as a class by bequeathing such property and capital to their descendants. This would seem to conceive what constitutes a dominant class in too narrowly 'economistic' terms. Although it is true that not being able to bequeath property and capital to one's descendants is a matter of importance, there are other advantages which may be conferred upon them so as to give them a very good chance of remaining in the upper reaches of the social pyramid. The difference is still real, but not such as to preclude the usage of the term 'class'.

capitalist ownership or control enters into it. As for the rest of the dominant class, its composition is mainly determined by the functions which its members perform. The middle-sized capitalist class of capitalist societies does not here exist. It may come to be reconstituted in one or other Communist country, for instance China, but in no Communist country does it now exist as a class. Petty trading and small-scale private farming do exist, but the 'petty bourgeoisie' of these societies is nevertheless overwhelmingly made up of the same kind of people as are to be found in the non-entrepreneurial part of the petty bourgeoisie of advanced capitalist societies, the people who exercise sub-managerial, supervisory and controlling functions at the lower reaches of society and the state. Finally, there is the vast majority of the population, forming a subordinate class of workers and peasants, whose individual power, responsibility and influence at all levels are exceedingly limited and whose 'input' in the decision-making process, though far greater than adverse propaganda depicts, is also limited and carefully controlled.

Class analysis is just as relevant to this kind of social and political structure as to any other. It is concerned with the nature and composition of the different classes in society (whatever these classes may be called); with the mechanisms whereby surplus labour is extracted and allocated; and with the struggles which the system generates. This is not to say that the questions, let alone the answers, are to be couched in the same terms as in the case of capitalist societies but, rather, that such questions are eminently applicable to Communist societies and that to pose them and answer them is indispensable for the understanding of these societies.

The purposes which surplus extraction is intended to serve in Communist regimes are decisively influenced by the absence of a capitalist (and landlord) class in their social and political structures. For it means that the people in control of the party and the state have a freedom of action in economic decision-making which is altogether denied their counterparts in capitalist countries, a freedom that is further enhanced in all other realms (including the process of production) by the nature of the political system itself.

As for the purposes of surplus extraction, it is no doubt the case that the people who are located at the upper reaches of the social pyramid seek to appropriate a part of the surplus congruent with their expectations within the given historical and social context. But what they appropriate, however noteworthy in comparison with what is available to the mass of the population, is a very small, even insignificant, part of the total product. The important point is that the people in control are able to decide the general purposes to which the bulk of the surplus should be devoted; and that they are able to do so without reference to the purposes, needs and wishes of a capitalist or landlord class or, for that matter, without much reference to anybody else either. No doubt, the people in power do take note of the grievances, wishes and demands of different parts of the population as refracted through a variety of agencies such as the press, trade unions and above all the party. But what they do about the grievances, wishes and demands that do reach them is largely a matter of their own choice: the state or, perhaps more accurately, the party leaders) in these regimes has a very high degree of autonomy.

This autonomy is used above all for the purpose naturally paramount for all dominant classes anywhere, namely the defence and strengthening of the social order over which they are in control. And in conditions of underdevelopment exacerbated by devastation due to foreign intervention and civil war, the people in power apply even greater 'pressure from above' upon the subordinate population for the achievement of their goals. In some notable instances, such as Stalin's rule in the Soviet Union in the late twenties and thirties, this amounted to 'revolution from above', with extreme state violence exercised against peasants, workers and society at large. This is a different version of class struggle from that to be found in capitalist societies, and whether it should be thus labelled is open to question. But the process nevertheless involves substantial pressure from above upon the subordinate population, usually accompanied by a considerable degree of state coercion. The purpose of this pressure is always claimed to be for the ultimate benefit of the population itself, and this in many instances is undoubtedly true. But this clearly does not obliterate the fact that it *is* a pressure exercised and imposed upon a population that has no great share in the decisions which are made on its behalf.

As for pressure from below in these regimes, its targets are not difficult to identify: they concern questions of wages, hours and conditions, and the 'relations of production' that govern the productive process; the availability, cost and quality of consumer goods and of welfare and collective services; bureaucracy, corruption and nepotism, and the manner in which power at all levels is exercised; the grievances and demands of ethnic, religious, political and other minorities; and a multitude of other matters of internal and international policy which may become subjects of controversy, dissent and challenge.

The questions which class analysis poses in this respect concern both the nature of the issues in contention and the manner in which conflicts are resolved or attenuated in these systems. A further question raised here by class analysis resembles that raised in regard to capitalist countries, even though the answer to it is likely to differ, namely what are the limits of reform, if any, in such systems, and who are likely to be the main protagonists of reform? One of the most hopeful features of these regimes, at least from a socialist perspective, is that pressure for reform does not come only from below, but is also engendered from above. How far and in what directions both sets of pressure go is bound to have a major impact on the future of socialism, not only in the countries concerned but far beyond them.

VIII

Something must also be said here of the challenge that has been posed to class analysis by feminists, members of racial or ethnic minorities, and others, on the ground that class analysis is incapable of explaining sexism, racism, nationalism and other such phenomena, and that it is irrelevant – indeed an obstacle – to the understanding of related matters of crucial importance to these groups.

These strictures seem to me misconceived on a number of grounds. There is, to begin with, the rather obvious but frequently overlooked fact that women, blacks and members of other minorities are also members of a class and are inevitably situated at some point of the social structure of their societies. Women, on this view, are part of the working class, as workers or as wives of workers, or of course as both; or they are members of the dominant class, also by virtue of their profession or business position, or by marriage. In one way or another, the point is also true for blacks and all other relevant groups in society.

It is perfectly legitimate for women, blacks and others to say and to feel with great intensity that they are, *above all*, women, blacks, or whatever, and that *this* beyond all else is what gives them their identity and defines their 'social being'. But their sense of a particular identity, however important in a number of different ways, not least politically, does not reduce the importance of class as an intrinsic part of their 'social being' – and, I would argue, as a *decisive* part of their 'social being'. It is reasonable and necessary to see 'social being' as a complex and contradictory entity in which many different identities coexist and often clash, and the closer the analysis gets to separate individuals the more complex and varied 'social being' is bound to reveal itself to be. All social analysis in this sense, and not only class analysis, has an inevitably 'reductionist' character. Even so, it remains the case that location in the social structure is crucial is determining the ways in which people experience discrimination, exploitation and oppression. The fact that they experience these as women, blacks, etc., does not in the least alter the validity of the point. Bourgeois women, and bourgeois blacks, do experience discrimination, and may be variously oppressed and exploited. But they experience discrimination, oppression and exploitation differently from women workers or black workers; and a black woman worker experiences them as a black, as a woman and as a worker. This testifies to the fact that 'social being' is indeed a multiple and complex set of elements, a kind of social DNA. But it is nevertheless class which suffuses and most deeply affects all other elements.

It has, however, been argued, notably by feminists but also by members of racial or ethnic minorities, that to speak of class domination and class subordination, and thus to divide society 'horizontally', is to obscure or altogether conceal the fact that women and blacks and others are not only subject to discrimination and oppression by members of the dominant class and the bourgeoisie but, in the various forms which sexism and racism assume in the working class and in the labour movement, by members of the subordinate class also. There is a lot in this, even though there are many forms of oppression, discrimination and exploitation available to employers that are not available to workers. But while there is no question that sexism and racism are to be found in the subordinate class, they are closely related to the nature of class society and are in this sense perfectly susceptible to class analysis.

The relation of sexism and racism to class society can be understood in two distinct ways: first, much of the discrimination which male white workers seek to exercise against women and blacks can easily be traced to what might be called economic motives, and must be seen as an expression of their class position and their desire to enhance or maintain their bargaining position *vis-à-vis* employers in the face of what they conceive to be a threat to that position. This is not intended as a justification but as an explanation. 'Social closure', on this view, has strong economic sources and is closely related to the competition between workers that capitalism imposes upon them. An instance of the phenomenon which does not involve women or blacks but a different set of protagonists is provided by the hostility which opposes Protestant to Catholic workers in Northern Ireland. It is tempting to see this struggle as a 'sectarian' one, based purely upon religious and ethnic grounds. But it is not particularly 'class reductionist' or an exaggerated form of 'economic determinism' to suggest that a basic cause of the antagonism is the attempt by Protestant workers to safeguard their already precarious and even dire material situation from what they take to be a major threat from an even more deprived minority, with both sides distinguished by religion, tradition, culture, historic memories and mutual grievances.

Undoubtedly, this economically-generated antagonism is rationalized and expressed in terms which are far removed from their economic roots. These terms soon acquire solidity and substance and therewith autonomy, and thus become powerful ideological constructs in their own right. People subscribe passionately to these constructs and come to define much of their 'social being' in the constructs' terms. Thus, Protestant workers come to see their Catholic counterparts not only as competitors but as the carriers of a particular kind of religious poison and as a threat to a cherished religious and national identity. They further rationalize their prejudices and fears by denouncing Catholic workers as lazy, shiftless and stupid. The process is a familiar one in many situations. The cord which attaches economic position to ideological construct is a very long one and runs through very rugged terrain. It is often buried deep, and it may snap altogether. But in relation to working-class manifestations of sexism, racism, etc., class situation cannot reasonably be left out of account.

The second point is closely related to the first, but distinct from it. It may well be said that there is prejudice and hatred and exclusion even where there is no plausible 'economic' source for them, for instance in the case of male violence against women, exercised by working-class as well as bourgeois men and against bourgeois as well as working-class women. This is true and important. But here too, it does not seem unduly 'reductionist' to argue that these are pathological expressions of the deep 'injuries of class', the multiple alienations and psychological deformations which are produced by class societies, with all the cruelties, brutalities, repressions and traumas which they engender. Men (and women) seek ways out of their 'private' troubles and problems, and do so in ways which are often irrational or sick or perverse. Adherence to fascist ideas and movements is the extreme manifestation of this in the twentieth century, but there are many other individual and collective manifestations to be found. The explanation of these phenomena requires the careful exploration of the social context in which they occur, of the social blockages which produce them and of the social pressures which they are expected, however misguidedly, to resolve. In other words, it requires class analysis.

To think otherwise requires resort to explanations which proceed from such notions as a given, ineluctable 'human nature' which makes human beings the creatures that they are and that they cannot ultimately help being. It requires reliance on some primal malediction which has ordained that aggression, domination and violence should be inscribed in the human condition, or in the male condition. To argue thus is to succumb to a dangerous and self-defeating irrationalism which is the enemy both of serious analysis and of rational and humane solutions to the real problems confronting the populations of class societies.

Nothing of this is intended to suggest that a formal proclamation of the abolition of class society, or even the actual beginning of its abolition, can at once end the processes of discrimination, exploitation and oppression which have always been part of the social life of class society and which have therefore acquired a formidable strength. The eradication of these evils is bound to be a prolonged enterprise, but there is every reason to think that the creation of a classless society, democratic, egalitarian and cooperative, would greatly attenuate these evils in a cumulative process that would eventually lead to their complete eradication.

In such a society, no aggregate of people would have such control over the means of domination as to turn itself into a dominant class. That control would be vested in society itself by way of mechanisms and institutions capable of ensuring the democratic administration of power and of preventing, by the same token, the resurrection of structures of domination. What is enshrined in the Marxist vision of a classless society, free from domination, is the conviction not that the achievement of such a society is easy, but that it is possible.

Nor does the history of the last hundred years tell us that such a vision is illusory. On the contrary, and without indulging in any vacuous eschatology, it tells us, I would argue, that pressure from below, despite all obstacles and setbacks, grinds away relentlessly, out of the conditions which produce it, at the prevailing structures of domination. It is the immense and global strength of this process which turns the achievement of a world free from domination and exploitation from a vision into a project.

Class analysis could only be made irrelevant by the coming into being of a classless society. There is a very long way to go before this is achieved. But it is likely to be achieved less slowly if more people, notably in the subordinate population, come to have an accurate view of social reality and of the conflicts which are at the centre of that reality. Class analysis, better than any other mode of analysis, makes such an understanding possible.

Bibliography

Engels, F., 1950: 'Preface', *The Eighteenth Brumaire of Louis Bonaparte*, in Marx and Engels, *Selected Works*, 3rd German edn. Moscow: Foreign Languages Publishing House.
Liebman, M., 1986: 'Reformism Yesterday and Social Democracy Today', in R. Miliband, J. Saville, M. Liebman and L. Panitch (eds), *The Socialist Register 1985/6*. London: Merlin Press.
Marx, K., 1976: *Capital*, vol. 1. London: Penguin Books and New Left Review.
    1981: *Capital*, vol. 3. London: Penguin Books and New Left Review.
Marx, K. and Engels, F., 1956: *Selected Correspondence*. London: Lawrence and Wishart.
    1976: 'Manifesto of the Communist Party' in their *Collected Works*, vol. 6. London: Lawrence and Wishart.
Miliband, R., 1982: *Capitalist Democracy in Britain*. London: Oxford University Press.
    1983: 'State Power and Class Interests', *New Left Review*, 138.
    1985: 'State Power and Capitalist Democracy', in S. Resnick and R. Wolff (eds), *Rethinking Marxism*. New York: Autonomedia.
Mills, C. W., 1956: *The Power Elite*. Oxford: Oxford University Press.
Wright, E. O., 1985: *Classes*. London: Verso.

Critical Theory[1]

AXEL HONNETH

It is now half a century since critical theory emerged under the direction of a single man and as the work of a circle of intellectuals; but it was not until the student movement turned back to the writings of the Institute for Social Research (*Institut für Sozialforschung*) that critical theory was recognized as a unified theoretical project. Since then it has occupied the intellectual imagination: historical research has retraced the history of that intellectual circle around Horkheimer from its beginnings in Frankfurt to its spread, via France, to the United States;[2] spurred on by the disillusioning accounts of its early members, philological analyses have brought to light the internal inconsistencies, indeed the whole disparity of the circle;[3] above all, younger authors, motivated by changes in the *Zeitgeist*, have continued to discover new themes which have thus far remained unnoticed in the old writings;[4] finally, however, the critical discussion that the Frankfurt School has stimulated for over twenty years has also revealed materially relevant deficiencies and theoretical aporias in the original project.[5] This process has in some cases led to the admission of a fundamental weakness in critical theory (see, e.g., Brandt: 1986).

Thus, for all the continual, indeed increasing, interest that critical theory

[1] Translated by John Farrell. I wish to thank Rolf Wiggershaus for helpful comments.

[2] See, among others, Dubiel: 1984; Jay: 1973; Wiggerhaus: 1986. In addition, the following provide comprehensive surveys: Bottomore: 1984; Brandt: 1981; Gmünder: 1985; Held: 1980; Jeyer: 1982; Kilminster: 1979; Slater: 1977; Tar: 1977.

[3] Institute members' accounts of their experiences at the institute exist primarily in interview form: see Habermas (1978) and Löwenthal (1980); an extract from Löwenthal is translated in Dubiel (1981). The first systematic investigations of the internal differences within the institute's circle are presented in Brandt (1981), Breuer (1985), Habermas (1986b) and Jay (1982).

[4] See, for example, Hörisch: 1980; see also Dews: 1984.

[5] Above all I am thinking of Benhabib (1981), Habermas (1984, ch. 4, section 2), Held (1980, part 3), Honneth (1985, part 1) and Wellmer (1971).

has attracted internationally,[6] a sober awareness of its theoretical achievements is what prevails today. Every new wave of interest has, with its research endeavours, removed from the old project a part of its initial fascination and gradually shaped it into a realistic theoretical approach that is open to verification. Every current attempt at a systematic reconstruction of critical theory has to proceed from the critical findings that this process has unearthed. Only with the awareness of all its deficiencies can one today productively continue the theoretical tradition originated by Horkheimer. In what follows I want to attempt such a systematic reconstruction of critical theory by supplementing the existing results with a further thesis, which is that the social-theoretical means whereby Horkheimer's goals might have been successfully realized were present solely in the works of those authors who held a more peripheral position in the Institute for Social Research. While Horkheimer, and later Adorno and Marcuse, grounded the idea of a philosophically oriented and at the same time empirically-founded theory of society firmly in the context of the contemporary sciences, they were not able to realize this claim, exemplary though it was, because they lacked an appropriate concept for the analysis of societal processes. On the other hand, Benjamin's, Neumann's, Kirchheimer's and, later, Fromm's material inquiries contained sociological insights and suggestions, which, taken together, could have provided pointers for such a societal concept. If the works of these authors had been taken more seriously with respect to their social-theoretical substance, then the philosophically-formulated objectives of critical theory could have been sociologically realized in a more fruitful manner.

In this essay I shall, following a brief sketch of the programmatic objectives in which critical theory was grounded by Max Horkheimer, identify the theoretically-based assumptions that prevented the 'inner circle' of the Institute for Social Research from successfully realizing the original concept. I shall then examine the social-theoretical alternative offered in the works of the 'outer circle' and, finally, after a brief glance at the post-war development of the institute, I shall consider implications of my thesis for Habermas's revision of critical theory.

I   Max Horkheimer and the Origins of Critical Theory

Among the many attempts undertaken in the period between the two world wars to develop Marxism in a productive manner, critical theory assumes an outstanding position. It was not so much its theoretical principles but, above all, its methodological objectives which distinguished this theory from comparable approaches; these objectives arose out of an unreserved and

---

[6] See the contributions in the following collections: Bonss and Honneth: 1982; Honneth and Wellmer: forthcoming.

programmatic acknowledgement of the specialist sciences. The systematic utilization of all social-scientific research disciplines in the development of a materialist theory of society was critical theory's principal goal; it hoped thereby to overcome the long-standing theoretical purism of historical materialism and make room for the possibility of a fruitful merger of academic social science and Marxist theory. This conception of the methodological objective found its most capable representative in Max Horkheimer, who was 'positivistic' enough to be able to acknowledge the value of the specialist sciences; in him the plan of an interdisciplinarily expanded Marxism grew to maturity.[7]

To realize this wide-ranging objective, an intellectual climate and geographical location were required which would attract scientists of different disciplines but of similar orientation; in addition, institutional facilities were needed in order to permit these scientists to work together under one roof. In the Frankfurt of the twenties such an intellectual climate existed; supported by a wealthy and open-minded bourgeoisie, forums of cultural life had emerged here: the newly-founded university, a liberal newspaper, a radio station happy to experiment and, finally, *Das Freie Jüdische Lehrhaus* (Free Jewish House of Instruction) – in all a cultural life that led to an exceptional concentration of intellectual energy.[8] In the Institute of Social Research the same city had gained a research centre which had the financial and organizational means to back social scientific projects. At this institute, founded at the instigation of Felix Weil in 1924 and affiliated to the university, research on the history of socialism was carried out in the first years.[9] Thus, in 1930, when Max Horkheimer was appointed to succeed Grünberg as director of this institute, it was receptive to the proposal that it should provide the means and facilities for the organizational realization of the programme for an interdisciplinary theory of society. Horkheimer used his inaugural address as the occasion to present for the first time in public the programme of a critical theory of society (Horkheimer: 1972d). In the journal *Zeitschrift für Sozialforschung* (or 'Studies in Philosophy and Social Science', as it was called in America), which was founded in 1932 and henceforth formed the intellectual centre of the institute's work,[10] Horkheimer, together with Herbert Marcuse, attempted to elaborate this approach in the following years.

The contemporary position of the human sciences formed the background of the somewhat programmatic articles in which the project of critical theory gradually assumed its methodological shape.[11] On the level of the history

[7] On Horkheimer's theoretical development, see Korthals: 1985; Küsters: 1980. On Horkheimer in general, see Schmidt: 1976.

[8] On this, see Schivelbusch: 1982.

[9] On the early history of the Institute for Social Research see, among others, Kluke (1972, esp. Book 4, ch. 2) and Migdal (1981).

[10] The collected edition of *Zeitschrift für Sozialforschung* (1970) is now available as a paperback (1980). On the history of this journal, see Schmidt's immensely informative Foreword to the new edition (Schmidt: 1980); see also Habermas: 1980.

of ideas, Horkheimer saw the the situation into which the effort to develop a theory of society is placed as characterized by a divergence of empirical research and philosophical thinking. For him, the Hegelian philosophy of history represented the last mould of a theoretical tradition in which both branches of knowledge were merged into a single mode of thought in such a way that the empirical analysis of reality coincided with the philosophico-historical conception of reason. In the course of the nineteenth century, however, the idealist premises on which this philosophy of history was based, as well as the unifying bond which had thus far held empirical research and philosophical reflection together, was dissolved. As a result, the two branches of the philosophy of history stood, unmediated, opposite each other, embodied in the new positivism and contemporary metaphysics. In positivism, empirical knowledge of reality is reduced to a mere search for facts, since such knowledge is separated from any philosophical self-confirmation; in the contemporary metaphysics of Max Scheler's and Nicolai Hartmann's philosophical projects, the reflection of reason atrophies to mere speculation on essence, since such reflection is independent of any theoretical reference to historico-empirical reality.[12]

For Horkheimer, the real problem of this historico-intellectual situation was its displacement of the very possibility of thinking in terms of a philosophy of history, for, in the abstract division between scientism and metaphysics – to which the post-Hegelian development of thinking had led – there is no place for the idea of a historically embodied reason on which the classical philosophy of history has always been based. Along with a philosophy of history, however, the possibility of a transcending critique is also removed from every theory of society: no longer are any cognitive means available to this theory to measure the given relations of a society against a transcending idea of reason. Therefore the foundation of a critical theory of society first presupposed the overcoming of that historico-intellectual fissure between empirical research and philosophy. Epistemologically, Horkheimer's and Marcuse's articles were directed at a systematic critique of positivism; methodologically, they were aimed at a concept of interdisciplinary research.

The materialist epistemology of the early Marx was the key to the institute's critique of positivism. Horkheimer adopted this approach, which initially was only sketched out in Marx's writings, from Lukács (see Jay: 1984, ch. 6); Marcuse, on the other hand, appropriated it from Heidegger.[13] But both of them proceeded from the presupposition that the empirical sciences – right through to their methodology – are determined by the

[11] Above all, I am thinking of the articles by Horkheimer (1972c; 1972d) and Marcuse (1968).

[12] On these two fronts against metaphysics and scientism see, above all, Horkheimer (1972d), but also Horkheimer (1972a).

[13] On the existential-ontological aspect of Marcuse's interpretation of Marxism, see Breuer (1977, ch. 2, sect. 2) and Schmidt (1968).

demands of societal labour; here, the securement of theoretical statements subserves the same interest of a mastery of physical nature by which the activity of labour is already guided on a pre-scientific level. As soon as this practical constitutional context of the sciences has been rendered transparent epistemologically, the misunderstanding emerges, however, to which positivism must inevitably lead: by justifying the sciences only on a methodological level, positivism cuts them off both from the consciousness of their own societal roots and from the knowledge of their practical objectives. In the denial of the practical framework of scientific theories Horkheimer and Marcuse saw, of course, not only the error of contemporary positivism but also the deficiency of the modern understanding of theory in general; Horkheimer retraces to as far back as Descartes the roots of that positivist consciousness which permits the sciences to appear as a pure undertaking completely detached from practical interests. 'Traditional theory' is the name he gives to this tradition of scientism which stretches across the entire period of modernity; this both he and Marcuse contrasted with 'critical theory' understood as a theory that is constantly aware of its social context of emergence as well as of its practical context of application.

Critical theory can fulfil the task thereby expected of it only if, at the same time, it has at its disposal a theory of history which is able to enlighten it about its own position and role in the historical process. Therefore, if only for epistemological reasons, the grounding of a critical theory of society demanded a reflection on the philosophico-historical level in a form for which no legitimate place was provided in the contemporary division between philosophy and the sciences. The rudiments of such a theory of history were already implicitly set out in the materialist epistemology which Horkheimer and Marcuse relied on in their critique of positivism; they elaborated these rudiments into a general framework of interpretation by extending them around the basic assumptions of historical materialism. In the thirties, Horkheimer and Marcuse still unwaveringly advocated the classical version of the Marxist theory of history According to this, a process of development of the forces of production is taken to be the central mechanism of societal progress; along with every expanded stage in the technical system of the mastery of nature, this process also forces a new stage in the social relations of production (see, e.g., Horkheimer: 1932). Critical theory should be included in this historical event not simply – like the empirical sciences – as a cognitive authority in the labour process, but rather as a critical authority in societal self-knowledge; following Horkheimer, Marcuse stated that in critical theory 'the possibilities, to which the societal situation itself has matured', attain consciousness (Marcuse: 1968). The societal position and the practical function of critical theory were evaluated in terms of the extent to which the potential for reason present in the productive forces had already been set free in the new forms of societal organization; just as, once, Hegel's philosophy of history was assigned to research critically, with idealist presuppositions, the empirical course of history with reference to the possibilities of reason embodied in it, so critical theory now assumed this same task on the basis of materialist premises.

If it is the case that these preliminary epistemological considerations moved along similar lines to a productivist philosophy of history advocated by Lukács and Korsch at that time,[14] then it was only in the next methodological step of critical theory that Horkheimer and Marcuse broke new ground; with this step they found what is today retrospectively called 'interdisciplinary materialism' (see, e.g., Bonss and Schindler: 1982). Both proceeded on the assumption that to the diagnosis on the philosophico-historical level, with which critical theory begins, there must be added empirical social research as a second current of reflection – hence the necessity for the cooperation of different disciplines. Neither for Horkheimer nor for Marcuse was it the case that it is exclusively the task of political economy empirically to examine society's condition in terms of a philosophy of history: a critical theory of society must make use of the entire spectrum of social scientific disciplines in order to be able to research appropriately the present conflict between the productive forces and relations of production. Horkheimer outlined the general model for the methodological relation between the philosophy of history and interdisciplinary research. It specifies a 'dialectical' dovetailing of both which was constituted such that 'philosophy, as a theoretical intention focused on the universal, the "essential", is in a position to give inspiring impulses to the specialist disciplines and, at the same time, is open enough to the world in order to allow itself to be impressed and changed by the advance of concrete studies' (Horkheimer: 1972d, p. 41).

outline of a critical theory of society and thereby determined the research programme of the institute for the thirties. The empirical problem, which he regarded as the focus of cooperation among the specialized disciplines, ensued for him from an application of the materialist philosophy of history to the contemporary situation: if the historical process in general progresses in such a way that the potential for reason embodied in the productive forces is released time and again in social conflicts, then, under the special conditions of the present, the question arises as to precisely which mechanisms prevent the outbreak of such conflicts. Just like many other Marxists of his generation, the young Horkheimer perceived the process of the increasing integration of the working class into the advanced capitalist societal system as the most striking developmental tendency of his time.[15] Horkheimer's perspective was so one-sidedly concentrated on this integrative achievement of advanced capitalism that he made it the point of reference for the entire research work of the institute; during the thirties, its interdisciplinary investigations were wholly concerned with the question, 'how [do] the mental mechanisms come about, by which it is possible that tensions between

[14] The best overview of the 'philosophy of history' assumptions of critical Marxism is still provided by Cerutti (1970).

[15] On the historical background of this thesis, see Mahnkopf: 1985, esp. ch. 6.

social classes, which feel impelled toward conflict because of the economic situation, can remain latent?' (Horkheimer: 1932, p. 136).

The formulation of that question demonstrates how Horkheimer had already conceived, in detail, the construction of interdisciplinary social analysis: the central discipline from then on was to be political economy; it alone is in a position to mediate materially between the philosophy of history and the specialist sciences because it investigates, from an empirical standpoint, the same process of capitalist production which appears, from a philosophico-historical perspective, as a stage in the realization of reason. If it is thus the case that political economy represents the theoretical backbone of a materialist social science, then, under the changed conditions, a second discipline must step alongside it. Since the potential for reason accumulated in the capitalist productive forces is no longer reflected in the class action of the proletariat as still assumed in the Marxist theory of revolution, an additional investigation of the 'irrational' binding forces that prevent that class from perceiving its actual interests is required. For Horkheimer, it was beyond question that this task could be accomplished only by means of a psychology informed by Freud. Finally, yet a third discipline must step between political economy and psychology because the social demands to conform do not strike the individual psyche unmediated, but rather only in a culturally refracted manner. As a concluding element of the research project he had sketched, Horkheimer envisaged a theory of culture that has to investigate the cultural conditions under which individual socialization in advanced capitalism takes place. From the imbrication of these three disciplines there ensues the tasks that Horkheimer assigned to critical theory in its first phase; they comprise the economic analysis of the post-liberal phase of capitalism, the social-psychological investigation of the societal integration of individuals, and the cultural-theoretical analysis of the mode of operation of mass culture. However, Horkheimer and his collaborators could only achieve a theoretical unity in his programme by using Marxist functionalism to establish a direct dependence between the individual elements of the investigation.

1 The economic analysis of post-liberal capitalism.
Horkheimer saw political economy as undertaking the central task of investigating the far-reaching process of change which had taken hold of capitalism since the end of its liberal phase. It was above all the emergence of National Socialism which raised the question of whether a changed organizational principle of capitalism was perhaps starting to emerge in the planned-economy features of the new economic system. Friedrich Pollock, a 'left-wing bourgeois' economist who grew up with Horkheimer, was entrusted with researching this area at the institute;[16] during the thirties he studied the newly emerging planned economy, and his findings were followed in

---

[16] On Pollock, see Dubiel: 1975.

their entirety by the 'inner circle' of the institute's members. Pollock's views are quintessentially expressed in the concept of 'state capitalism' (Pollock: 1941; 1975). He believed that, with National Socialism as well as with Soviet Communism, a planned-economy form of capitalism had taken shape in which the steering medium of the market had been supplanted by bureaucratic planning authorities. The management of the capitalist conglomerates had so seamlessly coalesced with the political power elites that full societal integration could henceforth take place in the form of centralized administrative domination. Originally undertaken as a specialized study, this analysis soon became the starting-point of a global theory of post-liberal capitalism (see, e.g., Horkheimer: 1972c); it provided the general framework within which the psychological and cultural-theoretical investigations could find their place.

2   The social-psychological investigation of societal integration.
Though the new organizational form of capitalist production could be explained by the theory of state capitalism, the question that could not be answered was why individuals, apparently without resistance, submit to a centrally-administered system of domination. Horkheimer delegated this task of social-psychological investigation to his friend Erich Fromm. With Fromm's arrival, the institute gained a crucial advocate of that intellectual movement of the Weimar Republic which strived for an integration of historical materialism and psychoanalysis.[17] Fromm, who had been practising as an analyst since 1926 and who was closely associated with *Das Freie Jüdische Lehrhaus*, was completely indebted to the 'Freudian Left' in his early studies.[18] Like Siegfried Bernfeld or Wilhelm Reich, he proceeded on the assumption that the integration of individuals into the capitalist system of domination comes about by way of the social formation of their psychosexual character. This general explanatory model, in which insights of psychoanalysis are linked with those of a Marxist sociology, was applied by Fromm in his investigations at the institute.[19] Its point of departure is the observation that the development of the state capitalist order entails a structural change in the bourgeois nuclear family; together with the economic basis of his authority, which was still accorded to him under liberal capitalist conditions, the male loses the unquestioned patriarchal authority which he previously possessed. The authoritative point of reference from

[17] On the 'Freudian Left', see Dahmer: 1973; on the Frankfurt School's reception of Freud, see Bonss: 1982.
[18] A complete overview of Fromm's theoretical development is given by Funk (1980).
[19] See, above all, Fromm: 1932; 1978. Fromm wrote the social-psychology part of the large-scale investigation, 'Authority and Family' (see Fromm: 1936); the pilot studies for this project, which Fromm undertook within the framework of an empirical investigation, 'German Works 1929', have recently been edited (Fromm: 1980). For a general background, see Bonss's Introduction to the latter work (Bonss: 1980).

which the child could develop and strengthen his ego is therefore lost, and the structural change of the family thus proceeds hand in hand with a weakening of the adolescent ego, as a consequence of which an authority-bound, easily manipulable personality-type emerges. Once again it was Horkheimer who gave a general form to the disparate and frequently speculative reflections of Fromm; the theory of the 'authoritarian personality', which combined the social-psychological investigations of the institute (Horkheimer: 1972b), was soon to be adopted by all the members of the 'inner circle'.

3 The cultural-theoretical analysis of mass culture.
The economic and the social-psychological approaches of the institute were related to one another by means of functionalist premises such that, taken together, the image they produce is of a self-contained integration of society. The economic structural analysis disclosed the developmental tendencies which allow capitalism to set a course for a planned-economy system of domination; from the alterations that this process of change entails in 'familial' socialization, social-psychological analysis then worked out the mechanisms by which individuals are smoothly adjusted to the new behavioural demands. The theory of culture, the third component of the research project envisaged by Horkheimer, would have been the place to force open the closed functionalism of such an analysis of society. Here, it could have been demonstrated that socialized subjects are not simply passively subjected to an anonymous steering process but, rather, actively participate with their own interpretative performances in the complex process of social integration. In fact, Horkheimer had, at the beginning, assigned a task to the analysis of culture that theoretically catered for this insight: like subcultural research today, it was to have empirically investigated those 'moral customs' and 'life-styles' in which the communicative everyday practice of social groups finds expression.[20] If Horkheimer had subsequently followed this line of research, then   as could be exemplarily demonstrated with the phenomenon of culture – that logically independent dimension of social action-orientations and value patterns, which cannot be viewed as a merely functional element in the reproduction of domination, would have become visible to him. Instead of this, however, and even before he was himself aware of the action-theoretic logic of his initial conceptual determinations, he had led the analysis of culture back into the functionalist reference system into which he had already previously integrated political economy and social psychology.[21] In this altered context, Horkheimer understood as 'culture'

[20] Thus, above all, in Horkheimer (1972d, esp. p. 43); the concept of culture that Horkheimer uses here is strongly reminiscent of E. P. Thompson's in his history of the English working-class.
[21] Programmatically, for instance, in Horkheimer (1972b); I have followed the re-ordering of Horkheimer's concept of culture from action-theoretic to institution-theoretic, in Honneth (1985, ch. 1).

(wherever works of art are not at issue) only that totality of cultural facilities and 'apparatuses' which further mediate the societal behavioural demands from the outside with the individual's psyche, which has become manipulable. Above all, the investigations that Theodor W. Adorno submitted on the emergence and effects of the culture industry move within the horizons of such a concept of culture, which is limited in terms of a theory of institutions.[22] In the institute, a type of cultural research was thus adopted in whose framework culture – as in the Marxist superstructural-basis doctrine – appears solely as a functional component of domination securement. Once again, Horkheimer's recourse to a functionalist system of reference can be traced back to the basic assumptions of his philosophy of history which formed the basis of his entire interdisciplinary research project; among these can be seen the theoretical premises that were necessarily the undoing of critical theory in its first phase.

II   The Theoretical Weaknesses of Critical Theory

If the different investigations that the members of the inner circle of the institute made in the course of the thirties are joined together into a theoretical whole, then what appears is the image of a totally integrated society; social life therein exhausts itself – as in the visions of theories of totalitarianism – in a closed circuit of the centralized exercise of domination, of cultural control and of individual conformity. If this image, given the societal circumstances with which the institute's members were confronted in the face of Fascism and Stalinism, may find a certain measure of historical justification, then, in contrast, from a systemic point of view it proves itself to be the result of a theoretically faulty construction. In the social-theoretical system of reference on which Horkheimer based his programme, that dimension of social action in which moral convictions and normative orientations form themselves independently is systematically excluded: this programme was so designed that only those social processes which can assume functions in the reproduction and expansion of social labour can find a place within it. This functionalist reductionism had its origins in the philosophico-historical premises on which Horkheimer's, but also Marcuse's and Adorno's, deliberations were generally based.

At the time, one thing was common to the philosophical works of all these authors: even though their thinking as a whole aimed radically to renew social philosophy, the basic convictions of their philosophy of history which they brought to bear in this attempt were nevertheless deeply rooted in the tradition of Marxism. Even where they attempt to rid themselves of this dogmatic residue, it is still done from the constantly retained perspective

---

[22] See, for example, Adorno: 1978; as far as I can see, the works of Leo Löwenthal, who was responsible for the theory of literature and culture at the institute, also belong in this framework: see, above all, Löwenthal: 1932.

of the Marxist philosophy of history. Neither the pioneering achievements of Durkheim and his school, nor the theoretical innovations of pragmatism, could ever have fallen on fertile ground here; the close circle of the institute remained constantly closed in the face of all attempts to consider the historical process other than from the point of view of the development of societal labour. There are two theoretical premisses which determine the conceptual framework of the philosophy of history within which the works of Horkheimer, Marcuse and Adorno, notwithstanding differences in detail, jointly move. First, all three assume that human reason or rationality must admit of being able to be understood as the intellectual faculty for the instrumental disposal over natural objects; to this extent, all three remain bound to the conceptual tradition of the philosophy of consciousness which construes human rationality according to the model of the cognitive relation of a subject to an object.[23] Second, all agree on the conclusion that can be drawn from the philosophico-historical premisses for a theory of history: namely, that historical development takes place above all as a process of unfolding precisely that potential for rationality which is set out in the instrumental disposal of man over natural objects. To this extent, they remain bound to the tendency already predominant in Marx, to instrumentalistically foreshorten human history to a developmental unfolding of the societal processing of nature (see Honneth: 1985, part 1, pp. 9ff.).

However shaped – in the details – by the influence of Lukács and Korsch,[24] Dilthey and Heidegger[25] or, finally, Benjamin,[26] it is this reductionist philosophy of history which served the research work of the institute as a general system of reference in its first decade. Not only are the theoretical deficits which have been identified in the normative foundations of early critical theory[27] grounded therein, but also the problems which we have followed in connection with Horkheimer's construction of an interdisciplinary theory of society. The functionalist style of Horkheimer's programme is the methodological consequence of the reductionism with which his philosophico historical referential model is imbued.[28] Because no other type of social action is conceded alongside of societal labour, Horkheimer can only take the instrumental forms of societal practice systematically into account on the level of his theory of society, and thus loses sight of that dimension of everyday practice in which socialized subjects generate and creatively develop common action-orientations in a communicative manner.

[23] On critical theory's premisses based on the philosophy of consciousness, see Habermas: 1984, pp. 366ff.

[24] On their influence on Horkheimer see, above all, Jay: 1984, ch. 6.

[25] On their influence on Marcuse, see Schmidt: 1968.

[26] On Walter Benjamin's influence on the early Adorno, see Buck-Morss: 1977.

[27] See, above all, Habermas (1984, chap. 4, sect. 2) and Benhabib (1986, pp. 147ff.); an 'interesting' rescue of Horkheimer's moral philosophy is undertaken by Schnädelbach (1986).

[28] I have developed this thesis at length in Honneth (1985, part 1, pp. 9ff.).

Only by considering this communicative sphere of social everyday practice could Horkheimer have discovered that societal reproduction never takes place in the form of a blind fulfilling of functional imperatives, but only by way of the integration of group-specific action norms. In his thinking the idea must break through that societies reproduce themselves in principle independent of the communicatively gained self-understanding of their members, in that they anchor the economic demands directly in the nature of the individual's needs with the help of systemic steering processes. As a consequence of such a conceptual model, the closed functionalism can finally emerge, and it is in this form that Horkheimer's programme of an 'interdisciplinary materialism' was ultimately presented.

Now in the institute itself, the idea of interdisciplinary social research enjoyed a lively and productive reception only up until the beginning of the forties. A general change of orientation was already perceptible in the articles that Horkheimer contributed to the last volume of the *Zeitschrift für Sozialforschung*[29] (which ceased publication in 1941), a change that not only implicated the philosophico-historical premises of critical theory but also the position of the specialist sciences within that theory. In these articles Horkheimer increasingly yielded to a pessimistic philosophy of history whose roots reach so far back into the early phase of his own intellectual biography that his writings of the thirties look, in retrospect, like a mere theoretical interlude (see Korthals: 1985). Just as at the time of his first reading of Schopenhauer, the dominating theme for Horkheimer now again became the destructive potential of human reason. True, the concept of work still formed the categorial foundation of this new conception of the philosophy of history, but instead of looking at the emancipatory possibilities stored in the process of the societal mastery of nature, Horkheimer now directed his glance at the devastating effects which the cognitive accomplishments presupposed in human labour-practice entail. It was the change from a positive to a negative concept of societal labour that introduced a new phase in the history of critical theory; the position thus far occupied by the productivist conception of progress was taken here by a critique of reason sceptical of progress and so radical that it must also doubt the cognitive value of the specialist disciplines.

Admittedly, it was not Max Horkheimer, but Theodor W. Adorno who was the outstanding representative of this new conception of critical theory. His thinking, like scarcely any others' of his time, was stamped with the historical experience of Fascism as a calamity for civilization;[30] this permitted him, from the very beginning, to view with scepticism what, by way of historical-materialistic ideas of progress, had gone into the original programme of the institute. In addition, his intellectual development had been so heavily influenced by artistic interests that he not unnaturally queried the narrow rationalism of the Marxist tradition of theory. Under the influence of

[29] I am thinking particularly of Horkheimer (1941; 1978).
[30] On this, see esp. Klein and Kippenburg: 1975.

Walter Benjamin, this reservation allowed him soon to undertake the first attempts to make aesthetic methods of interpretation fruitful for the materialist philosophy of history (see Buck-Morss: 1977, esp. ch. 6). Of course in Adorno's philosophy too, both conceptual themes – scepticism about progress, and the methodological place of honour for the aesthetic contents of experience – take effect only within the framework of those premisses of the philosophy of consciousness that had already been determining for Horkheimer's theoretical model. In the *Dialectic of Enlightenment* (1947), which they wrote together at the beginning of the forties and which subsequently gave the name to the new conception of critical theory, these dfferent themes and tendencies came together in a single book.

In its philosophico-historical approach, this book had already risen above the horizons of the institute's early programme: the totalitarian condition into which the world had fallen with the rise of Fascism is no longer to be explained by the conflict of productive forces and relations of production, but by the internal dynamic of the formation of human consciousness. Horkheimer and Adorno left the framework of theories of capitalism, within which the institute's social research had thus far moved, and instead presupposed the civilization process in its entirety as the system of reference for their theory, in which Fascism appears as the historical end-stage of a 'logic of disintegration' that is present even in the original form of existence of the species. The explanation of the mechanisms that have, right from the outset, forced the civilization process into this logic of disintegration constitutes the actual task of the *Dialectic of Enlightenment*; literary and philosophical works of the European history of ideas make up its primary material, and its style of argument is more that of the aphoristically-pointed essay than of an empirically designed investigation. The concept of the societal mastery of nature represents the only link with the original approach of critical theory, since it is as central for the new approach as it was for the philosophico-historical-based reference system of the empirical research programme. However, the same concept now receives a changed meaning:[31] in the *Dialectic of Enlightenment*, 'societal labour' no longer designates a form of emancipatory practice but, rather, the germ-cell of objectivizing thinking. For this form of a reified thinking that emerges concomitantly with the human processing of nature, Horkheimer and Adorno use the concept of 'instrumental rationality'; the central function assigned to this concept is to explain the origin and dynamics of the phylogenetic process of disintegration.

The new concept, which from then on characterized a key theme of critical theory, was indebted to a turning of Lukács's concept of reification in the direction of the anthropological. Horkheimer and Adorno understood the reifying thought forms, which Lukács derived from the abstraction imperatives of capitalist commodity exchange (Lukács: 1971), as an immanent component of humanity's instrumental disposal over nature. The ideas prompted by Alfred Sohn-Rethel's analysis of the abstraction of exchange

---

[31] I have followed this transformation of the concept of labour in Honneth (1982).

find their limits in the central premiss of the *Dialectic of Enlightenment*, i.e. that with the first act of the mastery of nature, the compulsion toward instrumental forms of thinking is already inevitably established.[32] If, for Horkheimer and Adorno, the emergence of instrumental rationality is thereby explained by the elementary structures of human labour, then they derive the historical dynamic of this rationality from the self-determined tendency with which its effects are shifted into the psychical and social life of the human species: the prehistoric efforts of instrumental thinking, by which humanity learns to assert itself over nature, are propagated step by step in the disciplining of the instincts, in the impoverishment of the sensual capabilities, and in the formation of social relations of domination. In this thesis, which essentially rests on a series of anthropological and ethnological arguments that only more recent textual interpretations have cast light on (see esp. Cochetti: 1985; Früchtl: 1986), the different parts of the *Dialectic of Enlightenment* reach an agreement about a common result: it amounts to nothing less than the claim that the entire civilization process of humanity is determined by a logic of gradual reification which is set in motion by the first act of the mastery of nature and is brought to its consequential completion in Fascism.

This philosophico-historical thesis can only be fully understood when, as its normative point of reference, an aesthetic personality-model is also considered in which humanity's freedom is defined as the ability to submit properly to nature. Because Horkheimer and Adorno view human emancipation as linked to the presupposition of a reconciliation with nature, they have to see in every act of the mastery of nature a step toward the self-alienation of the species. The arguments with which they substantiate the further influence of that initial reification in mental and social life issue from the same philosophical tradition of thought within which the aesthetic personality-model is also resident; this tradition is circumscribed by early German Romanticism on the one hand and by the philosophy of life on the other. This line of tradition forms, with respect to the history of theory, a background which the *Dialectic of Enlightenment* explicitly reveals only at few points;[33] the first to have critically referred to this background was Galvana della Volpe (1973) who viewed the book as nothing more than a product of 'late Romanticism'. However it is not, as della Volpe seems to assume, the romantic and life-philosophical themes that constitute the theoretical weakness of the *Dialectic of Enlightenment*, but rather the philosophico-historical framework within which these themes first gain significance.

As with the interdisciplinary research programme of the thirties, Horkheimer's and Adorno's theoretical work in the forties was also determined by a philosophy of history which reduces the historical process to a dimension of the mastery of nature. Though the 'philosophy of consciousness' premisses, which underlie such a theoretical reductionism, now appeared in a negativ-

---

[32] On this theme in general, see Müller: 1977; Schmucker: 1977.
[33] On this, see Habermas: 1987, pp. 130ff.; Honneth: 1984.

istic form, this normative re-evaluation nevertheless leaves the categorial thought-compulsions essentially untouched. Therefore, in the *Dialectic of Enlightenment*, Horkheimer and Adorno are forced to conceive of all social action according to the same pattern of the instrumental disposal of a subject over an object; this alone, and not the romantic tradition from which they draw, provides them with the basis for claiming the effectiveness of the same 'logic of reification' for the three dimensions of societal labour, the socialization of individuals and, finally, social domination. Because Horkheimer and Adorno, as can be shown in detail (see Honneth: 1985, ch. 2), conceptualized from the beginning both the process of the formation of individual needs and the process of the social exercise of domination according to the model of instrumental acts of disposal, they could, in retrospect, effortlessly see the civilization process as a whole dominated by the same instrumental rationality that underlies the act of the mastery of nature.

Not surprisingly, all creative accomplishments of interacting subjects and groups fall victim to this philosophico-historical reductionism; the entire sphere of communicative everyday practice is so decisively excluded from the investigation of the civilization process that social advances, such as occurred in this period, do not enter into the picture. One consequence, as can be seen in the *Dialectic of Enlightenment*, was the denial of another dimension of the civilizational progress which finds expression not in an increase of the forces of production, but in an expansion of judicial liberties and of the individual's scope for action (see Habermas: 1987, ch. 5); a second consequence was of a methodological kind and of no less significance for the further development of critical theory. Horkheimer and Adorno applied the philosophico-historical critique so generally that they had to comprehend every form of scientific knowledge, including social scientific research, as an element in the process of civilizational reification. They were thus forced to remove yet again the critical theory of society from the embrace of the empirical social sciences and return it to the exclusive domain of philosophy. With the *Dialectic of Enlightenment*, critical theory returned to the sphere of a philosophically self-contained theory from which, in the first place, it wished to free itself with the methodological thrust into interdisciplinary social research. From then on and into the post-war period, there was again a systematically unbridgeable gap between the philosophical and social scientific work of the institute. This gap was, once again, further widened by the philosophical investigations through which Adorno and Horkheimer continued their joint venture, although in separate ways, in the *Negative Dialectics* and the *Eclipse of Reason*.[34]

---

[34] On this movement toward a 're-philosophizing', see Adorno: 1973b; Dubiel: 1984, A sect. 4.3.3; Horkheimer: 1974.

III   The Social-Theoretical Alternative

The theoretical works of those who were briefly or indirectly or, in any case, more loosely associated with the institute[35] recede behind the pre-eminent importance which Horkheimer's, Adorno's, and Marcuse's writings acquired in the public image of critical theory. Given that this latter group of permanent institute members can be characterized only with difficulty as a homogeneous research circle, then this holds all the more for that group of three, or rather four, authors who, though they introduced all the important investigations in the research context of the institute, never merged their scientific identity with its programme and tradition. Thus, from the beginning, it was only their common marginal position which allows, in retrospect, Franz Neumann, Otto Kirchheimer, Walter Benjamin and, perhaps, Erich Fromm to be regarded as a single group. At first sight there is no interpretative foundation for contrasting them as an 'outer circle' with an 'inner circle' formed by Horkheimer, Adorno, Marcuse, Löwenthal and Pollock. Nor at first sight is there any common ground among the four authors in a sociological, or even social-philosophical, respect: Neumann and Kirchheimer – both were trained in jurisprudence and both reached political maturity in German social democracy – contributed investigations on theories of law and the state to the institute's work during the period of exile in New York;[36] Benjamin, an independent thinker, one of few found in our century, was, until his suicide in 1940, irregularly commissioned by the institute to research issues relating to theories of literature and culture;[37] Fromm, certainly at first a close associate of Horkheimer and fully commit-ted to the institute, took, when in exile in New York, a new course in the interpretation of psychoanalysis which caused relations with the institute to be broken off in 1939.[38]

Thus these different authors cannot be compared either in their theoretical orientations nor in their thematic alignments; what fundamentally unites them is the overall direction of their thinking which allowed them as a body to go beyond the functionalist reference system of the original programme of the institute. The spirit of contradiction of all four authors is ignited by Marxist functionalism, against which they oppose considerations that converge in an upward revaluation of individuals' and groups' own com-municative performances. True, this underlying impulse, which thrusts

[35] In the following I proceed from a distinction which Habermas introduced in his debate on critical theory (see Habermas: 1981, p. 558), and I shall attempt to clarify this essentially loose differentiation between a 'closed' and an 'outer' circle at the institute.

[36] An introductory survey is offered by Söllner (1979, pp. 86ff.). On Neumann, see Söllner (1978); on Kirchheimer, see the summary in Luthardt (1976).

[37] An introduction to Benjamin is offered by Witte (1985) and Wolin (1982).

[38] See, for a general introduction to Fromm, Bonss: 1982.

towards an overcoming of the philosophico-historical reductionism laid out in the categorial premisses of Marxism, is not expressly voiced in any of the works, but it is visible at every point where theoretical differences between representatives of the two groups within the institute begin to surface. It was not accidental divergence in object conception, but rather systemic differences in the model of a theory of society that separated the inner from the outer circle in every case.

Neumann's and Kirchheimer's knowledge of jurisprudence and political science was very fruitful in various investigations concerning the political form of integration of advanced capitalist societies. Their legal and scientific background meant that both were fully conversant with the view that law is a central steering mechanism of bourgeois society; they regarded constitutional law as the socially-generalized outcome of a political compromise which the classes, with varying degrees of power, had agreed upon under the conditions of private capitalism. This social-theoretical premiss constituted the background for the analyses in which Neumann, like Kirchheimer, investigated the formal constitutional alterations which accompany the economic structural change of capitalism.[39] The issue over which, as a group, they finally come into conflict with the institute's directorship concerned the organizational principles that underlay the new dominating order of National Socialism. Neumann and Kirchheimer advanced empirically-grounded objections to the 'state capitalism' thesis put forward by Horkheimer and Pollock. The social scientific investigations which they had conducted – from their American exile – on the situation in Germany (Kirchheimer: 1976b; 1976c; Neumann: 1978b) and their practical political experience of the end of the Weimar Republic, convinced them of the unbroken primacy of private capitalist interests over state management of the economy. Neumann and Kirchheimer could not therefore accept Pollock's thesis that, in National Socialism, state management of the market had merely devolved upon a centralized administrative bureaucracy; rather, they continued to argue that Fascism had not annulled the functional laws of the capitalist market as such but had simply placed them under the additional control of compulsory totalitarian measures. This thesis, with its doctrine of political compromise, was summarized in a single formula in the concept of the 'totalitarian monopolistic economy', which Neumann, in his investigation *Behemoth*, programmatically opposed to the concept of state capitalism (Neumann: 1966, pp. 221ff.).[40] This thesis claimed that National Socialist domination came about in the form of a socially restricted compromise which was freed from constitutional obligations and in which party, economic and administrative elites agreed upon

[39] See, above all, the following collections of essays: Neumann: 1978a; Kirchheimer: 1976a.

[40] On the debate within the institute on the analysis of Fascism see, among others, Rainer: 1984; Wilson: 1982.

political measures that, ultimately, had as their goal the improvement of monopolistic profit-opportunities.

It was not of course simply the empirical knowledge alone which allowed Neumann and Kirchheimer to follow the path of this analysis of Fascism, an analysis which has since been largely confirmed;[41] what equally contributes to the superiority of their interpretation as against the state-capitalism thesis are the social-theoretical conceptions implicit in their work. From the outset, Neumann and Kirchheimer perceived the societal order from a different perspective than the one that prevailed in the closer circle around Horkheimer; for the former, social integration represents a process which comes about not simply by means of the permanently unconscious fulfilling of societal functional imperatives, but also by way of political communication between social groups. Because of their concern about the position of the constitutional state, Neumann and Kirchheimer were for the first time confronted with the phenomenon of political legitimacy; as a result, they realized that the constitutional order of a society is always the expression of a generalizable compromise or consensus between political forces. The active participation in class conflicts that characterized the Weimar Republic led to a realistic assessment of the 'relative strength of social interests' (Kirchheimer: 1978): for Neumann and Kirchheimer, the power potential arising out of capitalist control of the means of production is not to be under-estimated. Finally, their experiences of Austro-Marxism[42] revealed to both of them the compromise character of a societal order as a whole: the institutions of a society are no more than momentary expressions of the social agreements which the different interest groups accept in accordance with their respective power potential.

In Neumann's and Kirchheimer's thinking all this comes together to form a concept of society whose centre is occupied by the comprehensive process of communication between social groups. This concept not only prevents the uncritical adoption of ideas that view all societal groups as completely integrated in the social order,[43] but above all sets up barriers against that Marxist functionalism toward which Horkheimer and his associates inclined. Neumann's and Kirchheimer's analyses always start from the interests and orientations that social groups themselves bring into societal reproduction on the basis of their class position. From the communicative process in which the different groups negotiate these interests among themselves through the utilization of their respective power potential, there emerges the fragile

---

[41] On the superiority of Neumann's and Kirchheimer's analysis of Fascism over the analysis offered by the theory of state capitalism, see Schäfer: 1977; Wilson: 1982.

[42] See the reference in Söllner (1979, pp. 101ff.); the influence of Austro-Marxism on the socialist theory of the state and of law in the Weimar Republic has not been extensively researched. A first approach, although it does not consider Neumann and Kirchheimer, is the investigation by Strom and Walter (1984).

[43] See, above all, Neumann: 1977.

compromise which finds expression in the institutional constitution of a society.

Because both Neumann and Kirchheimer thought in this way they could not assume that societal integration comes about by way of a steering process which simply extends into the symbolically mediated interests and orientation of social groups. For both of them it is the group-specific action perspectives and not the systemically produced motives of instinct that shape the social element out of which the integrative process of a society is formed. Thus Neumann's and Kirchheimer's concern is neither Marxist functionalism nor the assumption that totalitarianism is merely a delusional system (*Verblendungszusammenhang*) that has become total. Finally, if only for social-theoretical reasons, Neumann and Kirchheimer resist tendencies toward a centralism at the level of a theory of power – tendencies which can be found in Horkheimer and his associates because they consider the totalitarian state a homogeneous power centre, whereas for Neumann and Kirchheimer it is a self-evident assumption that state domination always grows out of an intertwinement of the power potentials of different interest groups.[44] The superiority of the social-theoretical approach, which is more implicitly than explicitly found in Neumann and Kirchheimer, is evident in the empirical richness and material diversity of their analyses of Fascism; precisely because they explain totalitarian domination in terms of an interplay of rival interest groups, their theories are still of value today.

Benjamin's intellectual path crossed the social-theoretical avenue of Neumann and Kirchheimer only at a single point: for him too, the conflict of social classes is both a continually effervescent experience and, at the same time, a theoretical premiss of every analysis of culture and society. Admittedly, Benjamin's interest lay not so much in a sociological investigation of society as in a diagnosis of the times in terms of a philosophy of history. The driving force behind this philosophy of history is the idea of a redemption of humanity from the guilt of social repression and domination; it draws its central insights from the tradition of Jewish Messianism and its social-theoretical view is formed by the ideas of historical materialism.[45] As a thinker who brought together very different theoretical traditions in his works, Benjamin had as close or as distant a connection to critical theory as to Gershom Scholem's Jewish hermeneutic and to Bertolt Brecht's materialist theory of literature. Of course, the interest in art as a theoretical source of knowledge linked him to Adorno from the very beginning (see Buck-Morss: 1977), and the preference for a micrological analysis of every-

[44] On this see, above all, Marramao: 1982; on the further development of Neumann's 'theory of intertwinement' in the post-war period, see Buchstein and Schlöer: 1983.

[45] There are few studies of Benjamin that are successful in demonstrating the unity behind his diverse thinking; of major significance is Habermas's interpretation (Habermas: 1983). See also Tiedemann: 1973.

day culture connected him to Siegfried Kracauer.[46]

It was on the question of the effects of the new media of modern mass culture on society and art generally that Benjamin came into conflict with the leading associates of the institute. Like Adorno and Horkheimer, Benjamin at first perceived the emergence of the culture industry as a process of destruction of the autonomous work of art: in so far as the products of artistic labour are technically reproducible, they lose that cultic aura which previously lifted them, like a sacred relic, out of the profane everyday world of the beholder (Benjamin: 1973b). The technical media of film, radio and photography destroy the aura surrounding the art product and expose it to a remote viewing by the public; the contemplative form of the solitary enjoyment of art is suppressed by the public methods of the collective experiencing of art. However, the differences of opinion in the institute were ignited not by the identification of these cultural developmental tendencies, but by the assessment of the receptive behaviour they engendered. In the destruction of aesthetic aura Adorno saw a process that forces the beholder to become a passive, reflectionless consumer and thereby renders aesthetic experiences impossible; mass art, which resulted from new reproduction technicized, represented for him nothing more than a 'de-aestheticization of art' (Entkunstung der Kunst).[47] Benjamin, on the other hand, saw in technicized mass art above all the possibility for new forms of collective perception; he pinned all his hopes on the fact that, in the public's remote experiencing of art, those illuminations and experiences, which had hitherto only occurred in the esoteric process of the solitary enjoyment of art, could from then on come about in more prosaic circumstances.

As in the debate about the state-capitalism thesis, it is not so much the individual empirical claims that still merit interest today, since subsequent developments and the state of international research have rendered these claims largely obsolete.[48] The social-theoretical considerations concealed behind the respective, competing positions are however instructive; thus, it becomes apparent that Benjamin and Adorno only arrived at differing assessments of technicized mass culture because they proceeded implicitly from different concepts of social integration. Not only an unwavering insistence on the knowledge value of only the esoteric work of art, but also the presupposition of a closed functionalism allowed Adorno to arrive at a strict rejection of the new art forms. He is so preoccupied with the idea of a systemic steering process of society which reaches into all cultural life-contexts that he cannot, under any circumstances, credit social groups with the creative performances which would be necessary in order to learn spontaneously new forms of world disclosure from the mass arts.[49] As we

[46] See the reference in Zohlen (1980).

[47] See, for example, the perspective in Adorno (1978); the 'de-aestheticization of art' is the heading under which he later considers the culture industry in Adorno (1973a, pp. 52ff.).

[48] On the current state of research, see the overview provided by Kellner (1982).

[49] See my critique in Honneth (1985, ch. 3).

have been able to observe, Adorno's theory of contemporary society begins with the claim of a system integration which has become total; thus he can regard the entire media of the culture industry only as a means of domination and must rate popular forms of art as phenomena of psychical regression.

Benjamin, however, cannot agree with the premises of this interpretation since he allows himself to be led, if not by an alternative model of social integration, then at least by other ideas about the composition of social experiences. Accordingly, social groups and classes are ascribed the ability to develop a collective imagination that finds expression in common experiences of perception and in common experiential contents; these collective worlds of perception are always sprinkled with far-fetched images which contain shocklike insights into the context of guilt and redemption of human history. Benjamin arrives at the notion of a pictorial imagination of social groups by way of an idiosyncratic absorption of, on the one hand, Ludwig Klages' anthropological theory and, on the other, Georges Sorel's conception of myth;[50] of course, he additionally fused both theoretical elements with insights which emphasize the significance of social interactional forms for the constitution of collective experiences. As a theorist of culture, Benjamin was thus primarily interested in the changes that the process of capitalist modernization occasion in the structures of social interaction, in the narrative forms of experience exchange and in the spatial conditions of communication, because these changes determine the social conditions under which the historical past enters the pictorial imagination of the masses and acquires immediate significance there. From such a perspective, which was the determining factor not only for individual articles by Benjamin but also for a whole series of his book reviews,[51] fragments of another image of social integration necessarily emerge: here, the experiential worlds of different groups and collectives represent not so much the mere material of domination but rather the logically independent forces themselves from which the movement of social life emerges.

If these observations are correct, Benjamin did not think functionalistically. True, he is not a theorist of society in the conventional sense of the term, for he showed little interest in an explanation of the mechanisms of the constitution of society. However, there are still enough social-theoretical elements in his analyses of culture to indicate the extent to which his conceptions went beyond the institute's functionalist level of thinking. For Benjamin, the socio-economic conditions of a society, the forms of com-

---

[50] Benjamin continually referred to Ludwig Klages's anthropological theory and, above all, to the conception of the pictorial imagination and dream consciousness; see here Benjamin (1985a). On the entire complex see, as an introductory but incomplete analysis, Fuld (1981).

[51] On his approaches to a history of forms of communication see, for example, Benjamin (1973a). Benjamin's interest in class-specific forms of experience and perception are evident in his book reviews: see, for example, Benjamin (1972; 1985b).

modity exchange and of production, can only represent the material by which the pictorial imaginations of social groups are ignited. Societal experiences are not merely the representations, charged with instinctual dynamic, of the functional imperatives of society, but rather the independent expression of an ability to develop a collective imagination. Therefore, social integration too is not simply to be conceived as a process that comes about by way of an administrative steering of individual attitudes and orientations. Rather, individual horizons of orientation always also represent extracts from those group-specific worlds that are independently formed in processes of communicative intercourse and that subsist on the forces of a pictorial imagination. These collective worlds stand together in a conflicting relationship whose respective historical form co-determines the course of societal reproduction; to be sure, Benjamin makes quite plain that it is the cultural struggle of social classes itself that determines the integrative ability of society. This, finally, also provides the motive that allowed Benjamin to reach a different assessment of modern mass art than Adorno: because he, unlike the latter, still credited oppressed groups with an ability to perceive creatively, he could pin all his hopes on the fact that mass-art forms unleash unthought-of potentials of the collective imagination and thereby lead to a politicization of the aesthetic.[52]

Like Neumann and Kirchheimer from the perspective of a theory of politics, Benjamin developed, from the perspective of a theory of culture, conceptions and considerations that went beyond the functionalist frame of reference of critical theory; the way this took place led in both cases not only to a more differentiated assessment of the integrative forms of capitalism, but also to preliminary insights into the communicative infrastructure of societies. All three were quick to realize that societal life-contexts are integrated by way of processes of social interaction; communications-theoretic insights of this kind are anticipated in the theory of the political compromise worked out by Neumann and Kirchheimer, as well as in the concept of social experience developed by Benjamin in his sociology of culture. Yet, not one of them used these insights as the foundation for an independent theory of society. The anti-functionalist elements found in their empirical investigations did not mature to that level of generality where they could have been transformed into an explicit critique of Marxist functionalism. Thus, the most sociologically productive research to be conducted under the auspices of the Institute for Social Research remained in the shadow of that philosophically ambitious but sociologically barren theoretical model which the members of the 'inner circle' had developed.

In Erich Fromm's thinking, communications-theoretic insights developed in the microsociological rather than macrosociological domain; the overcoming of the functionalist horizon of thinking, under which he himself had originally moved at the institute, was attained by way of a reinterpretation of psychoanalysis. The impetus for such a reinterpretation came during his

[52] See the contemporizing reference in Wellmer (1985, esp. pp. 41ff.).

exile in the United States which was forced upon him by Fascism in 1934. There, at first still attached to the institute which had resettled in New York, he became acquainted with the writings of those authors concerned with an interactionistic revision of the basic assumptions of psychoanalysis. Fromm willingly and rapidly took up the suggestions of this intellectual group, centred around Karen Horney and Harry Stack Sullivan,[53] on how to revise his theory of social psychology. The results of these revisions were published in 1941 in his book *Escape from Freedom*, in which the formation of the bourgeois personality is investigated within the framework of a now fundamentally altered conception of psychoanalysis. A revision of the psychoanalytical theory of instincts is at the core of the new conception. Fromm puts the assumption of humanity's pliable nature in that position which the hypothesis of a fixed, libidinally centred instinct-structure had assumed in Freudian theory; along with the instinctual impulses that constitute human needs he adds, besides 'self-preservation', 'social instincts' as well (Fromm: 1941, ch. 1). These two basic instincts form a drive-potential that, as a natural substratum, enters into every process of socialization; the shaping of the inner nature into historically-unique personality features takes place here in the medium of social interaction (Fromm: 1941, ch. 2).

With this fundamental change of direction Fromm severed his connections with the closed functionalism that had shaped his initial approach within social psychology; he now granted societal interaction not only a logically independent position of importance in the socialization process but moreover assigned it, albeit in the unfortunate form of a theory of instincts, the role of a constitutive driving force in social development. True, Fromm retained the 'milieu contextual-theoretic' orientation of his earlier investigations: that is, he continued to view personality development as primarily a 'dynamic conforming' of individual drive-potential to the behavioural imperatives that are admitted into the sociocultural milieux of different classes (see Bonss: 1982). However, because he now conceived the socialization operation as a whole as a process of communicative individualization, he was no longer able to assume that these social influences and expectations are deposited in a completely uninterrupted manner in the individual personality structure; rather, the behavioural demands of society take effect only by means of and through a medium that, in accordance with its entire structure, is aimed at the autonomy of the subject.[54] In principle, ego development thus takes place in the dovetailing of increasing individualization and growing socialization.

At the institute it was above all Adorno and Marcuse who reacted to Fromm's new theoretical approach; of course, because of more personal reasons, they did not develop their critique until he had already left the institute (see Bonss: 1982, pp. 394ff; Jay: 1973, pp. 101ff.). It was not so

[53] See, for example, Fromm (1971, pp. 193ff).
[54] See, above all, Fromm (1941, ch. 2).

much the interactionistic elements in Fromm's new theory as its revisions of the theory of instincts that encountered opposition in the closer circle of the institute's members. Adorno and Marcuse perceived the abandonment of the Freudian theory of the libido as the common characteristic and traitorous core of neo-analytical revisionism; they saw here a theoretical accommodation of psychoanalysis to the purposes of a conformist therapy.[55] Against this tendency they argued for the orthodox content of the Freudian theory of instincts; although Adorno nevertheless referred primarily to the Freudian dualism of the sexual and death instincts, Marcuse linked up with the aesthetic-revolutionary potential of the libido theory in his interpretation of psychoanalysis.[56] Thus, the conflict concerning the importance and content of the Freudian libido theory became centrally significant for the relationship of psychoanalysis and critical theory; from the beginning, Fromm's new social-theoretical approach, the really fruitful core of his revision of psychoanalysis, receded behind this conflict. Interactionism – the interactionism which as a common orientation underlies neo-analytical revisionism – was never taken seriously as a theoretical challenge by either Adorno or Marcuse. The social-theoretical premises of their own interpretations of psychoanalysis therefore remained concealed for a long time, and it is not until today that they have, through their problematic features, come to light.[57]

IV Jürgen Habermas and Critical Theory

The research work of the 'outer circle', all of which could have contributed to an overcoming of Marxist functionalism, remained without influence on the further development of critical theory; the institute's research links with the three survivors of that circle, Neumann, Kirchheimer and Fromm, broke definitively after the Second World War. Of course Adorno and Horkheimer had long severed connections not only with what were once some of their most productive associates, but also to a certain extent with their own past history. When the Institute for Social Research opened again in Frankfurt in 1950 it recommenced its research activity without any direct reference to the social-philosophical self-understanding of the thirties and forties. The unifying bond of a comprehensive theory that could have mediated between empirical research and philosophical reflection was broken in the post-war period. For that reason there was no longer an internal connection between

[55] See Adorno (1972b) and Marcuse (1966), especially the Epilogue, 'The Social Implications of Freudian "Revisionism"', in the latter work. See also Jacoby (1978), which is written from Adorno's and Marcuse's perspective.

[56] On these differences, see Bonss: 1982, pp. 397ff.

[57] For a critique of the social-theoretical premises of Adorno's interpretation of psychoanalysis see, above all, Jessica Benjamin (1977); I have attempted to continue this critique in Honneth (1985, pp. 99ff.).

the empirical studies conducted at the institute and the philosophical, cultural-critical research in which Horkheimer, Adorno and Marcuse (who remained in the United States) continued to pursue their original concerns. As a uniform, philosophically integrated school, critical theory was in ruins.

While a common denominator can scarcely be found for the empirical research projects of the institute,[58] the idea of a 'totally administered world' represents such a uniform point of reference, at least initially, for the social-philosophical works. As a theme, this idea runs through the cultural-critical studies of Horkheimer, Adorno and Marcuse,[59] where the central premises of the state-capitalism thesis became the general frame of reference for an analysis of post-war capitalism. The totalitarian perspective, which had already shaped the conception of society in the *Dialectic of Enlightenment*, now also determined the sociological investigations: because administrative social control and individual willingness to conform interlock seamlessly, societal life came to be seen as integrated in a stable and unassailable system of constraint. Of course, from their largely concurring diagnosis of the times, the three authors drew very different inferences for the project of a critical theory of society: in Horkheimer's thinking, a pessimism deriving from Schopenhauer – which had accompanied him from the very beginning – intensified to the point where it turned into a negative theology;[60] Adorno pressed ahead with a self-critique of conceptual thinking whose normative fixed point remained the idea of a mimetic rationality that is representatively preserved in the work of art;[61] only Marcuse reacted to the pessimistic diagnosis of the times with an attempt to rescue the lost idea of revolution by pushing reason under the threshold of the social and shifting it into the libidinal nature of human needs (see Habermas: 1985).

Notwithstanding the differences in objectives, the background of a philosophy of history remained common to the three approaches – a philosophy of history in which historical development is interpreted as a process of technical rationalization that comes to completion in the closed system of domination of contemporary society. It is a theory that at the beginning hardly disclosed itself as a new approach within critical theory which is the first to depart from the philosophical premises of this diagnosis of the times. Although Jurgen Habermas was early on associated with the

[58] See Institut für Sozialforschung (1955); in the fifties a concentration on industrial sociology was already emerging (see Institut für Sozialforschung: 1956; Pollock: 1957). In the seventies this concentration on projects within industrial sociology – in connection with Alfred Sohn-Rethel's theory – became almost total; see Brandt (1981) and, in general, Institut für Sozialforschung (1981).

[59] For Horkheimer, see the essays in his *Gesammelte Schriften* (1985, vols 7 and 8); for Adorno, see above all the studies and essays in his *Gesammelte Schriften* (1972a, vol. 8); for Marcuse see, among other of his works, Marcuse (1972).

[60] Immensely informative on Horkheimer's late work is Schmid Noerr (1985); see also Habermas: 1986b, esp. pp. 172ff.).

[61] On this, see Baumeister and Kulenkampff: 1973; on Adorno's later sociological work, see Honneth: 1985, ch. 3.

Institute for Social Research, he had at first, in his theoretical origins and orientation, little in common with the philosophical tradition of critical theory. In his scientific development, it was theoretical currents such as philosophical anthropology, hermeneutics, pragmatism and language analysis that had gained recognition, theoretical currents which were always foreign to the older generation around Adorno and Horkheimer – indeed the latter were hostile to these traditions of theory. Nevertheless, a theory has gradually emerged from Habermas's works which is so clearly motivated by the original objectives of critical theory that it may be accepted as the only serious new approach within this tradition today; the anti-functionalist impulses detected in the thinking of the marginal members of the institute have reached theoretical self-awareness in this theory and hence have become the frame of reference for a different conception of society.

The insight into the linguistic intersubjectivity of social action forms the foundation of this conception. Habermas reaches the fundamental premiss of his theory by way of a study of hermeneutic philosophy and of Wittgenstein's language analysis; from these he learns that human subjects are *ab initio*, i.e. always already, united with one another by means of reaching understanding in language (*sprachliche Verständigung*). The life-form of human beings distinguishes itself by an intersubjectivity anchored in the structures of language; therefore, for the reproduction of social life, the reaching of understanding in language between subjects represents a fundamental, indeed the most basic, presupposition.

In his thinking, Habermas lends weight to this thesis since he makes it the point of departure of a debate with the social-philosophical and sociological tradition: thus, in contemporary social philosophy, he criticizes the tendency toward a gradual reduction of all political-practical matters to questions of technically appropriate decisions (see Habermas: 1968). Contrary to social scientific functionalism, he argues that the reproductive tasks of a society are always determined by the normative self-understanding of communicatively-socialized subjects and that vital functions as such are by no means always encountered in human life-contexts (Habermas: 1982a). In this way he is ultimately led to a critique of Marxism that results in an 'action-theoretically extended' conception of history: if the human life-form distinguishes itself by the medium of achieving understanding in language then societal reproduction cannot be reduced to the single dimension of labour as propounded by Marx in his theoretical writings. Rather, in addition to the activity of processing nature, the practice of linguistically-mediated interaction must be viewed as an equally fundamental dimension of historical development (Habermas: 1972, parts 1–3, pp. 25ff.).

With this consideration Habermas has already implicitly broken with the basic assumptions of the philosophy of history that were thus far determining for the tradition of critical theory.[62] He no longer sees, as Adorno, Hork-

---

[62] On critical theory's communications-theoretic development – a term which encompasses Habermas's new approach – see Brunkhorst (1983), Honneth (1979) and Wellmer (1977); on Habermas's theory in its entirety, see McCarthy (1984).

heimer and Marcuse continued to do, the characteristic feature of human socialization in the operation of a continually expanding processing of nature, but rather in the fact that the collective securing of material existence is dependent, from the very beginning, on the simultaneous maintenance of a communicative agreement. Because human beings, in accordance with their nature, are only able to form a personal identity as long as they can grow into the intersubjectively bequeathed world of a social group and move therein, the interruption of the communicative process of reaching understanding would violate a presupposition of human survival which is just as fundamental as that of the collective appropriation of nature. Linguistic communication is the medium in which individuals can secure that mutuality in their action-orientations and conceptions of value which is necessary in order that the tasks of material reproduction can be societally mastered. However, the philosophy of history that had served critical theory as a theoretical system of reference abstracts from this dimension of social interaction; it was because of this abstraction that critical theory fell into the illusion of a Marxist functionalism in which all societal phenomena are considered in terms of the function they fulfil in the human processing of nature.

To be sure, the decisive step that Habermas has taken in the direction of an independent theory of society and thereby toward a new formulation of critical theory arises only by way of a loading of the two action concepts, 'labour' and 'interaction', with different categories of rationality. This step, rich in potential, results from Habermas's interest in incorporating the new distinction between two types of action into a theory of societal rationalization. A discussion of Marcuse's critique of technology provides the immediate occasion for this; Max Weber's concept of rationality, however, provides the theoretical framework (Habermas: 1971). Habermas conceives the two kinds of action distinguished in his critique of Marx not only as the pattern of specific forms of activity but also as the framework for special cognitive performances; to this extent, both fundamental dimensions of societal reproduction, 'labour' and 'interacton', have also to be able to be respectively distinguished by an independent form of knowledge production and an independent form of 'rationality'. However, Weber's concept of rationalization then proves itself to be too narrow: because, just as specific forms of rationality can be claimed for instrumental activities and technical knowledge, possibilities of rationalization must also be able to be shown for communicative practice and the knowledge embedded in it. Habermas summarizes the general thesis resulting from this critique of Weber in a conceptual framework borrowed from systems theory: although the species develops further – by way of the accumulation of technical and strategical knowledge – in the subsystems of purposive-rational action in which the tasks of societal labour and political administration are organized, it also continues to develop – by way of liberation from forces which impede communication – within the institutional framework in which the socially integrating norms are reproduced (Habermas: 1971, esp. pp. 92ff.).

All Habermas's extensions of his theory in the course of the seventies have followed the lines of this concept of society in which purposive-rationally organized action-systems are distinguished from a sphere of communicative everyday practice, with separate forms of rationalization being claimed for both social realms. Here, universal pragmatics serves further to clarify the linguistic infrastructure of communicative action (Habermas: 1979b); a theory of social evolution helps clarify the logic of development of societal knowledge and thereby the process of rationalization in both its forms;[63] and, finally, with the further reception of systems-theoretic conceptions, Habermas seeks to determine the mechanisms by which social action-realms become independent purposive-rationally organized systems (Habermas: 1982b).

Although these theoretical endeavours penetrate into the most diverging areas of science, nevertheless they are all aimed at the same objective, i.e. the communications-theoretic foundation of a critical theory of society. With their help Habermas seeks to prove that the rationality of communicative action is such a fundamental presupposition of societal development that the tendencies toward an instrumental reification diagnosed by Adorno and Horkheimer can be criticized as forms of societal rationalization that are one-sided, i.e. organized solely in a purposive-rational manner. In *The Theory of Communicative Action*,[64] which Habermas published in two volumes in 1981 (Habermas: 1981; 1984), this programme assumes a systematic form for the first time. The results of the different research work are brought together here to form a single theory in which the rationality of communicative action is reconstructed within the framework of a theory of speech acts; it is also further developed – in the passage on the history of sociological theory from Weber to Parsons – in order to lay the foundations of a theory of society; and, finally, it is made the point of reference for a critical diagnosis of the contemporary world.

In Habermas's theory, the concept of communicative rationality assumes the same key position which the concept of instrumental rationality held in the *Dialectic of Enlightenment*. Just as Adorno and Horkheimer developed the unfolding dynamics of a historical process – in which the present is comprehended as being in a state of crisis – from the rationality form of the mastery of nature, Habermas does so from the rationality potential of communicative action. The basic outline of his construction is that, in the communicative speech acts through which individual actions are coordinated, culturally invariant validity claims are stored and these are historically differentiated gradually in the course of a cognitive rationalization

---

[63] See the other essays in Habermas (1979a), and also Habermas (1979c).

[64] A brilliant presentation of the development which leads to the basic assumptions of this book is given by Bernstein (1985); see also my own presentation (Honneth: 1985, ch. 9).

process. Through decentring of the life-world knowledge that encompasses all communicative action, a cognitive attitude (as one aspect) is identified with which subjects relate to their environment solely from the point of view of success. Habermas sees, within such a historically-derived ability to act strategically, the social presupposition for the emergence of systemically-organized spheres of action.

As subjects learn to act in a manner oriented purely toward success, there emerges the possibility of coordinating social actions by non-linguistic media such as money or power[65] (instead of by processes of reaching understanding). The two spheres of action, which are detached from the communicative life-world because of the institutionalization of these steering media, are the domains of economic production and political administration. The economic system and the action sphere of the state are integrated from now on without recourse to the process of communicatively reaching an understanding. In modern societies they stand, as systems regulated in a manner free of norms, opposite those spheres of action which continue to be communicatively organized and in which the symbolic reproduction of social life proceeds.

On the basis of the historical decoupling of 'system' and 'life-world' Habermas justifies the introduction of the two-level concept of society, to which his construction leads. Here the process of communicatively reaching understanding is viewed also as the fundamental reproductive mechanism of modern societies but at the same time, the existence of such norm-free action spheres – accessible only by way of a systems-theoretic analysis – is presupposed as a historical product. Thus the interweaving of a theory of communication and a concept of system proves to be the essential component for a sociological theory of modernity: every analysis of those processes of reaching understanding by means of which societies today reproduce themselves in their life-worldly foundations requires the aid of systems analysis to investigate the systemic forms of material reproduction. Finally, from this dualistic construction Habermas derives the framework within which he attempts to develop his diagnosis of modernity; its central motive springs from the intention to interpret the process of the 'dialectic of enlightenment' in such a manner that the inevitable outcomes to which Adorno and Horkheimer were forced, can be avoided. The developed theory of society provides the discursive means for this, for, in light of this theory, the systemically-independent organizational complexes – in which Adorno and Horkheimer could only see the final stage of a logic of the mastery of nature – now prove to be the social products of a rationalization of the social life-world. It is not now the existence of purposive-rational organizational forms as such in social life that appears as a crisis-ridden tendency of the present, but just their incursion into that inner domain of society that is constitutively dependent on processes of communicatively reaching understanding. To this phenomenon of a 'colonization of the social lifeworld' Habermas thus

---

[65] On the introduction of the concept of system, see Habermas: 1981, pp. 229ff.

attaches his own diagnosis of a pathology of modernity: 'the rationalization of the lifeworld makes possible an increase in systems complexity which enlarges to such an extent that the released systemic imperatives outstrip the comprehension ability of the lifeworld which is instrumentalized by them' (Habermas: 1981, pp. 232ff.).

It is not difficult to see that the reasoning of this diagnosis of modernity is fully dependent on the two-level model of society – the point to which Habermas has further developed his communications-theoretic approach. Only because he sees modern societies divided into system and lifeworld, into purposive-rationally-organized functional contexts and communicatively-constituted spheres of action, can he understand the incursion of systemic forms of steering into the hitherto intact domains of a communicative everyday practice as the determining pathology of our times.

However, it is precisely the distinction between system and life-world which has recently met with opposition; with this distinction Habermas is in danger of yielding to the 'seductions of systems theory' and of again surrendering the actual potential of his communications-theoretic approach.[66] The outcome of the discussion which has been sparked off by this problem will determine the future of critical theory. This discussion will have to tackle the question of how the communications-theoretic turn – by means of which Habermas has overcome the instrumentalistic bottle-necks of the critical theory tradition – is to be developed further in a suitable theory of society. It may be that in the course of the discussion Neumann's, Kirchheimer's and Benjamin's sociological insights, which were not widely read at the time, can at last prove their theoretical potential for critical theory. It may well be that the theory of political compromise as well as Benjamin's concept of collective experiencing acquire – the moment they become components of a communicative theory of society – a systematic significance opposed to the dualism of system and lifeworld. The turn towards communication in critical theory thus might allow a recovery of a neglected aspect of its past.

[66] See McCarthy (1985); see also the contributions by Joas, Berger and Arnason in the collection of essays edited by Honneth and Joas (1986), as well as Honneth (1985, ch. 9). Habermas has in the mean time already replied to these critiques (Habermas: 1986a, esp. pp. 377ff.).

Bibliography

Adorno, T. W., 1972a: *Gesammelte Schriften.* Frankfurt-on-Main: Suhrkamp.
  1972b: 'Die revidierte Psychoanalyse', in his *Gesammelte Schriften*, vol. 8, pp. 20ff. Frankfurt-on-Main: Suhrkamp.
  1973a: Aesthetischen Theorie. Frankfurt-on-Main: Suhrkamp.
  1973b: *Negative Dialectics.* London.
  1978: 'On the Fetish Character in Music and the Regression of Listening', in A. Arato and E. Gebhardt (eds), *The Essential Frankfurt School Reader.* Oxford: Basil Blackwell, pp. 270ff.
Baumeister, T. and Kulenkampff, J., 1973: 'Geschichtsphilosophie und philosophische Ästhetik: Zu Adornos "Äesthetischer Theorie"', *Neue Hefte für Philosophie*, 5: 74ff.
Benhabib, S., 1981: 'Modernity and the Aporias of Critical Theory', *Telos*, 49: 39–
  1986: *Critique, Norm, and Utopia.* New York: Columbia University Press.
Benjamin, J., 1977: 'The End of Internalization: Adorno's Social Psychology', *Telos*, 32: 42ff.
Benjamin, W., 1972: 'Eine Chronik deutscher Arbeitsloser: Zu Anna Seghers Roman "Die Rettung"', in his *Gesammelte Schriften*, vol. 3. Frankfurt-on-Main: Suhrkamp pp. 530ff.
  1973a: 'The Storyteller: Reflections on the Work of Nikolai Leskov', in his *Illuminations.* London: Fontana pp. 83ff.
  1973b: 'The Work of Art in the Age of Mechanical Reproduction', in his *Illuminations.* London: Fontana pp. 219ff.
  1985a: 'Fragmente zur Moral und Anthropologie', in his *Gesammelte Schriften*, vol. 6. Frankfurt-on-Main: Suhrkamp pp. 54ff.
  1985b: 'Zu Knut Hamsun', in his *Gesammelte Schriften*, vol. 6. Frankfurt-on-Main: Suhrkamp pp. 142ff.
Bernstein, R. J. (ed.), 1985: 'Introduction', in *Habermas and Modernity.* Cambridge, England: Polity Press, pp. 1ff.
Bonss, W., 1980: 'Kritische Theorie und empirische Sozialforschung' in Fromm: 1980, pp. 7ff.
  1982: 'Psychoanalyse als Wissenschaft und Kritik: Zur Freudrezeption der Kritischen Theorie', in Bonss and Honneth: 1982.
Bonss, W. and Honneth, A. (eds), 1982: *Sozialforschung als Kritik.* Frankfurt-on-Main: Suhrkamp.
Bonss, W. and Schindler, N., 1982: 'Kritische Theorie als interdisziplinärer Materialismus', in Bonss and Honneth: 1982, pp. 31ff.
Bottomore, T., 1984: *The Frankfurt School.* London.
Brandt, G., 1981: 'Ansichten kritischer Sozialforschung 1930–1980', in Institute für Sozialforschung (ed.), *Gesellschaftliche Arbeit und Rationalisierung, Leviathan-Sonderheft*, 4: 9ff.
  1986: 'Max Horkheimer und das Projekt einer materialistischer Gesellschaftstheorie', in A. Schmidt and N. Altwicker (eds), *Max Horkheimer heute: Werk und Wirkung.* Frankfurt-on-Main: pp. 279ff.
Breuer, S., 1977: *Die Krise der Revolutionstheorie: Negative Vergesellschaftung und Arbeitsmetaphysik bei Herbert Marcuse.* Frankfurt-on-Main: Syndikat.
  1985: '*Horkheimer und Adorno: Differenzen in Paradigmakern der kritischen Theorie*', *Leviathan-Sonderheft*, 3:

Brunkhorst, H., 1983: 'Paradigmenkern und Theoriendynamik der kritischen Theorie der Gesellschaft', *Soziale Welt*, 34: 21ff.

Buchstein, H. and Schlöer, G., 1983: 'Politische Theorie in der Kritischen Theorie nach 1950: Franz L. Neumann', *Occasional Papers*, Faculty of Political Science, Free University of Berlin.

Buck-Morss, S., 1977: *The Origin of Negative Dialectics: Theodor W. Adorno, Walter Benjamin and the Frankfurt Institute*. New York: Free Press

Cerutti, F., 1970: 'Hegel, Lukács, Korsch: Zum dialektischen Selbstverständnis des kritischen Marxismus', in O. Negt (ed.), *Aktualität und Folgen der Philosophie Hegels*. Frankfurt-on-Main. pp. 195ff.

Cochetti, S., 1985: *Mythos und 'Dialektik der Aufklärung'*. Königstein: Königshausen und Neumann.

Dahmer, H., 1973: *Libido und Gesellschaft: Studien über Freud und die Freudsche Linke*. Frankfurt-on-Main: Suhrkamp.

Dews, P., 1984: 'Power and Subjectivity in Foucault', *New Left Review*, 144: 72ff.

Dubiel, H., 1975: 'Kritische Theorie und politische Ökonomie', in Pollock: 1975, pp. 7ff.
    1981: 'The Origins of Critical Theory: An Interview with Leo Löwenthal', *Telos*, 49.
    1984: *Theory and Politics*. Boston: MIT.

Erd, R., 1984: 'Franz L. Neumann und das Institut für Sozialforschung', in H. Joachim (ed.), *Recht, Demokratie und Kapitalismus: Aktualität und Probleme der Theorie Franz L. Neumanns*. Baden-Baden: pp. 111ff.

Fromm, E., 1932: 'Die psychoanalytische Charakterologie und ihre Bedeutung für die Sozialpsychologie', *Zeitschrift für Sozialforschung*, 1: 253ff.
    1936: 'Sozialpsychologischer Teil', in Institut für Sozialforschung, *Studien über Autorität und Familie: Forschungsbericht des Institut für Sozialforschung*. Paris: pp. 77ff.
    1941: *Escape from Freedom*. New York: Farrar and Rinehart.
    1971: 'Die Krise der Psychoanalyse', in *Analytische Sozialpsychologie und Gesellschaftstheorie* pp. 193ff. Frankfurt-on-Main: Suhrkamp.
    1978: 'The Method and Function of an Analytic Social Psychology', in A. Arato and E. Gebhardt (eds), *The Essential Frankfurt School Reader*. Oxford: Basil Blackwell pp. 477ff.
    1980: *Arbeiter und Angestellte am Vorabend des Dritten Reiches: Ein sozialpsychologische Unterschung*, researched and edited by W. Bonss. Stuttgart: DVA.

Fruchtl, J., 1986: *Mimesis – Konstellation eines Leitbegriffs bei Adorno*. Würzburg: Königshausen und Neumann.

Fuld, W., 1981: 'Walter Benjamins Beziehung zu Ludwig Klages', *Akzente*, 28: 274ff.

Funk, R., 1980: 'Zu Leben und Werk Erich Fromms', in Fromm, *Analytische Sozialpsychologie*, vol. 1 of *Gesamtausgabe*. Stuttgart: pp. ixff.

Gmünder, U., 1985: *Kritische Theorie: Horkheimer, Adorno, Marcuse, Habermas*. Stuttgart: Metzler-Verlag.

Geyer, C.-F., 1982: *Kritische Theorie: Max Horkheimer und Theodor W. Adorno*. Freiburg and Munich: Alber.

Habermas, J., 1968: *Theory and Practice*. Cambridge, England: Polity Press.
    1971: 'Technology and Science as "Ideology"', in his *Toward a Rational Society*. Cambridge, England: Polity Press, pp. 81ff.
    1972: *Knowledge and Human Interests*. Cambridge, England: Polity Press.
    1979a: *Communication and the Evolution of Society*. Cambridge, England: Polity Press.

1979b: 'What is Universal Pragmatics?', in his *Communication and the Evolution of Society*. Cambridge, England: Polity Press, pp. 1ff.

1979c: 'History and Evolution', *Telos*, 39: 5ff.

1980: 'The Inimitable *Zeitschrift für Sozialforschung*', *Telos*, 45: 114ff.

1981: *Theorie des Kommunikativen Handelns*, vol. 2, Frankfurt-on-Main: Suhrkamp.

1982a: 'Zur Logik der Sozialwissenschaften: Ein Literaturbericht', in his *Zur Logik der Sozialwissenschaften*. Frankfurt-on-Main: Suhrkamp pp. 89ff.

1982b: 'Eine Auseinandersetzung mit Niklas Luhmann: Systemtheorie oder kritische Theorie der Gesellschaft?', in his *Zur Logik der Sozialwissenschaften*. Frankfurt-on-Main: Suhrkamp pp. 396ff.

1983: 'Walter Benjamin: Consciousness-Raising or -Rescuing Critique', in his *Philosophical-Political Profiles*. Cambridge, England: Polity Press, pp. 129ff.

1984: *Reason and the Rationalization of Society*, vol. 1 of *Theory of Communicative Action*. Cambridge, England: Polity Press.

1985: 'Psychic Thermidor and the Rebirth of Rebellious Subjectivity', in R. J. Bernstein: 1985, pp. 67ff.

1986a: 'Entgegnung', in Honneth and Joas: 1986, pp. 327ff.

1986b: 'Bemerkungen zur Entwicklungsgeschichte des Horkheimerschen Werkes', in A. Schmidt and N. Altwicker (eds), *Max Horkheimer heute: Werk und Wirkung*. Frankfurt-on-Main: Fischer, pp. 163ff.

1987: *The Philosophical Discourse of Modernity*. Cambridge, England: Polity Press.

Habermas, J. *et al.*, 1978: 'Theory and Politics: A Discussion with Herbert Marcuse', *Telos*, 38: 124ff.

Held, D., 1980: *Introduction to Critical Theory*. London: Hutchinson

Honneth, A., 1979: 'Communication and Reconciliation: Habermas's Critique of Adorno', *Telos*, 39: 45ff.

1982: 'Work and Interaction', *New German Critique*, 26: 31ff.

1984: 'L'esprit et son object – parentés anthropologiques entre la "dialectique de la raison" et la critique de la civilisation dans la philosophie de la vie', in G. Raulet (ed.), *Weimar où l'explosion de la modernité*. Paris, pp. 97ff.

1985: *Kritik der Macht*. Frankfurt-on-Main: Suhrkamp.

Honneth, A. and Joas, H. (eds), 1986: *Kommunikatives Handeln: Beiträge zu Jürgen Habermas' 'Theorie des kommunikativen Handelns'*. Frankfurt-on-Main: Suhrkamp.

Honneth, A. and Wellmer, A. (eds), forthcoming: 'Die Frankfurter Schule und die Folgen: Ein internationales Symposium der Humboldt-Stiftung'. Berlin: De Gruyter.

Hörisch, J., 1980: 'Herrscherwort, Geld und geltende Sätze: Adornos Aktualisierung der Frühromantik und ihre Affinität zur poststrukturalistischen Kritik des Subjects', in B. Linder and W. M. Lüdke (eds), *Materialien zur ästhetischen Theorie Adornos*. Frankfurt-on-Main: Suhrkamp, pp. 397ff.

Horkheimer, M., 1932: 'Geschichte und Psychologie', *Zeitschrift für Sozialforschung*, 1: 125ff.

1941: 'Art and Mass Culture', *Zeitschrift für Sozialforschung*, 9: 290ff.

1972a: 'Notes on Science and the Crisis', in his *Critical Theory*. New York: Herder and Herder.

1972b: 'Authority and Family', in his *Critical Theory*. New York: Herder and Herder, pp. 47ff.

1972c: 'Traditional and Critical Theory', in his *Critical Theory*. New York: Herder and Herder, pp. 188ff.

1972d: 'Die gegenwärtige Lage der Sozialphilosophie und die Aufgabe eines

Instituts für Sozialforschung', in his *Sozialphilosophische Studien*, edited by W. Brede. Frankfurt-on-Main: S. Fischer, pp. 33ff.

1974: *Eclipse of Reason*. New York: Seabury.

1978: 'The End of Reason', in A. Arato and E. Gebhardt (eds), *The Essential Frankfurt School Reader*. Oxford: Basil Blackwell, pp. 26ff.

1985: *Gesammelte Schriften*. Frankfurt-on-Main: Fischer.

Institut für Sozialforschung (ed.), 1955: *Frankfurter Beiträge zur Soziologie*. Frankfurt-on-Main.

1956: *Betriebsklima, Frankfurter Beiträge*, vol. 3. Frankfurt-on-Main.

1981: *Gesellschaftliche Arbeit und Rationalisierung, Leviathan-Sonderheft*, 4.

Jacoby, R., 1978: *Soziale Amnesie: Eine Kritik der konformistischen Psychologie von Adler bis Laing*. Frankfurt-on-Main: Suhrkamp.

Jay, M., 1973: *The Dialectical Imagination*. Boston: Little, Brown & Co.

1982: 'Positive und Negative Totalität: Adornos Alternativentwurf zur interdisziplinären Forschung', in Bonss and Honneth: 1982, pp. 67ff.

1984: *Marxism and Totality: The Adventures of a Concept from Lukács to Habermas*. Cambridge, England: Polity Press.

Kellner, D., 1982: 'Kulturindustrie und Massenkommunikation: Die Kritische Theorie und ihre Folgen', in Bonss and Honneth: 1982, pp. 482ff.

Kilminster, R., 1979: *Praxis and Method: A Sociological Dialogue with Lukács, Gramsci and the Early Frankfurt School*. London.

Kirchheimer, O., 1976a: '*Von der Weimarer Republik zum Faschism: Die Auflösung der demokratischen Rechtsordnung*, edited by W. Luthardt. Frankfurt-on-Main: Suhrkamp.

1976b: 'Staatsgefuge und Recht des Drittens Reiches', in his *Von der Weimarer Republik zum Faschism: Die Auflösung der demokratischen Rechtsordnung*, edited by W. Luthardt. Frankfurt-on-Main. pp. 152ff.

1976c: 'Das Strafrecht im nationalsozialistischen Deutschland', in his *Von der Weimarer Republik zum Faschism: Die Auflösung der demokratischen Rechtsordnung*, edited by W. Lufthardt. Frankfurt-on-Main, pp. 186ff.

1978: 'Changes in the Structure of Political Compromise', in A. Arato and E. Gebhardt (eds), *The Essential Frankfurt School Reader*. Oxford: Basil Blackwell, pp. 49ff.

Klein, R. and Kippenburg, H. G., 1975: 'Zu einer Theorie der Geschichtserfahrung', *Saeculum*, 26: 128ff.

Kluke, P., 1972: *Die Stiftungsuniversität Frankfurt-am-Main 1914–1932*. Frankfurt-on-Main: Verlag Waldemar-Kramer.

Korthals, M., 1985: 'Die kritische Gesellschaftstheorie des frühen Horkheimer', *Zeitschrift für Soziologie*, 14 (4): 315ff.

Küsters, G.-W., 1980: *Der Kritikbegriff der Kritischen Theorie Max Horkheimers*. Frankfurt-on-Main and New York: Campus.

Löwenthal, L., 1932: 'Zur gesellschaftlichen Lage der Literatur', *Zeitschrift für Sozialforschung*, 1: 85ff.

1980: *Mitmachen wollte ich nie: Ein autobiographisches Gespräche mit Helmut Dubiel*. Frankfurt-on-Main: Suhrkamp.

Lukács, G., 1971: 'Reification and the Consciousness of the Proletariat', in his *History and Class Consciousness*. London: Merlin, pp. 83ff.

Luthardt, W., 1976: 'Bemerkungen zu Otto Kirchheimers Arbeiten bis 1933', in Kirchheimer: 1976a, pp. 7ff.

Mahnkopf, B., 1985: *Verbürgerlichung: Die Legende vom Ende des Proletariats*. Frankfurt-on-Main and New York: Campus.

Marcuse, H., 1966: *Eros and Civilization*. Boston: Beacon.
1968: 'Philosophy and Critical Theory', in his *Negations*. New York: Beacon.
1972: *One Dimensional Man*. London.
Marramao, G., 1982: 'Die Formveränderung des politischen Konflikts im Spät-kapitalismus: Zur Kritik des politiktheoretischen Paradigmas der Frankfurter Schule', in Bonss and Honneth: 1982, pp. 240ff.
McCarthy, T., 1984: *The Critical Theory of Jürgen Habermas*. Cambridge, England: Polity Press.
1985: 'Complexity and Democracy, or the Seducements of Systems Theory', *New German Critique*, 35: 27ff.
Migdal, U., 1981: *Die Frühgeschichte des Frankfurter Instituts für Sozialforschung*. Frankfurt-on-Main and New York: Campus.
Müller, R. W., 1977: *Geld und Geist: Zur Entstehungsgeschichte von Identitätsbewusstsein und Rationalität seit der Antike*, part 2. Frankfurt-on-Main.
Neumann, F. L., 1966: *Behemoth: The Structure and Practice of National Socialism 1933–1944*, part 2. New York: Oxford University Press.
1977: *Behemoth: Struktur und Praxis des Nationalsozialismus 1933–1944*. Cologne.
1978a: *Wirtschaft, Staat, Demokratie 1930–1954*, edited by A. Söllner. Frankfurt-on-Main.
1978b: 'Mobilisierung der Arbeit der Gesellschaftsordnung des Nationalsozialismus', in his *Wirtschaft, Staat, Demokratie: Aufsätze 1930–1954*, edited by A. Söllner. Frankfurt-on-Main: Suhrkamp, pp. 255ff.
Pollock, F., 1941: 'State Capitalism: Its Possibilities and Limitations', *Studies in Philosophy and Social Sciences*, 4 (2): 200ff.
1957: *The Economic and Social Consequences of Automation*. Oxford.
1975: 'Die gegenwärtige Lage des Kapitalismus und die Aussichten einer planwirtschaftlichen Neuordnung', in his *Stadien des Kapitalismus*, edited by H. Dubiel. Munich: C. H. Beck, pp. 20ff.
Schäfer, G., 1977: 'Franz Neumanns "Behemoth" und die heutige Faschismus-diskussion', 'Epilogue' in Neumann: 1977, pp. 665ff.
Schivelbusch, W., 1982: *Intellektuellendämmerung: Zur Lage der Frankfurter Intelligenz in den zwanziger Jahren*. Frankfurt-on-Main: Insel.
Schmid Noerr, G., 1985: 'Kritische Theorie in der Nachkriegs-Gesellschaft', 'Epilogue' in M. Horkheimer, *Gesammelte Schriften*, vols 7 and 8. Frankfurt-on-Main: Fischer, pp. 457ff.
Schmidt, A., 1968: 'Existential-Ontologie und historischer Materialismus bei Marcuse', in J. Habermas (ed.), *Antworten auf Herbert Marcuse*. Frankfurt-on-Main: Suhrkamp. pp. 17ff.
1976: *Die Kritische Theorie als Geschichtsphilosophie*. Munich and Vienna: Hanser.
1980: 'Die Zeitschrift für Sozialforschung Geschichte und gegenwärtige Bedeutung', in *Zeitschrift für Sozialforschung*, vol. 1. Munich: DTV, paperback edn, pp. 5ff.
Schmucker, J. F., 1977: *Adorno – Logik des Zerfalls*. Stuttgart.
Schnädelbach, H., 1986: 'Max Horkheimer und die Moralphilosophie des deutschen Idealismus', in A. Schmidt and N. Altwicker (eds), *Max Horkheimer heute: Werk und Wirkung*. Frankfurt-on-Main: Fischer. pp. 52ff.
Slater, P., 1977: *Origin and Significance of the Frankfurt School: A Marxist Perspective*. London.
Söllner, A., 1978: 'Franz L. Neumann – Skizzen zu einer intellektuellen und politischen Biographie', in Neumann: 1978a, pp. 7ff.

1979: *Geschichte und Herrschaft: Studien zur materialistischen Sozialwissenschaft 1929–1942*. Frankfurt-on-Main: Suhrkamp.

Strom, G. and Walter, F., 1984: *Weimarer Linkssozialismus und Austromarxismus*. Berlin.

Tar, Z., 1977: *The Frankfurt School*. New York.

Tiedemann, R., 1973: *Studien zur Philosophie Walter Benjamins*. Frankfurt-on-Main: Suhrkamp.

Volpe, G. della, 1973: 'Kritik eines spätromantischen Paradoxes', in his *Für eine materialistische Methodologie*. Berlin: Merve, pp. 117ff.

Wellmer, A., 1971: *Critical Theory of Society*. New York: Seabury.

1977: 'Communication and Emancipation: Reflections on the Linguistic Turn in Critical Theory', in J. O'Neill (ed.), *On Critical Theory*. London. pp. 231ff.

1985: 'Wahrheit, Schein, Versöhnung: Adornos ästhetische Rettung der Moderne', in his *Zur Dialektik von Moderne und Postmoderne*. Frankfurt-on-Main: Suhrkamp, pp. 9ff.

Wiggerhaus, R., 1986: *Die 'Frankfurter Schule' Geschichte, theoretische Entwicklung und politische Bedeutung*. Munich.

Wilson, M., 1982: *Das Institut für Sozialforschung und seine Faschismusanalysen*. Frankfurt-on-Main and New York: Campus.

Witte, B., 1985: *Walter Benjamin*. Reinbek bei Hamburg: Rowohlt.

Wolin, R., 1982: *Walter Benjamin: An Aesthetic Redemption*. New York: Columbia University Press.

Zeitschrift für Sozialforschung: 1970. Munich: DTV.

Zohlen, G., 1980: 'Text-Strassen: Zur Theorie der Stadtlektüre bei Siegfried Kracauer', in his *Text und Kritik: Siegfried Kracauer*. Munich: Heft 68, pp. 62ff.

Sociology and the Mathematical Method[1]

THOMAS P. WILSON

Language does not serve science very well as an analytic device. ... J. B. S. Haldane said that if someone could not use something in an equation then he did not really know what it meant, and Haldane's principle accounts for the universal use of mathematical notation in the sciences. The most important accomplishment of [*Culture and the Evolutionary Process*] is the explicit algebraic representation of a rich meaningful set of unambiguous processes with which to study cultural transmission.

Harpending: 1985

On the other hand, many, including myself, would like to argue that these notions about the sciences of man are sterile, that we cannot come to understand important dimensions of human life within the bounds set by this epistemological orientation

Taylor: 1971

The social sciences are concerned with such things as politics and government, law, crime and punishment, education, religion, the production and distribution of goods and services, class structure, organization and bureaucracy, war and revolution, race and ethnic relations, the family, similarities and differences between and within societies both contemporaneously and historically, and the like. The subject of this essay is the place of mathematics in the description and explanation of such phenomena. The issues, however, run very much deeper than can be addressed by a recital of the virtues of mathematics or a review of the literature in mathematical sociology. We are involved here with fundamental, enduring controversy over the nature of society and the social sciences. I want to take this occasion, then, to

---

[1] Parts of this essay are adapted from Wilson (1984) by permission.

reflect on these issues with specific reference to the place of the mathematical method in sociology.

There is a long-standing tension in the social sciences between two quite distinct and opposed ideas about the nature of social life and the possibilities of our knowledge of it. The dominant methodological position in sociology and economics since the Enlightenment has been that social phenomena should be understood following the intellectual model of the natural sciences. A corollary of this view is commitment to mathematics, not merely as perhaps a heuristic aid in data analysis, but as the proper idiom in which basic concepts and propositions should be formulated, phenomena described and data analysed, at least in principle and in the long run. However, there is also an equally venerable though perhaps less prominent tradition based on an idiographic, interpretative approach emphasizing the importance of meaning in social life and the necessity for understanding any particular datum in its singular and idiosyncratic context. On this view, mathematical methods are irrelevant if not positively misleading in the study of social phenomena. My purpose in this essay is to consider the issues raised by this persistent division of opinion, not with the intention of championing one side or the other, but rather of showing that the issue itself is misconceived. The conclusion I seek to establish is that although the 'natural science' model is inappropriate and misleading in the social sciences and mathematics cannot play the same fundamental role in the study of society as in understanding natural phenomena, nevertheless a purely idiographic approach is also ineffective and mathematics has an indispensable role to play in unravelling the complexities of social phenomenon. My thesis, then, is at odds with received wisdom on both sides.

Background

Since Galileo, mathematics has been recognized as the basic idiom in which the underlying concepts of the natural sciences can be formulated, at least in principle. This is not accidental: the connection between natural science and mathematics is essential and fundamental.[2] Consequently, an insistence that in principle the fundamental concepts and propositions in the social

---

[2] Even when no formal notation is used and the effort seems wholly descriptive and taxonomic, as has sometimes appeared to be the case in certain areas of biology, the mathematics of set theory is available if formal expression is wanted. The first epigraph notwithstanding, it is perfectly possible to reason rigorously and mathematically without specialized notation; notation is important, not in principle, but because it greatly facilitates dealing with complex matters. In simple cases, however, we do not need notation and indeed get along better without it. In the natural sciences it is always possible to adopt an explicit formalism for fundamental concepts and propositions, and this possibility is essential to the character of the natural sciences.

sciences can be formulated in an appropriate mathematical notation is equivalent to the claim that there is no essential methodological distinction between the natural and social sciences.

The idea that the social sciences should model themselves on the natural sciences circulated in a general way in the Enlightenment and was formulated as an explicit thesis by Auguste Comte and John Stuart Mill.[3] Since that time it has been the orthodox methodological position in the social sciences, particularly in economics and only slightly less so in sociology. However, there has also been continuing dissent from the conception of social science as the natural science of society. One important version of this opposition, originating in the hermeneutic and *geisteswissenschaftlich* traditions in the last century, holds that meaning and subjectivity are essential features of social life and that consequently the social sciences differ fundamentally from the natural sciences. This perspective has attracted renewed attention in recent years and has converged with ideas based on Wittgenstein's later writings in what is becoming known as the 'interpretative' approach in social science, which emphasizes the elucidation of subjective and cultural complexes of meaning.[4] In addition, there has long been a scattered literature drawing on a variety of phenomenological, humanist and other anti-positivist philosophical positions that is highly critical of what are viewed as the 'scientistic pretensions' of social science. And most recently, ethnomethodology has emerged as yet another perspec-

[3] Comte, it will be recalled, was opposed to the use of quantitative methods and coined the term 'sociology' when Quetelet usurped the label 'social physics' for his statistical studies of social phenomena. From a modern perspective, this seems incongruent with his insistence on what he understood to be the method of the natural sciences but is perhaps understandable in the context of his commitment to radical methodological holism and the nature of mathematics in the early nineteenth century.

[4] For example, see the collection edited by Rabinow and Sullivan (1979), and Giddens's discussions of hermeneutics, the *Geisteswissenschaften*, and the relations of these to critical theory (Giddens: 1976; 1977; 1979). The sense of the term 'interpretative' in this literature differs fundamentally from that in 'Conceptions of Interaction' (Wilson: 1970). 'Interpretative sociology' in the *geisteswissenschaftlich* tradition conceives of interpretation as a temporal process on the part of the social scientist, in which the 'hermeneutic circle' involves successive revisions of interpretations of social phenomena as each new level of understanding calls for revision of the basis on which that understanding is founded. This tradition emphasizes meaning and interpretation as methodological problems for the investigator. In contrast, in 'Conceptions of Interaction', interpretation is viewed as occurring in interaction between people and, as such, a phenomenon to be studied by sociologists. It is thought of not as the hermeneutic circle, but as the immediate process by which people ordinarily understand one another. The two senses of 'interpretative' are alike in treating meaning as a fundamental characteristic of social phenomena, but in other respects they differ in major and conflicting ways. In this essay I shall use the term 'interpretative' in the hermeneutic sense rather than that suggested in 'Conceptions of Interaction', since the former usage appears to have become established.

tive that rejects the natural science model for social science.[5]

Despite the objections from various quarters, however, it remains the dominant point of view in the social sciences that social science is, or at least ought to be, the natural science of society, and that explanations of social phenomena should be in terms of concepts and general laws that can, at least in principle, be expressed in mathematical form. Perhaps a major reason for this is that the critics of 'scientific' social science[6] appear to argue directly or indirectly for a vague and unsatisfactory idealism, subjectivism, or even outright ideologizing, in which the possibility of rational empirical inquiry into the conventional topics of social science is denied. While this accusation is unfair in many cases, it is accurate often enough to make social scientists' rejection of these criticisms understandable.

Nevertheless, though the goal of social science on the model of natural science has been pursued for two centuries with considerable energy and talent, the results have been disappointing. Even in economics, in which the attempt to use mathematics as a vehicle for substantive theory rather than as merely an aid in data analysis has been especially prominent, the contributions of mathematically-formulated theory to solid empirical understanding seem meagre relative to the magnitude and mathematical sophistication of the effort. More generally, irrespective of mathematical embodiment, the scientific achievements of social science are not impressive when one construes 'scientific' in the narrow sense of the natural sciences and distinguishes between programmatic claims and actual accomplishments.

One can, of course, try to explain this away by appealing to the frequently-alleged 'immaturity' of the social sciences, or by pleading the oft-claimed 'complexity' of social phenomena. However, we are well advised to greet such excuses with considerable scepticism. Just 66 years separated Copernicus's *De Revolutionibus* in 1543 from Kepler's *Astronomia Nova* in 1609, with Galileo's *Dialogo* following 23 years later in 1632 and Newton's *Principia* appearing 55 years after that in 1687: less than a century and a half in all. But two centuries have elapsed since Condorcet and three since Newton's contemporaries were inspired to think of applying his methods to the study

---

[5] The term 'ethnomethodology' does not identify a unified body of thought but rather a diverse array of often mutually incompatible approaches. Throughout this essay I shall use the term to refer to the tradition founded by Garfinkel (1967) and continued with the work of Sacks and his collaborators. For an overview, see Heritage: 1984; for discussion relevant to present concerns, see Maynard and Wilson: 1980; Wilson: 1982; 1985; Wilson and Zimmerman: 1980.

[6] The words 'science' and 'scientific' are problematic here. In a broad sense, they can be construed to refer to any form of rational empirical inquiry, including of course the natural sciences but also such fields as history and linguistics. However, the contemporary tendency is to understand 'science' as meaning natural science. In German it is possible to preserve the broad sense with the term *Wissenschaft*, but unfortunately this is usually rendered in English as 'science', which gives a misleading sense of the original. Perhaps the most prominent victim of this problem is Weber, who clearly did not advocate a natural science model for social science.

of social phenomena. Moreover, arguments about the greater complexity of social as compared to natural phenomena have worn thin in the years since Comte and Mill propounded them.

We must, then, re-examine the issues raised by the critics of the natural science model. While the retreat from rational empirical inquiry that these objections sometimes seem to imply is unacceptable, the disappointing results of the conventional programme for social science compel us to scrutinize its foundations more closely than is customary in the mainstream tradition. In particular, there are two sorts of issues, one logical and the other empirical, that require examination.

Logical Issues

It is generally a mistake for empirical scientists to appeal to philosophy for answers to the fundamental questions of their disciplines. Fashions in philosophy come and go, and scientists tend to be out-of-date amateurs. Nevertheless, social scientists especially have been prone to defend their methodological views on philosophical grounds, and so it is necessary to devote some attention to the formal arguments that have been advanced in support of a natural-science, mathematical approach to the study of social life. Then, having cleared away some of the undergrowth, we will turn to more-crucial empirical issues.

We can usefully narrow the focus by considering specifically what might be meant by 'the mathematical method' and the requirements for its employment. It is obvious, of course, that the natural sciences differ very significantly from one another in a great many respects, including both the extent to and the manner in which mathematics is used explicitly and self-consciously. Nevertheless, beneath this diversity there is a fundamental commonality in the way the natural sciences proceed that is the basis for the profound connection between mathematics and the scientific study of the material universe.

The crucial point is that the mathematical character of the natural sciences does not reside in the use of specialized notation or any particular variety of mathematics. Nor, moreover, can we find any fundamental similarity between the various natural sciences in the logical form of their theories that would clearly demarcate them from non-scientific fields of inquiry.[7] Rather, what is distinctive about the natural sciences and what builds into them a fundamentally mathematical character is the form of description that has emerged as an integral part of the scientific method as it has developed in physics, chemistry and biology. Specifically, the natural sciences attend to phenomena in an attitude divorced from the concrete

[7] See Gould: 1986. It should be noted that the 'history' in Gould's title refers to such fields as evolutionary biology and geology, not social history, and that his essay is directed to the diversity of methods within the natural sciences.

emotions, practical purposes, and the like, of particular observers as well as from whatever subjective states the objects of scientific description may possess. In short, description in the natural sciences employs what is known as an 'extensional' idiom, which attends only to the literal truth and falseness of statements and is concerned only with of what objects a given statement is true, i.e. with the statement's extension. This restriction, in addition to giving a specific sense of 'objectivity' appropriate to the natural sciences, provides the conditions necessary and sufficient for using mathematics to formulate the fundamental concepts and propositions of natural science. To develop this point in more detail, it will be useful to proceed indirectly by considering the strongest argument that has been advanced for the natural science model and a mathematical approach in the social sciences.

The extensionalist thesis

Most arguments aimed at establishing the necessity of a natural science approach in the social sciences are unpersuasive because they depend on doctrines heavily disputed or actually discarded in philosophy, or else they simply make claims or give examples of mathematical models without examining the basic questions. Thus, it is generally difficult to join issues in a clear and direct fashion. The major exception to this is an essay by Don Martindale (1963), which puts the case for the natural science model and a mathematical approach strongly and clearly. Martindale raises and addresses what is in fact the fundamental issue, and does so in a way that is directly relevant to our concerns.

After reviewing various objections to the use of mathematics in the social sciences, including particularly those associated with an interpretative approach, Martindale argues that

> with the emergence of symbolic logic in the twentieth-century world, it is no longer possible to reject the application of mathematics to social phenomena *in principle* under the reassuring illusion that one is still able to retain logic as appropriate to analysis. One must be prepared either to retain symbolic logic as a whole or reject it as a whole; this does not mean, of course, that all phases of it are equally useful to every problem. Moreover, if one rejects logic as inappropriate to social phenomena one must face the fact that no satisfactory substitutes for it have been developed, though this seems to have been the motive of various epistemological writings of Heidegger and other existentialists in their attempts to develop various prelogical 'mythic' and 'poetic' avenues to the 'truly true'. In a word, the twentieth-century developments in symbolic logic have rendered permanently obsolete all forms of the rejection of mathematics *in principle* as a tool of social science. (Martindale: 1963, p. 107)

The developments in symbolic logic that Martindale alludes to here result from the writings of Peano, Frege, Russell, Zermello and others whose work, around the turn of the century, created modern standard logic consisting of the predicate calculus with set theory.[8] Standard logic is a powerful idiom: it suffices in principle to express not only classical mathematics but scientific descriptions of natural phenomena, classifications and taxonomies, and the substance of the laws of nature. Moreover, no clear line can be drawn between mathematics in some narrow sense and standard logic itself. Martindale's argument, then, is that the only alternative to using standard logic in the social sciences is to abandon rational empirical inquiry into social life altogether, leaving the field to poets, myth-makers and, one might add, ideologues.

Prima facie, Martindale has presented a compelling case. If the only alternative to expression in standard logic is some form of non-rational discourse, then one must choose between the natural science model and the appropriateness of mathematical methods in principle, on the one hand, and abandonment of the attempt to understand social phenomena in a rational empirical manner, on the other. This expresses with unusual clarity the logical foundation for views that are widely held. Moreover, in one stroke it apparently cuts through all the debate about 'meaning', 'subjectivity' and 'interpretation': whatever importance 'meaning' may have in social life, it must be something that can in principle be captured in standard logic, or else it is beyond the reach of rational inquiry. Once matters are put this way, the basic issue seems to be decided, and the interpretative and other criticisms of the natural science model must apparently be set aside as naive and misguided.

For reasons that will become evident below, we refer to this as the 'extensionalist' thesis. It is intended to provide an a priori justification grounded in logic and the philosophy of science for the view that the natural science model is inescapable in the social sciences and that the fundamental concepts of social science are in principle amenable to mathematical statement. Thus, it seeks to establish rational philosophical foundations for conventional methodological wisdom in general and for a mathematical approach to social science in particular.

Critique of extensionalism

The extensionalist argument seems incontrovertible, and its conclusions inescapable. Certainly, the general point of view it expresses is widely accepted among social scientists, though often tacitly and unwittingly. Ironically, it is also a tacit presupposition of those who hold that any sort of social science is impossible and that consideration of social matters ought indeed to be left to poets, myth-makers and politicians. These opposed positions agree that the choice lies between the natural science model and

[8] There are a number of ways set theory can be formulated, not all of which are mutually compatible, and only some of which are suitable as a basis for empirical applications. For a characterization of set theories usable for this purpose, see Wilson: 1981.

abandonment of the effort toward rational empirical understanding of social life, and differ only in their view as to whether rational empirical understanding of social life can be had at all.

The critical assumption underlying the argument is that the only alternative to standard logic is ideology or some form of non-rational imagery such as poetry or myth. This doctrine, known in philosophy as 'extensionalism', is taken for granted in conventional methodological discussions in the social and behavioural sciences, as well as in the more extreme programmatic claims for behaviourism, sociobiology, the computer model in psychology, and artificial intelligence.

The term 'extensionalism' comes from the fact that standard logic satisfies the principle of *extensionality*: in standard logic, any two expressions true of the same objects, i.e. having the same extension, can be substituted freely for one another without changing the truth of the larger context. Thus, standard logic deals with the reference of an expression, what it is true of, rather than with its meaning. For example the terms 'viable creature with a heart' and 'viable creature with a kidney' are coextensive, since they are true of the same animals, though they differ in meaning. Consequently, within standard logic the terms 'viable creature with a heart' and 'viable creature with a kidney' are entirely equivalent, in the sense that any statement true of a viable creature with a kidney is also true of a viable creature with a heart, and any distinction that might be drawn on grounds of meaning cannot be represented within the idiom of standard logic itself.[9]

There is of course a large family of expressions, the intensional idioms, that have no place in standard logic. Examples include the so-called 'propositional attitudes', such as 'believes that', 'says that', 'wishes that', 'endeavours that', 'urges that', 'fears that', and related expressions such as 'wants', 'is looking for'; the modalities of necessity and possibility together with the closely related matters of counter-factual conditionals and laws of nature; and the concepts of meaning and proposition, as distinct from reference and sentence.[10] As Quine observes,

> the division between such idioms and the normally tractable [i.e. extensional] ones is notable. We saw how it divides referential from non-referential occur-

---

[9] Note, for example, that the first description warrants inspecting the creature for the presence of a heart, whereas the second warrants searching for a kidney, and these operations are quite different. However, because the two descriptions are extensionally equivalent, the assertion that a creature has a heart implies that it also has a kidney and so warrants looking for a kidney. In short, when viewed strictly logically, the differences between the two descriptions evaporate since we can always substitute one for the other without altering the truth of any larger extensional statement in which they are contained. Nevertheless, the fact remains that the two mean different things. Of course, not all differences in meaning turn on an operational criterion, but the example makes the point vividly here.

[10] The term 'intentional' is sometimes used, following Brentano and Husserl, for these expressions. See Quine: 1960, pp. 219–21.

rences of terms. Moreover it is intimately related to the division between behaviorism and mentalism, between efficient cause and final cause, and between literal theory and dramatic portrayal. (Quine: 1960, p. 219)

The extensionalist thesis, then, implies that the need for such intensional idioms is only apparent and practical, and that on any given occasion expressions involving them can be replaced by suitable extensional paraphrases. Of course, it is conceded, the extensional paraphrases will generally be intolerably cumbersome, and so non-extensional manners of speech are a practical necessity; but, according to the thesis, they are *only* manners of speech and the nature of reality is such that standard logic suffices in principle for all rational discourse.[11]

Extensionalism seems plausible from within the natural sciences, for extensional description is centrally important in physics, chemistry and biology. It is the foundation of what we know as 'scientific objectivity' as well as of the universality and generality of scientific concepts and laws. Even when the focus is on development over time, as in geology and evolutionary biology, the fundamental explanatory arguments depend on processes that operate universally (cf. Gould: 1986). Inevitably, when description involves intensional elements, issues of interpretation arise, not merely over the implications of the data, but over what the data are. The problem arises precisely because intensional idioms depend on some notion of meaning rather than a notion of truth, and systematic truth-conditions for intensional statements are elusive. To be sure, we decide the truth of intensional statements in everyday life, but we do so occasion-by-occasion and with careful attention to context and to the identity of the speakers and listeners, but the consequence is that intensional concepts cannot be seen as independent of their use in particular situations, whereas such abstraction is the essence of the natural sciences. However, the claim of extensionalism goes further and holds that standard logic, the language of natural science, is the language of *all* rational empirical discourse and that the ubiquitous reliance on intensional idioms is merely a practical convenience. It is this assumption that underlies the conclusion that the only alternative to the natural science model and a mathematical approach in the social sciences is to abandon rational empirical inquiry into social phenomena and settle for poetry, myth and ideology.

Nevertheless, for all its widespread acceptance, extensionalism is a false doctrine. One objection is that the claim that intensional idioms in rational discourse are dispensable in principle has yet to be convincingly illustrated in practice, so that the thesis remains an unredeemed promissory note. The more important difficulty with extensionalism, though, is that it depends

---

[11] The most careful and forceful argument for this view is given by Quine (1960; 1961). Although Quine's views have given rise to extensive debate, most of his critics argue with details of his position and overlook the more fundamental issue of extensionalism.

on concepts that cannot themselves be formulated extensionally, and thus it is caught in an internal contradiction.

The idea of standard logic is central to extensionalism, and if we do not understand what standard logic is, the thesis is unintelligible. We require, then, an explication of the concept of standard logic. However, if we are to adhere to extensionalist principles, that explication must itself be formulated within standard logic, and it is here that things fall apart. To understand the notation of standard logic we must understand the concept of truth, on which the basic elements of standard logic depend, namely truth-functional composition and logical quantification. The problem is that we cannot formulate the notion of truth within standard logic without at the same time opening the door to self-contradictory sentences such as the liar's:[12]

> this sentence is false.

Thus, in order to explain standard logic, we need a meta-language; and if the meta-language is also a version of standard logic, as required by the doctrine of extensionalism, we need a meta-meta-language to explain the meta-language, and so on. The infinite regress is known as the 'Tarski hierarchy', and its import here is that concepts central to standard logic itself cannot be formulated within that idiom.[13] We have then a paradox: extensionalism fails the extensionalist test for rational discourse.

The consequence of this is that the extensionalist thesis is untenable. The claim that in principle all rational discourse can be formulated in the idiom of standard logic is false: in particular, the claim itself cannot be stated in standard logic, since in order to understand what standard logic is, we require a notion of truth that cannot be expressed within standard logic.

The logical situation

Extensionalism is an untenable doctrine, and any argument that depends on it, whether or not explicitly, must be rejected. The implications of this

[12] It should be emphasized that the difficulty with the liar sentence is not the mere fact of self-reference, which, Hofstadter (1979) notwithstanding, is neither mysterious nor exceptional. For example, the statement 'this sentence has forty-eight letters and spaces' is completely unproblematic, and if we count the '-' between 'forty' and 'eight' as a letter or as a space, it is also true. Rather, the problem is with the term 'false', or equivalently, 'not true'.

[13] The same problem arises in other approaches to formulating the notion of truth for standard logic. For example, Kripke (1975) proposes a method that yields a definition of truth for the object language within the object language itself by permitting truth–value gaps in the object language; however, a meta-language is required to formulate this definition, and so the regress is not avoided. The crucial point is that while at any stage in the regress we can introduce another meta-language, we are always left with a notion of truth that is as yet unexplicated within standard logic. Consequently, the notion of truth to which the idea of this construction appeals in the first place is antecedent to standard logic and inexpressible within it.

are far-reaching, for much post-positivist philosophy of science, including much of what is currently in fashion among social science methodologists, still harbours an underlying commitment to extensionalism. For our concerns, the important consequence is that *a priori* arguments for the inescapability of a natural science approach to the study of social phenomena must be ruled out in so far as they imply extensionalism. In short, the philosophically-based self-assurance often expressed by advocates of the natural science model is distinctly out of place.

However, it is also important to observe that this critique does not, in itself, support the conclusion that the natural science model is inapplicable to the social sciences. Rather, it shows that the usual arguments advanced on behalf of the natural science model are bankrupt. Indeed, we should be suspicious of any a priori argument that seems to force the stronger conclusion that the natural science model is wrong for the social sciences, for generally such arguments also imply that natural science is impossible, which does not comport well with experience. In purely logical and philosophical terms, the suitability of the natural science model for the social sciences is undecided and probably will always remain so. To proceed, we must go beyond strictly logical and philosophical arguments and consider the phenomena with which social science is concerned.

The Phenomena of the Social Sciences

As we have noted, mathematics serves to describe the material universe, but only when that universe is viewed from a perspective that disregards the investigator's sentiments as well as any beliefs, purposes or feelings of the objects being studied. Thus, excluded from interest in the natural sciences are precisely those matters that require intensional expressions for their description and explanation. What is distinctive about the natural sciences, then, is not their mode of explanation, nor the logical form of their theories, but rather the demand that descriptions of phenomena be translatable into extensional terms.[14] To be sure, natural scientists employ natural language with all its dependence on intensional forms of expression

---

[14] A technical note may be in order here. One can adopt a 'black box' term that involves intensional notions in its empirical interpretation and use it as a primitive predicate: for example, '*x* believes that Cicero denounced Catiline'. Observe that while a variable, *x*, appears outside the clause governed by 'that', a variable cannot appear inside such a clause, as in the form '*x* believes that *y*', without precipitating problems of referential opacity (Quine: 1960; 1961) which destroy the fabric of standard logic. Thus moves along this line to extend standard logic to intensional discourse are futile since a separate primitive predicate is needed for each particular belief, desire, thought, etc., which makes it impossible to speak generally about beliefs and the like. For further discussion of such issues, see Quine (1953; 1960; 1961) and Wilson (1982). See also the discussion below, pp. 398–9.

when engaged in scientific activities. However, technical scientific descriptions and explanations of natural phenomena are among the few instances in which translation into an extensional idiom is a sanctionable ideal and it is this that is the basis for the fundamental role of mathematics in the natural sciences. The question, then, is whether social phenomena such as political and economic arrangements, conflict and change, can be captured in a wholly extensional idiom.[15]

The behaviourist programme

The central insight of radical behaviourism was the importance of eliminating all references to such matters as belief, knowledge, purpose and meaning precisely because these are not amenable to the kind of description required in natural science. However, the radical behaviourist programme has proved to be problematic in the behavioural and social sciences. The areas in which it has had significant success are those remotest from the central concerns of conventional social science, namely neurophysiology and physiological psychology, in which stimuli and responses can be described in physical, chemical and biological terms. But in the study of ordinary social phenomena, the rigorous methodological canons of radical behaviourism have had to be compromised. The result is a weak version of behaviourism that, while avoiding direct reference to belief, knowledge, purpose, meaning, and the like, and insisting on restricting attention to overt behaviour, nevertheless admits descriptions based on the irremediably intensional categories of ordinary language.[16] While the radical behaviourist programme itself is impeccable in formal terms, it has not been successful in providing a foundation for the study of social phenomena that follows the natural science model. We see, then, that the untenability of extensionalism does not prevent the formulation of a coherent programme for studying behaviour on the basis of the natural science model. However, rigorous pursuit of that programme has been successful only in so far as attention has been restricted

[15] It is important to emphasize that quantitative methods can be employed in the analysis of data, even when these are described with essential reliance on intensional terms, so long as descriptions are sufficiently clear to allow for classification and counting adequate for the purposes at hand. The mere use of quantitative techniques of data analysis, however, does not imply extensional description. See note 14.

[16] It is a commonplace that ordinary-language descriptions of behaviour impute knowledge, purpose and agency to the organism, and these are matters that defy extensional description. Consequently, the burden of proof here is on those who assert the positive claim that an uncompromising behaviourist methodology can in fact be employed in a sustained programme of research in the social sciences. It is not uncommon to find research called 'behaviourist' that relies heavily on everyday language for describing what the organisms in question are doing. The strong behaviourist and scientific claims often made in these cases are undermined by the tacit mentalism of everyday discourse.

to phenomena that can be defined neurophysiologically.[17] Consequently, a crucial question is whether this is accidental or instead reflects the fundamental nature of social phenomena.

The constitution of action

The heart of the problem is an important peculiarity of social life: in contrast to the phenomena addressed by physics, chemistry and biology, people in the normal course of everyday life produce their own descriptions of what they and others are doing.[18] A central issue here is the status of these indigenous descriptions: are they merely epiphenomenal, to be explained away by the same mechanisms that are also used to explain the rest of behaviour, or are people's descriptions of what they and others do in some way essential to the constitution of the phenomena the social sciences seek to describe and explain?

If indigenous descriptions are epiphenomenal, the way is perhaps open to successful prosecution of something like the radical behaviourist programme, for then what people do could be described independently of what they say. Indeed what they say would be nothing more than something else people do, to be described and explained in the same way as the rest of their behaviour. One could, then, describe both verbal and non-verbal behaviour in whatever terms were convenient for scientific purposes and proceed to look for causal relations between verbal and non-verbal behaviour, with verbal behaviour simply as another variable, dependent or independent according to which part of the causal chain one is studying.

However, things are otherwise. The phenomena classically of interest in the social sciences depend, essentially on indigenous descriptions. Even the most casual reflection makes it plain that social scientists' descriptions of phenomena are almost wholly parasitic on conventional descriptions used in everyday life. While social scientists may deal with such concepts as elasticity of demand or relative deprivation that seem far removed from ordinary life, these concepts are necessarily founded on actions people

---

[17] It should be emphasized that one cannot move from neurophysiology to social interaction without first describing social phenomena in neurophysiological terms. The difficulty is that while some responses such as anger apparently have well-defined neurophysiological descriptions, other phenomena require knowledge of the social context in order to be properly identified, for example aggression (Bandura: 1973).

[18] This could be dismissed as obvious, and one might point to the sociology of knowledge and sociological treatments of ideology, class consciousness, attitudes, and the like, as evidence that this characteristic of social life has not been neglected. However, social scientists have tended to avoid the fundamental theoretical and methodological issues it raises. The major exceptions to this arise in phenomenological approaches (e.g. Schütz: 1967) and, more centrally important here, ethnomethodology and conversation analysis (e.g. Garfinkel: 1967; Garfinkel and Sacks: 1970; Sacks: 1963).

recognize and describe, such as giving someone money or complaining about one's own lot in comparison with that of others. Moreover, we cannot comprehend a particular action, such as repaying a loan, and distinguish it from others such as making a gift or capitulating to extortion, without understanding the institutional context within which it occurs. We do not build up a pattern of society from descriptions of single actions that we can recognize independently of their institutional contexts, but rather develop an account in a hermeneutic fashion, forming ideas about overall patterns on the basis of particular events and then using these same ideas to understand more clearly the particular events that gave rise to them. Of course, when we are already familiar with a society because we live in it, this interpretative process can be quite unself-conscious and implicit, but the basic interdependence between descriptions of singular events and understandings of the larger social order remains. In short, the descriptive and measurement procedures actually employed in the social sciences without exception require the observer to be familiar with and competent in the use of the ways people describe their own and each others' actions.[19]

Moreover, this de facto dependence of social scientists' descriptions on indigenous ones is neither arbitrary nor an unfortunate residue handed down from a more benighted era. Instead, it reflects the nature of social phenomena. Detailed analysis of social interaction shows that people are oriented to what others say and do, and that they display that orientation in their own action.[20] In short, people produce descriptions for understanding and use as bases for further inference and action by themselves and others. It is clear that the way in which action is understood by people depends decisively on the social-structural context of the particular interaction. For example, whether an utterance is heard as an excuse or a request for help depends on the social categories the participants in a given situation see as relevantly applying to them on that occasion and on the activities they see as typically associated with those categories: in order to understand what they and others are doing, people necessarily invoke social-structural categories as an essential resource, which builds into every concrete interaction an essential trans-situational element. Hence, instead of being an

[19] This, of course, is well known and routinely conveyed to students in those parts of research training that deal with the actual details of how to formulate or interpret the results of a questionnaire, analyse historical documents or conduct field work. In fact, however, its implications for the viability of the natural science model have yet to be taken seriously by most sociological methodologists, who instead ignore it, presumably viewing it as merely a technical nuisance arising in the course of research but which can be idealized away for theoretical and methodological purposes. However, writers outside the mainstream consensus have raised this point (Cicourel: 1964; Garfinkel: 1967; Sacks: 1963; Wilson: 1970), and recently Giddens has emphasized it with his notion 'the double hermeneutic' (1984).

[20] The research literature is rapidly becoming very large. See Heritage (1984), Maynard and Wilson (1980), Wilson (1982; 1985), and Wilson and Zimmerman (1980) for discussion and references.

independent variable that affects action, social structure enters into the constitution of action itself. Finally, in using social categories this way to make sense of what they are doing, people endow social structure with precisely that external and constraining reality of which Durkheim spoke, even as they reproduce that social structure in their own interaction.[21]

The empirical situation

We have seen that the untenability of extensionalism does not prevent formulation of a coherent programme, such as radical behaviourism, for studying behaviour on the basis of the natural science model. However, rigorous pursuit of such a programme has historically been successful only at the cost of abandoning interest in the conventional topics of social science and turning instead to the investigation of neurophysiological phenomena. We see now that this is not an accident, for the phenomena of interest to the social sciences are *inherently* intensional. What people say, intend and know is central to what we are concerned with when we study any of the usual topics of the social sciences, such as social stratification, poverty, crime, ethnic and race relations, education, political processes, and so on. This, it must be emphasized, is not a question of logic or methodology, but, rather, a matter of empirical fact. As a consequence, we cannot expect mathematics to be an adequate medium for expressing the fundamental ideas in sociological theory, since mathematics presupposes extensionality.

The Place of Mathematical Models in Social Science

So far, the argument might seem to mandate rejection of any use of mathematics in social science. However, such a conclusion would be a mistake. What we have found untenable is the notion that mathematically-formulated concepts can play the same fundamental role in the social as in the natural sciences. But this does not mean that mathematical models have no role at all. Indeed, quite the opposite is the case: mathematical models have an essential place in our efforts to untangle the complexities of social reality.

The heuristic thesis

A useful point of departure is an instructive though no-doubt apocryphal anecdote. Once upon a time, the story goes, a certain professor of sociology

---

[21] Consequently, there can be no question of 'assembling' larger-scale social and institutional structures out of pre-identified individual behaviours, for those structures are built into the component individual actions that at the same time reproduce those same structures. The convergence with Giddens's notion of the duality of social structure (1979; 1984) is clear. However, Giddens is concerned to explore the implications for social theory broadly conceived, whereas the research referred to here deals with the concrete, observable mechanisms of social interaction.

was interested in the diffusion of messages by word of mouth. On the basis of his studies, he developed a mathematical model to predict the proportion of a population having heard a message after the elapse of a given amount of time from the introduction of the message to a single member of the population. One day, to illustrate the model to his class, the professor gave a simple message to one member of the class and allowed the students to mingle. Then at regular intervals he determined the number of students who had heard the message. Unfortunately, the results did not coincide at all well with the predictions of the model. However, the professor was not to be daunted, and so he established some rules governing to whom the students could talk and how often. After some tinkering, he eventually arrived at a set of rules such that the predictions of the model coincided satisfactorily enough with the data. This, he announced in triumph, proved the correctness of the model.

Presumably this tale was told as a caution against a certain kind of naivety in the design of experiments. However, for our purposes it is illuminating in another way. The important point to notice here is that once the rules had been settled and so long as the students followed them, the model gave a decent description of the way messages diffused in that population. Moreover, the rules gave definiteness to the notions of a 'message' and of having 'heard the message' in this context in a way that provided for the possibility of identifying unambiguously enough for the purpose at hand the students who had heard the message and counting them. Obviously, though, the model does not represent the fundamental facts of the situation, for the regularities it described depended on the rules and persisted only so long as those particular rules were followed. But, to repeat, so long as the rules were followed, the model gave an empirically adequate description that could be useful for various purposes. In addition to such practical applications as estimating the amount of time needed to spread the word on a particular matter, the model could be used to gain some insight into the implications of the rules underlying the regularities it represented.

This example is a basic paradigm for the relation of mathematical models to social life. It is true that we can represent certain aspects of social phenomena by mathematical models, sometimes very sophisticated ones, and in so doing contribute substantially to our understanding of how things work. However, the possibility of such a model arises from the fact that people in the course of their everyday lives employ social-structural categories as an essential resource in organizing their activities: it is on this fact that, directly or indirectly, both the concepts employed in and the regularities described by a mathematical model depend. The heuristic thesis, then, is that this is the general case.

It is crucially important here to note explicitly that use of a mathematical model does not imply that descriptions are untainted by intension. Rather, when we develop and apply such a model we arrange to package intensional idioms in such a way that, for the purpose at hand, we can proceed with formal calculations.[22] Perhaps the most important occasions for such packaging are coding operations and interpretations of computations. In the former, the raw stuff of social life is described using codes that, for example, can then be processed by computer and matched to symbols in the notation of a model. In the latter, the results are once again related to the social world. Between coding and interpretation, the data and the symbols of the model can be manipulated in a logically rigorous manner, but these computations have no meaning without the absorption of intension that occurs at the beginning and end. Quine makes this point in a slightly different way when arguing for a heuristic role for standard logic in dealing with practical affairs involving intensional idioms. However, he is also emphatic about the distinction between this use of standard logic and its employment in 'venturing to formulate the fundamental laws of a branch of science' (Quine: 1960, p. 221). In short, we can and must make use of mathematical models to sort out relations in our data and clarify our ideas about how one thing is related to another in a particular case. But we cannot look to mathematics as the idiom for formulating fundamental concepts and propositions that will yield a natural science of society.

Some potential counter-examples

Readers who have worked with mathematical models will undoubtedly be familiar with examples that, at first glance, appear to refute the heuristic thesis and instead seem to support the idea that mathematics can play a more fundamental role in the social sciences. It will be useful, then, to review briefly several of these, although not with an eye to complete coverage, nor with the intention of discussing any of them thoroughly. Rather, the purpose is to illustrate some typical candidate counter-examples to the heuristic thesis and the ways in which these fail to confound it. The considerations raised here, then, are intended to apply widely.

The most obvious place to look for counter-examples to the heuristic thesis is economic theory. Economists are prone to regard their enterprise as a positive science, taking it for granted that their assumptions are natural laws. Here if anywhere in the social sciences one finds sophisticated mathematical formulations of what appear to be the basic concepts of the field. However, there are two points to be noted about economic theory. First, as Max Weber among others observed, the basic concepts and postulates of classical and neo-classical economic theory reflect the categories and relations of the market and property institutions of capitalism. Consequently, the usefulness of economic analyses depends on the degree to which these institutions remain stable and effectively control behaviour. And to the extent that economic models are applied in areas in which their assumptions do not reflect institutionalized arrangements, we can anticipate strange

[22] See note 14.

results.[23]

Second, economic theories have a peculiar character. They consist of working out in detail, generally with the aid of considerable mathematical apparatus, the consequences of one or another set of assumptions. However, the relation of these assumptions to the empirical world is treated as variable, and the laws of economics are strict logical consequences of the conditions necessary for the theory to apply at all rather than empirical assertions that could be disconfirmed even when the conditions of applicability are satisfied. As a consequence, failure of economic predictions to correspond to data is not ordinarily construed to mean that the theory is wrong and must be modified or abandoned, but only that it did not apply to the situation in question. Thus, the theory of rational market behaviour is not viewed as disconfirmed when its predictions fail, for in that case it would have been jettisoned long ago; instead, the conclusion is that the actors were not behaving rationally or that there was no market. Models of this sort have their uses, of course, but one of them is not to justify claims to possessing a fundamental theory, or even strong empirical generalizations, of the sort characteristic of the natural sciences.[24] In sum, economic theory does not on inspection provide a clear counter-example to the heuristic thesis, but instead appears to sustain it.

Another example is network analysis.[25] The network approach makes an extremely important contribution as a corrective to the tendency in much sociological analysis, particularly of the quantitative sort, to focus on distributions of and correlations between attributes of individuals or groups. Moreover, much of the power of the approach lies in its use of mathematical models to characterize various properties of social networks. However, a social network exists only in so far as people or groups interact with one another in ways they take to be typical and required. Consequently, the models of network analysis depend ultimately on institutionalized patterns for their relevance and interpretation, and hence quite different institutional

[23] For example, Berk and Berk (1983; and personal conversations) show clearly that, while the 'new home economics' raises serious challenges for conventional sociological approaches to the family, it is also involved in obvious absurdities.

[24] In contrast, consider Ohm's law, which asserts that at normal temperatures and pressures the current flowing in a conductor is proportional directly to the voltage and inversely to the resistance. There are two things to note here. First, the relation is not asserted to hold at extreme temperatures and pressures, but under the stipulated conditions it is asserted to hold universally. Second, the relation between current, voltage and resistance does not follow logically from the conditions necessary for the law to apply in the first place but, rather, is an empirical assertion that might not hold even at moderate temperatures and pressures, though in fact it does. In contrast, the laws of economics are logical consequences of the conditions that must be satisfied if the theory is to be applied at all. This, it must be emphasized, does not mean that they are useless, but rather that they do not have the same character as laws of nature.

[25] See, for example, Wellman (1983) for a general overview and references.

patterns with fundamentally different dynamics may give rise to network relations that are indistinguishable. This of course does not diminish the usefulness of these models, but rather only emphasizes their heuristic status.

Finally, numerous mathematical models have been proposed in social psychology to represent various aspects of cognitive and affective phenomena. These are generally formulated as some form of computer model. While this is desirable from a formal point of view, since it requires that the model be clearly stated, it imposes the restriction that all descriptions must be treated as if they were extensional. Effective use of these models therefore depends on the user to absorb any considerations that depend on intensional elements such as meaning. This absorption occurs at the input stage, in such processes as coding observations, and at the output stage, as when substantive interpretations are given to factor loadings. In between, of course, the symbols can be manipulated in a manner that is independent of any such considerations, but the empirical relevance of the model and the cogency of the results depend crucially on the skill, sensitivity and insight with which these activities of meaning absorption are carried out. Again, this does not imply that models of this kind are pointless, but instead makes clear that their value is heuristic rather than as representations of fundamental processes.

Some conclusions

To say that a method is heuristic is not to patronize it. We need all the help we can get in understanding the intricacies of social phenomena, and mathematical models are powerful tools for the purpose. The virtues of mathematical models are well known and need no special emphasis here. However, several points are worth noting that become somewhat more salient when the role of mathematics is viewed as heuristic rather than fundamental.

First, in using a mathematical model to represent aspects of a social situation that are of particular interest, one gains the benefit of precise formulation. However, because we cannot now view such a model as capturing all that is important, even for the particular purposes at hand, we must be far more sensitive than has been customary in articulating the model with the historical and institutional context on which it is based, for otherwise we risk serious error in specifying the model. But this carries with it a further benefit, for it may well lead us to pursue qualitative inquiries that deepen our understanding of the context in addition to improving our model specification.

Second, a well-specified model can identify the quantitative, categorical and network data required to address adequately the questions that motivated our inquiry initially. The exercise of specifying a model can develop a set of sharply-focused empirical questions from a more general problem. However, if the model is viewed as heuristic, we are not so likely to miss the wood for the trees as when we mistake the model for the whole story.

Third, the line between mathematical models in some pure sense and the use of mathematics as an aid to data analysis becomes blurred once all mathematical models in the social sciences are recognized as having primarily a heuristic function. For example, one of the major points that has become clear in the rapid development of structural-equation modelling techniques is the importance of correctly specifying the causal structure, and this, it has been repeatedly emphasized in the textbooks, depends on an adequate theoretical understanding of the phenomenon. But exactly the same consideration arises with any mathematical model of social phenomena. To be sure, the models employed in statistical data analysis tend to be closer to the data and more *ad hoc* than models motivated by more general concerns, but this is neither an automatic liability nor a guarantee of superiority.

Finally, we must recognize more consistently than is now generally the case that the concepts and variables in terms of which a model is formulated are based directly or indirectly on the categories employed by the people we are studying to organize their activities for themselves. On the one hand, this fact provides the basis for non-arbitrary connections between the formalism of the model and the aspects of social reality it is supposed to represent. Clearly, attention to these connections is essential for correct specification of the model. On the other hand, it sets limits on the extent to which the substantive content of a model can be transported to other social situations having features that can be represented by the same formalism. For example, it may be that in each of two groups there is a network of relations that can be represented by a particular semi-lattice, but this means one thing if the relations in question are bureaucratic authority relations in both groups, or are bureaucratic authority relations in one and ritual gift-giving relations in the other. In the first case, numerous and tight parallels may exist between the two groups, whereas in the second, only the most superficial similarities may obtain.

Summary and Conclusion

In this essay I have examined some of the basic issues involved in attempting to employ mathematics as a tool in the social sciences. The main result is that mathematics cannot play the same role as a vehicle for expressing fundamental concepts and propositions in the social sciences as it does in the natural sciences. The reason for this is that the basic data of the social sciences, descriptions of social phenomena, are inherently intensional in character: the social sciences cannot insist on extensional description without abandoning their phenomena. This, however, does not mean that mathematics has no place in social science; rather, that mathematics plays a heuristic rather than a fundamental role in the study of social phenomena.

References

Bandura, A., 1973: *Aggression: A Social Learning Analysis*. Englewood Cliffs: Prentice-Hall.

Berk, R. A. and Berk, S. F., 1983: 'Supply-side Sociology of the Family: The Challenge of the New Home Economics', *Annual Review of Sociology*, 9: 375–95.

Cicourel, A. V., 1964: *Method and Measurement in Sociology*. Glencoe, Ill.: Free Press.

Føllesdal, D., 1970: 'Quine on Modality', in D. Davidson and J. Hintikka (eds), *Words and Objections: Essays on the Work of W. V. Quine*. Dordrecht: D. Reidel, pp. 175–85.

Garfinkel, H., 1984: *Studies in Ethnomethodology*. Cambridge, England: Polity Press. First published 1967.

Garfinkel, H. and Sacks, H., 1970: 'On Formal Structures of Practical Action', in J. C. McKinney and E. A. Tiryakian (eds), *Theoretical Sociology*. New York: Appleton-Century-Crofts, pp. 338–66.

Giddens, A., 1976: *New Rules of the Sociological Method*. New York: Basic Books.
1977: *Studies in Social and Political Theory*. New York: Basic Books.
1979: *Central Problems in Social Theory*. Berkeley and Los Angeles: University of California Press.
1984: *The Constitution of Society*. Cambridge, England: Polity Press.

Gould, S. J., 1986: 'Evolution and the Triumph of Homology, or Why History Matters', *American Scientist*, 74: 69.

Harpending, H., 1985: Review of R. Boyd and P. J. Richerson's *Culture and the Evolutionary Process*. (Chicago: University of Chicago Press, 1985), *Science*, 230: 931.

Heritage, J., 1984: *Garfinkel and Ethnomethodology*. Cambridge, England: Polity Press.

Hofstadter, D. R., 1979: *Gödel, Escher, Bach: An Eternal Golden Braid*. New York: Basic Books.

Kripke, S., 1975: 'Outline of a Theory of Truth', *Journal of Philosophy*, LXXII: 690–716.

Martindale, D., 1963: 'Limits to the Uses of Mathematics in the Study of Sociology', in J. C. Charlesworth (ed.), *Mathematics and the Social Sciences: The Utility and Inutility of Mathematics in the Study of Economics, Political Science, and Sociology*. Philadelphia, Pa.: American Academy of Political and Social Science.

Maynard, D. W. and Wilson, T. P., 1980: 'On the Reification of Social Structure', in S. G. McNall and G. N. Howe (eds), *Current Perspectives in Social Theory*, vol. 1. Greenwich, Conn.: JAI Press, pp. 287–322.

Quine, W. V., 1953: 'Three Grades of Modal Involvement', *Proceedings of the IXth International Congress of Philosophy*. Brussels: 65–81.
1960: *Word and Object*. Cambridge, Mass.: MIT Press.
1961: *From a Logical Point of View*. New York: Harper & Row.
1970: 'Reply to Føllesdal', in D. Davidson and J. Hintikka (eds), *Words and Objections: Essays on the Work of W. V. Quine*. Dordrecht: D. Reidel, p. 336.

Rabinow, P. and Sullivan, W. M. (eds), 1979: *Interpretative Sociology: A Reader*. Berkeley and Los Angeles: University of California Press.

Sacks, H., 1963: 'Sociological Description', *Berkeley Journal of Sociology*, 8: 1–16.

Schütz, A., 1967: *The Phenomenology of the Social World*. Evanston, Ill.: Northwestern University Press. First published 1932.

Taylor, C., 1971: 'Interpretation and the Sciences of Man', *Review of Metaphysics*, 25.

Wellman, B., 1983: 'Network Analysis: Some Basic Principles', in R. Collins (ed.), *Sociological Theory 1983*. San Francisco: Jossey-Bass, pp. 155–200.

Wilson, T. P., 1970: 'Conceptions of Interaction and Forms of Sociological Explanation', *American Sociological Review*, 35: 697–710.

    1981: 'General Models of Set Theory', *Notre Dame Journal of Formal Logic*, 22: 36–44.

    1982: 'Qualitative oder Quantitative Methoden in der Sozialforschung', *Kölner Zeitschrift für Soziologie und Sozialpsychologie*, 34: 487–508.

    1984: 'On the Role of Mathematics in the Social Sciences', *Journal of Mathematical Sociology*, 10: 221–39.

    1985: 'Social Structure and Social Interaction', Unpublished manuscript, Department of Sociology, University of California.

Wilson, T. P. and Zimmerman, D. H., 1980: 'Ethnomethodology, Sociology, and Theory', *Humboldt Journal of Social Relations*, 7: 52–88.

Index

414 *Index*

Hinkle, R., 38, 93n
Hirsch, E. D., 50, 51, 219
Hirschman, A., 43, 78
history/historical
assumptions of, 48–51
behaviourism and, 73–6
as discipline, 310
diversity of social practice, 386–9
philosophy of *see* critical theory and
systematics merged *see*
empiricism and theory
world-systems analysis and
progressive, 322–3; social
science, 313–15, 316–17, 321,
324
see also time
Hobbes, T., 227, 229
Hofstadter, D. R., 392n
Holton, G., 17–18, 69n, 263n
Homans, G., 44, 138n, 170
behaviourism, 5, 7, 10, 58–80
exchange theory, 41
historicity, 288
Honneth, A., 87n
on critical theory, 347–82
Hörisch, J., 347n
Horkheimer, M.: on critical theory
Habermas and, 370–72, 374–5
origins of, 348–56; cultural-
theoretical analysis of mass
culture, 353, 355–6, 366, 368;
economic analysis of post-liberal
capitalism, 353–4; social-
psychological investment of
societal integration, 354–5
social-theoretical alternatives,
362–3, 365–6
weaknesses of, 356–61
Horney, K., 369
hospitals, 106–7
Hughes, E., 85, 103, 104, 105–6
Hughes, J., 225n
human
action, *see* action
condition, Parsonian theory and,
123–7
nature, ineluctable, 345
humanism/humanities and attitude to
classics, 11, 13, 46–51
Hume, D., 140, 157

Hummell, H. J., 77
Husserl, E., 33–4, 129, 390n
Hymes, D. H., 200
hypostatization, 279

I, constitution of, 205–6, 207
idealism *see* interpretation
ideal-types, 178
procedures in Parsonian theory,
120, 128, 130–1
ideas, history of, 47n
see also critical theory
identification, syntheses of, 230
identity
formation of, 373; *see also*
socialization
in Parsonian theory, 122
ideology
as alternative to standard logic,
340
evaluation, 30–1
liberal and disciplines, 312
idiographic
and nomothetic schools, compared,
313–15, 323–4
procedures in Parsonian theory,
120–1, 129–31
imagination, collective, 367
Imhof, A. E., 130
immanent action, 90
immigrants, *see* ethnic minorities and
under United States
inclusion in analytical theorizing,
185, 189–91
income and class, 310
indexicality, 215, 249–50, 292
indifference, ethnomethodological,
231, 301
indigenous description,
epiphenomenal, 395–6
individual/individualism
collectivism and, Parsonian theory,
139–41
functionalism, 70–1
methodological, 67, 70, 73
pragmatism and, 86, 97, 99
Industrial Revolution, 23–4, 75, 319,
320–1
industrialization and literacy, 164
infinite versus singular context, 48

/301Ƨ678T>C1/